SEVENTEENTH-CENTURY VERSE AND PROSE

Seventeenth-Century
VERSE and PROSE

Volume Two: 1660–1700

HELEN C. WHITE

RUTH C. WALLERSTEIN

RICARDO QUINTANA

of the
University of Wisconsin

THE MACMILLAN COMPANY

Tenth Printing 1971

The Macmillan Company
866 Third Avenue, New York, New York 10022
Collier-Macmillan Canada, Ltd., Toronto, Ontario

Printed in the United States of America

PREFATORY NOTE

FOR THE CONVENIENCE of the reader with Volume II of this anthology in hand, we may restate several points from the preface to the whole.

In the choice of the text the principle followed has been to select the best seventeenth-century edition and reproduce it as accurately and directly as possible. The spelling and punctuation of the original have been kept, but all contractions, including the ampersand, have been expanded, purely typographical pecularities of seventeenth century printing, such as the long *s* and the old-fashioned use of *i* and *j* have been normalized, and the varieties of type have been reduced to two, roman and italic, with the italic reserved for special purposes. No attempt has been made to provide the apparatus for textual study.

To the libraries to which acknowledgments are made in Volume I the editors add with warm thanks the names of the Henry E. Huntington Library, the Newberry Library, and the libraries of Union Theological Seminary and Yale University. Acknowledgments for permission to reprint four texts will appear in the appropriate places.

In the selected bibliographies in the introductions and in the notes the following abbreviations are used for current periodicals and for notes:

ELH	*English Literary History*
ESEA	*Essays and Studies by Members of the English Association*
HLQ	*Huntington Library Quarterly*
JEGP	*Journal of English and Germanic Philology*
JHI	*Journal of the History of Ideas*
MLN	*Modern Language Notes*
MLQ	*Modern Language Quarterly*
MLR	*Modern Language Review*
MP	*Modern Philology*
NQ	*Notes and Queries*
OBS	*Oxford Bibliographical Society Proceedings & Papers*
PMLA	*Publications of the Modern Language Association of America*
PQ	*Philological Quarterly*
RES	*Review of English Studies*
SP	*Studies in Philology*
TLS	*London Times Literary Supplement*

TABLE OF CONTENTS

SEVENTEENTH-CENTURY VERSE AND PROSE

The Seventeenth Century

(1660–1700)

THE period of the Restoration—by which is here meant not merely the reign of Charles II (1660–1685) but the entire era extending down to the close of the seventeenth century—is somewhat more complex than many of the older critics and historians of literature were fully aware. Today it is generally appreciated that neither the drama nor the verse characteristic of these years gives us a wholly reliable index to the life that was going on, to the concerns of average Englishmen, to the temper of political leaders, philosophers, divines, scientists, and men of business. Whatever judgment, artistic or ethical, we are now disposed to pass upon Restoration comedy, we are no longer misled into assuming that what took place upon the stage was a faithful reflection of the manners of any save a very small group of fashionable folk, who in making virtues out of all that Puritanism had set its face against did not thereby win the admiration of many outside of their own closed circle. True enough, a decided if not overwhelming majority of the English people had rejected Puritanism, but by Puritanism they understood a political regime which had been established by dubious means, which had degenerated into something close to anarchy, and to which certain objectionable individuals and groups had attached themselves. They were willing, though with differing degrees of assent, to see Presbyterianism and Independency give way before a reëstablished Church of England. But the reaction against Puritanism did not embrace, as has sometimes been thought, a reaction against common decency and morality. No less than in the age of Shakespeare or the age of Milton, for all the changing outlook and temper, the concepts which most men applied to their own lives and to the fundamental issues of the time were basically ethical and religious.

In similar fashion we can be misled by the poetry of the Restoration if we allow ourselves to make sweeping generalizations concerning the character of the age on the basis of letters alone. The verse of Dryden reveals an obviously narrower range of sensibility, images, and verbal connotations than that of the metaphysical poets and, before them, of the Elizabethans. Dryden prided himself upon the quality of order and precision which he had attained, and what he thereby bestowed upon English verse can scarcely be overestimated. He was, of course, influenced to some degree in his views of literature and in his intentions as an artist by the theories and practices of seventeenth-century French writers, and, as we shall see presently, still more by those general currents of thought and feeling that are usually summed up under the term *neo-classical.* But to call Dryden neo-classical is one thing; it is something else again to proceed from there to a characterization of the entire period as an age of neo-classicism.

It is indeed probable that in any age the characteristics that give a literary period its critical name are by no means so universally dominant and pervasive as the necessities of historical discrimination would suggest. To the theorist surveying the chronological succession of literary movements and developments, it is natural and even sound to underscore the new and the different, since so much of literary progress is dependent upon the recognition and exploration of new avenues of development. And to the critical historian, charged with the duty of not only describing but summarizing and in some general way patterning the changing literary scene, it is tempting to emphasize the unique and the distinctive in dealing with the quite obvious fact that the total impression of one age is different from that of another. There are such things as dominant tendencies, however fortuitous the circumstances of their power, and influential spokesmen and examples, however irrelevant some of the sources of their effectiveness. This is peculiarly true of an age in which the circumstances of social prestige and patronage gave the Court and the aristocratic group so much weight and in considerable measure tended to isolate those who devoted themselves to belles lettres from the nation at large. And this concentration was reënforced by the outstanding position of one man, Dryden, whose unusual critical awareness and competence joined to his unquestioned creative preëminence in several fields made what he had to say on controverted literary topics of great contemporary influence and of enduring critical and historical interest. For these reasons it is of the first importance to understand the neo-classical.

But it should never be forgotten that if in the special sense suggested above this was the age of Dryden, it was also the age of Locke and Temple and Halifax, and even of Baxter and Bunyan. And, not to raise any questions of the sub-literary or the popular-literary, it is well to remember that Dryden's was by no means the only approach even to belles lettres, and still less to the general intellectual issues of the day with which the student of literature is necessarily concerned. To take only a few examples, was Locke neo-classical, or Sir Isaac Newton, or Halifax, or Temple? Viewed from the vantage point of such men, the Restoration period was an age of reason; but chiefly in the sense—as will presently become clear—that so many representative thinkers shared the assumption not only that the rational order in the universe is readily discoverable through intuition, but that something of this order lies in the heart of man and can be imparted to society, the State, and the Church. It was an age of reason, too, in its emphasis upon conceptual rather than symbolic thinking; in its Protestantism; in its increasingly utilitarian spirit. Such aspects of English thought and life are scarcely to be accounted for on the basis of literary or aesthetic theory.

Our approach to the Restoration must, in short, if it is in any way to take account of all the insights which modern criticism and cultural history have given us, be made from a great many directions and at more than one level. The day has passed when those whose chief concern is with the letters of the period—of this period or of any other—can afford, or indeed have any inclination, to isolate literary art from its immediate backgrounds, social, political, intellectual. This is not to say that the qualities of art are not *sui generis*, nor is it to confuse sociology with aesthetics. It is merely to be guided by an awareness, perhaps never keener than in our own day, that the human spirit reveals itself through time and history. There is a relationship between all aspects of an age, and though this relationship is too complex a thing (retaining even in analysis a measure of that vitality and viability which informed the actual events) ever to be diagrammed in the same way by two different observers, the matrix is not in doubt. The sections which follow, dealing with the political and religious background, with the intellectual climate, and with certain literary characteristics of the Restoration era, are not intended to be more than suggestive notes. Though they will serve, it is hoped, to alert the reader to the presence of various currents and focal centers of thought and feeling, their chief purpose is to emphasize the fact that the unity of the age is to be understoood only in terms of its complexities.

1. *Political and Religious Background*

It was in May, 1660, that Charles landed at Dover and made his triumphant progress up to London to be greeted along the way with strewn flowers, cheers, and other manifestations of relief and joy. The troubles and uncertainties of the past were over, so it was hoped, and peace and order lay ahead. The difficulty was that no one was quite sure what sort of order had now been restored or how it should be maintained. The King himself had, perhaps, as clear an idea as anyone. He desired a settlement of the religious problems on a broad basis, and a political arrangement which would assure him his throne while at the same time engaging the constructive energies of Parliament. But the forces which had brought about the downfall of his father, which had led to Commonwealth, Protectorate, and at last to that reaction against Puritanism to which the house of Stuart now owed its restoration, had not as yet settled into equilibrium. Charles, in the early days of his reign, was well-intentioned; he knew what he wanted for himself and for his subjects, but he was naïve to hope for peace and order on such easy terms. A new element in society had been emerging in England since the Tudors and its rise had been accelerated by the Civil Wars and the period of Puritan dominance. The middle class, which by the beginning of the eighteenth century was to be well established and conscious of itself, was as yet scarcely aware of its own identity; but its power had begun to make itself felt in various ways: in favor of property and commerce, against the concept of a rigidly unified and controlled state, and for Parliament in any future struggle between that body and the crown. In another sphere, the religious issues which had burned so fiercely from the time of Laud were not yet to be composed in any simple and ready fashion. The status of Roman Catholics was not a dead issue, as events were so grimly to prove; and upon the reëstablishment of the Church of England the rift between Anglican and Dissenter was widened, not narrowed. Finally, in regard to constitutional matters arising out of the day-to-day necessities of government, there were still no charted directions for the guidance of King, Parliament, or ministers. The principle of King in Parliament was, indeed, in the process of being established and with the accession of William and Mary in 1689 it was to be openly acknowledged by all, but that acknowledgment came only as the climax of a long struggle which saw Charles II pitting all his political acumen against Parliament and winning, and James II defying Parliament and losing his throne.

A bare chronicle of the most significant events in Restoration political history must include a reference to the war with Holland, known as the Second Dutch War, which broke out unofficially in the winter of 1663–1664, and, after a formal declaration of hostilities in March, 1665, was concluded by treaty in 1667. The causes of the war were entirely commercial, the after-effects, political. It was as a consequence of the general dissatisfaction attendant upon England's by no means distinguished record during these hostilities that Clarendon, Charles's first minister and the Duke of York's father-in-law, fell from office in 1667, and to escape the wrath of Parliament fled to the continent where he died in 1674. The vacuum thus created came in time to be filled by the famous "Cabal," an inner group of Privy Councilors (Clifford, Ashley, Buckingham, Arlington, Lauderdale), whose initials made up the term by which they came to be designated. Now that peace with Holland had been made, there were many representatives of the aristocratic and governing class who were quite clear as to the necessity of England's aligning herself with the Protestant forces of Europe against the growing power of Louis XIV. In 1668 it seemed that such a foreign policy was about to be embraced, and under Temple's diplomatic auspices the Triple Alliance was concerted between England, Sweden, and the Netherlands. By this time, however, Charles had begun to commit himself —and his Cabal—to an entirely different line. There are quite contradictory views as to the causes and motives which brought him to this course. Some would have it that he was forced to turn to Louis for the funds which his own Parliament persistently withheld. Others are of the belief that he was bent upon constructing a new political tyranny in alliance with Louis and continental absolutism. The results, in any case, were the Secret Treaty of Dover, signed in May, 1670, between Charles and Louis; the third Dutch War (1672–1674); Charles's Declaration of Indulgence (1672), which suspended the laws against Nonconformists and Roman Catholics; Parliament's angry rejoinder thereto in the form of the Test Act of 1673, which excluded from all civil and military offices those who would not take the sacrament according to the rites of the Church of England; and the sequence of events leading on to the formation of the Country or Opposition Party under the Earl of Shaftesbury, who had been a member of the now dissolved Cabal. The closing chapter in the history of Charles's reign begins in the autumn of 1678 with Titus Oates's dubious disclosures concerning a Popish Plot, and proceeds through a series of situations marked by a constantly rising tension to the royal dissolution of the Third Whig (or Oxford) Parliament on March 28, 1681. The last session of the Cavalier Parliament, which had first met seventeen years before in 1661, came during the closing days of 1678, when the hysteria excited by the Plot was at its height. In the Parliaments which followed—the so-called Whig Parliaments of 1679, 1680–1681, and 1681—the Opposition, which had now acquired the name of Whig while those of the Court Party were coming to be known as Tories—sought to put through legislation excluding the Catholic Duke of York from the succession. In this the Whigs would perhaps have come closer to success had not some of their own numbers—like, notably, Halifax—been increasingly repelled by the personality of Shaftesbury, the prime mover for Exclusion, with the result that on several occasions they aided in blocking the Exclusion Bill in Parliament. The King, meanwhile, bided his time. When he suddenly dissolved the Parliament which had met at Oxford in March, 1681, the Opposition was broken, and it was not many months before Shaftesbury fled abroad. With Lawrence Hyde, Earl of Rochester, as chief minister, the reign of Charles came to an end under conditions ironically different from those envisaged either by the King or his subjects fifteen years previously.

If Charles was a dangerous man—there are those who believe that he was—it was in no small part because he was a very clever one underneath his apparent indifference—clever, and within certain limits a most astute politician. His brother James provided a great contrast: principled, stubborn, completely inept in all of his relations with his subjects. Blind to recent history, he issued his Declaration of Indulgence in May, 1688. When Sancroft, Archbishop of Canterbury, and the six bishops resisted this, James ordered their prosecution. Their acquittal served as prelude to the action which was now concerted by men who for the moment thought of themselves as Englishmen rather than as spokesmen of any political party. James fled, the Convention met, and in February, 1689, William and Mary were proclaimed. The Bill of Rights in the political realm and the Toleration Act in the religious gave acknowledgment to principles which had perhaps been immanent in English society since 1660 but which only the force of events could bring to clear and open articulation.

In turning from the political to the religious backgrounds of the period, we should do well to remind ourselves that the entire seventeenth century in England was marked by a closer relationship between politics and religion than the modern mind can readily grasp. If there was somewhat less of this interdependence during the Restoration than in the half century preceding, if there were increasing signs that a development in the direction of a secularized society had now set in, religious and political concerns were still correlative to such an extent that it is difficult to understand them apart from one another.

The first years of the Restoration saw not only the reëstablishment of the Church of England but the accession to power in both the Church and Parliament of men who proceeded to deal with Puritanism in the most rigorous manner. The Clarendon Code (embracing the Corporation Act of 1661, the Act of Uniformity of 1662, the Conventicle Act of 1664, and the Five-Mile Act of 1665) was both a religious and a political instrument, insuring uniformity within the Church by steadfast refusal to consider the broader terms of comprehension which many had looked upon as being entailed in the Restoration, and signalizing in the nation at large the long-delayed triumph of that hereditary and governing class which had suffered various indignities throughout the Puritan regime. Perhaps it is too much to call the animating spirit behind this movement a persecuting one, but in some instances it bespoke a spirit of revenge and in most ways a narrowness of vision which if understandable seem all the more regrettable because they did not reflect the spirit of the nation as a whole.

For Anglicanism this policy carried with it certain obviously harmful consequences, for in driving the most resolute among the Puritans into dissent the Church thereby cut itself off from a psychic and spiritual energy the loss of which meant definite impoverishment. The intellectual intensity of a man like Baxter, the experiential intensity of a Bunyan—both of these were needed. For Puritanism the results were in many ways disastrous. Presbyterianism, with its aristocratic tradition of learning, found itself classed with enthusiastic sects drawn from the lower social orders. This loss of identity suffered by the older branches of Puritanism brought about, among other things, that drift towards Unitarianism so marked among the intellectual Nonconformists of the eighteenth century; while the depressed status accorded Dissenters as a whole was direct encouragement to seek for self-expression in material ways, always open to them.

There is perhaps no readier way to understand the position of the Church of England in regard, on the one hand, to the nation as a whole, and on the other to the Dissenters, than through the concept of the *via media*, set forth in countless Anglican sermons and books of the Restoration. As it was then defined, the "middle way" lay between the enthusiasm of dissent and the mere faith of Roman Catholicism—a faith, it was so charged, in despite of reason. There was strong appeal here not only to the innate Protestantism of so many Englishmen, but to a kind of moderate rationalism, widely entertained, which expressed itself both as contempt for the enthusiasm associated with the lesser sects and as trust in the rational foundations of belief. This being the case, the Church found tacit support among many whose respect for Anglicanism was merely hatred for Puritanism, but at the same time it drew into conformity a considerable number of earnest and learned men, chiefly at the universities, whose Puritanism had led them on to Christian rationalism. There were thus a good many forms of Anglicanism, more notably the wing that preached extreme royalism, passive obedience, and condign punishment of rebellious and murderous Puritans, and the moderate groups who would minimize the differences between English Protestants and who stood ready to redefine the terms of comprehension.

The idea of toleration in the seventeenth century was different from the nineteenth- or twentieth-century concept. To tolerate was to make large reservations concerning the fundamental rights of those outside the pale. In 1660 a State Church could possibly have been designed which, while preserving Episcopacy, would have offered more generous terms, or would at least have offered terms more generously, to those who had separated from the old Establishment. Total comprehension, however, could never have been effected, and in the absence of any strictly modern concept of complete religious freedom it was a question of out-and-out persecution or of some sort of toleration of those who deviated. In the light of history it is easy to see that the course which led to the Toleration Act of 1689 had in effect been set at the Restoration. Two factors, however, one political and the other broadly social, entered directly into the events and conditions which served to bring about the compromising settlement arrived at under William and Mary. The political factor was contributed by Charles and James, who in their desire to relieve their Roman Catholic subjects were under the necessity of including the dissenters within the scope of their several Indulgences. But when in 1673 Parliament countered with the Test Act, and when in 1688 the Archbishop of Canterbury and the seven bishops defied the royal order, the Dissenters refused all inducements to align themselves with the Stuarts against the Church of England. The Toleration Act, when it came, was not so much a reward for their faithfulness as an acknowledgment of a relationship between established Church and Dissent which was, after all, half kinship. The other factor, social in nature, which served to narrow the gap between the two Protestant elements is to be seen in the rise of the middle-class spirit with its prudential and utilitarian motives. It was said increasingly in the years immediately preceding the Revolution Settlement that continued hostility towards the Dissenters was bad for business and commerce. England, in short, was entering upon a new period in her culture in which the force and meaning of many of the older distinctions in religion were ceasing to have much validity.

2. *Intellectual Climate*

The seventeenth century constitutes one of the great epochs in the intellectual history of western culture. It was an age of genius in numerous fields of scientific investigation, notably mathematics, physics, mechanics, and astronomy. It produced Descartes, in whose philosophical statement the new picture of the universe was reflected. On the continent, under the influence of that *libertin* tradition fathered by Montaigne and others, there was a steady growth of the spirit of sceptical inquiry, directed at the condition of man in society and, as in the case of the inhabitants of the recently discovered continents, of man outside the European scheme of things. The pattern which is disclosed in the intellectual history of seventeenth-century England differs in certain notable respects from the continental. There was as great a release of energy, but owing to the fact that England was going through a period of radical readjustment in political and religious affairs this energy was directed somewhat differently than in France. Descartes can be understood without reference to his immediate social and political milieu; Hobbes and Locke cannot. The new science came to be as great a force in England as in any of the great European centers: Francis Bacon had kindled enthusiasm for a new method and a brave new world; Harvey and Gilbert, Sydenham and Boyle, and finally the incomparable Newton were to appear. But English science in the seventeenth century, no less than English philosophy, is set against a background into which the general interests of the age enter profoundly, as we can quickly enough convince ourselves by reading Boyle's works or Newton's theological writings. The shift in the world view which occurred between the beginning and end of the century could not be more striking than in England, but if the climate of opinion which had come to prevail by 1700 was one of reason and common sense, it was not a dominantly rationalistic one in the sense of being at odds with the controlling institutions of society and destructively critical of official views maintained by Church and State. The social and economic stability increasingly apparent from the Restoration onwards was the outward sign of the triumph of a new, middle-class civilization. It is the ethos of this civilization—at once speculative and practical, inquiring and yet entirely confident of itself and its future—that gives to English thought during the earlier phase of the Enlightenment so many of its distinguishing characteristics.

Since the present section, dealing with the climate of intellectual opinion, can in no case be more than a series of notes, something may be gained by taking Hobbes and Locke as central points and allowing certain ideas and intellectual attitudes of the Restoration to arrange themselves with regard to these two figures. And we may begin by asking certain questions covering both Hobbes and Locke. What are the implications of their political thought? How did they view the human situation? What were their attitudes towards literature?

As a political theorist Hobbes seems to draw energy from two different sources: his profound reaction against the disorders of his age, his fear of chaos, his fundamental conviction that man could, if he would, construct an enduring order; and his impulse as a philosopher to draw together into one great synthesis—and on the basis of what at first looks like complete materialism—the varied aspects of the human enterprise, social, political, intellectual, artistic. The result appears in his definition of authority, which is absolute and rests with the sovereign, who is to determine the moral code and the religion of the state. The implications residing in such a theory are too numerous for hasty summary, but a few may be cited. What has come to seem the chief significance of Hobbes does not lie so much in his doctrine of force, nor in the fashion in which he derived that doctrine both from psychology and physics, as in the fact that his observational point lay so far outside the circle of the traditional assumptions and values of English society. The thinkers of the Restoration were solidly allied against Hobbes, and it was in the process of refuting him that they brought to expression a set of doctrines concerning human nature and the state which embodied the principles and the spirit of the emerging society. Yet though Hobbes was in so many ways remote in spirit from this new society, it has more than once been pointed out that in his Leviathan the old scheme of social status and obligation has been quite supplanted by contractualism, in which respect he was voicing however unconsciously one of the controlling assumptions of middle-class civilization. But chiefly Hobbes's political analysis has come to symbolize that break with the past which was a profoundly psychic thing. The sense of an organic whole, a whole which defined all social relations as part of an order which imaged the larger one, was turning into something substantially different. Man was still a link in the great chain of being, but Milton's music of the Heavenly Spheres, which symbolized the harmony between man, the rest of the created world, and God, was fading out. In his increasing isolation man sensed a new self-sufficiency and a new self-confidence. The conceptualism of Hobbes—his description of experience by way of analysis and rational generalization—is highly significant. More than the old symbols were undergoing sterilization. The symbolic nature of experience was about to yield to those myths of the Enlightenment, that is, to reason and common sense.

To Hobbes the new situation presented itself as a perpetual challenge, an opportunity ever open. Because his own world was in crisis he proceeded to find in crisis the fundamental circumstances of all social life. His realistic analysis of human behaviour disclosed the drives which bring men into conflict with each other. But his conclusion was a surprising one: by means of our peculiarly human awareness of the conditions of existence we can work our way out of the disorders of natural life to the peace of the artificial state.

It is in his critical remarks and in his general attitude towards literature that Hobbes probably came closest to anticipating the spirit of the Enlightenment. His emphasis upon literary types and genres, his careful differentiations are significant. So is his insistence upon the depiction of the typical, the representative. The theory of imitation which was to do service throughout the age of the Enlightenment was here announced in its more important aspects. Literature taught and delighted. It dealt, each genre in its own way, with experiences that should be recognizably typical. And it was man-made, the result—like the ordered state—of an exercised craftsmanship and art. Hobbes's critical terms, which became the standard ones in English criticism, all called attention to the artificiality of literature, wherein indeed its glory lay: imagination—never creative in the Platonic way or in the manner described by nineteenth-century idealism—contrived the image which was the situation of poem or play and contributed the figurative language; judgment ensured propriety and common sense.

Though the principles enunciated by John Locke are in many respects not those of Hobbes, the two men differed far more widely in spirit and general outlook than is indicated by any specific points of disagreement. Locke's theory of government and the state was worked out over a long course of time and in the presence of that series of political crises occurring between 1670 and 1680—Locke was closely associated with Shaftesbury, living in the latter's home and acting both as physician and practical counsellor—but despite the fact that his ideas were formed during a period when so much still lay in the balance there is little in his writings which suggests an atmosphere of crisis. He is describing a society which has established itself beyond any power of *bouleversement*. The concept of force invoked by Hobbes does not appear. The individual has come into his own. In Locke's philosophical system single ideas occur first and then come together to form complex ones. Similarly in society as described by him the individual becomes fully mature before he enters into association with his fellows. Atomization can scarcely be carried further than in such concepts as these, but of course there was present in his thought much that did not appear in his analysis—a number of assumptions, that is, concerning the terms of contract between the state and its members which denote after all the presence of a common ground. Hobbes had shared with the older spokesmen for the ordered community a concept of an all-inclusive authority and control. In Locke middle-class individualism found its first convincing expositor.

On the subject of literature and the arts Locke said little, but that is enough to indicate his lack of interest if not his positive antagonism. His theory of ideas was, of course, to have a profound effect on eighteenth-century criticism, and the first chapters in the history of modern aesthetic inquiry are to be traced directly to his influence, but he himself felt none of Hobbe's excitement in the presence of man's artistic contructions, which he seems to have regarded as of only trifling significance. It is not here, but rather in his view of the human situation that Locke is expressing his profoundest convictions. We may explain much in Locke by reference to the empirical tradition, but we should never leave out of account the very large element of Protestanism present in all his thought, an element which was often the determining one. His rationalism developed many facets, but originally and fundamentally it was trust in the adequacy of human reason to interpret accurately the will of God as declared in Scripture. Such rationalism is directly in the Protestant tradition, as is likewise the sense of the limited nature of this reason: of the will of God we may know something, and though that be very little it is enough for all our purposes, our faith assuring us that what lies beyond our reason cannot be essentially irrational. The problems which Locke posed by his method of approach to the theory of knowledge, to morality, and to religion were all answered in the same spirit and from the same point of view. Man's status in the scale of created forms confers upon him only limited powers. Concerning God, the universe lying beyond the scope of our senses, and the ultimate moral values we must rest content with our practical knowledge. If only we will accept our human position, exploit fully the resources of reason and knowledge which have been granted us, and place our trust in God's love and the guidance given us by Christ we shall find our situation no mean one. The distance separating Hobbes's view and Locke's is measurable but great.

Though it would be impossible to take all Restoration thought into account by relating it to such themes as the foregoing, some of the more important movements readily suggest themselves. Three will be discussed briefly under the following heads: religious and ethical speculation; extreme rationalism and Deism; the impact of scientific thought upon certain other fields. The area of religious and ethical speculation is as vital as any that is to be distinguished in the complex of Restoration thought. In religion the reaction against Calvinistic doctrine, and in wider philosophic thought the reaction against Hobbesian materialism and egoism combined to establish a dominant kind of rationalism which found expression in the works of the Cambridge Platonists, in most of the Anglican clergy, and in representative writings in morality and ethics. We may perhaps go so far as to say that if there was ever an Age of Reason in England it existed during these decades of the Restoration—an Age of Reason by virtue of a conviction, both anti-Calvinistic and anti-Hobbesian, that the universe was one of order (as we should say, of value), that God's reason prevailed over His will, and that the light of reason which had been divinely infused into man showed him both the intelligent order that prevailed everywhere and his own moral duties. Other varieties of rationalism were, to be sure, dwelt upon. *Reason* sometimes indicated the rules of discourse, the "logic of the schools," or speculative understanding; sometimes it stood for the practical understanding, what could be known from the book of nature and from the various inborn senses of order, love, natural law, and conscience which were invoked so readily (to be rejected by Locke in the famous opening pages of the *Essay*); sometimes it was confined to that ethical reason which was regarded as distinct from the passions and the impelling will, and which guided us as God intended it to do so long as it held the passions in check. But more often than not it was used in a sense which served to center and organize that belief in the presence and dominance, everywhere, of meaning, order, love. And the most important development which was to occur within this area is to be traced in the increasing emphasis on God's benevolence and man's participation in the joy which motivates and accompanies such benevolence. It was thus that an Age of Reason prepared the way for the doctrine of charity, for humanitarianism, for sentiment, all of which were to be central during the eighteenth century.

Too much has perhaps been made of Deism as a factor in English thought. It must of course be reckoned with. It is constantly forcing itself upon our attention by way of personalities, books, and controversy, but it is doubtful whether it was at any point a main determinant, and to confuse it with French anticlericalism and religious criticism is to forget the nature of the English scene. Locke has sometimes been labelled a Deist. He himself always fought against this sort of classification through the use of controversial terms, and though it is readily apparent that Lockianism was made use of by later eighteenth-century Deists, we are to remember that Locke's theory of knowledge went dead against the main assumption of the Deists—the assumption concerning the adequacy of human reason to lead immediately, at all times, in all places, and without the aid of Revelation, to a belief in God and a sufficient knowledge of our mortal duty. As we look back upon the earlier Deists—Lord Herbert, Clifford, John Toland—we now see their principles as paralleling, some of the time, the ideas entertained by philosophers and divines who though rationalistic in many respects, some of which have been pointed out immediately above, were yet Christian rationalists, insistent, as was Locke, upon the need of Revelation and divine aid.

The relations in which Hobbes and Locke stood to the new science furnish us with a key to certain very important principles underlying the English scientific enterprise. Between Bacon and the youthful Hobbes there had been some sort of association, but the mature philosopher of Malmesbury was to take a course utterly different from that laid down by Baconianism. Hobbes was here the doctrinaire, settling the structure of the universe through ratiocination and assuming that scientific inquiry would proceed within such a determined scheme. Locke, though not strong in either science or mathematics, owed to his Oxford association with Boyle an insight such as Hobbes never attained into the nature of the metaphysical and epistemological problems attaching to the kind of scientific inquiry then taking place. In giving to human reason and to our knowledge of the ultimate universe the limitations inevitable to life upon this isthmus of a middle state, he was essentially in accord with great scientists like Boyle and Newton.

Something remains to be said about the general impact of scientific thought. Religion during the Restoration was scarcely ever at odds with scientific speculation, and through the argument from design it was shown in countless sermons, tracts, and lectures, particularly those given on the Boyle foundation, how the order and purpose revealed by scientific inquiry confirmed the grounds of religious and Christian faith. This was not precisely Locke's position, nor Bishop Berkeley's, but neither cautious empiricism nor an idealistic theory of knowledge could count for much against a set of assumptions in which so much of everyday thought and everyday good will came together.

The effect of science upon Restoration letters is most obviously apparent in the new prose style which was brought to perfection in this period. Many lines of influence converged, of course, to persuade the writers of the time to free their style of obscurities, baroque complexities, and erudite irrelevancies, to use the simple word instead of the unusual or highly colored one, to employ matter-of-fact imagery, practical similes. But there were other forces operating in this direction as well. The clear style was dwelt upon by a succession of Anglican divines, who described it in detail and urged its use in sermons and theological writing of all sorts as a corrective to Puritan enthusiasm and an outward sign of the rational approach to matters of the Christian faith. And the very nature of the more popular apostolate of the various Independent and Nonconformist preachers, to say nothing of the itinerant evangelists of the so-called Enthusiastic sects, necessitated the most rigorous attention to the elementary problems of communication. Simplicity and clarity of expression, and directness and homeliness of imaginative and emotional appeal were the indispensable condition of the appeal of preachers like Baxter, and still more Bunyan, to the masses of the population. In this movement the scientists played a highly important role, as the remarks on language delivered by Sprat in his *History of the Royal Society* serve to remind us.

No method such as has been put to use in the present section can be more than suggestive, nor can it be counted on not to pass over in silence certain lines of thought and certain specific ideas which were grantedly of major importance. The Enlightenment rested, from Descartes through Locke and on into the eighteenth century, upon a trust in rational intuition. Truth was to be known, that is, by the certitude which one experienced when one finally came upon it. The great shift which was to occur in modern European culture as the Enlightenment yielded to the spirit of the nineteenth century turned upon the abandonment of rational in favor of emotional intuition and certitude. Other criteria of truth which were entertained throughout the Enlightenment were simplicity and uniformity: the simple truth of early Christian time was placed in contrast with the false complexities of medievalism and Catholicism; the simplicity of the new astronomy as against the intricacies of the old confirmed the truth of the former; acceptance by the general sense of mankind was a certification of the natural and rational character of a theory or a belief. The contempt for enthusiasm—part of the great groundswell against the excesses of the sects if not of Puritanism as a whole—was often carried over into a kind of anti-intellectualism which sometimes took the form of a too great readiness to deride any form of intellectual endeavor not authorized by common sense. And finally, in the great literature that came to be written in the period between 1660 and the close of the eighteenth century, we find the myth concerning the normality of man. Every age and every society comes to some sort of agreement as to what is or should be normal, and proceeds to the prosecution of the deviates. The Enlightenment in England declared that all men were normal *in potentia*. Literature existed for their instruction and delight. Imagination was not emotional insight into absolute truth but merely that faculty by which the poet devised his fable and found appropriate language. It was judgment which assured the representative truth, the normality, of characters and manners. The theory of imitation was much more than a literary concept. It was the ultimate symbol, in this age which had discarded most symbols, of the human situation as it was then apprehended.

3. *Literary Patterns*

The dominant tone in which the attitudes of the Restoration embodied themselves in literature may first be approached through what is implied in the term neo-classicism. What that term means and how far it adequately describes some of the literary methods of the period is best answered in the work of the individual authors. But a few general considerations here will serve as a useful introduction to them. The term applies to aristocratic literature in particular. Classicism in spirit and in literary form, we may remind ourselves, was not new to England at the Restoration. The desire to civilize society and art by imitation of the spirit, the ideals, and above all the form and texture of the literature of Greece and Rome had exerted its first great influence on English literature as far back as Wyatt.

In him and in Sidney and, as Dryden loved to remember, in Ben Jonson, literary humanism or classicism had found its first great critical expression, directed against the prevailing literature. It looked to the models of expression and design which had flourished in Homer, Virgil, and the rest, which had been defined by Aristotle, Horace, and Quintilian, and which had been taught to wise citizens as a major part of their education by grammarians such as Priscian down to the dark ages. It demanded formal order and it sought to mature vulgar literature by imposing these models on it. But this classical outcry could be only partially heeded while the great intellectual and social energy of the Renaissance was expanding and was revitalizing and shaping to its own needs the world view and the still lively literary traditions of the middle ages, religious and philosophical, courtly and popular. How should the narrative pattern of Homer or Virgil affect anything but the merest arc of the surface of a *Faerie Queene*, swarming with the forms of medieval allegory and the transcendental philosophy of Florentine neo-Platonism and the images of the illuminated manuscripts?

Jonson himself, so classical a Renaissance figure and so proud an example to the Restoration, is worth pausing over for a moment. The formal unity of structure of his plays, and the universalized simplification of his comic characters as types can barely hoop in the exuberant abundance of the numbers and kinds of men he sets before us, the upsurge of their personalities, the peculiar mordancy rooted in medieval morality with which their creator castigates their sins. Yet it is the classical structure of his great plays which contributes so much to the final self-awareness and artistic detachment they bring us, and which gives its own sense of the universal, of the infinitude of life observable only in the particular finiteness of art and of typical men. His classicism is seen more clearly limiting itself in the fact that he expresses his view of character in the negative and disciplinary form of a portrayal of the abuses of reason. And in his critical notes the classicism is more simply dominant. His masters are those with whom *judgment* is a key word. That word supplants the complex steps of medieval and Platonic psychology by the idea of a simple, sufficient, immediate intuition by which man perceives the general in the particular, whether to make a moral judgment of what is normal and reasonable, or an artistic judgment of what in the parts is fitting to the whole. His poetry, finally, is classical in that it deals with social, moral, and critical reflections, seen in objective action: the good monarch and the great aristocracy, patrons of art and learning, working hand-in-hand with great scholars and great men of letters to create and maintain a great tradition.

But the neo-classicism of the Restoration is simpler and lighter. To Dryden, Jonson's language and wit will seem somewhat heavy and pedantic. Waller and Denham will be safer, more lucid models, and Suckling, the first master with Fletcher of "normal" diction, using the language of gentlemen talking together in the Court. The new classicism takes from the classics only what can best be accommodated to the new ideal of reason, and can best help to shape it. In aristocratic letters, it is an Augustan age.

Fresh translations of Virgil, Horace, Ovid, and the satirists occupy much of the time of Dryden and the amateurs of the Court, and intimate recollections and echoes of those poets and of Seneca, at least, among the moralists, fill the thought and the pages of the age. From them comes that simplified vision of Roman order and aristocratic responsibility, of Virgilian nobility and elegance, of Horatian self-possession, urbanity, and polished intimacy and naturalness that haunts the dreams of the educated men of the time, whatever their habitual practice. For the belief in a literary education and culture still prevails. The Renaissance had looked to literature as the force which sustained society by expressing, not without divine grace, its ideal vision of itself and by giving fame to noble men and deeds. The Age of Reason, with a more intimate actuality, hoped to see the great writers and the governing class, somewhat as in the age of Augustus, unite to form the ideal of taste, to define, illustrate, and give practical effect to manners, and through literature to lay its castigating finger upon the vices and follies into which men were led when reason, in the form of good sense, abdicated her function. The celebration of the monarchy was attempted by Dryden; but the royal family did not offer any genuinely grandiose symbol, and this is not one of the fields of Dryden's greatest poetry.

Altogether, the forms of poetry were limited and changed; the triumphs of the Restoration were in types of literature, both verse and prose, that had not reached such greatness before: satire, ode, epistle in verse or prose, didactic reflection in easy verse, lyric that is halved-Horace as Caesar said of Terence in relation to Menander. In heroic poetry, Dryden, in place of the epic he had longed to write, had to be content first to substitute his translation of Virgil and his occasional odes, and second to evoke the world of the epic as the contrasting background for his satires. Just over ten years before those satires, and while Dryden himself was in the midst of his heroic plays, *Paradise Lost* appeared and then shortly *Paradise Regained* and *Samson*. The Court recognized that *Paradise Lost* was a very great poem; but it is doubtful whether they saw its qualities or even the perfection of its classical form and style in anything like the same light as we. For example, Dryden's recognition of Milton's greatness did not keep him from "tagging" the verses of *Paradise Lost* with rhyme, nor from introducing something of Cartesian debate, in the manner of the political debate of his heroic plays, into the dialogue of the opera which he based on the great Puritan epic. In thinking of Milton in relation to the Court writers of the Restoration, one or two significant points arise. Between him and them there is something like a generation, just that generation in which the fear of enthusiasm and the idea of a very secular order and a purely lay scepticism were taking explicit shape. The nature of this change may be gauged by looking back for a moment to Waller. It had been an essential decision of his to write directly and objectively of man in the world of action as the classical poets and dramatists had done, and to set his hope in social discipline. But if in these ways he looks forward to Dryden, he retained an ideal of reason which was of the older, Miltonic age rather than of the Restoration. The great concepts of Reason and Nature and of Natural Law are present in both Waller and Milton, and it is the weakening of these concepts in Dryden and the literature of the Court which measures the distance between them and the great Puritan. Dryden cannot, of course, be gauged either in intellectual character or in scope of genius by the court wits. Yet it is in the climate of opinion which he and they share that he becomes the great architect of "neo-classical" literature, the simpler idea of reason based on empirical, skeptical observation.

Upon determining the meaning of the word "wit" much energy and skill were directed from about 1640 on; for the right use of reason meant an understanding of true wit as a natural and cosmopolitan use of the judgment. Cowley's and Hobbes's statements are landmarks (Volume I). Wit no longer concerned itself with the highest reaches, the thought and graces, the wonder that no virtue can digest into words, nor with mysteries hidden from the common mind. Its task was to free itself from poor clenches and other plays with word or poetic form, and from intricate, obscure, and multiple figure. Wit is now judgment made sensible in words, the same in all languages, finding out those differences in apparently like things which reveal the true and typical character of each and which in the end give man an objective attitude towards himself and the world. It sometimes perceives multiple meanings. These meanings do not signify the realms of the divine, the spiritual, the human. They mark rather the difference between insight and folly; they serve comedy and irony and give terseness to shining lucidity. To Restoration wit, exuberance and lyric diffuseness are also hindrances to swift, clear insight. Dryden's famous observation on Donne's lyrics that he was talking metaphysics to his mistress when he should have been making love to her sums up the thought of his age in favor of a lyric that should be no more than the clear and simple expression of a typical feeling; if dramatic, moving toward comedy of situation. Exuberance and diffuse description of sentiment or action and far-reaching figure had likewise to yield to discipline. Happily, we do not here have to consider the taming and caging in cold logic of Shakespeare's soaring thought and figures in the Restoration versions of his plays. We may rather fix our attention upon the transparent insights, the firm grasp upon certain central elements of order in human civilization which the age achieved, especially in developing the forms and the spirit of comedy and satire.

For these purposes the end-stopped heroic couplet became the overwhelmingly prevalent form of verse. Obviously orderly within a reasonable compass, even in tension, balanced, it enforced upon all its masters great definiteness and precision in thought and play of wit, combined as it was with a language whose ideal was the conversation of gentlemen. In the hands of Dryden, and more limitedly of Rochester and Sedley, the couplet proved an instrument marvelously flexible; easy, yet precise and energetic, in imposing form upon the insights drawn from common life.

Though we are not concerned with the drama, a word must be said of the influence neo-classical criticism exerted upon the stage not only by its emphasis upon the design and order of a work of art as a whole, a truly classical influence, but in two special developments—the conceptions of the rules of dramatic structure and the idea of decorum of character.

In alluding to this influence, we remind ourselves not only of the influence exerted by the study of the great works of Greece and Rome, and of Aristotle's *Poetics*, but also of the often more powerful influence of the neo-classical theory which had arisen in a century and a half of discussion; the body of "classical doctrine" which arose when certain supposed rules were drawn out of classical criticism, or when classical criticism thus drawn out was "explained" by the new theory of what was "reasonable." The term neo-classical criticism may thus mean either this body of doctrine, very remote from Aristotle, or a taste shaped by the spirit of the classics, particularly as defined by Horace in his *Art of Poetry*. The neo-classicism defined by us at first is that practical approach to life and letters which stems from Horace and the supposed pattern of culture under Augustus in Rome. It is, on the other hand, neo-classical "doctrine" that we have now in mind.

Restoration comedy owes much of its concentration and its skill in comic design to the ideal of the three unities, the simplification of themes, and the focus of the action in its final stages in a single place and within a brief time. In tragedy in England, the rules contributed to the monumental quality of *All for Love;* but serious drama never really simplified its action so that it could be amply realized within the formal time allotted to it. Dryden never transcended the shackles of time and place as Gustave Lanson said that Racine had done, by removing his action out of time and place into a psychological realm, and many of the real problems discussed in his essays are matters of the body of the drama and the energy of the imagination rather than of form. We shall, however, understand better what Dryden had to say of English tradition and of English taste in the themes and passions of the drama if we realize that he could not approach those problems of content, temper, and imaginative feeling quite directly. He felt bound to consider them rather as they were realized in the prescribed terms of formal structure.

The term *decorum* like the broader term *classicism* ought to signify two quite different things to the reader of Restoration literature. One is the profound ideal of the suitability of the parts, and particularly of the expression, of a work of art to the quality and purpose of the whole, so that its central insight stands forth lucidly and in perfect tone. This is the ideal which is to receive one of its great expressions in Pope's *Essay on Man* and which guides all Dryden's great poems. The other meaning of *decorum* embodies the conception that a particular social ideal is to be expressed didactically in literature; it is a sense special to neo-classicism.

For example, Aristotle had defined decorum of character as self-consistency and an integral relation between character and action. In the course of its evolution in the Renaissance, shaped by an overweening worship of the surface of things classical, this idea of Aristotle's came to mean, first, that characters ought to be treated in a modern interpretation just as they had been treated in classical works without variation of their characteristics. And, in the second place, that universality, integrity of character meant *moral* rightness, simply and didactically conceived, rather than psychological consistency. It is this second view which is important for us. When Sir Philip Sidney in the sixteenth century says in his *Defense of Poesy* that the poet shows characters as they ought to be rather than as they are, we can hardly be sure whether the "ought" signifies a psychological norm or a moral obligation. But under the pressure of a shifting social order and shifting social ideals, *decorum* comes clearly to mean something neither aesthetic nor ethical. It comes to mean suitability of manners, sentiments, and language to the ideal obligations or habits of a class, a class conceived not realistically but ideally, in a society which derives its ethical values from respect for an established political and social hierarchy. When Jeremy Collier, the high-flying and nonjuring Anglican clergyman, took up in 1698 the charges voiced by the Puritans of the 1640's against the immorality and profaneness of the stage, he had new weapons against them. His chief artillery was not a direct attack against the whole ethical and social vision of the drama, a more difficult task. Rather he excoriates the violation of decorum of character as we have described it: kings do not behave with kingly nobility, nor clergy as perfect ministers of God to the people. Dryden, commenting on Collier, kissed the rod for the lewdness in his plays and then rejected the idea of decorum Collier had used by appealing to more realistic social observation and a freer conception of the function of art in representing and criticising society. Still the idea of decorum played a part in some of his own criticism. And it is related to something significant in the sentiment of the age, something apparent in his own *Annus Mirabilis* and heroic plays, in his versions of Chaucer, and in his translation of Virgil, something that was to be most fully realized in Pope's Homer. In those works, the passion for *sententiae* or general reflections which overloads the poetry of Denham and Waller has become a passion for moral and social sentiments and sentimentalized emotion in the representation of the upper classes. By the time of Pope's *Iliad*, this sentimental representation attaches itself particularly to ideas of the hierarchy of government, to the obligations of leadership, to family duties and feelings, and to attitudes toward death.

With this conception of decorum of character goes also a related conception of decorum of language: the idea of a very special and elegant vocabulary for describing such persons, and of ornateness and figurative elaboration even in passages where no heightened emotion called it forth, other than the generally assumed elevation which, it was held, should form the texture of heroic poetry. The whole pattern of poetic language and of a remote, elegant, and formal world of ladies and gentlemen, ideal models and sources of manners, and exemplars of the more exalted emotions in a great society is already developed in Dryden, and we have therefore felt it important to define, though it is not illustrated in any of his work we have had room for except the fragment of his Virgil and perhaps a little in the tone of the ode on Mrs. Killigrew. It is a significant part of the sentiment of the age, akin to its expression of the heroic in Pindaric odes. In a sense very different from that applied to Crashaw, it has been called baroque.

In defining Court literature by considering how far it may be helpfully called neo-classical, we have necessarily put by an immense literary and cultural heritage which was not at all neo-classical. Dryden's art and the particular form which the classical models he studied take in adapting themselves to the climate of the Restoration and to the Age of Reason owe a great deal also to the heritage of a very great literature from the Renaissance. And there were immense social forces and literary and cultural traditions gaining fresh expression outside the world of the Court and little touched by neo-classical aims. Milton is too great to speak of in passing. Traherne is the last metaphysical poet only a little edited into classical neatness in what of his was published or prepared for publication. In Bunyan, the Puritan spirit achieved a great literary classic. Then too, Puritan mastery in the art of self-examination and in the diary as an instrument of that art, gives Pepys an essential training, as William Haller has observed, though only after the shift of religion and value which he made at the Restoration and only in the temper of the new age could the many facets of his personality have ripened and come to terms with themselves or defined themselves as they do here in the *Diary*. And will not Defoe still draw upon the same Puritan heritage for the singular gift which so illuminates his factual realism: his intensity in describing the effect of the minutiae of fact and outward situation upon a human consciousness in anguish and terror? The relation of Butler and Marvell to the Renaissance and classical heritage has its own character. Seeking the spirit of comedy, humor, and irony wherever she was to be found, they welcomed as readily in Rabelais and Cervantes as in Lucian her point of view and her modes of waging the eternal conflict against the illusions of egotism, complacency, and hardness.

The prose of the period reflects intimately and organically the growth of the new ideas of reason. But even while we must refer its tone, its expression, the shape of its sentences, and its ordonnance to the views of the functions of reason and the imagination held by its writers, yet in so far as it is an objective structure, a classical ideal helps to shape it. In France, the comparison of the new prose to the simplicity and the organic unity of the Greek temple was explicitly made. And we cannot doubt that the kinship was felt in England by others no less than, as one feels sure, by Dryden.

The idea of reason, then, would not have shaped itself as it did had not the literature of Greece and particularly Rome offered patterns of man and art in their norms. The formal analysis of literature was an integral part of this ideal of reason. And we shall enter most deeply into the age when we understand how it thought of the great types and of the styles as well as of the rules of structure of particular kinds. Epic, tragedy, the Pindaric ode, the Georgic were the heroic kinds and called for a harmony of tone, a consistency in the range of ideas and objects brought into play with the occasion and the character of the emotion dealt with. And so with the other literary types. The style in consequence will be high, low, or mean in accordance with this object; the diction and syntax familiar and easy or ceremonious; the figures grand in the heroes, appropriately mean in the comic, simple in the didactic.

Finally, underlying these literary forms and the conception of them was the spirit that informed them, and that may well be restated in closing. It is a thing more difficult to define and more consistently creative than the kinds and the rules, the idea of which might sometimes enlarge and sometimes bind and make rigid; and it was less explicitly discussed by the writers of the age, until the emphasis upon *authority* had passed into the ideal of taste. But it is the thing most constantly felt by neoclassical writers as the central fact of neoclassical literature, tying it very integrally with their own ideal in its broadest aspect. The sense of form, the idea that the structures built by men's imagination in a work of art have an ideal form likely to be the same in all ages and correspondent to the life of the imagination and to the judgment of the reader, is the manifestation in art of that sense of order so central to the age, an age which believed that the individual is most himself when he is most his norm; when he has the balance and poise arising from self-knowledge and control; and when he shapes his personality with constant reference to tradition and to the experience and values of the whole society in which he lives.

A Selected List of Books on the Background and the Literature of the Second Half of the Seventeenth Century in England

GENERAL

There are several recent treatments of this era from the point of view of literary history. An admirable statement is given by G. Sherburn in "The Restoration and Eighteenth Century (1660–1789)," one of the sections of *A Literary History of England*, ed. A. C. Baugh (1948). L. I. Bredvold contributes an excellent summary, "The Literature of the Restoration and the Eighteenth Century, 1660–1798," to *A History of English Literature*, ed. H. Craig (1950). There is a useful handbook by A. D. McKillop: *English Literature from Dryden to Burns* (1948). All three of the above contain bibliographical aids. C. V. Wedgwood, *Seventeenth-Century English Literature*, is a recent addition to the Home University Library (1950). Still useful are: R. Garnett, *The Age of Dryden* (1903); L. Cazamian, "Modern Times (1660–1932)," in *A History of English Literature* (rev. ed., 1935). Treating of specific aspects or of individuals are: A. Beljame, *Men of Letters and the English Public in the Eighteenth Century, 1660–1774: Dryden, Addison, Pope* (1881; Eng. tr., 1948); E. Dowden, *Puritan and Anglican* (1901); C. W. Previté-Orton, *Political Satire in English Poetry* (1910); H. Grierson, *Cross Currents in English Literature of the XVIIth Century* (1929); B. Dobrée, *Variety of Ways* (1932); J. H. Wilson, *Court Wits of the Restoration* (1948).

Vol. II of the *Cambridge Bibliography of English Literature*, ed. F. W. Bateson (4 vols., 1940) covers the period from 1660 to 1800 for both text and scholarship. Useful bibliographical compendia are to be found in V. de Sola Pinto, *The English Renaissance 1510–1688* (1938), and H. V. D. Dyson and J. Butt, *Augustans and Romantics 1689–1830* (1940). Of special studies, mention should be made of A. E. Case, *Bibliography of English Poetical Miscellanies, 1521–1750* (1935). An indispensable reference to modern scholarship in the field is "English Literature of the Restoration and Eighteenth Century: A Current Bibliography" (in *Philological Quarterly* since 1926). Other annual bibliographies are: *The Year's Work in English Studies* (pub. the English Association since 1921), *Annual Bibliography of English Language and Literature* (pub. the Modern Humanities Research Association since 1921), and the *PMLA* bibliography (pub. since 1923).

I. THE POLITICAL AND RELIGIOUS BACKGROUND

Bibliographies are: G. Davies, *Bibliography of British History, Stuart Period, 1603–1714* (1928), C. L. Grose, *A Select Bibliography of British History*, 1660–1760 (1939), and the shorter ones given by G. N. Clark in *The Later Stuarts, 1660–1714* (1934) and by D. Ogg in *England in the Reign of Charles II* (1934).

Historical treatments of this period of European culture are: D. Ogg, *Europe in the Seventeenth Century* (1925), G. N. Clark, *The Seventeenth Century* (1929), and P. Smith, *A History of Modern Culture*, Vol. II: *The Enlightenment* (1934). For England, the entire century is treated by G. M. Trevelyan, *England under the Stuarts* (15th ed., 1930), the first part by G. Davies, *The Early Stuarts* (1937), and the latter decades by G. N. Clark, *The Later Stuarts, 1660–1714* (1934), D. Ogg, *England in the Reign of Charles II* (1934), A. S. Turberville, *Commonwealth and Restoration* (1936), and G. M. Trevelyan, *The English Revolution, 1688–1689* (1938). Of more detailed treatments of particular themes and characters, there are: K. Feiling, *History of the Tory Party, 1640–1714* (1924), A. Bryant, *King Charles II* (1931), and A. Bryant, *Samuel Pepys* (3 vols., 1933–1938).

The political thought of the period is taken up by: G. P. Gooch, *Political Thought in England from Bacon to Halifax* (1914–1915), H. J. Laski, *Political Thought in England from Locke to Bentham* (1920), in *Social and Political Ideas of Some Great Thinkers of the Sixteenth and Seventeenth Centuries*, ed. F. J. C. Hearnshaw (1926), and in *Social and Political Ideas of Some English Thinkers of the Augustan Age, A. D. 1650–1750*, ed. F. J. C. Hearnshaw (1928). Special studies are: W. K. Jordan, *Development of Religious Toleration in England*, Vol. IV: 1640–1660 (1940), and J. Bowle, *Hobbes and his Critics: A Study in Seventeenth-Century Constitutionalism* (1951).

For the religious history of the period, the following are helpful guides:

For the Church of England: W. H. Hutton, *The English Church from the Accession of Charles I to the Death of Anne* (1913), and N. Sykes, *The Church of England and Non-Espicopal Churches in the Sixteenth and Seventeenth Centuries: An Essay towards an Historical Interpretation of the Anglican Tradition from Whitgift to Wake* (1948); while still useful is J. H. Overton, *Life in the English Church, 1660–1714* (1885).

For the nonconformists generally: H. W. Clark, *History of English Nonconformity*, Vol. II: "From the Restoration to the Close of the Nineteenth Century" (1913); C. E. Whitney, *Studies in English Puritanism from the Restoration to the Revolution, 1660–1688* (1931); and especially H. G. Plum, *Restoration Puritanism: A Study of the Growth of English Liberty* (1943).

There are many special studies of the various branches of Restoration nonconformity. Congregationalism: R. W. Dale, *History of English Congregationalism* (1907). Presbyterianism: A. H. Drysdale, *History of the Presbyterians in England* (1889). The Baptists: W. T. Whitley, *History of British Baptists* (1923), A. C. Underwood, *History of the English Baptists* (1947). Unitarianism: H. McLachlan, *The Unitarian Movement in the Religious Life of England* (1934), R. V. Holt, *The Unitarian Contribution to Social Progress in England* (1938), and for the earlier phases, E. M. Wilbur, *A History of Unitarianism: Socinianism and Its Antecedents* (1945). The Quakers: W. C. Braithwaite, *The Beginnings of Quakerism* (1912) and *The Second Period of Quakerism* (1916); A. Lloyd, *Quaker Social History, 1669–1738* (1950), and A. Raistrick, *Quakers in Science and Industry: Being an Account of the Quaker Contributions to Science and*

Industry during the 17th and 18th Centuries (1950).

Various aspects of the religious-social life and thought of the times have received special study, notably by R. B. Schlatter, *The Social Ideas of Religious Leaders, 1660–1668* (1940). Other treatments are: R. A. Knox, *Enthusiasm: A Chapter in the History of Religion, With Special Reference to the Seventeenth and Eighteenth Centuries* (1950), G. V. Portus, *Caritas Anglicana, Or An Historical Inquiry into Those Religious and Philanthropical Societies that Flourished between 1678 and 1740* (1912), E. D. Bebb, *Nonconformity and Social and Economic Life, 1660–1800* (1935), M. G. Jones, *The Charity School Movement: A Study of Eighteenth Century Puritanism in Action* (1938), I. Parker, *Dissenting Academies in England: Their Rise and Progress and their Place among the Educational Systems of the Country* (1914), and H. McLachlan, *English Education under the Test Acts: The History of the Nonconformist Academies, 1662–1820* (1931).

2. THE INTELLECTUAL CLIMATE

For the general background of European thought, two studies are of unusual value: E. Cassirer, *Die Philosophie der Aufklärung* (1932), trans. as *The Philosophy of the Enlightenment* (1951); and P. Hazard, *La crise de la conscience europée ne, 1680–1715* (1934).

English thought is treated by: B. Willey, *The Seventeenth Century Background* (1934), and M. H. Carré, *Phases of Thought in England* (1949). What was once the standard statement is still useful though often lacking in modern emphasis: L. Stephen, *History of English Thought in the Eighteenth Century* (3rd ed., 1902). Studies of particular themes and aspects are: A. Lovejoy, *The Great Chain of Being* (1936) and *Essays in the History of Ideas* (1948), L. Whitney, *Primitivism and the Idea of Progress in English Popular Literature of the Eighteenth Century* (1934), O. Elton, "Reason and Enthusiasm in the Eighteenth Century," in *Essays and Studies by Members of the English Association* X (1924), 122–135, R. F. Jones, *Ancients and Moderns* (1936), R. F. Jones and others, *The Seventeenth Century: Studies in the History of English Thought and Literature from Bacon to Pope* (1951), and D. G. James, *The Life of Reason: Hobbes, Locke, Bolingbroke* (1949).

The religious and ethical speculation of the post-Restoration decades has been studied from various points of view by: J. Tulloch, *Rational Theology and Christian Philosophy in England in the Seventeenth Century* (1872), H. R. McAdoo, *The Structure of Caroline Moral Theology* (1949), G. R. Cragg, *From Puritanism to the Age of Reason: A Study of Changes in Religious Thought within the Church of England, 1660 to 1700* (1950), F. J. Powicke, *The Cambridge Platonists; A Study* (1926), E. Cassirer, *Die Platonische Renaissance in England und die Schule von Cambridge* (1932), W. C. de Pauley, *The Candle of the Lord: Studies in the Cambridge Platonists* (1937), J. A. Passmore, *Ralph Cudwoth: An Interpretation* (1951), R. Niebuhr, *The Children of Light and the Children of Darkness* (1944), and R. S. Crane, "Suggestions toward a genealogy of the 'Man of Feeling,'" *ELH* I (1934), 205–230.

The more extreme rationalism of the era is considered by: F. R. Tennant, *Miracle and Its Philosophical Presuppositions* (1925), J. Orr, *English Deism: Its Roots and Its Fruits* (1934), J. M. Creed and J. S. B. Smith, *Religious Thought in the Eighteenth Century Illustrated from Writers of the Period* (1934), O. M. Griffiths, *Religion and Learning. A Study in English Presbyterian Thought from the Bartholomew Ejections (1662) to the Foundation of the Unitarian Movement* (1935), and E. C. Mossner, *Bishop Butler and the Age of Reason: A Study in the History of Thought* (1936).

Modern scholarship in the scientific thought of the period and its spreading influence is dealt with bibliographically in the

"Critical Bibliography of the History and Philosophy of Science and of the History of Civilization" (in *Isis* since 1913), and by F. A. Dudley, *The Relations of Literature and Science: A Selected Bibliography, 1930–1949* (1949). For the general reader the best introductions to seventeenth-century science and its impact on general thought are: W. C. Dampier, *A History of Science and Its Relations with Philosophy and Religion* (4th ed., 1949), A. N. Whitehead, *Science and the Modern World* (1925), and E. A. Burtt, *The Metaphysical Foundations of Modern Physical Science* (1925). The Royal Society is treated by: H. B. Wheatley, *The Early History of the Royal Society* (1905), W. Huggins, *The Royal Society or, Science in State and in the Schools* (1906), H. Lyons, *The Royal Society, 1660–1940* (1944). Studies of especial interest are: M. Nicolson, *The Microscope and English Imagination* (1935), *A World in the Moon: A Study of the Changing Attitude toward the Moon in the Seventeenth and Eighteenth Centuries* (1936), and "Cosmic Voyages," *ELH* VII (1940), 83–107; W. E. Houghton, "The English Virtuoso in the Seventeenth Century," *JHI* III (1942), 51–73, 190–219; three articles by R. F. Jones, "Science and English Prose Style in the Third Quarter of the Seventeenth Century," "Science and Language in England of the Mid-Seventeenth Century," and "Science and Criticism in the Neo-Classical Age of English Literature," all reprinted in R. F. Jones, *The Seventeenth Century: Studies in the History of English Thought and Literature from Bacon to Pope* (1951); and G. N. Clark, *Science and Social Welfare in the Age of Newton* (rev. ed., 1949). Other studies which might be given here are listed below, in the section concerning literary patterns, in connection with the effect of science on the verse and the prose style of this period.

3. LITERARY PATTERNS

The most comprehensive survey of the taste of the period is by B. S. Allen, *Tides in English Taste (1619–1800)* (1937). More specialized but helpful is W. J. Bate, *From Classic to Romantic: Premises of Taste in Eighteenth-Century England* (1946). A biographical treatment is: J. W. Draper, *Eighteenth Century English Aesthetics: A Bibliography* (1931). Important aspects are dealt with by: G. Williamson, "The Restoration Revolt against Enthusiasm," *SP* XXX (1933), 571–603; and in two articles by D. F. Bond, "Distrust of the Imagination in English Neo-Classicism," *PQ* XIV (1935), 54–69, and "The Neo-Classical Psychology of the Imagination," *ELH* IV (1937), 245–264.

The French background of neo-classicism is treated by: R. Bray, *La formation de la doctrine classique en France* (1927). Varied approaches to English neo-classicism are to be found in: L. I. Bredvold, "The Rise of English Classicism: Study in Methodology," *CL* II (1950), 253–268; S. Vines, *The Course of English Classicism* (1930); and two articles by P. S. Wood, "Native Elements in English Neo-Classicism," *MP* XXIV (1926), 201–208, and "The Opposition to Neo-Classicism in England, 1660–1700," *PMLA* XLIII (1928), 182–197.

Rhetorical theories and practices are taken up by: D. L. Clark, *Rhetoric and Poetry in the Renaissance* (1922), R. C. Wallerstein, "The Development of the Rhetoric and Metre of the Heroic Couplet," *PMLA* L (1935), 166–209, G. Williamson, "The Rhetorical Pattern of Neo-Classical Wit," *MP* XXXIII (1935), 55–81, and H. T. Swedenberg, Jr., *The Theory of the Epic in England, 1650–1800* (1944).

Three modern studies of the influence of science upon the poetry of the age are illuminating: M. H. Nicolson, *Newton Demands the Muse: Newton's 'Optics' and the Eighteenth Century Poets* (1946), and *The Breaking of the Circle: Studies in the Effect of the "New Science" upon Seventeenth Century Poetry* (1950); D. Bush, *Science and English Poetry: A Historical Sketch, 1590–1950* (1950).

The best collection of English literary criticism and still the most helpful general discussion of the critical patterns developing during the period are afforded by: *Critical Essays of the Seventeenth Century*, ed. J. E. Spingarn (3 vols., 1908–1909). Other editions and collections serving special purposes are: *The Critical Works of John Dennis*, ed. E. N. Hooker (2 vols., 1939–1943), and *Dramatic Essays of the Neoclassical Age*, ed. H. H. Adams and B. Hathaway (1950). There are general treatments by: J. E. Routh, *The Rise of Classical English Criticism to the Death of Dryden* (1915), and J. W. H. Atkins, *English Literary Criticism: 17th and 18th Centuries* (1951). A helpful short introduction to the subject is: R. S. Crane, "Neo-Classical Criticism," *Dictionary of World Literature* (1943). French background and influence are authoritatively discussed by: A. F. B. Clark, *Boileau and the French Classical Critics in England, 1660–1830* (1925).

An indispensable study of seventeenth-century English prose is G. Williamson, *The Senecan Amble: A Study in Prose from Bacon to Collier* (1951). The articles by R. F. Jones, cited in connection with science and the intellectual climate in section 2 above, bear directly on the nature of the prose of the century. The fullest treatment of prose style in English sermons is: W. F. Mitchell, *English Pulpit Oratory from Andrewes to Tillotson: A Study of Its Literary Aspects* (1932). Other discussions of this important subject are: R. F. Jones, "The Attack on Pulpit Eloquence in the Restoration: An Episode in the Development of the Neo-Classical Standard for Prose," reprinted in R. F. Jones, *The Seventeenth Century: History of English Thought and Literature from Bacon to Pope* (1951), C. F. Richardson, *English Preachers and Preaching, 1640–1670: A Secular Study* (1928), and C. Smyth, *The Art of Preaching, 747–1939* (1940).

Edward Hyde, Earl of Clarendon

EDWARD HYDE was born in 1609 in a family of country gentry. He entered Oxford in 1622 and took his B.A. in 1626. In 1625 he came to London to study law, was called to the bar in 1633, and rose rapidly to distinction. His friends during these years were Ben Jonson, Selden, Waller, Hales of Eton, and presently Falkland. In the early Parliamentary conflict of Charles's reign, 1628–1640, he sided with the popular party against the King's advisers until the demands of that party, and particularly their attack upon the bishops and the Episcopal Church, seemed to him to violate the long-established institutions of government. He then became secretly the King's adviser, often unheeded. In 1645 he became openly Chancellor of the Exchequer and was knighted. Through 1645 he prepared Charles's principal state papers looking to adjustment of the difficulties with Parliament. In 1646, after the defeat of the Royalists in the West, he fled with the Prince of Wales, who was in his charge, to Scilly and thence to the Island of Jersey, where he remained in exile after the Prince went on to France, steadfastly refraining from any effort to compromise with the new order. And there he began to write his *History of the Rebellion* from his immediate recollections and from many documents which he was able to procure. He brought it at this time down to 1644.

In 1648 he was asked to join the Prince on the continent and became his principal adviser in shaping the policies and forming the connections that helped to make possible the Restoration when the time was ripe. On his return with Charles he was created Baron Hyde, and at the coronation, Earl of Clarendon. At first, as Chancellor of the Exchequer, he was virtually head of Charles's government, working in a spirit of reconciliation though not, as it proved, one suited to the times. Gradually, partly because he sought to reëstablish exactly the constitution which in his view had existed in the Common Law before the war, and because he was out of touch with the economic and social revolution, partly for many reasons into which we need not go here, he became enormously unpopular both with the Court (which understood neither his ideals of conduct nor his restraint), and with the Country Party, and was deserted by the King. To avoid possible impeachment for treason, he resigned and left the country in November, 1667. Formal banishment by Parliament followed, and after years of illness, danger, and wandering he died at Rouen in France in 1674.

In the early days of his banishment, in July, 1668, he began to write his life for his children, to vindicate himself and his political creed. Here he depended probably entirely upon recollection. In 1670, however, when he had written down to 1660, his son Laurence was allowed to visit him, bringing with him the earlier manscript. In the course of a year Clarendon completed his *History of the Rebellion* by weaving together, with additions where they were needed, the original history and major portions of the life. It was first published from a transcript, 1702–1704. The best edition, from the original manuscript, is that by Macray, 1888. The parts of the life not incorporated into the history and a continuation begun in 1672 were published as *The Life of Clarendon* in 1759. The proceeds from these volumes have been used in accordance with his will to establish and support the famous Clarendon Press at Oxford, of which University he was a great chancellor from 1660 until his exile.

As Clarendon's many other writings are state papers rather than literature, we give no account of them. The list is readily available in the major essay on him by Sir Charles Firth in *The Dictionary of National Biography*. It contains also an estimate, not favorable, of several biographies of him. Firth has analysed the composition, the views, and the historical validity of the *History* in "Clarendon's *History of the Rebellion*," *English Historical Review*, XIX (1904), 26–54, 246–262, 464–483. There are comments on his work in the histories of the period by Gardiner and Ranke, and a brief but pregnant notice in Toynbee's *Study of History*. H. G. Wormald's *Clarendon. Politics, History and Religion* (1951) has taken issue with some of their views, reinterpreting Clarendon in the light of a fresh view of the history of his times. D. Nichol Smith's edition of *Characters from the Histories and Memoirs of the Seventeenth Century, with an Essay on the Character* (1918) contains a number of the characters from the *History*. J. Bowle *Hobbes and his Critics* (1951) brings out the conservatism shown by Clarendon in his answer to Hobbes.

Though Clarendon's immediate focus varied as he worked, in his middle years and in his old age, on the first draft of the *History* and on his *Life*, his work assumes a single massive design from which its universally acknowledged greatness arises. He wished to analyse for the instruction of posterity by what means the great society into which he had entered as a youth had been destroyed; and to define and vindicate the ultimate basis of that society in law, in order that its restoration might be secured. Incidentally he wished to vindicate Charles I as a constitutional monarch ruined by his evil advisers. Clarendon's conception of the law or "constitution" which underlay English society, and to which judgment about particular issues ought to be referred, is twofold. It is the Common Law and tradition of England by which the great institutions of church and state and their related functions have been defined; and it is in some sense the great medieval and Renaissance conception of law, the law of Hooker, the ideal of reason and moral law in man reflecting order in the universe, a law to which Common Law seeks implicitly to give the best practical expression.

This is his underlying assumption for the history of the events and above all of the men who are his immediate concern. For Clarendon sees the course of events as determined by the men who played leading parts in them. His portraits were expanded, treated with greater freedom and edge, and their number increased in the work of the later years and the final history. He had, like the great Greek and the great Roman historian to whom he owed so much, Thucydides and Tacitus, been an intimate part of the men and events he described; and he had leisure and recollection to weigh them. His characters embody his considered estimate of human nature in particular men, set forth simply, but with careful artistic finish. The great modern historians of the period necessarily remind us that Clarendon takes no account of the great religious revolution which lay immediately behind the Civil War, seems not to have understood it. Yet it is easy to forget that the forces of economic and social history live only as they enter into and form part of the characters and motives of men. To us, at least, Clarendon gives one of the most engaging, penetrating, and enduring forms of literature: the comment of a man of integrity, wide views, deep experience, shrewdness, and passionate concern, and literary sophistication upon his fellows in a critical moment of history.

from THE HISTORY OF THE REBELLION AND CIVIL WARS IN ENGLAND[1]

III. 34 The other, sir H. Vane, was a man of great natural parts and of very profound dissimulation, of a quick conception and very ready, sharp, and weighty expression. He had an unusual aspect, which, though it might naturally proceed both from his father and mother, neither of which were beautiful persons, yet made men think there was somewhat in him of extraordinary; and his whole life made good that imagination. Within a very short time after he returned from his studies in Magdalen college in Oxford, where, though he was under the care of a very worthy tutor, he lived not with great exactness, he spent some little time in France and more in Geneva, and after his return into England contracted a full prejudice and bitterness against the Church, both against the form of the government and the liturgy, which was generally in great reverence, even with many of those who were not friends to the other. In this giddiness, which then much displeased, or seemed to displease, his father, who still appeared highly conformable[2] and exceedingly sharp against those who were not, he transported himself into New England, a colony within few years before planted by a mixture of all religions which disposed the professors[3] to dislike the government of the Church; who were qualified by the King's charter to choose their own government and governors, under the obligation that every man should take the oaths of allegiance and supremacy; which all the first planters[4] did when they received their charter, before they transported themselves from hence, nor was there in many years after the least scruple amongst them of complying with those obligations; so far men were, in the infancy of their schism, from refusing to take lawful oaths. He was no sooner landed there but his parts made him quickly taken notice of, and very probably his quality, being the eldest son of a Privy Councillor,[5] might give him some advantage; insomuch that, when the next season came for the election of their magistrates, he was chosen their governor, in which place he had so ill fortune (his working and unquiet fancy raising and infusing a thousand scruples of conscience which they had not brought over with them nor heard of before) that, he unsatisfied with them and they with him, he transported himself into England; having sowed such seed of dissension there as grew up too prosperously, and miserably divided the poor colony into several factions and divisions, and persecutions of each other, which still continue to the great prejudice of that plantation:[6] insomuch as some of them, upon the ground of[7] their first expedition, Liberty of Conscience, have withdrawn themselves from their jurisdiction, and obtained other charters from the King, by which, in other forms of government, they have enlarged their plantations, within new limits adjacent to the other.[8] He was no sooner returned into England than he seemed to be much reformed in those extravagancies, and, with his father's approbation and direction, married a lady of a good family, and by his father's credit with the earl of Northumberland, who was High Admiral of England, was joined presently and jointly with sir William Russell in the office of Treasurer of the Navy, (a place of great trust and profit,) which he equally shared with the other, and seemed a man well satisfied and composed[9] to the government. When his father received the disobligation from the lord Strafford by his being created baron of Raby, the house and land of Vane, (and which title he had promised himself,) which was unluckily cast upon him, purely out of contempt, they sucked in all the

[1] Text: ed. by W. D. Macray, 1888, reprinted by permission of the Clarendon Press, Oxford

[2] conforming to the established church

[3] those who subscribed to the religions

[4] colonists

[5] His father, Sir Harry Vane the Elder, was Privy Councillor to Charles I.

[6] colony

[7] on the principle of

[8] New Hampshire and Rhode Island

[9] disposed

thoughts of revenge imaginable;[10] and from thence he[11] betook himself to the friendship of Mr. Pimm[12] and all other discontented or seditious persons, and contributed all that intelligence which will be hereafter mentioned, as he himself will often be, that designed the ruin of the earl, and which grafted him in the entire confidence of those who promoted the same; so that nothing was concealed from him, though it is believed that he communicated his own thoughts to very few.

. . . . .

VII. 267 He [Vane] was indeed a man of extraordinary parts, a pleasant wit, a great understanding, which pierced into and discerned the purposes of other men with wonderful sagacity, whilst he had himself *vultum clausum*,[13] that no man could make a guess of what he intended. He was of a temper not to be moved, and of rare dissimulation, and could comply when it was not seasonable to contradict without losing ground by the condescension; and if he were not superior to Mr. Hambden,[14] he was inferior to no other man in all mysterious artifices.[15] There need no more be said of his ability than that he was chosen to cozen and deceive a whole nation which excelled in craft and dissembling:[16] which he did with notable pregnancy and dexterity, and prevailed with a people, which could not be otherwise prevailed upon than by advancing their idol presbytery, to sacrifice their peace, their interest, and their faith, to the erecting a power and authority that resolved to persecute presbytery to an extirpation,[17] and very near brought their purpose to pass.

. . . . .

III. 148–152 The first design that was entertained against the Church, and which was received in the House of Commons with a visible countenance[18] and approbation of many who were neither of the same principles or purposes,[19] was a short bill that was brought in to take away the bishops' votes in Parliament and to leave them out in all commissions of the peace[20] and with relation to any temporal affairs. This was contrived with great deliberation and preparation to dispose men to consent to it, and to this many of the House of Peers were much disposed, and amongst them none more than the earl of Essex and all the popular[21] lords; who observed that they[22] seldom carry any thing which directly opposed the King's interest by [reason of] the number of the bishops, who for the most part unanimously concurred against it, and opposed many of their other designs: and they believed that it could do the Church no harm by[23] the bishops' having fewer diversions from their spiritual charges.

149. In the House of Commons they used that and other arguments to remove the prejudice from it;[24] and, as there were many who were persuaded that the passing that bill would be no prejudice and were as unwilling that the bishops should be justices of peace and in any other secular commissions as the lords were that they should sit with them, so they prevailed with others, who heartily desired that there might be no such diminution of their honour and authority, by persuading them that there was so great concurrence[25] towards the passing this bill, and so great a combination throughout the nation against the whole government of the Church and a resolution to destroy it absolutely: in which the Scots were so resolutely en-

[10] Sir Henry Vane the elder had purchased the estate of Raby and hoped if he won a title, to take its name from that estate; but Strafford, when he was created Earl of Wentworth, took as his second title Baron Raby, thus excluding Vane's hope.

[11] that is, young Harry Vane

[12] Pym, one of the leaders of the Parliamentary opposition to the King

[13] "a closed countenance"

[14] another Parliamentary leader

[15] tricks

[16] the Scots, who were used to help the Parliamentary opposition against the King

[17] destruction, total rooting out

[18] support [19] that is, with each other

[20] list of those commissioned to sit as justices of the peace (magistrates)

[21] favoring the party of the people

[22] the House of Lords

[23] could do no harm because the bishops would

[24] the prejudice against the bill

[25] agreement

gaged that they discoursed in all companies that it was impossible for a firm peace to be preserved between the nations if bishops were not taken away, and that the army would never march out of the kingdom[26] till that were brought to pass: but that if this bill were once passed, a greater number in both Houses would be so well satisfied that the violenter party would be never able to prosecute their desires. And this reason did prevail over many men of excellent judgments and unquestionable affections,[27] who did in truth at that time believe that the passing this Act was the only expedient to preserve the Church: insomuch as when it was brought into the House it found a better reception than was expected, and some men, who others thought would have opposed it, spake on its behalf, expressing their desire that it might pass.

150. There was a difference in opinion in this debate between two persons who had been never known to differ in the House, and the entire friendship they had for each other was very remarkable; which administered much pleasure to very many who loved neither of them. When the bill was put to the question, Mr. Hyde[28] (who was from the beginning known to be an enemy to it) spake very earnestly for the throwing it out; said, 'It was changing the whole frame and constitution of the kingdom, and of the Parliament, itself; that from the time that Parliaments began there had never been one Parliament when the bishops were not part of it: that if they were taken out of the House, there would be but two estates left;[29] for that they as the clergy were the third estate, and being taken away, there was nobody left to represent the clergy: which would introduce another piece of injustice, which no other part of the kingdom could complain of, who were all represented in Parliament, and were therefore bound to submit to all that was enacted because it was upon the matter[30] with their own consent: whereas, if the bishops were taken from sitting in the House of Peers, there was nobody who could pretend to [re]present the clergy; and yet they must be bound by their determinations.'[31]

151. When he had done, the lord Falkland, who always sat next to him, (which was so much taken notice of, that if they came not into the House together, as usually they did, every body left the place for him that was absent,) suddenly stood up, and declared himself to be of another opinion; and that, 'as he thought the thing itself to be absolutely necessary for the benefit of the Church, which was in so great danger, so he had never heard that the constitution of the kingdom would be violated by the passing that Act; and that he had heard many of the clergy protest that they could not acknowledge that they were [re]presented by the bishops. However, we might presume that if they could make that appear, that they were a third estate, that the House of Peers (amongst whom they sat and had yet their votes) would reject it.'[32] And so, with some facetiousness answering some other particulars, concluded for the passing the Act.

152. The House was so marvellously delighted to see the two inseparable friends divided in so important a point, that they could not contain[33] from a kind of rejoicing, and the more because they saw Mr. Hyde was much surprised with the contradiction; as in truth he was, having never discovered the least inclination in the other toward such a compliance: and therefore they entertained an imagination and hope that they might work the lord Falkland to a farther concurrence with them. But they quickly found themselves disappointed, and that, as there was not the least inter-

[26] the Scotch army which had come down into England, determined to see a Presbyterian Church established in place of the Episcopal

[27] good disposition (towards the King and the Episcopal Church)

[28] Clarendon himself

[29] In England there were three classes regarded as forming the body politic: Clergy, Barons and Knights, Commons; finally the three were fixed as Lords Temporal, Lords Spiritual (represented by the bishops), and Commons.

[30] practically speaking

[31] i.e., the clergy must be bound by what Parliament determined

[32] the bill

[33] contain themselves

ruption of the close friendship between the other two, so, when the same argument came again into debate about six months after, the lord Falkland changed his opinion, and gave them all the opposition he could: nor was he reserved in acknowledging that he had been deceived, and by whom, and confessed to his friends, with whom he would deal freely, that Mr. Hambden had assured him that if that bill might pass there would be nothing more attempted to the prejudice of the Church: which he thought, as the world then went, would be no ill composition.[34]

. . . . .

VII. 217–234 But I must here take leave a little longer to discontinue this narration; and if the celebrating the memory of eminent and extraordinary persons, and transmitting their great virtues for the imitation of posterity, be one of the principal ends and duties of history, it will not be thought impertinent in this place to remember a loss which no time will suffer to be forgotten, and no success or good fortune could repair. In this unhappy battle was slain the lord viscount Falkland:[35] a person of such prodigious parts of learning and knowledge, of that inimitable sweetness and delight in conversation, of so flowing and obliging a humanity and goodness to mankind, and of that primitive simplicity and integrity of life, that if there were no other brand upon this odious and accursed civil war than that single loss, it must be most infamous and execrable to all posterity.

Turpe mori, post te, solo non posse dolore.[36]

218. Before this Parliament his condition of life was so happy that it was hardly capable of improvement. Before he came to twenty years of age he was master of a noble fortune, which descended to him by the gift of a grandfather, without passing through his father or mother, who were then both alive, and not well enough contented to find themselves passed by in the descent. His education for some years had been in Ireland, where his father was Lord Deputy; so that when he returned into England to the possession of his fortune, he was unentangled with any acquaintance or friends, which usually grow up by the custom of conversation[37] and therefore was to make a pure election[38] of his company, which he chose by other rules than were prescribed to the young nobility of that time. And it cannot be denied, though he admitted some few to his friendship for the agreeableness of their natures and their undoubted affection to him, that his familiarity and friendship for the most part was with men of the most eminent and sublime parts, and of untouched reputation in point of integrity; and such men had a title to his bosom.

219. He was a great cherisher of wit and fancy and good parts in any man, and, if he found them clouded with poverty or want, a most liberal and bountiful patron towards them, even above his fortune; of which in those administrations he was such a dispenser as if he had been trusted with it to such uses, and if there had been the least of vice in his expense he might have been thought too prodigal. He was constant and pertinacious in whatsoever he resolved to do, and not to be wearied by any pains that were necessary to that end. And therefore, having once resolved not to see London (which he loved above all places) till he had perfectly learned the Greek tongue, he went to his own house in the country, and pursued it with that indefatigable industry that it will not be believed in how short a time he was master of it, and accurately read all the Greek historians.

220. In this time, his house being within ten miles of Oxford,[39] he contracted familiarity and friendship with the most polite and accurate[40] men of that university; who found such an immenseness of wit and such a solidity of judgment in him, so in-

[34] settlement

[35] Lucius Cary, second viscount

[36] "It is shameful not to be able to die, after thee, of grief alone." Lucan, *Pharsalia*, ix, 108

[37] habit of social intercourse

[38] choice; see Volume I, Ben Jonson's ode *To the . . . memorie of . . . Sir Lucius Cary and Sir. H. Morison*

[39] Great Tew, near Burford, actually about sixteen miles

[40] cultivated men and careful scholars

finite a fancy bound in by a most logical ratiocination,[41] such a vast knowledge that he was not ignorant in any thing, yet such an excessive humility as if he had known nothing, that they frequently resorted[42] and dwelt with him, as in a college situated in a purer air; so that his house was a university bound in a lesser volume, whither they came not so much for repose as study, and to examine and refine those grosser propositions which laziness and consent made current in vulgar[43] conversation.

221. Many attempts were made upon him by the instigation of his mother (who was a lady of another persuasion in religion, and of a most masculine understanding, allayed[44] with the passion and infirmities of her own sex) to pervert him in his piety to the Church of England, and to reconcile him to that of Rome; which they prosecuted[45] with the more confidence, because he declined no opportunity or occasion of conference with those of that religion, whether priests or laics, having diligently studied the controversies, and exactly read all or the choicest of the Greek and Latin Fathers,[46] and having a memory so stupendous that he remembered on all occasions whatsoever he read. And he was so great an enemy to that passion and uncharitableness which he saw produced by difference of opinion in matters of religion, that in all those disputations with priests and others of the Roman Church he affected[47] to manifest all possible civility to their persons, and estimation of their parts; which made them retain still some hope of his reduction,[48] even when they had given over offering farther reasons to him to that purpose. But this charity towards them was much lessened, and any correspondence with them quite declined, when by sinister arts they had corrupted his two younger brothers, being both children, and stolen them from his house and transported them beyond seas, and perverted his sisters: upon which occasion he writ two large discourses against the principal positions of that religion, with that sharpness of style and full weight of reason that the Church is deprived of great jewels in the concealment of them, and that they are not published to the world.[49]

222. He was superior to all those passions and affections which attend vulgar minds, and was guilty of no other ambition than of knowledge, and to be reputed a lover of all good men; and that made him too much a contemner of those arts, which must be indulged in the transactions of human affairs. In the last short Parliament he was a burgess[50] in the House of Commons; and from the debates, which were then managed with all imaginable gravity and sobriety, he contracted such a reverence to parliaments that he thought it really impossible that they could ever produce mischieve or inconvenience to the kingdom, or that the kingdom could be tolerably happy in the intermission of them. And from the unhappy and unseasonable dissolution of that convention,[51] he harboured, it may be, some jealousy and prejudice of[52] the Court, towards which he was not before immoderately inclined; his father having wasted a full fortune there in those offices and employments by which other men use to obtain a greater. He was chosen again this Parliament[53] to serve in the same place, and in the beginning of it declared himself very sharply and severely against those exorbitancies[54] which had been most grievous to the State; for he was so rigid an observer of established laws and rules that he could not endure the least breach or deviation from them, and thought no mischieve so intolerable as the presumption of ministers of state to break positive rules[55] for reason of

[41] process of thought [42] resorted to

[43] common, popular [44] alloyed

[45] carried out

[46] the early writers of the church (up to the fifth century)

[47] disposed himself

[48] of reducing or persuading him to their point of view

[49] his *Discourse of Infallibility* published 1645; again, with an answer to a reply, 1651; with several other treatises, 1660

[50] member of Parliament (for Newport in the Isle of Wight)

[51] meeting of Parliament

[52] suspicion and prejudice against

[53] the "Long Parliament"

[54] excessive demands on the part of the King and his advisers

[55] laws or explicit decrees

state, or judges to transgress known laws upon the title of[56] conveniency or necessity; which made him so severe against the earl of Strafford and the lord Finch,[57] contrary to his natural gentleness and temper: insomuch as they who did not know his composition to be as free from revenge as it was from pride, thought that the sharpness to the former might proceed from the memory of some unkindnesses, not without a mixture of injustice, from him towards his father. But without doubt he was free from those temptations, and was only misled by the authority of those who he believed understood the laws perfectly, of which himself was utterly ignorant; and if the assumption, which was scarce controverted, had been true, that an endeavour to overthrow the fundamental laws of the kingdom had been treason, a strict understanding might make reasonable conclusion, to satisfy his own judgment, from the exorbitant parts of their several charges.[58]

223. The great opinion he had of the uprightness and integrity of those persons who appeared most active,[59] especially of Mr. Hambden, kept him longer from suspecting any design against the peace of the kingdom; and though he differed commonly from them in conclusions, he believed long their purposes were honest. When he grew better informed what was law, and discerned a desire to control that law by a vote of one or both Houses, no man more opposed those attempts, and gave the adverse party[60] more trouble by reason and argumentation; insomuch as he was, by degrees, looked upon as an advocate for the Court, to which he contributed so little, that he declined those addresses, and even those invitations, which he was obliged almost by civility to entertain.[61] And he was so jealous of the least imagination that he should incline to preferment,[62] that he affected even a morosity to the Court and to the courtiers; and left nothing undone which might prevent and divert the King's or Queen's favour towards him, but the deserving it. For when the King sent for him once or twice to speak with him, and to give him thanks for his excellent comportment in those councils, which his majesty graciously termed doing him service, his answers were more negligent and less satisfactory than might be expected; as if he cared only that his actions should be just, not that they should be acceptable, and that his majesty should think they proceeded only from the impulsion of conscience, without any sympathy in his affections; which from a stoical[63] and sullen nature might not have been misinterpreted, yet from a person of so perfect a habit of generous and obsequious compliance with all good men might very well have been interpreted by the King as more than an ordinary averseness to his service: so that he took more pains, and more forced his nature to actions unagreeable and unpleasant to it, that he might not be thought to incline to the Court, than any man hath done to procure an office there. And if anything but not doing his duty could have kept him from receiving a testimony of the King's grace and trust at that time, he had not been called to his Council; not that he was in truth averse to the Court or from receiving public employment; for he had a great devotion to the King's person, and had before used some small endeavour to be recommended to him for a foreign negociation, and had once a desire to be sent ambassador into France; but he abhorred an imagination or doubt should sink into the thoughts of any man that, in the discharge of his trust and duty in

[56] in the name of, on the grounds of

[57] Strafford, Earl of Wentworth, Charles's famous minister, condemned by Bill of Attainder and executed in 1641; Finck, one of the judges against John Hampden on the question of King's right to ship money, who declared that no acts of Parliament could bind the King from commanding his subjects or their money

[58] He might have concluded from their exorbitant charges that they meant, treasonously, to overthrow the fundamental laws(?).

[59] in opposition to Strafford

[60] the party adverse to the King and, as Clarendon believed, to the constitution or laws

[61] consider, receive

[62] advancement or office from the King

[63] here in an unfavorable sense: a person who affected to be above feeling, as in stoic philosophy

Parliament, he had any bias to the Court, or that the King himself should apprehend that he looked for a reward for being honest.

224. For this reason, when he heard it first whispered that the King had a purpose to make him a councillor, for which in the beginning there was no other ground but because he was known sufficient,[64] (*haud semper errat fama, aliquando et elegit,*[65]) he resolved to decline it, and at last suffered himself only to be overruled by the advice and persuasions of his friends to submit to it. Afterwards, when he found that the King intended to make him his Secretary of State, he was positive to refuse it;[66] declaring to his friends that he was most unfit for it, and that he must either do that which would be great disquiet to his own nature, or leave that undone which was most necessary to be done by one that was honoured with that place, for that the most just and honest men did every day that which he could not give himself leave to do. And indeed he was so exact and strict an observer of justice and truth, *ad amussim,*[67] that he believed those necessary condescensions and applications to the weakness of other men, and those arts and insinuations which are necessary for discoveries and prevention of ill, would be in him a declension from the rule which he acknowledged fit and absolutely necessary to be practised in those employments; and was so precise in the practick principles[68] he prescribed to himself, (to all others he was as indulgent,) as if he had lived *in republica Platonis, non in fæce Romuli.*[69]

225. Two reasons prevailed with him to receive the seals,[70] and but for those he had resolutely avoided them. The first, the consideration that it [his avoiding them] might bring some blemish upon the King's affairs, and that men would have believed that he had refused so great an honour and trust because he must have been with it obliged to do somewhat else not justifiable. And this he made matter of conscience, since he knew the King made choice of him before other men especially because he thought him more honest than other men. The other was, lest he might be thought to avoid it out of fear to do an ungracious thing to the House of Commons, who were sorely troubled at the displacing sir Harry Vane, whom they looked upon as removed for having done them those offices[71] they stood in need of; and the disdain of so popular an incumbrance[72] wrought upon him next to the other. For as he had a full appetite of fame by just and generous actions, so he had an equal contempt of it by any servile expedients: and he so much the more consented to and approved the justice upon sir Harry Vane, in his own private judgment, by how much he surpassed most men in the religious observation of a trust, the violation whereof he would not admit of any excuse for.

226. For these reasons, he submitted to the King's command, and became his Secretary, with as humble and devout an acknowledgment of the greatness of the obligation as could be expressed, and as true a sense of it in his heart. Yet two things he could never bring himself to whilst he continued in that office, that was, to his death; for which he was contented to be reproached, as for omissions in a most necessary part of his place. The one, employing of spies, or giving any countenance or entertainment to them; I do not mean such emissaries as with danger would venture to view the enemy's camp, and bring intelligence of their number or quartering, or such generals as such an observation can comprehend, but those who by communication of guilt or dissimulation of manners wound themselves into such trusts and secrets as enabled them

[64] able

[65] "Reputation is not always wrong, sometimes selects wisely." Tacitus, *Life of Agricola*, 9. The sentence comes from a character portrait of Agricola which concludes that he was expected to receive an office, not on his own solicitation but "upon his being thought equal to the station."

[66] determined in refusing

[67] "precisely"

[68] principles of action

[69] "in the republic of Plato, not in the dregs of Romulus" (Rome). Cicero, *Letters to Atticus*, ii, 1

[70] of office as Secretary of State

[71] services

[72] a hindrance so based on mere popular feeling

to make discoveries for the benefit of the State. The other, the liberty of opening letters upon a suspicion that they might contain matter of dangerous consequence. For the first, he would say, such instruments[73] must be void of all ingenuity and common honesty before they could be of use, and afterwards they could never be fit to be credited; and that no single preservation could be worth so general a wound and corruption of human society as the cherishing such persons would carry with it. The last, he thought such a violation of the law of nature[74] that no qualification by office could justify a single person in the trespass; and though he was convinced by the necessity and iniquity of the time that those advantages of information were not to be declined, and were necessarily to be practised, he found means to shift it from himself, when he confessed he needed excuse and pardon for the omission: so unwilling he was to resign any thing in his nature to an obligation in his office. In all other particulars he filled his place plentifully, being sufficiently versed in languages to understand any that is used in business and to make himself again understood. To speak of his integrity, and his high disdain of any bait that might seem to look towards corruption, *in tanto viro injuria virtutum fuerit*.[75]

227. Some sharp expressions he used against the archbishop of Canterbury,[76] and his concurring in the first bill to take away the votes of bishops in the House of Peers, gave occasion to some to believe, and opportunity to others to conclude and publish, that he was no friend to the Church and the established government of it, and troubled his very friends much, who were more confident of the contrary than prepared to answer the allegations.

228. The truth is, he had unhappily contracted some prejudice to the archbishop; and having only known him enough to observe his passion, when it may be multiplicity of business or other indisposition had possessed him, did wish him less entangled and engaged in the business of the Court or State, though, (I speak it knowingly,) he had a singular estimation and reverence of his great learning and confessed integrity, and really thought his letting himself to[77] those expressions which implied a disesteem of him, or at least an acknowledgement of his infirmities, would enable him to shelter him from part of the storm he saw raised for his destruction; which he abominated with his soul.

229. The giving his consent to the first bill for the displacing the bishops did proceed from two grounds: the first, his not understanding the original of their right and suffrage there: the other, an opinion that the combination against the whole government of the Church by bishops was so violent and furious, that a less composition than the dispensing with their intermeddling in secular affairs would not preserve the order.[78] And he was persuaded to this by the profession of many persons of honour, who declared they did desire the one and would then not press the other; which in that particular misled many men. But when his observation and experience made him discern more of their intentions than he before suspected, with great frankness he opposed the second bill that was preferred for that purpose; and had, without scruple, the order itself in perfect reverence, and thought too great encouragement could not possibly be given to learning, nor too great rewards to learned men; and was never in the least degree swayed or moved by the objections which were made against that government, holding them most ridiculous, or affected to the other[79] which those men fancied to themselves.

230. He had a courage of the most clear and keen temper, and so far from fear that he was not without appetite of danger; and therefore upon any occasion of action he always engaged his person in those troops which he thought, by the forwardness of the commanders, to be most like to be farthest engaged; and in all such encounters he had about him a strange cheerfulness and companiableness, without

[73] persons used as instruments for this purpose

[74] of our basic ethical insight and responsibility

[75] "were an injury to his virtues in speaking of such a man." Tacitus, *Agricola*, 9

[76] Laud

[77] allowing himself

[78] the episcopacy

[79] or disposed toward the other government (i.e., Presbyterianism)

at all affecting the execution[80] that was then principally to be attended, in which he took no delight, but took pains to prevent it where it was not, by resistance, necessary: insomuch that at Edgehill,[81] when the enemy was routed, he was like to have incurred great peril by interposing to save those who had thrown away their arms, and against whom it may be others were more fierce for their having thrown them away: insomuch as a man might think he came into the field only out of curiosity to see the face of danger, and charity to prevent the shedding of blood. Yet in his natural inclination he acknowledged he was addicted to the profession of a soldier; and shortly after he came to his fortune, and before he came to[82] age, he went into the Low Countries with a resolution of procuring command and to give himself up to it, from which he was converted by the complete inactivity of that summer: and so he returned into England, and shortly after entered upon that vehement course of study we mentioned before, till the first alarum from the north;[83] and then again he made ready for the field, and though he received some repulse in the command[84] of a troop of horse, of which he had a promise, he went a volunteer with the earl of Essex.

231. From the entrance into this unnatural war, his natural cheerfulness and vivacity grew clouded, and a kind of sadness and dejection of spirit stole upon him which he had never been used to; yet being one of those who believed that one battle would end all differences, and that there would be so great a victory on one side that the other would be compelled to submit to any conditions from the victor, (which supposition and conclusion, generally sunk into the minds of most men, prevented the looking after many advantages which might then have been laid hold of,) he resisted those indispositions, *et in luctu bellum inter remedia erat.*[85] But after the King's return from Brainford,[86] and the furious resolution of the two Houses not to admit any treaty for peace, those indispositions which had before touched him grew into a perfect habit of uncheerfulness; and he, who had been so exactly unreserved and affable to all men that his face and countenance was always present and vacant[87] to his company, and held any cloudiness and less pleasantness of the visage a kind of rudeness or incivility, became on a sudden less communicable, and thence very sad, pale, and exceedingly affected with the spleen. In his clothes and habit, which he had intended before always with more neatness and industry and expense than is usual to so great a mind, he was not now only incurious[88] but too negligent; and in his reception of suitors, and the necessary or casual addresses to his place, so quick and sharp and severe, that there wanted not some men (who were strangers to his nature and disposition) who believed him proud and imperious, from which no mortal man was ever more free.

232. The truth is, as he was of a most incomparable gentleness, application, and even a demissness[89] and submission to good and worthy and entire men,[90] so he was naturally (which could not but be more evident in his place which objected[91] him to another conversation and intermixture than his own election[92] had done) *adversus malos injucundus,*[93] and was so ill a dissembler of his dislike and disinclination to ill men that it was not possible for such not to discern it. There was once in the House of Commons such a declared acceptation[94] of the good service an eminent member had done to them, and as they said, to the whole kingdom, that it was moved, he being present, that the Speaker might in the name of the whole House give him thanks, and then that every member might, as a testimony of his particular acknowledgment, stir or move his hat towards him; the which (though not ordered) when very many did, the lord

[80] bloodshed
[81] the first battle of the Civil War [82] of
[83] by the incursion of the Scotch
[84] repulse as to being given command
[85] "and war was one of the remedies of his [Agricola's] grief." Tacitus, *Agricola,* 29
[86] 1643

[87] disengaged [88] not fine
[89] dejectedness
[90] men of integrity
[91] exposed [92] choice
[93] "severe toward the worthless" Tacitus, *Agricola,* 22
[94] acceptance

Falkland, (who believed the service itself not to be of that moment, and that an honourable and generous person could not have stooped to it for any recompense,) instead of moving his hat, stretched both his arms out and clasped his hands together upon the crown of his hat, and held it close down to his head; that all men might see how odious that flattery was to him, and the very approbation of the person, though at that time most popular.

233. When there was any overture or hope of peace he would be more erect and vigorous, and exceedingly solicitous to press any thing which he thought might promote it; and sitting amongst his friends, often, after a deep silence and frequent sighs, would, with a shrill and sad accent, ingeminate[95] the word *Peace*, *Peace*, and would passionately profess that the very agony of the war, and the view of the calamities and desolation the kingdom did and must endure, took his sleep from him, and would shortly break his heart. This made some think, or pretend to think, that he was so much enamoured on peace that he would have been glad the King should have bought it at any price; which was a most unreasonable calumny; as if a man that was himself the most punctual and precise in every circumstance that might reflect upon conscience or honour could have wished the King to have committed a trespass against either. And yet this senseless scandal made some impression upon him, or at least he used it for an excuse of the daringness of his spirit; for at the leaguer[96] before Gloster, when his friends passionately reprehended him for exposing his person unnecessarily to danger, (as he delighted to visit the trenches and nearest approaches, and to discover what the enemy did,) as being so much beside[97] the duty of his place that it might be understood against it, he would say merrily, that his office could not take away the privileges of his age, and that a Secretary in war might be present at the greatest secret of danger; but withal alleged seriously that it concerned him to be more active in enterprises of hazard than other men, that all might see that his impatiency for peace proceeded not from pusillanimity or fear to adventure his own person.

234. In the morning before the battle,[98] as always upon action, he was very cheerful, and put himself into the first rank of the lord Byron's regiment, who was then advancing upon the enemy, who had lined the hedges on both sides with musketeers; from whence he was shot with a musket on the lower part of the belly, and in the instant falling from his horse, his body was not found till the next morning, till when there was some hope he might have been a prisoner; though his nearest friends, who knew his temper, received small comfort from that imagination. Thus fell that incomparable young man, in the four and thirtieth year of his age, having so much despatched the business of life that the oldest rarely attain to that immense knowledge and the youngest enter not into the world with more innocence; and whosoever leads such a life need not care upon how short warning it be taken from him.

[95] utter twice, twin forth
[96] siege [97] outside
[98] the first battle of Newberry, September 20, 1643

Samuel Butler

SAMUEL BUTLER (1613–1680) was born in Strensham, a village in Worcestershire, the son of substantial yeomen farmers. He attended the King's School in Worcester, but left at the age of fourteen to serve as secretary to one of the local gentry. Very little has ever come to light concerning the earlier period of his life, but he probably continued to make his living by acting as secretary to well-to-do patrons, and it is known that he was once in the employment of the Countess of Kent and later, in 1661, of the Earl of Carbery. The appearance of *Hudibras*, Part I, late in 1662 (it was dated 1663) was the beginning of a new period in his life, for the tremendous success of the burlesque poem quickly established him in Restoration society as one of the foremost writers of the age. The second part of *Hudibras* followed in about a year, but it was not until 1677 that Part III (dated 1678) made its belated appearance. After his death, Butler was often cited as a signal example of royal ingratitude, and the charge was made that Charles II had through indifference neglected to bestow any suitable acknowledgment on the poet whose satiric portrait of the Puritans served the reëstablished state so admirably. Certainly, Butler received no spectacular rewards from the crown, but it is now known that Charles, as a matter of fact, signed several orders of money in Butler's favor—whether these were ever paid is another matter—and it may well be that the patronage which the Duke of Buckingham extended to Butler came as a result of the King's intercession. In any case, Butler was in the employment of Buckingham for several years and accompanied him to France on a diplomatic journey in 1670. Butler is said, too, to have assisted the Duke in the composition of the *Rehearsal*. Almost all of Butler's certain work, *Hudibras* excepted, seems to fall between 1667 and 1680, the year of his death, and includes a number of shorter satiric poems—of these the best known is *The Elephant in the Moon*, directed at certain members of the Royal Society—and almost two hundred *characters* in prose. Practically all of this material remained in manuscript form until the appearance in 1759 of Thyer's *Genuine Remains in Verse and Prose of Mr. Samuel Butler*, where a good part of it was made available to eighteenth-century readers. Why Butler should have chosen to suppress during his own lifetime such a large portion of his writings—assuming the choice was indeed his—is but one of many unanswered questions concerning the circumstances of his life and the general nature of his career as Restoration satirist.

Hudibras was published as follows: Part I in 1663; Part II in 1664; Parts I and II together (and with the addition of the *Heroical Epistle of Hudibras to Sidrophel* and annotations) in 1674; Part III in 1678. Many spurious publications were fathered on Butler, including three volumes of *Posthumous Works* which appeared early in the eighteenth century. A quantity of previously unpublished material was given by Thyer in *The Genuine Remains in Verse and Prose of Mr. Samuel Butler* (2 vols., 1759). The standard modern edition of Butler is that in three volumes in the "Cambridge English Classics," for which A. R. Waller has edited *Hudibras* and

Characters and Passages from Note-Books, René Lamar, *Satires and Miscellaneous Poetry and Prose*. Zachary Grey's edition of *Hudibras* (2 vols., 1774) is still valuable for its annotations.

The enormous popularity which *Hudibras* enjoyed throughout the post-Restoration period is not difficult to account for. The savage repudiation of the Puritans expressed itself not only in the retaliatory and restrictive laws of the Clarendon Code, but also in a general attitude of contempt accompanied by a malicious delight in caricaturing the late rulers of the land. In the characters of Hudibras and Ralpho—Presbyterian and Independent—Butler, a master of caricature, presented the age with two incomparable portraits of Puritan hypocrisy and knavery, and his amazing bill of particulars—for which the anti-Puritan satire of two decades was drawn upon—his verbal wit, and his command of contemptuous rhythm and rhyme assured the contemporary success of his burlesque poem. *Hudibras*, in fact, continued to be universally read right down through the eighteenth century, and thus served to keep alive something of the fierce antipathies of the earlier period. Though there are some who would deny Butler any claim to true artistry, most readers have been ready to acknowledge his wit and his power of sustained improvisation, which show throughout the first two parts of *Hudibras* (the third part is pretty much of a misfire). The entire concept lying behind the burlesque poem was, furthermore, a striking contribution to English satiric writing. Scarron, in France, had already established travesty—in his *Virgile Travesti*—as a definite type of satiric poetry; Cervantes, long before, had exploited the possibilities of anti-romance; and almost simultaneously with the appearance in Restoration England of the new heroic tragedy the ironic possibilities of anti-heroic treatment had begun to suggest themselves. But though Butler may have placed himself under obligation to many writers, he succeeded in creating a new variety of low burlesque poetry which in its peculiar way—or rather ways, for the levels of intention and irony are multiple—is an imaginative triumph. Dryden for one, though acknowledging Butler's powers with characteristic generosity, took issue with this kind of low satire, in contradistinction to which he set up that refined and polished manner of high burlesque poetry so perfectly illustrated by his own *MacFlecknoe*. Not a little of Butler was to live on, however, in Swift and other eighteenth-century masters of comic incongruity.

Of the depth and sincerity of Butler's own anti-Puritanism there can be no question. From the beginning of the first Civil War he seems to have regarded the supporters of Parliament as fools and knaves, and we know that parts of *Hudibras* were written as early as the 1640's. But if Butler was anything he was an everlasting realist; he insisted upon seeing things as they were and analysing the undesirable facts. And what he lived to witness during the years following the Restoration caused a moral revulsion in him as strong as that which had previously been induced by the follies and sins of the Puritan usurpers. His *Satyr upon the Licentious Age of Charles the Second*, while inferior as satiric verse, is a most significant commentary upon the age. The most successful of his minor verse pieces is *The Elephant in the Moon*, wherein Butler has good sport at the expense of certain members of the Royal Society, here depicted as lacking the basic qualities of intellectual honesty and as greedily pursuing "things wonderful, instead of true." It is not an attack on the new experimental science as such, but rather another expression in imaginative-satiric terms of one of Butler's favorite themes, namely the futility of ill-judged or meanly motivated intellectual curiosity. The notebook of Butler's which has come down to us under the title of *Miscellaneous Observations and Reflections on Various Subjects* reveals clearly enough the theoretical bent of his mind, the seriousness with which he looked upon himself as a moral commentator, and his readiness to discuss the function and craft of satire in terms of the new criticism stemming from Hobbes and others.

Butler's most substantial work, after *Hudibras,* is his set of prose *characters.* Since they remained unpublished in his own day they had no effect upon his contemporaries. They are, however, not only the finest *characters* produced during the latter part of the century but an adequate medium for the later Butler, for whom satiric wit, while never ceasing to be in one sense a matter of words, figurative language, and verbal rhythms, had taken on more and more the aspect of truth, moral and intellectual, explored philosophically and represented by way of its infinite divergencies. He is least theoretical in *characters* like *A Bumpkin or Country-Squire*—social comedies in little, pointing directly towards the *Tatler* and *Spectator. A Ranter* is one of many sketches in which he is continuing the tradition of the controversial *character,* established as a well-recognized type during the period of triumphant Puritanism. *A Philosopher* is a good example of the satiric statement which carries with it much of its underlying intellectual theory. But Butler's triumph in the medium of the prose *character* is surely *A Modern Politician,* remarkable for its length, its wonderfully sustained tension, its moral earnestness, and the mastery of irony which it bespeaks from beginning to end.

Most of the significant modern discussions of Butler are to be found in articles, of which the following may be mentioned: René Lamar, "Du nouveau sur l'auteur d' 'Hudibras': Samuel Butler en Worcestershire," *La Revue Anglo-Américaine,* I (1923–1924), 213–227; E. S. De Beer, "The Later Life of Samuel Butler," *RES* IV (1928), 159–166; R. Quintana, "The Butler-Oxenden Correspondence," *MLN* XLVIII (1933), 1–11; R. Quintana, "Samuel Butler: A Restoration Figure in a Modern Light," *ELH* XVIII (1951), 7–31. References to other recent works of Butler scholarship and criticism will be found in the last article cited above. As an introduction to his edition of the *Satires and Miscellaneous Poetry and Prose* René Lamar provides a useful bibliography of the earlier appearances of Butler's works.

from HUDIBRAS

The First Part[1]

The Argument of the First Canto

Sir Hudibras *his passing worth,*
The manner how he sally'd forth:
His Arms and Equipage are shown;
His Horse's Vertues, and his own.
Th' Adventure of the Bear *and* Fiddle.
Is sung, but breaks off in the middle.

CANTO I

When *civil* fury first grew high,
And men fell out they knew not why,
When hard *Words, Jealousies,* and *Fears,*
Set Folks together by the Ears,
And made them fight, like mad or drunk,
For Dame *Religion* as for Punk,
Whose honesty they all durst swear for,
Though not a man of them knew wherefore:
When *Gospel-Trumpeter* surrounded,

[1] Text: *Hudibras. The First and Second Parts,* 1678. Zachary Grey's edition of *Hudibras* (2 vols., 1774) is notable for the fullness of its annotations. In the footnotes which here follow, the initial *G* indicates that Grey's explanatory material has been drawn upon. The symbol *B* indicates one of Butler's own notes, a number of which he appended for the first time to the 1674 edition of the first and second parts

With long-ear'd rout[2] to Battel sounded,
And Pulpit, Drum Ecclesiastick,
Was beat with fist, instead of a stick:[3]
Then did Sir *Knight* abandon dwelling,
And out he rode a Colonelling.
  A Wight he was, whose very sight wou'd
Entitle him *Mirror of Knighthood;*
That never bent his stubborn knee
To any thing but Chivalry,
Nor put up blow, but that which laid
Right worshipful on Shoulder-blade:
Chief of Domestick Knights and Errant,
Either for Chartel[4] or for Warrant:
Great on the Bench, Great in the Saddle,
That could as well bind o'er, as swaddle.[5]
Mighty he was at both of these,
And styl'd of *War* as well as *Peace.*
(So some Rats of amphibious nature,
Are either for the Land or Water)
But here our Authors make a doubt,
Whether he were more wise, or stout.
Some hold the one, and some the other:
But howsoe'er they make a pother,
The difference was so small, his Brain
Outweigh'd his Rage but half a Grain:
Which made some take him for a Tool
That Knaves do work with, call'd a Fool.
And offer to lay wagers that
As *Mountaigne* playing with his Cat,[6]
Complains she thought him but an Ass,
Much more she would Sir *Hudibras.*
(For that's the Name our valiant Knight
To all his Challenges did write.)
But they're mistaken very much,
'Tis plain enough he was no such.
We grant, although he had much wit,
H' was very shie of using it,
As being loath to wear it out,
And therefore bore it not about.
Unless on Holy-days, or so,
As Men their best Apparel do.
Beside, 'tis known he could speak *Greek,*
As naturally as Pigs squeek:
That *Latine* was no more difficile,
Than to a Black-bird 'tis to whistle.
Being rich in both, he never scanted
His Bounty unto such as wanted;
But much of either would afford,
To many that had not one word.
For *Hebrew* Roots, although th' are found
To flourish most in barren ground,[7]
He had such plenty as suffic'd
To make some think him circumcis'd:
And truely so perhaps, he was
'Tis many a Pious Christians case.
  He was in *Logick* a great Critick,
Profoundly skill'd in Analytick.[8]
He could distinguish, and divide
A Hair 'twixt *South* and *South-West* side:
On either which he would dispute,
Confute, change hands, and still confute.
He'd undertake to prove by force
Of Argument, a Man's no Horse.
He'd prove a Buzard is no Fowl,
And that a *Lord* may be an Owl,
A Calf an *Alderman,* a Goose a *Justice,*
And Rooks *Committee-men,* and *Trustees;*[9]
He'd run in Debt by Disputation,
And pay with Ratiocination.
All this by Syllogism, true
In mood and figure,[10] he would do.
  For *Rhetorick* he could not ope
His mouth, but out there flew a Trope:
And when he hapned to break off
I' th' middle of his speech, or cough,

[2] *G:*"Their ears appeared to greater advantage from the shortness of their hair; whence they got the name of Roundheads . . . "

[3] *G:*"Alluding to their vehement action in the pulpit, and their beating it with their fists, as if they were beating a drum."

[4] *G:*letter of defiance, challenge to a duel

[5] *G:*bang, cudgel. *B:*"Bind over to the Sessions, as being a Justice of the Peace in his Country, as well as Colonel of a Regiment of Foot, in the Parliaments Army, and a Committee-man."

[6] *B:*"*Mountaigne* in his Essays supposes his Cat thought him a Fool, for loosing his time, in playing with her."

[7] Grey cites Sir Thomas Browne's *Vulgar Errors* (5.22): "That children in the school of Nature, without institution, would naturally speak the primitive language of the world, was the opinion of the ancient heathens, and continued since by Christians, who will have it our Hebrew tongue, as being the language of Adam."

[8] *B:*"*Analytique* is a part of *Logick* that teaches to Decline and Construe *Reason,* as *Grammar* does *Words.*"

[9] *G:*committee-men appointed by Parliament were sometimes called rooks (i.e., cheats, swindlers) as a result of the way in which "they harassed and oppressed the country in a most arbitrary and scandalous manner . . . "

[10] *G:*in logic, "a due disposal of a middle term of a syllogism with the two extremes"

H' had hard words, ready to shew why,
And tell what Rules he did it by[11]
Else when with greatest Art he spoke,
You'd think he talk'd like other folk,
For all a Rhetoricians Rules,
Teach nothing but to name his Tools.
His ordinary Rate of Speech
In loftiness of sound was rich,
A *Babylonish* dialect,[12]
Which learned Pedants much affect.
It was a parti-colour'd dress
Of patch'd and pyball'd Languages:
'Twas English cut on *Greek* and *Latin*,
Like Fustian heretofore on Sattin.
It had an odd promiscuous Tone,
As if h' had talk'd three parts in one.[13]
Which made some think when he did gabble,
Th' had heard three Labo'rers of *Babel;*
Or *Cerberus* himself pronounce
A Leash[14] of Languages at once.
This he as volubly would vent.
As if his stock would ne'er be spent.
And truly to support that charge
He had supplies as vast and large.
For he could coin or counterfeit
New words[15] with little or no wit:
Words so debas'd and hard, no stone[16]
Was hard enough to touch them on.
And when with hasty noise he spoke 'em,
The Ignorant for currant took 'em.
That had the Orator who once,[17]
Did fill his Mouth with Pibble Stones
When he harangu'd, but known his Phrase,
He would have us'd no other ways.
In *Mathematicks* he was greater
Than *Tycho Brahe*,[18] *or Erra Pater:*[19]
For he, by *Geometrick* scale,
Could take the size of *Pots of Ale;*[20]
Resolve by Signs and Tangents streight,
If *Bread* or *Butter* wanted weight;
And wisely tell what hour o' th' day
The Clock doth strike, by *Algebra.*
Beside he was a shrewd *Philosopher*,
And had read every Text and gloss over:
What e'er the crabbed'st Author hath
He understood b' implicit Faith,
What ever *Sceptick* could inquire for;
For every *why* he had a *wherefore;*
Knew more than forty of them do,
As far as words and terms could go.
All which he understood by Rote,
And as occasion serv'd, would quote;
No matter whether right or wrong:
They might be either said or sung.
His Notions fitted things so well,
That which was which he could not tell;
But oftentimes mistook th' one
For th' other, as great Clerks have done.
He could reduce all things to Acts,[21]
And knew their Natures by Abstracts,
Where Entity and Quiddity
The Ghosts of defunct Bodies flie;
Where Truth in Person does appear,[22]

[11] Grey cites the story given in a French historical work (Marville, *Mélanges d'histoire*) of a sermon printed at Bruges about 1500 in which each place where the preacher had coughed with oratorical effectiveness was marked with a *hem hem.*

[12] *B:*"A confusion of Languages, such, as some of our Modern *Virtuosi* use to express themselves in."

[13] *G:*alluding to the old catches in three parts

[14] in sporting language, a set of three hounds, hawks, etc.

[15] *G:*the Presbyterians coined a number of words and expressions: out-goings, workings-out, gospel-walking-time, etc.

[16] *G* passes along the suggestion that *stone* might be emended to read *tone.*

[17] *B:*"Demosthenes, who is said to have a defect in Pronounciation, which he cur'd by using to speak with little stones in his mouth."

[18] Danish astronomer (1546–1601)

[19] *G:*a reference to William Lilly, the English astronomer (1602–1681), publisher during the 1640's of almanacs foretelling victories for the forces of Parliament. Lilly is the Sidrophel of *Hudibras*, Part II.

[20] *G:*Hudibras, as a justice of the peace, had the right to inspect weights and measures.

[21] *B:*"The old Philosophers thought to extract Notions out of Natural things, as Chymists do Spirits and Essences; and when they had refin'd them into the nicest subleties, gave them as insignificant Names, as those Operators do their Extractions: But (as *Seneca* says) the subtler things are render'd, they are but the nearer to Nothing. So are all their definitions of things by Acts, the nearer to Nonsense."

[22] *B:*"Some Authors have mistaken Truth for a Real thing, when it is nothing but a right Method of putting those Notions, or Images of things (in the understanding of Man) into the same state and order, that their Originals hold in Nature, and therefore *Aristotle* says, *unumquodque sicut se habet secundum esse, ita se habet secundum veritatem.* Met. I. 2."

Like words congeal'd in Northern Air.[23]
He knew *what's what*, and that's as high
As *Metaphysick* Wit can fly,
In *School Divinity* as able
As he that hight *Irrefragable;*[24]
Profound in all the Nominal
And real ways beyond them all;
And with as delicate a Hand,
Could twist as tough a Rope of Sand.
And weave fine Cobwebs, fit for Skull[25]
That's empty when the Moon is full;
Such as take Lodgings in a Head
That's to be left unfurnished.
He could raise Scruples dark and nice,
And after solve 'em in a trice:
As if Divinity had catch'd
The Itch, of purpose to be scratch'd;
Or, like a Mountebank, did wound
And stab her self with doubts profound,
Only to shew with how small pain
The sores of faith are cur'd again;
Although by woful proof we find,
They always leave a Scar behind.
He knew the Seat of Paradise,[26]
Could tell in what degree it lies:
And as he was dispos'd, could prove it,
Below the Moon, or else above it
What *Adam* dreamt of when his Bride
Came from her Closet in his side:
Whether the Devil tempted her
By a *High Dutch* Interpreter:[27]
If either of them had a Navel;[28]
Who first made Musick malleable:[29]
Whether the Serpent at the fall
Had cloven Feet, or none at all.
All this without a Gloss or Comment,
He would unriddle in a moment:
In proper terms, such as men smatter
When they throw out and miss the matter.
  For his *Religion* it was fit
To match his Learning and his Wit:
'Twas *Presbyterian* true blew,
For he was of that stubborn Crew
Of Errant Saints, whom all men grant
To be the true Church *Militant:*
Such as do build their Faith upon
The holy Text of *Pike* and *Gun;*
Decide all Controversies by
Infallible *Artillery;*
And prove their Doctrine Orthodox
By Apostolick *Blows* and *Knocks;*
Call Fire and Sword and Desolation,
A *godly-thorough-Reformation,*[30]
Which always must be carry'd on,
And still be doing, never done:
As if Religion were intended
For nothing else but to be mended.
A Sect, whose chief Devotion lies
In odd perverse Antipathies;
In falling out with that or this,
And finding somewhat still amiss:
More peevish, cross, and splenetick,
That Dog distract, or Monky sick.
That with more care keep Holy-day
The wrong,[31] than others the right way:
Compound for Sins, they are inclin'd to;
By damning those they have no mind to;
Still so perverse and opposite,
As if they worshipp'd God for spight,
The self-same thing they will abhor
One way, and long another for.
Free-will they one way disavow,
Another, nothing else allow.
All Piety consists therein
In them, in other Men all Sin.
Rather than fail, they will defie

[23] *B*:"Some report, that in *Nova Zemble*, and *Greenland*, Mens words are wont to be Frozen in the Air, and at the Thaw may be heard."

[24] Alexander of Hales, English theologian (died 1245), was called Doctor Irrefragabilis or the Invincible Doctor.

[25] *G*:"For the skull of lunatics."

[26] *B*:"There is nothing more ridiculous than the various opinions of Authors about the Seat of Paradise; Sir *Walter Rawleigh* has taken a great deal of pains to collect them; in the beginning of his *History of the World;* where those who are unsatisfied, may be fully inform'd."

[27] *B*:"*Gropius Becanus* [1518–1572, author of *Origines Antverpianae* (1569)] endeavours to prove that High-Dutch was the Language that *Adam* and *Eve* spoke in *Paradise*."

[28] *B*:"*Adam* and *Eve* being Made, and not Conceiv'd, and Form'd in the Womb, had no Navel, as some Learned Men have suppos'd, because they had no need of them."

[29] *B*:"Musick is said to be invented by *Pythagoras,* who first found out the Proportion of Notes, from the sounds of Hammers upon an Anvil."

[30] Grey cites from Clement Walker's *History of Independency* (1648, 1649, 1651) one of the many stories concerning atrocities said to have been committed by the forces of Parliament upon people worshipping in accordance with the Anglican service.

[31] *G*:Certain Presbyterians are said to have kept a fast on Christmas.

That which they love most tenderly,
Quarrel with *minc'd Pies*, and disparage
Their best and dearest friend, *Plum-porridge;*
Fat *Pig* and *Goose* it self oppose,
And blaspheme *Custard* through the *Nose*.
Th' Apostles of this fierce Religion,
Like *Mahomet's*, were Ass and Widgeon,[32]
To whom our Knight, by fast instinct
Of Wit and Temper was so linkt,
As if Hipocrisie and Non-sence
Had got th' Advouson[33] of his Conscience.
  Thus was he gifted and accouter'd,
We mean on th' inside, not the outward:
That next of all we shall discuss;
Then listen Sirs, it followeth thus:
  His tawny *Beard* was th' equal grace
Both of his Wisdom and his Face;
In Cut and Dy so like a Tile,
A sudden view it would beguile:
The upper part thereof was Whey,
The nether Orange mixt with Grey.
This hairy Meteor did denounce
The fall of Scepters and of Crowns;
With grizly type did represent
Declining Age of Government;
And tell with Hieroglyphick Spade,[34]
Its own grave and the State's were made.
Like *Sampson's* Heart-breakers,[35] it grew
In time to make a Nation rue;
Though it contributed its own fall,
To wait upon the publick downfall.
It was Canonick, and did grow
In Holy Orders by strict vow;[36]
Of Rule as sullen and severe,
As that of rigid *Cordeliere:*
'Twas bound to suffer Persecution
And Martyrdome with resolution;
T' oppose it self against the hate
And vengeance of th' incensed State:
In whose defiance it was worn,
Still ready to be pull'd and torn,
With red-hot Irons to be tortur'd,
Revil'd, and spit upon, and martyr'd.
Maugre all which, 'twas to stand fast,
As long as Monarchy should last.
But when the State should hap to reel,
'Twas to submit to fatal Steel,
And fall, as it was consecrate
A Sacrifice to fall of State;
Whose thred of life the fatal Sisters
Did twist together with its Whiskers,
And twine so close, that time should never,
In life or death, their fortunes sever;
But with his rusty Sickle mow
Both down together at a blow.
  So learned *Taliacotius*[37] from
The brawny part of Porter's Bum,
Cut supplemental Noses, which
Would last as long as Parent breech:
But when the Date of *Nock*[38] was out,
Off dropt the Sympathetick Snout.
  His *Back*, or rather Burthen show'd
As if it stoop'd with its own load.
For as *Æneas* bore his Sire,
Upon his Shoulders through the Fire:
Our Knight did bear no less a Pack
Of his own Buttocks on his Back:
Which now had almost got the Upper-
Hand of his Head, for want of Crupper.
To poize this equally, he bore
A *Paunch* of the same bulk before:
Which still he had a special care
To keep well cramm'd with thrifty fare;
As White-pot,[39] Butter-milk, and Curds,
Such as a Countrey house affords;
With other Victual, which anon,
We further shall dilate upon,
When of his Hose we come to treat,
The Cub-bord where he kept his meat,
  His *Doublet* was of sturdy Buff,
And though not Sword, yet Cudgel-proof;
Whereby 'twas fitter for his use,
That fear'd no blows but such as bruise.
  His *Breeches* were of rugged Woollen,
And had been at the Siege of *Bullen*,[40]
To old King *Harry* so well known,
Some Writers held they were his own.

[32] *B*:"*Mahomet* had a tame Dove that used to pick Seeds out of his Ear, that it might be thought to Whisper and Inspire him. His Ass was so intimate with him, that the Mahometans believe it carry'd him to Heaven, and stays there with him to bring him back again."

[33] right of presenting a nominee to a vacant ecclesiastical benefice

[34] *G*:"Alluding to the picture of Time and Death."

[35] *G*:lovelocks

[36] *B*:"He made a Vow never to cut his *Beard*, until the Parliament had subdued the King, of which Order of Phanatique Votaries, there were many in those times."

[37] *B*:"*Taliacotius* was an *Italian* Chirugeon, that found out a way to repair lost and decay'd Noses."

[38] notch or nick; and Oliver Cromwell

[39] *G*:Devonshire white-pot

[40] *G*:Henry VIII laid seige to Boulogne in 1544.

Through they were lin'd with many a piece,
Of Ammunition-Bread and Cheese,
And fat Black-puddings, proper food
For Warriers that delight in Blood;
For, as we said, he always chose
To carry Vittle in his Hose.
That often tempted Rats, and Mice,
The Ammunition to surprize:
And when he put a Hand but in
The one or th' other Magazine,
They stoutly in defence on't stood
And from the wounded Foe drew bloud,
And till th' were storm'd and beaten out,
Ne'r left the fortifi'd Redoubt;
And though Knights Errant, as some think,
Of old did neither eat nor drink,
Because when thorough Desarts vast
And Regions Desolate they past,
Where Belly-timber above ground
Or under was not to be found,
Unless they graz'd, there's not one word
Of their Provision, on Record:
Which made some confidently write,
They had no stomachs but to fight,
'Tis false: for *Arthur* wore in Hall
Round Table like a Farthingal,
On which, with Shirt pull'd out behind,
And eke before his good Knights din'd.
Though 'twas no Table, some suppose,
But a huge pair of round Trunk-hose;
In which he carry'd as much meat
As he and all his Knights could eat;
When laying by their Swords and Truncheons,
They took their Breakfast, or their Nuncheons;
But let that pass at present, lest
We should forget where we digrest;
As learned Authors use, to whom
We leave it, and to th' purpose come,
His Puissant Sword unto his side
Near his undaunted Heart was ty'd,
With Basket-hilt, that wou'd hold broth,
And serve for Fight, and Dinner both.
In it he melted Lead for Bullets,
To shoot at Foes, and sometimes Pullets;
To whom he bore so fell a Grutch,
He ne'er gave quarter t' any such.
The trenchant blade, *Toledo* trusty,
For want of fighting was grown rusty,
And eat into it self, for lack
Of some body to hew and hack.
The peaceful Scabbard where it dwelt,
The Rancor of its Edge had felt:
For of the lower end two handful,
It had devoured 'twas so manful;
And so much scorn'd to lurk in case,
As if it durst not shew its face.
In many desperate Attempts
Of Wars, Exigents, Contempts,
It had appear'd with Courage bolder
Than Sergeant *Bum*, invading shoulder.[41]
Oft had it ta'en possession,
And Pris'ners too, or made them run.
This Sword a *Dagger* had his Page.
But was but little for his age:
And therefore waited on him so,
As Dwarfs upon Knights Errant do.
It was a serviceable Dudgeon,
Either for fighting or for drudging;
When it had stab'd or broke a head,
It would scrape Trenchers, or chip Bread,
Toast Cheese or Bacon, though it were
To bait a Mouse-trap, 'twould not care.
'Twould make clean shooes, and in the Earth
Set Leeks and Onions, and so forth.
It had been Prentice to a Brewer,
Where this and more it did endure.
But left the Trade, as many more
Have lately done on the same score.[42]
In th' Holsters, at his Saddle-bow,
Two aged Pistols he did stow,
Among the surplus of such meat
As in his Hose he could not get.
They were upon hard Duty still,
And every night stood Sentinel,
To guard the Magazine i' th' Hose
From two legg'd and from four legg'd Foes.
Thus clad and fortifi'd, Sir Knight
From peaceful home set forth to fight.
But first with nimble active force
He got on th' outside of his *Horse*.
For having but one stirrup ty'd
T' his Saddle, on the further side,
It was so short, h' had much adoe
To reach it with his desperate Toe.
But after many strains and heaves
He got up to the Saddle eaves.
From whence he vaulted into th' Seat
With so much vigor, strength, and heat,
That he had almost tumbled over

[41] *G*: The reference is to the manner in which a sergeant or bailiff lays his hand on the shoulder of a debtor being placed under arrest.

[42] *B*: "*Oliver Cromwell* and Colonel *Pride* had been both Brewers."

With his own weight, but did recover,
By laying hold of Tail and Mane,
Which oft he us'd instead of Reyn.
But now we talk of mounting Steed,
Before we further do proceed,
It doth behove us to say something,
Of that which bore our valiant *Bumkin*.
The Beast was sturdy large and tall,
With Mouth of Meal and Eyes of Wall:
I would say Eye, for h' had but one,
As most agree, though some say none.
He was well stay'd, and in his Gate
Preserv'd a grave majestick state.
At Spur or Switch no more he skipt,
Or mended pace, than *Spaniard* whipt:[43]
And yet so fiery, he would bound,
As if he griev'd to touch the Ground:
That *Cæsar's* Horse, who, as Fame goes,
Had Corns upon his Feet and Toes,[44]
Was not by half so tender-hooft,
Nor trode upon the ground so soft.
And as that Beast would kneel and stoop,
(Some write) to take his Rider up:
So *Hudibras* his ('tis well known,)
Would often do, to set him down.
We shall not need to say what lack
Of Leather was upon his back:
For that was hidden under pad,
And breech of Knight gall'd full as bad.
His strutting Ribs on both sides show'd
Like furrows he himself had plow'd:
For underneath the skirt of Pannel,
'Twixt every two there was a Channel.
His dragling Tail hung in the Dirt,
Which on his Rider he would flirt
Still as his tender side he prickt,
With arm'd heel or with unarm'd kickt:
For *Hudibras* wore but one Spur,
As wisely knowing, could he stir
To active trot one side of's Horse,
The other would not hang an Arse.
A Squire he had whose name was *Ralph*,
That in th' adventure went his half.
Though Writers (for more statelier tone)
Do call him *Ralpho*, 'tis all one:
And when we can with Meeter safe,
We'll call him so, if not plain *Ralph*,
For Rhime the Rudder is of Verses,
With which like Ships they stear their courses.
An equal stock of Wit and Valour
He had laid in, by birth a Taylor.
The mighty *Tyrian* Queen that gain'd
With subtle shreds a Tract of Land,[45]
Did leave it with a Castle fair
To his great Ancestor, her Heir:
From him descended cross-leg'd Knights,
Fam'd for their Faith and Warlike Fights[46]
Against the bloudy Caniball,
Whom they destroy'd both great and small.
This sturdy Squire had as well
As the bold *Trojan* Knight, seen hell,[47]
Not with a counterfeited Pass
Of Golden Bough, but true Gold-lace.
His knowledge was not far behind
The Knights, but of another kind,
And he another way came by't,
Some call it *Gift*, and some *New light;*
A liberal Art, that costs no pains
Of Study, Industry, or Brains.
His Wits were sent him for a Token,
But in the Carriage crackt and broken
Like Commendation Nine-pence, crookt
With to and from my Love,[48] it lookt,
He ne'r consider'd it, as loath
To look a Gift-horse in the Mouth;
And very wisely would lay forth
No more upon it than 'twas worth.
But as he got it freely, so
He spent it frank and freely too.
For Saints themselves will sometimes be,
Of Gifts that cost them nothing, free.
By means of this, with *hem* and *cough*,
Prolongers to enlightned Snuff,
He could deep Mysteries unriddle,
As easily as thread a Neele;
For as of Vagabonds we say,
That they are ne'r beside their way:
What e'r men speak by this *New Light*,

[43] *G*: refers to the fable of the Spaniard under the lash

[44] *B*: "Julius Cæsar had a Horse with Feet like a Man's *Utebatur equo insigni, pedibus prope Humanis, & in modum Dignitorum ungulis fissis*. Sueton *in* Jul. Cap. 61."

[45] *B*: "*Dido* Queen of *Carthage*, who bought as much Land as she could compass with an Oxes Hide, which she cut into small Thongs and cheated the owner of so much ground, as serv'd her to build *Carthage* upon."

[46] *G*: refers to tailors and knights templars (who "had their effigies laid on their tombs, with the legs across")

[47] *B*: "*Aeneas* whom *Virgil* reports to use a Golden Bough, for a Pass to Hell, and Tailors call that place Hell, where they put all they steal."

[48] *G*: a bent ninepenny piece of silver, given to a sweetheart as a love token (a "commendation"), and called *To my Love and from my Love*

Still they are sure to be i' th' right.
'Tis a *Dark-Lanthorn* of the Spirit,
Which none see by but those that bear it.
A Light that falls down from on high,
For Spiritual Trades to couzen by:
An *Ignis Fatuus*[49] that bewitches,
And leads Men into Pools and Ditches,
To make them *dip* themselves, and sound
For Christendom and dirty Pond;
To dive like Wild-foul for Salvation,
And fish to catch Regeneration.
This Light inspires, and plays upon
The nose of Saint like Bag-pipe drone,
And speaks through hollow empty Soul,
As through a Trunk, or whisp'ring hole,[50]
Such language as no mortal Ear
But spiritual Eve-droppers can hear.
So *Phœbus* or some friendly Muse
Into small Poets song infuse;
Which they at second-hand reherse
Through Reed or Bag-pipe, Verse for Verse.
  Thus *Ralph* became infallible,
As three or four-leg'd Oracle,
The ancient Cup, or modern Chair,
Spoke truth point-blank, though unaware:
  For mystick Learning, wondrous able
In Magick *Talisman*, and *Cabal*,[51]
Whose Primitive Tradition reaches
As far as *Adam's* first green Breeches:[52]
Deep-sighted in Intelligences,
Idea's, Atomes, Influences;
And much of *Terra Incognita*,
Th' intelligible World could say;[53]
A deep occult Philosopher,
As learn'd as the *Wild Irish* are,[54]
Or Sir *Agrippa*,[55] for profound
And solid Lying much renown'd:
He *Anthroposophus*,[56] and *Floud*,[57]
And *Jacob Behmen*[58] understood;
Knew many an Amulet and Charm,
That would do neither good nor harm:
In *Rosy-Crucian* Lore as Learned,
As he that *Veré adeptus* earned.[59]
He understood the speech of Birds
As well as they themselves do words:
Could tell what subtlest *Parrots* mean,
That speak and think contrary clean;
What *Member* 'tis of whom they talk
When they cry *Rope*, and *Walk Knave, walk*.[60]
He'd extract numbers out of matter,
And keep them in a Glass, like water,
Of Sov'raign pow'r to make men wise;
For dropt in blere, thick-sighted Eyes,
They'd make them see in darkest night,
Like Owls, though pur-blind in the light.
By help of these (as he profest)
He had *First Matter* seen undrest:
He took her naked all alone,
Before one Rag of *Form* was on.

[49] a will-o'-the-wisp

[50] *G*:"Alluding probably to the mistaken notion, that the oracles at Delphos and other places were delivered in that manner . . . "

[51] *B*:"Talisman is a Device to destroy any sort of Vermin by casting their Images in Metal, in a precise minute, when the Stars are perfectly inclin'd to do them all the mischief they can. This has been experimented by some modern *Virtuosi*, upon Rats, Mice, and Fleas, and found (as they affirm) to produce the Effect with admirable success.

"*Raymund Lully* interprets *Cabal*, out of the *Arabick*, to signifie *Scientia superabundans*, which his Comentator *Cornelius Agrippa*, by over magnifying, has render'd a very superfluous Foppery."

[52] *B*:"The Author of *Magia Adamica* endeavours to prove the Learning of the antient *Magi*, to be deriv'd from that knowledge which God himself taught *Adam* in *Paradise*, before the Fall."

[53] *B*:"The Intelligible world, is a kind of *Terra del Fuego*, or *Psittacorum Regio*, discover'd only by the Philosophers, of which they talk, like Parrots, what they do not understand."

[54] *B*:"No Nation in the World is more addicted to this occult Philosophy, than the Wild Irish, as appears by the whole practice of their Lives, of which see *Cambden* in his description of *Ireland*."

[55] Cornelius Agrippa (died 1535), German theologian and occultist

[56] Thomas Vaughan's *Anthroposophia Theomagica; or a discourse of the nature of man and his state after death* (1650)

[57] Robert Fludd (1574–1637), English Rosicrucian

[58] Jakob Böhme (1575–1624), German mystic

[59] *B*:"The Fraternity of the *Rosy-Crucians* is very like the Sect of the antient *Gnostici* who call'd themselves so, from the excellent Learning they pretended to, although they were really the most ridiculous Sots of all Mankind.

"*Vere Adeptus*, is one that has Commnec'd in their Fanatique extravagance."

[60] The references, says Grey, are to certain ludicrous tracts of the 1642–1660 period, such as *Walk, knaves, walk* (1659).

The *Chaos* too he had descr'yd,
And seen quite through, or else he ly'd:
Not that of Past-board which men shew
For Goats at Fair of *Barthol'mew;*
But its great Gransire, first o' th' name,
Whence that and *Reformation* came:
Both Cousin-Germans, and right able
T' inveigle and draw in the Rabble.
But *Reformation* was, some say,
O' th' younger house to *Puppet-Play*.
He could foretell whats'ever was
By consequence to come to pass.
As Death of Great Men, Alterations,
Diseases, Battels, Inundations.
All this without th' Eclipse of Sun,
Or dreadful Comet, he hath done
By inward Light, a way as good,
And easie to be understood.
But with more lucky hit than those
That use to make the Stars depose,
Like Knights o' th' Post,[61] and falsly charge
Upon themselves what others forge:
As if they were consenting to
All mischief in the World men do:
Or like the Dev'l, did tempt and sway 'em
To Rogueries, and then betray 'em.
They'l search a Planet's house, to know,
Who broke and robb'd a house below:
Examine *Venus*, and the *Moon*
Who stole a Thimble and a Spoon:
And though they nothing will confess,
Yet by their very looks can guess,
And tell what guilty Aspect bodes,
Who stole, and who receiv'd the Goods.
They'l question *Mars*, and by his look
Detect who 'twas that nimm'd a Cloke:
Make *Mercury* confess and peach
Those Thieves which he himself did teach.
They'l find i' th' Phisiognomies
O' th' Planets all mens destinies.
Like him that took the Doctor's Bill,
And swallow'd it instead o' th' Pill.[62]
Cast the Nativity o' th' Question,
And from Positions to be guest on,
As sure as if they knew the Moment
Of Natives birth, tell what will come on 't.[63]
They'l feel the Pulses of the Stars,
To find out Agues, Coughs, Catarrhs;
And tell what *Crysis* does divine
The Rot in Sheep, or Mange in Swine:
In Men what gives or cures the Itch,
What makes them Cuckolds, poor or rich:
What gains or loses, hangs or saves;
What makes men great, what fools or knaves;
But not what wise, for only of those
The Stars (they say) cannot dispose,
No more than can the Astrologians.
There they say right, and lik true *Trojans*.
This *Ralpho* knew, and therefore took
The other course, of which we spoke.
  Thus was th' accomplish'd Squire endu'd
With Gifts and Knowledge, per'lous shrew'd.
Never did trusty Squire with Knight,
Or Knight with Squire jump more right.
Their Arms and Equipage did fit,
As well as Virtues, Parts, and Wit.
Their Valors too were of a Rate,
And out they sally'd at the Gate.
Few miles on horseback had they jogged,
But fortune unto them turn'd dogged.
For they a sad adventure met,
Of which we now prepare to Treat:
But e'er we venture to unfold
Atchievements so resolv'd and bold,
We should as learned Poets use,
Invoke the assistance of some *Muse;*
However Criticks count it sillier
Than Juglers talking t' a Familiar.
We think 'tis no great matter which,
They're all alike, yet we shall pitch
On one that fits our purpose most,
Whom therefore thus do we accost.
  Thou that with Ale or viler Liquors,
Didst inspire *Withers*, *Prin*, and *Vickars*,[64]
And force them, though it were in spight
Of Nature, and their Stars, to write;
Who, as we finde in sullen Writs,

[61] A knight of the post was one who made a living giving false evidence.

[62] *G*: "The countryman's swallowing the paper on which the prescription was written, upon the physician's ordering him to take it, was literally true."

[63] *G*: In case the exact hour and minute of a child's birth had been forgotten, an astrologer would undertake to read the child's future by basing his calculations on the moment at which he was consulted.

[64] *B*: "This *Vickars* was a Man of as great Interest and Authority in the late Reformation, as *Pryn* or *Withers*, and as able a Poet; He Translated *Virgils Æneids* into as horrible Travesty in earnest, as the French *Scaroon* did in Burlesque, and was only outdone in his way by the Politick Author of *Oceana*."

And cross-graind Works of modern Wits,
With Vanity, Opinion, Want,
The wonder of the Ignorant,
The Praises of the Author, penn'd
By himself, or wit-ensuring friend,
The Itch of Picture in the Front,
With Bays, and wicked Rhime upon 't
All that is left o' th' forked Hill[65]
To make men scribble without skill,
Canst make a Poet, spight of fate,
And teach all People to translate;
Though out of Languages in which
They understand no Part of Speech:
Assist me but this once, I'mplore,
And I shall trouble thee no more.
  In Western Clime there is a Town
To those that dwell therein well known;
Therefore there needs no more be sed here
We unto them refer our Reader:
For brevity is very good,
When w'are, or are not understood.
To this Town People did repair
On days of Market or of Fair,
And to crack'd Fiddle, and hoarse Tabor
In merriment did drudge and labor:
But now a sport more formidable
Had rak'd together Village rabble.
'Twas an old way of Recreating,
Which learned Butchers call *Bear-baiting:*
A bold advent'rous exercise,
With ancient *Heroe's* in high prize;
For Authors do affirm it came
From *Istmian* or *Nemean* game;
Others derive it from the *Bear*
That's fixt in Northern Hemisphere,
And round about the Pole does make
A circle like a Bear at stake,
That at the Chain's end wheels about,
And over-turns the Rabble-rout.
For after solemn Proclamation
In the Bear's name (as is the fashion,
According to the Law of Arms,
To keep men from inglorious harms)
That none presume to come so near
As forty foot of stake of Bear;
If any yet be so fool-hardy,
T'expose themselves to vain Jeopardy;
If they come wounded off and lame
No honour's got by such a maim.
Although the Bear gain'd much b'ing bound
In honour to make good his ground.
When he's engag'd, and take no notice,
If any press upon him, who 'tis,
But let them know at their own cost
That he intends to keep his post.
This to prevent, and other harms,
Which always wait on feats of Arms,
(For in the hurry of a Fray
'Tis hard to keep out of harm's way)
Thither the Knight his course did stear,
To keep the peace 'twixt *Dog* and *Bear;*
As he believ'd h' was bound to doe,
In Conscience and Commission too.
And therefore thus bespoke the Squire;
  We that are wisely mounted higher[66]
Then Constables, in Curule wit,[67]
When on Tribunal bench we sit,
Like Speculators, should foresee
From *Pharos*[68] of Authority,
Portended Mischiefs farther then
Low Proletarian Tithing-men.
And therefore being inform'd by bruit,
That *Dog* and *Bear* are to dispute;
For so of late men fighting name,
Because they often prove the same;
(For where the first does hap to be
The last does *coincidere*)
Quantum in nobis, have thought good,
To save th' expence of Christian blood,
And try if we by Mediation
Of Treaty and accommodation
Can end the quarrel, and compose
The bloudy Duel without blows.
Are not our Liberties, our Lives,
The Laws, Religion, and our Wives
Enough at once to lie at stake,
For *Cov'nant* and the *Causes* sake;
But in that quarrel *Dogs* and *Bears*
As well as we must venture theirs?
This Feud by *Jesuits* invented,
By *evil Counsel* is fomented,
There is a *Machiavilian* Plot,
(Though ev'ry *Nare olfact* it not)

[65] *G*:Parnassus, with its two tops

[66] *B*:"This Speech is set down as it was deliver'd by the Knight in his own words: but since it is below the Gravity of Heroical Poetry, to admit of Humor, but all men are oblig'd to speak wisely alike. And too much of so extravagant a Folly would become tedious, and impertinent, the rest of his Harangues have only his Sense exprest in other words, unless in some few places where his own words could not be so well avoided."

[67] The Roman magistrate sat in a curule chair.

[68] the famous lighthouse in Alexandria harbor

A deep design in 't to divide
The well-affected that confide,
By setting Brother against Brother,
To claw and curry one another.
Have we not enemies *plus satis*,
That *Cane & angue pejus* hate us?[69]
And shall we turn our fangs and claws
Upon our selves without a cause?
That some occult design doth lie
In bloudy *Cynarctomachy*[70]
Is plain enough to him that knows
How Saints lead Brothers by the Nose.
I wish my self a Pseudo-Prophet,
But sure some mischief will come of it:
Unless by providential wit
Or force we averruncate it.[71]
For what design, what interest
Can Beast have to encounter Beast?
They fight for no espoused *Cause;*
Frail *Priviledge, Fundamental Laws,*
Nor for a *thorough Reformation,*
Nor *Covenant,* nor *Protestation;*
Nor *Liberty of Consciences,*
Nor Lords and Commons *Ordinances;*
Nor for the *Church,* nor for *Church Lands,*
To get them in their own no Hands;
Nor *evil Counsellors* to bring
To Justice that seduce the King;
Nor for the worship of us men,
Though we have done as much for them.
Th' *Egyptians* worshipp'd *Dogs,* and for
Their faith made fierce and zealous Warr.
Others ador'd a *Rat,* and some
For that Church suffer'd Martyrdome.
The *Indians* fought for the truth
Of th' *Elephant,* and *Monkey's* Tooth:[72]
And many, to defend that faith,
Fought it out *mordicus*[73] to death.
But no Beast ever was so slight,
For Man, as for his God, to fight.
They have more wit, alas! and know
Themselves and us better than so.
But we, we onely do infuse
The Rage in them like *Boute-feus.*[74]
'Tis our example that instills
In them th' infection of our ills.
For as some late Philosophers
Have well observed, Beasts that converse
With Man, take after him, as Hogs
Get Pigs all th' year, and Bitches Dogs.
Just so by our example Cattle
Learn to give one another Battel.
We read in *Nero's* time, the Heathen,
When they destroy'd the *Christian Brethren,*
They sow'd them in the skins of Bears,
And then set Dogs about their Ears:
From whence, no doubt, th' invention came
Of this lewd Antichristian Game.
  To this, quoth *Ralpho,* Verily,
The Point seems very plain to be.
It is an Antichristian Game,
Unlawful both in thing and name;
First for the *Name,* The word *Bear-baiting,*
Is Carnal, and of man's creating:
For certainly there's no such word
In all the *Scripture* on Record.
Therefore unlawful and a sin,
And so is (secondly) the *thing.*
A vile *Assembly* 'tis, that can
No more be prov'd by Scripture than
Provincial, Classick, National;[75]
Mere humane Creature-Cobwebs all.
Thirdly, it is Idolatrous:

[69] "who hate us worse than dogs and snakes"

[70] literally, "dog-and-bear-fighting;" *B*: "cynarctomarchy signifies nothing in the World, but a Fight between *Dogs* and *Bears,* though both the Learned and Ignorant agree, that in such words very great Knowledge is contained: and our Knight as one, or both of those, was of the same opinion."

[71] *B*: "Another of the same kind, which though it appear ever so Learned, and Profound, means nothing else but the weeding of Corn."

[72] *B*: "The History of the White Elephant, and the Monkeys Tooth, which the *Indians* ador'd, is written by Monsieur *Le Blanc.* This Monkey's Tooth was taken by the Portuguese from those that worship'd it, and though they offer'd a vast Ransom for it, yet the Christians were perswaded by their Priests, rather to burn it. But as soon as the fire was kindled, all the People present were not able to indure the horrible stink that came from it, as if the Fire had been made of the same Ingredients, with which Seamen use to compose that kind of Granado's, which they call Stinkards."

[73] by holding fast (literally, with the teeth)

[74] a linstock, a firebrand; *B*: "*Bout-feus* is a French word, and therefore it were uncivil to suppose any English Person (especially of Quality) ignorant of it, or so ill-bred as to need an Exposition."

[75] *G*: the classical, provincial, and national assemblies of the Presbyterians

For when men run a-whoring thus
With their Inventions whatsoe'r
The thing be, whether *Dog* or *Bear*,
It is Idolatrous and *Pagan*
No less than worshipping of *Dagon.*
Quoth *Hudibras*, I smell a *Rat;*
Ralpho, thou dost prevaricate.
For though the *Thesis* which thou lay'st
Be true *ad amussim*[76] as thou say'st:
(For that *Bear-baiting* should appear
Jure Divino[77] lawfuller
Than *Synods*[78] are, thou dost deny,
Totidem verbis so do I)
Yet there's a fallacy in this:
For if by sly *Homœosis*,[79]
Thou would'st Sophistically imply
Both are unlawful, I deny.
And I (quoth *Ralpho*) do not doubt
But *Bear-baiting* may be made out
In Gospel-times, as lawful as is
Provincial or *Parochial Classis:*
And that both are so near of kin,
And like in all as well as sin,
That put them in a bag and shake 'em,
Your self o' th' sudden would mistake 'em,
And not know which is which, unless
You measure by their wickedness:
For 'tis not hard t' imagine whether
O' th' two is worst, though I name neither.
Quoth *Hudibras*, thou offer'st much,
But are not able to keep touch.
Mira de lente, as 'tis i' th' Adage,
Id est, to make a Leak a Cabbage.[80]
Thou canst at best but overstrain
A Paradox, and th' own hot brain:
For what can *Synods* have at all
With *Bears* that's Analogical?
Or what relation has debating
Of Church-Affairs with *Bear-baiting?*
A just comparison still is,
Of things *ejusdem generis.*[81]
And then what *Genus* rightly doth,
Include and comprehend them both?
If *Animal*, both of us may
As justly pass for *Bears* as they.
For we are Animals no less.
Although of different *Specieses.*
But, *Ralpho* this is no fit place,
Nor time to argue out the Case:
For now the Field is not far off,
Where we must give the world a proof
Of Deeds, not Words, and such as suit
Another manner of Dispute.
A Controversie that affords
Actions for Arguments, not Words:
Which we must manage at a rate
Of Prowess and Conduct adæquate;
To what our place and fame doth promise,
And all the godly expect from us.
Nor shall they be deceiv'd, unless
W' are slurr'd and outed by success:
Success, the Mark no mortal Wit,
Or surest hand can always hit:
For whatsoe're we perpetrate,
We do but row, we 'are steer'd by Fate,
Which in success oft disinherits,
For spurious Causes, noblest merits.
Great Actions are not always true Sons
Of great and mighty Resolutions:
Nor doth the bold'st attempts bring forth
Events still equal to their worth;
But sometimes fail, and in their stead,
Fortune and Cowardice succeed,
Yet we have no great cause to doubt,
Our actions still have born us out.
Which though th' are known to be so ample,
We need no copy from example,
We' are not the onely person durst
Attempt this Province, nor the first.
In Northern Clime a valorous Knight
Did whilom kill his Bear in fight,
And wound a Fidler: we have both
Of these the objects of our Wroth,
And equal Fame and Glory from
Th' Attempt or Victory to come.
'Tis sung, There is a valiant *Marmaluke*[82]
In foreign Land, yclep'd—[83]
To whom we have been oft compar'd
For Person, Parts, Address and Beard:
Both equally reputed stout,
And in the same Cause both have fought.
He oft in such Attempts as these
Came off with glory and success.
Nor will we fail in th' execution,
For want of equal Resolution.

[76] exactly [77] by Divine law

[78] in the Presbyterian Church, an ecclesiastical court

[79] *G*:"An explanation of a thing by something resembling it."

[80] Grey refers to Erasmus's adage, "Egregia de lente," about the "remarkable lentil," i.e., to talk much and prove nothing.

[81] of the same kind

[82] *G*:a soldier serving one of the Turkish Sultans

[83] Sir Samuel Luke according to tradition

Honour is, like a Widow, won
With brisk Attempt and putting on;
With ent'ring manfully, and urging;
Not slow approaches, like a Virgin.
  This said, as once the *Phrygian* Knight,[84]
So ours, with rusty steell, did smite
His *Trojan* Horse, and just as much
He mended pace upon the touch;
But from his empty stomach groan'd
Just as that hollow Beast did sound,
And angry answer'd from behind,
With brandish'd Tail and blast of Wind.
So have I seen with armed heel,
A Wight bestride a *Commonweal;*[85]
Whil'st still the more he kick'd and spurr'd,
The less the sullen Jade has stirr'd.

PROSE CHARACTERS[1]

A MODERN POLITICIAN

Makes new Discoveries in Politics, but they are, like those that *Columbus* made of the new World, very rich but barbarous. He endeavours to restore Mankind to the original Condition, it fell from, by forgetting to discern between Good and Evil; and reduces all Prudence back again to its first Author the Serpent, that taught *Adam* Wisdom; for he was really his Tutor, and not *Samboscor*, as the *Rabbins* write. He finds the World has been mistaken in all Ages, and that Religion and Morality are but vulgar Errors, that pass among the Ignorant, and are but mere Words to the Wise. He despises all learning as a Pedantic little Thing; and believes Books to be the Business of Children, and not of Men. He wonders how the Distinction of Virtue and Vice came into the World's Head; and believes them to be more ridiculous than any Foppery of the Schools. He holds it his Duty to betray any Man, that shall take him for so much a Fool as one fit to be trusted. He stedfastly believes, that all Men are born in the State of War, and that the civil Life is but a Cessation, and no Peace, nor Accommodation: And though all open Acts of Hostility are forborn by Consent, the Enmity continues, and all Advantages by Treachery or Breach of Faith are very lawful—That there is no Difference between Virtue and Fraud among Friends, as well as Enemies; nor any thing unjust, that a Man can do without Damage to his own Safety or Interest—That Oaths are but Springes to catch Woodcocks withal; and bind none but those, that are too weak and feeble to break them, when they become ever so small an Impediment to their Advantages—That Conscience is the effect of Ignorance, and the same with that foolish Fear, which some Men apprehend, when they are in the dark and alone—That Honour is but the Word, which a Prince gives a Man to pass his Guards withal, and save him from being stopped by Law and Justice the Sentinels of Governments, when he has not Wit nor Credit enough to pass of himself—That to shew Respect to Worth in any Person is to appear a Stranger to it, and not so familiarly acquainted with it as those are, who use no Ceremony; because it is no new Thing to them, as it would appear if they should take Notice of it—That the easiest Way to purchase a Reputation of Wisdom and Knowledge is to slight and undervalue it; as the readiest Way to buy cheap is to bring down the Price: for the World will be apt to believe a Man well provided with any necessary or useful Commodity, which he sets a small Value upon—That to oblige a Friend is but a kind of casting him in Prison, after the old *Roman* Way, or modern *Chinese*, that chains the Keeper and Prisoner together: for he that binds another Man to himself, binds himself as much to him, and lays a restraint upon both. For as Men commonly never forgive those that forgive them, and always hate those that purchase their Estates (tho' they pay dear and more than any Man else would give) so they never willingly endure those, that have laid any Engagement upon them, or

[84] *G:* "Alluding to Laocoon, who, suspecting the treachery of the Grecians, smote their wooden horse with a spear . . . "

[85] *G:* "Alluding probably to that harmless inoffensive person Richard Cromwell, who was dispossessed of the government as Protector in a small time . . . "

[1] Text: *The Genuine Remains in Verse and Prose*, 1759

at what rate soever purchased the least Part of their Freedom.—And as Partners for the most Part cheat or suspect one another; so no Man deals fairly with another, that goes the least Share in his Freedom.

To propose any Measure to Wealth or Power is to be ignorant of the Nature of both: for as no Man can ever have too much of either; so it is impossible to determine what is enough; and he, that limits his Desires by proposing to himself the Enjoyment of any other Pleasure, but that of gaining more, shews he has but a dull Inclination, that will not hold out to his Journey's End. And therefore he believes that a Courtier deserves to be beg'd himself, that is ever satisfied with begging: for Fruition without Desire is but a dull Entertainment; and that Pleasure only real and substantial, that provokes and improves the Appetite, and increases in the Enjoyment. And all the greatest Masters in the several Arts of thriving concur unanimously, that the plain downright Pleassure of Gaining is greater and deserves to be prefered far before all the various Delights of Spending, which the Curiosity, Wit, or Luxury of Mankind in all Ages could ever find out.

He believes, there is no Way of thriving so easy and certain as to grow rich by defrauding the Public: for public Thieveries are more safe and less prosecuted than private, like Robberies committed between Sun and Sun, which the County pays, and no one is greatly concerned in. And as the Monster of many Heads has less Wit in them all than any one reasonable Person: so the Monster of many Purses is easier cheated than any one indifferent crafty Fool. For all the Difficulty lies in being trusted; and when he has obtained that, the Business does itself; and if he should happen to be questioned and called to an Accompt, a Baudy Pardon is as cheap as a Paymaster's Fee, not above fourteen Pence in the Pound.

He thinks, that when a Man comes to Wealth or Preferment, and is to put on a new Person, his first Business is to put off all his old Friendships and Acquaintances as Things below him, and no Way consistent with his present Condition; especially such as may have Occasion to make use of him, or have Reason to expect any civil Returns from him: for requiting of Obligations received in a Man's Necessity is the same Thing with paying of Debts contracted in his Minority, when he was under Age, for which he is not accountable by the Laws of the Land. These he is to forget as fast as he can, and by little Neglects remove them to that Distance, that they may at length by his Example learn to forget him: for Men, who travel together in Company, when their Occasions lye several Ways, ought to take leave and part. It is a hard Matter for a Man that comes to Preferment not to forget himself; and therefore he may very well be allowed to take the Freedom to forget others: for Advancement, like the Conversion of a Sinner, gives a Man new Values of Things and Persons, so different from those he had before, that that, which was wont to be most dear to him, does commonly after become the most disagreeable. And as it is accounted noble to forget and pass over little Injuries; so it is to forget little Friendships, that are no better than Injuries when they become Disparagements, and can only be importune and troublesome, instead of being useful, as they were before. All Acts of Oblivion have, of late Times, been found to extend, rather to loyal and faithful Services done, than Rebellion and Treasons committed. For Benefits are like Flowers, sweet only and fresh when they are newly gathered, but stink when they grow stale and wither; and he only is ungrateful, who makes returns of Obligations; for he does it merely to free himself from owing so much as Thanks. Fair Words are all the Civility and Humanity, that one Man owes to another; for they are obliging enough of themselves, and need not the Assistance of Deeds to make them good: for he that does not believe them has already received to much, and he that does, ought to expect no more. And therefore promises ought to oblige those only to whom they are made, not those who make them; for he that expects a Man should bind himself is worse than a Thief, who does that Service for him, after he has robbed him on the High-way—Promises are but Words, and Words Air, which no Man can claim a Propriety in, but is equally free to all, and incapable of being confined; and if it were not, yet he who pays Debts, which he can possibly avoid, does but part with his Money for nothing, and pays more for the mere Reputation of Honesty and Conscience than it is worth.

He prefers the Way of applying to the Vices and Humours of great Persons before all other Methods of getting into Favour: for he that can be admitted into these Offices of Privacy and Trust seldom fails to arrive at greater; and with greater Ease and Certainty than those, who take the dull Way of plain Fidelity and Merit. For Vices, like Beasts, are fond of none but those that feed them; and where they once prevail, all other Considerations go for nothing. They are his own Flesh and Blood, born and bred out of him; and he has a stronger natural Affection for them than all other Relations whatsoever—And he, that has an Interest in these, has a greater Power over him than all other Obligations in the World. For though they are but his Imperfections and Infirmities, he is the more tender of them; as a lame Member, or diseased Limb is more carefully cherished than all the rest, that are sound and in perfect Vigour. All Offices of this kind are the greatest Endearments, being real Flatteries enforced by Deeds and Actions, and therefore far more prevalent than those, that are performed but by Words and Fawning; though very great Advantages are daily obtained that Way—And therefore he esteems Flattery as the next most sure and successful Way of improving his Interests. For Flattery is but a kind of civil Idolatry, that makes Images it self of Virtue, Worth, and Honour in some Person, that is utterly void of all, and then falls down, and worships them. And the more dull and absurd these Applications are, the better they are always received: for Men delight more to be presented with those Things they want, than such as they have no need nor use of. And though they condemn the Realities of those Honours and Renowns, that are falsely imputed to them, they are wonderfully affected with their false Pretences. For Dreams work more upon Men's Passions, than any waking Thoughts of the same Kind; and many, out of an ignorant Superstition, give more Credit to them, than the most rational of all their vigilant Conjectures, how false soever they prove in the Event—No wonder then if those, who apply to Men's Fancies and Humours, have a stronger Influence upon them than those, that seek to prevail upon their Reason and Understandings, especially in things so delightful to them as their own Praises, no Matter how false and apparently incredible: for great Persons may wear counterfeit Jewels of any Caract, with more Confidence and Security from being discovered, than those of meaner Quality; in whose Hands the Greatness of their Value (if they were true) is more apt to render them suspected. A Flatterer is like *Mahomet's* Pigeon, that picks his Food out of his Master's Ear, who is willing to have it believed, that he whispers Oracles into it; and accordingly sets a high Esteem upon the Service he does him, though the Impostor only designs his own Utilities—For Men are for the most Part better pleased with other Men's Opinions, though false, of their Happiness, than their own Experiences; and find more Pleasure in the dullest Flattery of others than all the vast Imaginations they can have of themselves, as no Man is apt to be tickled with his own fingers; because the Applauses of others are more agreeable to those high Conceits, they have of themselves, which they are glad to find confirmed, and are the only Music, that sets them a dancing, like those that are bitten with a Tarantula.

He accounts it an Argument of great Discretion, and as great Temper, to take no Notice of Affronts and Indignities put upon him by great Persons. For he that is insensible of Injuries of this Nature can receive none; and if he lose no Confidence by them, can lose nothing else; for it is greater to be above Injuries, than either to do, or revenge them; and he, that will be deterred by those Discouragements from prosecuting his Designs, will never obtain what he proposes to himself. When a Man is once known to be able to endure Insolencies easier than others can impose them, they will raise the Siege, and leave him as impregnable; and therefore he resolves never to omit the least Opportunity of pressing his Affairs, for Fear of being baffled and affronted; for if he can at any Rate render himself Master of his Purposes, he would not wish an easier, nor a cheaper Way, as he knows how to repay himself, and make others receive those Insolencies of him for good and current Payment, which he was glad to take before—And he esteems it no mean Glory to shew his Temper of such a Compass, as is able to reach from the highest Arrogance to the meanest, and most dejected Submissions. A Man, that has endured all Sorts of Affronts, may be allowed, like an Apprentice that has served out his Time, to set up for himself, and put them off upon others; and if the most common and approved Way of growing rich is to gain by the Ruin and loss of those, who are in necessity, why should not a Man be allowed as well to make himself appear great by debasing those, that are below him? For Insolence is no inconsiderable Way of improving Greatness and Authority in the Opinion of the World. If all Men are born equally fit to govern, as some late Philosophers affirm, he only has the Advantage of all others, who has the best Opinion of his own Abilities, how mean soever they really are; and, therefore, he stedfastly believes, that Pride is the only great, wise, and happy Virtue that a Man is capable of, and the most compendious and easy Way to Felicity—For he, that is able to persuade himself impregnably, that he is some great and excellent Person, how far short soever he falls of it, finds more Delight in that Dream than if he were really so; and the less he is of what he fancies himself to be, the better he is pleased, as Men covet those things, that are forbidden and denied them, more greedily than those, that are in their Power to obtain; and he, that can enjoy all the best Rewards of Worth and Merit without the Pains and Trouble that attend it, has a better Bargain than he, who pays as much for it as it is worth. This he performs by an obstinate implicit believing as well as he can of himself, and as meanly of all other Men; for he holds it a kind of Self-Preservation to maintain a good Estimation of himself: And as no Man is bound to love his Neighbour better than himself; so he ought not to think better of him than he does of himself; and he, that will not afford himself a very high Esteem, will never spare another Man any at all. He who has made so absolute a Conquest over himself (which Philosophers say is the greatest of all Victories) as to be received for a Prince within himself, is greater and more arbitrary within his own Dominions, than he that depends upon the uncertain Loves or Fears of other Men without him.—And since the Opinion of the World is vain, and for the most Part false, he believes it is not to be attempted but by Ways as false and vain as it self; and therefore to appear and seem is much better and wiser, than really to be, whatsoever is well esteemed in the general Value of the World.

Next Pride he believes Ambition to be the only generous and heroical Virtue in the World, that Mankind is capable of. For as Nature gave Man an erect Figure, to raise him above the groveling Condition of his fellow Creatures the Beasts: so he, that endeavours to improve that, and raise himself higher, seems best to comply with the Design and Intention of Nature. Though the Stature of Man is confined to a certain Height, yet his Mind is unlimited, and capable of growing up to Heaven: And as those, who endeavour to arrive at that Perfection, are adored and reverenced by all, so he, that endeavours to advance himself as high as possibly he can in this World, comes nearest to the Condition of those holy and divine Aspirers. All the purest Parts of Nature always tend upwards, and the more dull and heavy downwards: so in the little World the noblest Faculties of Man, his Reason and Understanding, that give him a Prerogative above all other earthly Creatures, mount upwards—And therefore he, who takes that Course and still aspires in all his Undertakings and Designs, does but conform to that which Nature dictates—Are not the Reason and the Will, the two commanding Faculties of the Soul, still striving which shall be uppermost? Men honour none but those that are above them, contest with Equals, and disdain Inferiors. The first Thing that God gave Man, was Dominion over the rest of his inferior Creatures; but he, that can extend that over Man, improves his Talent to the best Advantage. How are Angels distinguished but by *Dominions*, *Powers*,

Thrones, and *Principalities?* Then he, who still aspires to purchase those, comes nearest to the Nature of those heavenly Ministers, and in all Probability is most like to go to Heaven—No Matter what Destruction he makes in his Way, if he does but attain his End: for nothing is a Crime, that is too great to be punished; and when it is once arrived at that Perfection, the most horrid Actions in the World become the most admired and renowned. Birds, that build highest are most safe; and he, that can advance himself above the Envy or Reach of his Inferiors, is secure against the Malice and Assaults of Fortune. All Religions have ever been persecuted in their primitive Ages, when they were weak and impotent; but, when they propagated and grew great, have been received with Reverence and Adoration by those, who otherwise had proved their crullest Enemies; and those, that afterwards opposed them, have suffered as severely as those, that first profest them. So Thieves, that rob in small Parties, and break Houses, when they are taken are hanged: but, when they multiply and grow up into Armies, and are able to take Towns, the same things are called heroic Actions, and acknowledged for such by all the World. *Courts of Justice*, for the most Part, commit greater Crimes than they punish, and do those that sue in them more Injuries than they can possibly receive from one another; and yet they are venerable, and must not be told so, because they have Authority and Power to justify what they do, and the Law (that is, whatsoever they please to call so) ready to give Judgment for them. Who knows, when a *Physician* cures or kills? and yet he is equally rewarded for both, and the Profession esteemed never the less worshipful—And therefore he accounts it a ridiculous Vanity in any Man to consider, whether he does right or wrong in any Thing he attempts; since the Success is only able to determine, and satisfy the Opinion of the World, which is the one, and which the other. As for those Characters and Marks of Distinction, which *Religion*, *Law*, and *Morality* fix upon both, they are only significant and valid, when their Authority is able to command Obedience and Submission; but when the greatness, Numbers, or Interest of those, who are concerned, outgrows that, they change their Natures; and that, which was Injury before, becomes Justice, and Justice Injury. It is with Crimes, as with Inventions in the Mechanics, that will frequently hold true to all Purposes of the Design, while they are tried in little; but, when the Experiment is made in great, prove false in all Particulars, to what is promised in the Model: So Iniquities and Vices may be punished and corrected, like Children when they are little and impotent; but when they are great and sturdy, they become incorrigible, and Proof against all the Power of Justice and Authority.

Among all his Virtues there is none, which he sets so high an Esteem upon as Impudence, which he finds more useful and necessary than a Vizard is to a Highwayman. For he, that has but a competent Stock of this natural Endowment, has an Interest in any Man he pleases, and is able to manage it with greater Advantages than those, who have all the real Pretences imaginable, but want that dextrous Way of solliciting, by which, if the worst fall out, he is sure to lose Nothing, if he does not win. He that is impudent is shot-free, and if he be ever so much overpowered can receive no hurt; for his Forehead is impenetrable and of so excellent a Temper, that nothing is able to touch it, but turns Edge and is blunted. His Face holds no Correspondence with his Mind, and therefore whatsoever inward Sense or Conviction he feels, there is no outward Appearance of it in his Looks, to give Evidence against him; and in any Difficulty, that can befal him, Impudence is the most infallible Expedient to fetch him off, that is always ready, like his Angel Guardian, to relieve and rescue him in his greatest Extremities; and no outward Impression, nor inward neither (though his own Conscience take Part against him) is able to beat him from his Guards. Though Innocence and a good Conscience be said to *a brazen Wall*, a *brazen Confidence* is more impregnable,

He admires good Nature as only good greater Affliction to an innocent Man to be suspected, than it is to one, that is guilty and impudent, to be openly convicted of an apparent Crime. And in all the Affairs of Mankind, a brisk Confidence, though utterly void of Sense, is able to go through Matters of Difficulty with greater Ease, than all the Strength of Reason less boldly inforced; as the *Turks* are said by a small slight handling of their Bows, to make an Arrow without a Head pierce deeper into hard Bodies, than Guns of greater Force are able to do a Bullet of Steel. And though it be but a Cheat and Imposture, that has neither Truth nor Reason to support it, yet it thrives better in the World than Things of greater Solidity; as Thorns and Thistles flourish on barren Grounds, where nobler Plants would starve: And he, that can improve his barren Parts by this excellent and most compendious Method, deserves much better, in his Judgment, than those, who endeavour to do the same thing by the more studious and difficult Way of downright Industry and Drudging. For Impudence does not only supply all Defects, but gives them a greater Grace than if they had needed no Art; as all other Ornaments are commonly nothing else, but the Remedies, or Disguises of Imperfections—And therefore he thinks him very weak, that is unprovided of this excellent and most useful Quality, without which the best natural or acquired Parts are of no more use, than the *Guanches* Darts, which, the Virtuosos say,[2] are headed with Butter hardned in the Sun. It serves him to innumerable Purposes, to press on and understand no Repulse, how smart or harsh soever; for he, that can sail nearest the Wind, has much the Advantage of all others; and such is the Weakness or Vanity of some Men, that they will grant that to obstinate Importunity, which they would never have done upon all the most just Reasons and Considerations imaginable; as those, that watch Witches, will make them confess that, which they would never have done upon any other Account.

He believes a Man's Words and his Meaning should never agree together: For he, that says what he thinks, lays himself open to be expounded by the most ignorant; and he, who does not make his Words rather serve to conceal, than discover the Sense of his Heart, deserves to have it pulled out, like a Traytor's, and shewn publicly to the Rabble. For as a King, they say, cannot reign without dissembling; so private Men, without that, cannot govern themselves with any Prudence or Discretion imaginable—That is the only politic Magic, that has Power to make a Man walk invisible, give him access into all Men's Privacies, and keep all others out of his; which is as great an Odds, as it is to discover, what Cards those he plays with have in their Hands, and permit them to know nothing of his. And therefore he never speaks his own Sense, but that which he finds comes nearest to the Meaning of those he converses with; as Birds are drawn into Nets by Pipes that counterfeit their own Voices. By this means he possesses Men, like the *Devil*, by getting within them before they are aware, turns them out of themselves, and either betrays, or renders them ridiculous, as he finds it most agreeable either to his Humour, or his Occasions.

As for Religion, he believes a wise Man ought to possess it, only that he may not be observed to have freed himself from the Obligations of it, and so teach others by his Example to take the same Freedom: For he, who is at Liberty, has a great Advantage over all those, whom he has to deal with, as all Hypocrites find by perpetual Experience—That one of the best Uses, that can be made of it, is to take Measure of Men's Understandings and Abilities by it, according as they are more or less serious in it; for he thinks, that no Man ought to be much concerned in it but Hypocrites, and such as make it their Calling and Profession; who, though they do not *live by their Faith*, like the Righteous, do that which is nearest to it, get their living by it; and that those only take the surest Course, who make their best Advantages of it in this World, and trust to Providence for the next, to which purpose he believes it is most properly to be relied upon by all Men.

He admires good Nature as only good to those who have it not, and laughs at Friendship as a ridiculous Foppery, which all wise Men easily outgrow; for the more

[2] Thyer, editor of the *Genuine Remains*, notes the following: "What *Butler* refers to is recorded by *Sprat* in his History of the Royal Society. . . . "

a Man loves another, the less he loves himself. All Regards and civil Applications should, like true Devotion, look upwards, and address to those that are above us, and from whom we may in Probability expect either Good or Evil; but to apply to those, that are our Equals, or such as cannot benefit or hurt us, is a far more irrational Idolatry than worshipping of Images or Beasts. All the Good, that can proceed from Friendship, is but this, that it puts Men in a Way to betray one another. The best Parents, who are commonly the worst Men, have naturally a tender Kindness for their Children, only because they believe they are a Part of themselves, which shews, that Self-love is the Original of all others, and the Foundation of that great Law of Nature, Self-Preservation; for no Man ever destroyed himself wilfully, that had not first left off to love himself—Therefore a Man's Self is the proper Object of his Love, which is never so well employed, as when it is kept within its own Confines, and not suffered to straggle. Every Man is just so much a Slave as he is concerned in the Will, Inclinations, or Fortunes of another, or has any thing of himself out of his own Power to dispose of; and therefore he is resolved never to trust any Man with that Kindness, which he takes up of himself, unless he has such Security as is most certain to yield him double Interest: For he that does otherwise, is but a *Jew* and a *Turk* to himself, which is much worse than to be so to all the World beside. Friends are only Friends to those who have no need of them, and when they have, become no longer Friends; like the Leaves of Trees, that clothe the Woods in the Heat of Summer, when they have no need of Warmth, but leave them naked when cold Weather comes; and since there are so few that prove otherwise, it is not Wisdom to rely on any.

He is of Opinion, that no Men are so fit to be employed and trusted as Fools, or Knaves; for the first understand no Right, the others regard none; and whensoever there falls out an Occasion, that may prove of great Importance, if the Infamy and Danger of the Dishonesty be not too apparent, they are the only Persons, that are fit for the Undertaking. They are both equally greedy of Employment, the one out of an Itch to be thought able, and the other honest enough to be trusted, as by Use and Practice they sometimes prove: For the general Business of the World lies, for the most Part, in *Rotines* and Forms, of which there are none so exact Observers, as those, who understand nothing else to divert them; as Carters use to blind their Fore-horses on both Sides, that they may see only forward, and so keep the Road the better; and Men, that aim at a Mark, use to shut one Eye, that they may see the surer with the other. If Fools are not notorious, they have far more Persons to deal with of their own Elevation (who understand one another better) than they have of those, that are above them, which renders them fitter for many Businesses than wiser Men, and they believe themselves to be so for all: For no Man ever thought himself a Fool, that was one, so confident does their Ignorance naturally render them; and Confidence is no contemptible Qualification in the Management of human Affairs—And as blind Men have secret Artifices and Tricks to supply that Defect, and find out their Ways, which those, who have their Eyes and are but hoodwinked, are utterly unable to do: so Fools have always little Crafts and Frauds in all their Transactions, which wiser Men would never have thought upon; and by those they frequently arrive at very great Wealth, and as great Success, in all their Undertakings—For all Fools are but feeble and impotent Knaves, that have as strong and vehement Inclinations to all Sorts of Dishonesty as the most notorious of those Engineers, but want Abilities to put them in Practice; and as they are always found to be the most obstinate and intractable People to be prevailed upon by Reason or Conscience; so they are as easy to submit to their Superiors, that is Knaves, by whom they are always observed to be governed, as all Corporations are wont to choose their Magistrates out of their own Members. As for Knaves, they are commonly true enough to their own Interests; and while they gain by their Employments, will be careful not to disserve those, who can turn them out when they please, what Tricks soever they put upon others; and therefore such Men prove more useful to them, in their Designs of Gain and Profit, than those, whose Consciences and Reason will not permit them to take that Latitude.

And since Buffoonery is, and has always been so delightful to great Persons, he holds him very improvident, that is to seek in a Quality so inducing, that he cannot at least serve for want of a better; especially since it is so easy, that the greatest Part of the Difficulty lyes in Confidence, and he, that can but stand fair, and give Aim to those that are Gamesters, does not alway lose his Labour, but many times becomes well esteemed for his generous and bold Demeanor; and a lucky Repartee hit upon by Chance may be the making of a Man. This is the only modern Way of running at Tilt, with which great Persons are so delighted to see Men encounter one another, and break Jests, as they did Lances heretofore; and he that has the best Beaver to his Helmet, has the greatest Advantage; and as the former past upon the Account of Valour, so does the latter on the Score of Wit, though neither, perhaps, have any great Reason for their Pretences, especially the latter, that depends much upon Confidence, which is commonly a great Support to Wit, and therefore believed to be its betters, that ought to take place of it, as all Men are greater than their Dependents—So pleasant it is to see Men lessen one another, and strive who shall shew himself the most ill-natured and ill-mannered. As in Cuffing all Blows are aimed at the Face; so it fares in these Rencounters, where he, that wears the toughest Leather on his Visage, comes off with Victory, though he has ever so much the Disadvantage upon all other Accounts—For a Buffoon is like a Mad-Dog, that has a Worm in his Tongue, which makes him bite at all that light in his Way; and as he can do nothing alone, but must have somebody to set him that he may throw at, he that performs that Office with the greatest Freedom, and is contented to be laughed at, to give his Patron Pleasure, cannot but be understood to have done very good Service, and consequently deserves to be well rewarded; as a Mountebank's *Pudding*, that is content to be cut, and slashed, and burnt, and poisoned, without which his Master can shew no Tricks, deserves to have a considerable Share in his Gains.

As for the Meanness of these Ways, which some may think too base to be employed to so excellent an End, that imports nothing: for what Dislike soever the World conceives against any Man's Undertakings, if they do but succeed and prosper, it will easily recant its Error, and applaud what it condemned before; and therefore all wise Men have ever justly esteemed it a great Virtue to disdain the false Values, it commonly sets upon all Things, and which it self is so apt to retract—For as those, who go up Hill, use to stoop and bow their Bodies forward, and sometimes creep upon their Hands; and those, that descend, to go upright: so the lower a Man stoops and submits in these endearing Offices, the more sure and certain he is to rise; and the more upright he carries himself in other Matters, the more like in probability to be ruined—And this he believes to be a wiser course for any Man to take than to trouble himself with the Knowledge of Arts or Arms: For the one does but bring a Man an unnecessary Trouble, and the other as unnecessary Danger; and the shortest and more easy Way to attain to both, is to despise all other Men, and believe as stedfastly in Himself as he can, a better and more certain Course than that of Merit.

What he gains wickedly he spends as vainly; for he holds it the greatest Happiness, that a Man is capable of, to deny himself nothing, that his Desires can propose to him, but rather to improve his Enjoyments by glorying in his Vices: for Glory being one End of almost all the Business of this World, he who omits that in the Enjoyment of himself and his Pleasures, loses the greatest Part of his Delight. And therefore the Felicity, which he supposes other Men apprehend that he receives in the Relish of his Luxuries, is more delightful to him than the Fruition itself.

A BUMPKIN, OR COUNTRY-SQUIRE

Is a Clown of Rank and Degree. He is the Growth of his own Land, a Kind of *Antocthanus,*[3] like the *Athenians,* that sprung out of their own Ground; or Barnacles that grow upon Trees in *Scotland:* His homely Education has rendered him a Native only of his own Soil, and a Foreigner to all other Places, from which he differs in Language, Manner of Living, and Behaviour, which are as rugged as the Coat of a Colt that has been bred upon a Common. The Custom of being the best Man in his own Territories has made him the worst every where else. He assumes the upper End of the Table at an Ale-House, as his Birthright; receives the Homage of his Company, which are always subordinate, and dispenses Ale and Communication, like a Self-conforming Teacher in a Conventicle. The chief Points, he treats on, are the Memoirs of his Dogs and Horses, which he repeats as often as a Holder-forth, that has but two Sermons; to which if he adds the History of his Hawks and Fishing, he is very painful and laborious. He does his endeavour to appear a Drole, but his Wit being, like his Estate, within the Compass of a Hedge, is so profound and obscure to a Stranger, that it requires a Commentary, and is not to be understood without a perfect Knowledge of all Circumstances of Persons, and the particular Idiom of the Place. He has no Ambition to appear a Person of civil Prudence or Understanding, more than in putting off a lame infirm Jade for sound Wind and Limb; to which Purpose he brings his Squirehood and Groom to vouch; and, rather than fail, will outswear an Affidavit-Man. The Top of his Entertainment is horrible strong Beer, which he pours into his Guests (as the *Dutch* did Water into our Merchants, when they tortured them at *Amboyna*) till they *confess* they can drink no more; and then he triumphs over them as subdued and vanquished, no less by the Strength of his Brain, than his Drink. When he salutes a Man, he lays violent Hands upon him, and gripes and shakes him, like a Fit of an Ague: and, when he accosts a Lady, he stamps with his Foot, like a *French* Fencer, and makes a Longee at her, in which he always misses his Aim, too high or too low, and hits her on the Nose or Chin. He is never without some rough-handed Flatterer, that rubs him, like a Horse, with a Curry-Comb, till he kicks and grunts with the Pleasure of it. He has old Family Stories and Jests, that fell to him with the Estate, and have been left from Heir to Heir time out of Mind: With these he entertains all Comers over and over, and has added some of his own Times, which he intends to transmit over to Posterity. He has but one Way of making all Men welcome, that come to his House, and that is, by making himself and them drunk; while his Servants take the same Course with theirs, which he approves of as good and faithful Service, and the rather, because, if he has Occasion to tell a strange improbable Story, they may be in a Readiness to vouch with the more Impudence, and make it a Case of Conscience to lye, as well as drink for his Credit. All the heroical Glory he aspires to, is but to be reputed a most potent and victorious Stealer of Deer, and beater-up of Parks, to which Purpose he has compiled Commentaries of his own great Actions, that treat of his dreadful Adventures in the Night, of giving Battle in the Dark, discomfiting of Keepers, horsing the deer on his own Back, and making off with equal Resolution and Success. He goes to Bawdy-Houses, to see Fashions; that is, to have his Pocket pick't, and the Pox into the Bargain.

[3] An autochthon is a human being sprung from the land he inhabits.

A PHILOSOPHER

Seats himself as Spectator and Critic on the great Theater of the World, and gives Sentence on the Plots, Language, and Action of whatsoever he sees represented, according to his own Fancy. He will pretend to know what is done behind the Scene, but so seldom is in the Right, that he discovers nothing more than his own Mistakes. When his Profession was in Credit in the World, and Money was to be gotten by it, it divided itself into Multitudes of Sects, that maintained themselves and their Opinions by fierce and hot Contests with one another; but since the Trade decayed and would not turn to Account, they all fell of themselves, and now the World is so unconcerned in their Controversies, that three Reformado Sects joined in one, like *Epicuro-Gassendo-Charltoniana*,[4] will not serve to maintain one Pedant. He makes his Hypotheses himself, as a Taylor does a Doublet without Measure, no Matter whether they fit *Nature*, he can make *Nature* fit them, and, whether they are strait or wide, pinch or stuff out the Body accordingly. He judges of the Works of *Nature* just as the Rabble do of State-Affairs: They see things done, and every Man according to his Capacity guesses at the Reasons of them, but knowing nothing of the Arcana or secret Movements of either, they seldom or never are in the Right; howsoever they please themselves, and some others, with their Fancies, and the further they are off Truth, the more confident they are they are near it; as those, that are out of their Way, believe, the further they have gone, they are the nearer their Journey's End, when they are furthest of all from it. He is confident of immaterial Substances, and his Reasons are very pertinent, that is, *substantial* as he thinks, and *immaterial* as other do. Heretofore his Beard was the Badge of his Profession, and the Length of that in all his Polemics was ever accounted the Length of his Weapon; but when the Trade fell, that fell too. In *Lucius*'s time they were commonly called *Beard-Wearers;* for all the Strength of their Wits lay in their Beards, as *Sampson*'s did in his Locks: But since the World began to see the Vanity of that *Hair-brained* Cheat, they left it off, to save their Credit.

A RANTER

Is a *Fanatic* Hector, that has found out by a very strange Way of new Light, how to transform all the *Devils* into *Angels of Light;* for he believes all Religion consists in Looseness, and that Sin and Vice is *the whole Duty of Man*. He put off the *old Man*, but puts it on again upon the *new one*, and makes his *Pagan* Vices serve to preserve his *Christian* Virtues from wearing out; for if he should use his Piety and Devotion always it would hold out but a little while. He is loth that Iniquity and Vice should be thrown away, as long as there may be good Use of it; for if that, which is wickedly gotten, may be disposed to pious Uses, why should not Wickedness itself as well? He believes himself Shot-free against all the Attempts of the *Devil*, the *World*, and the *Flesh*, and therefore is not afraid to attack them in their own Quarters, and encounter them at their own Weapons. For as strong Bodies may freely venture to do and suffer that, without any Hurt to themselves, which would destroy those that are feeble: So a Saint, that is strong in Grace, may boldly engage himself in those great Sins and Iniquities, that would easily damn a weak Brother, and yet come off never the worse. He believes Deeds of Darkness to be only those Sins that are committed in private, not those that are acted openly and owned. He is but an *Hypocrite* turned the wrong Side outward; for, as the one wears his Vices within, and the other without, so when they are counter-changed the *Ranter* becomes an *Hypocrite*, and the *Hypocrite* an able *Ranter*. His Church is the *Devil's* Chappel; for it agrees exactly both in Doctrine and Discipline with the best reformed Baudy-Houses. He is a Monster produced by the Madness of this latter Age; but if it had been his Fate to have been whelped in old *Rome* he had past for a Prodigy, and been received among raining of Stones and the speaking of Bulls, and would have put a stop to all public Affairs, until he had been expiated. *Nero* cloathed *Christians* in the Skins of wild Beasts; but he wraps wild Beasts in the Skins of *Christians*.

[4] Dr Walter Charleton (1619–1707), prominent member of the Royal Society, was author of *Physiologia Epicuro-Gassendo-Charltoniana, or a Fabrick of Science Natural upon the Hypothesis of Atoms* (1654).

Henry More

HENRY MORE was born in October of 1614 at Grantham in Lincolnshire, the youngest of a family of twelve. His father was a gentleman of "fair estate and fortune," who bred his son to a strict Calvinism but who read Spenser's *Faerie Queene* to him on winter evenings, with appreciation of the "phansy" as well as the morality. The Calvinism lasted through Grantham Grammar School, but when More went to Eton in 1628 he came to question and presently to reject the key doctrine of Predestination. The Spenserianism was to stay with him and color all his own poetic style.

After three years of perfecting his Latin and Greek at Eton, More was admitted at the end of 1631 to Christ's College, Cambridge. Under the guidance of a quite un-Calvinistic tutor, Robert Gell, More plunged into the reading of philosophy. The common university experience of scepticism was More's; only in his case the issue was not the existence of God, but the meaning of his own existence. Seeking a more divine knowledge than that of the usual philosophical exercises of the university of his day, More began to read Plato and the writings of the neo-Platonists, and he was filled with the enthusiasm of a great discovery. At the same time he began to read the *Theologia Germanica* with its more practical and inward mystical emphasis. Under the stimulus of the quite Platonic belief that he who would apprehend the Real must make himself spiritually ready for that undertaking, More devoted himself to a very ascetic course of spiritual discipline, at the end of which he found a spiritual peace that was to last. This happy issue, it has been suggested, may have been due, in part at least, to the influence of the great leader and inspirer of Platonic studies in the Cambridge of those years, Benjamin Whichcote of Emmanuel, who began to give the Sunday afternoon lecture in Trinity Church in 1637.

What is certain is that More made up his mind to devote his life to philosophical studies. He had received his B.A. in 1635. In 1639 he received his M.A. and became a fellow of Christ's College, and apparently somewhere about the same time took orders. Although he is said to have received many offers of preferment, including the suggestion of a bishopric, More remained at Cambridge (except for a brief period of retirement from 1666 to 1668) for the rest of his life. He was an enthusiastic and a successful teacher, even in his earliest teaching years acting as tutor to a number of young men of rank and promise. But apparently none of these young men evoked the interest which the sister of one of his students, Ann Finch, presently Lady Conway, inspired. A young woman of unusual qualities of mind and spirit, Lady Conway became not only his devoted pupil but his intimate friend, patroness, and inspiration. Her splendid home at Ragley became his favorite retreat for studying and writing, and here he enjoyed the society of various intellectual figures of the day, ranging from the half-scientist, half-adventurer Van Helmont to Jeremy Taylor, to say nothing of the remarkable assortment of medical and religious helpers who tried to assuage the sufferings of the mysterious illness which afflicted Lady Conway.

But great as was his influence as a university teacher, it was carried further afield when in 1642 he published *Psychodia Platonica: or a Platonicall Song of the Soul.* The Spenserian stanzas of this work brought to a good many seeking spirits of that day More's allegorical presentation of the neo-Platonists' answers to the ancient riddles of the origin and destiny of the soul. This was the beginning of a period of great literary activity that continued to the day of his death. Four years later in 1646 he published *Democritus Platonissans: or an Essay upon the Infinitie of Worlds,* a remarkable verse exposition of the idea of infinity and a trumpet call to his generation to enter into the freedom of a new intellectual world with all its exhilarating prospects for the human spirit. Both publications with some further additions were collected in the *Philosophical Poems* of 1647.

After that More's main energies went into a series of prose works, both Latin and English, of which the most important were *An Antidote against Atheism* (1653), *Conjectura Cabbalistica* (1653), *Enthusiasmus Triumphatus* (1656), *The Immortality of the Soul* (1659), *An Explanation of the Grand Mystery of Godliness* (1660), *Enchiridium Ethicum* (1667), and *Divine Dialogues* (1668), the latter unquestionably the most popular of all his writings. In the later years of his life More yielded to the contemporary passion for highly complicated allegorical scriptural interpretation that was to engulf even the scientific mind of Sir Isaac Newton. And a good part of those years went into the enterprise of translating his English philosophical works into Latin. All through his life he maintained an extensive correspondence with many of the leading intellectual figures of his day, Descartes, Hartlib, Glanvill, William Penn, and many others.

From the purely literary point of view, More's work still remains obscure. He is too intent on the explanation of his ideas to give his allegory the necessary sense of reality; passion and music alike are wanting to large stretches of his verse; his syntax is often contorted and involved; and his diction ranges from sentimental archaism to highly theoretic and often dangerously private coinage. And much of his prose is heavy and over-involved, over-subtle and over-abstract. And just as in his earlier choice of the Spenserian stanza More showed little talent for choosing the right medium for his limitations as a poet, so in his choice of the dialogue form for his most popular prose work, he took no account of his own lack of dramatic sense and want of vitalizing detail. But difficult as his work often is, there is a good deal in More to repay study. There is real intellectual passion in his verse and in a surprising number of passages, metaphysical energy and splendor. There is a large and spacious spirit in his prose, and grace and urbanity in the expression of the exchange of views in the *Dialogues*. He is at home on the heights and yet keeps enough ethical sympathy to transport the responsive reader for a little to that lofty realm.

From the point of view of insight into his time and place More is of real importance. He is the literary voice of a very interesting and important intellectual and religious movement, that of the Cambridge Platonists, and he is a very original and considerable thinker in his own right.

The Cambridge Platonists, like Lord Falkland earlier in the century, sought a rational approach to the religious controversies of the day that were threatening not only the peace of society but the life of religion itself. The first of the men usually denominated the Cambridge Platonists, Benjamin Whichcote, the great university preacher of the Commonwealth, was not only weary of the emphasis of the time on dogmatic controversy, but convinced of the unimportance of many of the issues on which men were so bitterly fighting each other. He felt that the emphasis should be shifted from doctrinal agreement to Christian sympathy and charity, and that decisions on institutions and morals should be made on the basis of reason and Scripture taken broadly, not literally, text by text. He was aware, too, of the inroads which scepticism was making on faith, and he appealed to reason against both enthusiasm and atheism. The speculative character of the movement was emphasized in Whichcote's followers, Smith and Cudworth, but as Tulloch long ago pointed out, it reached its ripest personal-religious development in More.

Against many of the philosophers, old and new, More insisted that religion and philosophy should cooperate, that reason, the guide alike of the philosopher and the theologian, was the only sure foundation of truth. In Platonism of the Plotinian type and in Scripture, More found the vindication of his own deepest insight and surest personal intuition, the existence of a realm of spiritual beauty transcending the physical realm. But More was no mere backward-looking academic. He was aware early in life of the impact of the scientific thinking that was in process of transforming the intellectual world of his day, and he was clearly ambitious of fitting it into a new synthesis of philosophical knowledge, spiritual insight, and religious revelation.

This is particularly apparent in More's relation to Descartes. Miss Nicolson has shown what an important part More played in the welcome to Cartesian ideas and in the interpretation of them to England. This is especially evident in the introduction to *Democritus Platonissans* in which More names Descartes in the preface and takes a position on the infinity of worlds in the poem itself that was clearly influenced by his work. The idea itself, as A. O. Lovejoy shows (*The Great Chain of Being*, 1948), though it was to have so revolutionary an influence on seventeenth-century thinking on cosmography, did not owe its origin to the astronomers but to Platonistic speculations on the nature of the creator and the consequences of the purely metaphysical principle of plenitude. Bruno had already found in the idea of the infinity of worlds a moving revelation of the creative energy manifest in the universe, and this exhilaration More clearly shares in *Democritus Platonissans*.

But of even greater influence was the psychological emphasis of Descartes, and particularly was this true for More to whom the proof of the existence of God from the idea of God in the mind of man was a peculiarly congenial one. There seems to be no question that in the beginning at least Cartesianism reassured More on his reasoning as to the validity of his profoundest insights about the nature of man and his universe. But as E. A. Burtt has pointed out in *The Metaphysical Foundations of Modern Science* (rev. 1932, repr. 1949), More like Hobbes found it impossible to rest content with the Cartesian dualism. He could not, however, accept Hobbes's solution. He agreed that nothing could exist without extension, but he boldly claimed extension for spirit. Unlike matter, spirit was for More freely penetrable and able in turn to penetrate and to move matter. From the notion of the incorporeal substance in the human being More moved to the idea of a spirit of nature holding together the different parts of the material universe. And from the all-pervading harmony and order of the world More argued the existence of a spiritual substance higher than the spirit of nature, and defined that spiritual substance in terms not only of the Plotinian Absolute but of the Christian God.

For the religious motive was always the dominant motive in More's speculations; and in his religious constitution, for all the mystical loftiness of his thinking, there was always a strongly practical vein. It is significant that when he came to his most popular work, the *Divine Dialogues*, he published the last two of the dialogues, the fourth and fifth, dealing with the more practical theme of the Kingdom of God, before the more speculative dialogues on the nature of God and his Providence. And the *Dialogues* as a whole are set in a frame-work of very immediate and practical preoccupation with the problems of the author's time and place. The attack on Rome is in line with the Anglican controversy of the period. And the characterization of two of the participants in the Fourth Dialogue, "Hylobares, A young, witty and well-moralized *Materialist*," and "Cuphophron, A zealous, but Airy-minded, *Platonist* and *Cartesian*, or *Mechanist*," reveals More's concern over the effect of contemporary currents of thought on young men like his university students.

In 1878 Grosart printed the *Complete Poems* in the Chertsey Worthies Library. Otherwise, so far as modern editing is concerned, only selections of More's work are available. For the poetry G. Bullough's *Philosophical Poems* (1931) affords a substantial selection and a good critical introduction. F. I. MacKinnon's *Philosophical Writings of Henry More* (1925) prints representative selections from the *Antidote against Atheism*, *The Immortality of the Soul*, and *Enchiridium Metaphysicum*, with a helpful introduction, bibliography, and outline summary of More's philosophy. The 1690 English translation of *Enchiridion Ethicum* was reproduced by the Facsimile Text Society in 1930.

R. Ward's *Life* (1710), edited by M. F. Howard, was reprinted in 1911; a good deal of valuable material on More's personality and relations as well as his life has been made available in M. Nicolson's *Conway Letters* (1930). There are introductory sketches of More in E. A. George, *Seventeenth Century Men of Latitude* (1908) and F. J. Powicke, *Cambridge Platonists* (1926), and more critical studies in the books of G. P. H. Pawson (1930) and W. C. de Pauley (1937) on the Cambridge Platonists. The general religious position of More and his fellow-Platonists is most fully presented in J. Tulloch, *Rational Theology and Christian Philosophy*, II, (1872), and his contribution to toleration is treated in W. K. Jordan, *Development of Religious Toleration*, IV (1940). More's attempt to link seventeenth-century religion with science is studied in detail in P. R. Anderson, *Science in Defence of Liberal Religion* (1933), and his relations to Descartes and Cartesianism in M. Nicolson, "Early Stages of Cartesianism in England," *SP* XXVI, 356–374 and E. A. Burtt, *Metaphysical Foundations of Modern Physical Science* (1925; rev. 1932).

DEMOCRITUS PLATONISSANS[1]

or

An Essay upon the Infinity of Worlds out of Platonick[2] Principles

TO THE READER

Reader,

I Present to thee here in its proper place what I have heretofore offered to thee upon lesse advantage, but upon so little, no where (I conceive) as that I should despair of thy acceptance, if the overstrangenesse of the Argument prove no hinderance. INFINITIE of WORLDS! A thing monstrous[3] *if assented to, and to be startled at,*[4] *especially by them, whose thoughts this one have alwayes so engaged, that they*

[1] Text: *Philosophical Poems* (1647)

[2] of Platonism, the philosophical system of the Greek philosopher, Plato (427–347 B.C.), a system famous for its analysis of the relations between the permanent and self-moved and the transient and variable, its theory of ideas, and its definition of Reality in terms of the True, the Beautiful, and the Good; actually of this system as developed by the followers of Plato, notably by Plotinus, (205–270), the leader of the Alexandrian neo-Platonists

[3] marvellous

[4] shocked at, frightened at

can find no leisure to think of any thing else. But I onely make a bare proposall[5] *to more acute judgements, of what my sportfull phancie,*[6] *with pleasure hath suggested: following my old designe of furnishing mens minds with variety of apprehensions*[7] *concerning the most weighty points of Philosophie, that they may not seem rashly to have settled in the truth, though it be the truth: a thing as ill beseeming*[8] *Philosophers, as hastie prejudicative*[9] *sentence Politicall Judges. But if I had relinquished here my wonted*[10] *self, in proving Dogmaticall, I should have found very noble Patronage for the cause among the ancients,* Epicurus,[11] Democritus,[12] Lucretius,[13] etc. *Or if justice may reach the dead do them the right,*[14] *as to shew,*[15] *that though they be hooted at, by the Rout*[16] *of the learned, as men of monstrous conceits,*[17] *they were either very wise or exceeding fortunate to light on so probable and specious*[18] *an opinion, in which notwithstanding there is so much difficulty and seeming inconsistencie.*

Nay and that sublime and subtill Mechanick[19] *too,* Des-Chartes,[20] *though he seem to mince*[21] *it must hold infinitude of worlds, or which is as harsh, one infinite one. For what is his* mundus indefinitè extensus,[22] *but* extensus infinitè?[23] *Else it sounds onely* infinitus quoad nos,[24] *but* simpliciter finitus.[25] *But if any space be left out unstuff'd with Atoms,*[26] *it will hazard the dissipation*[27] *of the whole frame*[28] *of Nature into disjoynted*[29] *dust; as may be proved by the Principles of his own Philosophie. And that there is space where-ever God is, or any actuall*[30] *and self-subsistent Being, seems to me no plainer then one of their* κοιναὶ ἔννοιαι.[31]

For mine own part, I must confesse these apprehensions do plainly oppose what heretofore I have conceived; but I have sworn more faithfull friendship with Truth then with my self. And therefore without all remorse lay battery against mine own edifice: not sparing to shew how weak that is, that my self now deems not impregnably strong. I have at the latter end of the last Canto of Psychathanasia,[32] *not without triumph concluded, that the world hath not continued* ab aeterno[33] *from this ground:*[34]

....Extension
That's infinite implies a contradiction.

And this is in answer to an objection against my last argument of the souls Immortalitie, viz. *divine goodnesse. Which I there make the measure of his providence. That ground limits the Essence of the world as well as its duration, and satisfies the curiositie*[35] *of the Opposer,*[36] *by shewing the incompossibilitie*[37] *in the Creature,*

[5] setting forth, statement
[6] playful fancy
[7] conceptions [8] becoming
[9] prejudging [10] customary
[11] Epicurus, Greek philosopher (342?–270 B.C.), who taught that pleasure is the only good, and the end of all morality, but the life of pleasure must be a life of virtue
[12] celebrated Greek philosopher (460?–362? B.C.), called the "Laughing Philosopher" from his continual laughter at the follies of mankind, noted for his enthusiasm for scientific experiment and speculation and for his theory of atoms
[13] Titus Lucretius Carus (96?–55 B.C.), Roman poet and Epicurean philosopher, who developed further the atomic theory of Democritus
[14] justice [15] show [16] pack
[17] ideas [18] fair
[19] a philosopher who explains phenomena by the assumption of mechanical action
[20] René Descartes (1596–1650), French philosopher, who sought mathematical certitude in metaphysical demonstration and developed the distinction between thought and extension, mind and matter to such a point that only the continual intervention of God could harmonize them
[21] minimize it
[22] indefinitely extended
[23] infinitely [24] with respect to us
[25] plainly limited
[26] according to Democritus one of the ultimate particles of matter of which the universe is formed
[27] scattering [28] structure
[29] disconnected [30] existing in fact
[31] Common Notions, or Innate Conceptions
[32] the second part of *A Platonick Song of the Soul,* treating the immortality of souls, especially man's soul
[33] endured "from eternity"
[34] fundamental principle
[35] the inquisitiveness
[36] the one who opposes the defender of a thesis in an academic disputation
[37] total incompatibility

not want of goodnesse in the Creatour to have staid[38] *the framing of the Universe. But now roused up by a new Philosophick furie, I answer that difficultie by taking away the Hypothesis of either the world or time being finite: defending the infinitude of both. Which though I had done with a great deal of vigour and life, and semblance*[39] *of assent, it would have agreed*[40] *well enough with the free heat*[41] *of Poesie, and might have passed for a pleasant flourish:*[42] *but the severity of my own judgement and sad*[43] *Genius,*[44] *hath cast in many correctives and coolers*[45] *into the Canto it self: so that it cannot amount to more then a discussion. And discussion is no prejudice*[46] *but an honour to the truth: for then and never but then is she victorious. And what a glorious Trophee*[47] *shall the finite world erect when it hath vanquished the Infinite; a Pygmee a Giant!*

H. M.

The Argument of Democritus Platonissans, *or* The Infinitie of Worlds

'Gainst boundlesse time th' objections made,
And wast[48] *infinity*
Of Worlds, are with new reasons weigh'd,
Mens judgements are left free.

Hence, hence unhallowed[49] ears and hearts more hard
Then winter clods fast froze[50] with Northern wind.
But most of all, foul tongue I thee discard
That blamest all that thy dark strait'ned[51] mind,
Cannot conceive:[52] But that no blame thou find;
Whate're my pregnant Muse brings forth to light,
She'll not acknowledge to be of her kind,[53]
Till Eagle-like she turn them to the sight
Of the eternall Word[54] all deckt with glory bright.

Strange sights do straggle[55] in my restlesse thoughts,
And lively[56] forms with orient[57] colours clad
Walk in my boundlesse mind, as men ybrought[58]
Into some spacious room, who when they've had
A turn or two, go out, although unbad.
All these I see and know, but entertain
None to my friend but who's most sober sad;
Although, the time my roof doth them contain
Their presence doth possesse[59] me till they out[60] again.

And thus possest, in silver trump I sound
Their guise,[61] their shape, their gesture and array,[62]
But as in silver trumpet nought is found
When once the piercing sound is past away,
(Though while the mighty blast therein did stay,

[38] stopped [39] appearance [40] been in harmony with [41] noble enthusiasm [42] boast
[43] serious [44] quality of mind [45] anything that cools emotions [46] injury
[47] monument or memorial of victory [48] uncultivated [49] not formally consecrated
[50] frozen [51] contracted in intelligence [52] comprehend [53] descended of her
[54] a title of Christ from the English translation of *Logos* in the Johannine writings (John 1.1, 14, etc.)
[55] intrude where they have no right to be [56] living [57] brilliant
[58] past participle, a conscious archaism of Spenser and his imitators
[59] engross [60] with ellipsis of *go* [61] manner [62] attire

Its tearing noise so terribly did shrill,
That it the heavens did shake, and earth dismay)
As empty I of what my flowing quill
In heedlesse hast elswhere, or here, may hap[63] to spill.

For 'tis of force and not of a set[64] will.
Ne dare my wary mind afford assent
To what is plac'd above all mortall skill.[65]
But yet our various thoughts to represent
Each gentle wight[66] will deem[67] of good intent.[68]
Wherefore with leave th' infinitie I'll sing
Of Time, of Space: or without leave; I'm brent[69]
With eagre[70] rage, my heart for joy doth spring,
And all my spirits[71] move with pleasant trembeling.

An inward triumph doth my soul up-heave[72]
And spread[73] abroad through endlesse 'spersed[74] air.
My nimble mind this clammie clod doth leave,
And lightly stepping on from starre to starre
Swifter then lightning, passeth wide and farre,
Measuring[75] th' unbounded Heavens and wastfull[76] skie;
Ne ought she finds her passage to debarre,
For still the azure Orb[77] as she draws nigh
Gives back,[78] new stars appear, the worlds walls 'fore her flie!

For what can stand that is so badly staid?[79]
Well may that fall whose ground-work is unsure.
And what hath wall'd the world but thoughts unweigh'd
In freer reason? That antiquate,[80] secure,[81]
And easie dull conceit of corporature,[82]
Of matter, quantitie, and such like gear[83]
Hath made this needlesse, thanklesse[84] inclosure,
Which I in full disdain quite up will tear
And lay all ope,[85] that as things are they may appear.

. . . . .

Wherefore who'll[86] judge the limits of the world
By what appears unto our failing[87] sight
Appeals to sense,[88] reason down headlong hurld
Out of her throne by giddie[89] vulgar[90] might.
But here base senses dictates they will dight[91]
With specious title of Philosophie,
And stiffly[92] will contend their cause is right
From rotten rolls[93] of school[94] antiquity,
Who constantly denie corporall Infinitie.

[63] happen [64] fixed [65] understanding [66] generous being [67] judge
[68] purpose [69] burned (archaic form) [70] sharp [71] faculties [72] exalt
[73] expand [74] dispersed [75] taking the measure of [76] unfrequented
[77] in the old astronomy, one of the concentric hollow spheres surrounding the earth; here the sky
[78] retreats [79] supported [80] antiquated [81] over-confident
[82] corporality, materiality [83] stuff, rubbish [84] deserving no thanks [85] open
[86] whoever will [87] inadequate [88] sensation [89] foolish [90] ignorant [91] adorn
[92] stubbornly [93] documents on rolls of parchment [94] Scholastic

But who can prove their corporalitie[95]
Since matter which thereto's essentiall
If rightly sifted's[96] but a phantasie,[97]
And quantitie who's deem'd[98] Originall[99]
Is matter, must with matter likewise fall.
What ever is, is Life and Energie[100]
From God, who is th' Originall of all;
Who being everywhere doth multiplie
His own broad shade[101] that endlesse throughout all doth lie.

He from the last projection of light
Ycleep'd[102] *Shamajim,*[103] which is liquid fire
(It *Aether*[104] eke[105] and centrall *Tasis*[106] hight[107])
Hath made each shining globe[108] and clumperd mire[109]
Of dimmer Orbs.[110] For Nature doth inspire
Spermatick[111] life, but of a different kind.
Hence those congenit[112] splendour doth attire
And lively heat, these darknesse dead doth bind,
And without borrowed rayes they be both cold and blind.

All these be knots of th' universall stole[113]
Of sacred *Psyche;*[114] which at first was fine,
Pure, thin, and pervious[115] till hid powers did pull
Together in severall points and did encline[116]
The nearer parts in one clod[117] to combine,
Those centrall[118] spirits that the parts did draw
The measure[119] of each globe did then define,
Made things impenetrable[120] here below,
Gave colour, figure, motion, and each usuall law.

And what is done in this Terrestriall[121] starre
The same is done in every Orb beside.
Each flaming Circle[122] that we see from farre
Is but a knot in *Psyches* garment tide.
From that lax shadow cast throughout the wide

[95] the quality of being embodied
[96] examined closely
[97] fantasy; figment of imagination
[98] supposed [99] source
[100] neo-Platonic term which More defines as "the rayes of an essence, or the beams of a vitall Centre"
[101] unsubstantial image of something real
[102] named (literary archaism) [103] Hebrew for *liquid fire*
[104] "the fluid fiery nature of heaven" (More)
[105] also [106] Greek for *extension*
[107] called [108] planetary or celestial body
[109] clotted bog [110] heavenly bodies
[111] "all magnetick power whatsoever that doth immediately rule and actuate any body" (More)
[112] congenital [113] robe
[114] from the Greek for *soul* or *spirit* [115] permeable
[116] incline [117] clot
[118] of "the depth, or inmost Being of any thing, from whence its Acts and Energies flow forth" (More)
[119] proposition [120] inscrutable
[121] earthly star, *i.e.*, the earth [122] the orb of a heavenly body

And endlesse world, that low'st projection
Of universall life each thing's deriv'd
What er'e appeareth in corporeall fashion;[123]
For body's but this spirit, fixt, grosse by conspissation.[124]

And that which doth con[s]pissate[125] active is;
Wherefore not matter but some living sprite[126]
Of nimble[127] nature which this lower mist
And immense field of Atoms doth excite,[128]
And wake into such life as best doth fit
With his own self. As we change phantasies[129]
The essence of our soul not chang'd a whit[130]
So do these Atomes change their energies
Themselves unchanged into new Centreities.[131]

And as our soul's not superficially
Colourd by phantasms,[132] nor doth them reflect
As doth a looking-glasse such imag'rie
As it to the beholder doth detect:[133]
No more are these lightly or smear'd or[134] deckt
With form or motion which in them we see,
But from their inmost Centre they project
Their vitall rayes,[135] not merely passive be,
But by occasion[136] wak'd rouse up themselves[137] on high.

So that they're life, form, sprite, not matter pure,
For matter pure is a pure nullitie,[138]
What nought can act is nothing, I am sure;
And if all act,[139] that is they'll not denie
But all that is is form:[140] so easily
By what is true, and by what they embrace[141]
For truth, their feigned[142] Corporalitie
Will vanish into smoke, But on I'll passe,
More fully we have sung this in another place.[143]

. . . . .

I will not say our world is infinite,
But that infinity of worlds there be.
The Centre of our world's the lively light
Of the warm sunne, the visible Deity

[123] In a note on the ninth stanza of the second canto of *Psychozoia* More himself thus sums up the Plotinian doctrine of the creation of the corporeal world which underlies this whole passage: "So she [Psyche] keeping steddily her own station, . . . like a plentifull flame shining out in the extreme margins of the fire begot a fuliginous darknesse; which she seeing streightway actuated with life and form, . . . so that darknesse becoming a variously adorned aedifice is not disjoyned from its builder, but dependeth thence as being the genuine and true energie of the soul of the World."

[124] dense by condensation [125] make dense [126] spirit [127] acting rapidly
[128] set in motion, quicken [129] fantasies, images impressed on the mind by sense objects
[130] jot [131] central qualities [132] mental images
[133] lay bare [134] or . . . or: either . . . or
[135] life-giving rays: "the rayes of an essence is its energie" (More)
[136] a juncture of circumstances [137] lift up themselves [138] nought
[139] active principles [140] the essential determinant principle that makes a thing what it is
[141] adopt [142] imagined [143] in his poem *Psychozoia*

Of this externall Temple. *Mercurie*[144]
Next plac'd and warm'd more thoroughly by his rayes,
Right nimbly 'bout his golden head doth fly:
Then *Venus*[145] nothing slow about him strayes[146]
And next our *Earth* though seeming sad full sprightly[147] playes.

And after her *Mars*[148] rangeth[149] in a round[150]
With fiery locks and angry flaming eye,
And next to him mild *Jupiter*[151] is found,
But *Saturn*[152] cold wons[153] in our outmost sky.
The skirts[154] of his large Kingdome surely ly
Near to the confines of some other worlds
Whose Centres are the fixed starres[155] on high,
'Bout which as their own proper[156] Suns are hurld
Joves, *Earths*, and *Saturns;* round on their own axes twurld.

Little or nothing are those starres to us
Which in the azure Evening gay[157] appear
(I mean for influence but judicious
Nature and carefull Providence her dear
And matchlesse work did so contrive whileere,[158]
That th' Hearts or Centres in the wide world pight[159]
Should such a distance each to other bear,
That the dull Plants with collated light.[160]
By neighbour suns might cheared be in dampish[161] night.

And as the Planets in our world (of which
The sun's the heart and kernell) do receive
Their nightly light from suns that do enrich
Their sable[162] mantle with bright gemmes, and give
A goodly splendour, and sad men relieve[163]
With their fair twinkling rayes, so our worlds sunne
Becomes a starre elsewhere, and doth derive
Joynt[164] light with others, cheareth all that won
In those dim duskish[165] Orbs round other suns that run.

This is the parergon[166] of each noble fire[167]
Of neighbour worlds to be the nightly[168] starre,
But their main work is vitall heat t' inspire[169]

[144] the smallest planet of the solar system and the nearest to the sun, named for the Latin god of commerce

[145] a planet moving in an orbit between that of Mercury and the earth, named for the Roman goddess of love

[146] roams [147] gayly

[148] the fourth planet in order from the sun, named for the Roman god of war, conspicuous for its red light

[149] roves [150] circle

[151] the largest of the planets of the solar system, named for the Roman god of the heavens

[152] the sixth major planet from the sun and the most distant known to the ancients, named for the ancient Roman god of the seed-sowing

[153] dwells [154] borders

[155] stars which seem always to hold the same position in the heavens [156] particular

[157] bright [158] erewhile, some time ago [159] placed [160] light bestowed [161] misty

[162] black [163] ease [164] common [165] partly obscure [166] bywork

[167] from *fires of heaven* for the stars [168] occurring every night [169] breathe into

Into the frigid spheres that 'bout them fare,[170]
Which of themselves quite dead and barren are
But by the wakening warmth of kindly dayes,
And the sweet dewie nights they well declare[171]
Their seminall virtue,[172] in due courses[173] raise
Long hidden shapes[174] and life, to their great Makers praise.

These with their suns I several worlds do call,
Whereof the number I deem infinite:
Else[175] infinite darknesse were in this great Hall
Of th' endlesse Universe; For nothing finite
Could put that immense shadow unto flight.
But if that infinite Suns we shall admit,
Then infinite worlds follow in reason right.
For every Sun with Planets must be fit,[176]
And have some mark for his farre-shining shafts[177] to hit.

But if he shine all solitarie, alone,
What mark is left? what aimed[178] scope[179] or end
Of his existence? wherefore every one
Hath a due number of dim Orbs that wend[180]
Around their centrall fire. But wrath[181] will rend
This strange composure[182] back'd with reason stout.
And rasher tongues right speedily will spend[183]
Their forward[184] censure, that my wits run out
On wool-gathering,[185] through infinite spaces all about.

. . . . .

And if these globes be regions of life
And severall kinds of plants therein do grow,
Grasse, flowers, hearbs, trees, which the impartiall knife
Of all consuming Time still down doth mow,
And new again doth in succession[186] show;[187]
Which also's done in flies, birds, men and beasts;
Adde sand, pearls, pebbles, that the ground do strow,
Leaves, quills, hairs, thorns, blooms, you may think the rest
Their kinds[188] by mortall penne cannot be well exprest:

And if their kinds no man may reckon well,
The summe of successive particulars[189]
No mind conceive nor tongue can ever tell.
And yet this mist of numbers (as appears)
Belongs to one of these opacous[190] sphears,
Suppose[191] this *Earth;* what then will all those Rounds[192]

[170] range [171] manifest [172] power of producing offspring
[173] series [174] excellences of form [175] otherwise [176] fitted [177] beams
[178] aimed at [179] mark for shooting at, purpose [180] take their way
[181] strong indignation [182] intellectual production [183] express [184] ready
[185] indulging in wandering fancies [186] progeny [187] bring forward
[188] classes of the remainder? [189] individuals [190] opaque
[191] assume as a basis of argument [192] globes

Produce? No *Atlas*[193] such a load upbears.
In this huge endlesse heap o'rewhelmed, drown'd,
Choak'd, stifled, lo! I lie, breathlesse, even quite confound.[194]

Yet give me space a while but to respire,[195]
And I my self shall fairly well out-wind;[196]
Keep this possession[197] true, unhurt, entire,
That you no greater difficulty find
In this new old opinion here defin'd
Of infinite worlds, then one world doth imply.
For if we do with steddy patience mind[198]
All is resolv'd int' one absurdity,
The grant[199] of something greater then infinitie.

. . . . .

Who dare gainsay[200] but God is every where
Unbounded, measurelesse, all Infinite;
Yet the same difficulties meet us here
Which erst[201] us met and did so sore affright
With their strange vizards.[202] This will follow right[203]
Where ever we admit Infinity
Every denominated[204] part proves streight[205]
A portion infinite, which if it be,
One infinite will into myriads[206] multiply.

But with new argument to draw more near
Our purpos'd[207] end. If God's omnipotent
And this omnipotent God be every where,
Where e're he is then can he eas'ly vent[208]
His mighty virtue[209] thorough all extent.[210]
What then shall hinder but[211] a roscid[212] air
With gentle heat eachwhere[213] be 'sperst and sprent[214]
Unlesse omnipotent power we will empair,
And say that empty space his working can debare.[215]

Where now this one supposed world is pight
Was not that space at first all vain[216] and void?
Nor ought said; no, when he said, *Let't be light.*[217]
Was this one space better then all beside,
And more obedient to what God decreed?
Or would not all that endlesse Emptinesse
Gladly embrac'd (if he had ever tride)[218]
His just command? and what might come to passe
Implies no contradictious inconsistentnesse.

[193] in Greek mythology a Titan punished for warring on Zeus by having to support the heavens on his head and hands
[194] confounded [195] come up to the surface to breathe [196] extricate [197] conviction
[198] remember [199] acknowledgment [200] deny [201] first [202] countenances
[203] straightway [204] constituted [205] straightway [206] countless numbers [207] proposed
[208] pour out [209] power [210] its compass [211] prevent that [212] dewy
[213] everywhere [214] sprinkled [215] stop [216] empty
[217] See Gen. 1.3. [218] put to the test

Wherefore this precious sweet Ethereall dew
For ought we know, God each where did distill,
And thorough all that hollow Voidnesse threw
And the wide gaping drought therewith did fill,
His endlesse overflowing goodnesse spill
In every place; which streight he did contrive
Int' infinite severall[219] worlds, as his best skill.[220]
Did him direct and creatures could receive:
For matter infinite needs infinite worlds must give.

The Centre of each severall world's a Sunne
With shining beams and kindly warming heat,
About whose radiant crown the Planets runne,
Like reeling moths around a candle light.
These all together, one world I conceit.[221]
And that even infinite such worlds there be,
That inexhausted[222] Good that God is hight[223]
A full[224] sufficient reason is to me,
Who simple[225] Goodnesse make the highest Deity.[226]

Als[227] make himself the key of all his works
And eke the measure of his providence;
The piercing eye of truth to whom nought lurks[228]
But lies wide ope unbar'd[229] of all pretence.
But frozen hearts! away! flie farre from hence,
Unless you'l thaw at this celestiall fire
And melt into one mind and holy sense[230]
With Him that doth all heavenly hearts inspire,
So may you with my soul in one assent conspire.[231]

But what's within, uneath[232] is to convey
To narrow vessels that are full afore.[233]
And yet this truth as wisely as I may
I will insinuate,[234] from senses[235] store
Borrowing a little aid. Tell me therefore
When you behold with your admiring[236] eyes
Heavens Canopie all to be spangled o're
With sprinkled stars, what can you well devize[237]
Which causen[238] may such carelesse order in the skies?

A peck of peasen[239] rudely[240] poured out
On plaister flore, from hasty heedlesse hond
Which lie all carelesse scattered about,
To sight[241] do in as seemly order stond,[242]
As those fair glistering[243] lights in heaven are found.
If onely for this world they were intended,
Nature would have adorn'd this azure Round
With better Art, and easily have mended
This harsh disord'red order, and more beauty lended.

[219] different [220] sense of what is fitting [221] conceive [222] unexhausted [223] called
[224] entirely [225] pure [226] character of God [227] also [228] is concealed [229] laid bare
[230] feeling [231] accord [232] hard [233] before [234] suggest [235] sensations
[236] wondering [237] imagine [238] archaic form of *cause* [239] peas [240] roughly
[241] to the eye [242] stand [243] sparkling

But though these lights do seem so rudely throwen
And scattered throughout the spacious sky,
Yet each most seemely[244] sits in his own Throne
In distance[245] due and comely Majesty;
And round their lordly seats their servants high
Keeping a well-proportionated[246] space
One from another, doing chearfully
Their daily task. No blemish may deface
The worlds in several[247] dekt with all art and grace:

. . . . .

Now sith[248] so farre as sense can ever try[249]
We find new worlds, that still new worlds there be,
And round about in infinite numbers lie,
Further then reach of mans weak phantasie
(Without suspition of temerity)
We may conclude; as well as men conclude
That there is air farre 'bove the mountains high,
Or that th' Earth a sad[250] substance doth include
Even to the Centre with like[251] qualities indu'd.

For who did ever the Earths Centre pierce,
And felt or sand or gravell with his spade
At such a depth? what Histories rehearse
That ever wight did dare for to invade
Her bowels but one mile in dampish shade?
Yet I'll be bold to say that few or none
But deem this globe even to the bottome made
Of solid earth, and that her nature's one
Throughout, though plain[252] experience hath it never shown.

But sith sad earth so farre as they have gone
They still descry, eas'ly they do inferre
Without all check of reason, were they down
Never so deep, like substance would appear,
Ne dream of any hollow horrour[253] there.
My mind with like uncurb'd facility
Concludes from what by sight is seen so clear:
That ther's no barren wast vacuity
Above the worlds we see, but still new worlds there ly,

And still and still[254] even to infinity:
Which point since I so fitly have propos'd,
Abating[255] well the inconsistency[256]
Of harsh[257] infinitude therein suppos'd
And prov'd by reasons[258] never to be loos'd[259]
That infinite space and infinite worlds there be;

[244] so as to present a stately appearance [245] aloofness [246] adjusted in proportion
[247] each in his own place [248] seeing that [249] ascertain [250] solid [251] the same
[252] direct [253] horror of emptiness [254] and ever more and more [255] demolishing
[256] incongruity [257] forbidding [258] statements of facts as arguments
[259] to be made insecure, weakened

This load laid down, I'm freely[260] now dispos'd
A while to sing of times infinity;
May infinite Time afford me but his smallest fee.[261]

For smallest fee of time will serve my turn
This part for to dispatch, sith endlesse space
(Whose perplext[262] nature well mans brains might turn,
And weary wits disorder and misplace)[263]
I have already passed:[264] for like case[265]
Is in them both. He that can well untie
The knots that in those infinite worlds found place,
May easily answer each perplexity
Of these worlds infinite matters endlesse durancie.[266]

The *Cuspis*[267] and the *Basis*[268] of the *Cone*[269]
Were both at once dispersed every where;
But the pure *Basis* that is God alone:
Else would remotest sights as big appear
Unto our eyes as if we stood them near.
And if an Harper harped in the Moon,
His silver sound would touch our tickled[270] ear:
Or if one hollowed[271] from highest Heaven aboven,
In sweet still Evening-tide, his voice would hither roame.[272]

This all would be if the *Cuspe* of the *Cone*
Were very[273] God. Wherefore I rightly 't deem
Onely a Creaturall[274] projection,
Which flowing yet from God hath ever been,
Fill'd the vast empty space with its large stream.
But yet it is not totall[275] every where
As was even now by reason rightly seen:
Wherefore not God, whose nature doth appear
Entirely omnipresent, weigh'd with judgement clear.

A reall infinite matter, distinct
And yet proceeding from the Deitie
Although with different form as then untinct[276]
Has ever been from all Eternity.
Now what delay can we suppose to be,
Since matter alway[277] was at hand prepar'd
Before the filling of the boundlesse sky
With framed[278] Worlds; for nought at all debar'd,[279]
Nor was His strength ungrown, nor was His strength empair'd.

[260] without constraint [261] allotted portion [262] involved
[263] put in a wrong place [264] passed judgment on
[265] the same position of matters [266] duration
[267] the point, "the last projection of life from *Psyche*" [Spirit], according to More
[268] God, as More presently explains
[269] More has in mind here a right circular cone, which he explains as follows: "And because all from him [God] descends . . . with abatement or contraction, I give the name of *Cone* to the Universe."
[270] excited by a thrilling sensation [271] hallooed [272] make its way [273] rightly called
[274] of the nature of a created being [275] relating to the whole, entire [276] unaffected
[277] always [278] formed [279] excluded

How long would God be forming of a fly?
Or the small wandring moats that play in th' sun?
Least moment well will serve none can deny,
His *Fiat*[280] spoke[281] and streight the thing is done.
And cannot He make all the World as soon?[282]
For in each Atom of the matter wide[283]
The totall Deity doth entirely won,
His infinite presence doth therein reside,
And in this presence infinite powers do ever abide.

Wherefore at once from all eternity
The infinite number of these Worlds He made,
And will conserve to all infinitie,
And still drive on their ever moving trade,[284]
And steddy hold what ever must be staid;
Ne must one mite be minish'd[285] of the summe,
Ne must the smallest atom ever fade,
But still remain though it may change its room;[286]
This truth abideth strong from everlasting doom.[287]

. . . . .

Witnesse ye Heavens if what I say's not true,
Ye flaming Comets wandering on high,
And new fixt[288] starres found in that Circle blue,
The one espide in glittering *Cassiopie*,[289]
The other near to *Ophiuchus*[290] thigh.
Both bigger then the biggest starres that are,
And yet as farre remov'd from mortall eye
As are the furthest, so those Arts[291] declare
Unto whose reaching sight Heavens mysteries lie bare.

Wherefore these new-seen lights were greater once
By many thousand times then this our sphear
Wherein we live, 'twixt good and evil chance.
Which to my musing mind doth strange appear
If those large bodies then first shaped were.
For should so goodly things so soon decay?
Neither did last the full space of two[292] year.
Wherefore I cannot deem that their first day
Of being, when to us they sent out shining ray,

. . . . .

[280] Latin for *let it be done* [281] spoken [282] in as short a time [283] extensive
[284] course [285] withdrawn [286] assigned place [287] ordinance, decree

[288] The discovery and reporting of new stars in the unchanging heavens by Tycho Brahe, Kepler, and Galileo was one of the most genuinely revolutionary aspects of the "new philosophy."

[289] In 1572 Tycho Brahe observed the first of the new stars in the constellation of Cassiopeia.

[290] Another new star observed first in Ophiuchus, or Serpentarius, in 1604, became the subject of Kepler's famous treatise, *De Stella Nova.*

[291] branches of learning

[292] The star of 1572 (October or November) disappeared from view in March, 1574, and that of 1604 (October) had vanished by March of 1606.

And like[293] I would adventure to pronounce[294]
Of all the Comets that above the Moon,
Amidst the higher Planets rudely dance
In course perplex,[295] but that from this rash doom
I'm bet off[296] by their beards[297] and tails farre strown
Along the skie, pointing still opposite
Unto the sunne, however they may roam;
Wherefore a cluster of small starres unite
These Meteors some do deem, perhaps with judgement right.

And that these tayls are streams of the suns light
Breaking through their near[298] bodies as through clouds.
Besides the Optick glasse[299] has shown to sight
The dissolution of these starrie crouds.
Which thing if't once be granted and allow'd,[300]
I think without all contradiction
They may conclude these Meteors are routs[301]
Of wandering starres, which though they one by one
Cannot be seen, yet joyn'd cause this strange vision.[302]

. . . . .

But for the new fixt starres there's no pretence,
Nor beard nor tail to take occasion[303] by,
To bring in that unluckie inference
Which weaken might this new built mysterie.[304]
Certes in raging fire they both did frie.
A signe whereof you rightly may aread
Their colours changeable varietie,
First clear and white, then yellow, after red,
Then blewly pale, then duller still, till perfect dead.

And as the order of these colours went
So still decreas'd that Cassiopean starre,[305]
Till at the length to sight it was quite spent:[306]
Which observations strong reasons are,
Consuming fire its body did empare[307]
And turn to ashes. And the like will be
In all the darksome[308] Planets wide and farre.
Ne can our Earth from this state standen free
A Planet as the rest, and Planets fate must trie.[309]

. . . . .

The burning bowels of this wasting ball[310]
Shall gullup[311] up great flakes of rolling[312] fire,
And belch out pitchie flames, till over all

[293] in like manner [294] proclaim [295] intricate, difficult to clear up
[296] beaten off, driven away [297] the tail of a comet, seeming to precede the nucleus
[298] closely attached [299] telescope [300] admitted as probable [301] troops
[302] object of sight [303] take advantage
[304] In the intervening stanzas, More canvasses various other suggested explanations of the phenomena he has been discussing.
[305] the nova of Tycho Brahe's discovery [306] destroyed [307] impair [308] dark
[309] undergo [310] the earth [311] gullop, belch [312] increasing

Having long rad'd,[313] Vulcan[314] himself shall tire
And (th' earth an asheap made) shall then expire:
Here Nature laid asleep in her own Urn[315]
With gentle rest right easly will respire,
Till to her pristine task she do return
As fresh as Phenix[316] young under th' Arabian Morn.

. . . . . .

Ne ought we doubt how Nature may recover
In her own ashes long time buried.
For nought can ever consume that centrall power
Of hid spermatick[317] life, which lies not dead
In that rude heap, but safely covered;[318]
And doth by secret force suck from above
Sweet heavenly juice, and therewith nourished
Till[319] her just[320] bulk, she doth her life emprove,[321]
Made mother of much[322] children that about her move.

Witnesse that uncouth[323] bird of Arabie[324]
Which out of her own ruines doth revive
With all th' exploits of skilfull Chymistrie,
Such as no vulgar wit[325] can well believe.
Let universall Nature witnesse give
That what I sing 's no feigned forgerie.[326]
A needlesse task new fables to contrive,
But what I sing is seemly[327] verity
Well suting[328] with right reason and Philosophie.

But the fit time of this mutation
No man can finden[329] out with all his pains.
For the small sphears of humane reason run
Too swift within his narrow compast[330] brains.
But that vast Orb of Providence contains
A wider period; turneth still and slow.
Yet at the last his aimed end he gains.
And sure[331] at last a fire will overflow
The aged Earth, and all must into ashes go.

Then all the stately works and monuments
Built on this bottom shall to ruine fall.
And all those goodly Statues shall be brent
Which were erect to the memoriall[332]
Of Kings, and Kaesars, ne[333] may better 'fall[334]
The boastfull works of brave Poetick pride
That promise life and fame perpetuall;
Ne better fate may these poore lines abide.[335]
Betide[336] what will to what may live no lenger[337] tide![338]

[313] made red [314] Roman god of the fiery element [315] Nature is her own funeral urn.
[316] mythical bird, fabled to live for centuries in the Arabian desert and then burn itself to ashes and rise from the ashes with restored youth
[317] spermatical [318] concealed [319] so as to reach [320] rightful, proper [321] improve
[322] a great number of [323] strange [324] the Phoenix [325] ordinary intellect
[326] fictitious fabrication [327] fair [328] suiting, fitting [329] archaic form of *find*
[330] circumscribed [331] assuredly [332] memory [333] nor [334] befall
[335] expect [336] happen [337] longer [338] time

This is the course that never-dying Nature
Might ever hold from all Eternitie
Renuing still the faint decayed creature
Which would grow stark[339] and drie as aged tree,
Unlesse by wise preventing[340] Destinie
She were at certain periods of years
Reduced[341] back unto her Infancie,
Which well fram'd argument (as plainly appears)
My ship from those hard rocks and shelves right safely stears.

Lo! now my faithfull muse hath represented
Both frames[342] of Providence to open view,
And hath each point in orient colours painted
Not to deceive the sight with seeming shew
But earnest to give either part their due;
Now urging th' uncouth strange perplexitie
Of infinite worlds and Time, then of a new[343]
Softening that harsher inconsistency
To fit the immense goodnesse of the Deity.

And here by curious men 't may be expected
That I this knot[344] with judgement grave decide,
And then proceed to what else was objected.
But, ah! What mortall wit may dare t' areed[345]
Heavens counsels in eternall horrour hid?
And Cynthius pulls me by my tender ear,
Such signes I must observe with wary heed:
Wherefore my restlesse Muse at length forbear.[346]
Thy silver sounded Lute hang up in silence here.

from DIVINE DIALOGUES[1]

Containing Several Disquisitions and Instructions touching the Attributes of GOD and His PROVIDENCE in the WORLD

THE FOURTH DIALOGUE

Philotheus, Bathynous, Sophron, Philopolis, Euistor, Hylobares, Cuphophron.[2]

Philoth. Our Conference hitherto, O *Philopolis*, has been spent either in proving briefly the *Existence of God*, or in clearing[3] of his *Attributes*, or in defending[4] of his Providence: which was but a necessary preparation to them that doubt of these things, for the due understanding of the Mysteries of his Kingdome. For if there be no God nor any Divine Providence, there

[339] rigid [340] anticipating, precautional
[341] brought back [342] structures
[343] over again [344] knotty point
[345] reveal
[346] cease

[1] Text: 1668

[2] More's own cast of speakers for his dialogue:

The proper Characters of the Persons in the ensuing Dialogues, *with some Allusion to their Names.*

Philotheus, A zealous and Sincere Lover of God and *Christ* and of the whole Creation.
Bathynous, The Deeply-thoughtful or profoundly-thinking man.
Sophron, The Sober and wary man.
Philopolis, The pious and loyal Politician.
Euistor, A man of Criticism, Philologie and *History*.
Hylobares, A young, witty and well-moralized *Materialist*.
Cuphophron, A zealous, but Airy-minded, *Platonist and Cartesian*, or *Mechanist.*
Ocymo, *Cuphophron's* Boy, so called from his Nimbleness.

[3] demonstrating or explaining

[4] vindicating

can be no Kingdome of God upon Earth, as *Hylobares* well noted at first. And indeed if the Providence of God be not everywhere, it is a very suspicable[5] business that it is in truth no-where. Whence appears the necessity of admitting such Hypotheses as will make sense of all occurrences and appearances of things which we meet withall in what-ever Nations of the Earth or parts of the Universe. And such I conceive were those that were suggested in our two last days Conferences: With which if Hylobares (who seemed to be the onely man dissettled[6] touching these Points) be fully satisfied, I am now ready to serve you, *Philopolis*, according to the best of my skill, touching[7] your demands[8] concerning the *Kingdome of God*.

Philop. I humbly thank you, *Philotheus*, and my eager desire to hear you discourse of so important a Theme, and my jealousie[9] that we shall be much streighɩned[10] in time, makes me beg of you that, without any farther delay, you would be pleased to fall upon the matter.

Hyl. Which *Philotheus* will doe the more couragiously, *O Philopolis*, after I have briefly acknowledged my thanks for, and also have declared the steddy[11] efficacy of, his yesterday's discourse. For though I was highly exalted through the sense and power of his Reason, yet I do not now flag again as the day before, but, having a full and comprehensive view of things, I finde in my self a permanent assent to[12] Truth as well now I am cool and calm as then when I was most transported; and, which is a wonderful accession[13] to all this, this firm and full satisfaction I have thus unexpectedly received touching the Existence of God, and the unexceptionableness[14] of his Providence, draws in along with it a more hearty and settled belief of all the fundamental Points of Christian Religion, so far forth as the Scripture has declared them. So that that of Christianity, which hung more loosely and exteriourly in my mind before, methinks I have now imbibed[15] into the very centre of my heart and soul, and do without all hesitancy close with[16] the truth thereof. Whence, I hope, I shall be the more idoneous[17] Auditour of this higher Discourse of yours, *O Philotheus*, touching the Kingdome of God.

Philoth. I am exceeding[18] glad, O *Hylobares*, that my former Discourses have had this excellent effect upon you; though it be no more then I hoped for, and have often experimented[19] in others, and most feelingly in my self, who could never doubt of Christianity when I had once satisfied my self of the truth of those Points you profess your self now at length so fully satisfied in. Which I must confess makes me prone to think, that those that either slight or misbeliev Christianity, so far forth as the Scripture has declared the same, do not seriously or settledly[20] believe there is a God or a Divine Providence, but are of a light, Sceptical, confounded[21] and heedless spirit, and take more pleasure to seem able to talk, then to find themselves of any determinate[22] judgement, though in things of the greatest moment.

Cuph. The greatest Wits of the World have been such persons as you seem so freely to perstringe,[23] *O Philotheus*, that is to say, *Sceptical* or *Aporetical*.[24] Witness not onely the whole Sect of the *Academici*,[25] but that Miracle for wit and eloquence *Plato*[26] himself, that sweetly-singing Swan,[27] as *Socrates*[28] had him represented to him in a dream.[29] Is there any thing more pleasant then this melifluous Dialogues? and yet ordinarily nothing con-

[5] open to suspicion [6] disturbed, unsettled
[7] regarding [8] questions
[9] solicitude or anxiety [10] restricted
[11] firm [12] mental acceptance of
[13] addition [14] perfect satisfactoriness
[15] assimilated [16] agree with [17] fit
[18] exceedingly [19] experienced
[20] in a settled manner [21] confused
[22] determined [23] censure
[24] of aporetic nature, full of doubts and objections
[25] the name of which the Ancients gave to those who embraced the system of Plato
[26] See above, p. 61, footnote 2.
[27] in classical mythology, because of its pure white plumage, the symbol of faultlessness or excellence in contrast to the crow or goose; also, because of the belief that the swan sings shortly before its death, used as a symbol for the singer and the poet
[28] Greek philosopher (469–399 B.C.), famous for his inductive method of inquiry and instruction, and his insistence on knowledge as the foundation of virtue
[29] Diog. Laert. *in vita Platon.* [III. 5.] [More's note]

cluded but is a mere *Sceptical* or *Aporetical* chace of wit, a game wherein nothing is taken or aimed at but mere ingenious[30] pastime.

Philoth. Such wilde-goose chaces in matters of less moment, *O Cuphophron*, may be more plausible[31] or tolerable: but in Points of greater consequence to speak eloquently on both sides, and then to be able to conclude nothing, nor, it may be, so much as desirous thereof, is not so much like the famed melody of the Swan's voice, as like the clapping of her wings one against another, and so making a fluttering noise for a time, but after casting both behind her back, not at all regarding whether the right or left wing were stronger.

Hyl. A flourish,[32] *O Cuphophron*, that every Goose can make as well as a Swan. But for my part, *Philotheus*, I desire nothing more then a settledness of mind in matters of the highest consequence, such as the *Existence of God*, the *Immortality of the Soul*, the *benignity of Providence*, and the like: and therefore I think my self infinitely happy in that full satisfaction I have received from your excellent Reasonings, I find them so firm and permanent.

Philoth. And I wish they may long so abide, *Hylobares*.

Hyl. Why, what can dissettle them, *Philotheus?*

Philoth. Nothing, unless dissettledness of Life. If you fix[33] in the *Divine Life*, which is fixable no-where but in the *Divine Body*, then the reasons of *Divine Truth* will take root in this ground, and so prove permanent indeed. But if they grow not up from this ground, they will be but as a Flower in your hand or a Feather in your cap, and having no vital Cognation[34] with the Subject they are in, they will easily be blown away or wither.

Hyl. I had thought the Soul had been so Divine a thing of it self, that the Cognation betwixt it and the reasons of Divine Truth had been sufficient, if once received, firmly to retain them.

Philoth. O no, *Hylobares:* The Soul by sympathizing[35] too much with this earthly and brutish Body becomes brutish her self, and loses her *Divinity;* else all would be alike capable[36] of Divine Truth. But the recuperation[37] of the Divine Body[38] by virtue of her true and real Regeneration is also the recovery of her *Divinity*.

Hyl. But what do you mean by this Divine Body, *O Philotheus?*

Philoth. The same which the Pythagoreans[39] mean by their τὸ αὐγοειδὲς σῶμα,[40] which is also called *Ethereal*, or *Heavenly*.

Euist. That is no wonder, that the *Heavenly Body* and the *Divine* should be all one, whenas[41] Aristotle[42] himself calls Heaven τὸ θεῖον σῶμα, the Divine body.[43]

Hyl. But how shall we be able to attain to this *Divine Body*, O Philotheus, in which, so far as I see, is the Root and Substance of Truth, forasmuch as the Life is in it?

Philoth. Reason without this is but a dead σκιουραθία[44] or umbratile[45] Imagination, a faint and ineffectual thing, evanid,[46] fugitive and flitting:[47] but Reasons flourishing out of this stock are the immarcescible[48] Flowers of the Paradise of God.

Hyl. Wherefore, Philotheus, I am the more desirous to know how we may come by this *Divine* or *Paridisiacal*[49] Body.

Philoth. By a firm and lively Faith in the Power and Spirit of the Lord *Jesus*, whereby he is able to mortifie[50] and subdue

30 intellectual 31 praiseworthy

32 brag, or boast

33 take up one's position mentally

34 kinship, relationship

35 agreeing, harmonizing

36 able to perceive or comprehend

37 recovery

38 More immediately proceeds to explain what he means by this term.

39 followers of Pythagoras, a sixth-century B.C. Greek philosopher, organized into a secret society, with an esoteric teaching of which number was the key principle

40 "the brilliant or luminous body"

41 seeing that

42 Greek philosopher and scientist (384–322 B.C.), famous for his development of Plato's idea of the first cause as a self-knowing Reason, and his explanation of the world of nature and of man

43 *De Cælo, lib.* 2.*c*.3. [More]

44 literally, *painting with the shadows*

45 of a shadowy nature, insubstantial

46 transient, evanescent

47 fleeting 48 imperishable

49 celestial, of the heavenly Paradise

50 deprive of life

all sin in us and extinguish all Selfishness, so that we become utterly dead to our selves, and as little concerned for our selves in any externall gratification of worldly Honour, carnal Pleasure, mundane Power, or any thing that is grateful[51] to the mere Animal Life, as if we were not at all in being. If we stand firm in this Faith, and second[52] it with constant and sincere Devotion, and inward[53] breathings[54] toward the prize set before us, adding thereto a due and discreet Temperance and circumspection in all our externall deportments,[55] that we neither act nor speak anything from the promptings of the Selfish Principle, or any way to gratifie our corrupt Animality; this method will in due time bring us to a perfect state of self-deadness: which death being finished, there does most certainly succeed a spiritual Resurrection from the dead into the *Life* which is truly *Divine*, and which is not found but in the *Divine Body*. So that by our sincere Devotions and breathings toward God we imbibe both the Divine Life and the Divine Body at once; which is the true spiritual birth of *Christ*,[56] *whom as many as receive, they become the Sons of God;*[57] as being born, *not of bloud, nor of the will of the flesh, but of God*.[58] And this also is the *inward*[59] *man* of which *Paul* professes that, *though the outward perish, is yet* (in the true Saints of God) renewed *day by day*. Wherefore he that is arrived to this *Substantiality*[60] *of life* will be fixt in all useful Divine Truths, and the Reasons that grow on such a Root will be found solid and permanent by him that has the Root: but where they are merely verbal and imaginarie, and float onely in the Brain, the Heart being *animal* and *brutish*, they may easily prove very weak, fugitive, and vanishing. Not that they are so in themselves, but may appear so to those who have onely the Picture of the Flower in their Brain, not the Root in their Heart, in which is the Pavilion[61] of Life, and inmost Tabernacle[62] of God in the Soul. He that lives in this *dispensation* of *life*,[63] *O Hylobares*, can never be dissettled in his thoughts touching the Existence of God, and his Providence, or the Immortality of the Soul. For he cannot be prone to suspect[64] the Soul's capacity of living separate from the Body, whiles he perceives her to live at that distance and defiance with the Body already, while she is in it; nor at all doubt of the Existence of God, whose power, spirit, impulse and energie he so distinctly perceives in his own Soul. For such is the nature of the Divine Life, that none that feels it but must confess it not to belong to any creature as such, but to be the very Power and Spirit of God actuating[65] the Soul. How can he then doubt of Him, whose power and presence he so sensibly[66] feels? Wherefore this *Dispensation of Life*, *Hylobares*, is all in all to him that desires to philosophize with steddiness and solidity.

Hyl. These are great and magnificent things which you declare, O *Philotheus*, but yet such as seem to me neither incredible nor unimitable.[67] And therefore, God willing, I shall endeavour, as well as I can, to steer my course according to the Rules you have intimated, and make it my main scope[68] to attain to that state which you call the *Dispensation of Life:* For I see all is very vain and shadowy without it. But in the meantime I must crave pardon of *Philopolis*, that I have occasioned *Philotheus* to mis-spend so much of that time that he thought too little for his own design and for the present purpose in hand.

Philop. Philotheus speaks so savourly[69] and edifyingly of every subject he is put upon, that it is ever pitty to interrupt him. But, sith[70] he has now desisted of himself, if he please at length to enter upon the Subject I first of all propounded, it will very much gratifie my desires.

[51] acceptable, pleasing
[52] support, reënforce
[53] pious, spiritual
[54] aspirations [55] manners, ways
[56] Christ born in the spirit of man (?)
[57] Joh. 1.12 (Here as usual, the Scriptural citation is More's.)
[58] II Cor. 4.16. [59] spiritual
[60] existence as a substance
[61] temporary shelter
[62] from the Jewish tabernacle or temple, dwelling-place of Jehovah or God
[63] religious order or system
[64] have doubts about
[65] quickening, vivifying
[66] intensely
[67] not to be imitated [68] object
[69] pleasantly [70] since

Hyl. It is therefore now, *Philopolis*, very seasonable to propound your *Quere's*[71] to him.

Philop. My First Quere, O *Philotheus*, was, *What the kingdome of God is;* the Second, *When it began*, and *where it has been or is now to be found;* the Third, *What progress it has hitherto made in the world;* the Fourth and last, *What success it is likely to have to the end of all things.* These are the Quere's, *Philotheus*, which I at first propounded, concerning which if you please to instruct us plainly and intelligibly, though not so accurately and scholastically,[72] we shall think our selves eternally obliged to you for your pains.

Philoth. I shall doe my best I can to serve you herein, *Philopolis*, and that as briefly and perspicuously as I can, with all plainness of speech, and without any affectation of Scholastick Scrupulosities,[73] being desirous onely to be understood and to convince. And the God of Heaven assist us in this our discourse of his heavenly Kingdome, that we may so understand the Mysteries of it, as that we may faithfully endeavour the promoting the Interest thereof both in our selves and in all men, to the Glory of God and Salvation of the World, Amen.

Philop. Amen, I pray God.

Philoth. Your first Quere, O *Philopolis*, though it be very short, yet is exceeding comprehensive, and, by reason of the multifarious[74] signification of the terms, involves much matter[75] in it at once; which yet I shall endeavour to comprise[76] and take in as well as I can by this brief Definition of the *Kingdome of God* in general. *The Kingdome of God is the Power of God enjoyning, exciting, commissioning,* or *permitting his creatures to act according to certain Laws, which, considering all circumstances,* or *upon the compute*[77] *of the whole, are for the best.*

Philop. I partly understand you, *Philotheus*, and conceive[78] you intend such a Definition of the *Kingdome of God* as takes in the *Kingdome of Nature* also, and respects those Laws whereby both the brute Animals are guided and the senseless[79] Plants and dead Meteors and Elements, according to the extent of your defence hitherto of *Divine Providence* running from the highest and most Intellectual Orders of things, even to those Material Beings which are framed[80] and actuated by the *Spirit of Nature*, or *Seminal*[81] *Soul of the World.*[82]

Sophr. Why, that is no more then the Scripture itself will warrant him to doe, *Philopolis*. The Psalmist is very frequent in[83] such expressions. *The Lord has prepared his throne in Heaven and his Kingdome ruleth over all. Bless ye the Lord, all his Hosts, ye Ministers of his that doe his pleasure. Bless the Lord all his works in all places of his dominion. Bless the Lord, O my Soul.* This in the 103. Psalm. And in the 148. Psalm he makes all the several degrees[84] of the Creation from Heaven to Earth, from Angels to Brutes, Plants and Meteors, the Hosts of God, and exhorts them all to *praise the name of the Lord: For he spake the word, and they were made; he commanded, and they were created: he hath made them fast for ever and ever; he hath given them a Law which shall not be broken.* And again in the 119. Psalm, *O Lord, thy word endureth for ever in Heaven, thy Truth also remaineth from one generation to another. Thou hast laid the foundation of the Earth, and it abideth; they continue this day according to thy ordinance: for all things serve thee.* Whence it is plain that the Dominion of God and his Kingdome reaches as far as the whole comprehension[85] of the Creation.

Cuph. Why then, in some places, O *Sophron*, the Kingdome of God will be

[71] queries
[72] like a Schoolman, a scholastic philosopher
[73] scruples, instances of scrupulousness, or being meticulous in matters of right and wrong
[74] much diversified
[75] substance of meaning as distinguished from form of expression
[76] comprehend [77] judgment
[78] understand, take your meaning to be
[79] incapable of sensation
[80] given shape
[81] with the power of producing offspring
[82] in the Plotinian system, the source of the life and energy of the corporeal world
[83] addicted to
[84] steps in an ascent or descent
[85] inclusion of the whole

coincident[86] with the Kingdome of the Devil.

Bath. Why, *Cuphophron,* what greater inconvenience[87] is there in that, then that the *Kingdome of Nature* and the *Kingdome of God* should be coincident, which you seem not to gainsay?

Cuph. Methinks it sounds very odly: and besides, we may conceive a subordination[88] betwixt the *Kingdome of God* and the *Kingdome of Nature;* but the *Kingdome of God* and the *Kingdome of the Devil* seem to be in utter opposition one to another, and therefore in no capacity of being parts of the same Kingdome.

Bath. That is wittily urged, O *Cuphophron,* as to the exteriour sound of the words; but look into the intrinsecall[89] nature of things, and set the Beasts of the field and the Devils of Hell one by another, and tell me the difference that uncapacitates[90] the one from being the members of the Kingdome of God more then the other. Is it because the Devils have more subtiltie then the Beasts of the field? This were reprochfully to intimate the Kingdome of God to be a City of Fools. Is it because the one is Spiritual, the other Corporeal? This reason would also exclude the good Angels, the choicest part of God's Kingdome. Is it because the Devils are lapsed?[91] Yet their Lapse is but into the *Animal life,* whose deepest root and fountain is *Self-love* or *Selfishness,* which stands in opposition to that other fountain or root of the *Divine Life,* which is the *pure Love of God,* or of that which is simply and absolutely Good. But Self-love or Selfishness is equally the Root of Life in Brutes as in Devils. Whence it seems manifest, that in reality the Devils are as capable of being part of the Kingdome of God as the Brutes.

Cuph. The difference, O *Bathynous,* seems to be this, That the Brutes retain the integrity[92] of their nature, but the Devils have degenerated from their first condition, and forsook their station[93] God had placed them in.

Bath. I confess, O *Cuphophron,* that the Lapse of the fallen Angels is great, but yet they never sunk beneath the utmost[94] Circuit[95] of the Dominion of Providence, or that *Divine Nemesis*[96] that is continually interwoven into all the degrees of the Creation. So that nothing that is not exterminated out of all Being, but necessarily is subject to the Laws of some order or other of the Creation it has cast it self into. As if some noble Familie should by taking ill courses[97] lose all that Honour and Riches that were left them by their Ancestours, and in process of time become mere Gally-slaves, they do not cease to be still Subjects of the Prince of that Countrey in which they experience these varieties of Fortune; so the Angels degenerating into Devils do not cease to be under the Dominion of God, but find their *Nemesis* in his Dominion. *For there is neither strength nor counsell against the Almighty,*[98] nor can any one out-wit the reaches of his Providence. Gaolers and Prisoners and Hangmen, and all manner of Executioners, are as well Subjects of the Prince as those men of noble rank and quality.[99]

Sophr. All instruments of the *Wrath of God* are part of his Dominion as well as those of his *Love:* For, as the Son of *Sirach*[100] tells us, *There be spirits that are created for vengeance, which in their fury lay on sore strokes; in the time of Destruction they pour out their force, and appease the wrath of him that made them. Fire and Hail and Famine and Death, all these were created for vengeance: Teeth of wild Beasts and Scorpions, Serpents and the Sword punishing the wicked to destruction: All these rejoyce in his commands,*

[86] occupying the same place or portion of space, or occurring at the same time and occupying the same space of time

[87] incongruity, absurdity

[88] arrangement in a series of successively dependent ranks

[89] intrinsical [90] incapacitates

[91] fallen [92] original perfect state

[93] assigned position

[94] outermost [95] circumference

[96] retributive justice, personified here with the name of the Greek goddess of retributive justice

[97] falling into bad conduct

[98] Prov. 21.30.

[99] good social position

[100] Jesus, the son of Sirach of Jerusalem (fl. ca. 200 B.C.), author of Ecclesiasticus

and are ready upon earth to execute his will, when need requires.[101] To this purpose he speaks, and methinks[102] plainly insinuates that the Infernal Powers[103] themselves (of which these are many times but the externall weapons) are part of the Army of the Lord of Hosts.[104]

Bath. It is impossible to be otherwise, O *Sophron;* for it is repugnant[105] to the Wisedome and Omnipotency of God, to suffer any thing to be that is in no wise subject to his Power and Dominion.

Hyl. Gentlemen, methinks you are too-too solicitous in searching and setting out the *Extent* of *Boundaries* of the Kingdome of God, whenas it were a more curious[106] Point, and no less pertinent to the present Quere, [*What the Kingdome of God is,*] to define what *species* of Dominion or Power it is that he thus universally exercises over the Creation.

Cuph. Is it not *absolute* and *unlimited Sovereignty*, *Hylobares,* which we from the *Greeks* call Tyranny?

Sophr. No, by no means, *Cuphophron.* If you understood what Tyranny is, you would find your Assertion as contradictious[107] as blasphemous.

Euist. Sophron saies very true, *Hylobares;* for Aristotle[108] defines Tyranny μοναρχιαν πρὸς το συμφέρον τὸ τοῦ μοναρχοῦντος,[109] and elsewhere[110] in his Politicks[111] describing it more copiously, he saies, it is such a Government in one person as, being unaccountable to any, rules over his equals, or those that are better then himself, doing all things for his own Interest, and not for the Interest of them that he rules. Which things are utterly incompetible[112] to God, who is infinitely better then all the Creation, and is onely capable of doing them good, but not of receiving any good from them.

Cuph. I minded not how *Tyranny* is defined in your learned Authours, *Euistor,* but look'd upon the word as significative of such a Sovereignty as is absolute and unlimited, and that in one person, who is tied to no Law, but acts merely according to the suggestions and sentiments of his own heart.

Euist. And, to tell you the truth, the Criticks, O *Cuphohron,* teach us that the word τὐραννος anciently[113] signified no worse then[114] so, that is to say, an absolute Monarch, a person invested with absolute Sovereignty or Power.

Philoth. If *Cuphophron* meant no otherwise then so, *Euistor,* his meaning was sound and good, though his expression not so warrantable.[115] *For it is very unsafe and scandalous to apply ill-sounding words to the Divine Majesty, though lined*[116] *underneath with a tacit well-meaning.* But to say that that *species* of Dominion which God exercises over his Creatures is absolute Sovereignty, or a power of doing all things according of[117] the suggestions or sentiments of his own mind, this is a sober and true declaration touching the Dominion of God.

Hyl. But I beseech you, *Philotheus,* wherein is this vast unlimited Sovereignty of God founded? in his Omnipotency, or in what is it? For some say absolute and irresistible Power can doe no wrong.

Philoth. That's a thing, *Hylobares,* I could yet never understand, that the most omnipotent Power that is imaginable can ever have a right to doe what is wrong, that is to say, to create any evil that is truly so upon the full compute of all circumstances, or in the entire[118] comprehension[119] of the whole Oeconomy[120] of the Universe, No *Power,* though never so *omnipotent,* can claim a right to such an act, no more then any *Intellect,* never so *omniscient,* can claim a right of authentickly[121] thinking that true which is really false.

[101] Ecclesiastic. 39.28, etc. [33–37]
[102] it seems to me
[103] the powers of evil, or of hell
[104] in the Bible used both for earthly and heavenly armies
[105] contradictory [106] precise, subtle
[107] self-contradictory
[108] [Politic.] lib. 3. *cap.* 7. [More]
[109] "monarchy ruling in the interest of the monarch"
[110] *Politic. lib.* 4.*c.*10. [More]
[111] famous treatise on the kinds of government
[112] inappropriate to
[113] in ancient times
[114] than [115] justifiable
[116] reënforced [117] according to
[118] complete [119] understanding
[120] economy, management
[121] really

But in answer to your main question, wherein the Right of this absolute Soveraignty in God is founded, I must tell you both distinctly and compendiously[122] at once, That to *infinite, permanent* and *immutable Goodness* of right belongs as well *Omnisciency* as *Omnipotency*, the one as her *Secretary*, the other as her *Satellitium.*[123] But the *infinitely-good God* is not onely *of right*, but *by nature*, both *Omniscient* and *Omnipotent.* And from these three, his infiinite *Goodness, Wisedome* and *Power*, issue out all the Orders[124] of the Creation in the whole Universe. So that all the Creatures being his, and his Goodness being so perfect, immutable and permanent, as never out of any humour,[125] (as I may so speak) vacillancy,[126] or supine indifferency,[127] to be carried otherwise then to what is the best, and his Wisedome never at a loss to discern, nor his Power to execute it; we see the clearest foundation imaginable of the *Right* of that *absolute Sovereignty* we acknowledge in God. For is there not all reason, that he that is so immutable Good, that it is repugnant[128] that he should ever will any thing but what is absolutely for the best, should have a full right of acting merely according to the suggestions and sentiments of his own minde, it being impossible but that they should be for the best, he having proportionable[129] *Wisedome* also and *Power* adjoyned to this infinite *Goodness*, to contrive and execute his holy, just and benign designs?

Philop. In my apprehension, *Philotheus*, this is marvellously[130] plain, and such as I wanted[131] no instruction in. And therefore let me intreat you to draw nearer to the main point in hand, which is the Kingdome of God properly so called. For, methinks, we have done hitherto, as if some having a design to observe more particularly some one Kingdome in the Map of the World, suppose *England, France*, or *Spain*, should forget their intended purpose, and lose time in taking a vagary[132] through all *Europe* at least, if not all the four quarters[133] of the World. I desire, *Philotheus*, to understand what that Kingdome[134] of God is that is amongst *Men*, being less curious touching that part of his Dominion that he exercises over *Angels*, whether lapsed or unlapsed, or that Power he exserts upon the Kingdome of Nature, whether Animals or Plants or other inferiour creatures. *Quæ supra nos nihil ad nos:*[135] and there is in some sense the like reason concerning those *things below us.* I desire my prospect[136] may be enlarged onely towards those things that are on the same levell with my self: which I press the more earnestly, because of the streightness[137] of the time I fear we shall be cast into.

Philoth. I commend your providence,[138] *Philopolis*, and desire you to persist in this freedome of calling us back to those subjects you have the greatest mind[139] to be satisfied in, as often as we stray: For this last Evening is wholly dedicated to your service. But however, for all the haste I affect[140] to enter upon that Point you chiefly aim at, namely, What the Kingdome of God is signally[141] so called, I must first mention a Division,[142] before I fall[143] upon that Definition. For the Kingdome of God, as it respects Men also, is either *Internall* or *Externall;* according as our Saviour has declared, *Neither shall they say, Lo here, or Lo there; for behold, the Kingdome of God is within you.*[144]

Cuph. I suppose this Kingdome is muchwhat[145] the same with the Philosophicall Kingdome of the *Stoicks*,[146] who make

[122] summarily
[123] retinue or company of planets
[124] ranks, grades [125] whim, caprice
[126] vacillation [127] indolent apathy
[128] contradictory [129] commensurate
[130] in a marvellous manner [131] lacked
[132] stroll [133] four points of the compass
[134] kingship
[135] "Whatever things are above us are no affair of ours."
[136] mental view
[137] straitness, insufficiency [138] foresight
[139] you are most strongly disposed
[140] incline to
[141] in a striking manner
[142] distinction
[143] take up
[144] Luke 17.21.
[145] pretty much
[146] a school of Greek philosophers, founded by Zeno around 300 B.C., who held that since the world is governed by divine law, the wise man will accept his destiny, unmoved by pleasure or pain

their wise man a King and Emperour, and what not? and count it their chief happiness to have a full dominion over their Passions, especially the more grim and harsh ones, that they may enjoy themselves in quiet.

Philoth. O no, *Cuphophron*, there is no sameness at all betwixt this *Kingdome of the Stoicks* and the *Kingdome of God*. For this Kingdome of the *Stoicks* is the Kingdome of *Selfishness, and Self-love* sways the Sceptre there and wears the Diademe: But in the Kingdome of God, God himself, who is that pure, free, and perfectly-*unselfed*[147] *Love*, has the full dominion of the Soul, and the ordering and rule of all the Passions. It is a wonderful thing to consider how multifarious[148] the Impostures and false pretensions to the *inward Kingdome* are discovered to be by those that are really possessed thereof; how one Passion (as suppose *Pride* or *Covetousness*) subdues all the rest unto it self, and rules instead of the *Divine Love;* how *all the Passions* are brought into a demure[149] subjection to the sense of some *externall Interest*, especially if it bear the *Title* of *Sacred* or *Holy;* and how men may be disciplin'd or educated thereto, as Setting-dogs[150] for the Game, whenas[151] the Soul in such a case has subdued all her affections, onely to surrender her self a more absolute slave to the will of those men whose business it is to bring the World into blinde obedience (by studied Impostures and Hypocrisies) to such Laws as are made for their carnal[152] interest, and, instead of propagating the Kingdome of God, to plant the Kingdome of the Devil or Antichrist[153] amongst men. Let the Soul in such cases as these have never so great a command over her affections, this is no *Kingdome of God*, but a presumptuous and tyrannical Usurpation of some petty[154] Masters against the Right of his Kingdome. Unless this *internall Kingdome* be established in the *Love* and *Peace* and *Patience of the Lord Jesus*, it is but the Reign of mere self-seeking Nature, or the Kingdome of the Devil. *The Kingdome of God in the Soul is the Empire of the Divine Love*, which equally affects[155] the good of all men, *rejoyces with them that rejoyce, and weeps with them that weep:*[156] It is that state of the Soul whereby a man *loves God with all his heart and soul, and his neighbour as himself,*[157] and *deals with others as himself would be dealt with;*[158] whereby a man earnestly desires the common good of all men, and finds himself concern'd in repelling or preventing any publick evil. To be brief, It is the Rule of the Spirit of God in the Soul, who takes the rains[159] of all our Powers, Faculties and Affections into his own hand, and curbs them and excites[160] them according to his own most holy will, that is carried to no particular Self-interest, but ever directs to that which is simply and absolutely the best. This also is the Kingdome of *Christ* in the Inward man, the mystical *Melchizedek,*[161] who is first *King of Righteousness,*[162] as the word signifies, that is, of impartial Rectitude and Uprightness, without all Self-respects[163] and then *King of Salem,*[164] that is, *Prince of Peace*. Finally it is that Kingdome which consists not in externall Superstitions,[165] but, as the Apostle[166] speaks, *in righteousness, and peace, and joy in the Holy Ghost.*[167]

Philop. This *Internall Kingdome of God*, O *Philotheus*, is so lovely and desirable, that I cannot but request you to intimate the means of acquiring it, before you proceed to the *Externall*.

Philoth. O how I love you, *Philopolis*, for this motion,[168] forasmuch as I perceive that it cannot proceed from any vain[169] curiosity, but from a sincere desire of entring into life and holiness! The most effectual means in the general[170] is inti-

[147] selfless (from which all of self has been removed)
[148] many and various [149] settled
[150] dogs to indicate the game
[151] inasmuch as [152] sensual
[153] a great adversary, who will fill the world with wickedness but will be defeated forever by Christ at his second coming
[154] inferior [155] aims at
[156] Rom. 12.15. [157] Matt. 22.37.
[158] Matt. 7.12. [159] reins [160] quickens
[161] a pre-Levitical priest-king in the Old Testament
[162] Heb. 7.2.
[163] personal or selfish ends
[164] supposed to be Jerusalem
[165] irrational religious practices
[166] St. Paul [167] Rom. 14.17.
[168] suggestion [169] foolish
[170] in the main, *or* generally

mated[171] up and down in the Gospels by our Blessed Saviour. As where he compares the Kingdome of Heaven to a *Treasure hid in the field*, and to a *single Pearl of great price*, for which one *sells all he has to purchase it;*[172] and where he tells us that the *Kingdome of God suffers violence*, and that *the violent take it by force;*[173] and again, where he declares that he *that lays his hand to the plough, and looketh back, is not fit for the Kingdome of God,*[174] and in like passages. For all these signifie thus much to us, that whosoever would acquire so excellent a state of the Soul as this which we call the Kingdome of God, he must forthwith quit all things else whatsoever that stand in competition with it; That he must with all imaginable earnestness of spirit and with a kind of holy violence reach at it, and endeavour[175] the taking of it through all dangers, hardships and resistences[176] whatsoever, as he that would scale the walls of a City to obtain the Crown; and, lastly, That this pursuit be without any intermissions[177] or lazy relapses into the power of the World or the Flesh again, but that it be peremptory,[178] constant and continued, till we have wone the prize, and finde all that fulfilled in us which we desired or expected; which is the perfect subduing of all our corruptions, and the establishing of the Reign of the true *Melchizedek* in us, the *living Righteousness* of God, and the replenishing of our hearts with purity, peace, and joy in the Holy Ghost.

Philop. This is excellently good in the general, O *Philotheus*. But have you no farther directions more particularly to recommend to us?

Philoth. Truth lies in a little room, especially that of it that is most usefull, O *Philopolis*. And therefore I will trouble you with no farther instructions then what are comprized in these few Principles. As first, That we have a firm and unshaken Faith in the Power of God, and in the assistence of the Spirit of the Lord *Jesus*, for the subduing all Envy, Pride, Lust, all Worldliness and Selfishness, and what-ever is contrary to the Kingdome of God in us, that we may have a comfortable[179] conquest over these and all like corruptions through him that strengthens us. This is the first necessary Principle we ought to be imbued with, if we mean seriously to set our selves to the atchieving so great and weighty an enterprise: This, I say, is the first necessary Principle, namely, *A full and firm belief that the Atchievement is possible.* The second is, That we believe it to be our duty to arrive to this blessed state, and not to satisfie our selves with any condition on this side of it, much less, out of any Antinomian[180] Sophistrie or Witchcraft,[181] to phansie our selves released from all obligation to any real and living Righteousness in us; but to be entirely obedient to the voice of Wisedome and Truth, *Be ye perfect, as your Father which is in Heaven is perfect;*[182] and to remember, that it was the end[183] of *Christ's* coming into the world, *to pluck up every plant that was not of his Father's planting,*[184] and to raise such a seed[185] upon earth as *have neither spot nor wrinkle, nor any such thing, but are holy*[186] *and without blemish.* If either of these two Principles be wanting, the defect will be notorious in the success.[187] For who can with any courage attempt such difficulties as he thinks either impossible to be overmastered, or not his duty to grapple with. Wherefore being sound in these, *Philopolis*, he must adde *Meditation, Circumspection,* and *Devotion.* Meditation in private especially. Circumspection in his dealing with externall objects, whether men or things, that he be not carried away unawares against those rules and resolutions he made to himself in private, but ever stand upon his guard; and if he be assaulted with any temptation, to call to Heaven for succour, and to trust in the strength of God against the surprize. Which I think is the true meaning of *praying continually*. But in a more particular manner, to adde to your private Meditation the fervency of Devotion, and earnestly to beg of God, that he would every day more and more discover to you

[171] made known [172] Matt. 13.44, 45 [46].
[173] Matt. 11.12. [174] Luke 9.62.
[175] attempt strenuously [176] oppositions
[177] temporary pauses [178] resolved
[179] satisfactory

[180] holding that under the "law of grace" the moral law is not binding on the Christian
[181] magic influence [182] Matt. 5.48.
[183] purpose [184] Matt. 15.13.
[185] progeny [186] Eph. 5.27. [187] result

the ugliness of Sin, and the amiableness[188] of Righteousness, and that your hatred may be more keenly edged[189] against the one, and your love more highly inflamed towards the other; that the work of the Heart may go on, and not those umbratile skirmishes of the Brain in Phancie and exteriour Reason, but that we may effectually feel the difference of the contrary actings of the *Powers* of the *Kingdome of Light* and the *Kingdome of Darkness* charging one another in the field, *Life* against *life* and *Substance* against *Substance*, till Hell and Death be absorpt[190] into victory, and the evil Nature be quite consumed into a glorious flame of Love and Triumph, These all are the Mysteries of the *Heart*, O *Philopolis* not of the *Head*, which, in comparison, is but an outward Shop of Phancies and fine Pictures; but the transactions of *substantial life and Reality* are in that other part, which is the *Secret Tabernacle of God*, and hidden *Temple* for most effectual Prayer. For the *Heart* is the *proper Pavilion* of either the *spirit of the World,*[191] *or the Spirit of God*, which kindles there the holy desire and thirst after Righteousness: Which vehement, sincere and cordial desire, the true gift and fruit of the Spirit, is the very *soul* and *substance of Prayer*, and a certain *Divine Magick* that draws all the heavenly Powers into the centre of our Souls, imbibing the comfortable dews of Paradise, to the ineffable refreshing of the Garden of God. Through this sluce[192] is let in all the nourishment to the new Birth,[193] and it is the fear of the first living seed thereof. Whence the *Centre of our Soul* in the *Heart*[194] requires more diligent observation then that more *peculiar*[195] *one* in the *Head*. For though this seems more peculiarly ours, yet the other joyns us with that which is more to us then we are to our selves, whether it be the *spirit of the world* or of *God*, and makes us feelingly communicate with *Life* and *Substance;* whenas the other without this would onely lead us into *a field of Shadows and Dreams*.

Wherefore, O *Philopolis*, he that is a Candidate for the Kingdome of God, let him above all things cultivate the Heart; for through this onely is the Inlet into the Kingdome of Light.[196] *Blessed are the pure in heart; for they shall see God. Blessed are they that hunger and thirst after righteousness; for they shall be satisfied.*[197] *I stretch forth my hands unto thee; my Soul gaspeth unto thee, as a thirsty Land where no water is.*[198] And again, *Blessed is the man whose strength is in thee, in whose heart are thy ways; Who passing through the valley of* Baca *make it a Well, and the rain filleth the pools with water. They go from strength to strength, till every one of them appear before God in Sion.*[199] By which is intimated, that firm Faith and holy desire brings us at last to the fruition of God and his Kingdome.

To all which I need not adde, for a conclusion, the perpetuall and constant performance of what-ever we find our selves able and bound in duty to perform. For he that has this Faith and sincere desire can never sin against the Power of God and the Dictates of his own Conscience. This, *Philopolis*, is a brief, but faithfull, direction for the obtaining that great prize, *the Kingdome of God within us*.

Philop. And I am infinitely obliged to you, *Philotheus*, for your hearty and serious Instructions in so important a Mysterie. I hope they will never slip out of my mind.

[188] loveableness [189] incited
[190] from past participle of Latin *absorbere*, *absorptus*
[191] of those concerned only with the mundane and irreligious
[192] sluice [193] spiritual regeneration
[194] the seat of the emotions
[195] individual [196] Kingdom of God
[197] Matt. 5.6, 8. [198] Ps. 143.6.
[199] Ps. 84.5, 6, 7.

Richard Baxter

RICHARD BAXTER was born at Rowton in the parish of High Ercall near Shrewsbury on November 12, 1615. His father was a Puritan gentleman, and his mother came of an old yeoman family. He would seem to have been educated at home until his fifteenth year when he was sent to the Donnington Free School in the parish of Wroxeter. Apparently the desire of his parents to keep their only child near them led them to set aside Richard's university aspirations and accept the invitation of the Chaplain to the Council at Ludlow Castle to study with him. After a year and a half at Ludlow Castle, which ever after seemed to Baxter a world of temptations, the Chaplain persuaded his neglected student to go up to London for Court acquaintance and preferment. So after three months at home Richard went up to Whitehall to stay with the older brother of George Herbert, Sir Henry Herbert, the Master of the Revels. But a month of the Court of Charles I was enough for Baxter, and he returned home to spend the next four years there reading and studying as much as his health would permit.

In his own apprehensive meditations about another world Baxter became aware of an overwhelming desire to awaken the careless of this world to thought of that other realm so much in his own mind, and discovered in himself a capacity for persuasion that gave him confidence in his call to preaching. The fact that he lacked the recognized academic degrees made him pause, but the thought that he might save even one or two souls seemed to him more than worth the risk of ridicule for his lack of academic honors. The problem of subscription to the Book of Common Prayer which troubled so many Puritans seems to have bothered him little, for he had been brought up in conformity with the customs of the Church of England. An opportunity to teach school at Dudley presented itself; so on December 23, 1638, he was ordained deacon by the Bishop of Worcester and licensed to teach. He apparently judged it presumptuous to aspire to pastoral charge, but he began to preach at once. He was now brought into contact with Nonconformists and so forced to look more closely into a position which he had apparently pretty much taken for granted. His new Nonconformist friends were apparently not so much concerned about Episcopacy as about certain matters of ceremony which the Puritans had long objected to, and to these Baxter now addressed himself with characteristic thoroughness. The result of his studies was a moderate position on the Book of Common Prayer; he found in it nothing to justify proscribing its use as unlawful when nothing better was possible, but plenty of what he called "disorder and defectiveness." While now as always separation seemed to Baxter intolerable, he sympathized with the sufferings of the Nonconformists at the hands of the bishops.

Less than a year later he went as assistant to the pastor of Bridgnorth to give his whole time to preaching, the great passion of this part of his life. The "Etcetera Oath" of 1640 in the interest of the maintenance of the hierarchical status quo forced Baxter a little farther on his way when he found himself one of the Nonconforming majority of the ministers of Shropshire who voted against it. But he found the population of Bridgnorth so unresponsive to the call to conversion that before his second year was out he was glad to accept the invitation of the town of Kidderminster to become their lecturer or preacher. The stipend offered was small, and the vicarage was in the possession of a "reader," incapable of preaching, but the offer appealed to Baxter, the least self-seeking of men. The town was poor and the population, many of them weavers, ignorant and unhealthy and rude, much given to drunkenness. But there was a small company of the converted among them who might prove helpful to the preacher in his efforts to win the rest. Here in April of 1641 Baxter began the work that was to make him famous, devoting himself to the preaching that he, like his fellow Puritans, judged the most important work man could do, with a moral passion and persuasiveness that drew men from miles around.

So he had worked for about fifteen months when the progress of the dispute between King and Parliament forced him to take sides, which he did for the Parliament, to no small extent moved by the desire to rescue the King from those who had misled him into war against his Parliament. The town rabble raised by Royalist gentlemen in the neighborhood made things so threatening that Baxter thought it prudent to withdraw to Gloucester, and from there he went to Coventry, where he preached without payment to the soldiers of the Parliamentary forces there and devoted himself to his studies. But anxiety for friends led him to Naseby Field in the middle of June, 1645, and there coming into close contact with Cromwell's army, he was astonished to learn that the reports that the sectaries had taken over and were in possession of the Army were true. He had refused an earlier invitation to make "a gathered church" of Cromwell's first troop and be their pastor because he disapproved of separation; so now he felt some responsibility for the situation which he judged not yet past recovery. He accepted Colonel Whalley's invitation to be chaplain to his regiment, and spent eighteen months with them, disputing valiantly with the Anabaptists and Independents and Arminians in possession of the army at large. But a complete breakdown of his health put an end to his army career. In his convalescence at the home of sympathetic friends the tireless Baxter began the most famous of his works, *The Saints' Everlasting Rest*. He was now invited back to Kidderminster, ostensibly to his old post of lecturer but actually, though he did not know it, to be vicar. Again, he behaved with his characteristic generosity to his predecessor, leaving him in possession of his vicarage and his "fifths." And he set himself with fresh energy to his old work of spiritual reform and of leadership of the Puritan clergy in the neighborhood, sweetening the "Discipline" which he proceeded to enforce, with charity to the poor and tireless patience with the aspiring.

But though the throngs that flocked to hear him preach necessitated the building of five galleries in the church, Baxter came to feel that even preaching was not so effective as the catechizing to which he began to devote a major portion of his time and effort from the end of 1655. This more personal instruction and exhortation of his parishioners seemed to him the most effective way he had yet found of reaching the human conscience and meeting the needs and circumstances of the individual life. And the fame which Baxter achieved as a pastor, extended by his book *Gildas Salvianus: the Reformed Pastor*, widened his correspondence with requests for help from other ministers faced with the problems of the pastoral office.

Meanwhile Baxter had been achieving a position of leadership in a movement for unification of the outstanding parties to the disputes as to the nature of the Church of England, the Erastian, the Episcopal, the Presbyterian, and the Independent. As early as 1652 he had proposed to the monthly meeting of ministers at his house a scheme which he thought might achieve unity in the essentials of Christian observance, leaving liberty in matters that seemed to him of more doubtful certainty. A larger meeting at Worcester directed him to draw up such a plan, and, as one might expect, the first item in the resulting scheme was the Discipline. The Worcestershire Association that was to make a beginning in putting this plan into action was described by Baxter as made up not of Presbyterians or Independents but of "mere Catholicks." Similar associations were formed in other parts of England and Wales, and Baxter began to have hopes of bringing the Independents in and even of finding a way of association with the Anabaptists. As a result of these and similar activities Baxter was recognized as a leader of wide influence and was consulted by those who on the death of Cromwell were planning the return of the King.

Upon the accomplishment of the Restoration Baxter was, with a number of other leading Presbyterian divines, made one of the King's Chaplains, and he took a prominent part in the conferences looking to agreement that followed. But when the King proposed that the plans for indulgence of Independents and Anabaptists be widened so as to include others, even Socinians and Catholics, Baxter protested. He had already rejected the offer of a bishopric because of his disapproval of the old diocesan type of government, but he still hoped for a settlement which would associate Presbyters with the Bishop and give the individual minister what he considered proper authority in his own parish. However, the tide had set in the direction of what Baxter considered the restoration of Prelacy. In May of 1661 the National Vow and Covenant was by order of Parliament burned, and by July the Savoy conference of Bishops and Divines from which he had hoped for an agreement broke up, and Baxter, as he complained, found himself called by what to him was the odious name of Presbyterian when he considered that all he had been asking for was "Primitive Episcopacy."

Baxter returned to Kidderminster to see if he could reach an agreement with the reinstated vicar that would let him continue his preaching, but the vicar refused, and shortly thereafter the bishop of the diocese refused to let him preach. So Baxter left Kidderminster and went to London where it was possible for him to preach a lecture. He himself went to the parish church wherever he was and urged his Kidderminster faithful to do so. But when the Uniformity Act became law on May 19, 1662, he felt called upon to make clear his dissent, though he still considered himself a loyal member of the Church of England. He was now effectively silenced; so he devoted himself to study and writing. In September of 1662 he married Margaret Charlton, a devoted parishioner and very rare spirit with whom he had fallen deeply in love, and his happiness with her did much to sweeten the years of frustration and persecution that lay ahead. She died in 1681.

In 1668 Baxter took advantage of the interval between the expiration of the first Conventicle Act and the coming into effect of the second to throw the service which he held at his home in Acton open to the public. At the request of the Rector of Acton the meeting was suppressed and Baxter arrested and put in jail for six months. In 1672 the Royal Declaration of Indulgence for all Nonconformists made it possible for Baxter to preach again, but Parliament forced the King to withdraw it in 1673. In the years that followed Baxter was often the victim of the persecutions that vexed the Protestant Dissenters, until in 1685 he was charged with sedition and attack on the Anglican liturgy and tried before Judge Jeffreys in Westminster Hall. He was fined and thrown into prison, where he stayed for eighteen months. Upon his release he settled down in London, preaching when his health allowed, and writing, until his death in 1691.

Baxter wrote voluminously on many of the issues of religious doctrine and practice controverted in his day, and on a wide range of topics concerning Christian conduct and experience, to the number, it is said, of nearly one hundred and seventy separate works. Most of these writings are very difficult of access today. W. Orme published *The Practical Works of Richard Baxter* in 1830. *The Saints' Everlasting Rest* (1650), ed. W. Young, was reprinted in 1907. *Chapters from A Christian Directory*, selected by J. Tawney with a preface by C. Gore, was published in 1925, and *The Reformed Pastor* (1656), ed. J. T. Wilkinson, in 1939. There are annotated bibliographies of Baxter's works by A. B. Grosart (1868) and A. G. Matthews (1932).

Today Baxter's autobiographical writings are probably the best-known portion of his work. An abridgement of the *Reliquiae Baxterianae: or, Mr. Richard Baxter's Narrative of the Most Memorable Passages of His Life and Times*, (ed. M. Sylvester, 1696) by J. M. Lloyd Thomas appeared in 1925; it is also available in Everyman's Library (1931). Baxter's memoir of his wife, *A Breviate of the Life of Margaret Baxter* (1681), was reprinted by J. T. Wilkinson as *Richard Baxter and Margaret Charlton, a Puritan Love Story* in 1928.

The standard biography is by F. J. Powicke (2 vols., 1924–1926). A brief study is A. R. Ladell, *Richard Baxter, Puritan and Mystic* (1925). I. Morgan, *The Nonconformity of Richard Baxter* (1945) is a detailed analysis of Baxter's general religious position, and C. F. Kemp, *A Pastoral Triumph* (1948) is a study by an expert in pastoral work of Baxter's ministry at Kidderminster.

from THE SAINTS EVERLASTING REST[1]

THE FIRST PART

CHAP. IV

What This Rest Containeth

But all this is onely the outward[2] Court, or at least not the holiest[3] of all: Now we have ascended these steps, may we look within the vail?[4] May we shew what this Rest containeth, as well as what it presupposeth? But alass, how little know I of that, whereof I am about to speak! Shall I speak before I know? But if I stay till I clearly know, I shall not come again to speak. The glimpse which *Paul*[5] saw, contained that which could not, or must not be uttered, or both.[6] And if *Paul* had had a tongue to have uttered it, it would have done no good, except his hearers had ears to hear it. If *Paul* had spoke the things of Heaven in the language of Heaven, and none understood that language, what[7] the better? Therefore I'l speak, while I may, that little, very little which I do know of it, rather then be wholy silent: The Lord reveal it to me, that I may reveal it to you: and the Lord open some light, and shew both you and me his Inheritance;[8] Not as to Balaam[9] onely, whose eyes the vision of God opened, to see the goodliness of Jacobs tents, and Israels tabernacles, where he had no portion; but from whence must come

[1] Text: 1650

[2] as in the temple at Jerusalem in the Bible

[3] the tabernacle (See Heb. 9.3.)

[4] screening the tabernacle

[5] Saul of Tarsus, converted to Christianity by a vision on the road to Damascus, the apostle to the Gentiles and the author of a number of Epistles

[6] II Cor. 12.4. [Here as throughout, unless otherwise indicated, the Scriptural references are Baxter's.]

[7] in what respect

[8] the blessings to be enjoyed by His chosen people

[9] son of Beor of Pethor of Mesopotamia, given to prophecy, killed in battle by the Hebrews

his own destruction:[10] Nor as to Moses,[11] who had onely a discovery, in stead of possession, and saw the Land, which he never entered:[12] But as the pearl was revealed to the Merchant in the Gospel, who rested not till he had sold all he had and bought it:[13] and as Heaven was opened to blessed *Stephen*, which he was shortly to enter, and the glory shewed him, which should be his own possession.[14]

. . . . .

Sect. I

There is Contained in this Rest.

1. A Cessation from Motion or Action; not of all action, but of that which hath the nature of a Means, and implies the absence of the End. When we have obtained[15] the Haven, we have done sailing. When the workman hath his wages, it is implyed, he hath done his work. When we are at our journeys end, we have done with the way. All Motion ends at the Center;[16] and all Means cease, when we have the End. Therefore prophecying ceaseth, tongues fail, and knowledg shall be done away;[17] that is, so far as it had the nature of a Means, and was imperfect:[18] And so faith may be said to cease; not all faith, (for how shall we know all things past which we saw[19] not but by beleeving? how shall we know the last Judgment, the resurrection of the body, before hand, but by beleeving? how shall we know the life everlasting, the Eternity of the joys we possess, but by beleeving? But all that faith which as a Means referred to the chief End, shall cease. There shall be no more prayer, because no more necessity, but the full enjoyment of what we pray'd for. Whether the soul pray for the bodies resurrection, for the last judgment, etc. or whether soul and body pray for the eternal continuance of their joys, is to me yet unknown: Otherwise we shall not need to pray for what we have; and we shall have all that is desirable. Neither shall we need to fast, and weep, and watch any more being out of the reach of sin and temptations. Nor will there be use[20] of Instructions and Exhortations: Preaching is done; The Ministry of man ceaseth; Sacraments useless; The Laborers called in, because the harvest is gathered; the tares[21] burned, and the work is done; The Unregenerate past hope; the Saints past fear, for ever: Much less shall there be any need of laboring for inferior ends, as here we do; seeing they will all devolve[22] themselves into the Ocean of the ultimate End, and the lesser good be wholy swallowed up of[23] the Greatest.

Sect. II

2. This Rest containeth a perfect freedom from all the Evils that accompanied us through our course, and which necessarily follow[24] our absence from the chief good. Besides our freedom from those eternal flames, and restless miseries, which the neglect of Christ and Grace must remedilesly endure;[25] an inheritance which both by birth and actual merit, was due to us, as well as to them. As God will not know the wicked, so as to own[26] them; so neither will Heaven know iniquity to receive it: for there entereth nothing that defileth, or is unclean; all that Remains without.[27] And doubtless there is not such a thing as Grief and Sorrow known there: Nor is there such a thing, as a pale face, a languid body, feeble joynts, unable[28] infancy, decrepit age, peccant[29] humors, dolorous sickness, griping fears, consuming cares, nor whatsoever deserves

[10] Num. 24.15, 16 [31].5.

[11] the great lawgiver and leader who brought the children of Israel out of Egypt, and who died before they entered the Promised Land

[12] Deut. 34.1, 2, 3, 4.

[13] Matt. 13.44, 45, 46.

[14] Acts 7.55, 56.

[15] reached

[16] fixed or unmoving center of rotation or revolution

[17] put away, dismissed

[18] [I] Cor. 13.8.

[19] knew

[20] need for using

[21] vetch or darnel, occurring as weeds in the corn (See Matt. 13.25–30.)

[22] roll down

[23] by

[24] result from

[25] be subjected to

[26] acknowledge

[27] Rev. 21.27.

[28] incompetent

[29] morbid (disease-producing)

the name of evil. Indeed a gale of Groans and Sighs, a stream of Tears, accompanyed us to the very Gates, and there bid us, farewel, for ever: We did weep and lament, when the world did rejoice; but our Sorrow is turned into Joy, and our Joy shall no man take from us.[30] God were not the chief and perfect good, if the full fruition[31] of him did not free us from all Evil. But we shall have occasion to speak more fully of this in that which follows.

3. This Rest containeth, the Highest Degree of the Saints personal perfection; both of Soul and Body. This necessarily qualifies them to enjoy the Glory, and throughly to partake[32] the sweetness of it. Were the Glory never so great, and themselves not made capable[33] by a personal perfection suitable thereto, it would be little to them. There's necessary a right disposition of the Recipient, to a right enjoying, and affecting:[34] This is one thing that makes the Saints Joys there so great; Here, Eye hath not seen nor Ear heard, nor Heart conceived what God hath layd up for them that wait[35] for him:[36] For the Eye of flesh is not capable of seeing it, nor this Ear of hearing it, nor this Heart of understanding it; But there the Eye, and Ear, and Heart are made capable; else how do they enjoy it? The more perfect the sight is, the more delightful the beautiful object. The more perfect the Appetite, the sweeter the Food. The more musical the Ear, the more pleasant the Melody. The more perfect the Soul, the more Joyous those Joys, and the more Glorious to us is that Glory. Nor is it onely our sinful imperfection, that is here to be removed; nor onely that which is the fruit of sin; but that which adhered to us in our pure naturals.[37] *Adams*[38] dressing the Garden,[39] was neither sin nor the fruit of sin: Nor is either to be less Glorious then the Stars, or the Sun in the Firmament of our Father: Yet is this the dignity to which the Righteous shall be advanced.[40] There is far more procured by Christ, then was lost by *Adam*. It's the misery of wicked men here, that all without them is mercy, excellent mercies; but within them a heart full of sin shuts the door against all and makes them but the more miserable. When all's well within, then all's well indeed. The neer[41] Good, is the best; and the neer evil and enemy, the worst. Therefore will God, as a special part of his Saints Happiness, perfect themselves, as well as their condition.

. . . . .

Sect. IV

4. This Rest containeth, as the principal part, our nearest fruition of God the Chiefest Good. And here, *Reader*, wonder not If I be at a loss; and if my apprehensions[42] receive but little[43] of that which is in my expressions. If to the beloved Disciple[44] that durst speak and enquire into Christs secrets, and was filled with his Revelations,[45] and saw the new *Jerusalem*[46] in her Glory, and had seen Christ, *Moses* and *Elias*[47] in part of theirs;[48] If it did not appear to him what we shall be, but only in general, that when Christ appears, we shall be like him,[49] no wonder if I know little. When I know so little of God, I cannot know much what it is to enjoy him. When it is so little I know of mine own soul, either it's quiddity,[50] or quality, while it's here in this Tabernacle,[51] how little must I needs know of the Infinite Majesty, or the state of this soul, when it's advanced to that enjoyment? If I know so little of Spirits and Spirituals,[52] how little of the Father of Spirits? Nay, if I never saw that creature, which contains not something unsearchable; nor the worm so small, which afforded not matter for Questions

[30] John 16.20, 21, 22. [31] enjoyment
[32] take part in [33] able to comprehend
[34] moving of the emotions
[35] look forward to [36] [Isa. 64.4.]
[37] natural gifts [38] the first man
[39] the Garden of Eden
[40] Gen. 2.15., Dan. 12.3.
[41] close at hand [42] perceptions
[43] have but little conferred upon them
[44] St. John
[45] The Revelation of Saint John the Divine
[46] the spiritual church
[47] Elijah, Old Testament prophet, who was taken to heaven in a chariot of fire (Elias in the New Testament)
[48] the Transfiguration (See Matt. 17.1–3.)
[49] I John 3.2.
[50] the real nature or essence of a thing
[51] tabernacle of the body
[52] inhabitants of the spiritual realm

to puzzle the greatest Phylosopher that ever I met with, no wonder then if mine eye fail when I would look at God, my tongue fail me in speaking of him, and my heart in conceiving.[53] As long as the Athenian Superscription doth so too well suite[54] with my sacrifices, [*To the unknown God*,][55] and while I cannot contain the smallest rivelet; It's little I can contain of this immense Ocean. We shall never be capable of clearly knowing, till we are capable of fully enjoying, nay nor till we do actually enjoy him. What strange conceivings,[56] hath a man born blind, of the Sun, and its light? or man born deaf of the nature of sounds and musick? So do we yet want that sense, by which God must be clearly known. I stand and look upon a heap of Ants, and see them all with one view, very busie to little purpose; They know not me, my being, nature, or thoughts, though I am their fellow creature: How little then must we know of the great Creator, though he with one view[57] continually beholds us all. Yet a knowledg we have, though imperfect, and such as must be done a way: A Glimpse the Saints behold, though but in a glass; Which makes us capable of some poor, general, dark apprehensions of what we shall behold in Glory. If I should tell a Worldling but what the holiness and Spiritual Joys of the Saints on earth are, he cannot know it; for grace[58] cannot be clearly known without grace:[59] how much less could he conceive it, Should I tell him of this Glory? But to the Saints[60] I may be somewhat more encouraged to speak; for Grace giveth them a dark[61] knowledg, and slight taste of Glory.

As all Good whatsoever is comprised in God, and all in the creature are but drops of this Ocean: So all the Glory of the blessed is comprised in their enjoyment of God; and if there be any mediate[62] Joys there, they are but drops from this. If men and Angels should study to speak the blessedness of that estate in one word, what can they say beyond this, That it is the nearest[63] enjoyment of God? Say they have God, and you say they have all, that's worth a having. O the full joys offered to a beleever in that one sentence of Christs, I would not for all the world, that one verse had been left out of the Bible: *Father, I will that those Whom thou hast given me, be with me Where I am, that they may behold my Glory which thou hast given me*, John 17.24. Every word full of Life and Joy. If the Queen of Sheba[64] had cause to say of Solomons[65] Glory, *Happy are thy men, happy are these thy servants that stand continually before thee and that hear thy wisdom;*[66] then sure they that stand continually before God, and see his Glory, and the Glory of the Lamb, are somewhat more then happy. . . .

. . . . .

Sect. V

5. This Rest containeth A Sweet and constant Action of all the Powers of the Soul and Body in this fruition of God.

. . . . .

[53] *O qui perpetua mundum ratione gubernas, Terrarum cœlique sator, qui tempus ab ævo; Ire jubes stablisque manens das cuncta moveri; Principium, rector, dux, semita, terminus idem; Tu requies tranquilla piis; te cernere, finis.* Boetius. *Vide Gerson. part.* 3. *Alphabet. divini Amoris; cap.* 14. *egregie de attributis et excellentiis divinis expatiantem.* [Baxter's note]

[O Thou, who dost guide the world in enduring order, Creator of earth and heaven, who from eternity dost bid time to pass, and thyself remaining unmoved makest all things to be moved; beginning, guide, leader, way, end, Thou quiet rest to the pious, whose end is to behold thee. Boethius. See Gerson, part 3 of the *Alphabet of Divine Love*, chapter 14, notably treating of the divine attributes and excellences.]

[54] harmonize with

[55] to which St. Paul refers in his sermon on Mars Hill (See Acts 17.22–23.)

[56] conceptions [57] glance

[58] the favor of God

[59] the divine influence which operates in men's souls to strengthen them

[60] Elect [61] indistinct

[62] serving as a means to an end

[63] most intimate

[64] who came to test King Solomon's wisdom

[65] ancient Hebrew King, famous for his wisdom and his building

[66] I Kings 10.8.

Certain it is, it shall be the everlasting work of those Blessed Saints, to stand before the Throne of God and the Lamb,[67] and to praise him for ever and ever. As their Eyes and Hearts shall be filled with his Knowledg, with his Glory, and with his Love; so shall their mouthes be filled with his praises. Go on[68] therefore, Oh ye Saints, while you are on Earth, in that Divine Duty. Learn, Oh learn that Saint-beseeming[69] work; for in the mouthes of his Saints, his praise is comely. Pray, but still praise; Hear,[70] and Read, but still praise:[71] Praise him in the presence of his people; for it shall be your Eternal work: Praise him, while his Enemies deride and abuse you: You shall praise him, while they shall bewail it and admire you. Oh Blessed Employment! to sound forth for ever, *Thou art worthy O Lord to receive Honor, Glory, and Power, Revel.* 4.11. And *worthy is the Lamb who was slain, to receive Power, and Riches, and Wisdom, and Strength, and Honor, and Glory, and Blessing; for he hath Redeemed us to God by his blood out of every kinred,*[72] *and tongue, and people, and Nation; and hath made us unto our God Kings and Priests, Revel.* 5.12, 9, 10. *Alleluja: Salvation, and Honor, and Glory, and Power unto the Lord our God: Praise our God all ye his servants, and ye that fear him, small, and great. Alleluja: for the Lord God omnipotent reigneth, Revel.* 19. 1, 5, 6. Oh Christians! this is the blessed Rest; A Rest without Rest: For *they Rest not day and night, saying, Holy, Holy, Holy, Lord God Almighty which was, and is, and is to come, Revel.* 4.8. Sing forth his praises now, ye Saints; It is a work our Master Christ hath taught us. And you shall for ever sing before him, the song of Moses,[73] and the song of the *Lamb, Great and marvellous are thy works, Lord God Almighty, Just and true are thy Ways, thou King of Saints, Revel.* 15.3.

. . . . .

Sect. VI

And if the Body shall be thus employed, Oh how shall the Soul be taken up? As its powers and capacities are greatest, so its action strongest, and its enjoyment sweetest. As the bodily senses have their proper aptitude and action, whereby they receive and enjoy their objects so doth the Soul in its own action enjoy its own object: By knowing, by thinking and Remembering, by Loving, and by delightful joying; this is the Souls enjoying. By these Eyes it sees, and by these Arms it embraceth. If it might be said of the Disciples with Christ on Earth, much more that behold him in his Glory, *Blessed are the Eyes that see the things you see, and the Ears that hear the things that you hear: for many Princes and great ones have desired (and hoped) to see the things that you see, and have not seen them, etc. Mat.* 13.16.17.

Knowledg of it self is very desireable, even the knowledg of some evil (though not the Evil itself:) As far as the Rational Soul[74] exceeds the Sensitive,[75] so far the Delights of a Philosopher, in discovering the secrets of Nature, and knowing the mystery of Sciences, exceeds the Delights of the Glutton, the Drunkard, the unclean, and of all voluptuous sensualists whatsoever: so excellent is all Truth. What then is their Delight, who know the God of Truth? What would I not give, so that all the uncertain questionable[76] Principles in *Logick, Natural Philosophy, Metaphysicks,* and *Medicine,* were but certain in themselves, and to me? And that my dull, obscure notions of them were but quick[77]

[67] a favorite animal for sacrifice in the Old Testament, used figuratively for Christ in the New

[68] persevere

[69] becoming

[70] hear sermons and instructions

[71] Ps. 33.1, 2., and 147.1.

[72] kindred, tribe

[73] the song which Moses and the Children of Israel sang after the drowning of Pharaoh and his hosts in the Red Sea (See Gen. 15.1–18.)

[74] one of the three kinds of soul in Scholastic philosophy, the reasoning soul, alone of the three, capable of existing outside of the body

[75] another kind of Scholastic soul, that which is concerned with sensation

[76] doubtful

[77] alive

and clear! Oh, what then should I not either perform, or part with, to enjoy a clear and true Apprehension of the most True God? How noble a faculty of the Soul is this Understanding?[78] It can compass the Earth: It can measure the Sun, Moon, Stars, and Heaven: It can foreknow each Eclipse to a minute, many years before: Yea, but this is the top of all its excellency, It can know God who is infinite, who made all these; a little here, and more, much more hereafter. Oh the wisdom and goodness of our Blessed Lord! He hath created the Understanding with a Natural Byas, and inclination to Truth, as its object; and to the Prime[79] Truth, as its Prime Object: and lest we should turn aside to any Creature, he hath kept this as his own Divine Prerogative, not communicable to any Creature, *viz.* to be the Prime Truth. And though I think not (as some[80] do) that there is so neer a close,[81] between the Understanding and Truth, as may produce a proper Union or Identity: Yet doubtless it's no such cold touch, or disdainful embrace, as is between these gross earthly Heterogeneals.[82] The true, studious, contemplative man, knows this to be true; who feels as sweet embraces between his Intellect and Truth, and far more, then ever the quickest sense[83] did in possessing its desired object. But the true, studious, contemplative Christian, knows it much more; who sometimes hath felt more sweet embraces between his Soul and Jesus Christ, then all inferior Truth can afford. I know some Christians are kept short this way, especially the careless in their watch and walking; and those that are ignorant or negligent in the dayly actings of Faith, who look[84] when God casts in Joys while they lie idle, and labor not to fetch them in by beleeving: But for others, I appeal to the most of them; Christian, dost thou not sometime,[85] when, after long gazing heavenward, thou hast got a glimpse of Christ, dost thou not seem to have been with *Paul* in the third Heaven, whether in the body or out,[86] and to have seen what is unutterable? Art thou not, with *Peter*[87] almost beyond thy self? ready to say, *Master it's good to be here?*[88] Oh that I might dwell in this Mount![89] Oh that I might ever see what I now see! Didst thou never look so long upon the Sun of God, till thine Eyes were dazled with his astonishing glory? and did not the splendor of it make all things below seem black and dark to thee, when thou lookest down again? Especially in thy day of suffering for Christ; (when he usually appears most manifestly to his people): Didst thou never see one walking in the midst of the fiery furnace with thee, like to the Son of God? If thou do know him, value him as thy life, and follow on to know him,[90] and thou shalt know incomparably more then this. Or if I do but renew thy grief to tell thee of what thou once didst feel, but now hast lost; I counsel thee to *Remember whence thou art fallen, and Repent, and do the first works, and be watchful, and strengthen the things which remain,*[91] and I dare promise thee (because God hath promised,) thou shalt see, and know, that which here thine Eye could not see, nor thy Understanding conceive. Beleeve me Christians, yea, beleeve God, You that have known most of God in Christ here, it is as nothing to that you shall know; It scarce, in comparison of that, deserves to be called Knowledg. The difference betwixt our knowledg now,

[78] *Scalig. Exercit.* 107 *Sect.* 3 *Dicit Voluntatem nihil aliud esse quam intellectum extentum, ad habendum et faciendum id quod cognoscit.* [Julius Caesar Scaliger, *Exercitationes* on *Jerome Cardan, De Subtilitate,* 107, sect. 3: he says that free will is nothing other than the understanding extended for the having and the bringing to pass of what it has perceived.] . . . And for my part I think not, that the Soul is divisible into several faculties, but rather . . . the Understanding and Will be the same with the Soul and one another; Or distinct Acts of the same Soul; not faculties. [Baxter's note]

[79] the first, the principal, here God

[80] Lord Brook, *Union of the Soul and Truth* [Baxter's note]

[81] junction

[82] heterogeneous persons

[83] capability of feeling

[84] await the time [85] now and then

[86] [II Cor. 12.2–4.]

[87] Simon, name changed to Peter by Christ, the chief of the Apostles and the founder of the church among the Jews

[88] [Matt. 17.1–4.]

[89] of the Transfiguration

[90] Hosea 6.2, 3. [91] Rev. 2.5 and 3.2.

and our knowledg then will be as great, as that between our fleshly bodies now, and our spiritual glorified bodies then.[92] For as these bodies, so that knowledg must cease, that a more perfect may succeed. Our silly childish thoughts of God, which now is the highest we reach to, must give place to a manly knowledg. All this saith the Apostle,[93] I *Cor.* 13.8, 9, 10, 11, 12. *Knowledg shall vanish away: For we know in part, etc. But when that which is perfect is come, then that which is in part shall be done away. When I was a childe, I spake as a childe, I thought as a childe, I understood as a childe, but when I became a man, I put away childish things. For now we see through a glass darkly, but then face to face: Now I know in part, but then I shall know, even as also I am known.*

Marvel not therefore, Christian, at the sence of that place of *John* 17.3. how it can be life eternal to know God, and his Son Christ: You must needs know, that to enjoy God and his Christ, is eternal Life; and the souls enjoying is in knowing.[94] They that savor[95] only of earth, and consult[96] with flesh, and have no way to try[97] and judg but by sense, and never were acquainted with this Knowledg of God, nor tasted how gracious he is, these think it's a poor happiness to know God: let them have health and wealth, and worldly delights, and take you the other. Alas poor men! they that have made tryal of both, do not grudg you your delights, nor envy your happiness, but pity your undoing[98] folly, and wish, O that you would come near, and taste, and try, as they have done, and then judg; Then continue in your former mind, if you can. For our parts, we say with that knowing Apostle (though the speech may seem presumptuous) I *John* 5.19, 20. *We know that we are of God, and the Whole World lieth in wickedness: And We know that the Son of God is come, and hath given us an understanding, that we may know him that is True; and we are in him that is True, in his Son Jesus Christ: This is the true God, and Eternal Life.* Here one verse contains the sum of most that I have said. *The Son of God is come* (to be our Head and Fountain of Life) *and so hath given us an understanding* (that the Soul may be personally qualified and made capable) *to know him* (*God*) *that is True,* (the Prime Truth), *and we are* (brought so near in this enjoyment, that) *we are in him that is True* (not properly by an essential[99] or personal union, but we are in him, by being) *in his Son Jesus Christ. This* (we have mentioned) *is the* (only) *True God* (and so the fittest object for our understanding, which chuseth Truth), *and* (this knowing of him, and being in him, in Christ) *is eternal life.*

. . . . . .

Sect. VII

And doubtless the Memory will not be Idle, or useless, in this Blessed work. If it be but by looking back, to help the soul to value its enjoyment, Our knowledg will be enlarged, not diminished; therefore the knowledg of things past shall not be taken away. And what is that knowledg, but Remembrance? Doubtless from that height, the Saint can look behind him and before him. And to compare past with present things, must needs raise in the Blessed Soul an unconceiveable esteem and sense of its Condition.[100] To stand on that Mount,[101] whence we can see the Wilderness and *Canaan*[102] both at once, to stand in Heaven, and look back on Earth, and weigh them together in the ballance of a comparing sense and judgment, how must it needs transport the soul, and make it cry out, Is this the purchase that cost so dear, as the blood of God? No wonder: O blessed price! and thrice, blessed Love, that invented[103] and Condescended! Is this the end of Believing? Is this the end of the Spirits workings? Have the Gales of Grace

[92] See I Cor. 15.44. [93] St. Paul
[94] *Scoti glossa est vera,* viz. *ut Cognoscant te Amando et Fruendo.* ["That gloss of Scotus is true, namely, that they may come to know thee in loving and in enjoying."] *Vide Scotum in* 4. *senten. distinct.* 48. *Q.* I p. 256. [Baxter's note]
[95] show traces of the influence
[96] take counsel [97] test
[98] ruinous [99] absolute
[100] situation, circumstances
[101] Mount Nebo (See Deut. 34.1–4.)
[102] the Promised Land
[103] created

blown me in such a Harbour? Is it hither that Christ hath enticed my Soul? O blessed way, and thrice blessed end! Is this the Glory which the Scripture spoke of, and Ministers preached of so much? Why now I see the Gospel indeed is good tydings, even tydings of peace and Good things; tydings of great Joy to all Nations![104] Is my mourning, my fasting, my sad humblings, my heavy[105] walking, groanings, complainings, come to this? Is my praying, watching, fearing to offend, come to this? Are all my afflictions, sickness, languishing, troublesom physick, fears of Death, come to this? Are all Satans Temptations, the worlds Scorns and Jeers, come to this? (And now if there be such a thing as Indignation left, how will it here let fly?) O vile nature, that resisted so much, and so long, such a blessing! Unworthy Soul! Is this the place thou camest so unwillingly towards? Was Duty wearisom? Was the world too good to lose? Didst thou stick at,[106] leaving all, denying all, and suffering any thing, for this? Wast thou loath to dye, to come to this? O false Heart! that had almost betrayed me to Eternal flames, and lost me this glory! O base flesh, that would needs have been pleased, though to the loss of this felicity! Didst thou make me to question the truth of this Glory? Didst thou shew me Improbabilities, and draw me to distrust the Lord? Didst thou question the Truth of that Scripture which promised this? Why my soul! art thou not now ashamed, that ever thou didst question that Love that hath brought thee hither? That thou wast Jealous[107] of the faithfulness of thy Lord? That thou suspectest his Love, when thou shouldst only have suspected thy self? That thou didst not Live continually transported with thy Saviours Love? and that ever thou quenchedst a motion[108] of his Spirit? Art thou not ashamed of all Thy hard thoughts of such a God? Of all thy mis-interpreting of, and grudging at those providences,[109] and repining at those ways that have such an end? Now thou art sufficiently convinced, that the ways thou calledst Hard, and the Cup thou calledst Bitter, were necessary: That thy Lord had sweeter ends, and meant thee better then thou wouldst believe: And that thy Redeemer was saving thee, as well when he crossed thy desires, as when he granted them; and as well when he broke thy Heart, as when he bound it up. Oh no thanks to thee, unworthy Self, but shame, for this received Crown: But to Jehovah[110] and the Lamb be Glory for ever.

Thus, as the memory of the wicked will eternally promote their torment, to look back on the pleasures enjoyed, the sin committed, the Grace refused, Christ neglected, and time lost: So will the Memory of the Saints for ever promote their Joys. And as it's said to the wicked, *Remember that thou in thy life time receivedst Thy good things:* So will it be said to the Christian, *Remember that thou in thy life time receivedst thine evils; but now thou art comforted, as they are tormented.*[111] And as here the Remembrance of former good is the occasion of encreasing our grief, (*I remembred God, and Was troubled; I called to Remembrance my Songs in the night*, Psal. 77.3, 6.) So there the Remembrance of our former sorrows addeth life to our Joys.

. . . . .

Sect. VIII

But Oh the full, the near, the sweet enjoyment, is that of the Affections, Love and Joy: It's near; for Love is of the Essence of the Soul, and Love is the Essence of God: *For God is Love*, I *John* 4.8, 16. How near therefore is this Blessed Closure?[112] The Spirits phrase is, *God is Love, and he that dwelleth in Love, dwelleth in God, and God in him*, Vers. 16. The acting[113] of this affection wheresoever, carryeth much delight along with it: Especially when the object appears deserving, and the Affection is strong. But O what will it be, when perfected Affections, shall have the strongest, perfect, incessant actings,[114]

[104] Luke 1.19. and 2, 10. Acts 13.32.
[105] bowed down with grief
[106] The comma obviously belongs after the next two words.
[107] doubtful [108] prompting, instigation
[109] provisions
[110] God, the Almighty, from His principal Old Testament name
[111] Luke 16.25. [112] end
[113] activity [114] performances

upon the most perfect object, the ever Blessed God? Now the poor soul complains, Oh that I could love Christ more! but I cannot, alas, I cannot: Yea, but then thou canst not chuse but love him: I had almost said, forbear if thou canst. Now thou knowest little of his Amiableness,[115] and therefore lovest little: Then thine eye will affect thy heart, and the continual viewing of that perfect beauty, will keep thee in continual ravishments of Love. Now thy Salvation is not perfected, nor all the mercies purchased, yet given in: But when the top stone[116] is set on, thou shalt with shouting cry, Grace, Grace: Now thy sanctification is imperfect, and thy pardon and Justification[117] not so compleat as then it shall be:[118] Now thou knowest not what thou enjoyest, and therefore lovest the less; But when thou knowest much is forgiven, and much bestowed, thou will Love more. Doth *David*,[119] after an imperfect deliverance, sing forth his Love? *Psal.* 116.1. *I love the Lord, because he hath heard my voyce, and supplications.* What think you will he do eternally? And how will he love the Lord, who hath lifted him up to that Glory? Doth he cry out, *O how I love thy Law!*[120] *My delight is in the Saints on earth, and the excellent*, Psal. 16.3. How will he say then, *O how I love the Lord! and the King of Saints, in whom is all my delight?* Christians, doth it not now stir up your love, to remember all the experiences of his Love? To look back upon a life of mercies? Doth not kindness melt you? And the Sun-shine of Divine Goodness warm your frozen hearts? What will it do then, when you shall live in Love, and have All, in him, who is All? O the high delights of Love! of this Love! The content that the heart findeth in it! The satisfaction it brings along with it! Surely Love is both work and wages.

And if this were all, what a high favour, that God will give us leave to love him! That he will vouchsafe to be embraced by such Arms, that have embraced Lust and Sin before him! But this is not all: He returneth Love for Love; nay, a thousand times more: As perfect as we shall be, we cannot reach his measure of Love. Christian, thou wilt be then brim full of Love; yet love as much as thou canst, thou shalt be ten thousand times more beloved. Dost thou think thou canst overlove him? What! love more then Love it self? Were the Arms of the Son of God open upon the Cross, and an open passage made to his Heart by the Spear, and will not Arms and Heart be open to thee in Glory? Did he begin to love before thou lovedst, and will he not continue now? Did he love thee an enemy? thee a sinner? thee who even loathedst they self? and own thee when thou didst disclaim thy self? And will he not now unmeasurably love thee a Son? thee a perfect Saint? thee who returnest some love for Love? Thou wast wont injuriously to Question his Love: Doubt of it now if thou canst. As the pains of Hell will convince the rebellious sinner of Gods wrath, who would never before believe it: So the Joys of Heaven will convince thee thoroughly of that Love, which thou wouldst so hardly be perswaded of. He that in love wept over the old Hierusalem[121] neer her Ruines;[122] with what love will he rejoyce over the new Hierusalem[123] in her Glory? O methinks I see him groaning and weeping over dead *Lazarus*, till he force the Jews that stood by to say, *Behold how he loved him:*[124] Will he not then much more by rejoycing over us, and blessing us, make all (even the damned, if they see it) to say, Behold how he loveth them? Is his Spouse while black, yet comely? Is she his Love, his Dove, his undefiled? Doth she ravish his heart with one of her eyes? Is her Love better then wine?[125] O believing soul, study a little, and tell me, What is the Harvest which these first fruits foretel? and the Love which these are but the earnest of? Here, O here,

[115] loveableness

[116] the stone which caps or crowns

[117] the action by which man is freed from the penalty of sin and accounted righteous by God

[118] I know it's commonly said, That Justification hath no degrees; but yet it is taken for several Acts, whereof that of Christ absolving and acquitting us at the last Judgment is the most compleat Justification. [Baxter's note]

[119] greatly sinning and greatly repenting King of Israel and psalmist

[120] Ps. 119.97.

[121] Jerusalem

[122] [Luke 13.34.]

[123] the spiritual church

[124] John 11.33, 35, 36.

[125] Cant. 1.5 and 5.2 and 6.9. and 4.9, 10, etc.

is the Heaven of Heaven! This is the Saints fruition of God![126] In these sweet, mutual, constant actings and embracements of Love, doth it consist? To Love, and be beloved: *These are the Everlasting Arms that are underneath*, Deut. 33.27. *His left hand is under their heads, and with his right hand doth he embrace them,* Cant. 2.6. Reader, stop here, and think a while, what a state this is; Is it a small thing in thine eyes to be beloved of God? to be the Son, the Spouse, the Love, the delight of the King of Glory? Christian, believe this, and think on it; Thou shalt be eternally embraced in the Arms of that Love, which was from everlasting, and will extend to everlasting: Of that Love, which brought the Son of Gods Love from Heaven to Earth, from Earth to the Cross, from the Cross to the Grave, from the Grave to Glory: That Love, which was weary, hungry, tempted, scorned, scourged, buffetted, spit upon, crucified, pierced; which did fast, pray, teach, heal, weep, sweat, bleed, dye: That Love will eternally embrace thee. When perfect created Love, and most perfect uncreated love meet together, O the blessed meeting! It will not be like *Joseph*[127] and his Brethren, who lay upon one anothers necks weeping; It will break forth into a pure Joy, and not such a mixture of joy and sorrow as their weeping argued: It will be Loving and rejoycing, not loving and sorrowing: Yet will it make *Pharoahs*[128] (Satans) court to ring with the News, that *Josephs* Brethren are come; that the Saints are arrived safe at the bosom of Christ, out of the reach of hell for ever. Neither is there any such love as *Davids*[129] and *Jonathans;*[130] shutting up in sorrows, and breathing out its last into sad lamentations for a forced separation: No; Christ is the powerful attractive, the effectual Loadstone, who draws to it all like it self; *All that the Father hath given him, shall come unto him;* even the Lover, as well as the Love, doth he draw; *and they that come unto him, he will in no wise cast out, John chap.* 6. *vers.* 37, 39. For know this, Beleever, to they everlasting comfort; that if these Arms have once embraced thee, neither sin, nor hell, can get thee thence for ever. The Sanctuary is inviolable, and the Rock impregnable, whither thou art fled, and thou art safe lockt up to all Eternity. Thou hast not now to deal with an unconstant creature, but with him, with whom is no varying, nor shadow of change, even the Immutable God. If thy happiness were in thine own hand, as *Adams*, there were yet fear; But it's in the keeping of a faithful Creator. Christ hath not bought thee so dear, to trust thee with they self any more. His Love to thee will not be as thine was on earth to him, seldom[131] and cold, up and down, mixed (as Aguish bodies) with burning and quaking, with a Good day and a bad: No; Christian, he that would not be discouraged by thine enmity, by thy loathsom, hateful nature, by all thy unwillingness, unkinde Neglects, and churlish resistances; he that would neither cease nor abate his Love for all these, Can he cease to love thee, when he hath made thee truly Lovely? He that keepeth thee so constant in thy love to him, that thou canst challenge *tribulation, distress, persecution, famine, nakedness, peril, or sword to separate thy Love from Christ if they can, Rom.* 8.35. How much more will himself be constant? Indeed he that produced these mutual embracing Affections, will also produce such a mutual constancy in both, that thou mayst confidently be perswaded, as *Paul* was before thee, *That neither Death, nor Life, nor Angels, nor Principalities, nor Powers,*[132] *nor things present, nor things to come, nor*

[126] As so often in Christian symbolism, the Beloved of Canticles is taken as a figure of the faithful soul.

[127] the son of Jacob and Rachel, who was sold by his jealous brethren into slavery in Egypt, where he rose to high office and so was able to save his family in time of famine (See Gen. 37; 39–43.)

[128] the general name for the kings of Egypt in the Old Testament

[129] the great king who united the entire kingdom of Israel and made it strong; famous, also, as a psalmist (See I Sam. 16 to I Kings 2.)

[130] eldest son of King Saul, famous for his friendship with David, and his loyalty to him in the face of his father's enmity (See I Sam. 18 ff.)

[131] infrequent

[132] two of the nine orders of angels in medieval angelology

heighth, nor depth, nor any other creature, shall be able to separate us from the Love of God, which is in Christ Jesus our Lord, Vers. 38, 39. And now are we not left in the Apostles admiration?[133] *What shall We say to these things?* Infinite Love must needs be a mystery to a finite capacity. No wonder if Angels desire to pry into this mystery: And if it be the study of the Saints here, to know the heighth, and bredth, and length, and depth of this Love, though it passeth[134] knowledg:[135] This is the Saints Rest in the Fruition of God by Love.

. . . . .

Sect. IX

Lastly, The Affection of Joy hath not the least share in this Fruition. It's that, which all the rest lead to, and conclude in: even the unconceiveable Complacency which the Blessed feel in their seeing, knowing, loving, and being beloved of God. The delight of the Senses Here, cannot be known by expressions, as they are felt! How much less this Joy? This is the *white stone,*[136] *which none knoweth but he that receiveth:*[137] And if there be any Joy which the stranger medleth[138] not with,[139] then surely this, above all, is it. All Christs ways of mercy tend to, and end in the Saints Joys. He wept, sorrowed, suffered, that they might rejoyce: He sendeth the Spirit[140] to be their Comforter; He multiplieth promises, he discovers[141] their future happiness; that their Joy may be full: He aboundeth to them in mercies of all sorts; he maketh them lie down in green pastures, and leadeth them by the still waters; yea,[142] openeth to them the fountain of Living[143] Waters; That their Joy may be full: That they may thirst no more; and that it may spring up in them to everlasting life:[144] Yea, he causeth them to suffer, that he may cause them to rejoyce; and chasteneth them, that he may give them Rest;[145] and maketh them (as he did himself) *to drink of the brook in the Way, that they may lift up the head. Psal.* 110.7. And lest after all this they should neglect their own comforts,[146] he maketh it their duty, and presseth it on them, commanding them to *rejoyce in him alway, and again to rejoyce.*[147] And he never brings them into so low a condition, wherein he leaves them not more cause of Joy then of Sorrow. And hath the Lord such a care of our comfort Here? where, the Bridegroom[148] being from us, we must mourn?[149] Oh, what will that Joy be, where the Soul being perfectly prepared for Joy, and Joy prepared by Christ for the Soul, it shall be our work, our business, eternally to rejoice. And it seems the Saints Joy shall be greater then the Damneds torment; for their Torment is the torment of creatures, prepared for the Devil and his Angels: But our Joy is the Joy of our Lord; even our Lords own Joy shall we enter:[150] *And the same Glory, which the Father giveth him, doth the Son give to them, Joh.* 17.22. And *to sit with him in his Throne, even as he is sit down in his Father's Throne, Revel.* 3.21. What sayst thou to all this, O thou sad and drooping Soul? Thou that now spendest thy days in sorrow, and thy breath in sighings, and turnest all thy voyce into groanings; who knowest no garments but sackcloth, no food but the bread and water of Affliction; who minglest thy bread with tears, and drinkest the tears which thou weepest, what sayest thou to this great change? From All Sorrow to more then All Joy? Thou poor Soul, who prayest for Joy, waitest for Joy, complainest for want of Joy, longest for Joy; why, then thou shalt have full Joy, as much as thou canst hold, and more then ever thou thoughtest on, or thy heart desired: And in the mean time walk carefully, watch constantly, and then let God

[133] wonder [134] transcends

[135] Pet. 1.12. Eph. 3.18 [19].

[136] an allusion to the use among the ancients of a white stone as a memorial of a fortunate event

[137] Rev. 2, 17. [138] mixes, joins

[139] Prov. 14.10.

[140] the Holy Spirit, the Second Person of the Trinity

[141] reveals [142] verily

[143] that live or have life

[144] John 15.11 and 16.24 and 17.13.

[145] Ps. 94.12, 13. [146] encouragements

[147] I Thes. 5.16, Ps. 32.11 and 33.1, etc.

[148] figuratively of Christ in relation to the church

[149] Matt. 9.15. [150] Matt. 25.

measure out thy times and degrees of Joy. It may be he keeps them till thou have more need: Thou mayst better lose thy comfort, then thy safety: If thou shouldst dye full of fears and sorrows, it will be but a moment and they are all gone, and concluded in Joy unconceiveable: As the Joy of the Hypocrite, so the fears of the upright, are but for a moment. And as their hopes are but golden[151] dreams, which, when death awakes them, do all perish, and their hopes dye with them; so the Saints doubts and fears are but terrible dreams, which, when they dye, do all vanish: and they awake in Joyful Glory. For *Gods Anger endureth but a moment*, but *in his favor is Life; weeping may endure for a night*, (darkness and sadness go together,) *but Joy cometh in the morning, Psal.* 30.5. Oh blessed morning, thrice blessed morning! Poor, humble, drooping Soul, how would it fill thee with Joy now, if a voyce from Heaven should tell thee of the Love of God? of the pardon of thy sins? and should assure thee of thy part in these Joys? Oh, what then will thy Joy be, when thy actual Possession shall convince thee of thy Title, and thou shalt be in Heaven before thou art well aware; When the Angels shall bring thee to Christ, and when Christ shall (as it were) take thee by the hand, and lead thee into the purchased possession, and bid thee welcom to his Rest, and present thee unspotted before his Father, and give thee thy place about his Throne? Poor Sinner; what sayest thou to such a day as this? Wilt thou not be almost ready to draw back, and to say, What, I Lord? I the unworthy Neglecter of thy Grace! I the unworthy dis-esteemer of thy blood, and slighter of thy Love! must I have this Glory? Make me a hired servant, I am no more worthy to be called a son: But Love will have it so; therefore must thou enter into his Joy.

. . . . .

Sect. X

And it is not Thy Joy onely; it is a Mutual Joy, as well as a Mutual Love: Is there such Joy in Heaven at thy Conversion, and will there be none at thy Glorification? Will not the Angels welcom thee thither? and congratulate thy safe Arrival? Yea, it is the Joy of Jesus Christ: For now he hath the end[152] of his undertaking, labor, suffering, dying, when we have our Joys; When he is Glorified in his Saints, and admired in all them that beleeve.[153] We are his seed, and the fruit of his Souls travel, which when he seeth, he will be satisfied, *Isa.* 53.10, 11. This is Christs Harvest, when he shall reap the fruit of his labors, and when he seeth it was not in vain, it will not repent him concerning his sufferings; but he will rejoyce over his purchased inheritance, and his people shall rejoyce in him.

Yea, the Father himself puts on Joy too, in our Joy: As we grieve his Spirit, and weary him with our iniquities; so is he rejoyced in our Good: Oh how quickly Here, doth he spy a Returning Prodigal, even afar off?[154] how doth he run? and meet him? and with what compassion falls he on his neck, and kisseth him? and puts on him the best robe, and ring on his hands, and shoes on his feet, and spares not to kill the fatted Calf, that they may eat and be merry: This is indeed a happy meeting; But nothing to the Embracements, and the Joy, of that last and great Meeting.

Yea, more yet; as God doth mutually Love and Joy, so he makes this His Rest, as it is our Rest. Did he appoint a Sabbath because he rested from six days work, and saw all Good and very Good?[155] What an eternal Sabbatism[156] then, when the work of Redemption, Sanctification, Preservation, Glorification are all finished, and his work more perfect then ever, and very Good indeed?[157] Oh Christians, write these words in letters of Gold, *Zeph.* 3.17. *The Lord thy God in the midst of thee, is mighty: He will Save; He will Rejoyce over thee with Joy: He will Rest in his Love; He will Joy over thee with Singing.* Oh, well may we then Rejoyce in our God with Joy, and Rest in our Love, and Joy in him with Singing. See *Isai.* 65.18, 19.

And now, look back upon all this: I say

[151] joyous
[152] purpose for which he undertook it
[153] [II] Thes. 1, 10.
[154] an allusion to Christ's parable of the prodigal son whom his father warmly welcomed on his return (Luke 15.11–32.)
[155] [Gen. 1.31 and 2.3.]
[156] Sabbath rest
[157] So the Lord is said to Rejoice and to take pleasure in his people, Psal. 147.11. and 149.4. [Baxter's note]

to thee, as the Angel to *John,* What hast thou seen?[158] Or, if yet thou perceive not, draw neerer, Come up hither; Come and see: Dost thou fear thou hast been all this while in a Dream? Why, these are the true sayings of God. Dost thou fear (as the Disciples) that thou hast seen but a Ghost in stead of Christ?[159] a Shadow in stead of Rest? Why, come neer, and feel; a Shadow contains not those Substantial[160] Blessings, nor rests upon the Basis of such Foundation-Truth, and sure word of Promise, as you have seen these do. Go thy way now, and tell the Disciples,[161] and tell the humble drooping Souls thou meetest with, That thou hast, in this glass, seen Heaven; That the Lord indeed is risen, and hath here appeared to thee; and behold he is gone before us into Rest: and that he is now preparing a place for them, and will come again and take them to himself, that where he is, there they may be also. *Joh.* 14.3. Yea, go thy ways, and tell the unbeleeving world, and tell thy unbeleeving heart; if they ask, What is the hope thou boastest of, and what will be thy Rest? Why, this is my Beloved, and my Friend, and this is my Hope, and my Rest. Call them forth, and say, *Behold what Love the Father hath bestowed upon us, that we should be the Sons of God,* I *Joh.* 3.1. and that we should enter into our Lords own Rest.

. . . . .

Sect. XI

But alass, my fearful heart dare scarce proceed: Methinks I hear the Almighties voyce saying to me, as *Elihu,*[162] *Job.* 38.2. *Who is this that darkeneth counsel by words without knowledg?*

But pardon, O Lord, thy Servants sin: I have not pryed into unrevealed things; nor with audacious wits curiously searched into thy counsels: but indeed I have dishonored thy Holiness, wronged thine Excellency, disgraced thy Saints Glory, by my own exceedingly disproportionable[163] pourtraying. I bewail from heart, that my conceivings fall so short, my Apprehensions are so dull, my thoughts so mean, my Affections so stupid, and my expressions so low and unbeseeming such a Glory. But I have onely heard by the hearing of the Ear, Oh let thy Servant see thee, and possess these Joys, and then I shall have more suitable conceivings, and shall give thee fuller Glory, and abhor my present self, and disclaim and renounce all these Imperfections. *I have now uttered that I understood not; things too wonderful for me, which I knew not. Yet I beleeved, and therefore spake.*[164] Remember with whom thou hast to do: what canst thou expect from dust, but Levity? or from corruption, but defilement? Our foul hands will leave where they touch, the marks of their uncleanness; and most on those things that are most pure. I know *thou wilt be sanctified in them that come nigh thee, and before all the people thou wilt be glorified:*[165] And if thy Jealousie excluded from that Land of Rest thy servants *Moses* and *Aaron,*[166] because they sanctified thee not in the midst of *Israel,*[167] what then may I expect? But though the weakness and unreverence[168] be the fruit of mine own corruption; yet the fire is from thine Altar, and the work of thy commanding. I looked not into thine Ark,[169] nor put forth my hand unto it without thee. Oh therefore wash away these stains also in the blood of the Lamb; and let not Jealousie burn us up: lest thou affright thy people away from thee, and make them in their discouragement to cry out, *How shall the Ark of God come to us? Who is able to stand before this holy Lord God?*[170] *Who shall approach and dwell with the consuming fire?* Imperfect, or none, must be thy Service here. Oh take thy Sons excuse, *The spirit is willing, but the flesh is weak.*[171]

158 [Rev. 1.19.]
159 Luke 24.37, 38, 39.
160 solid
161 Mark 16.7.
162 one of Job's friends
163 disproportionate, inadequate
164 Job 24.3.
165 Levit. 10.2, 3.
166 elder brother of Moses and Miriam, and his great support (See Num. 20.24.)
167 Num. 20.12, Deut. 32.51.
168 irreverence
169 the coffer containing the tables of the law
170 II Sam. 6.8. [9.] I Sam. 6.20.
171 Matt. 16.48.

John Evelyn

JOHN EVELYN was born at Wotton in Surrey on October 31, 1620, of a good family which had enriched itself by the making of gunpowder. In his early education he enjoyed a degree of indulgence which he afterward regretted but also an opportunity to cultivate his taste for drawing and designing. In February of 1637 he was admitted to the Middle Temple, and in the following May as a Fellow Commoner he entered Balliol College, Oxford, where to the regular academic studies he added dancing, vaulting, and music. In April of 1640 he went to London to reside in the Middle Temple, but the prospect of public affairs was dark for a young man of strong Royalist and Church sympathies. Although a younger son, Evelyn seems always to have had sufficient resources to do pretty much what he chose, to have enjoyed unusual opportunities of access to cultivated society at home and abroad, and to have possessed both the taste and the address to make the most of his opportunities.

So now in July of 1641 he turned to foreign travel, visiting Holland and Belgium, seeing some military service, and receiving academic honors. October found him back in England, and in November he joined the royal army in time for the retreat from the battle of Brentford. It did not take Evelyn long to conclude that there was nothing he could do in the royal cause but ruin his family; so he retired to Wotton for a quiet life of study and gardening. It was not so easy, however, for a man in his position to avoid compromising himself; so in November of 1643 he returned to the Continent, now setting about his travels in earnest, and recording his impressions in the diary which eventually was to prove his chief claim to remembrance. In the course of the next four years Evelyn visited France, Italy, and Switzerland, and studied French, German, and Spanish, chemistry and anatomy; he learned to play the theorbo and the lute, and everywhere he visited gardens and collections of curiosities and paintings and sculpture, and explored famous buildings, especially the ruins of antiquity. And although the sums at his disposal were modest for the traveling "milor" of the time, he brought home a creditable collection of ancient treasures. On June 7, 1647, he married the very young daughter of the English ambassador in Paris, and later that year he came home to England. The opening of the year 1649 found him settled at Sayes Court at Deptford, which was to be his home for the greater part of the remainder of his life, and the same month saw his first publication, a translation from the French.

Evelyn spent a good part of the next couple of years abroad, but recognizing the hopelessness of the Royalist cause after Worcester, he came back to England in the beginning of 1652 to settle permanently. A year later he had completed the purchase of Sayes Court, and had promptly set about the beautifying of it. His reputation as a man of wide and cosmopolitan culture was already established, and this he proceeded to justify with a series of publications, largely translations. Meanwhile the Royalist prospects had grown so dim that Evelyn seriously proposed founding a sort of scientific convent to which he and his wife would retire. The Restoration of Charles

II changed all that, and Evelyn found himself in high favor at Court. He declined military preferment as he was later to decline knighthood. But in 1660 he became a fellow of the newly-founded Royal Society and on the King's nomination, a member of the Council—and a very active and serviceable member he proved to be.

In May of 1662 Evelyn became one of the Commissioners for reforming the streets and the traffic of London, and this service was followed by a series of appointments to commissions: for an inquiry into the uses of the revenues of Gresham College, on Sewers, on the regulation of the Mint, for the care of the sick and the wounded and the prisoners of the war with Holland—the series culminating in his appointment to the Council of Trade and Plantations in 1671, and to the Commission of the Privy Seal in 1685. He died in 1706.

But though Evelyn thus demonstrated his sense of civic duty and his conviction of the scholar's obligation to action, it was as a virtuoso that the ingenious Mr. Evelyn commanded the admiration of his time. And the reason for that reputation is nowhere to be better found than in the list of his publications. For they extend through his life, reflecting the variety of his interests and the versatility of his talents. The first, a translation from the French of the Sieur de la Mothe le Vayer, *Of Liberty and Servitude*, was published, with a preface that made no secret of his Royalist sympathies, in January, 1649, as Evelyn himself said, "a few days before his Majesty's decollation." The last, *Acetaria, A Discourse of Sallets*, was published in 1699. Between the two lie some twenty-eight publications, both translations and originals. Among the translations were the first English version, a verse translation, of the first book of Lucretius' *De Rerum Natura*, published in 1656; a translation of *Le Jardinier Francois* of M. Nicolas de Bonnefons, in 1658, his first venture into gardening literature, to which he was to make so distinguished a contribution; *Instructions Concerning Erecting of a Library* by Gabriel Naudaeus, the great French librarian, published in 1661; *A Parallel of the Antient Architecture with the Modern* of Roland Fréart, Sieur de Chambray, published in 1664, and the same writer's *An Idea of the Perfection of Painting*, in 1668; and *The Compleat Gard'ner* of Monsieur de la Quintinye, the Chief Director of the French King's gardens in 1693. On his own he wrote in behalf of the Royalist cause, on the smoke menace to London, on the history and art of chalcodography and engraving in copper, on solitude as preferred to public employment, on certain famous impostors who had claimed contemporary interest, on the economic relations of England and Holland, and on coins and medals. But his most important work from the point of view of his own time was in the fields of gardening and forestry. He had an abundance of practical experience in both fields at Wotton and at Sayes Court, which he made a showplace which even royalty condescended to visit. His most famous and most influential work, *Sylva, or a Discourse of Forest-Trees, and the Propogation of Timber*, was published in 1664. To the title work was annexed *Pomona, or, an Appendix concerning Fruit-Trees in Relation to Cider*, and *Kalendarium Hortense, or Gard'ners Almanac*. This work had reached a fourth edition by 1706, the year of its author's death. In 1666 Evelyn published *The English Vineyard*, a report of the advice and experience of the King's Gardener, John Rose. *A Philosophical Discourse of Earth, Relating to the Culture and Improvement of it for Vegetation* was first presented to the Royal Society in 1675 and published in 1676.

But the diary on which Evelyn's latter-day fame rests, was not printed until 1818. Evelyn had revised it himself only to October, 1664. In 1818 a selection was made with tacit alterations and published by the nominal editor, the distinguished antiquary William Bray, and William Upcott who would seem to have done most of the work. A second edition of this publication with improvements appeared in 1819, and a third, said to have been superintended by Upcott, in 1827. H. B. Wheatley tried to obtain access to the original manuscript but had to be content with the 1827 Bray text for his editions of 1879 and 1906. There are also editions by John Forster (4 vols., 1850–1852), Austin Dobson (3 vols., 1906), Globe (1908), and Everyman's Library (2 vols., n.d.). A modern edition of the whole text by E. S. de Beer is in progress.

A number of other works have been published posthumously, the most notable of which is *The Life of Mrs. Godolphin*, first published in 1847 and republished a number of times since (ed. Sampson, Oxford, 1939).

The *Diary* of Evelyn is not, as Dr. Keynes has pointed out, a diary in the strict sense. While there are probably some day-to-day entries, Evelyn seems on the whole to have written up his diary at intervals, sometimes using notes made at the time, but often writing from memory. The resultant work is far more objective and formal than the famous diary of his friend Pepys; indeed, a good many entries give every appearance of being very carefully considered and planned essays. And from first to last the whole tone of the diary is different from Pepys', as the man was different. While Evelyn was a thorough man of the world, free of the fashionable as well as the most sophisticated society, he was also a man for whom his religion meant a good deal and who took its restraints and its prescriptions quite seriously. It is a counter-poise, therefore, to the picture of Restoration society often taken for granted that among those whose company Charles II obviously enjoyed was one who so clearly faced his King's personal shortcomings.

A general account of Evelyn is available in A. Ponsonby, *John Evelyn* (1933). C. Marburg, *Mr. Pepys and Mr. Evelyn* (1935) surveys both the relations of the two diarists to each other and the comparable areas of their lives and interests, and prints thirty-seven letters which had not been printed before, with finding lists for the letters exchanged between the two men. G. Keynes, *John Evelyn* (1937) presents not only "A Study in Bibliophily" but also a bibliography of Evelyn's writings. Special aspects are studied in the following: E. G. Craig, "John Evelyn and the Theatre," *Books and Theatres* (1925), 1–68; M. Denny, "The Early Program of the Royal Society and John Evelyn," *MLQ* I (1940); G. B. Parks, "John Evelyn and the Art of Travel," *HLQ* X (1947); and W. G. Hiscock, "John Evelyn's Library at Christ Church," *TLS* (April 6, 1951).

from THE DIARY OF JOHN EVELYN[1]

Oct[ober] 25th [1644]. [Florence.] We went to the Portico[2] where the famous statues of Judith and Holofernes[3] stand, also the Medusa,[4] all of copper; but what is most admirable is the Rape of a Sabine with another man under foot, the confusion and turning of whose limbs is most admirable. It is of one entire marble, the worke of John di Bologna,[5] and is most stupendous; this stands directly against the greate piazza,[6] where, to adorne one fountaine, are erected four marble statues and

[1] Text: Wheatley, 4 vols., reprinted by permission of W. E. Parker, Price Waterhouse & Co. for Simpkin Marshall Ltd., London, and Charles Scribner's Sons, New York, 1906

[2] now known as the *Loggia dei Lanzi*

[3] by Donatello, placed before the Palazzo Vecchio in 1498 as a warning to tyrants

[4] Perseus by Benvenuto Cellini

[5] Giovanni da Bologna (1524–1608)

[6] Piazza della Signoria

eight of brasse, representing Neptune and his family of sea-gods,[7] of a Colossean[8] magnitude, with four sea-horses in Parian[9] marble of Lamedrati,[10] in the midst of a very great basin; a work, I think, hardly to be parallel'd. Here is also the famous statue of David by M. Angelo;[11] Hercules and Cacus by Baccio Bandinelli;[12] the Perseus in copper by Benevento,[13] and the Judith of Donatelli,[14] which stand publickly before the old palace[15] with the Centaur of Bologna,[16] huge Colossean figures. Neere this stand Cosmo di Medici on horseback,[17] in brasse on a pedistal of marble, and four copper bass relievos[18] by John di Bologna, with divers inscriptions; the Ferdinand the First[19] on horseback is of Peitro Tacca.[10] The brazen boare,[21] which serves for another public fountaine, is admirable.

After dinner we went to the church of the Annunciata,[22] where the Duke[23] and his court were at their devotions, being a place of extraordinary repute for sanctity: for here is a shrine[24] that dos greate miracles [proved] by innumerable votive tablets, etc., covering almost the walles of the whole church. This is the image of Gabriel who saluted the Blessed Virgin, and which the artist finish'd so well that he was in despaire of performing the Virgin's face so well, whereupon it was miraculously don for him whilst he slept; but others say it was painted by St. Luke himselfe.[25] Whoever it was, infinite is the devotion of both sexes to it. The altar is set off with four columns of oriental alabaster, and lighted by thirty greate silver lamps. There are innumerable other pictures by rare masters. Our Saviour's Passion in brasse tables inserted in marble is the worke of John di Bologna and Baccio Bandinelli.

To this church joynes a convent[26] whose cloister is painted in *fresca*[27] very rarely. There is also neere it an hospital for 1000 persons, with nurse children,[28] and several other charitable accom'odations.

At the Duke's Cavalerizzo,[29] the Prince has a stable of the finest horses of all countries, Arabs, Turks, Barbs,[30] Gennets,[31] English, etc., which are continualy exercis'd in the *manège*.[32]

Nere this is a place where are kept several wild beasts, as wolves, catts, beares, tygers, and lions. They are loose in a deep wall'd court, and therefore to be seene with more pleasure than at the Tower of London,[33] in their grates.[34] One of the lions leaped to a surprising height to catch a joynt of mutton which I caused to be hung downe. . . .

[January] 17th [1652/1653]. I began to set out the ovall garden at Sayes Court,[35] which was before a rude orchard and all the rest one intire field of 100 acres, without any hedge, except the hither holly hedge joyning to the banke of the mount walk.[36] This was the beginning of all the

[7] Tritons [8] colossal
[9] from the island of Paros, famous for its marble
[10] actually by Bartolommeo Ammanati, sixteenth-century Florentine sculptor
[11] Michelangelo
[12] a rival of Michelangelo
[13] Benvenuto Cellini
[14] Donatello
[15] Palazzo Vecchio
[16] Hercules slaying the centaur Nessus, in marble, by Giovanni da Bologna
[17] Grand Duke Cosimo I, in bronze by Giovanni da Bologna
[18] bas-reliefs
[19] Grand Duke of Florence (1587–1609)
[20] seventeenth-century sculptor, pupil of Giovanni da Bologna
[21] also by Pietro Tacca
[22] Santissima Annunziata, begun in the thirteenth century
[23] Duke Ferdinand II (1621–1670)
[24] the Cappella della Vergine Annunziata
[25] a thirteenth-century fresco behind the altar
[26] an old Servite monastery
[27] fresco
[28] Spedale degli Innocenti, or Foundling Hospital, famous for the Andrea della Robbia medallions of infants in swaddling clothes
[29] cavalerizza, or riding school
[30] Barbary horse
[31] jennet, small Spanish horse
[32] art of horsemanship
[33] The Tower Menagerie was one of the sights of London.
[34] grated cages
[35] Sayes Court, Deptford, the purchase of which Evelyn completed the next month, and the garden of which he was to make one of the show-places of the region
[36] raised walk

succeeding gardens, walks, groves, enclosures, and plantations there.

[January] 30th [1652/1653]. At our own parish church a stranger preach'd. There was now and then an honest orthodox man got into the pulpit, and tho' the present incumbent was somewhat of the Independent,[37] yet he ordinarily preach'd sound doctrine, and was a peaceable man, which was an extraordinary felicity in this age.

[March] 18th [1655]. Went to London on purpose to hear that excellent preacher Dr. Jeremy Taylor[38] on 14 Matt. v. 17. shewing what were the conditions of obtaining eternal life: also concerning abatements[39] for unavoidable infirmities, how cast[40] on the accompts of the crosse. On the 31st I made a visit to Dr. Jer. Taylor to conferr with him about some spiritual matters, using him thenceforward as my ghostly[41] father. I beseech God Almighty to make me ever mindful of, and thankful for, his heavenly assistances.

Jan[uary] 27th [1657/1658]. After six fits of a quartan[42] ague with which it pleased God to visite him, died my deare Son Richard, to our inexpressible griefe and affliction, 5 yeares and 3 days old onely, but at that tender age a prodigy for witt[43] and understanding; for beauty of body a very angel; for endowment of mind of incredible and rare hopes.[44] To give onely a little taste of them, and thereby glory to God, sense of God; he had learn'd all his catechisme who out of the mouths of babes and infants does sometimes perfect his praises:[45] at 2 years and a halfe old he could perfectly reade any of the English, Latine, French, or Gottic[46] letters, pronouncing the three first languages exactly. He had before the 5th yeare, or in that yeare, not onely skill to reade most written hands, but to decline all the nouns, conjugate the verbs regular, and most of the irregular; learn'd out "Puerilis"[47] got by heart almost the entire vocabularie of Latine and French primitives[48] and words, could make congruous syntax, turne English into Latine, and *vice versâ*, construe and prove[49] what he read, and did the government and use of relatives, verbs, substantives, elipses, and many figures and tropes, and made a considerable progress in Comenius's[50] Janua;[51] began himselfe to write legibly, and had a stronge passion for Greeke. The number of verses he could recite was prodigious, and what he remember'd of the parts of playes, which he would also act; and when seeing a Plautus[52] in one's hand, he ask'd what booke it was, and being told it was comedy, and too difficult for him, he wept for sorrow. Strange was his apt and ingenious application of fables and morals, for he had read Æsop;[53] he had a wonderful disposition to mathematics, having by heart divers propositions of Euclid[54] that were read to him in play, and he would make lines and demonstrate them. As to his piety, astonishing were his applications of Scripture upon occasion, and his early, [sic] and understood the historical part of the Bible and New Testament to a wonder, how Christ came to redeeme mankind, and how, comprehending these necessarys himselfe, his godfathers were discharg'd of their promise.[55] These and the like illumi-

[37] Puritans who, as against the Established Church, held that each congregation should rule itself

[38] the author of *Holy Living* and *Holy Dying*

[39] deductions [40] reckoned

[41] spiritual

[42] fever occurring every fourth day

[43] wisdom [44] promise

[45] Matt. 21.16. [46] Gothic

[47] *Sententiae Pueriles*, the famous collection of moral sayings for teaching children elementary Latin

[48] root words [49] test

[50] Peter Comenius, Bishop of Moravia, famous seventeenth-century educational reformer

[51] *Ianua Linguae Reserata*, or *The Gate of Languages Unlocked*

[52] M. Accius Plautus, the great Roman comic poet of the second century B.C.

[53] a Phyrgian philosopher and fabulist of the sixth century B.C., to whom is ascribed a collection of fables that probably extends beyond his work

[54] the great Alexandrian mathematician who flourished about 300 B.C.; also his treatise on geometry

[55] to see that he received the necessary education in Christian fundamentals

nations, far exceeding his age and experience, considering the prettinesse of his addresse and behaviour, cannot but leave impressions[56] in me at the memory of him. . . .

[October] 22nd [1658]. Saw the superb funerall of the Protector.[57] He was carried from Somerset House in a velvet bed of state[58] drawn by six horses, houss'd with the same[59]; the pall[60] held by his new Lords; Oliver lying in effigie in royal robes, and crown'd with a crown, sceptre, and globe,[61] like a king. The pendants[62] and guidons[63] were carried by the officers of the army; the Imperial banners, achievements,[64] etc., by the heraulds in their coates; a rich caparison'd horse, embroider'd all over with gold; a knight of honour arm'd cap-a-pie,[65] and after all, his guards, souldiers, and innumberable mourners. In this equipage[66] they proceeded to Westminster: but it was the joyfullest funerall I ever saw, for there were none that cried but dogs, which the soldiers hooted away with a barbarous noise, drinking and taking tobacco in the streetes as they went. . . .

[May] 29th [1660]. This day his Majestie Charles the Second came to London after a sad and long exile and calamitous suffering both of the King and Church, being 17 yeares. This was also his birthday, and with a triumph[67] of above 20,000 horse and foote, brandishing their swords and shouting with inexpressible joy; the wayes strew'd with flowers, the bells ringing, the streetes hung with tapissry,[68] fountaines running with wine; the Maior, Aldermen, and all the Companies in their liveries, chaines of gold, and banners; Lords and Nobles clad in cloth of silver, gold, and velvet; the windowes and balconies all set[69] with ladies; trumpets, music, and myriads of people flocking, even so far as from Rochester,[70] so as they were seven houres in passing the citty, even from 2 in the after-noone till 9 at night.

I stood in the Strand and beheld it, and bless'd God. And all this was don without one drop of bloud shed, and by that very army which rebell'd against him; but it was the Lord's doing, for such a restauration was never mention'd in any history antient or modern, since the returne of the Jews from the Babylonish captivity; nor so joyfull a day and so bright ever seene in this nation, this hapning when to expect or effect it was past all human policy.

[October] 17th [1660]. Scot,[71] Scroope,[72] Cook,[73] and Jones,[74] suffered for reward of their iniquities at Charing Crosse, in sight of the place[75] where they put to death their natural Prince, and in the presence of the King his sonn, whom they also sought to kill. I saw not their execution, but met their quarters[76] mangl'd and cutt and reeking as they were brought from the gallows in baskets on the hurdle.[77] Oh the miraculous providence of God!

[November] 26th [1661]. I saw Hamlet Prince of Denmark played, but now the old plays began to disgust this refined age, since his Majestie's being so long abroad.

[November] 27th [1662]. Went to London to see the entrance of the Russian Ambassador, whom his Majesty order'd to be received with much state,[78] the Emperor not only having ben kind to his Majesty

[56] a strong emotional effect
[57] Oliver Cromwell
[58] a splendidly-decorated bed for the laying-out of the corpse of a distinguished person
[59] with velvet coverings attached to the saddles
[60] heavy cloth covering the coffin
[61] golden ball carried as a symbol of authority
[62] hanging shields with armorial bearings
[63] pennants [64] funeral shields, hatchments
[65] from head to foot [66] state
[67] triumphal procession [68] tapestry
[69] adorned with
[70] thirty-three miles from London
[71] Thomas Scott, Regicide, Secretary of State to the Commonwealth
[72] Adrian Scroope, Regicide, major in Parliamentary army, member of the Protector's Council for Scotland
[73] John Cook, Regicide, Solicitor-General for the Commonwealth
[74] John Jones, Regicide, major in the Parliamentary army, member of the first two Councils of State of the Commonwealth, brother-in-law to Cromwell
[75] Whitehall
[76] The sentence for treason was to be hanged, drawn, and quartered.
[77] sled on which criminals were drawn to execution
[78] pomp

in his distress, but banishing all commerce with our nation during the rebellion.

First the Citty Companies[79] and Train'd Bands[80] were all in their stations: his Majesty's Army and Guards in greate order. His Excellency came in a very rich coach, with some of his chiefe attendants; many of the rest on horseback, clad in their vests[81] after the eastern manner, rich furrs, caps, and carrying the presents, some carrying hawkes, furrs, teeth, bows, etc. It was a very magnificent shew. . . .

Sept[ember] 2nd [1666]. This fatal night about ten, began the deplorable fire neere Fish streete in London.

[September] 3rd [1666]. I had public prayers at home. The fire continuing, after dinner I took coach with my Wife and Sonn and went to the Bank side in Southwark, where we beheld that dismal spectacle, the whole citty in dreadfull flames neare the water side; all the houses from the Bridge, all Thames streete, and upwards towards Cheapeside, downe to the Three Cranes, were now consum'd: and so returned exceeding astonished[82] what would become of the rest.

The fire having continu'd all this night (if I may call that night which was light as day for 10 miles round about, after a dreadfull manner) when conspiring with a fierce eastern wind in a very drie season; I went on foote to the same place, and saw the whole south part of the city burning from Cheapeside to the Thames, and all along Cornehill (for it likewise kindl'd back against the wind as well as forward), Tower streete, Fen-church streete, Gracious streete,[83] and so along to Bainard's Castle, and was now taking hold of St. Paul's church,[84] to which the scaffolds contributed exceedingly. The conflagration was so universal, and the people so astonish'd, that from the beginning, I know not by what despondency or fate, they hardly stirr'd to quench it, so that there was nothing heard or seene but crying out and lamentation, running about like distracted creatures without at all attempting to save even their goods; such a strange consternation there was upon them, so as it burned both in breadth and length, the churches, public halls, Exchange, hospitals, monuments, and ornaments,[85] leaping after a prodigious manner, from house to house and streete to streete, at greate distances one from the other; for the heat with a long set of faire and warm weather had even ignited the aire and prepar'd the materials to conceive the fire, which devour'd after an incredible manner houses, furniture, and every thing. Here we saw the Thames cover'd with goods floating, all the barges and boates laden with what some had time and courage to save, as on the other, the carts, etc., carrying out to the fields, which for many miles were strew'd with moveables of all sorts, and tents erecting[86] to shelter both people and what goods they could get away. Oh the miserable and calamitous spectacle! such as happly the world had not seene since the foundation of it, nor be outdon till the universal conflagration[87] thereof. All the skie was of a fiery aspect, like the top of a burning oven, and the light seene above 40 miles round about for many nights. God grant mine eyes may never behold the like, who now saw above 10,000 houses all in one flame; the noise and cracking and thunder of the impetuous flames, the shreiking of women and children, the hurry of people, the fall of towers, houses, and churches, was like an hideous storme, and the aire all about so hot and inflam'd that at the last one was not able to approach it, so that they were forc'd to stand still and let the flames burn on, which they did for nere two miles in length and one in breadth. The clowds also of smoke were dismall and reach'd upon computation neer 50 miles in length. Thus I left it this afternoone burning, a resemblance of Sodom,[88] or the last day. It forcibly call'd to my mind that passage—

[79] London trade guilds
[80] companies of trained citizen soldiers
[81] long cassock-like garments
[82] bewildered as to
[83] Gracechurch Street
[84] It is estimated that hardly a sixth part of the old walled City escaped.
[85] decorations [86] being erected
[87] a reference to a widely-held theory as to the end of the world
[88] most important of the cities in the plain of Siddim; its destruction by fire from heaven (Gen. 10.19; 13.10–13; 19.1–29) often referred to in the Bible as a warning to sinners

non enim hic habemus stabilem civitatem:[89] the ruines resembling the picture of Troy.[90] London was, but is no more! Thus I returned.

[October] 18th [1666]. . . . This night was acted my Lord Broghill's[91] tragedy called "Mustapha" before their Majesties at Court, at which I was present, very seldom going to the public theaters for many reasons, now as they were abused to an atheistical liberty,[92] fowle and undecent women[93] now (and never till now) permitted to appeare and act, who inflaming severall young noblemen and gallants, became their misses,[94] and to some their wives; witness the Earl of Oxford,[95] Sir R. Howard,[96] Prince Rupert,[97] the Earle of Dorset,[98] and another greater person than any of them, who fell into their snares, to the reproch of their noble families, and ruine of both body and soule. I was invited by my Lord Chamberlaine[99] to see this tragedy, exceedingly well written, tho' in my mind I did not approve of any such pastime in a time of such judgments and calamities.

[April] 18th [1666/1667]. I went to make court to the Duke[100] and Duchess of Newcastle[101] at their house in Clerkenwell, being newly come out of the north. They receiv'd me with great kindnesse, and I was much pleas'd with the extraordinary fanciful habit, garb, and discourse of the Duchess.[102]

[April] 25th [1666/1667]. Visited again the Duke of Newcastle, with whom I had ben acquainted long before in France, where the Duchess had obligation to my Wive's mother,[103] for her marriage there; she was sister to Lord Lucas,[104] and maid of honour then to the Queene Mother;[105] married in our chapel at Paris. My wife being with me, the Duke and Dutchess both would needs bring her to the very Court.

[April] 27th [1666/1667]. I had a greate deale of discourse with his Majestie at dinner. In the afternoone I went againe with my Wife to the Dutchess of Newcastle, who receiv'd her in a kind of transport,[106] suitable to her extravagant humour[107] and dresse, which was very singular.

[May] 30th [1666/1667]. To London to wait on the Dutchess of Newcastle (who was a mighty pretender to learning, poetrie, and philosophie, and had in both published divers bookes) to the Royal Society, whither she came in greate pomp, and being receiv'd by our Lord President[108] at the dore of our meeting roome, the mace, etc. carried before him, had sev-

[89] "For here have we no continuing city" (Heb. 13.14.)

[90] after its destruction at the hands of the Greeks (The ten-years' siege of Troy by the Greeks to recover Helen was the most celebrated of ancient wars, and its total destruction at the end of the period, a classic symbol of civic disaster.)

[91] Richard, Lord Broghill, later Earl of Orrery, and the author of a number of plays

[92] license as if there were no God

[93] Margaret Hughes, Nell Gwynn, etc.

[94] mistresses

[95] Aubrey de Vere, 20th Earl of Oxford

[96] Sir Robert Howard, Member of Parliament, Auditor of the Exchequer, and dramatist

[97] son of the Prince Palatine Frederick and Elizabeth, daughter of James I, famous Royalist general and cavalry leader in the Civil War

[98] Charles Sackville, Lord Buckhurst, later Earl of Dorset; see pp. 433–36.

[99] Edward Montagu, 2nd Earl of Manchester, Parliamentary general who played a prominent part in the King's Restoration, Lord Chamberlain and Speaker of the House of Lords

[100] William Cavendish, First Duke of Newcastle, one of the most generous supporters of Charles I and Charles II, author of a book on horsemanship, and a dabbler in playwriting

[101] Margaret Cavendish, Duchess of Newcastle, author of poems, plays, an historically important autobiography, and *The Life of William Cavendish, Duke of Newcastle* (1667)

[102] For Pepys' opinion of the same lady see p. 378.

[103] wife of Sir Richard Browne, "his Majesty's Resident with the French king"

[104] Lieutenant of the Tower

[105] Henrietta Maria

[106] ecstacy

[107] mood

[108] William, Viscount Brouncker, Commissioner of the Navy, first President of the Royal Society

eral experiments shewed to her. I conducted her Grace to her coach, and return'd home.

[January] 18th [1670/1671]. This day I first acquainted his Majesty with that incomparable young man Gibbon,[109] whom I had lately met with in an obscure place by meere accident as I was walking neere a poor solitary thatched house, in a field in our parish, neere Says Court. I found him shut in; but looking in at the window I perceiv'd him carving that large cartoon or crucifix[110] of Tintoret,[111] a copy of which I had myselfe brought from Venice, where the original painting remaines. I asked if I might enter; he open'd the door civilly to me, and I saw him about such a work as for the curiosity[112] of handling, drawing, and studious[113] exactnesse, I never had before seene in all my travells. I questioned him why he worked in such an obscure and lonesome place; he told me it was that he might apply himselfe to his profession without interruption, and wondred not a little how I had found him out. I asked if he was unwilling to be made knowne to some greate man, for that I believe it might turn to his profit; he answer'd he was yet but a beginner, but would not be sorry to sell off that piece; on demanding the price he said £100. In good earnest the very frame was worth the money, there being nothing in nature so tender and delicate as the flowers and festoons about it, and yet the worke was very strong; in the piece was more than 100 figures of men, etc. I found he was likewise musical, and very civil,[114] sober, and discreete in his discourse. There was onely an old woman in the house. So desiring leave to visite him sometimes, I went away.

Of this young artist, together with my manner of finding him out, I acquainted the King, and begg'd that he would give me leave to bring him and his worke to Whitehall, for that I would adventure my reputation with his Majesty that he had never seene any thing approch it, and that he would be exceedingly pleased, and employ him. The King said he would himselfe go see him. This was the first notice his Majestie ever had of Mr. Gibbon.

[December] 20th [1673]. I had some discourse with certaine strangers, not unlearned, who had ben born not far from Old Nineveh;[115] they assur'd me of the ruines being still extant, and vast and wonderfull were the buildings, vaults, pillars, and magnificent fragments; but they could say little of the Toure of Babel[116] that satisfied me: but the description of the amœnitie[117] and fragrancy of the country for health and cherefullnesse delighted me, so sensibly they spake of the excellent aire and climate in respect of our cloudy and splenetic[118] country.

Oct[ober] 4th [1683]. . . . Following his Majesty this morning thro' the gallerie, I went, with the few who attended him, into the Dutchesse of Portsmouth's[119] *dressing-roome* within her bed-chamber, where she was in her morning loose garment, her maids combing her, newly out of her bed, his Majesty and the gallants standing about her; but that which engag'd my curiosity was the rich and splendid furniture of this woman's apartment, now twice or thrice pull'd down and rebuilt to satisfie her prodigal and expensive pleasures, whilst her Majestys[120] does not exceede some gentlemen's ladies in furniture and accommodation. Here I saw the new fabriq of French tapissry, for designe, tendernesse[121] of worke, and incomparable imitation of the best paintings, beyond any thing I had

[109] Grinling Gibbons, famous wood carver

[110] at that time used for any representation of the Crucifixion, including paintings

[111] Jacopo Robusti, Il Tintoretto, sixteenth-century Italian painter

[112] artistic workmanship

[113] studied [114] modest

[115] ancient capital of Assyria on the Tigris, often referred to by the prophets Jonah and Nahum, the book which bears the name of the latter beginning: "The burden of Nineveh"

[116] brick structure erected in the plain of Shinar to prevent the very confusion it brought about (See Gen. 11.4–9.)

[117] amenity, from Latin *amoenitas*, pleasantness

[118] gloomy, producing low spirits and melancholy

[119] Louise de Querouaille, agent of Louis XIV and mistress of Charles II, who played an influential part in the palace intrigues of the time

[120] Katherine of Braganza [121] delicacy

ever beheld. Some pieces had Versailles, St. Germain's, and other palaces of the French King, with huntings, figures, and landskips,[122] exotiq fowls, and all to the life rarely don. Then for Japan[123] cabinets, screenes, pendule[124] clocks, greate vases of wrought plate, tables, stands, chimney furniture, sconces, branches, braseras,[125] etc., all of massie[126] silver, and out[127] of number, besides some of her Majestys best paintings.

Surfeiting of this, I din'd at Sir Stephen Fox's,[128] and went contented home to my poor, but quiet villa. What contentment can there be in the riches and splendor of this world, purchas'd with vice and dishonour!

Feb[ruary] 4th [1684/1685]. . . . Prayers were solemnly made in all the churches, especially in both the Court Chapells, where the chaplaines reliev'd one another every halfe quarter of an houre from the time he began to be in danger till he expir'd, according to the forme prescribed in the Church offices. Those who assisted his Majesty's devotions were, the Abp. of Canterbury,[129] the Bishops of London,[130] Durham,[131] and Ely,[132] but more especialy Dr. Ken,[133] the Bp. of Bath and Wells. It is sayd they exceedingly urg'd the receiving the holy sacrament, but his Majesty told them he would consider of it, which he did so long 'till it was too late. Others whisper'd that the Bishops and Lords, except the Earles of Bath[134] and Feversham,[135] being order'd to withdraw the night before, Hurlston,[136] the priest, had presumed to administer the Popish offices.[137] He gave his breeches and keys to the Duke,[138] who was almost continually kneeling by his bed-side, and in teares. He also recommended to him the care of his natural children, all except the Duke of Monmouth,[139] now in Holland, and in his displeasure. He intreated the Queene to pardon him (not without cause); who a little before had sent a Bishop to excuse her not more frequently visiting him, in reguard of her excessive griefe, and withall, that his Majesty would forgive it if at any time she had offended him. He spake to the Duke to be kind to the Dutchesse of Cleaveland,[140] and especialy Portsmouth, and that Nelly[141] might not starve.

Thus died King Charles II. of a vigorous and robust constitution, and in all appearance promising a long life. He was a Prince of many virtues, and many greate imperfections; debonaire,[142] easy of accesse, not bloudy nor cruel; his countenance fierce, his voice greate, proper[143] of person, every motion became him; a lover of the sea, and skillful in shipping; not affecting[144] other studies, yet he had a laboratory, and knew of many empyrical[145] medicines, and the easier mechanical[146] mathematics; he lov'd planting and building, and brought in a politer way of living, which pass'd to luxury and intolerable expence. He had a particular talent in telling a story, and facetious passages, of which he had in-

[122] landscapes
[123] of Japanese lacquered work
[124] pendulum [125] braziers
[126] solid [127] beyond
[128] first person to inform Charles of Cromwell's death, knighted (1665), Paymaster of the Forces
[129] William Sancroft, distinguished anti-Calvinist controversialist, later opponent of James II's religious measures, and Non-Juror
[130] Henry Compton, who later opposed James II's religious policy, and signed the invitation to William of Orange
[131] Nathaniel, 3rd Baron Crewe of Stene, a favorite of the Duke of York, Dean of the Chapel Royal
[132] Francis Turner, chaplain to the Duke of York, Bishop of Rochester (1683), of Ely (1684), and Non-Juror
[133] Thomas Ken, famous for his saintly character and his hymns and other devotional writings
[134] a Lord of the Bedchamber
[135] Captain of the Guard
[136] Father Huddleston, who had aided Charles II's escape from Worcester
[137] Catholic rites
[138] the Duke of York
[139] James, the son of Charles II by Lucy Walters, Duke of Monmouth (See Evelyn's account of Monmouth, pp. 113–14 below.)
[140] Barbara Villiers, wife of Roger Palmer, Earl of Castlemaine (1661), mistress of Charles II, Duchess of Cleveland
[141] Nell Gwynn
[142] gracious [143] well-formed
[144] not showing a liking for
[145] empiric, as distinguished from scientific, depending on experience and observation
[146] practical as opposed to speculative

numerable; this made some buffoons and vitious wretches too presumptuous and familiar, not worthy the favour they abus'd. He tooke delight in having a number of little spaniels follow him and lie in his bed-chamber, where he often suffer'd the bitches to puppy and give suck, which render'd it very offensive, and indeede made the whole Court nasty and stinking. He would doubtlesse have ben an excellent Prince had he ben less addicted to women, who made him uneasy, and allways in want to supply their unmeasurable profusion, to the detriment of many indigent persons who had signaly serv'd both him and his father. He frequently and easily chang'd favorites, to his greate prejudice. As to other public transactions and unhappy miscarriages, 'tis not here I intend to number them; but certainly never had King more glorious opportunities to have made himselfe, his people, and all Europe happy, and prevented innumerable mischiefs, had not his too easy nature resign'd him to be manag'd by crafty men, and some abandon'd and profane wretches who corrupted his otherwise sufficient parts, disciplin'd as he had ben by many afflictions during his banishment, which gave him much experience and knowledge of men and things; but those wicked creatures took him off from all application becoming so greate a King. The history of his reigne will certainely be the most wonderfull for the variety of matter and accidents, above any extant in former ages: the sad tragical death of his father, his banishment and hardships, his miraculous restauration, conspiracies against him, parliaments, wars, plagues, fires, comets,[147] revolutions abroad happening in his time, with a thousand other particulars. He was ever kind to me, and very gracious upon all occasions, and therefore I cannot, without ingratitude, but deplore his losse, which for many respects, as well as duty, I do with all my soul.

. . . . .

I can never forget the inexpressible luxury[148] and prophaneness, gaming and all dissoluteness, and as it were total forgetfullnesse of God (it being Sunday evening) which this day se'nnight[149] I was witnesse of, the King sitting and toying with his concubines, Portsmouth, Cleaveland, and Mazarine,[150] etc., a French boy[151] singing love songs, in that glorious gallery, whilst about 20 of the greate courtiers and other dissolute persons were at basset[152] round a large table, a bank of at least 2000 in gold before them, upon which two gentlemen who were with me made reflexions with astonishment. Six days after was all in the dust! . . .

[July] 15th [1685]. I went to see Dr. Tenison's library[153] [in St. Martin's].

Monmouth was this day brought to London and examin'd before the King,[154] to whom he made great submission, acknowledged his seduction by Ferguson the Scot,[155] whom he nam'd the bloudy villain. He was sent to the Tower, had an interview with his late Dutchesse,[156] whom he receiv'd coldly, having lived dishonestly with the Lady Henrietta Wentworth[157] for two yeares. He obstinately asserted his conversation with that debauch'd woman to be no sin, whereupon, seeing he could not be persuaded to his last breath, the divines who were sent to assist him thought not fit to administer the Holy Communion to him. For the rest of his faults he profess'd greate sorrow, and so died without any apparent feare; he would not make

[147] dreaded then as presaging disaster

[148] lechery

[149] the space of seven nights and days; a week ago

[150] Hortensia Mancini, niece of Cardinal Mazarin, Duchess of Mazarin, foremost rival of the Duchess of Portsmouth

[151] Evelyn mentions hearing him at Lord Rochester's on January 28, 1685, and describes him as famed for his singing

[152] a card game resembling faro

[153] a library which Dr. Tenison, the vicar of St. Martin's (afterward Archbishop of Canterbury) founded for the public use

[154] James II

[155] Robert Ferguson, political pamphleteer in support of Monmouth and the Protestant cause, reputed one of the authors of the Rye House plot, an adviser in the plans for insurrection of Argyle and Monmouth

[156] Lady Anne Scott, daughter and heiress of the 2nd Earl of Buccleuch

[157] Henrietta Maria, Baroness Wentworth, mistress of the Duke of Monmouth, who generously supported his attempt on the throne, and died less than a year after his execution

use of a cap or other circumstance,[158] but lying downe, bid the fellow[159] do his office better than to the late Lord Russell,[160] and gave him gold; but the wretch made five chopps before he had his head off; which so incens'd the people, that had he not been guarded and got away, they would have torn him to pieces.

The Duke made no speech on the scaffold (which was on Tower Hill) but gave a paper containing not above 5 or 6 lines, for the King, in which he disclaims all title to the crown, acknowledges that the late King, his father, had indeede told him he was but his base sonn, and so desir'd his Majesty to be kind to his wife and children. This relation I had from Dr. Tenison (Rector of St. Martin's), who, with the Bishops of Ely and Bath and Wells, were sent to him by his Majesty, and were at the execution.

Thus ended this quondam[161] Duke, darling of his father and the ladies, being extreamly handsome and adroit; an excelent souldier and dancer, a favourite of the people, of an easy nature, debauch'd by lust, seduc'd by crafty knaves who would have set him up only to make a property,[162] and took the opportunity of the King being of another religion, to gather a party of discontented men. He fail'd, and perish'd. . . .

May 26th [1703]. This day died Mr. Sam. Pepys, a very worthy, industrious and curious[163] person, none in England exceeding him in knowledge of the navy, in which he had passed thro' all the most considerable offices, Clerk of the Acts and Secretary of the Admiralty, all which he perform'd with great integrity. When King James II. went out of England, he laid down his office, and would serve no more, but withdrawing himselfe from all public affaires, he liv'd at Clapham with his partner Mr. Hewer,[164] formerly his clerk, in a very noble house and sweete place, where he enjoy'd the fruits of his labours in greate prosperity. He was universally belov'd, hospitable, generous, learned in many things, skill'd in music, a very greate cherisher of learned men of whom he had the conversation.[165] His library[166] and collection of other curiosities were of the most considerable, the models of ships especially. Besides what he publish'd of an account of the Navy, as he found and left it, he had for divers yeares under his hand the History of the Navy, or *Navalia* as he call'd it; but how far advanc'd, and what will follow of his, is left, I suppose, to his sister's son Mr. Jackson, a young gentleman whom Mr. Pepys had educated in all sorts of usefull learning, sending him to travel abroad, from whence he return'd with extraordinary accomplishments, and worthy to be heir. Mr. Pepys had been for neere 40 yeares so much my particular friend, that Mr. Jackson sent me compleat mourning, desiring me to be one to hold up the pall at his magnificent obsequies, but my indisposition hinder'd me from doing him this last office.

158 appurtenance
159 Jack Ketch, the famous executioner
160 William, Lord Russell, one of Shaftesbury's Council of Six, executed for the Insurrection Plot, July 1683
161 sometime
162 make a tool of him
163 eager for knowledge
164 William Hewer, Deputy Judge Advocate of the Fleet (1677), Commissioner of the Navy (1685), Member of Parliament (1685)
165 company
166 which he gave to Magdalen College, Cambridge

Andrew Marvell

WE HAVE ventured to divide our selection from Marvell between this and the preceding volume because his work in the two periods is so different and because (even if the division between the two volumes is a mere convenience of format) Marvell as the chief satirist of the first half of the Restoration has a prescriptive place among the founders of the satire of the Age of Reason, and he is best appreciated when set among them. In 1659, having previously served for several years as assistant to Milton in the Latin secretaryship, and having been the great panegyrist of Cromwell, he was elected a member of Parliament for his native town of Hull. He was then thirty-eight, and he sat in Parliament, voting as a member of the Country or opposition party and writing home careful accounts of his activities to his constituents (Margoliouth, *Poems and Letters*, Vol. II) until his death in 1678. Except for his lines on Cromwell's death he had presumably not written since about 1654. Those lines show an increased simplicity of statement.

The endeavor of Clarendon and others to fasten a rigid code of conformity and repression on England, the slackened weakness of the country contrasted with her triumphant energy and commanding position under Cromwell and Blake—a weakness signalized when the Dutch sailed into the Medway—, the apparent indolence of Charles II, and the character of his Court and his personal life, and the Catholicism of his brother James, then Duke of York, called forth from men of many sorts before the first ten years of the Restoration were past a number of satires (many collected later into *Poems on Affairs of State*) anonymous as for a hundred years under strenuous censorship attacks on government had been; rough, coarse, often violent; but vigorous, and the best of them inventive enough in their plots or devices. Of these, so many were attributed to Marvell that he must have been well known to have written a number of them. All that may possibly be attributed to him have been printed by H. Margoliouth in his great edition. The likelihood of attribution, with details of publication, is there studied by him; and there is a full commentary on the prose satires by P. Legouis in his comprehensive study, *André Marvell.* They are edited by A. B. Grosart in *The Complete Works*, The Fuller Worthies Library, Vols. 24–27 (1872–1875). See also Previté-Orton (general bibliography).

Marvell's prose satires originated as strictly controversial literature. The earliest and greatest, *The Rehearsal Transprosed* (1672) and *The Rehearsal Transprosed*, Part II (1673), are answers, loosely in the form of running commentaries, the first to a group of writings by Samuel Parker directed toward the suppression of the Dissenters, and the second to Parker's and other answers to Marvell's first part.[1]

[1] Parker's principal works to which Marvell alludes are: *A Discourse of Ecclesiastical Politie* (that is, church government), 1672; *A Defense and Continuation of the Ecclesiastical Politie*, 1671; *Bishop Bramhall's Vindication of Himself and of the Episcopal Clergy . . . together with a Preface showing what grounds there are for fears and jealousy of Popery*, 1672 (Preface by Parker); *A Reproof to the Rehearsal Transprosed*, 1672. Legouis supplies a full list of the pamphlets in the controversy.

Actual commentary, however, bears in these satires only a small proportion to a broad discussion of the issue and a sweeping mockery of Parker's views, history, and character. Marvell's deliberate intention is to destroy Parker's influence by comedy and raillery. The pamphlets are overlong and somewhat random in direction but with an underlying sustained unity of invention and point of view. His witty achievement was hailed joyously by King and Court, and by such an historian, later, as Burnett. Swift singled it out as proving that a genius could do enduring work even in the negative form Marvell had chosen. *The Rehearsal* was followed by a further discussion of issues in another controversy, *Mr. Smirke: Or the Divine in Mode . . . Together with a Short Historical Essay, concerning General Councils, Creeds, and Impositions in Matters of Religion*, 1676, a work in two parts of which the second is a piece of brilliantly ironic historical writing against the multiplication of dogma and on behalf of the severe limitation of discussion of the Christian mysteries. His last satire was *An Account of the Growth of Popery and Arbitrary Government in England*, 1677.

Samuel Parker had been a Puritan, had complied with the Anglican Church, and was now, with a very bright and quick mind, but with superficiality, narrowness, and complaisance, pushing himself into preferment (he was ultimately Bishop of Oxford) by attacks upon the Dissenters and upon Charles's indulgence toward them. On lines that Marvell did not err in calling close to the arguments of Hobbes, Parker urged the absolute control of the sovereign over all ecclesiastical matters, and the need of his requiring complete conformity even in insignificant rites and forms. Marvell had always had a keen sense of the danger of self-righteousness in the Presbyterians and other Puritans and of ignorant and short-visioned unrest among some of the sects. But nothing was more inward to his mind than the belief in liberty of conscience, supported by the grace of God. The strong limits which he placed upon speculative thought looked to the affirmation and emphasis of that ethical insight and self-awareness which was *right reason*. Parker's stress upon mere manners seemed to him a denial of the central religious consciousness. And in defending now the struggle of the members of the sects towards light, he was recognizing in others the centrality of that subtle play of the sensibility out of which his own great poetry had sprung. He had, too, a deep and humble sense of the history of the hard years 1640–1660 in which he had begun to share when he returned from the Continent in 1646. In regard to the Civil War, he felt that the cause of the country gentlemen of the Long Parliament who opposed the King was too good to have been fought for, and that men ought to have trusted the King. But he would have men learn generosity from the lesson of that tragedy resulting from intransigence in which all England had been caught, and he scorned one who could forget his own origins and activities, or overlook or seek to suppress the human aspirations which had been seething in that troubled time. More largely, his satires are informed by a realistic view of history and the human situation as a whole, liberal, though disillusioned and ironic. And the serious passages which intersperse their comedy place Marvell among the ranks of modern historians who are then beginning to study the emergence of government as a process in history. Order, he holds, is to be broken only under the most intolerable strains. Nonetheless government derives its power from the consent of the governed, and is a process quite secondary and mediate to securing the larger life of men as men.

His method is broadly burlesque. It is significant that he greatly admired Butler. Stimulated by Parker's arbitrariness and the inflation of his style, he identifies him with the Bayes of the recent brilliant burlesque attack upon heroic drama in *The Rehearsal*. But "burlesque" by no means suggests the scope and comic penetration of his raillery, the play of his irony. The sustained parallels and literary allusions—to Bayes, to Rabelais, to Don Quixote, and others—recurring ever and again with fresh surprise create something like a continuous comedy peering through the surface, as the continued references to Parker's prognostications in our selection illustrate. The acute and numerous parallels drawn from the whole course of history and from a vast learning would be pedantic were they not so wittily handled and so carefully directed. Marvell sees down the years a single struggle of simple human integrity against power, selfishness, and passion. And the evocation of homely—often very coarse—but lively imagined scenes in Parker's life parallels scenes drawn from Roman or other history, uniting in a common effect to establish the two universal realms, the one of wisdom and the other of the folly in which Parker has his habitat. Marvell's poetry uses symbol and play upon word to lift us from the realm of immediate experience to the realm of spirit and thought; in his prose, the same devices are given deliberate comic inversion. He can reduce Parker into a mean and ludicrous context by a single vulgar figure or by the sudden literal interpretation of a word beside its habitual figurative sense.

Marvell's own language is quiet, "reasonable," familiar, or even the other side of familiarity. But it is a quietness that at its best seems to anticipate Swift's. It is capable occasionally, when urged by scorn or concentration of meaning, of a piercing succinctness of definition. Of formal rhythms it has none. But at high points a music born of generous indignation weights every word.

from THE REHEARSAL TRANSPROS'D[1]

[Marvell is answering Parker's arguments for the extreme repression of the Dissenters. In this passage, he imagines what the Protestants of the Continent, with whom England had traditionally allied herself intellectually and politically, would think of Parker's work, should it come abroad.]

Neither will the Gravity therefore of their Judgments take the measures, I hope, either of the Education at our Universities, or of the Spirit[2] of our Divines, or of the Prudence, Piety, and Doctrine of the Church of *England*, from such an Interloper. Those Gardens of ours use to bear much better fruit. There may happen sometimes an ill Year, or there may be such a Crab-stock as cannot by all ingrafting be corrected. But generally it proves otherwise. Once perhaps in a hundred years there may arise such a Prodigy in the University (where all Men else learn better Arts and better Manners) and from thence may creep into the Church (where the Teachers at least ought to be well instructed in the knowledge and practice of Christianity) so prodigious[3] a Person I say may even there be hatch'd, as shall neither know or care how to behave himself to God or Man; and who having never seen the receptacle of Grace or Conscience at an Anatomical Dissection, may conclude therefore that there is no such matter, or no such obligation among Christians; who shall persecute the Scripture it self, unless it will conform to his Interpretation; who shall strive to put the World into Blood, and animate Princes to be the Executioners of their own Subjects for well-doing. All this is possible; but comes to pass as rarely and at as long periods in our Climate, as the birth of a false Prophet. But unluckily, in this fatal Year of Seventy two, among all the Calamities that Astrologers foretel, this also hath befaln us. I would not hereby confirm his vanity, as if I also believed that any Scheme of Heaven[4] did influence his actions, or that he were so considerable as that the Comet[5] under which they say

[1] Text: The Second Impression with Additions and Amendments, 1672

[2] Text: *spitit*

[3] abnormal, of the nature of a prodigy

[4] positions of the stars at any given time, for astrological computation

[5] probably that of 1664, just before the plague (Grosart)

we yet labour, had fore-boded the appearance of his Preface. No, no: though he be a creature most noxious, yet he is more despicable. A Comet is of far higher quality, and hath other kind of imployment. Although we call it an Hairy-Star, it affords no prognostick of what breeds there: but the Astrologer that would discern our Author and his business, must lay by his Telescope, and use a Microscope. You may find him still in Mr. *Calvin's* head.[6] . . .

from PART II[7]

[Marvell begins with an objection to the violence of Parker's writing as unsuited to discussion about religion or by a churchman. He goes on . . .]

And yet nevertheless, and all that has been said before being granted, it may so chance that to write, and that Satyrically, and that a second time and a third; and this too even against a Clergy-man, may be not only excusable but necessary. That I may spare a tedious recapitulation, I shall prove all the rest upon the strongest instance, that is in the case of a Clergy-man. For it is not impossible that a man by evil arts may have crept into the Church, thorow the Belfry or at the Windows. 'Tis not improbable that having so got in he should foul the Pulpit, and afterwards the Press with opinions destructive to Humane Society and the Christian Religion. That he should illustrate so corrupt Doctrines with as ill a conversation,[8] and adorn the lasciviousness of his life with an equal petulancy of stile and language. In such a concurrence of misdemeanors what is to be done? Why certainly, how pernicious soever this must be in the example and consequence, yet, before any private man undertake to obviate it, he ought to expect the judgment of the Diocesan[9] and the method of the Ecclesiastical Discipline. There was in the ancient times of Christianity a wholsome usage, but now obsolete, which went very far in preventing[10] all these occasions. For whosoever was to receive Ordination, his name was first published to the Congregation in the same way as the Banes[11] of those that enter into Matrimony: and if any could object a sufficient cause against him that was proposed, he was not to be admitted to the Ministry. He that would be a Preacher was to be first himself commented upon by the People, and in the stile of those ages was said *Praedicari*.[12] But since that circumspection has been devolved into[13] the single oversight of the later Bishops, it cannot be otherwise, but some one or other may sometimes escape into the Church, who were much fitter to be shut out of Doors. Yet then if our great Pastors should but exercise the Wisdom of common Shepheards, by parting with one to stop the infection of the whole Flock, when his rottenness grew notorious; or if our Clergy would but use the instinct of other creatures, and chase the blown[14] Deer out of their Heard; such mischiefs might quickly be remedied. But on the contrary it happens not seldome that this necessary duty (which is so great a part of true *Ecclesiastical Politie*) is not only neglected, but that persons so dangerous are rather incouraged by their Superiors, and he that, upon their omission, shall but single out one of them, yet shall be exposed to the general out-cry of the Faculty,[15] and be pursued with Bell, Book, and Candle, as a declared and publick enemy of the Clergy. Whereas they ought to consider that by this way of proceeding, they themselves do render that universal which was but individual, and affix a personal crime upon their whole Order, and, for want of separating from one obnoxious, do contribute to the causes of separation, justifying so far that Schism which they condemn. In this Case, and supposing such a failer[16] of justice in those whose Province it is to prevent or punish, I ask again what is to be done? Why certainly the next thing had been to admonish him in partic-

[6] Parker was strongly opposed to Calvinism, and Marvell had earlier in this tract deplored his attack on Calvin.

[7] Text: first edition, 1673

[8] habit of life

[9] wait for the judgment of the bishop of his diocese

[10] anticipating

[11] banns; notice of intended marriage read in church to allow any objection to be made

[12] commented on

[13] passed down by the revolution of time

[14] out of breath

[15] the whole body of the clergy

[16] failure

ular as a Friend does his Friend, or one Christian another. But he that hath once Printed an ill book has thereby condens'd his words on purpose lest they should be carried away by the wind; he has diffused his poyson so publickly in design that it might be beyond his own recollection;[17] and put himself deliberately past the reach of any private admonition. In this Case it is that I think a Clergy-man is laid open to the Pen of any one that knows how to manage it; and that every person who has either Wit, Learning or Sobriety is licensed, if debauch'd to curb him, if erroneous to catechize him, and if foul-mouth'd and biting, to muzzle him. For they do but abuse themselves who shall any longer consider or reverence such an one as a Clergy-man, who as oft as he undresses degrades himself and would never have come into the Church but to take Sanctuary. Rather, wheresoever men shall find the footing of so wanton a Satyr[18] out of his own bounds, the neighbourhood ought, notwithstanding all his pretended capering Divinity, to hunt him thorow the woods with hounds and horn home to his harbour.

How far and whether at all the *Author of the Ecclesiastical Politie* is culpable on these accounts, I must refer to the Readers judgment upon perusal of my first and this my second book, though I could much rather wish that men would be at leisure to take the length of him out of his own discourses. But, had he not appear'd so to me, I should never have molested him, adventur'd my self, or interessed[19] the Publick by writing in this manner. For I am too conscious of mine own imperfections to rake into and dilate upon the failings of other men; and though I carry always some ill Nature about me, yet it is I hope no more than is in this world necessary for a Preservative; but as for the Clergy, the memory of mine own extraction,[20] and much more my sense of the Sanctity of their function ingage me peculiarly to esteem and honour them. Insomuch that for their sakes I bear much respect even to their *poor* wives, of whom I may say (as Bishop *Bramhall*[21] comparing the Readers with the Preachers, and who understood both) that *if they come short* of other Women *in point of Efficacy*, *yet they have the advantage* of other Women *in point of Security*. And though I am not so inamour'd of them as to worship 'em for *Goddesses;* yet I am so far from rejecting them as *Dish-clouts*, that what the *Author of Eccles. Politie* affirms of the Clergy of the Church of *England*, *I dare averre* concerning their Wives, *that taking them under all their disadvantages they are at this very time vastly the furthest off from being justly contemptible* (*to mention no other Order or Profession of Women*) *of any Clergy-mens Wives in the world. The pre-eminence is so evident that it clears the comparison from all possible suspition of being proud or odious.*[22]

Being of this temper there could be no great appearance of my being overforward to come out in Print in such a Stile against one of his cloath, unless upon some very extraordinary occasion. And such this occasion seemed to me, and so urgent and justifiable that it might absolve me in any Readers opinion. For this sharpness of Stile does indeed for the most part naturally flow from the humour of the Writer: and therefore 'tis observable that few are guilty of it but either those that write too young, (when it resembles the acidity of juices strain'd from the fruits before they be matured) or else those that write too old (and then 'tis like the sowrness of liquors which being near corrupting turn eager[23]). And both these are generally disrellish'd: or if men do admit them for sawce, yet he must be very thirsty that will take a draught of 'm; whereas the generousest wine drops from the grape naturally without pressing, and though piquant hath its sweetness. And though I cannot arrogate so much as even the similitude of those good qualities to my Writing, yet I dare say that never was there a more pregnant ripeness in the causes. For having read one, two, three, and now four books of the same Author, and of the

[17] gathering together again
[18] goat-footed, irresponsible, wood-land creature in Greek myth
[19] interested
[20] his father being a clergyman

[21] 1594–1663; bishop of Armagh
[22] Marvell seems to imply a jibe at Parker, whom he repeatedly accuses of having a mistress rather than a wife.
[23] vinegarish

same subject, which was no less then that weighty matter of *Ecclesiastical Politie* and all its dependances,[24] I observed first, that there was no name to them; a thing of very ill example. For every one that will treat of so nice and tender argument ought to affix his name, thereby to make himself responsible to the publick for any dammage that may arise by his undertaking. Otherwise though he has a License in his pocket, or be perhaps himself the Licenser, it is but a more authoriz'd way of libelling; and it looks too like a man that shall lay a train of Gun-powder, and then retire to some obscure place from whence after he has applyed his mach, he may solace himself with the mischief; or though it be not so design'd, yet the effect is not more probably to stop a flame than to propagate it, and in stead of preserving, to subvert and blow up the Government: Whereas if men were obliged to leave that anonymous and sculking method both of Writing and Licensing, they would certainly grow more careful what opinions they vented, what expressions they used, and we might have miss'd many books that have of late come out by the same authority contrary to all good manners, and even to the Doctrine of our Church under which they take protection. Had there been no other cause but this, it might have sufficed, and when *Ecclesiastical Politie* march'd *Incognito*, and Theology went on mumming,[25] it was no less allowable for any one to use the license of Mascarade to show him, and the rest of 'm the consequence of such practice.

But beside this, when I perused his books, and others of the same patern, I saw that they plainly incroached upon other mens vocations, and that a sort[26] of Divines, among whom he alwayes acted the highest parts, had clann'd together to set up above those of the King and Duke[27] a new Company of Comedians. Such was their Dramatick and Scenical way of scribling, and they did so teem with new Plays perpetually, that there was no Post nor Pillar[28] so sacred that was exempt, no not even the walls of *Pauls*[29] it self much less the *Temple-gate*[30] from the pasting up of the Titles. Insomuch that I have seen a Lacquey[31] that could not read, having been sent to take down the Play for the afternoon, has by mistake brought away the Title of a new book of Theology. Yet if they did it well, they might perhaps in time get some custom; but alas those great men in the Pulpit how ridiculous do they appear on a Stage, and he that has all his life been cramp'd in a Reading pew at what a loss must he be when he comes to tread in whatsoever Theater! They are so unfit to bear a part among any Civil and Judicious Company, that, whatsoever place they may hold in the Church, I am confident they must make all their friends to be but receiv'd into the *Nursery*.[32] And had not Mr. *Killegrew*[33] foreseen that they must of course within a little time fall to dirt of themselves, he would ere this to be sure have trounced the *Author of the Ecclesiastical Politie*, for intrenching upon his Patent. But he knew they were below his neglect and the *Pit*[34] would quickly do their business, and not only hiss but palt[35] them off the Stage. And I, that had sate so long more quiet than all the rest of the Spectators, could not at last restrain my self from using also the liberty of the House and revenging the expense of my time and money, by representing the *Author of the* Comedy call'd the *Ecclesiastical Politie* in that Farse of mine own the *Rehearsal Transpros'd*.

Neither yet was this all that deserved reprehension in his Writings, He useth such a Ruffian-like stile, and upon which, to my knowledge, he peculiarly values

[24] matters depending on it

[25] disguising in a show

[26] company

[27] the two London theatrical companies, the King's and the Duke's

[28] on which placards or sheets were posted, especially at booksellers' shops

[29] St. Paul's Cathedral

[30] entrance to the group of buildings once belonging to the Knights' Templars but in Marvell's time, Inns of Court, where lawyers studied

[31] man-servant

[32] theatre set up in 1663 as a school for young actors

[33] Thomas Killigrew, manager of the King's Company, was also joint patentee or manager of the Nursery.

[34] the main auditory of the theatre

[35] drive with missiles

himself, that any one would suspect he had travell'd and convers'd all his life time either among the Nation of the *Bravo's*[36] and *Filoux*,[37] or else been educated in the Academy of the *Venetian* Galleys which he himself was in his second book so apprehensive of, that he never rested until he had found in his third how to supply them with Slaves out of the Non-conformists.[38] But I perceive since that men of his parts can arrive at those perfections sitting but in their Closets and over-hearing the Water-men[39] which others after long Voyages and observation neither would nor could ever attain to. Then the Arrogance which runs through all his books is insupportable, boasting proudly of himself, vilifying and censuring others to such a degree that as I never heard any thing equal, so neither any thing like it but the Mountebanks[40] abroad, who after a deal of Scaffold Pageantry to draw audience, entertain them by decrying all others with a Panegyrick[41] of their own Balsam. There is scarce any sort and rank of men ancient or modern, scarce any particular person though of the most established and just reputation, but he does if he meet them not hale them into his way to invey against them and trample upon them, nay even such as have but a book, or two, or three before (perhaps a page, perhaps a line) been happy in his good opinion. And this he does for the most part in the most bitter manner that is possible: I know not whether I may properly call it Satyrical, but let it go so for once, for what he wants in wit he supplyes however in good will, and where the Conceit[42] is deficient, he makes it out alwayes with railing. He scarce ever opens his mouth, but that he may bite, nor bites, but that from the *Vesicles*[43] of his Gums he may infuse a venom. Had he been but innocently dull, he might have been sure no man would have medled with him: but when there was no end of his buttering one book upon another, and he still writ worse and worse, with less vigour alwayes, but more virulence, that perpetual grating did indeed set my teeth on edge, and I thought that even the most candid Readers would out of their equity not take it amiss if at last he did by hearing ill himself, lose part of that pleasure which he had so frequently taken in traducing and speaking hitherto ill of others. For no man needs Letters of Mart[44] against one that is an open Pirate of other mens Credit: and I remember within our time one *Simons*, who rob'd alwayes upon the *Bricolle*,[45] that is to say, never interrupted the Passengers but still set upon the Thieves themselves after, like Sir *John Falstaff*, they were gorged with a booty; and by this way, so ingenious, that it was scarce criminal, he lived secure and unmolested all his dayes with the reputation of a Judge rather than an High-way man. But my greatest incentive was, as I told him in my former Pamphlet, the perniciousness of the whole design of his books; tending, in my opinion, to the disturbance of all Government, the misrepresenting of the generous and prudent Counsels of His Majesty, and raising a mis-intelligence[46] betwixt Him and His People; beside his calumniating the whole foraign Protestancy, his stirring up of persecution against those at home, and his mangling even of Religion it self and Christianity: And to this purpose he suited befitting Principles, and to those a Language as harmonious: seeming to have forgot not only all Scripture rules, but even all Scripture expressions; unless where he either distorts them to his own interpretation, or attempts to make them ridiculous to others; Insomuch, that, of all the books that ever I read, I must needs say I never saw a Divine guilty of so much ribaldry and prophaneness. Which though it was a matter of such Decency to his undertaking that I account it to have been even Necessary, yet in the whole I look'd upon as so uncanonical and impious, that it would bear an higher and more deserved accusation than that of *Onias* the Son of

[36] bullies [37] vagabonds

[38] The galleys were driven by slave rowers.

[39] men who ply the Thames in boats, for passengers

[40] those who set up stages on the street to sell drugs from

[41] elaborate praise

[42] thought, usually worked out wittily

[43] cavity, small sac, as of a poisonous snake

[44] of marque; license to fit out a private vessel and proceed against enemy shipping

[45] the bound of a ball from the side of an enclosed tennis court

[46] misunderstanding

Simeon the *Just*,[47] for officiating in a Womans Zone[48] instead of the Priestly girdle, and for the sacred Pectoral[49] wearing his Mistress Stomacher.[50] I must confess that when all these things centred together upon my imagination, and I saw that none of his Superiors offer'd to interpose against an evil so great in it self, and as to me appear'd so publick in the consequence and mischief, I could hold no longer, and I, though the most unfit of many, assumed upon him the Priviledge (if any such Priviledge there be) of an English *Zelote*.[51] . . .

. . . . .

[Marvell explains that he at first respected the office of his opponent as a clergyman, but that the abusive quality of Parker's and other answers inspired by him made it necessary to show that the man and his work were of a piece.]

Whoever shall go back to trace his Original, will quickly be at a stand[52] and find themselves so soon involved in the Fabulous Age, that they will run astray and be benighted in his History before noon. They will find his *Saturn*[53] to have reign'd much later than *William* the *Conqueror;* or if, like a true born *Arcadian*,[54] he derive himself from before the Moon, it must be understood concerning the last Change. I cannot yet learn, though he hath imployed me long about it, who was his Grandfather: but, as modern as he must have been, 'tis the certainer Heraldry to extract him from a *Vesicle*[55] *of the Earth*, and let him go for the Grand-son of a *Pimple*. For no Prince how great soever begets his Predecessors, and the noblest Rivers are not Navigable to the Fountain. Even the Parentage of the *Nile* is yet in obscurity, and 'tis a dispute among Authors whether *Snow* be not the head of his Pedigree. I read indeed as long ago as in the Reign of *Edward* the *4th*,[56] concerning one *Henry Parker*, a Carmelite Friar, who having preach'd against the secular grandeur and pomp of the Clergy in those times, was forced to make a publick Recantation at *Pauls-Cross*.[57] But this is too obsolete: and though otherwise the Analogy might easily be propagated, yet I suppose the honest Monk kept to his vow of Continence: and besides, should the *Author of the Ecclesiastical Politie*, descend from that Line, it would make too great a Solecism[58] in his Scutcheon.[59] There was also in the latter end of Queen *Elizabeth*, and beginning of King *James*, one *Robert Parker, the Author* of another kind of *Ecclesiastical Politie*, a Learned, but severe Non-conformist, who writ also the book *de Cruce*,[60] for which he was forced to cross the Seas. But neither can I find him to come within the proportion of time or Scale of his Genealogy. Therefore to come nearer, I find in the Reign of the late King *Charles* one *Humfrey Parker*, Yeoman, who together with Mr. *Chancey*, for opposing the Rails about the Communion Table at *Ware* was sentenced to make a solemn submission and acknowledgment of his fault, as he did accordingly. There are several Arguments that might incline me to think the *Author of the Ecclesiastical Politie* is com'd of his Succession, and one particularly, because in the Record I read that this *Humfrey* took a Journey upon this occasion into *Northampton shire*, the seat of the Answerers[61] Family. But that which seems to come nearest home to him and the Chronology of his Grandfather, is in the year 1640 in a Petition from the City of *London*

[47] The story is told in the Apocrypha in Macabees.

[48] kind of girdle

[49] breast plate worn by the high-priest of the Jews

[50] covering worn under lacing of bodice

[51] member of one of the extreme dissenting sects

[52] be perplexed how to proceed

[53] the original progenitor or father of the gods

[54] The Arcadians, a pastoral people of ancient Greece, included in their nature worship along with the moon a culture deity or founder whom they believed older than the moon.

[55] sac, cavity [56] 1461–1483

[57] at St. Paul's Cathedral; Henry Parker wrote *Dives et Pauper*, 1493

[58] irregularity (commonly of grammar)

[59] armorial bearing, coat-of-arms

[60] Puritan divine, 1564?–1614. His *De Politeia Ecclesiastica*, written in exile, is a treatise on Presbyterianism; on the title of *de Cruce* Marvell appears in error.

[61] See introduction.

and several Counties to the then Parliament; complaining among other things of *Martin Parkers* Ballads, in disgrace of Religion, to the increase of all vice, and withdrawing of people from reading, studying and hearing the Word of God and other good books. 'Tis not at all unlikely that this, as an hereditary provocation, hath stuck upon him ever since, and that he swore at the Altar, when he was but nine years old, to be aveng'd for this affront to his lineage. We see often that the signature[62] of the Grand father revives upon the child, and, as some Rivers diving for a while under ground, makes a Bridge of the Parents to spring up again at that interval. Hence doubtless hath proceeded all his peek[63] against the Non-conformists: hence that unquenchable *Nemesis*[64] against the City; hence it is that he hath taken upon him to defend in gross[65] at this time the whole mass of enormityes, right or wrong, then complain'd of in that Petition: all this mischief for a Ballad-makers sake of the kindred. The Duke of *Muscovy*[66] indeed declared War against *Poland*, because he and his Nation had been vilifyed by a *Polish* Poet: but the *Author of the Ecclesiastical Politie* would it seems disturb the peace of Christendom for the good old cause of a superannuated Chanter of *Saffron-hill* and *Pyecorner*.[67] But though indeed he doth not write his books in the *Smithfield* Meetre, yet they are all Blank Ballad, and the subject and consequence *to the disgrace of Religion, the increase of all vice, and with-drawing people from reading, studying, and hearing the Word of God, and other good books is exactly the same*. So that he may when he will put in for Letters of Administration in the Prerogative Court,[68] and enter his Claim too with the Heralds:[69] for every one will yield him to be the next of kin to that Author; or let him but produce his own Writings, 'tis Evidence sufficient. If it should prove otherwise, the fault is in his own obscurity, that hath left all the Neighbourhood and me in the dark; and let him make what shift he will to procure himself a[70] Grandfather, for I have taken pains enough, I am sure, to help him to one.

But however for that matter, let the worst come to the worst, he had a Mother undeniably and probably a Father: Otherwise he would be shrowdly disappointed, and in a worse case then *Prince Prettyman* lamenting,[71]

What Oracle this Secret can evince,
Sometimes a Fishers Son, sometimes a Prince:
It is a secret great, as is the world,
In which I like the Soul am toss'd and hurl'd:

And he might with good reason exclaim more pathetically—*Bring in my Father, why d'ye keep him from me? Although a Fisherman, he is my Father.*

Was ever Son yet brought to this distress,
To be for being a Son made fatherless?
Oh you just Heavens! rob me not of a Father:
The being of a Son take from me rather.

His Mother is said to have been an honest Yeoman's Daughter, and to have been his Fathers Servant, with whom she lived with good reputation and so ever since her marriage; except what disgrace may have reflected from her issue, which being her grief and misfortune ought not to be her scandal. But though he came of a good Mother, he had a very ill Sire. He was a man bred toward the Law, and betook himself, as his best practice, to be a Sub Committee[72] man, or, as the stile[73] ran, one of the Assistant Committee in *Northampton-shire*. In the rapine of that employment, and what he got by picking the teeth of his Masters he sustain'd himself, till he had raked together some little estate. And then being a man for the purpose, and that had begun his fortune out of the sequestration[74] of the Estates of the Kings party, he to perfect it the more, proceeded to take away their Lives; not in the hot and Military way (which diminishes always the

[62] characteristic form or marking
[63] pique [64] spirit of vengeance
[65] in the mass
[66] Russia, or a province of what is now Russia; Moscow
[67] poorer districts, one in old London, one just outside the area (Grosart)
[68] a court for the probate of wills
[69] for the coat-of-arms
[70] u in the original text
[71] from *The Rehearsal*
[72] one of the committee sitting on sequestration of the lands of royalists
[73] title [74] fine or deprivation

offence) but in the cooler blood and sedentary execution of an High Court of Justice. Accordingly he was preferr'd to be one of that number that gave Sentence against the three Lords, *Capel*, *Holland*, and *Hamilton*,[75] who were beheaded. By this Learning in the Law he became worthy of the degree of a Serjeant, and sometimes to go the Circuit[76] till for misdemeanor he was Petition'd against. But for a taste of his abilities, and the more to re-ingratiate himself, he printed in the year 1650, a very remarkable book called *The Government of the People of* England, *precedent and present the same. Ad subscribentes confirmandum, Dubitantes informandum, Opponentes convincendum;*[77] and underneath, *Multa videntur quæ non sunt, Multa sunt quæ non videntur.*[78] Under that ingraven, two Hands joyn'd with the Motto, *Ut uniamur*,[79] and beneath a Sheaf of Arrows with this Device, *Vis unita fortior*,[80] and to conclude, *Concordia parvae res crescunt Discordia dilabuntur.*[81] A most Hieroglyphical Title[82] and sufficient to have supplyed the Mantlings and Atchievements[83] of the Family! By these Parents he was sent to *Oxford*, with intention to breed him up to the Ministry. There in a short time he enter'd himself into the Company of some young Students who were used to Fast and Pray weekly together, but for their refection[84] fed sometimes on a Broth from whence they were commonly call'd *Grewellers:*[85] only it was observed that he was wont still to put more *Graves* than all the rest in his Porrige. And after that he pick'd acquaintance not only with the Brotherhood at *Wadham Colledge*, but with the *Sisterhood* too at another old *Elsibeths*,[86] one *Elizabeth Hamptons*, a plain devout Woman, where he train'd himself up in hearing their Sermons and Prayers, receiving also the Sacrament in the House, till he had gain'd such proficience that he too began to exercise[87] in that Meeting, and was esteem'd one of the *preciousest* young men in the University. But when thus, after several years approbation, he was even ready to have taken the charge not of an *admiring*[88] *drove* or *heard*, as he now calls them, but of a Flock upon him, by great misfortune, the King came in by the miraculous providence of God influencing the distractions of some, the good affections of others, and the weariness of all towards that happy Restauration after so many sufferings to his Regal Crown and Dignity. Nevertheless, he broke not off yet from his former habitudes,[89] and though it were now too late to obviate this inconvenience, yet he persisted, as far as in him was, that is by praying, caballing,[90] and discoursing to obstruct the restoring of the Episcopal Government, Revenues, and Authority. Insomuch that finding himself discountenanced on those accounts by the then Warden of *Wadham*, he shifted Colledges to *Trinity*,[91] and, when there, went away without his Degree, scrupling forsooth the Subscription[92] then required. From thence he came to *London*, where he spent[93] a considerable time in creeping into all Corners and Companies, Horoscoping[94] up and down concerning the duration of the Government:

[75] tried as royalists and beheaded outside Westminster Hall, March 9, 1649

[76] one of a higher group of lawyers, from whom judges were chosen, and sometimes to form part of the court that moved about to hold a series of sessions

[77] "to confirm those who subscribe, to inform the doubting, to convince opponents"

[78] "Many things shall seem so which are not; many are so which do not appear."

[79] "that we may be made one"

[80] "united power is stronger"

[81] "in peace small fortunes grow; by discord they are dissipated"

[82] symbolic, the Egyptian writing being supposed a system of symbols or emblems

[83] details of coat-of-arms [84] repast

[85] gruellers; the broth being oat meal and water enriched, as Marvell adds, with fat (graves) from the bottom of a roasting pot

[86] Marvell had earlier made great mock of Parker's calling Queen Elizabeth old Elizabeth in reference to a law he wished to prove obsolete.

[87] to expound the Scripture (a term special to the Dissenters)

[88] wondering [89] habits

[90] petty plotting

[91] colleges of Oxford

[92] feeling scruples against the articles of religion required to be assented to

[93] original text: spnnt

[94] reckoning the position of the stars to make prophecy

not considering any thing as best, but as most lasting and most profitable. And after having many times cast a figure,[95] he at last satisfyed himself that the Episcopal Government would indure as long as this King lived, and from thence forward cast about how to be admitted into the Church of *England*, and find the High-way to her preferments. In order to this he daily inlarged, not only his Conversation but his Conscience, and was made free of some of the Town-vices: imagining like *Muleasses* King of *Tunes* (for I take witness that on all occasions I treat him rather above his quality than otherwise) that by hiding himself among the Onyons, he should escape being traced by his Perfumes. Ignorant and mistaken man, that thought it necessary to part with any virtue to get a Living; or that the Church of *England* did not require and incourage more sobriety, than he could ever be guilty of: whereas it hath alwayes been fruitful of men, who, together with obedience to that Discipline, have lived to the envy of the Non-conformists in their conversation, and without such could never either have been preserved so long or after so long a dissipation have ever recover'd. But neither was this yet in his opinion sufficient: and therefore he resolved to try a shorter path which some few men have trode not unsuccessfully: that is, to print a book, if that would not do, a second, if not that, a third of an higher extraction and so forward, to give experiment against their former party of a keen stile and a Ductile[96] judgement. His first Proof piece was in the year 1665, the *Tentamina Physico theologica:* a tedious transcript of his Common place book, wherein there is very little of his own, but the arrogance and the unparallel'd censoriousness that he exercises over all other Writers, beside his undutiful inveying even then against the *Vesicles of the Earth* for meer bubbles, as he did shortly after against his Fathers Memory, and in his Mothers presence before several witnesses, for a couple of *whining Phanaticks*. However he accounted it a safe book, on all sides, it being of so trite and confessed an argument that few judicious men would read it to examine the errours: and in so rough and scabbed a *Latine*, that a man must have long nails, and those sharper than ordinary, to distinguish betwixt the Skin and the Disease, the Faults and the Grammar. To omit his usual volume and circumference of periods;[97] which though he takes alwayes to be his chiefest strength, yet indeed, like too great a Line, weakens the defense, and requires too many men to make it good. But the Cause being against Atheism, he was secure that none would attaque him. For whether there be any Atheists is some controversie, and he is Compurgator[98] for most of 'm: or if there be such, yet they know the Bastions are all undermined and they should be blown up as soon as enter'd. But let him shew me any Atheist that he hath reduced by his book, unless he may pretend to have converted some (as in the old *Florentine* Wars) by meer tyring them out, and perfect weariness. In this Treatise however it was difficult for him to have hedged in the Nonconformists: only here and there he sprinkles a glittering ore, to give hopes of a vein underneath of such metal as might by a skilful hand be founded[99] into any figure; and having shown as he thought sufficiently that he believ'd there was a God, he imagin'd that thenceforward, write what, and against whom he would, it might pass as indisputably; that all would be current which past his Touch-stone;[100] that as his Predecessor *Midas*[101] turn'd into Gold whatsoever he touched, so every thing by his handling should be transmuted to Orthodoxy. When he had Cook'd up these musty Collections, he makes his first invitation to his *old Acquaintance* my Lord Arch-bishop of *Canterbury*, who had never seen before nor heard of him. But I must confess he furbishes up his Grace in so glorious an Epistle, that, had not my Lord been long since proof against the most Spiritual Flattery, the Dedication

[95] plotted out the positions of the stars and their significance

[96] pliant

[97] Marvell in the first part had mocked Parker's elaborate theoretical style.

[98] one who puts them to trial by oath

[99] cast

[100] stone which would tell by touch whether an object was gold

[101] King of Lydia who according to legend had this power, a disastrous one

only without ever reading the book, might have served to have fix'd him from that instant as his Favourite. Yet all this I perceive did not his work, but his Grace was so unmindful, or rather so prudent, that the Gentleman thought it necessary to spur up again the next year with another new book to show more plainly what he would be at. This he dedicates to Doctor *Bathurst*[102] and to evidence from the very Epistle that he was ready to renounce that very Education the Civility[103] of which he is so tender of as to blame me for disordering it, he picks occasion to tell him: *to your prevailing advise, Sir, do I owe my first rescue from the Chains and Fetters of an unhappy Education.* But in the book which he calls, a *free and impartial Censure of the Platonick Philosophy* (censure[104] 'tis sure to be whatsoever he writes) he speaks out, and demonstrates himself ready and equipp'd to surrender not only the Cause, but betray his party without making any Conditions for them, and to appear forthwith himself in the head of the contrary Interest. Which supposing the dispute to be just, yet in him was so mercenary, that none would have descended to act his part but a Divine of Fortune. And even Lawyers take themselves excused from being of Counsel for the King himself, in a Cause where they have been entertain'd[105] and instructed by their Client. But so flippant he was, and forward in this book, that, in despight of all Chronology, he could introduce *Plato* to invey against *Calvin*, and from the Platoniques he could miraculously hook in a Discourse against the Non-conformists. After this feat of activity he was ready to leap over the Moon: no scruple of Conscience could stand in his way, and no preferment seemed too high for him; For about this time, I find that having taken a turn at *Cambridge*, to qualifie himself, he was received within doors to be my Lord Archbishops other Chaplain, and into some degree of favour:[106] which, considering the difference of their humours and ages, was somewhat surprizing. But, whether indeed in times of heat and faction the most temperate Spirits may sometimes chance to take delight in one that is spightful, and make some use of him; or whether it be that even the most grave and serious persons do for relaxation divert themselves willingly by whiles[107] with a Creature that is unlucky, mimical and gamesome; so it was. And thenceforward the nimble Gentleman danced upon Bell-ropes, vaulted from Steeple to Steeple, and cut Capers out of one Dignity to another. Having thus dexterously stuck his Groat[108] in *Lambeth*[109] Wainscot it may easily be conceived he would be unwilling to lose it, and therefore he concern'd himself highly, and even to jealousie in upholding now that Palace, which if falling, he would out of instinct be the first should leave it. His Majesty about that time labouring to effect his constant promises of Indulgence to his people,[110] the Author therefore walking with his own shadow in the evening took a great fright lest all were agoe.[111] And in this conceit[112] being resolv'd to make good his Figure,[113] and that one Government should not last any longer than the other, he set himself to write those dangerous Books which I have now to do with: wherein, he first makes all that he will to be Law, and then whatsoever is Law to be Divinity. And I shall appeal to all Readers, and I hope make it good, that never in any age, by any man (that I may not say any Church-man) have there been published Discourses either so erroneously founded, or so foully managed, or of so pernicious consequence. In conclusion, this is that man who insists so much and stirrops himself[114] upon the Gravity of his Profession, and the Civility of his Education: which if he had in the least observed in respect

[102] President of Trinity College, Oxford and Dean of Wells Cathedral; responsible for Parker's turn to the Episcopal church

[103] refinement

[104] *censure* means both judgment and blame

[105] engaged

[106] In 1667 Parker became chaplain to Archbishop Sheldon and came to reside at Lambeth. Many preferments followed rapidly.

[107] at odd times

[108] small coin; perhaps here, put his bet up

[109] the London residence of the Archbishop of Canterbury

[110] allowance of religious freedom, contrary to the Church of England

[111] gone [112] thought

[113] See note 96.

[114] rises in the stirrup, prides himself (?)

either to himself or others, I should, I could never have made so bold with him. And nevertheless, it being so necessary to represent him in his own likeness that it may appear what he is to others, and to himself, if possibly he might at last correct his indecencies, I have not committed any fault of stile, nor even this tediousness, but in his imitation. I have not used any harsh expressions but what were suitable to that Civility of Education which he practises, and that Gravity of Profession which he hath set up of: and even therein I have taken care, beside what my nature hath taken care for, to shoot below the mark, and not to retaliate to the same degree; being willing, as I must yield him the preference for many good qualities, so in his worst however to give him the precedence. And yet withall that it hath been thus far the odiousest task that ever I undertook, and has look'd to me all the while like the cruelty of a Living Dissection, which, however, it may tend to publick instruction, and though I have pick'd out the most noxious[115] Creature to be anatomiz'd, yet doth scarse excuse or recompence the offensiveness of the scent and fouling of my fingers. Therefore I will here break off abruptly, leaving many a vein not laid open, and many a passage not search'd into; . . .

[After taking up a number of minor points, Marvell comes to the general issue of the king's power and the purpose of the laws. The power of the magistrates does most certainly issue, he holds, from the divine authority. But "the modester question . . . would be, how far it is advisable for a prince to exert and push the rigor of that power which no man can deny him." Christianity supports government, but where the magistrate clashes with the rules and ends of Christianity, he subverts his own power. Christianity obliges men to a very hard duty, being of the inner life. Thus Marvell attacks Parker's doctrine of absolute submission to the sovereign and proceeds to consider the nature and habit of the laws.]

. . . . .

I should be very sory to disseminate in a matter so weighty, any Errour, nay even an unseasonable or dangerous Truth; none being more desirous or more sensible of the Necessity of Publick Obedience. And therefore as I have consulted none to make them conscious[116] or culpable of what mistake I may run into, so if any shall convince me of one herein, I shall ingenuously retract it. But if this appear to be sufficient in reason for the preserving of Government, 'tis probable that it will prove to be so likewise in fact, and that there is no further provision made for the Magistrate. I do suppose therefore that the true stress and force of Laws lyes in their aptitude and convenience for the general good of the People; and no Magistrate is so wanton as to make Laws meerly out of the pleasure of Legislation, but out of the prospect of some utility to the Publick. Few Subjects are so capable[117] as to imagine any further Obligation: neither does that opinion lean towards Atheism, but proceeds rather from an honorable apprehension concerning God; that he could not institute Government to the prejudice of mankind, or exact obedience to Laws that are destructive to the Society. Therefore, as long as the Magistrate shall provide Laws that appear useful in the experiment, the whole people will stand by him to exact obedience from the refractory, and pursue them like a Common Enemy. But if it fall out otherwise, that the Laws are inconvenient in the practice, men are so sensible of that, and so dull in Divinity, that, should the Legislator persist never so much, he would danger[118] to be left in the field very single; and should you, Mr. *Necessity Bayes,*[119] inculcate your heart out, the Auditory would scarce be converted. Indeed how is it possible to imagine, and to what purpose, that ever any Magistrate should make Laws but for a general advantage? and who again but would be glad to abrogate them when he finds them pernicious to his Government? And therefore it is very usual to make at first Probationary Laws, and for some term of years only; that both the

[115] harmful

[116] sharing knowledge; Parker had accused Marvell of expressing Milton's views, and Marvell later in the tract explicitly defends Milton

[117] understanding

[118] so the text: be in danger

[119] a reference to *The Rehearsal*

Law-giver and the Subject may see at leisure how proper they are and suitable to the effect for which they were intended. And indeed all Laws however are but Probationers[120] of time; and, though meant for perpetuity, yet, when unprofitable, do as they were made by common consent, so expire by universal neglect,[121] and without Repeal grow Obsolete. There is again beside the Convenience of a Law, another security in the Penalty. For because few Laws are so perfect or convenient, but that some man will out of a vicious temper or interest transgress them; the Penalties too of Pecuniary Mulcts,[122] or of Life, or Limme, or Liberty and whatsoever else are necessary, and doubtless the Magistrate does therein hold the ballance of Justice, and weigh the punishment as near as may be, that it should be proportionable to the offence. And out of that care it is, that Governors make the same fault sometimes capital, otherwhiles Pecuniary,[123] other, Imprisonment, *etc.* but that, whatsoever it is, being once undergone, all men reckon that the Magistrate and Justice are satisfied. For indeed how can Humane Laws bind beyond the declared intention of the Magistrate in them. They who obey them find therein their Convenience and Reward they who break them the Punishment: and upon those two wheels all Government hath turned. But to make all Obedience matter of Salvation, is a Note that I believe no Tyrant ever thought of: and it would be some trouble to calculate, when a Law is alter'd here upon Earth, and the same offence shall one year be Capital, and the next year perhaps thought fit to be Finable; how far the Judicature of Heaven takes the same measures, as it is a sin, in the Damnation: Or suppose the Crime be pardon'd here, why should not the Malefactor plead it too in Heaven? . . .

[120] text, Probatiouers [121] text, negrect

[122] fines [123] of money

John Bunyan

JOHN BUNYAN, the son of a brazier or mender of pots and pans of Elstow near Bedford, was baptized on November 30, 1628. While Bunyan was himself later to describe his parents as of "that rank that is meanest and most despised of all the families in the land," they were certainly not beggars, and he himself received the minimum schooling of the poor, learning to read and write. He early manifested gifts of leadership among his careless contemporaries, and a talent for words that would seem to have found its first expression in profanity. From 1644 to 1647 he served in the Commonwealth army, and presently he married a wife of godly parentage, who brought to the new household only a couple of books of piety destined, however, to exert a considerable influence on Bunyan's own work.

Bunyan's first religious attraction seems to have been to the Established Church, but he continued to indulge in such sports as tip-cat, bell-ringing, and dancing, even on the Sabbath. His conscience was awake, however, and an almost obsessive sensitiveness to the spell of words, particularly phrases from the Scriptures which he was now reading assiduously, drove him along the classic road of anguish for sin and terror of deserved damnation to faith and assurance of salvation, and so to conversion. In 1655 Bunyan was received into the fellowship of the Particular Open-Communion Baptists at Bedford and thereupon settled in that town. Like so many other religious enthusiasts of the day Bunyan proceeded to combine his calling of itinerant tinker with lay preaching on behalf of his sect, an avocation in which he soon made his mark.

But Bunyan was not content just to preach; he began to write, too. It is significant of the religious situation of the time that Bunyan's first printed book was in controversy with the Quakers. Upon the Restoration of Charles II, Bunyan had warning that he was to be seized for unauthorized preaching, but he chose to stand by his principles. He was jailed, and although he was apparently at first given a good deal of liberty, that was soon curtailed, and he was effectively cut off from preaching. He thereupon proceeded to carry on his ministry by writing tracts on prayer and on Christian behavior at home and in the world, *Prison Meditations* in jingling verse, etc. In such works Bunyan became known to a wider public than he had been able to reach with his voice, and with the added prestige of the martyr for independent religious principles. By the time of the publication in 1666 of *Grace Abounding*, the story of his conversion, Bunyan was clearly able to speak with the authority of a recognized leader of the Saints.

Bunyan's second imprisonment from 1666–1672 seems to have afforded him more liberty, which he used for the service of his Church but he published little. At the end of this period in January, 1672, Bunyan's congregation ratified him as their pastor, and in March Bunyan took advantage of Charles II's Declaration of Indulgence not only to sue for his freedom but to secure a license as a preacher. This was granted, and Bunyan proceeded to extend the field of his preaching with great success. To the passion of his first preaching and the sharpness of his controversy Bunyan now seems to have added a wider humanity and breadth of spirit. But his prosperity was short-lived, for in 1675 the withdrawal of the Declaration of Indulgence brough fresh persecution of the Dissenters and a return to prison for John Bunyan. For diversion the prisoner began to write the story of his spiritual experience in allegorical form, and apparently to his surprise found that the great story came out of his mind with ease and abundance. Indeed, the story of his whole life's experience may be said to have been released in the freedom of the allegory of *The Pilgrim's Progress.* It was published in 1678, and its success with the public for which it was destined, the humble and the pious, was immediate. Two years later in 1680 Bunyan gave the opposite side in *The Life and Death of Mr. Badman*, and two years after that he published the immensely complicated and ingenious allegory of *The Holy War*, in which the visions of Revelation jostle the political vicissitudes of the seventeenth century as seen by the millenarian imagination. In 1684 the more serene and gracious humanism of Bunyan's later years found its final expression in the second part of *The Pilgrim's Progress*, a work half of appeasement and half of admonishment of the incipient feminism of some of the women Saints of the time.

The death of Charles II in 1685 made it possible for Bunyan to preach more freely, and this he continued to do with great applause from the Open-Communion Baptists and the more liberal Independents until his death in 1688. He was buried in Bunhill Fields, the famous burial place of the Dissenting great.

Bunyan's *The Pilgrim's Progress* is perhaps the outstanding example of a book that won its first fame among the humble and only then slowly made its way with the literary. Its present position among the acknowledged classics of the English language is the more remarkable because of the contrast between the social and cultural position of its humble and untutored author and the traditionally educated, not to say learned, and artistically-sophisticated orientation of the typical seventeenth-century writer. The "work of the Spirit" or "natural genius" might furnish an adequate explanation to the predilections of an earlier time, but the twentieth-century scholar was bound to wonder whether the genius had been either so untutored or so independent of human aid as Bunyan had claimed.

The resemblances between *The Holy War* and Thomas Bernard's *The Isle of Man* had been noticed in Bunyan's own time, but the full extent of Bunyan's possible literary relations of a conventional type was not apparent until 1904 when J. B. Wharey published *Sources of Bunyan's Allegories*, a study of Bunyan's resemblances to Spenser and Milton and to earlier allegorical traditions. This study made it quite clear that in a lifetime of considerable reading Bunyan had come in contact directly or indirectly with a much more considerable range of learning, human and divine, than his own Scripture-centered prefaces would suggest. The alertness and responsiveness of Bunyan to the religious movements of his time was further developed in what is still the standard life, John Brown, *John Bunyan: His Life, Times and Work* (1885; rev. F. M. Harrison, 1928), and in G. B. Harrison, *John Bunyan: a Study in Personality* (1928). In 1933 G. R. Owst in his epoch-making *Literature and Pulpit in Medieval England* called attention to some striking resemblances between the preaching of the friars and Bunyan's work and suggested the possibility of some as yet unexplored continuities between popular medieval and popular seventeenth-century preaching.

But it remained for W. Y. Tindall to work out the general orientation of Bunyan, his relation to his milieu, and the character of that milieu in *John Bunyan, Mechanick Preacher* (1934). Mr. Tindall, in possession of an extensive background of the popular preaching and propaganda of the time on the radical religious front, demonstrated that Bunyan far from being an isolated and unsupported genius was in fact the voice of a great religious, social, and literary movement, the key to which was to be found in the "mechanick" preacher, the humble, unlettered working-man who combined the pursuit of his secular calling with the preaching of whatever brand of radical sectarian Christianity he believed would save the world. To the Saints to whom he "opened" the Word of God, such a preacher seemed the realization of the primitive Apostolic ideal and the vindication of the freedom of the Holy Spirit, using the meanest of human instruments for the achievement of the divine purpose and demonstrating the value of God-given human gifts without benefit of formal education and in defiance of the artificial hierarchies of society.

The nature of his relations to his fellow Saints made the "mechanick" preacher sensitive to their thoughts and feelings and responsive to their interests and tastes. And particularly after the social and economic disappointments of the mid-century the "mechanick" preacher became the voice of the social unrest of the sects, using traditional Biblical symbols for cautious expression of frustrated rebellion. Above all, he met his auditory on their own ground, using the simplest and clearest of language, intermingling the vulgarities of barn and shop and marketplace with Biblical grandeur and assuaging the familiar miseries of humble life with apocalyptic hopes and visions.

In this tradition Bunyan composed and published a variety of works ranging from controversial tracts and hair-splitting scriptural controversies to verses for children and allegories for men and women. The most passionately personal of his works, *Grace Abounding*, followed the pattern of the classic Enthusiastic preacher's autobiography of the time, the first part treating his conversion, the second, his call and devotion to the ministry. And the incredibly complex allegory of *The Holy War* reflected not only the too familiar vicissitudes of the inner struggles of conversion but the millenarian hopes and aspirations that agitated the ecclesiastical and political scene of those years. *The Life and Death of Mr. Badman*, one of the most popular of Bunyan's works in every sense, combined two of the classic types of the time, the moral dialogue and the story of divine judgment, and as Mr. Tindall has shown, drew heavily on earlier examples. Likewise his *Book for Boys and Girls* used the work of popular emblematists like Wither and Quarles.

But it was in *The Pilgrim's Progress* that his power to transmute the conventions of his tradition was most dramatically illustrated. Not only his allegorical sources, but the commonplaces of the experience of his fellow Saints in conversion, in witness, in trial and persecution, in mutual reassurance and fortification, are transmuted with the sureness that comes from an established tradition. In these great works of Bunyan the innermost heart and life of a large section of seventeenth-century England finds expression, and a rich sub-literary or semi-literary development of popular writing reaches its peak in a literary genius of the first rank.

There is no modern edition of Bunyan's collected works, but there are two nineteenth-century editions, by G. Offor (1852) and H. Stebbing (1859). *Grace Abounding* has been edited by J. Brown and published with *The Pilgrim's Progress* (1888, 1907). It is also available in Everyman's Library (1928). *The Pilgrim's Progress* has found a number of distinguished editors, among whom are: J. Brown (1887), C. H. Firth (1898), J. B. Wharey (1928), who has produced the most scholarly text, and F. M. Harrison (1938). In 1932 F. M. Harrison published *A Bibliography of the Works of John Bunyan.*

Among recent works on Bunyan the most considerable is H. Talon, *John Bunyan: L'Homme et L'Oeuvre* (1948), a thorough and carefully documented study of his work (An English translation appeared in 1951.). Among recent shorter studies are to be noted: C. E. Dugdale, "Bunyan's Court Scenes," University of Toronto Pubs., (1941); R. Sharrock, "Spiritual Autobiography in *The Pilgrim's Progress,*" *RES* XXIV (1948); and M. Hussey, "Bunyan's 'Mr. Ignorance,'" *MLR* XLIV (1949). There is also an essay on Bunyan in F. R. Leavis, *The Common Pursuit* (1951).

from GRACE ABOUNDING TO THE CHIEF OF SINNERS[1]

[After a brief account of his early life and his marriage, Bunyan develops at length the story of his sinfulness, his repentance, and his seeking and striving for assurance of salvation, until he falls into a despair that his sin is not of the nature of theirs for whom Christ died, and therefore he does not share in man's redemption.]

. . . Thus, by the strange and unusual assaults of the Tempter, was my Soul like a Broken Vessel, driven as with the Winds, and tossed sometimes headlong into despair; sometimes upon the Covenant of Works, and sometimes to wish that the new Covenant, and the conditions thereof, might so far forth as I thought my self concerned, be turned another way, and changed. *But in all these, I was but as those that jostle against the Rocks; more broken, scattered and rent.* Oh, the unthought of imaginations, frights, fears and terrors, that are affected by a thorough application of guilt, wielding[2] to desperation! *This is the man that hath his dwelling among the tombs, with the dead; that is always crying out, and cutting himself with stones,* Mar. 5.1.2.3. But I say, all in vain; Desperation will not comfort him, the Old Covenant will not save him: Nay, Heaven and Earth shall pass away before one jot[3] or title[4] of the Word and law of Grace shall fail, or be removed. This I saw, this I felt, and under this I groaned; yet this advantage I got thereby, namely, a farther confirmation of the certainty of the way of Salvation, and that the Scriptures were the Word of God. Oh! I cannot now express what then I saw and felt of the steadiness of Jesus Christ, the Rock of Man's Salvation: What was done, could not be undone, added to, nor altered. I saw, indeed, that sin might drive the Soul beyond Christ, even the sin which is unpardonable; but woe to him that was so driven, for the Word would shut him out.

Thus was I always sinking, whatever I did think, or do. So one day I walked to a neighbouring Town, and sate down upon a Settle[5] in the Street, and fell into a very deep pause[6] about the most fearful state my sin had brought me to; and after long musing,[7] I lifted up my head, but me-thought I saw, as if the Sun that shineth in the Heavens did grudge to give light; and as if the very stones in the Street, and tiles upon the Houses, did bend themselves against me; me-thought that they all combined together, to banish me out of the World; I was abhorred of them, and unfit to dwell among them, or be partaker of their benefits, because I had sinned against the Saviour. Oh, how happy now was every creature, over I was! For they stood fast, and kept their station,[8] but I was gone and lost.

Then breaking out in the bitterness of my Soul, I said to my self, with a grievous sigh *How can God comfort such a wretch as I?* I had no sooner said it, but this returned upon me as an echo doth answer a voice, *This sin is not unto death.* At which I was as if I had been raised out of a Grave, and cried out again, *Lord, how couldst thou find out such a word as this?* For I was filled with admiration[9] at the fitness, and also at the unexpectedness of the sentence. The fitness of the word, the rightness of the timing of it, the power, and sweetness, and light, and glory that came with it also, was marvellous to me to find. I was now, for the time out of doubt, as to that about which I was so much in doubt before: My fears before *were*, that my sin was not pardonable, and so that I had no

[1] Text: 1692 [2] driving [3] the iota
[4] tittle, dot over the *i* [5] bench
[6] suspense [7] meditation
[8] assigned portion [9] astonishment

right to pray, to repent, *etc.* or that if I did, it would be of no advantage, or profit to me. But now, thought I, if *this sin* is not unto death, then it is pardonable; therefore from this I have encouragement to come to God by Christ for mercy; to consider the promise of forgiveness, as that which stands with open arms to receive me, as well as others. This therefore was a great easement[10] to my mind; to wit, that my sin was pardonable, that it was not the sin unto death, (I *Joh.* 5.16.17) None but those that know what my trouble (by their own experience) was, can tell what relief came to my Soul by this consideration: It was a release to me from my former bonds, and a shelter from the former storm: I seemed now to stand upon the same ground with other sinners, and to have as good right to the Word[11] and Prayer as any of they.[12]

Now, I say, I was in hopes that my sin was not unpardonable, but that there might be hopes for me to obtain forgiveness. But, Oh, how Satan now did lay about[13] him, for to bring me down again! But he could by no means do it, neither this day, nor the most part of the next; for this good sentence stood like a mill post[14] at my back: Yet towards the evening of the next day, I felt this word[15] begin to leave me, and to withdraw its supportation[16] from me, and so I returned to my old fears again, but with a great deal of grudging[17] and peevishness, for I feared the sorrow of despair; nor could my faith now longer retain this word.

But the next day at evening, being under many fears, I went to seek the Lord, and as I prayed, I cried, and my Soul cried to him in these words, with strong Cries; *O Lord, I beseech thee, shew me, that thou hast loved me with an everlasting love*, Jer. 31.3. I had no sooner said it, but with sweetness this returned upon me, as an eccho, or sounding again, *I have loved thee with an everlasting love.* Now I went to bed in quiet; also when I awaked the next morning, it was fresh upon my Soul; and I believed it.

But yet the Tempter[18] left me not, for it could not be so little as an hundred times, that he, that day, did labour to break my peace. Oh, the combats and conflicts that I did then meet with, as I strove to hold by this word! That of *Esau* would fly in my face like Lightning: I should be sometimes up and down twenty times in an hour; yet God did bear me up, and keep my heart upon this word; from which I had also, for several days together, very much sweetness, and comfortable hopes of pardon: For thus it was made out unto me, *I loved thee whilst thou wast committing this sin I loved thee before, I love thee still; and I will love thee for ever.*

Yet I saw my sin most barbarous, and a filthy[19] crime, and could not but conclude, and that with great shame and astonishment, that I had horridly abused[20] the holy Son of God; wherefore I felt my soul greatly to love and pity him, and my bowels[21] to yearn towards him; for I saw he was still my friend, and did reward me good for evil; yea, the love and affection that then did burn within, to my Lord and Saviour Jesus Christ, did work, at this time, such a strong and hot desire of revengement[22] upon my self, for the abuse[23] I had done unto him, that, to speak as I then thought, had I had a thousand Gallons of blood within my veins, I could freely then have spilt it all at the command and feet of this my Lord and Saviour.

And as I was thus in musing, and in my studies,[24] considering how to love the Lord, and to express my love to him, that saying came in upon me, *If thou, Lord, shouldst mark iniquity, O Lord, who should stand? but there is forgiveness with thee, that thou mayest be feared*, Psal. 130.4. These were good words to me, especially the latter part thereof, to wit,[25] that there is forgiveness with the Lord that he might be feared; that is, as then I understood it, that he might be loved, and had in rever-

[10] relief [11] the Gospel message
[12] sometimes used for *them* in more informal English of the time
[13] strike out vigorously
[14] post on which a windmill was supported; hence something thick and massive
[15] short utterance, divine communication
[16] countenance
[17] complaining and fretfulness
[18] Satan [19] morally foul
[20] wronged
[21] as seat of emotions; hence heart
[22] retribution, punishment [23] injury
[24] anxious thought [25] that is, namely

ence; for it was thus made out to me, *That the great God did set so high an esteem upon the love of his poor Creatures, that rather than he would go without their love, he would pardon their transgressions.*

And now was that word fulfilled on me, and I was also refreshed by it; *Then shall they be ashamed and confounded, and never open their mouth any more because of their shame, when I am pacified towards them for all that they have done, saith the Lord God*, Ezek. 16.36. Thus was my Soul at this time (and, as I then did think for ever) set at liberty from being afflicted with my former guilt and amazement.[26]

But before many weeks were over, I began to despond again, fearing lest, notwithstanding all that I had enjoyed, yet I might be deceived, and destroyed at the last; for this consideration came strong into my mind, *That whatever comfort and peace I thought I might have from the word of the promise of Life, yet unless there could be found in my refreshment a concurrence and agreement in the Scriptures, let me think what I will thereof, and hold it never so fast, I should find no such thing at the end; for the Scriptures cannot be broken.* Joh. 10.35.

Now began my heart again to ake, and fear I might meet with disappointment at the last. Wherefore I began with all seriousness to examine my former comfort, and to consider whether one that had sinned as I had done, might with confidence trust upon the faithfulness of God, laid down in those words by which I had been comforted; and on which I had leaned my self: But now were brought those sayings to my mind, *For it is impossible for those who were once enlightened, and have tasted the heavenly Gift, and were made partakers of the Holy Ghost, and have tasted the good Word of God, and the Powers of the World to come, if they shall fall away, to renew them again unto Repentance. Heb. 6. For if we sin wilfully, after we have received the knowledge of the truth, there remains no more sacrifice for sin, but a certain fearful looking for of Judgment and fiery indignation, which shall devour the adversaries*, Heb. 10. *Even as* Esau, *who for one morsel of meat, sold his Birth right: For you know how that afterwards, when he would have inherited the blessing, he was rejected, for he found no place of repentance, though he sought it carefully with tears*, Heb. 12.

Now was the Word of the Gospel forced from my Soul; so that no promise or encouragement was to be found in the Bible for me: And now would that saying work upon my spirit to afflict me, *Rejoyce not, O Israel, for Joy as other people*, Hos. 9.1. For I saw indeed, there was cause of rejoycing for those that held to Jesus; but as for me, I had cut my self off by my transgressions, and left my self neither foot-hold, nor hand-hold, amongst all the stays and props in the precious Word of Life.

And truly, I did now feel my self to sink into a gulf, as an house whose foundation is destroyed, I did liken my self, in this condition, unto the case of some child that was fallen into a Mill-pit; who, though it could make some shift to scrabble[27] and sprawl in the water, yet because it could find neither hold for hand nor foot, therefore at last it must die in that condition. So soon as this fresh assault had fastned on my Soul, that Scripture came into my heart, *This for many days*, Dan. 10.14. And indeed, I found it was so; for I could not be delivered, nor brought to peace again, until well-nigh two years and an half were compleatly finished. Wherefore these words, though in themselves, they tended to discouragement, yet to me, who feared this condition would be eternal, they were at sometimes as an help and refreshment to me.

For, thought I, *many days* are not forever, *many days* will have an end; therefore seeing I was to be afflicted, not a few, but *many days*, yet I was glad it was but *for many days*. Thus I say, I could re-call my self sometimes and give my self an help; for as soon as ever the words came into my mind, at first, I knew my trouble would be long; yet this would be but sometimes, for I could not always think on this, nor ever be helped by it, though I did.

Now while these Scriptures lay before me, and laid sin anew at my door, that saying In *Luke* 18.1. with others, did encour-

[26] frenzy

[27] struggle

age me to prayer: Then the Temtper [sic] again laid at me very sore; suggesting, *That neither the Mercy of God, nor yet the Blood of Christ, did at all concern me, nor could they help me for my sin; therefore it was but in vain to pray.* Yet, thought I, *I will pray: But,* said the Tempter, *your sin is unpardonable. Well,* said I, *I will pray. 'Tis to no boot,*[28] said he. *Yet,* said I, *I will pray.* So I went to prayer to God; and while I was at prayer, I uttered words to this effect, *Lord, Satan tells me, that neither thy Mercy, nor Christ's Blood is sufficient to save my Soul: Lord, shall I honour thee most, by believing thou wilt nor canst? Lord, I would fain honour thee, by believing thou wilt and canst.*

And as I was thus before the Lord, that Scripture fastned on my heart, [*O man great is thy faith,*] Mat. 15.28. even as if one had clapped me on the back, as I was on my knees before God: Yet I was not able to believe this, that this was a prayer of faith, till almost six months after; for I could not think that I had faith, or that there should be a word for me to act[29] faith on; therefore I should still be, as sticking in the jaws of desperation, and went mourning up and down, in a sad condition.

There was nothing now that I longed for more, than to be put out of doubt, as to this thing in question, and as I was vehemently desiring to know if there was indeed hopes for me, these words came rolling into my mind, *Will the Lord cast off for ever? and will he be favourable no more? Is his mercy clean gone for ever? doth his promise fail for evermore? Hath God so gotten*[30] *to be gracious? hath he in Anger shut up his tender mercies?* Psal. 77.7, 8, 9. And all the while they run in my mind, me thought,[31] I had this still as the answer, *'Tis a question whether he hath, or no; it may be, he hath not.* Yea, the interrogatory[32] seemed to me, to carry in it a sure affirmation that indeed he had not, nor would so cast off, but would be favourable; that his promise doth not fail, and that he had not forgotten to be gracious, nor would in anger shut up tender mercy: Something also there was upon my heart at the same time, which I cannot now call to mind; which with this Text, did sweeten my heart, and make me conclude, that his mercy might not be quite gone, nor clean gone for ever.

. . . . .

[Yet the alternations of comfort and torment did still continue for some time.]

At another time, though, just before, I was pretty well and savoury in my Spirit,[33] yet suddenly there fell upon me a great cloud of darkness, which did so hide from me the things of God and Christ, that I was as if I had never seen or known them in my life: I was also so over-run in my Soul with a senseless, heartless frame-of-spirit,[34] that I could not feel my Soul to move or stir after *Grace* and *Life* by *Christ;* I was as if my loyns were broken, or as if my hands and feet had been tied or bound with Chains. At this time also I felt some weakness to seize upon my outward man, which made still the other affliction the more heavy and uncomfortable to me.

After I had been in this condition some three or four days, as I was sitting by the fire, I suddenly felt this Word to sound in my Heart, *I must go to Jesus;* at this my former darkness and Atheism fled away, and the blessed things of Heaven were set within my view. While I was on this sudden thus overtaken with Surprize; Wife, said I, is there ever such a Scripture, *I must go to Jesus?* she said she could not tell; therefore I sat musing still to see if I could remember such a place; I had not sat above two or three minutes, but that came bolting in upon me, *And to an innumerable Company of Angels;* and withal, *Hebrews* the twelfth, about the Mount *Sion* was set before mine Eyes, *Heb.* 12.22, 23, 24.

Then with Joy I told my Wife, *O now I know, I know!* but that night was a good night to me, I never had but few better; I longed for the company of some of God's People, that I might have imparted unto them what God had shewed me: Christ was a precious Christ to my Soul that Night, I could scarce lie in my Bed for Joy,

[28] advantage [29] carry out in action
[30] obvious misprint for *forgotten*
[31] it seemed to me
[32] question
[33] full of spiritual savor or delightfulness
[34] disposition of spirit

and Peace, and Triumph, through Christ; this great Glory did not continue upon me until Morning, yet the twelfth of the Author to the *Hebrews*, Heb. 12.22, 23. was a blessed Scripture to me for many days together after this.

The Words are these, *You are come to Mount* Sion, *to the City of the living God, to the Heavenly* Jerusalem, *and to an innumerable company of Angels, to the general Assembly and Church of the first born which are written in Heaven, to God the Judge of all, and to the Spirits of just men made perfect, and to Jesus the Mediator of the New Testament, and to the blood of sprinkling, that speaketh better things than that of* Abel. Thorow this blessed Sentence, the Lord led me over and over, first to this Word, and then to that, and shewed me wonderful glory in every one of them. These words also have oft since this time been great refreshment to my Spirit. Blessed be God for having mercy on me.

from THE PILGRIMS PROGRESS[35]

In the similitude[36] of a DREAM

As I walk'd through the wilderness of this world, I lighted on a certain place, where was a Denn;[37] And I laid me down in that place to sleep: And as I slept I dreamed a Dream. I dreamed, and behold *I saw a Man cloathed with Raggs, standing in a certain place, with his face from*[38] *his own House, a Book*[39] *in his hand, and a great burden*[40] *upon his back.*[41] I looked and saw him open the Book, and Read therein; and as he Read, he wept and trembled: and not being able longer to contain,[42] he brake out with a lamentable cry; saying *what shall I do?*

I saw also that he looked this way, and that way, as if he would run; yet he stood still, because as I perceived, he could not tell which way to go. I looked then, and saw a Man named *Evangelist*[43] coming to him, and asked, *Wherefore dost thou cry?* He answered, Sir, I perceive, by the Book in my hand, that I am Condemned to die,[44] and after that to come to Judgement; and I find that I am not willing to do the first,[45] nor able to do the second.[46]

Then said *Evangelist*, Why not willing to die? since this life is attended with so many evils? The Man answered, Because I fear that this burden that is upon my back, will sinck me lower then the Grave; and I shall fall into *Tophet*.[47] And Sir, if I be not fit to go to Prison, I am not fit (I am sure) to go to Judgement, and from thence to Execution; And the thoughts of these things make me cry.

Then said *Evangelist*, If this be thy condition, why standest thou still? He answered, Because I know not whither to go. Then he gave him a *Parchment-Roll*, and there was written within, *Fly from the wrath to come.*[48]

The Man therefore Read it, and looking upon *Evangelist* very carefully; said, Whither must I fly? Then said *Evangelist*, pointing with his finger over a very wide Field, Do you see yonder Wicket-gate?[49] The Man said, No. Then said the other, Do you see yonder shining light?[50] He said, I think I do. Then said *Evangelist*, Keep that light in your eye, and go up directly

[35] Text: 1678

[36] *I have used similitudes. Hosea 12.10.* [Bunyan's note on title page]

[37] cavern

[38] averted from

[39] the Bible [40] load

[41] Isa. 64.6; Luke 14.33; Ps. 38.4; Hab. 2.2; Act. 16.31. (Here as usual the Biblical citations are Bunyan's own.)

[42] restrain himself

[43] used in Bunyan's time for itinerant preachers, trying to bring the gospel to the unconverted

[44] Heb. 9.27. [45] Job 26[6].21, 22.

[46] Ezek. 22.14.

[47] [a site in the valley of Hinnom in the Old Testament, earlier defiled by human sacrifice, and later used for the burning of the refuse of Jerusalem] Isa. 30.33.

[48] Matt. 37.[3.7.]

[49] Matt. 7.[13.] Ps. 119[105].

[50] II Pet. 1.29.[19.]

thereto, so shalt thou see the Gate; at which when thou knockest, it shall be told thee what thou shalt do.[51]

So I saw in my Dream, that the Man began to run; Now he had not run far from his own door, but his Wife and Children perceiving it, began to cry after him to return: but the Man put his fingers in his Ears,[52] and ran on crying, Life, Life, Eternal Life: so he looked not behind him, but fled towards the middle of the Plain.[53]

The Neighbours also came out to see him run,[54] and as he ran some mocked, others threatned; and some cried after him to return: Now among those that did so, there were two that were resolved to fetch him back by force: The name of the one was *Obstinate*, and the name of the other Pliable. Now by this time the Man was got a good distance from them; But however they were resolved to pursue him; which they did and in little time they over-took him[.] Then said the Man, Neighbours, *Wherefore are you come?* They said, To perswade you to go back with us; but he said, That can by no means be: You dwell, said he, in the City of *Destruction* (the place also where I was born,) I see it to be so; and dying there, sooner or later, you will sink lower then the Grave, into a place that burns with Fire and Brimstone; Be content[55] good Neighbours, and go along with me.

What! said *Obstinate*, *and leave our Friends, and our comforts behind us!*

Yes, said *Christian*, (for that was his name) because that all is not worthy to be compared with a little of that that I am seeking to enjoy,[56] and if you will go along with me, you shall fare as I my self; for there where I go, is enough, and to spare;[57] Come away, and prove[58] my words.

Obst. *What are the things you seek, since you leave all the World to find them?*

Chr. I seek an *Inheritance, incorruptible, undefiled, and that fadeth not away;*[59] and it is laid up[60] in Heaven, and fast[61] there, to be bestowed at the time appointed, on them that diligently seek it.[62]

Ob. *Tush,* said *Obstinate*, *away with your Book; will you go back with us, or no?*

Ch. No, not I, said the other; because I have laid my hand to the plow.[63]

Ob. *Come then, Neighbour* Pliable, *let us turn again, and go home without him; There is a Company of these Craz'd-headed Coxcombs,*[64] *that when they take a fancy*[65] *by the end, are wiser in their own eyes then seven men that can render a Reason.*

Pli. Then said *Pliable*, Don't revile; if what the good *Christian* says is true, the things he looks after, are better then ours: my heart inclines to go with my Neighbour.

Obst. *What! more Fools still? be ruled by me and go back, who knows whither such a brain-sick fellow will lead you? go back, Go back, and be wise.*

Ch. Come with me Neighbour *Pliable*, there are such things to be had which I spoke of, and many more Glories besides; If you believe not me, read here in this Book; and for the truth of what is exprest therein, behold all is confirmed by the blood[66] of him that made it.[67]

Pli. *Well Neighbour* Obstinate (*said* Pliable) *I begin to come to a point; I intend to go along with this good man, and cast in my lot with him: But my good Companion, do you know the way to this desired place?*

Ch. I am directed by a man whose name is *Evangelist* to speed me to a little Gate that is before us, where we shall receive instruction about the way.

Pli. *Come then good Neighbour, let us be going, then they went both together.*

Obst. And I will go back to my place, said *Obstinate*. I will be no Companion of such miss-led fantastical[68] Fellows.

Now I saw in my Dream, that when *Ob-*

[51] *Christ and the way to him cannot be found without the Word.* [Bunyan's marginal note]

[52] Luke 14.26. [53] Gen. 19.17.

[54] *They that fly from the wrath to come, are A Gazing-Stock to the world.* Jer. 20.10. [Bunyan's note]

[55] calm, willing [56] II Cor. 4.18.

[57] Luke 15. [58] test [59] I Pet. 1.4.

[60] put away for safety [61] secure

[62] Heb. 11.16. [63] Luke 9.62. [64] fools

[65] delusion [66] Christ's redeeming blood

[67] Heb. 13.20 2[2].

[68] people with such wild notions

stinate was gon back, *Christian* and *Pliable* went talking over the Plain . . .

. . . . .

[At Pliable's request Christian proceeds to tell him what, according to his book, the place they are seeking will be like.]

Now I saw in my Dream, that just as they had ended this talk, they drew near to a very *Miry Slough*, that was in the midst of the Plain, and they being heedless, did both fall suddenly into the bogg. The name of the Slow was *Dispond*.[69] Here therefore they wallowed for a time, being grieviously bedaubed with the dirt; And *Christian*, because of the burden that was on his back, began to sink in the Mire.

Pli. *Then said* Pliable, *Ah Neighbour Christian, where are you now?*

Ch. Truly, said *Christian*, I do not know.

Pli. At that *Pliable* began to be offended; and angerly, said to his Fellow. *Is this the happiness you have told me all this while of? if we have such ill speed*[70] *at our first setting out, What may we expect, 'twixt this, and our journeys end? May I get out again with my life, you shall possess the brave*[71] *Country alone for me.* And with that he gave a desperate struggle or two, and got out of the Mire, on that side of the Slow which was next to his own House: So away he went, and *Christian* saw him no more.

Wherefore *Christian* was left to tumble[72] in the Slow of *Dispond* alone, but still he endeavoured to struggle to that side of the Slow, that was still further from his own House, and next to the Wicket gate; the which he did, but could not get out, because of the burden that was upon his back; But I beheld in my Dream, that a Man came to him, whose name was *Help*, and asked him, *What he did there?*

Chr. Sir, said *Christian*, I was directed this way by a Man called *Evangelist;* who directed me also to yonder Gate, that I might escape the wrath to come:[73] And as I was going thither, I fell in here.

Help. *But why did you not look for the steps?*[74]

Ch. Fear followed me so hard, that I fled the next[75] way, and fell in.

Help. *Give me thy hand: so he gave him his hand*, and he drew him out upon sound ground,[76] and bid him go on his way.

Then I stepped to him that pluckt him out; and said; Sir, Wherefore, since over this place, is the way from the City of *Destruction*, to yonder *Gate*, is it, that *this* Plat[77] is not mended, that poor Travellers might go thither with more security? And he said unto me, this *Miry slow*, is such a place as cannot be mended: It is the descent whither the scum and filth that attends conviction for sin, doth continually run, and therefore is it called the *Slough of Dispond:* for still as the sinner is awakened about his lost condition, there ariseth in his soul many fears, and doubts, and discouraging apprehensions, which all of them get together, and settle in this place: And this is the reason of the badness of this ground.

It is not the pleasure of the King, that this place should remain so bad;[78] his Labourers also, have by the direction of His Majesties Surveyors, been for above this sixteen hundred years, imploy'd about this patch of ground, if perhaps it might have been mended: yea, and to my knowledge, saith he, *Here* hath been swallowed up, at least, Twenty thousand Cart Loads; Yea Millions of wholesom Instructions, that have at all seasons been brought from all places of the Kings Dominions; (and they that can tell, say, they are the best Materials to make good ground of the place;) If so be it might have been mended, but it is the *Slough of Dispond* still; and so will be, when they have done what they can.

True, there are by the direction of the Law-giver, certain good and substantiall Steps, placed even through the very midst of this *Slough;*[79] but at such time as this place doth much spue out its filth, as it doth against[80] change of weather, these steps are hardly seen; or if they be, Men through the diziness of their heads, step besides; and then they are bemired to purpose,[81] notwithstanding the steps be there;

[69] despondency [70] success
[71] grand [72] wallow
[73] [See Matt. 3.7.]
[74] *The Promises* [Bunyan's note]
[75] the nearest [76] Ps. 40.2.

[77] spot [78] Isa. 35.3, 4.
[79] *The Promises of forgiveness and acceptance to life by faith in Christ.* [Bunyan's note]
[80] in anticipation of
[81] effectively

but the ground is good when they are once got in at the Gate.[82]

. . . . .

[Christian arrived at the Gate, and then went on to the House of the Interpreter. There he saw a number of very instructive sights; and with these in his mind as a stimulus to fresh effort, he resumed his journey.]

Now I saw in my Dream, that the high way up which *Christian* was to go, was fenced on either side with a Wall, and that Wall is called *Salvation.* Up this way therefore did burdened *Christian* run, but not without great difficulty, because of the load on his back.

He ran thus till he came at a place somewhat ascending; and upon that place stood a *Cross,* and a little below in the bottom, a Sepulcher. So I saw in my Dream, that just as *Christian* came up with the *Cross,* his burden loosed[83] from off his Shoulders, and fell from off his back; and began to tumble; and so continued to do, till it came to the mouth of the Sepulcher, where it fell in, and I saw it no more.

Then was Christian glad and lightsom,[84] and said with a merry heart, *He hath given me rest, by his sorrow; and life, by his death.*[85] Then he stood still a while, to look and wonder; for it was very surprizing to him, that the sight of the Cross should thus ease him of his burden. He looked therefore, and looked again, even till the springs that were in his head sent the waters down his cheeks.[86] Now as he stood looking and weeping behold three shining ones came to him, and saluted him, with *Peace be to thee:* so the first said to him, *Thy sins be forgiven.* The second, stript him of his Rags, and cloathed him with change of Raiment. The third also set a mark in his fore-head, and gave him a Roll with a Seal upon it, which he bid him look on as he ran, and that he should give it in at the Cœlestial Gate: so they went their way. Then *Christian* gave three leaps for joy, and went out singing.

. . . . .

[Christian now meets a series of highly symbolic but very lifelike characters, Simple, Sloth, etc., who represent various mistaken approaches to the undertaking in which he is engaged. He is refreshed at a house for Pilgrims and so strengthened to pass through the Valley of Humiliation and achieve the victory in the combat with Apollyon. Then he goes through the Valley of the Shadow of Death to find, when he comes out, Faithful for a companion with whom to talk over the meaning of his experience. Talkative joins them but soon wearies of Faithful's searching questions as to the reality of his religious professions and leaves them.]

Then I saw in my Dream, that when they were got out of the Wilderness, they presently saw a Town before them, and the name of that Town is *Vanity;* and at the Town there is a *Fair* kept, called *Vanity-Fair:* It is kept all the Year long, it beareth the name of *Vanity-Fair,* because the Town where tis kept, *is lighter then* Vanity; and also, because all that is there sold, or that cometh thither, is *Vanity.* As is the saying of the wise, *All that cometh is vanity.*[87]

This Fair is no new erected business, but a thing of Ancient standing; I will shew you the original of it.

Almost five thousand years agone, there were Pilgrims walking to the Cœlestial City, as these two honest[88] persons are; and *Beelzebub, Apollyon,* and *Legion,* with their Companions, perceiving by the path that the Pilgrims made, that their way to the City lay through *this Town* of *Vanity,* they contrived here to set up a Fair; a Fair wherein should be sold of *all sorts of Vanity,* and that it should last all the year long. Therefore at *this Fair* are all such Merchandize sold, as Houses, Lands, Trades, Places, Honours, Preferments,[89] Titles, Countreys, Kingdoms, Lusts, Pleasures and Delights of all sorts, as Whores, Bauds, Wives, Husbands, Children, Masters, Servants, Lives, Blood, Bodies, Souls, Silver, Gold, Pearls, precious Stones, and what not.

And moreover, at this Fair there is at all times to be seen Juglings, Cheats, Games,

[82] I Sa[m]. 12.23.
[83] came unfastened [84] free of care
[85] *When God releases us of our guilt and burden, we are as those that leap for joy.* [Bunyan's note]
[86] Zech. 12.10.
[87] Isa. 40.17. Eccl. I. chap. 2.11, 17.
[88] respectable
[89] promotions, appointments (especially ecclesiastical)

Plays, Fools, Apes, Knaves, and Rogues, and that of all sorts.

Here are to be seen, and that for nothing, Thefts, Murders, Adultries, False-swearers, and that of a blood-red colour.[90]

And as in other fairs of less moment, there are the several Rows and Streets, under their proper names, where such and such Wares are vended: So here likewise, you have the proper Places, Rows, Streets, (*viz.* Countreys, and Kingdoms,) where the Wares of this Fair are soonest to be found. Here is the *Britain* Row, the *French* Row, the *Italian* Row, the *Spanish* Row, the *German* Row, where several sorts of Vanities are to be sold. But as in other *fairs* some one Commodity is as the chief of all the *fair*, so the Ware of *Rome* and her Merchandize is greatly promoted in *this fair:* Only our *English* Nation, with some others, have taken a dislike thereat.

Now, as I said, the way to the Cælestial City lyes just thorow *this Town*, where this lusty[91] Fair is kept; and he that will go to the City, and yet not go thorow this Town, *must* needs *go out of the World*.[92] The Prince of Princes himself, when here, went through *this Town* to his own Countrey, and that upon a *Fair-day too:* Yea, and as I think, it was *Beelzebub*[93] the chief Lord of this *Fair*, that invited him to buy of his *Vanities;* yea, would have made him Lord of the *Fair*, would he but have done him Reverence as he went thorow the *Town*. Yea, because he was such a person of Honour, *Beelzebub* had him from *Street* to *Street*, and shewed him all the Kingdoms of the World in a little time, that he might, if possible, alure that Blessed One, to *cheapen*[94] and *buy* some of his *Vanities*.[95] But he had no mind[96] to the Merchandize, and therefore left the *Town*, without laying out so much as one Farthing[97] upon these *Vanities*. This *Fair* therefore is an Ancient thing, of long standing, and a very great *Fair*.

Now these Pilgrims, as I said, must needs go thorow this *fair:* Well, so they did; but behold, even as they entred into the *fair*, all the people in the *fair* were moved, and the Town itself as it were in a Hubbub about them; and that for several reasons: For,

First, The Pilgrims were cloathed with such kind of Raiment, as was diverse[98] from the Raiment of any that Traded in that *fair*. The people therefore of the *fair* made a great gazing[99] upon them: Some said they were Fools, some they were Bedlams,[100] and some they are Outlandish-men.[101]

Secondly, And as they wondred at their Apparel, so they did likewise at their Speech, for few could understand what they said;[102] they naturally spoke the Language of *Canaan*,[103] but they that kept the *fair*, were the men of this World: So that from one end of the fair to the other, they seemed Barbarians[104] each to the other.

Thirdly, But that which did not a little amuse the Merchandizers,[105] was, that these Pilgrims set very light by[106] all their Wares, they cared not, so much as to look upon them: and if they called upon them to buy, they would put their fingers in their ears, and cry, *Turn away mine eyes from beholding vanity;* and look upwards, signifying that their Trade[107] and Traffick[108] was in Heaven.[109]

One chanced mockingly, beholding the carriages[110] of the men, to say unto them, What will ye buy? but they, looking gravely upon him, said, *We buy the Truth*.[111] At that, there was an occasion taken to despise[112] the men the more; some

[90] in reference to oaths by Christ's blood, etc. (?)
[91] merry
[92] I Cor. 5.10. *Christ went through this fair.* [Bunyan's note]
[93] in the Bible the Prince of the Devils
[94] bargain for
[95] Matt. 4.8.; Luke 4, 5.6, 7.
[96] inclination to
[97] the quarter of a penny
[98] different in character
[99] gazed conspicuously
[100] inmates of Bethlehem Hospital for the insane, London; especially discharged patients licensed to beg
[101] foreign
[102] I Cor. 2.7, 8.
[103] the Land of Promise of the Israelites; hence heaven
[104] foreigners, whose language and customs are different
[105] dealers in commodities
[106] accounted of very small value
[107] occupation
[108] buying and selling
[109] Ps. 119.37.; Phil. 3.19, 20.
[110] manner of carrying themselves
[111] Prov. 23, [23].
[112] show contempt for

mocking, some taunting, some speaking reproachfully, and some calling upon others to smite them. At last things came to an hubbub and great *stir* in the fair, in so much that all order was confounded. Now was word presently brought to the *great one*[113] of the *fair*, who quickly came down, and deputed some of his most trusty friends to take these men into examination, about whom the *fair* was almost overturned. So the men were brought to examination; and they that sat upon[114] them, asked them whence they came, whether[115] they went, and what they did there in such an unusual Garb? The men told them, that they were Pilgrims and Strangers in the World, and that they were going to their own Countrey, which was the Heavenly *Jerusalem;* and that they had given none[116] occasion[117] to the men of the Town, nor yet to the Merchandizers, thus to abuse them, and to let[118] them in their Journey. Except it was, for that, when one asked them what they would buy, they said they would *buy the Truth*. But they that were appointed to examine them, did not believe them to be any other then Bedlams and Mad, or else such as came to put all things into a confusion in the *fair*. Therefore they took them and beat them, and besmeared them with dirt, and then put them into the Cage, that they might be made a Spectacle to all the men of the *fair*.

. . . . .

Then a convenient time being appointed, they brought them forth to their Tryal in order to[119] their condemnation. When the time was come, they were brought before their Enemies and arraigned; the Judge's name was Lord *Hategood*. Their Indictment was one and the same in substance, though somewhat varying in form; the Contents whereof was this.

That they were enemies to, and disturbers of their Trade; that they had made Commotions and Divisions in the Town, and had won a party to their own most dangerous opinions, in contempt of the Law of their Prince.

Then *Faithful* began to answer, That he had only set himself against that which had set it self against him that is higher then the highest.[120] And said he, As for disturbance, I make none, being my self a man of Peace; the Party[121] that were won to us, were won by beholding our Truth and Innocence, and they are only turned from the worse to the better. And as to the King you talk of, since he is *Beelzebub*, the Enemy of our Lord, I defie him and all his Angels.

Then Proclamation was made, that they that had ought to say for their Lord the King against the Prisoner at the Bar, should forthwith appear and give in their evidence. So there came in three Witnesses, to wit,[122] *Envy*, *Superstition*, and *Pickthank*.[123] They was[124] then asked, If they knew the Prisoner at the Bar? and what they had to say for their Lord the King against him.

Then stood forth *Envy*, and said to this effect; My Lord, I have known this man a long time, and will attest upon my Oath before this honourable Bench, That he is—

Judge. Hold, give him his Oath; So they sware him. Then he said, My Lord, This man, notwithstanding his plausible[125] name, is one of the vilest men in our Countrey; He neither regardeth[126] Prince nor People, Law nor Custom: but doth all that he can to possess[127] all men with certain of his disloyal notions, which he in the general[128] calls Principles of Faith and Holiness. And in particular, I heard him once my self affirm, *That Christianity, and the Customs of our Town of* Vanity, *were Diametrically opposite*[129] *and could not be reconciled*. By which saying, my Lord, he doth at once, not only condemn all our laudable doings, but us in the doing of them.

Judg. Then did the Judge say to him, Hast thou any more to say?

Env. My Lord I could say much more, only I would not be tedious to the Court. Yet if need be, when the other Gentlemen have given in their Evidence, rather then any thing shall be wanting that will dispatch[130] him, I will enlarge my Testimony

[113] lord [114] sat in judgment upon
[115] whither [116] not one
[117] excuse [118] obstruct
[119] for the purpose of [120] God
[121] company [122] that is
[123] flatterer, sycophant
[124] plural
[125] pleasing [126] has respect for
[127] put in possession [128] in general terms
[129] in opposition [130] get rid of

against him. So he was bid stand by. Then they called *Superstition*, and bid[131] him look upon the Prisoner; they also asked, What he could say for their Lord the King against him? Then they sware him so he began.

Super. My Lord, I have no great acquaintance[132] with this man, nor do I desire to have further knowledge of him; However this I know, that he is a very pestilent fellow, from some discourse[133] that the other day I had with him in this *Town;* for then talking with him, I heard him say, That our Religion was naught,[134] and such by which a man could by no means please God: which sayings of his, my Lord, your Lordship very well knows, what necessarily thence will follow, *two wit*, That we still do worship in vain, are yet in our Sins, and finally shall be damned; and this is that which I have to say.

Then was *Pickthank* sworn, and bid say what he knew, in behalf of their Lord the King against the Prisoner at the Bar.

Pick. My Lord, and you Gentlemen all, This fellow I have known of a long time, and have heard him speak things that ought not to be spoke. For he hath railed[135] on our noble Prince *Beelzebub*, and hath spoke contemptibly[136] of his honourable Friends, whose names are the Lord *Oldman*,[137] the Lord *Carnal delight*, the Lord *Luxurious*, the Lord *Desire of Vain-glory*, my old Lord *Lechery*, Sir *Having Greedy*,[138] with all the rest of our Nobility;[139] and he hath said moreover, that if all men were of his mind, if possible, there is not one of these noble Men should have any longer a being[140] in this Town. Besides, he hath not been afraid to rail on you, my Lord, who are now appointed to be his Judge, calling you an ungodly Villian, with many other such like vilifying terms, by which he hath bespattered most of the Gentry of our Town. When this *Pickthank* had told his tale, the Judge directed his speech to the Prisoner at the Bar, saying, Thou Runagate,[141] Heretick, and Traitor, hath thou heard what these honest[142] Gentlemen have witnessed against thee?

Faith. *May I speak a few words in my own defence?*

Judg. Sirrah, Sirrah, thou deservest to live no longer, but to be slain immediately upon the place; yet that all may see our gentleness towards thee, let us see what thou hast to say.

Faith. 1. I say then in answer to what Mr. *Envy* hath spoken, I never said ought[143] but this, *That what*[144] *Rule, or Laws, or Custom, or People, were flat against the Word of God, are diametrically opposite to Christianity*. If I have said a miss in this, convince me of my errour, and I am ready here before you to make my recantation.

2. As to the second, to wit, Mr. *Superstition*, and his charge against me, I said only this, *That in the worship of God there is required a divine Faith; but there can be no divine Faith, without a divine Revelation of the will of God: therefore whatever is thrust*[145] *into the worship of God, that is not agreeable*[146] *to a divine Revelation, cannot be done but by an humane*[147] *Faith, which Faith will not profit*[148] *to Eternal life*.

3. As to what Mr. *Pickthank* hath said, I say, (avoiding terms, as that I am said to rail, and the like) That the Prince of this Town, with all the Rablement[149] his Attendants, by this Gentlemen named, are more fit for a being in Hell, then in this Town and Countrey; *and so the Lord have mercy upon me*.

Then the Judge called to the Jury (who all this while stood by, to hear and observe) Gentlemen of the Jury, you see this man about whom so great an uproar hath been made in this Town: you have also heard what these worthy Gentlemen have witnessed against him; also you have heard his reply and confession: It lieth[150] now in

[131] bade [132] personal knowledge
[133] conversation [134] an evil thing
[135] uttered abusive language
[136] contemptuously
[137] *theologically*, unregenerate human nature
[138] greedy for possessions (?)
[139] *Sins are all Lords and Great ones* [Bunyan's note]
[140] position [141] apostate
[142] worthy [143] aught, anything
[144] whatever [145] interpolated
[146] conformable
[147] belonging to man as distinguished from God
[148] advance [149] rabble
[150] rests

your brests[151] to hang him, or save his life. But yet I think meet[152] to instruct you into our Law.

There was an Act made in the days of *Pharaoh* the Great, Servant to our Prince, that lest those of a contrary Religion should multiply and grow too strong for him, their Males should be thrown into the River.[153] There was also an Act made in the days of *Nebuchadnezzar* the Great, another of his Servants, That whoever would not fall down and worship his golden Image, should be thrown into a fiery Furnace.[154] There was also an Act made in the days of *Darius*, That who so, for some time, called upon any God but his, should be cast into the Lions Den.[155] Now the substance of these Laws this Rebel has broken, not only in thought (which is not to be born) but also in word and deed; which must therefore needs be intolerable.

For that of *Pharaoh*, his Law was made upon a supposition,[156] to prevent mischief, no Crime being yet apparent; but here is a Crime apparent. For the second and third, you see he disputeth against our Religion; and for the Treason he hath confessed, he deserveth to die the death.

Then went the Jury out, whose names were Mr. *Blind-man*, Mr. *No-good*, Mr. *Malice*, Mr. *Love-lust*, Mr. *Live-loose*, Mr. *Heady*, Mr. *High-mind*,[157] Mr. *Enmity*, Mr. *Lyar*, Mr. *Cruelty*, Mr. *Hate-light*, and Mr. *Implacable*, who every one gave in his private Verdict against him among themselves, and afterwards unanimously concluded to bring him in Guilty before the Judge. And first Mr. *Blind-man*, the foreman, said, *I see clearly that this man is an Heretick*. Then said Mr. *No-good*, *Away with such a fellow from the Earth*. *Ay*, said Mr. *Malice*, *for I hate the very looks of him*. Then said Mr. *Love-lust*, *I could never indure*[158] *him*. *Nor I*, said Mr. *Live-loose*, *for he would alwayes be condemning my way*. *Hang him, hang him*, said Mr. *Heady*. *A sorry Scrub*,[159] said Mr. *High-mind*. *My heart riseth against him*, said Mr. *Enmity*. *He is a Rogue*, said Mr. *Lyar*. *Hanging is too good for him*, said Mr. *Cruelty*. *Lets dispatch him out of the way*, said Mr. *Hate-light*. Then said Mr. *Implacable*, *Might I have all the World given me, I could not be reconciled to him, therefore let us forthwith*[160] *bring him in guilty*[161] *of death:* And so they did, therefore he was presently Condemned, To be had[162] from the place where he was, to the place from whence he came, and there to be put to the most cruel death that could be invented.

They therefore brought him out, to do with him according to their Lay;[163] and first they Scourged him, then they Buffetted him, then they Lanced his flesh with Knives; after that, they Stoned him with Stones, then prickt him with their Swords, and last of all they burned him to Ashes at the Stake. Thus came *Faithful* to his end. Now, I saw that there stood behind the multitude, a Chariot and a couple of Horses, waiting for *Faithful*, who (so soon as his adversaries had dispatched him) was taken up into it, and straight-way was carried up through the Clouds, with sound of Trumpet, the nearest way to the Cœlestial Gate. But as for *Christian*, he had some respit, and was remanded back to prison, so he there remained for a space: But he that over-rules all things, having the power of their rage in his own hand, so wrought it about,[164] that *Christian* for that time escaped them, and went his way.

Well Faithful, *thou hast faithfully profest*
Unto thy Lord: with him thou shalt be blest;
When Faithless *ones, with all their vain delights,*
Are crying out under their hellish plights
Sing, Faithful, *sing; and let thy name survive,*
For though they kill'd thee, thou art yet alive.

Now I saw in my Dream, that *Christian* went not forth alone, for there was one whose name was *Hopeful*, (being made so by the beholding of *Christian* and *Faithful* in their words and behaviour, in their sufferings at the *fair*) who joyned himself unto him, and entering into a brotherly convenant, told him that he would be his Companion. Thus one died to make[165] Testimony to the Truth, and another rises

[151] hearts [152] proper [153] Exod. 1.
[154] Dan. 3. [155] Dan. 6.
[156] suspicion, expectation
[157] haughty, arrogant

[158] endure [159] person of mean presence
[160] immediately [161] deserving
[162] taken [163] arrangement
[164] brought it about [165] render

out of his Ashes to be a Companion with *Christian.* This *Hopeful* also told *Christian,* that there were many more of the men in the *fair* that would take their time and follow after.

So I saw that quickly after they were got out of the *fair,* they overtook one that was going before them, whose name was *By-ends;*[166] so they said to him, What Countrey-man,[167] Sir? and how far go you this way? He told them, That he came from the Town of *Fair-speech,* and he was going to the Cœlestial City, (but told them not his name.)

From Fair-speech, *said* Christian; *is there any that be good live there?*

By-ends. Yes, said *By-ends,* I hope.

Chr. *Pray Sir, what may I call you?*

By-ends. I am a Stranger to you, and you to me; if you be going this way, I shall be glad of your Company; if not, I must be content.

Chr. *This Town of Fair-*speech, *I have heard of it, and, as I remember, they say its a Wealthy place.*

By-ends. Yes, I will assure you that it is, and I have very many Rich Kindred there.

Chr. *Pray who are your Kindred there, if a man may be so bold?*

By-ends, To tell you Truth, I am a Gentleman of good Quality;[168] yet my Great Grand-father was but a Water-man,[169] looking one way, and Rowing another; and I got most of my Estate by the same occupation.

Chr. *Are you a Married man?*

By-ends. Yes, and my Wife is a very Virtuous woman, the Daughter of a Virtuous woman: She was my Lady *Fainings*[170] Daughter, therefore she came of a very Honourable Family, and is arrived to such a pitch[171] of Breeding, that she knows how to carry[172] it to all, even to Prince and Peasant. 'Tis true, we somewhat differ in Religion from those of the stricter sort, yet but in two small points: First, we never strive against Wind and Tide. Secondly, we are alwayes most zealous when Religion goes in his Silver Slippers; we love much to walk with him in the Street, if the Sun shines, and the people applaud it.

Then Christian stept a little a toside[173] to his Fellow *Hopeful,* saying, It runs in my mind that this is one *By-ends* of *Fair-speech,* and if it be he, we have as very[174] a Knave in our Company, as dwelleth in all these parts. Then said *Hopeful, Ask him; methinks*[175] *he should not be ashamed of his name.* So *Christian* came up with him again, and said, Sir, you talk as if you knew something more then[176] all the World doth, and if I take not my mark[177] amiss, I deem[178] I have half a guess of you: Is not your name Mr. *By-ends* of *Fair-speech?*

By-ends. That is not my name, but indeed it is a Nick-name that is given me by some that cannot abide me, and I must be content to bear it as a reproach, as other good men have born theirs before me.

Chr. *But did you never give an occasion to men to call you by this name?*

By-ends. Never, never! The worst that ever I did to give them an occasion to give me this name, was, That I had alwayes the luck to jump in my Judgement with the present way of the times, whatever it was, and my chance was to get[179] thereby; but if things are thus cast[180] upon me, let me count them a blessing, but let not the malicious load me therefore with reproach.

Chr. *I thought indeed that you was the man that I had heard of, and to tell you what I think, I fear this name belongs to you more properly then you are willing we should think it doth.*

By-ends. Well, If you will thus imagine, I cannot help it. You shall find me a fair Company-keeper,[181] if you will still admit me your associate.

Chr. *If you will go with us, you must go against Wind and Tide, the which, I perceive, is against your opinion: You must also own Religion in his Rags, as well as when in his Silver Slippers, and stand by him too, when bound in Irons, as well as when he walketh the Streets with applause.*

By-ends. You must not impose,[182] nor Lord it over my Faith; leave me to my liberty, and let me go with you.

Chr. *Not a step further, unless you will do in what I propound,*[183] *as we.*

Then said *By-ends,* I shall never desert

[166] from *by-end,* a secret selfish purpose
[167] from what district? [168] social position
[169] boatman [170] Feigning [171] apex
[172] gain the advantage [173] aside to (?)

[174] unqualified [175] it seems to me
[176] than [177] target [178] judge [179] gain
[180] raked up and uttered as a reproach
[181] reveller [182] intrude upon [183] propose

my old Principles, since they are harmless and profitable. If I may not go with you, I must do as I did before you overtook me, even go by my self, untill some overtake me that will be glad of my Company.

Then *Christian* and *Hopeful* out-went[184] him.

. . . . .

[They went on, through the Plain of Ease, to the River of God, and along the river to By-Path Meadow. There they fell into the hands of Giant Despair but escaped, and went on to the Delectable Mountains. From there they set out along the Highway to the Cœlestial City, talking together of faith. Once they were entrapped by Flatterer but released by a "shining One," who chastized them to teach them the way they should go. They resisted the drowsy air of the Inchanted Ground with talk of Hopeful's spiritual history until they came into the Country of Beulah within sight of the City. As they started to go up to the City, there came to meet them two men "in Raiment that shone like Gold."]

Christian then and his Companion asked the men to go along with them, so they told them they would; but, said they, you must obtain it[185] by your own faith. So I saw in my Dream that they went on together till they came within sight of the Gate.

Now I further saw that betwixt them and the Gate was a River,[186] but there was no Bridge to go over, the River was very deep; at the sight therefore of this River, the Pilgrims were much stounded,[187] but the men that went with them, said, You must go through, or you cannot come at the Gate.[188]

The Pilgrims then, began to enquire if there was no other way to the Gate; to which they answered, Yes, but there hath not any, save two, to wit, *Enoch*[189] and *Elijah*,[190] been permitted to tread that path, since the foundation of the World, nor shall, untill the last Trumpet shall sound.[191] The Pilgrims then, especially *Christian*, began to dispond in his mind, and looked this way and that, but no way could be found by them, by which they might escape the River. Then they asked the men, if the Waters were all of a depth. They said, No; yet they could not help them in that Case,[192] for said they: *You shall find it deeper or shallower, as you believe in the King of the place.*

They then addressed themselves to the Water; and entring, *Christian* began to sink, and crying out to his good Friend *Hopeful;* he said, I sink in deep Waters, the Billows go over my head, all his Waves go over me, *Selah*.[193] Then said the other, Be of good chear, my Brother, I feel the bottom, and it is good. Then said *Christian*, Ah my friend, the sorrows of death have compassed me about, I shall not see the Land that flows with Milk and Honey.[194] And with that, a great darkness and horror fell upon *Christian*, so that he could not see before him; also here he in great measure lost his senses, so that he could neither remember nor orderly talk of any of those sweet refreshments[195] that he had met with in the way of his Pilgrimage. But all the words that he spake, still tended to discover that he had horror of mind, and hearty fears that he should die in that River, and never obtain entrance in at the Gate: here also, as they that stood by, perceived, he was much in the troublesome thoughts of the sins that he had committed, both since and before he began to be a Pilgrim. 'Twas also observed, that he was troubled with apparitions of Hogoblins[196] and Evil Spirits. For ever and anon[197] he would intimate so

184 outstripped 185 arrival at the City

186 *Death* [Bunyan's note]

187 stupefied with bewilderment

188 *Death is not welcome to nature though by it we pass out of this World into glory.* [Bunyan's note]

189 Old Testament figure, who because of his faithfulness was directly translated by God (See Gen. 5.18–24.)

190 a famous prophet in the Old Testament, who was carried to heaven in a chariot of fire (See II Kings 2.)

191 I Cor. 15.51, 52.

192 *Angels help us not comfortably through death.* [Bunyan's note]

193 a word of unknown significance, often recurring in the Psalms, probably a musical or liturgical sign

194 Christians *conflict at the hour of death.* [Bunyan's note]

195 here used in a spiritual sense

196 hobgoblins, terrifying apparitions

197 every now and then

much by words. *Hopeful* therefore here had much adoe[198] to keep his Brothers head above water, yea sometimes he would be quite gone down, and then ere a while[199] he would rise up again half dead.

. . . . . .

Then they both took courage, and the enemy[200] was after that as still as a stone, untill they were gone over. *Christian* therefore presently found ground to stand upon; and so it followed that the rest of the River was but shallow. Thus they got over. Now upon the bank of the River, on the other side, they saw the two shining men again, who there waited for them. Wherefore being come up out of the River, thy [sic] saluted them saying, *We are ministering Spirits, sent forth to minister for those that shall be Heirs of Salvation.* Thus they went along towards the Gate, now you must note that the City stood upon a mighty hill, but the Pilgrims went up that hill *with ease*, because they had these two men to lead them up by the Arms; also they had left their *Mortal* Garments behind them in the River;[201] for though they went in with them, they came out without them. They therefore went up here with much agility and speed, though the foundation upon which the City was framed was higher then the Clouds. They therefore went up through the Regions of the Air, sweetly talking as they went, being comforted,[202] because they safely got over the River, and had such glorious Companions to attend them.

. . . . . .

Now while they were thus drawing towards the Gate, behold a company of the Heavenly Host[203] came out to meet them: To whom it was said, by the other two shining Ones, These are the men that have loved our Lord, when they were in the World; and that have left all for his holy Name, and he hath sent us to fetch them, and we have brought them thus far on their desired Journey; that they may go in and look their Redeemer in the face with joy. Then the Heavenly Host gave a great shout, saying, *Blessed are they that are called to the Marriage Supper of the Lamb:*[204] and thus they came up to the Gate.

Now when they were come up to the Gate, there was written over it, in Letters of Gold, *Blessed are they that do his commandments, that they may have right to the Tree of life; and may enter in through the Gates into the City.*[205]

Then I saw in my Dream, that the shining men bid them call at the Gate, the which when they did, some from above looked over the Gate; to wit, *Enoch*, *Moses*,[206] and *Elijah*, *etc.* to whom it was said, These Pilgrims, are come from the City of *Destruction*, for the love that they bear to the King of this place: and then the Pilgrims gave in unto them each man his Certificate, which they had received in the beginning; Those therefore were carried into the King, who when he had read them, said, Where are the men? to whom it was answered, They are standing without the Gate, the King then commanded to open the Gate; *That the righteous Nation*, said he, *that keepeth Truth may enter in.*[207]

Now I saw in my Dream, that these two men went in at the Gate; and loe, as they entered, they were transfigured, and they had Raiment put on that shone like Gold. There was also[208] that met them with Harps and Crowns, and gave them to them; The Harp to praise withall, and the Crowns in token of honour; Then I heard in my Dream that all the Bells of the City Rang for joy: and that it was said unto them, *Enter ye into the joy of your Lord.*[209] I also heard the men themselves, that they

[198] much trouble
[199] presently
[200] the Devil
[201] *They have put off mortality.* [Bunyan's note]
[202] heartened
[203] multitude (See Luke 2.13.)
[204] Rev. 19.
[205] Re[v]. 22.14.
[206] the great lawgiver and leader of the Children of Israel whom the Lord buried in an unknown grave
[207] Isa. 26.2.
[208] some pronominal word like *those* omitted but understood here
[209] See Matt. 25.21.

sang with a loud voice, saying, *Blessing, Honour, Glory and Power, be to him that sitteth upon the Throne, and to the Lamb for ever and ever.*[210]

Now just as the Gates were opened to let in the men, I looked in after them; and behold, the City shone like the Sun, the Streets also were paved with Gold, and in them walked many men, with Crowns on their heads, Palms in their hands, and golden Harps to sing praises withall.[211]

There were also of them that had wings, and they answered one another without intermission, saying, *Holy, Holy, Holy, is the Lord.* And after that, they shut up the Gates: which when I had seen, I wished my self among them.

. . . . .

[210] Rev. 5.13, 14.

[211] therewith

Sir William Temple

SIR WILLIAM TEMPLE (1628–1699) came of a family closely associated with Irish affairs, his grandfather having gone over to Ireland in 1609 to assume the post of Provost of Trinity College, Dublin, his father holding office as Master of the Rolls both before and after the Restoration. Because of the death of his mother in 1638 and his father's absence in Ireland, Temple was brought up by his uncle, Dr. Henry Hammond, an eminent Anglican divine. In 1644 he was entered as a fellow-commoner at Emmanuel College, Cambridge, where he had as tutor Ralph Cudworth, the Platonist. Temple took no degree, but in 1648, apparently with the intention of preparing himself for the diplomatic service, set out upon his foreign travels. On his way to France he stopped at the Isle of Wight, where he met his future wife, Dorothy Osborne, en route to join her royalist father in France. Temple spent much of the ensuing four years in France, Holland, and Flanders, and it was during this period that he wrote a number of early essays and prose romances—the latter for the amusement of Dorothy Osborne, whose letters to him, likewise of this period, have charmed so many since the first of them were published in 1836. After long opposition by both families, Temple and Dorothy were married on Christmas Day, 1654. Temple's first period of diplomatic service began in 1665, when he was sent on a mission to the Bishop of Munster. Following his appointment to the residency at Brussels—shortly after which he was made a Baronet—he helped negotiate the famous Triple Alliance of 1668, by which England, Holland, and Sweden united to form a common front against France. It was not Charles's intention, however, to bring about a permanent rift with France, and through the Secret Treaty of Dover with France (1670) plans were devised which in 1672 resulted in England's declaring war against Holland. Temple, now English ambassador at the Hague, was recalled in 1671. The next three years he spent in retirement, writing a number of pamphlets on public affairs, of which the most notable was the *Observations upon the United Provinces of the Netherlands*, published in 1672 with the intention of presenting a sympathetic view of Holland. Temple's second period of public service, which began in 1674 when he was called upon to help negotiate peace with Holland, included two embassies to the Hague and ended with his retirement from public life early in 1681. He had returned to England early in 1679, and in the ensuing months had worked for national unity in the face of the bitter partisanship of those days and the turmoil raised by the Plot. But his council of moderation—he was deeply mistrustful of the Monmouth faction and of Shaftsbury, its leader—led nowhere, his scheme for the reorganization of the Privy Council miscarried, and though elected to the second Whig Parliament in 1679, he refused to stand for election in 1681, and retired to his house at Sheen, near Richmond. In 1679 he had published his first *Miscellanea*, containing a number of essays among which was one, *Upon the Original and Nature of Government*, intended among other things to acquit him of the charge of having, as a member of the Privy Council, favored absolutism in government. During his final period (1681–1699), residing at Sheen and later at Moor Park in Surrey, he composed his *Memoirs* and the greater part of his essays. He seems to have played no part in the events leading up to the Revolution, but King William, who as prince of Orange had come to know and admire Temple when the latter was Ambassador at the Hague, is said to have made two or three visits to Sheen in an unsuccessful attempt to persuade the retired statesman to reënter public life as Secretary of State. It may well be that the publication in 1691 of one book of Temple's *Memoirs* was the result of the author's desire to display to the English people the King's admirable conduct in the '70's. In 1689 Swift, recommended no doubt by his relatives in Ireland, became a member of the Temple household, acting as secretary at three different periods extending down to Temple's death in January, 1699, and undertaking—against those who were attacking Temple's essay *Upon the Ancient and Modern Learning*—the defense of his patron in *The Battle of the Books* and *A Tale of a Tub*, largely composed at Moor Park but not published until 1704.

The chief publications during Temple's lifetime were the *Observations upon the United Provinces* (1672), *Miscellanea, the first part* (1679), *Miscellanea, the second part* (1690), and *Memoirs . . . 1672 to . . . 1679* (1691; known as *Memoirs, Part* II). Swift, his literary executor, brought out *Miscellanea, the third part* (1701), three volumes of *Letters* (1700, 1703), and Part III of the *Memoirs* (1709; Part I never appeared). The first collected edition of Temple's works appeared in 1720, the four-volume edition of 1814 being still the standard one. Several of the essays have appeared in modern editions: J. A. Nicklin, *Essays of Sir William Temple* (1903); A. F. Sieveking, *Sir William Temple Upon the Gardens of Epicurus, With Other XVIIth Century Garden Essays* (1908); J. E. Spingarn gave *Of Poetry* and *Upon Ancient and Modern Learning* in Vol. III of *Critical Essays of the Seventeenth Century* (1909); F. J. Fielden reprinted *Of Poetry, Of Popular Discontents,* and *Of Health and Long-Life* in *Sir William Temple, Three Essays* (1939). G. N. Clark has edited (1932) the *Observations on the United Provinces.* In 1930 appeared *The Early Essays and Romances of Sir William Temple Bt.*, edited by G. C. Moore Smith. Both as a writer and as a man Temple would perhaps have a stronger appeal for us today if he had not come to be bracketed with Halifax. It is only natural that these two should now be associated in our minds, for their paths sometimes crossed in public life, they held similar views regarding domestic and foreign affairs, they were in certain ways temperamentally akin, and they happen to have been two of the foremost prose writers—from a literary point of view, that is—of the post-Restoration era. Halifax is certainly the more striking figure, just as his *Advice to a Daughter* is more to the modern taste than anything written by Temple. But the comparison is really not a just one, nor is it altogether fair to Temple. Despite their several points of likeness they entertained substantially different interests and as writers worked to different ends.

Temple's work falls into two readily distinguishable groups. In a tract like the *Observation upon the United Provinces of the Netherlands*, in the essay *Upon Government*, and in the *Memoirs* we have the straightforward, practical prose of a diplomat, statesman, and public servant. The writings of this kind, taken together, give a clear view of Temple's position regarding the issues of the time, and of his theories about governments and societies. He believed that England's welfare lay in alliance with the Dutch. At home, he mistrusted faction, and though he had reason to doubt Charles II's political wisdom if not his integrity, he seems to have hoped, as did Halifax, for a recognition on the part of both King and Parliament of a common ground and a common duty. The *Observations* is interesting as one of the earliest attempts to interpret a foreign people sympathetically, and also by reason of its completely naturalistic approach to questions pertaining to the cultural characteristics of different nations and societies. Though the *Essay upon Government* does not figure prominently, if indeed at all, in modern discussions of seventeenth-century political thought, it probably comes as close as any other statement of the period —the period, that is, between Hobbes and Locke—to giving the middle-of-the-road opinion on such matters as the origin and nature of government. Locke rejected as unhistorical all forms of the patriarchal theory, which found in the organization of the family and in the authority resting on the head of the family the true explanation of the origin of government. This patriarchal theory could be used by a writer like Filmer, whose *Patriarcha*, published in 1680, is the main object of Locke's attack in his *First Treatise*, to bolster up quite reactionary claims; but Temple was drawn to it, as were many of the Anglican clergy of these years, by a sense of history and an awareness of the psychological facts of social life, and in these respects he proved to be somewhat more scientific, more naturalistic, than those who thought in terms of "contract." Temple's public writings are those, in short, of a man who was decidedly more of a theorist than Halifax and correspondingly less of a willing and successful pragmatist. Faced with a turn of events which went against his principles, he went into permanent retirement in 1681, and even the accession of William III, his friend of long standing, could not tempt him back into public life. Temple's conduct here has often been interpreted unsympathetically, but to attribute it wholly to injured pride and egoistic disillusionment is to forget that he loved the peace of his gardens, loved his books, and like many others who have been touched by the philosophic spirit had no doubt that it was as important that some give themselves over to the quiet and dispassionate consideration of man's condition as that others should mix in current politics.

The rest of Temple's writings consist of his literary essays. A few of these he had ventured to publish, along with a good deal of quite different material, in his early volume of miscellanies (1679), but it was only after his retirement in 1681 that he turned to the essay as his chief medium of expression. The *Miscellanea* of 1690 he may well have regarded as his chief work. It is clear, at any rate, that he packed into the four long essays which make up this volume the fruits of a decade's reading and speculation. What he said in a later essay seems to apply precisely to those which appeared together in 1690: "I have chosen those Subjects of these Essays wherein I take Human Life to be most concerned . . . and wherein, though I may not be able to inform Men more than they know, yet I may perhaps give them the Occasion to consider more than they do." In the first essay, *Upon the Ancient and Modern Learning*, he is seeking to refute those who find progressive improvement in the arts and in civilization. It is here that Temple gives his clearest statement of the cyclical theory of history which he opposed to the progressive. *Upon the Gardens of Epicurus*, the latter pages of which undertake to summarize what a gentleman should know about gardening, begins with a discussion of moral theories, emphasizes the prime importance of moral speculation, which Temple sets up against "natural philosophy," and discusses in a personal tone reminiscent of Montaigne the writer's own preference for the Epicurean "tranquillity of mind and indolence of body." The third and fourth essays, *Of Heroic Virtue* and *Of Poetry*, are complementary studies of two "endowments of nature"—the only two endowments which men have regarded as divine. The essay on gardening best illustrates his indebtedness to Montaigne, the father of the modern familiar, personal essay. If in prose style Temple was perhaps as much indebted to Bacon and Browne, it is clear that intellectually and temperamentally he was deeply affected by that *libertin* tradition stemming from Montaigne. It is to be observed that he always brushed aside any view of man's social institutions or cultural and artistic achievements which was not wholly historical and naturalistic. Temple professed contempt for all "natural philosophy" save "what we owe to the mathematics," but by virtue of his own approach to the history of civilization and his eagerness to bring into focus all the data bearing upon the varied cultures of the world his place is actually with the early social scientists of our modern era. It is unfortunate that of the two essays chiefly concerned with literature, *Upon the Ancient and Modern Learning* should, by reason of the controversy it stirred up, have assumed a prominence which it does not deserve. *Of Poetry* is a vastly superior performance and one of the notable critical essays of the period, particularly remarkable for its range of information and its early application of the methods of comparative literature. Poetic art, we are told, is no more supernatural in its nature than is heroic virtue: it is invention, albeit of a kind and a degree depending upon the elevation of genius. Temple's emphasis upon invention would seem to come straight out of Hobbes, as his terminology (wit, fancy, coldness of good sense, soundness of judgment) unquestionably does. The discussion of humour, which occurs towards the end of the essay, proved to be one of his most fruitful observations.

The most recent full-length study is by Homer E. Woodbridge, *Sir William Temple, The Man and his Work* (1940). The *Memoirs of the Life, Works, and Correspondence of Sir William Temple, Bart.* (2 vols., 1836) by Thomas P. Courtney is still of value. Clara Marburg's *Sir William Temple, A Seventeenth Century "Libertin"* (1932) gives an analysis from the point of view of intellectual history. Comments by A. F. Sieveking, J. E. Spingarn, and F. J. Fielden are to be found in the modern editions noted above.

from UPON THE GARDENS OF EPICURUS; OR OF GARDENING IN THE YEAR 1685[1]

The same Faculty of Reason, which gives Mankind the great Advantage and Prerogative over the rest of the Creation, seems to make the greatest Default of Humane Nature; and subjects it to more Troubles, Miseries, or at least Disquiets of Life, than any of its Fellow-Creatures: 'Tis this furnishes us with such variety of Passions, and consequently of Wants and Desires, that none other feels; and these followed by infinite Designs and endless Pursuits, and improved by that restlessness of thought, which is natural to most Men, give Him a condition of Life suitable to that of His Birth; so that as He alone is born crying, He lives complaining, and dies disappointed.

Since we cannot escape the pursuit of Passions, and perplexity of Thoughts, which our Reason furnishes us, there is no way left, but to endeavour all we can, either to subdue or to divert them. This last is the common business of common men, who seek it by all sorts of Sports, Pleasures, Play, or Business. But because the two first are of short continuance, soon ending with weariness, or decay of Vigour and Appetite, the return whereof must be attended, before the others can be renewed; and because Play grows dull, if it be not enlivened with the Hopes of Gain, the general Diversion of Mankind seems to be Business, or the pursuit of Riches in one kind or other, which is an amusement, that has this one advantage above all others, that it lasts those Men who engage in it, to the very ends of their Lives; none ever growing too old for the Thoughts and Desires of increasing his Wealth and Fortunes, either for Himself, his Friends, or his Posterity.

In the first and most simple Ages of each Country, the Conditions and Lives of men

[1] Text: *Miscellanea, the Second Part,* third edition, 1692

seem to have been very near of Kin with the rest of the Creatures; they lived by the Hour, or by the Day, and satisfied their Appetite with what they could get, from the Herbs, the Fruits, the Springs they met with when they were hungry or dry; then, with what Fish, Fowl or Beasts they could kill, by Swiftness or Strength, by Craft or Contrivance, by their Hands or such Instruments as Wit helped, or Necessity forced them to invent. When a man had got enough for the day, He laid up the rest for the morrow, and spent one day in labour, that He might pass the other at ease; and lured on by the Pleasure of this Bait, when He was in Vigour, and His Game fortunate, He would provide for as many days as He could, both for Himself and His Children, that were too young to seek out for themselves. Then He cast about, how by sowing of Grain, and by Pasture of the tamer Cattel, to provide for the whole year. After this, dividing the Lands necessary for these Uses, first among Children, and then among Servants, He reserved to Himself a Proportion of their Gain, either in the native Stock, or something equivalent, which brought in the use of Money; and where this once came in, none was to be satisfied, without having enough for Himself and His Family, and all His and their Posterity for ever; so that I know a certain Lord who professes to value no Lease, though for an hundred or a thousand years, nor any Estate or Possession of Land that is not for ever and ever.

From such small Beginnings have grown such vast and extravagant Designs of poor mortal men: Yet none could ever answer the naked Indian, Why one man should take pains, and run Hazards by Sea and Land all his Life, that his Children might be safe and lazy all theirs: And the Precept of taking no care for to morrow, though never minded as impracticable in the World, seems but to reduce Mankind to their natural and original Condition of Life. However by these ways and degrees the endless increase of riches seems to be grown the perpetual and general amusement or business of Mankind.

Some few in each Country make those higher Flights after Honour and Power, and to these ends sacrifice their Riches, their Labour, their Thought, and their Lives; and nothing diverts nor busies Men more, than these pursuits, which are usually covered with the Pretences, of serving a Mans Country, and of Publick Good. But the true service of the Publick is a business of so much Labour and so much Care, that though a good and wise man may not refuse it, if He be called to it by His Prince or His Country, and thinks He can be of more than vulgar use, yet He will seldom or never seek it, but leaves it commonly to men, who under the disguise of Publick Good, pursue their own designs of Wealth, Power, and such Bastard Honours as usually attend them, not that which is the true and only true Reward of Virtue.

The pursuits of Ambition, though not so general, yet are as endless as those of Riches, and as extravagant; since none ever yet thought he had Power or Empire enough: And what Prince soever seems to be so great, as to live and reign without any further desires or fears, falls into the Life of a private man, and enjoys but those Pleasures and Entertainments, which a great many several Degrees of private Fortune will allow, and as much as Humane Nature is capable of enjoying.

The Pleasures of the Senses grow a little more choice and refined; those of Imagination are turned upon embellishing the Scenes He chooses to live in; Ease, Conveniency, Elegancy, Magnificence, are sought in Building first, and then in furnishing Houses or Palaces: The admirable imitations of Nature are introduced by Pictures, Statues, Tapestry, and other such atchievements of Arts. And the most exquisite delights of Sense are pursued, in the Contrivance and Plantations of Gardens, which, with Fruits, Flowers, Shades, Fountains, and the Musick of Birds that frequent such happy places, seem to furnish all the pleasures of the several Senses, and with the greatest, or at least the most natural Perfections.

Thus the first Race of *Assyrian* Kings, after the Conquests of *Ninus* and *Semiramis,*[2] passed their Lives, till their Empire fell to the *Medes*. Thus the *Caliphs* of

[2] legendary Assyrian figures, Ninus being accounted the founder of Nineveh, and his wife, Semiramis, said to have built the hanging gardens of Babylon

Egypt, till deposed by their *Mamalukes*.[3] Thus passed the latter parts of those great Lives of *Scipio*, *Lucullus*, *Augustus*, *Diocelsian*.[4] Thus turned the great Thoughts of *Henry* the Second of *France*, after the end of his Wars with *Spain*. Thus the present King of *Morocco*, after having subdued all his Competitors, passes His Life in a Country Villa, gives Audience in a Grove of Orange-trees planted among purling Streams. And thus the King of *France*,[5] after all the Successes of his Councils or Arms, and in the mighty Elevation of His present Greatness and Power, when He gives Himself leisure from such Designs or Pursuits, passes the softer and easier parts of His time in Countrey Houses and Gardens, in building, planting or adorning the Scenes, or in the common Sports and Entertainments of such kind of Lives. And those mighty Emperors, who contented not themselves with these pleasures of common Humanity, fell into the Frantick or the Extravagant; they pretended to be Gods, or turned to be Devils, as *Caligula*[6] and *Nero*,[7] and too many others known enough in Story.

Whilst Mankind is thus generally busied or amused, that part of them, who have had either the Justice or the Luck, to pass in common Opinion for the wisest and the best part among them, have followed another and very different Scent; and instead of the common designs of satisfying their Appetites and their Passions, and making endless Provisions for both, they have chosen what they thought a nearer and a surer way to the ease and felicity of Life, by endeavouring to subdue, or at least to temper their Passions, and reduce their Appetites to what Nature seems only to ask and to need. And this design seems to have brought Philosophy into the World, at least that which is termed Moral, and appears to have an End, not only desirable by every man, which is the Ease and Happiness of Life, but also in some degree suitable to the force and reach of humane Nature: For as to that part of Philosophy, which is called Natural, I know no end it can have, but that of either busying a man's Brains to no purpose, or satisfying the Vanity, so natural to most men, of distinguishing themselves by some way or other, from those that seem their Equals in Birth, and the common advantages of it; and whether this distinction be made by Wealth or Power, or appearance of Knowledge, which gains Esteem and Applause in the World, is all a case. More than this, I know no Advantage Mankind has gained by the progress of Natural Philosophy, during so many Ages it has had Vogue in the World, excepting always, and very justly, what we owe to the Mathematicks, which is in a manner, all that seems valuable among the Civilized Nations, more than those we call Barbarous, whether they are so or no, or more so than our selves.

How ancient this Natural Philosophy has been in the World, is hard to know; for we find frequent mention of ancient Philosophers in this kind, among the most ancient now extant with us. The first who found out the Vanity of it, seems to have been *Solomon*, of which Discovery he has left such admirable Strains in *Ecclesiastes*. The next was *Socrates*, who made it the business of His Life to explode it, and introduce that which we call Moral in its place, to busie Human Minds to better purpose. And indeed, whoever reads with Thought what these two, and *Marcus Antoninus*,[8] have said upon the Vanity of all that mortal man can ever attain to know of Nature, in its Originals or Operations, may save himself a great deal of Pains, and justly conclude, That the knowledge of such things is not our Game; and (like the pursuit of a Stag by a little Spaniel) may serve to amuse and to weary us, but will never be hunted down. Yet I think those Three I have named, may justly pass for

[3] The Mamaluke dynasties of Egyptian sultans extended from 1250 to 1517.

[4] Scipio: Scipio Africanus (237–183 B.C.), victorious over Hannibal. Lucullus: Lucius Licinius, a Roman general and famous epicure of the first century B.C. Augustus: the first Roman Emperor (27 B.C.–14 A.D.). Diocletian: Roman Emperor (245–313), who enjoyed gardening after abdicating in 305

[5] Henry II (1519–1559), was King 1547–1559

[6] Roman emperor 37–41

[7] Roman emperor 54–68

[8] i.e., Marcus Aurelius (121–180), emperor of Rome 161–180, eminent Stoic philosopher and author of the *Meditations*

the wisest Triumvirate that are left us, upon the Records of Story or of Time.

After *Socrates*, who left nothing in writing, many Sects of Philosophers began to spread in *Greece*, who entred boldly upon both Parts of Natural and Moral Philosophy. The first with the greatest Disagreement, and the most eager Contention that could be upon the greatest Subjects: As, Whether the World were Eternal, or produced at some certain time? Whether if produced, it was by some Eternal Mind, and to some end, or by the fortuituous Concourse of Atoms, or some Particles of Eternal Matter? Whether there was one World or many? Whether the Soul of man was a part of some Æthereal and Eternal Substance, or was Corporeal? Whether if Eternal, it was so before it came into the Body, or only after it went out? There were the same Contentions about the Motions of the Heavens, the Magnitude of the Cœlestial Bodies, the Faculties of the Mind, and the Judgment of the Senses. But all the different Schemes of Nature that have been drawn of old, or of late by *Plato*, *Aristotle*, *Epicurus*, *Des-Cartes*, *Hobs*, or any other that I know of, seem to agree but in one thing, which is, The want of Demonstration or Satisfaction, to any thinking and unpossessed Man; and seem more or less probable one than another, according to the Wit and Eloquence of the Authors and Avocates that raise or defend them; like Juglers Tricks, that have more or less appearance of being real, according to the dextrousness and skill of Him that plays 'em; whereas perhaps if we were capable of knowing Truth and Nature, these fine Schemes would prove like Rover Shots, some nearer and some further off, but all at great distance from the Mark, it may be none in sight.

Yet in the midst of these and many other such Disputes and Contentions in their Natural Philosophy, they seemed to agree much better in their Moral, and upon their Enquiries after the Ultimate End of man, which was his Happiness; their Contentions or Differences seem'd to be rather in Words, than in the Sense of their Opinions, or in the true meaning of their several Authors or Masters of their Sects: All concluded, that Happiness was the Chief Good, and ought to be the Ultimate End of Man; that as this was the end of Wisdom, so Wisdom was the way to Happiness. The Question then was, In what this Happiness consisted. The Contention grew warmest between the Stoicks and Epicureans, the other Sects in this point siding in a manner with one or the other of these, in their Conceptions or Expressions. The Stoicks would have it to consist in Virtue, and the Epicureans in Pleasure; yet the most reasonable of the Stoicks made the pleasure of Virtue to be the greatest Happiness; and the best of the Epicureans made the greatest Pleasure to consist in Virtue; and the difference between these two, seems not easily discovered: All agreed, the greatest Temper, if not the total subduing of Passion, and exercise of Reason, to be the state of the greatest Felicity: To live without Desires or Fears, or those Perturbations of Mind and Thought, which Passions raise: To place true Riches in wanting little, rather than in possessing much; and true Pleasure in Temperance, rather than in satisfying the Senses: To live with indifference to the common Enjoyments and Accidents of Life, and with Constancy upon the greatest Blows of Fate or of Chance; not to disturb our Minds with sad Reflections upon what is past, nor with anxious Cares or raving Hopes about what is to come; neither to disquiet Life with the Fears of Death, nor Death with the Desires of Life; but in both, and in all things else, to follow Nature, seem to be the Precepts most agreed among them.

Thus Reason seems only to have been called in, to allay those Disorders which it self had raised, to cure its own Wounds, and pretends to make us wise no other way, than by rendring us insensible. This at least was the Profession of many rigid Stoicks, who would have had a wise Man, not only without any sort of Passion, but without any Sense of Pain, as well as Pleasure, and to enjoy Himself in the midst of Diseases and Torments, as well as of Health and Ease; a Principle, in my mind, against common Nature and common Sense, and which might have told us in fewer Words, or with less Circumstance, that a Man to be wise, should not be a Man; and this perhaps might have been easie enough to believe, but nothing so hard as the other.

The Epicureans were more intelligible in their Notion, and fortunate in their Expression, when they placed a man's Happiness in the Tranquility of Mind, and Indolence of Body; for while we are composed of both, I doubt both must have a Share in the good or ill we feel. As Men of several Languages, say the same things in very different Words; so in several Ages, Countries, Constitutions of Laws and Religion, the same thing seems to be meant by very different expressions; What is called by the Stoicks Apathy, or Dispassion; by the Scepticks, Indisturbance; by the Molinists,[9] Quietism; by common men, Peace of Conscience; seems all to mean but great Tranquillity of Mind, though it be made to proceed from so diverse Causes, as Human Wisdom, Innocence of Life, or Resignation to the Will of God. An old Usurer had the same Notion, when He said, No man could have Peace of Conscience, that run out of his Estate; not comprehending what else was meant by that Phrase, besides true Quiet and Content of Mind; which however expressed, is, I suppose, meant by all, to be the best account that can be given of the Happiness of man, since no man can pretend to be happy without it.

I have often wondred, how such sharp and violent Invectives came to be made so generally against *Epicurus*,[10] by the Ages that followed Him, whose Admirable Wit, Felicity of Expression, Excellence of Nature, Sweetness of Conversation, Temperance of Life, and Constancy of Death, made Him so beloved by His Friends, admired by his Scholars, and honoured by the *Athenians*. But this Injustice may be fastned chiefly upon the envy and malignity of the Stoicks at first, then upon the Mistakes of some gross Pretenders to His Sect (who took Pleasure only to be sensual) and afterwards, upon the Piety of the Primitive Christians, who esteemed his Principles of Natural Philosophy, more opposite to those of our Religion, than either the *Platonists*, the *Peripateticks*,[11] or *Stoicks* themselves: Yet I confess, I do not know why the account given by *Lucretius* of the Gods, should be thought more impious, than that given by *Homer*, who makes them not only subject to all the weakest Passions, but perpetually busie in all the worst or meanest Actions of men. . . .

. . . . .

. . . But all the different Sects of Philosophers, seem to have agreed in the Opinion, of a wise Man's abstaining from Publick Affairs. . . . They thought that sort of Business too gross and material for the abstracted fineness of their Speculations. They esteemed it too sordid and too artificial for the cleanness and simplicity of their Manners and Lives. They would have no part in the Faults of a Government, and they knew too well, that the Nature and Passions of men made them incapable of any that was perfect and good, and therefore thought all the Service they could do to the State they live under, was to mend the Lives and Manners of particular men that composed it. . . . But above all, they esteemed Publick Business the most contrary of all others, to that Tranquility of Mind, which they esteemed and taught, to be the only true Felicity of man.

For this Reason *Epicurus* passed His Life wholly in his Garden; there He Studied, there He Exercised, there He taught his Philosophy; and indeed, no other sort of Abode seems to contribute so much, to both the Tranquility of Mind, and Indolence of Body, which He made His Chief Ends. The Sweetness of Air, the Pleasantness of Smells, the Verdure of Plants, the Cleanness and Lightness of Food, the Exercises of working or walking, but above all, the Exemption from Cares and Sollicitude, seem equally to favour and improve, both Contemplation and Health, the Enjoyment of Sense and Imagination, and thereby the Quiet and Ease both of the Body and Mind.

Though *Epicurus* be said to have been the first that had a Garden in *Athens*, whose Citizens before Him, had theirs in their Villaes or Farms without the City; yet the use of Gardens seems to have been

[9] Molinism is the name given the doctrines stemming from Luis Molina (1535–1600), a Spanish Jesuit.

[10] 342?–270 B.C.

[11] i.e., the Aristotelians

the most ancient and most general of any sorts of Possession among Mankind, and to have preceded those of Corn, or of Cattel, as yielding the easier, the pleasanter, and more natural Food. As it has been the Inclination of Kings, and the choice of Philosophers, so it has been the common Favourite of publick and private Men, a pleasure of the greatest and the Care of the meanest, and indeed an Employment and a Possession, for which no Man is too high nor too low. . . .

OF POETRY[12]

The two common Shrines, to which most Men offer up the Application of their Thoughts and their Lives, are Profit and Pleasure, and by their Devotions to either of these, they are vulgarly distinguished into Two Sects, and called either Busie or Idle Men. Whether these Terms differ in meaning, or only in sound, I know very well may be disputed, and with appearance enough, since the Covetous Man takes perhaps as much Pleasure in his Gains as the Voluptuous does in his Luxury, and would not pursue his Business unless he were pleased with it, upon the last Account of what he most wishes and desires, nor would care for the encrease of his Fortunes, unless he proposed thereby, that of his Pleasures too, in one kind or other, so that Pleasure may be said to be his end, whether he will allow to find it in his pursuit or no. Much ado there has been, many Words spent, or (to speak with more respect to the antient Philosophers) many Disputes have been raised upon this Argument, I think to little purpose, and that all has been rather, an Exercise of Wit than an Enquiry after Truth, and all Controversies that can never end, had better perhaps never begin. The best is to take Words as they are most commonly spoken and meant, like Coyn as it most currantly passes, without raising scruples upon the weight or the allay, unless the cheat or the defect, be gross and evident. Few things in the World or none, will bear too much refining, a Thred too fine Spun will easily break, and the Point of a Needle too finely Filed. The usual acceptation, takes Profit and Pleasure, for two different things, and not only calls the Followers or Votaries of them, by several Names of Busie and of Idle Men, but distinguishes the Faculties of the mind, that are Conversant about them, calling the Operations of the first, Wisdom, and of the other, Wit, which is a *Saxon* Word, that is used to express, what the *Spaniards* and *Italians* call *Ingenio,* and the *French, Esprit,* both from the *Latin,* but I think Wit more peculiarly signifies that of *Poetry,* as may occur upon Remarks of the *Runick* Language.[13] To the first of these are Attributed, the Inventions or Productions of things generally esteemed the most necessary, useful, or profitable to Human Life, either in private Possessions or publick Institutions: To the other, those Writings or Discourses, which are the most Pleasing or Entertaining, to all that read or hear them; Yet according to the Opinion of those that link them together, As the Inventions of Sages and Law-givers themselves, do please as well as profit those who approve and follow them, so those of Poets, Instruct and Profit as well as Please such as are Conversant in them, and the happy mixture of both these, makes the excellency in both those compositions, and has given occasion for esteeming, or at least for calling, Heroick Virtue and Poetry, Divine.

The Names given to Poets, both in *Greek* and *Latin,* express the same Opinion of them in those Nations; The *Greek* signifying Makers or Creators,[14] such as raise admirable Frames and Fabricks out of nothing, which strike with wonder and with pleasure, the Eyes and Imaginations of those who behold them; The *Latin* makes the same Word, common to Poets and to Prophets. Now as Creation, is the first Attribute and highest Operation of Divine Power, so is Prophecy the greatest

[12] Text: *Miscellanea, the Second Part,* third edition, 1692

[13] Temple's "Remarks of the Runish Language" will be found in latter passages of this essay on p. 159 and pp. 166–167.

[14] The Greek ποιητής [poiētēs] means a maker, the creator of a poem; the Latin *vates* means a prophet, a poet.

Emanation of Divine Spirit in the World. As the Names in those Two Learned Languages, so the Causes of Poetry, are by the Writers of them, made to be Divine, and to proceed from a Cœlestial Fire or Divine Inspiration, and by the vulgar Opinions, recited or related to in many passages of those Authors, the Effects of Poetry were likewise thought Divine and Supernatural, and Power of Charms and Enchantments were ascribed to it.

Carmina vel Coelo possunt deducere Lunam,
Carminibus Circe Socios mutavit Ulyssis,
Frigidus in pratis cantando rumpitur Anguis.[15]

But I can easily admire Poetry, and yet without adoring it, I can allow it to arise from the greatest Excellency of natural Temper, or the greatest Race of Native Genius, without exceeding the reach of what is Human, or giving it any Approaches of Divinity, which is, I doubt debased or dishonoured, by ascribing to it any thing, that is in the compass of our Action, or even Comprehension, unless it be raised by an immediate influence from it self. I cannot allow Poetry to be more Divine in its effects, than in its causes, nor any Operation produced by it, to be more than purely natural, or to deserve any other sort of wonder, than those of Musick, or of Natural Magick, however any of them have appeared to minds little Versed in the Speculations of Nature, of occult Qualities, and the Force of Numbers or of Sounds. Whoever talks of drawing down the Moon from Heaven, by the force of Verses or of Charms, either believes not himself, or too easily believes what others told him, or perhaps follows an Opinion, begun by the Practise of some Poet, upon the facility of some People, who knowing the time when an Eclypse would happen, told them, he would by his Charms call down the Moon at such an hour, and was by them thought to have performed it.

When I read that Charming Description in *Virgil's* Eighth Ecclogue, of all sorts of Charms and Fascinations by Verses, by Images, by Knots, by Numbers, by Fire, by Herbs, imployed upon occasion of a violent Passion, from a jealous or disappointed Love: I have recourse to the strong Impressions of Fables and of Poetry, to the easy mistakes of Popular Opinions, to the Force of Imagination, to the Secret Virtues of several Herbs, and to the Powers of Sounds: And I am sorry, the Natural History, or Account of Fascination, has not imployed the Pen of some Person, of such excellent Wit, and deep Thought and Learning, as *Casaubon,* who Writ that curious and useful Treatise of *Enthusiasm,*[16] and by it discovered the hidden or mistaken Sources of that Delusion, so frequent in all Regions and Religions of the World, and which had so fatally spread over our Country in that Age, in which this Treatise was so seasonably published. 'Tis much to be lamented, That he lived not to compleat that Work, in the Second Part he promised; or that his Friends neglected the publishing it, if it were left in Papers, though loose and unfinished. I think a clear Account of Enthusiasm and Fascination, from their natural Causes, would very much deserve from Mankind in general, as well as from the Commonwealth of Learning; might perhaps prevent many publick disorders, and save the Lives of many innocent, deluded or deluding People, who suffer so frequently, upon Account of Witches and Wizards. I have seen many miserable Examples of this kind, in my youth at home, and tho' the Humor or Fashion, be a good deal worn out of the World, within Thirty or Forty Years past, yet it still remains in several remote Parts of *Germany, Sweden,* and some other Countries.

But to return to the Charms of Poetry, if the forsaken Lover, in that Ecclogue of *Virgil,* had expected only from the Force of her Verses, or her Charms, what is the Burthen of the Song, To bring *Daphnis* home from the Town where he was gone and engaged in a new Amour; if she had

[15] "Magic songs can draw down the moon from heaven; by magic songs Circe changed Ulysses' comrades; the cold snake in the meadow is made to burst by singing magic songs." Virgil, *Eclogues,* viii. 69–71.

[16] Dr. Meric Casaubon (Florence Étienne Méric Casaubon, 1599–1671) was the author of *A Treatise Concerning Enthusiasme, As it is an Effect of Nature: but is mistaken by many for either Divine Inspiration, or Diabolical Possession* (London, 1655).

pretended only to revive an old fainting Flame, or to damp a new one that was kindling in his Breast, she might, for ought I know, have compassed such Ends, by the Power of such Charms, and without other than very Natural Enchantments. For there is no Question, but true Poetry may have the Force, to raise Passions and to allay them, to change and to extinguish them, to temper Joy and Grief, to raise Love and Fear, nay to turn Fear into Boldness, and Love into Indifference, and into Hatred it self; and I easily believe, That the disheartened *Spartans*, were new animated, and recovered their lost Courage, by the Songs of *Tyrtæus*,[17] that the Cruelty and Revenge of *Phalaris*,[18] were changed by the Odes of *Stesichorus*,[19] into the greatest Kindness and Esteem, and that many men were as passionately Enamoured, by the Charms of *Sappho's*[20] Wit and Poetry, as by those of Beauty, in *Flora*[21] or *Thais;*[22] for 'tis not only Beauty gives Love, but Love gives Beauty to the Object that raises it; and if the possession be strong enough, let it come from what it will, there is always Beauty enough in the Person that gives it. Nor is it any great Wonder, that such Force should be found in Poetry, since in it are assembled all the Powers of Eloquence, of Musick, and of Picture, which are all allowed to make so strong Impressions upon Humane Minds. How far Men have been affected with all or any of these, needs little Proof or Testimony; The Examples have been known enough in *Greece* and in *Italy*, where some have fallen down right in Love, with the Ravishing Beauties of a lovely Object, drawn by the Skill of an admirable Painter; nay, Painters themselves, have fallen in Love with some of their own Productions, and doated on them, as on a Mistress or a fond Child, which distinguishes among the *Italians*, the several Pieces that are done by the same Hand, into several Degrees of those made, *Con Studio, con Diligenza*, or *Con Amore;* whereof the last are ever the most excelling. But there needs no more Instances of this Kind, than the Stories related, and believed by the best Authors, as known and undisputed; Of the two young *Græcians*, one whereof ventured his Life, to be lock'd up all Night in the Temple, and satisfie his Passion with the Embraces and Enjoyment of a Statue of *Venus*, that was there set up, and designed for another sort of Adoration; The other pined away and dyed for being hindred his perpetually gazing, admiring, and embracing a Statue at *Athens*.

The Powers of Musick, are either felt or known by all Men, and are allowed to work strangely upon the Mind and Body, the Passions and the Blood, to raise Joy and Grief, to give Pleasure and Pain, to cure Diseases, and the Mortal Sting of the *Tarantula*, to give Motions to the Feet as well as the Heart, to Compose disturbed Thoughts, to assist and heighten Devotion it self. We need no Recourse to the Fables of *Orpheus*[23] or *Amphion*,[24] or the Force of their Musick upon Fishes and Beasts, 'tis enough that we find the Charming of Serpents, and the Cure or Allay of an evil Spirit or Possession, attributed to it in Sacred Writ.

For the Force of Eloquence, that so often raised and appeased the Violence of Popular Commotions, and caused such Convulsions in the *Athenian* State, no Man needs more, to make him Acknowledge it, than to consider *Cæsar*, one of the greatest and wisest of mortal Men, come upon the Tribunal, full of Hatred and Revenge, and with a determined Resolution to Condemn *Labienus*,[25] yet upon the Force of *Cicero's* Eloquence, (in an Oration for his De-

[17] a Spartan poet of the seventh century B.C., whose verses are said to have saved the Spartans from defeat in the Second Messian War

[18] Greek tyrant of Argigentum in Sicily during the sixth century

[19] a Greek poet of Sicily, who flourished about the beginning of the sixth century

[20] Greek poetess of Lesbos, who also flourished about the beginning of the sixth century

[21] Roman goddess of flowers

[22] Greek courtesan of the late fourth century B.C., mistress of Alexander the Great

[23] a poet and musician of classical mythology, able to charm beasts and inanimate nature with the music of his lyre

[24] According to Greek mythology he built a wall around Thebes by playing on his charmed lyre and thus causing the stones to fall into place.

[25] The speech of Cicero's in question was in defence not of Labienus but of Quintus Ligarius.

fence) begin to change Countenance, turn pale, shake to that degree, that the Papers he held, fell out of his hand, as if he had been frighted with Words, that never was so with Blows, and at last change all his Anger into Clemency, and acquit the brave Criminal, instead of condemning him.

Now if the Strength of these three mighty Powers, be united in Poetry, we need not wonder, that such Virtues, and such Honours have been attributed to it, that it has been thought to be inspired, or has been called Divine, and yet I think it will not be disputed, that the Force of Wit, and of Reasoning, the Height of Conceptions and Expressions, may be found in Poetry as well as in Oratory, the Life and Spirit of Representation or Picture, as much as in Painting, and the Force of Sounds as well as in Musick; and how far these three natural Powers together may extend, and to what Effect, (even such as may be mistaken for Supernatural or Magical) I leave it to such Men to consider, whose Thoughts turn to such Speculations as these, or who by their native Temper and Genius, are in some degree disposed to receive the Impressions of them. For my part, I do not wonder, that the famous Doctor *Harvey*,[26] when he was reading *Virgil*, should sometimes throw him down upon the Table, and say he had a Devil; nor that the learned *Meric Casaubon*,[27] should find such Charming Pleasures and Emotions, as he describes, upon the reading some Parts of *Lucretius*;[28] that so many should cry, and with down-right Tears, at some Tragedies of *Shake-spear*, and so many more should feel such Turns or Curdling of their Blood, upon the reading or hearing some excellent Pieces of Poetry, nor that *Octavia*[29] fell into a Swound, at the recital made by *Virgil* of those Verses[30] in the Sixth of his *Æneides*.

This is enough to assert the Powers of Poetry, and discover the Ground of those Opinions of old, which derived it from Divine Inspiration, and gave it so great a share in the supposed Effects of Sorcery or Magick. But as the Old Romances, seem to lessen the Honour of true Prowess and Valour in their Knights, by giving such a part in all their Chief Adventures to Enchantment, so the true excellency and just esteem of Poetry, seems rather debased than exalted, by the Stories or Belief of the Charms performed by it, which among the *Northern* Nations, grew so strong and so general, that about Five or Six Hundred Years ago, all the *Runick* Poetry came to be decryed, and those antient Characters, in which they were Written, to be abolished by the Zeal of Bishops, and even by Orders and Decrees of State, which has given a great Maim, or rather an irrecoverable Loss to the Story of those *Northern* Kingdoms, the Seat of our Ancestors, in all the *Western* Parts of *Europe*.

The more true and natural Source of Poetry may be discovered, by observing to what God this Inspiration was ascribed by the Antients, which was *Apollo* or the Sun, esteemed among them the God of Learning in general, but more particularly of Musick and of Poetry. The Mystery of this Fable, means I suppose, that a certain Noble and Vital Heat of Temper, but especially of the Brain, is the true Spring of these Two Arts or Sciences: This was that Cœlestial Fire, which gave such a pleasing Motion and Agitation to the minds of those Men, that have been so much admired in the World, that raises such infinite images of things so agreeable and delightful to Mankind: By the influence of this Sun, are produced those Golden and Inexhausted Mines of Invention, which has furnished the World with Treasures so highly esteemed, and so universally known and used, in all the Regions that have yet been discovered. From this arises that Elevation of Genius, which can never be produced by any Art or study, by Pains or by Industry, which cannot be taught by Precepts or Examples, and therefore is agreed by all, to be the pure and free Gift of Heaven or of Nature, and to be a Fire kindled out of some hidden spark of the very first Conception.

[26] Dr. William Harvey (1578–1657), famous as discoverer of the circulation of the blood

[27] See footnote 16 above.

[28] Roman philosophical poet (96?–55 B.C.), author of *De Rerum Natura*, which sets forth Epicurean theories

[29] sister of the Emperor Augustus and second wife of Mark Antony

[30] descriptive of Æneas's descent to the underworld

But tho' Invention be the Mother of Poetry, yet this Child, is like all others, born naked, and must be Nourished with Care, Cloathed with Exactness and Elegance, Educated with Industry, Instructed with Art, Improved by Application, Corrected with Severity, and Accomplished with Labor and with Time, before it Arrives at any great Perfection or Growth: 'Tis certain that no Composition requires so many several Ingredients, or of more different sorts than this, nor that to excel in any qualities, there are necessary so many Gifts of Nature, and so many improvements of Learning and of Art. For there must be an universal Genius, of great Compass as well as great Elevation. There must be a spritely Imagination or Fancy, fertile in a thousand Productions, ranging over infinite Ground, piercing into every Corner, and by the Light of that true Poetical Fire, discovering a thousand little Bodies or Images in the World, and Similitudes among them, unseen to common Eyes, and which could not be discovered, without the Rays of that Sun.

Besides the heat of Invention and liveliness of Wit, there must be the coldness of good Sense and soundness of Judgment, to distinguish between things and conceptions, which at first sight, or upon short glances, seem alike; to choose among infinite productions of Wit and Fancy, which are worth preserving and cultivating, and which are better stifled in the Birth, or thrown away when they are born, as not worth bringing up. Without the Forces of Wit, all Poetry is flat and languishing; without the succors of Judgment, 'tis wild and extravagant. The true wonder of Poesy is, That such contraries must meet to compose it, a Genius both Penetrating and Solid; in Expression both Delicacy and Force; and the Frame or Fabrick of a true Poem, must have something both Sublime and Just, Amazing and Agreeable. There must be a great Agitation of Mind to Invent, a great Calm to Judge and correct, there must be upon the same Tree, and at the same Time, both Flower and Fruit. To work up this Metal into exquisite Figure, there must be imploy'd the Fire, the Hammer, the Chizel and the File. There must be a general Knowledge both of Nature and of Arts, and to go the lowest that can be, there are required *Genius*, Judgment, and Application; for without this last, all the rest will not serve turn, and none ever was a great Poet, that applyed himself much to any thing else.

When I speak of Poetry, I mean not an Ode or an Elegy, a Song or a Satyr, nor by a Poet the Composer of any of these, but of a just Poem: And after all I have said, 'tis no wonder, there should be so few that appeared, in any Parts or any Ages of the World, or that such as have, should be so much admired, and have almost Divinity ascribed to them, and to their Works.

Whatever has been among those, who are mentioned with so much Praise or Admiration by the Antients, but are lost to us, and unknown any further than their Names, I think no Man has been so bold among those that remain to question the Title of *Homer* and *Virgil*, not only to the first Rank, but to the supream Dominion in this State, and from whom, as the great Law-givers as well as Princes, all the Laws and Orders of it, are, or may be derived. *Homer* was without Dispute, the most Universal *Genius* that has been known in the World, and *Virgil* the most Accomplish't. To the first must be allowed, the most fertile Invention, the richest Vein, the most general Knowledge, and the most lively Expression: To the last, The noblest Idea's, the justest Institution, the wisest Conduct, and the choycest Elocution. To speak in the Painters Terms, we find in the Works of *Homer*, the most Spirit, Force, and Life; in those of *Virgil*, the best Design, the truest Proportions, and the greatest Grace; The Colouring in both seems equal, and indeed, in both is admirable. *Homer* had more Fire and Rapture, *Virgil* more Light and Swiftness;[31] or at least the Poetical Fire was more raging in one, but clearer in the other, which makes the first more amazing, and the latter more agreeable. The Oare was richer in one, but in t'other more refined, and better allay'd, to make up excellent Work. Upon the whole, I think it must be confessed, that *Homer*

[31] F. J. Fielden points out in his edition (*Sir William Temple: Three Essays*) that *sweetness*, which is the reading at this point of the earlier text of 1690, is preferable.

was of the two, and perhaps, of all others, the vastest, the sublimest, and the most wonderful *Genius;* and that he has been generally so esteemed, there cannot be a greater Testimony given, than what has been by some observed that not only the Greatest Masters, have found in his Works, the best and truest Principles of all their Sciences or Arts, but that the noblest Nations, have derived from them, the Original of their several Races, though it be hardly yet agreed, Whether his Story be True, or Fiction. In short, these two immortal Poets, must be allowed to have so much excelled in their kinds, as to have exceeded all Comparison; to have even extinguished Emulation, and in a manner confined true Poetry, not onely to their two Languages, but to their very Persons. And I am apt to believe so much of the true *Genius* of Poetry in general, and of its Elevation in these two Particulars, that I know not, whether of all the Numbers of Mankind, that live within the Compass of a Thousand Years; for one Man that is born capable of making such a Poet as *Homer* or *Virgil*, there may not be a Thousand born Capable of making as great Generals of Armies, or Ministers of State, as any the most Renowned in Story.

I do not here intend to make a further Critick upon Poetry, which were too great a Labour, nor to give Rules for it, which were as great a Presumption: Besides, there has been so much Paper blotted upon these Subjects, in this Curious and Censuring Age, that 'tis all grown tedious or Repetition. The Modern *French* Wits (or Pretenders) have been very severe in their Censures, and exact in their Rules, I think to very little Purpose; For I know not, why they might not have contented themselves, with those given by *Aristotle* and *Horace*, and have Translated them rather than Commented upon them, for all they have done has been no more, so as they seem, by their Writings of this kind, rather to have valued themselves, than improved any body else. The Truth is, there is something in the *Genius* of Poetry, too Libertine to be confined to so many Rules; and whoever goes about to subject it to such Constraints, loses both its Spirit and Grace, which are ever Native, and never learnt, even of the best Masters. 'Tis as if to make excellent Honey, you should cut off the Wings of your Bees, confine them to their Hive or their Stands, and lay Flowers before them, such as you think the sweetest, and like to yield the finest Extraction; you had as good pull out their Stings, and make arrant Drones of them. They must range through Fields, as well as Gardens, choose such Flowers as they please, and by Proprieties and Scents they only know and distinguish: They must work up their Cells with Admirable Art, extract their Honey with infinite Labour, and sever it from the Wax, with such Distinction and Choyce, as belongs to none but themselves to perform or to judge.

It would be too much Mortification, to these great Arbitrary Rulers, among the *French* Writers, or our own, to Observe the worthy Productions that have been formed by their Rules, the Honour they have received in the World, or the Pleasure they have given Mankind. But to comfort them, I do not know, there was any great Poet in *Greece*, after the Rules of that Art layd down by *Aristotle*, nor in *Rome*, after those by *Horace*, which yet none of our Moderns pretend to have outdone. Perhaps *Theocritus*[32] and *Lucan*,[33] may be alledg'd against this Assertion, but the first offered no further, than at Idils or Ecologues; and the last, though he must be avowed for a true and a happy *Genius*, and to have made some very high Flights, yet he is so unequal to himself, and his Muse is so young, that his Faults are too noted, to allow his Pretences. *Fœliciter audet*,[34] is the true Character of *Lucan*, as of *Ovid*,[35] *Lusit amabiliter*.[36] After all, the utmost that can be atchieved, or I think pretended, by any Rules in this Art, is but to hinder some men from being very ill Poets, but not to make any man a very

[32] Greek pastoral poet of the third century B.C.

[33] Roman poet (39–65 A.D.), author of the epic, *Pharsalia*

[34] "He is audacious to happy effect." Horace, *Epistles*, II. i. 166

[35] (43 B.C.–17 A.D.), Latin poet, best known for the *Metamorphoses*

[36] "He ridiculed without ill-feeling." Horace, *Epistles*, II. i. 148

good one. To judge who is so, we need go no further for Instruction, than three Lines[37] of *Horace:*

Ille meum qui Pectus inaniter angit,
Irritat, mulcet, falsis terroribus implet,
Ut Magus, *et modo me* Thebis, *modo ponit* Athenis.

He is a Poet,

Who vainly anguishes my Breast,
Provokes, allays, and with false Terror fills,
Like a Magician, and now sets me down
In Thebes, *and now in* Athens.

Whoever does not affect and move the same present Passions in you, that he represents in others, and at other times, raise Images about you, as a Conjurer is said to do Spirits, Transport you to the Places and to the Persons he describes, cannot be judged to be a Poet, though his Measures are never so just, his Feet never so smooth, or his Sounds never so sweet.

But instead of Critick, or Rules concerning Poetry, I shall rather turn my Thoughts to the History of it, and observe the Antiquity, the Uses, the Changes, the Decays, that have attended this great Empire of Wit.

It is I think generally agreed, to have been the first sort of Writing that has been used in the World; and in several Nations to have preceded the very Invention or Usage of Letters. This last is certain in *America*, where the first *Spaniards* met with many strains of Poetry, and left several of them Translated into their Language, which seem to have flowed from a true Poetick Vein, before any Letters were known in those Regions. The same is probable of the *Scythians*, the *Grecians*, and the *Germans*. *Aristotle* says,[38] the *Agathyrsi* had their Laws all in Verse; and *Tacitus*,[39] that the *Germans* had no Annals nor Records but what were so; and for the *Grecian* Oracles delivered in them, we have no certain Account where they began, but rather reason to believe it was before the Introduction of Letters from *Phœnicia* among them. *Pliny* tells it,[40] as a thing known, that *Pherecides* was the first who Writ Prose in the *Greek* Tongue, and that he lived about the time of *Cyrus;* whereas *Homer* and *Hesiod* lived some Hundreds of Years before that Age; and *Orpheus*, *Linus*, *Musæus*, some Hundreds before them: And of the *Sybils*, several were before any of those, and in times as well as places, whereof we have no clear Records now remaining. What *Solon* and *Phthagoras* Writ, is said to have been in Verse, who were something older than *Cyrus;* and before them, were *Archilochus*, *Simonides*, *Tyrtæus*, *Sappho*, *Stesichorus* and several other Poets famous in their times. The same thing is reported of *Chaldæa*, *Syria* and *China;* among the ancient *Western Goths* (our Ancestors) the *Runick* Poetry, seems to have been as old as their Letters; and their Laws, their Precepts of Wisdom as well as their Records, their Religious Rites as well as their Charms and Incantations, to have been all in Verse.

Among the *Hebrews*, and even in Sacred Writ the most antient, is by some Learned Men esteemed to be the Book of *Job*, and that it was Written before the time of *Moses*, and that it was a Translation into *Hebrew* out of the old *Chaldæan* or *Arabian* Language. It may probably be conjectured, that he was not a *Jew*, from the place of his abode, which appears to have been Seated between the *Chaldæns* of one side, and the *Sabæns* (who were of *Arabia*) on the other, and by many Passages, of that admirable and truly inspired Poem, the Author seems to have lived in some Parts near the Mouth of *Euphrates* or the *Persian* Gulf, where he contemplated the Wonders of the Deep as well as the other Works of Nature, common to those Regions. Nor is it easy to find any Traces of the *Mosaical* Rites or Institutions, either in the Divine Worship, or the Morals related to, in those Writings: For not only Sacrifices and Praises, were much more antient in Religious Service, than the Age of *Moses;* But the Opinion of one Deity, and Adored without any Idol or Representations was Professed and Received among the antient *Persians* and *Hetruscans* and *Chaldæans*. So that if *Job* was an *Hebrew*,

[37] *Epistles,* II. i. 211–213
[38] *Problems,* xix. 28
[39] *Germania,* II
[40] *Natural History,* VII. 57.14

'tis probable he may have been of the Race of *Heber* who lived in *Chaldæa*, or of *Abraham* who is supposed to have left that Country for the Profession or Worship of one God, rather than from the Branch of *Isaac* and *Israel*, who lived in the Land of *Canaan*. Now I think it is out of Controversy, that the Book of *Job* was Written Originally in Verse, and was a Poem upon the Subject of the Justice and Power of God, and in Vindication of His Providence, against the common Arguments of Atheistical Men, who took occasion to dispute it, from the usual Events of Human things, by which so many ill and impious Men seem Happy and Prosperous in the course of their Lives, and so many Pious and Just Men, seem Miserable or Afflicted. The *Spanish* Translation of the *Jews* in *Ferrara*,[41] which pretends to render the *Hebrew* (as near as could be) word for word; and for which, all Translators of the Bible since, have had great Regard, gives us the Two first Chapters, and the Last from the seventh Verse in Prose, as an Historical Introduction and Conclusion of the Work, and all the rest in Verse, except the Transitions from one Part or Person of this Sacred Dialogue to another.

But if we take the Books of *Moses* to be the most antient in the *Hebrew* Tongue, yet the Song of *Moses* may probably have been Written before the rest; as that of *Deborah*, before the Book of *Judges*, being Praises sung to God, upon the Victories or Successes of the *Israelites*, related in both. And I never read the last, without observing in it, as True and Noble Strains of Poetry and Picture, as in any other Language whatsoever, in spight of all Disadvantages from Translations into so different Tongues and common Prose. If an Opinion of some Learned Men both Modern and Antient could be allowed, that *Esdras* was the Writer or Compiler of the first Historical Parts of the Old Testament, though from the same Divine Inspiration as that of *Moses* and the other Prophets, then the Psalms of *David* would be the first Writings we find in *Hebrew;* and next to them, the Song of *Solomon* which was written when he was young, and *Ecclesiastes* when he was old: So that from all sides, both Sacred and Prophane, It appears that *Poetry* was the first sort of Writing known and used in the several Nations of the World.

It may seem strange, I confess, upon the first thought, that a sort of Style so regular and so difficult, should have grown in use, before the other so easy and so loose: But if we consider, what the first end of Writing was, it will appear probable from Reason as well as Experience; For the true and General End, was but the Help of Memory, in preserving that of Words and of Actions, which would otherwise have been lost, and soon vanish away, with the Transitory Passage of Human Breath and Life. Before the Discourses and Disputes of Philosophers, began to busie or amuse the *Græcian* Wits, there was nothing Written in Prose, but either Laws, some short Sayings of Wise men, or some Riddles, Parables, or Fables, wherein were couched by the Antients, many Strains of Natural or Moral Wisdom and Knowledge; and besides these, some short Memorials of Persons, Actions, and of Times. Now 'tis obvious enough to conceive, how much easier, all such Writings should be Learnt and Remembred, in Verse than in Prose, not only by the Pleasure of Measures and of Sounds, which gives a great Impression to Memory, but by the order of Feet which makes a great Facility of Tracing one Word after another, by knowing what sort of Foot or Quantity, must necessarily have preceded or followed the Words we retain and desire to make up.

This made Poetry so necessary, before Letters were invented, and so convenient afterwards; and shews, that the great Honor and general Request, wherein it has always been, has not proceeded only, from the Pleasure and Delight, but likewise from the Usefulness and Profit of Poetical Writings.

This leads me naturally to the Subjects of Poetry, which have been generally, Praise, Instruction, Story, Love, Grief, and Reproach. Praise, was the Subject of all the Songs and Psalms mentioned in Holy Writ, of the Hymns of *Orpheus*, of *Homer* and many others; Of the *Carmina Secularia* in *Rome*, Composed all and De-

[41] *Biblia en Lengua Española*, a version of the Old Testament published at Ferrara in 1553

signed for the Honor of their Gods; of *Pindar*,[42] *Stesichorus*,[43] and *Tyrtaus*,[44] in the Praises of Virtue or Virtuous Men. The Subject of *Job*, is Instruction concerning the Attributes of God and the Works of Nature. Those of *Simonides*, *Phocillides*, *Theognis*,[45] and several other of the smaller *Greek* Poets, with what passes for *Pythagoras*,[46] are Instructions in Morality: The first Book of *Hesiod*[47] and *Virgils Georgicks*, in Agriculture, and *Lucretius*[48] in the deepest natural Philosophy. Story, is the proper Subject of *Heroick* Poems, as *Homer* and *Virgil* in their inimitable *Illiads* and *Æneids;* And *Fable*, which is a sort of Story, in the *Metamorphosis* of *Ovid*.[49] The *Lyrick* Poetry has been chiefly Conversant about Love, tho' turned often upon Praise too; and the Vein of Pastorals and Eclogues has run the same course, as may be observed in *Theocrytus*,[50] *Virgil*,[51] and *Horace*,[52] who was I think, the first and last of true *Lyrick* Poets among the *Latins:* Grief has been always the Subject of *Elegy*, and Reproach that of *Satyr*. The *Dramatick* Poesy has been Composed of all these, but the chief end seems to have been Instruction, and under the disguise of Fables, or the Pleasure of Story; to shew the Beauties and the Rewards of Virtue, the Deformities and Misfortunes, or Punishment of Vice: By Examples of both, to Encourage one, and Deter Men from the other; to Reform ill Customs, Correct ill Manners, and Moderate all violent Passions. These are the general Subjects of both Parts; tho' Comedy give us but the Images of common Life, and Tragedy those of the greater and more extraordinary Passions and Actions among Men. To go further upon this Subject, would be to tread so beaten Paths, that to Travel in them, only raises Dust, and is neither of Pleasure nor of Use.

For the Changes that have happened in Poetry, I shall observe one Antient, and the others that are Modern will be too Remarkable, in the Declines or Decays of this great Empire of Wit. The first Change of Poetry was made, by Translating it into Prose, or Cloathing it in those loose Robes, or common Veils that disguised or covered the true Beauty of its Features, and Exactness of its Shape. This was done first by *Æsop*[53] in *Greek*, but the Vein was much more antient in the *Eastern* Regions, and much in Vogue, as we may observe, in the many Parables used in the old Testament, as well as in the New. And there is a Book of Fables, of the sort of *Æsop's*, Translated out of *Persian*,[54] and pretended to have been so, into that Language out of the antient *Indian;* But though it seems Genuine of the *Eastern* Countries, yet I do not take it to be so old, nor to have so much Spirit as the *Greek*. The next Succession of Poetry in Prose, seems to have been in the *Miletian* Tales, which were a sort of little Pastoral Romances; and though much in request in old *Greece* and *Rome*, yet we have no Examples that I know of them, unless it be the *Longi Pastoralia*,[55] which gives a Tast of the great Delicacy and Pleasure, that was found so generally in those sort of Tales. The last Kind of Poetry in Prose, is that which in latter Ages has over-run the World, under the Name of Romances, which tho' it seems Modern, and a Production of the *Gothick* Genius, yet the Writing is antient. The remainders

[42] (522?–443 B.C.), Greek lyric poet

[43] (640?–550 B.C.), likewise a Greek lyric poet

[44] See footnote 17 above.

[45] Simonides of Ceos flourished at the beginning of the fifth century B.C., Phocylides and Theognis during the sixth century B.C.

[46] The Greek philosopher and mathematician (sixth century B.C.), left no writings, his theories having been handed down by his followers.

[47] Greek poet of the eighth century B.C., author of *Works and Days*

[48] See footnote 28 above.

[49] See footnote 35 above.

[50] See footnote 32 above.

[51] 70–19 B.C. [52] 65–8 B.C.

[53] Æsop, to whom *Æsop's Fables* has been traditionally ascribed, is said to have lived from about 620 B.C. through the first part of the following century.

[54] *Le Livre des Lumières, ou la Conduite des Roys, composé par le sage Pilpay* (Paris, 1644), a translation of the Persian version of certain Arabic fables, the latter being derived from the Indian fables of Pilpay

[55] *Daphnis and Chloe*, the Greek pastoral romance, attributed to Longus, a Greek writer who flourished sometime in the early part of the Christian era

of *Petronius Arbiter,*[56] seem to be of this kind, and that which *Lucian*[57] calls his True History: But the most antient that passes by the Name, is *Heliodorus,*[58] Famous for the Author's chusing to lose his Bishoprick, rather than disown that Child of his Wit. The true Spirit or Vein of antient Poetry in this kind, seems to shine most in Sir *Philip Sidney*, whom I esteem both the greatest Poet and the Noblest Genius of any that have left Writings behind them, and published in ours or any other modern Language; a Person born capable not only of forming the greatest *Ideas*, but of leaving the noblest Examples, if the length of his Life had been equal to the excellence of his Wit and his Virtues.

With him I leave the Discourse of antient Poetry, and to discover the Decays of this Empire, must turn to that of the modern, which was introduced after the Decays, or rather Extinction of the old, as if true Poetry being dead, an Apparition of it walked about. This mighty Change, arrived by no smaller Occasions, nor more ignoble Revolutions, than those which destroyed the antient Empire and Government of *Rome*, and Erected so many New ones upon their Ruins, by the Invasions and Conquests, or the general Inundations of the *Goths*, *Vandals*, and other Barbarous or Northern Nations, upon those Parts of *Europe*, that had been subject to the *Romans*. After the Conquests made by *Caesar* upon *Gaul*, and the nearer Parts of *Germany*, which were continued and enlarged in the times of *Augustus* and *Tiberius*[59] by their Lieutenants or Generals, great Numbers of *Germans* and *Gauls* resorted to the *Roman* Armies and to the City it self, and habituated themselves there, as many *Spaniards*, *Syrians*, *Græcians* had done before upon the Conquest of those Countries. This mixture, soon Corrupted the Purity of the *Latin* Tongue, so that in *Lucan,*[60] but more in *Seneca,*[61] we find a great and harsh Allay, entered into the Style of the *Augustan* Age. After *Trajan* and *Adrian*[62] had subdued many *German* and *Scythian* Nations, on both sides of the *Danube*, the Commerce of those barbarous People grew very frequent with the *Romans;* and I am apt to think, that the little Verses ascribed to *Adrian*, were in imitation of the *Runick* Poetry. The *Scythicas Pati Pruinas* of *Florus,*[63] shews their Race or Clymate, and the first Rhyme that ever I read in *Latin*, with little Allusions of Letters or Syllables, is in that of *Adrian* at his Death;

O Animula, vagula, blandula,
Quae nunc abibis in loca,
Palidula, lurida, timidula,
Nec ut soles dabis jocoa.[64]

'Tis probable the old Spirit of Poetry, being lost or frighted away by those long and bloody Wars with such barbarous Enemies, this New Ghost began to appear in its room, even about that Age, or else that *Adrian*, who affected that piece of Learning as well as others, and was not able to reach the old Vein, turned to a new one, which his Expeditions into those Countries made more allowable in an Emperor, and his Example recommended to others. In the time of *Boetius,*[65] who lived

[56] Petronius Arbiter, to whom the *Satyricon* has been ascribed, lived in the first century A.D.

[57] Greek satirist of the second century A.D., author of *The True History*

[58] a Greek writer of the third century A.D., (not, as Temple believed, the Heliodorus who was a bishop) author of *Ethiopica*, an early Greek romance

[59] Augustus, emperor from 27 B.C. to 14 A.D.; Tiberius, emperor from 14 to 37 A.D.

[60] 39–65 A.D. See footnote 33 above.

[61] 4 B.C.?–65 A.D.

[62] Trajan, emperor from 98 to 117 A.D.; Adrian, emperor from 117 to 138 A.D.

[63] The phrase "Scythicas Pati Pruinas" ("to endure the Scythian snows") is from a poem addressed to the Emperor Adrian, probably by the poet and rhetorician Publius Annius Florus.

[64] The Emperor's famous verses, *Adriani Morientis ad Animam*, were translated by Pope:

Ah, fleeting Spirit! wandring fire,
That long hast warm'd my tender breast,
Must thou no more this frame inspire,
No more a pleasing cheerful guest?
Whither, ah whither, art thou flying,
To what dark undiscover'd shore?
Thou seem'st all trembling, shiv'ring, dying,
And Wit and Humour are no more!

[65] Boetius, or Boethius (480?–524), Roman philosopher, author of *De Consolatione Philosophiae* (*The Consolation of Philosophy*)

under *Theodorick*[66] in *Rome*, we feel the *Latin* Poetry smell rank of this *Gothick* Imitation, and the old vein quite seared up.

After that Age, Learning grew every day more and more obscured, by that Cloud of Ignorance, which coming from the *North*, and increasing with the Numbers and Successes of those barbarous People, at length over-shadowed all *Europe* for so long together. The *Roman* Tongue began it self to fail or be disused, and by its Corruption made way for the Generation of three New Languages, in *Spain*, *Italy* and *France*. The Courts of the Princes and Nobles, who were of the Conquering Nations, for several Ages used their *Gothick*, or *Franc*, or *Saxon* Tongues, which were mingled with those of *Germany*, where some of the *Goths* had sojourned long, before they proceeded to their Conquests of the more *Southern* or *Western* Parts. Wherever the *Roman* Colonies had long remained, and their Language had been generally spoken, the common People used that still, but vitiated with the base allay of their Provincial Speech. This in *Charlemain's*[67] time was called in *France*, *Rustica Romana;* and in Spain during the *Gothick* Reigns there, *Romance;* but in *England*, from whence all the *Roman* Souldiers, and great Numbers of the *Britains* most accustomed to their Commerce and Language, had been drained, for the Defence of *Gaul* against the barbarous Nations that Invaded it about the time of *Valentinian*,[68] that Tongue being wholly extinguish't, (as well as their own) made way for the intire use of the *Saxon* Language. With these Changes, the antient Poetry was wholly lost in all these Countries, and a new sort grew up by degrees, which was called by a new Name of Rhimes with an easy Change of the *Gothick* Word *Runes*, and not from the *Greek*, *Rythmes*, as is vulgarly supposed.

Runes, was properly the Name of the Antient *Gothick* Letters or Characters, which were Invented first or introduced by *Odin*, in the Colony or Kingdom of the *Getes* or *Goths*, which he Planted in the *North-West* Parts, and round the *Baltick* Sea, as has been before related.[69] But because all the Writings, they had among them for many Ages, were in Verse, it came to be the common Name of all sorts of Poetry among the *Goths*, and the Writers or Composers of them, were called *Runers* or *Rymers*. They had likewise another Name for them, or for some sorts of them, which was *Vüses* or *Wises*, and because the Sages of that Nation, expressed the best of their Thoughts, and what Learning and Prudence they had, in these kind of Writings, they that succeeded best and with most Applause were termed Wise-men, the good Sense, or Learning, or useful Knowledge contained in them, was called Wisdom, and the pleasant or facetious Vein among them was called Wit, which was applied to all Spirit or Race of Poetry, where it was found in any Men, and was generally pleasing to those that heard or read them.

Of these *Runes*, there were in use among the *Goths* above a hundred several sorts, some Composed in longer, some in shorter Lines, some equal and others unequal, with many different Cadencies, Quantities, or Feet, which in the pronouncing, make many different sorts of Original or Natural Tunes. Some were Framed with Allusions of Words, or Consonance of Syllables, or of Letters, either in the same Line or in the Dystick, or by alternate Succession and Resemblance, which made a sort of Gingle, that pleased the ruder Ears of that People. And because their Language was composed most of Monosyllables, and of so great Numbers, many must end in the same Sound; another sort of *Runes* were made, with the Care and Study of ending two Lines, or each other of four Lines, with Words of the same sound, which being the easiest, requiring less Art, and needing less Spirit (because a certain Chime in the Sounds supplied that want, and pleased common Ears); this in time grew the most general among all the

[66] Theodoric the Great invaded Italy in 488.

[67] Charlemagne, 742–814

[68] Roman emperor from 364 to 375

[69] "as has been before related": Temple's reference is to the fourth section of his essay *Of Heroic Virtue*, which, like the essays *Upon the Gardens of Epicurus* and *Of Poetry*, appeared in *Miscellanea, the Second Part.*

Gothick Colonies in *Europe*, and made Rhymes or Runes pass for the modern Poetry, in these Parts of the World.

This was not used only in their modern Languages, but during those ignorant Ages, even in that barbarous *Latin* which remained and was preserved among the *Monks* and *Priests*, to distinguish them, by some shew of Learning from the Laity, who might well admire it, in what Degree soever, and Reverence the Professors, when they themselves could neither Write nor Read even in their own Language; I mean not only the Vulgar Lay-men, but even the Generality of Nobles, Barons, and Princes among them; and this lasted, till the antient Learning and Languages began to be restored in *Europe*, about Two Hundred Years ago.

The common vein of the *Gothick Runes* was what is Termed *Dithyrambick*, and was of a raving or rambling sort of Wit or Invention, loose and flowing, with little Art or Confinement to any certain Measures or Rules; yet some of it wanted not the true Spirit of Poetry in some Degree, or that natural Inspiration which has been said to arise from some Spark of Poetical Fire, wherewith particular Men are born. And such as it was, it served the turn, not only to please, but even to Charm the Ignorant and Barbarous Vulgar, where it was in use. This made the *Runers* among the *Goths*, as much in request and admired, as any of the antient and most celebrated Poets were among the Learned Nations; for among the blind, he that has one Eye is a Prince. They were as well as the others thought inspired, and the Charms of their *Runick* Conceptions, were generally esteemed Divine or Magical at least.

The subjects of them were various, but commonly the same with those already observed in the true antient Poetry. Yet this Vein was chiefly imployed, upon the Records of Bold and Martial Actions, and the Praises of Valiant Men that had fought Successfully or Dyed Bravely, and these Songs or Ballads were usually sung at Feasts, or in Circles of Young or Idle Persons, and served to inflame the Humor of War, of Slaughter and of Spoils among them. More refined Honour or Love, had little Part in the Writings, because it had little in the Lives or Actions of those fierce People and bloody Times. Honour among them consisted in Victory, and Love in Rapes and in Lust.

But as the true Flame of Poetry was rare among them, and the rest was but Wild Fire that Sparkled or rather Crackled a while, and soon went out with little Pleasure or Gazing of the Beholders; Those *Runers* who could not raise Admiration by the Spirit of their Poetry, endeavoured to do it by another, which was that of Enchantments; This came in to supply the Defect of that sublime and Marvellous, which has been found both in Poetry and Prose among the Learned Antients. The *Gothick Runers* to Gain and Establish the Credit and Admiration of their Rhymes, turned the use of them very much to Incantations and Charms, pretending by them, to raise Storms, to Calm the Seas, to cause Terror in their Enemies, to Transport themselves in the Air, to Conjure Spirits, to Cure Diseases, and Stanch Bleeding Wounds, to make Women kind or easy, and Men hard or invulnerable; as one of their most antient *Runers*, affirms of himself and his own Atchievments, by Force of these Magical Arms. The Men or Women who were thought to perform such Wonders or Enchantments, were, from *Vïses* or *Wises*, the Name of those Verses wherein their Charms were conceived, called *Wizards* or *Witches*.

Out of this Quarry, seem to have been raised, all those Trophees of Enchantment, that appear in the whole Fabrick of the old *Spanish* Romances, which were the Productions of the *Gothick* Wit among them during their Reign, and after the Conquests of *Spain*, by the *Saracens*, they were applied to the long Wars between them and the Christians. From the same may perhaps be derived, all the visionary Tribe of *Fairies*, *Elves*, and *Goblins*, of *Sprites* and of *Bul-beggars*, that serve not only to fright Children into whatever their Nurses please, but sometimes, by lasting Impressions, to disquiet the sleeps and the very Lives of Men and Women, till they grow to Years of Discretion, and that God knows is a Period of time, which some People Arrive to but very late, and perhaps others never. At least this belief prevailed so far among the *Goths* and their Races, that all sorts of Charms, were not only Attributed to their *Runes* or *Verses*, but to their very Characters; so that about the Eleventh Century, they were forbidden and abolished in *Sweden*, as they had been before in *Spain*, by Civil and Ecclesiastical Commands or Constitutions, and what has been since recovered of that Learning or Language, has been fetcht as far as *Ysland* it self.

How much of this Kind, and of this Credulity remained even to our own Age, may be observed by any Man that Reflects so far as Thirty or Forty Years; how often Avouched, and how generally Credited were the Stories of *Faires*, *Sprites*, *Witchcrafts*, and *Enchantments;* In some Parts of *France*, and not longer ago, the common People believed certainly, there were *Lougaroos*, or Men turned into Wolves; and I remember several *Irish* of the same mind. The Remainders are woven into our very Language, *Mara* in old *Runick* was a *Goblin* that seized upon Men asleep in their Beds, and took from them all Speech and Motion. Old *Nicka* was a Sprite that came to strangle People who fell into the Water: *Bo* was a fierce *Gothick* Captain, Son of *Odin*, whose Name was used by his Souldiers when they would Fright or Surprise their Enemies; and the Proverb of Rhyming, *Rats to Death*, came I suppose from the same Root.

There were not longer since than the time I have mentioned, some Remainders of the *Runick* Poetry among the *Irish*. The Great Men of their Septs, among the many Offices of their Family, which continued always in the same Races, had not only a *Physician*, a *Hunts-man*, a *Smith*, and such like, but a *Poet*, and a *Tale-teller:* The first Recorded and Sung the Actions of their Ancestors, and Entertained the Company at Feasts; The Latter, Amuzed them with Tales when they were Melancholy and could not sleep: And a very Gallant Gentleman of the *North* of *Ireland* has told me, of his own Experience, That in his Wolf-Huntings there, when he used to be abroad in the Mountains three or four Days together, and lay very ill a Nights, so as he could not well sleep, they would bring him one of these *Tale-tellers*, that when he lay down, would begin a Story of a King, or a Gyant, a Dwarf and a Damosel, and such rambling stuff, and continue it all Night long in such an even Tone, that you heard it going on, whenever you awaked; and he believed nothing any Physitians give, could have so good and so innocent effect, to make Men Sleep, in any Pains or Distempers of Body or Mind. I remember in my youth, some Persons of our Country to have said Grace in Rhymes, and others their constant Prayers; and 'tis vulgar enough, that some Deeds or Conveyances of Land, have been so, since the Conquest.

In such poor wretched Weeds as these, was Poetry cloathed during those shades of Ignorance that over-spread all *Europe*, for so many Ages after the Sunset of the *Roman* Learning and Empire together, which were Succeeded by so many New Dominions, or Plantations of the *Gothick* Swarms, and by a New Face of Customs, Habit, Language, and almost of Nature: But upon the dawn of a New Day, and the Resurrection of other Sciences, with the Two Learned Languages among us, This of Poetry began to appear very early, tho' very unlike it self, and in shapes as well as Clothes, in Humor and in Spirit very different from the Antient. It was now all in Rhyme, after the *Gothick* Fashion, for indeed none of the several Dialects of that Language or Allay, would bear the Composure of such Feet and Measures, as were in use among the *Greeks* and *Latins*, and some that attempted it, soon left it off, despairing of Success. Yet in this New Dress, Poetry was not without some Charms, especially those of Grace and Sweetness, and the Oar begun to shine in the Hands and Works of the first Refiners. *Petrarch, Ronsard, Spencer,*[70] met with much Applause upon the Subjects of Love, Praise, Grief, Reproach. *Ariosto*[71] and *Tasso*,[72] entered boldly upon the Scene of *Heroick* Poems, but having not Wings for so high Flights, began to Learn of the old Ones, fell upon their Imitations, and

[70] Petrarch, 1304–1374; Ronsard, 1524–1585; Edmund Spencer, 1552?–1599

[71] 1474–1533, author of the epic poem, *Orlando Furioso*

[72] 1544–1595, author of the epic poem, *Gerusalemme Liberata*

chiefly of *Virgil*, as far as the Force of their Genius, or Disadvantage of New Languages and Customs would allow. The Religion of the Gentiles, had been woven into the Contexture of all the antient Poetry, with a very agreeable mixture, which made the Moderns affect, to give that of Christianity, a place also in their Poems. But the true Religion, was not found to become Fiction so well, as a false had done, and all their Attempts of this kind, seemed rather to debase Religion, than to heighten Poetry. *Spencer* endeavoured to Supply this, with Morality, and to make Instruction, instead of Story, the Subject of an *Epick* Poem. His Execution was Excellent, and his Flights of Fancy very Noble and High, but his Design was Poor, and his Moral lay so bare, that it lost the Effect; 'tis true, the Pill was Gilded, but so thin, that the Colour and the Taste were too easily discovered.

After these three, I know none of the Moderns that have made any Atchievments in *Heroick* Poetry worth Recording. The Wits of the Age, soon left off such bold Adventures, and turned to other Veins, as if not worthy to sit down at the Feast, they contented themselves with the Scraps, with Songs and Sonnets, with Odes and Elegies, with Satyrs and Panegyricks, and what we call Copies of Verses upon any Subjects or Occasions, wanting either Genius or Application for Nobler or more Laborious Productions, as *Painters* that cannot Succeed in great Pieces, turn to Miniature.

But the modern Poets, to value this small Coyn, and make it pass, tho' of so much a baser Metal than the old, gave it a New Mixture from Two Veins, which were little known or little esteemed among the Ancients. There were indeed certain *Fairyes* in the old Regions of Poetry, called *Epigrams*, which seldom reached above the Stature of Two, or Four, or Six Lines, and which Being so short, were all turned upon Conceit, or some sharp Hits of Fancy or Wit. The only Ancient of this kind among the *Latins*, were the *Priapeia*, which were little Voluntaries or Extemporaries, Written upon the ridiculous Woodden Statues of *Priapus*, among the Gardens of *Rome*. In the decays of the *Roman* Learning and Wit as well as Language, *Martial*, *Ausonius*,[73] and others fell into this Vein, and applied it indifferently to all Subjects, which was before Restrained to one, and Drest it something more cleanly than it was Born. This Vein of Conceit, seemed proper for such Scraps or Splinters, into which Poetry was broken, and was so eagerly followed, as almost to over-run all that was Composed in our several modern Languages; The *Italian*, the *French*, the *Spanish* as well as *English*, were for a great while full of nothing else but Conceit: It was an Ingredient, that gave Taste to Compositions which had little of themselves; 'twas a Sauce that gave Point to Meat that was Flat, and some Life to Colours that were Fading, and in short, those who could not furnish Spirit, supplied it with this Salt, which may preserve Things or Bodys that are Dead; but is, for ought I know, of little use to the Living, or necessary to Meats that have much or pleasing Tasts of their own. However it were, this Vein first over-flowed our modern Poetry, and with so little Distinction or Judgment that we would have Conceit as well as Rhyme in every Two Lines, and run through all our long Scribbles as well as the short, and the whole Body of the Poem, whatever it is: This was just as if a Building should be nothing but Ornament, or Cloaths nothing but Trimming; as if a Face should be covered over with black Patches, or a Gown with Spangles, which is all I shall say of it.

Another Vein which has entred and helpt to Corrupt our modern Poesy, is that of Ridicule, as if nothing pleased but what made one Laugh, which yet come from Two very different Affections of the Mind; for as Men have no Disposition to Laugh at things they are most pleased with, so they are very little pleased with many things they Laugh at.

But this mistake is very general, and such modern Poets, as found no better way of pleasing, thought they could not fail of it, by Ridiculing. This was Encouraged by finding Conversation run so much into the same Vein, and the Wits in Vogue to take up with that Part of it, which was formerly left to those that were called Fools, and were used in great Families,

[73] Martial, famous for his Latin epigrams, lived in the first century A.D.; Ausonius, poet and scholar, lived in the fourth century A.D.

only to make the Company Laugh. What Opinion the *Romans* had of this Character, appears in those Lines of *Horace:*

Absentem qui rodit amicum,
Qui non defendit alio culpante, solutos
Qui captat risus hominum famamque; dicacis
Fingere qui non visa potest, Commissa tacere
Qui nequit, Hic Niger est, Hunc tu Romane
caveto.[74]

And 'tis pity the Character of a Wit, in one Age, should be so like that of a Black in another.

Rablais[75] seems to have been Father of the Ridicule, a Man of Excellent and Universal Learning as well as Wit, and tho' he had too much Game given him for *Satyr* in that Age, by the Customs of Courts and of Convents, of Processes and of Wars, of Schools and of Camps, of Romances and Legends; Yet he must be Confest to have kept up his Vein of Ridicule by saying many things so Malicious, so Smutty, and so Prophane, that either a Prudent, a Modest, or a Pious Man, could not have afforded, tho' he had never so much of that Coyn about him, and it were to be wished, that the Wits who have followed his Vein, had not put too much Value upon a Dress, that better Understandings would not wear (at least in publick) and upon a compass they gave themselves, which other Men would not take. The Matchless Writer of *Don Quixot*[76] is much more to be admired, for having made up so excellent a Composition of Satyr or Ridicule, without those Ingredients, and seems to be the best and highest Strain that ever was, or will be reached by that Vein.

It began first in Verse, with an *Italian* Poem, called *La Secchia Rapita*,[77] was pursued by *Scarron*[78] in *French* with his *Virgil* Travesty, and in *English* by Sir *John Mince*,[79] *Hudibras*,[80] and *Cotton*,[81] and with greater height of *Burlesque* in the *English*, than I think in any other Language. But let the Execution be what it will, the Design, the Custom, and Example are very pernicious to Poetry, and indeed, to all Virtue and Good Qualities among Men, which must be disheartened, by finding how unjustly and undistinguish't they fall under the lash of Raillery, and this Vein of Ridiculing the Good as well as the Ill, the Guilty and the Innocent together. 'Tis a very poor, tho' common Pretence to merit, to make it appear by the Faults of other Men. A mean Wit or Beauty may pass in a Room, where the rest of the Company are allowed to have none; 'tis something to sparkle among Diamonds, but to shine among *Pebbles*, is neither Credit nor Value worth the pretending.

Besides, these two Veins brought in, to supply the Defects of the modern Poetry, much Application has been made to the smoothness of Language or Style, which has at the best, but the Beauty of Colouring in a Picture, and can never make a good one, without Spirit and Strength. The Academy[82] set up by Cardinal *Richlieu*,[83] to amuse the Wits of that Age and Country, and divert them from raking into his Politicks and Ministery, brought this in Vogue, and the *French* Wits have for this last Age, been in a manner, wholly turned to the Refinement of their Language, and indeed with such Success, that it can hardly be excelled, and runs equally through their Verse and their Prose. The same Vein has been likewise much Cultivated in our modern *English* Poetry, and by such poor Recruits, have the broken Forces of this Empire been of late made up, with what Success I leave to be judged

[74] "He who calumniates his absent friend, or who does not defend him when another attacks; who seeks to rain laughter and to gain the reputation of a wit; who is capable of inventing things he never saw, is unable to keep secret what has been confided to him,—he is a dangerous man [literally, he is black]. Roman, beware of him." Horace, *Satires*, I. iv. 81–85

[75] François Rabelais, 1494?–1553

[76] Miguel de Cervantes, 1547–1616

[77] "The Rape of the Bucket," a mock heroic epic by the Italian poet Alessandro Tassoni (1565–1635)

[78] Paul Scarron (1610–1660) wrote a burlesque epic, *Virgile Travesti.*

[79] Sir John Minnes or Mince or Mennes (1599–1671), co-author with James Smith of *Wits Recreation* (1640), *Musarum Deliciae* (1655), and *Wit Restored* (1658)

[80] i.e., Samuel Butler, author of *Hudibras*

[81] Charles Cotton (1630–1687) paraphrased Scarron in *Scarronides* (1664).

[82] the *Académie Française*

[83] 1585–1642

by such, as consider it in the former Heights, and the present Declines both of Power and of Honour, but this will not discourage, however it may affect, the true Lovers of the Mistriss, who must ever think her a Beauty in Rags as well as in Robes.

Among these many Decays, there is yet one sort of Poetry, that seems to have succeeded much better with our Moderns, than any of the rest, which is *Dramatick*, or that of the Stage: In this the *Italian*, the *Spanish*, and the *French*, have all had their different Merit, and received their just Applauses. Yet I am deceived, if our *English*, has not in some kind excelled both the Modern and the Antient, which has been by Force of a Vein Natural perhaps to our Country, and which with us, is called Humour, a Word peculiar to our Language too, and hard to be Expressed in any other; nor is it (that I know of) found in any Foreign Writers, unless it be *Moliere*,[84] and yet his it self, has too much of the Farce, to pass for the same with ours. *Shakespear* was the first that opened this Vein upon our Stage, which has run so freely and so pleasantly ever since, that I have often wondered, to find it appear so little upon any others; being a Subject so proper for them, since Humour is but a Picture of particular Life, as Comedy is of general; and tho' it represents Dispositions, and Customs less common, yet they are not less natural than those that are more frequent among Man; for if Humour it self be forced, it loses all the Grace, which has been indeed the Fault of some of our Poets most Celebrated in this kind.

It may seem a Defect in the antient Stage, that the Characters introduced were so few, and those so common, as a Covetous Old Man, an Amorous Young, a Witty Wench, a Crafty Slave, a Bragging Souldier: The Spectators met nothing upon the Stage, but what they met in the Streets and at every Turn. All the Variety is drawn only from different and uncommon Events; whereas if the Characters are so too, the Diversity and the Pleasure must needs be the more. But as of most general Customs in a Country, there is usually some Ground, from the Nature of the People or the Clymat, so there may be amongst us, for this Vein of our Stage, and a greater variety of Humor in the Picture, because there is a greater variety in the Life. This may proceed from the Native Plenty of our Soyl, the unequalness of our Clymat, as well as the Ease of our Government, and the Liberty of Professing Opinions and Factions, which perhaps our Neighbors may have about them, but are forced to disguise, and thereby they may come in time to be extinguish't. Plenty begets Wantonness and Pride, Wantonness is apt to invent, and Pride scorns to Imitate; Liberty begets Stomack or Heart, and Stomack will not be Constrained. Thus we come to have more Originals, and more that appear what they are, we have more Humour because every Man follows his own, and takes a Pleasure, perhaps a Pride to shew it.

On the contrary, where the People are generally poor, and forced to hard Labour, their Actions and Lives are all of a Piece; where they serve hard Masters, they must follow his Examples as well as Commands and are forced upon Imitation in small Matters, as well as Obedience in great: So that some Nations look as if they were cast all by one Mould, or Cut out all by one Pattern, (at least the common People in one, and the Gentlemen in another): They seem all of a sort in their Habits, their Customs, and even their Talk and Conversation, as well as in the Application and Pursuit of their Actions and their Lives.

Besides all this, there is another sort of Variety amongst us, which arises from our Clymat, and the Dispositions it Naturally produces. We are not only more unlike one another, than any Nation I know, but we are more unlike our selves too, at several times, and owe to our very Air, some ill Qualities as well as many good: We may allow some Distempers Incident to our Clymat, since so much Health, Vigor and Length of Life have been generally Ascribed to it; for among the *Greek* and *Roman* Authors themselves, we shall find the *Britains* observed, to Live the longest, and the *Ægyptians* the shortest, of any Nations that were known in those Ages. Besides, I think none will Dispute the Native Courage of our Men, and Beauty of our Women, which may be elsewhere as

[84] 1622–1673

great in Particulars, but no where so in General; they may be (what is said of Diseases) as Acute in other Places, but with us, they are Epidemical. For my own Part, who have Conversed much with Men of other Nations, and such as have been both in great Imployments and Esteem, I can say very impartially, that I have not observed among any, so much true Genius as among the *English;* No where more Sharpness of Wit, more Pleasantness of Humour, more Range of Fancy, more Penetration of Thought or Depth of Reflexion among the better Sort: No where more Goodness of Nature and of Meaning, nor more Plainness of Sense and of Life than among the common Sort of Country People, nor more blunt Courage and Honesty, than among our Sea-men.

But with all this, our Country must be confest, to be what a great Foreign Physitian called it, The Region of Spleen, which may arise a good deal from the great uncertainty and many suddain Changes of our Weather in all Seasons of the Year: And how much these Affect the Heads and Hearts, especially of the finest Tempers, is hard to be Believed by Men, whose Thoughts are not turned to such Speculations. This makes us unequal in our Humours, inconstant in our Passions, uncertain in our Ends, and even in our Desires. Besides, our different Opinions in Religion and the Factions they have Raised or Animated, for Fifty Years past, have had an ill Effect upon our Manners and Customs, inducing more Avarice, Ambition, Disguise (with the usual Consequences of them) than were before in our Constitution. From all this it may happen that there is no where more true Zeal in the many different Forms of Devotion, and yet no where more Knavery under the Shews and Pretences. There are no where so many Disputers upon Religion, so many Reasoners upon Government, so many Refiners in Politicks, so many Curious Inquisitives, so many Pretenders to Business and State-Imployments, greater Porers upon Books, nor Plodders after Wealth. And yet no where more Abandoned Libertines, more Refined Luxurists, Extravagant Debauches, Conceited Gallants, more Dabblers in Poetry as well as Politicks, in Philosophy and in Chymistry. I have had several Servants far gone in Divinity, others in Poetry; have known in the Families of some Friends, a Keeper deep in the *Rosycrucia* Principles,[85] and a Laundress firm in those of *Epicurus*.[86] What Effect soever such a Composition or Medly of Humours among us may have upon our Lives or our Government, it must needs have a good one upon our Stage, and has given admirable Play to our Comical Wits. So that in my Opinion there is no Vein of that sort either Antient or Modern, which Excels or Equals the Humour of our Plays. And for the rest, I cannot but observe, the Honour of our Country, that the good Qualities amongst us, seem to be Natural, and the ill ones more Accidental, and such as would be easily Changed by the Examples of Princes, and by the Precepts of Laws; such I mean as should be Designed to Form Manners, to Restrain Excesses, to Encourage Industry, to Prevent Mens Expences beyond their Fortunes, to Countenance Virtue, and Raise that True Esteem due to Plain Sense and Common Honesty.

But to Spin off this Thread which is already Grown too Long: What Honour and Request the antient Poetry has Lived in, may not only be Observed from the Universal Reception and Use in all Nations from *China* to *Peru*, from *Scythia* to *Arabia*, but from the Esteem of the Best and the Greatest Men as well as the Vulgar. Among the *Hebrews*, *David* and *Solomon* the Wisest Kings, *Job* and *Jeremiah* the Holiest Men, were the best Poets of their Nation and Language. Among the *Greeks*, the Two most Renowned Sages and Law-givers were *Lycurgus*[87] and *Solon*,[88] whereof the Last is known to have Excelled in Poetry, and the First was so great a Lover of it, That to his Care and Industry we are said (by some Authors) to owe the Collection and Preservation of

[85] the occult principles of the Rosicrucian Society (reputedly founded in the fifteenth century by one Christian Rosenkreutz), popularized by a well-known book by the Abbé de Villars, *Comte de Gabalis, ou Entretiens sur les Sciences secrètes* (1670)

[86] 342?–270 B.C.

[87] the traditional Spartan lawgiver of the ninth century B.C.

[88] the Athenian lawgiver (638?–559 B.C.)

the loose and scattered Pieces of *Homer*, in the Order wherein they have since appeared. *Alexander* is reported neither to have Travelled nor Slept, without those admirable Poems always in his Company. *Phalaris*[89] that was Inexorable to all other Enemies, Relented at the Charms of *Stesichorus*[90] his Muse. Among the *Romans*, the Last and Great *Scipio*,[91] passed the soft Hours of his Life in the Conversation of *Terence*,[92] and was thought to have a Part in the Composition of his Comedies. *Cæsar* was an Excellent Poet as well as Orator, and Composed a Poem in his Voyage from *Rome* to *Spain*, Relieving the Tedious Difficulties of his March, with the Entertainments of his Muse. *Augustus* was not only a Patron, but a Friend and Companion of *Virgil* and *Horace*, and was himself, both an Admirer of Poetry, and a pretender too, as far as his Genius would reach, or his busy Scene allow. 'Tis true, since his Age, we have few such Examples of great Princes favouring or affecting Poetry, and as few perhaps of great Poets deserving it. Whether it be, that the fierceness of the *Gothick* Humours, or Noise of their perpetual Wars frighted it away, or that the unequal mixture of the Modern Languages would not bear it; Certain it is, That the great Heights and Excellency both of Poetry and Musick, fell with the *Roman* Learning and Empire, and have never since recovered the Admiration and Applauses that before attended them. Yet such as they are amongst us, they must be confest to be the Softest and Sweetest, the most General and most Innocent Amusements of common Time and Life. They still find Room in the Courts of Princes, and the Cottages of Shepherds. They serve to Revive and Animate the dead Calm of poor or idle Lives, and to Allay or Divert the violent Passions and Perturbations of the greatest and the busiest Men. And both these Effects are of equal use to Humane Life; for the Mind of Man is like the Sea, which is neither agreeable to the Beholder nor the Voyager, in a Calm or in a Storm, but is so to both, when a little Agitated by gentle Gales; and so the Mind, when moved by soft and easy Passions or Affections. I know very well, that many who pretend to be Wise, by the Forms of being Grave, are apt to despise both Poetry and Musick, as Toys and trifles too light for the Use or Entertainment of serious Men. But whoever find themselves wholly insensible to these Charms, would I think do well, to keep their own Counsel, for fear of Reproaching their own Temper, and bringing the Goodness of their Natures, if not of their Understandings, into Question: It may be thought at least an ill Sign, if not an ill Constitution, since some of the Fathers went so far as to esteem the Love of Musick a sign of Predestination, as a thing Divine, and Reserved for the Felicities of Heaven it self. While this World lasts, I doubt not, but the Pleasure and Request of these Two Entertainments, will do so too, and happy those that content themselves with these or any other so Easy and so Innocent, and do not trouble the World or other Men, because they cannot be quiet themselves, though no body hurts them.

When all is done, Humane Life is at the greatest and the best, but like a froward Child, that must be Play'd with, and Humor'd a little, to keep it quiet, till it falls asleep, and then the Care is over.

[89] See footnote 18 above.

[90] See footnote 19 above.

[91] "Scipio the Younger" (185–129 B.C.), adopted grandson of "Scipio the Elder" (Scipio Africanus, victor over Hannibal)

[92] the Latin playwright (190?–159 B.C.)

Anglican Sermons

THE seventeenth century was the great age of English pulpit oratory. But it was also the transitional period between two phases of English Protestantism, and the sermons representative of the Jacobean and Caroline eras stand in marked contrast with those preached from Anglican pulpits during the four decades following the Restoration. The contrast is of course a multiple one, involving not only stylistic and rhetorical characteristics but all the complexities of imaginative sensibility and of philosophical and theological orientation. By common consent the three post-Restoration divines who stand forth as masters of the art of the sermon are Barrow, South, and Tillotson. Not too dissimilar in style, they represent not only the general movement towards a simplified prose but the theological trend in the direction of a kind of rationalism. In both respects they differ sharply from the two great representatives of the earlier, golden period of seventeenth-century Anglicanism, Donne and Andrewes. Yet in spite of the many things which as Restoration divines they held in common, in spite of the fact that collectively they stand for an Anglicanism which seems closer to the spirit of Locke than of Hooker, it would be a mistake to identify them too closely with one another. They were three individuals, differing in temperament and in views, each illustrating certain attitudes and interests characteristic of post-Restoration Anglican thought and sentiment.

Isaac Barrow (1630–1677)

Barrow was born in London, the son of Thomas Barrow, linendraper to Charles I and a staunch royalist. He received his early education at Charterhouse School, entering Trinity College, Cambridge, in 1645. Despite the Puritanism which was then dominant at Cambridge, Barrow remained true to the loyalties of his family and declined to take the Covenant. Proceeding to the B.A. in 1648, he was elected fellow of his college in 1649, took his M.A. in 1652, travelled abroad for some four years, and upon his return home in 1659 received episcopal ordination from Bishop Brownrigg. By this time he had become a notable scholar, distinguished both for his classical and mathematical studies. The Restoration quickly brought him full recognition: in 1660 he was appointed Regius Professor of Greek at Cambridge; in 1662, professor of geometry at Gresham College; and in 1663, the first Lucasian Professor of Mathematics at Cambridge. As a mathematician he was considered by his contemporaries second only to Newton, in whose favor Barrow resigned his Lucasian Professorship in 1669. He was chaplain to Charles II, and received the D.D. by royal mandate in 1670. Two years thereafter he became Master of Trinity, serving as such during the five remaining years of his life.

His writings as a divine fall into three groups, represented by the controversial *Treatise on the Pope's Supremacy* (1680), the *Brief Exposition on the Creed* (1697), and his sermons. His fame has come to rest almost entirely upon his sermons, but it should be remembered that because many of these were written with no thought of pulpit delivery (he is said to have seen in print only his famous Spital Sermon, delivered in 1671, *On the Duty and Reward of Bounty to the Poor*) the

Restoration had scant opportunity to know him as a preacher. The two aspects which strike the modern student of his sermons most forcibly concern his rhetorical art and his thought. His style is clear, fluent, vigorous, and his figurative language is effective but for the most part unobtrusive. His ideal is said to have been Chrysostom. He gives us consistently the practical emphasis of the moralist, though with this he combines a high degree of intellectuality. Each of his sermons, as has often been remarked, resembles the demonstration of a mathematical theorem. In regard to his position as theologian and philosopher, he has never been classed as one of the Cambridge Platonists, nor should he be. Like them he endeavored, however, to minimize unimportant differences. He went so far in reaction against Calvinism as to make the Atonement universal. He held Hobbes's doctrine that men are naturally enemies to one another a "monstrous paradox," maintaining the contrary, the Aristotelian principle, that man is naturally a sociable creature. But Barrow is chiefly to be remembered as an early and one of the clearest expounders of the doctrine of beneficence, which was one of the most important contributions of Anglican thought to the so-called Age of Reason.

Robert South (1634–1716)

South, like Barrow, was the son of a London merchant. At Westminster School, to which he was admitted as a King's scholar in 1647, he studied under the famous Richard Busby. He was elected a student of Christ Church, Oxford, matriculating late in 1651, taking the B.A. in 1655, and the M.A. two years later. As a student at Oxford he was known for his Anglican principles, and there was some opposition to his proceeding to the M.A. because of his use of the Book of Common Prayer. After travelling on the continent he received episcopal ordination in 1658, and upon returning to Oxford preached a notorious assize sermon in which he attacked the Independents. Shortly after the Restoration he was appointed Public Orator of Oxford University, a post which he retained until 1677. He was domestic chaplain to Lord Clarendon, and when Clarendon fell in 1667 South became chaplain to the Duke of York. In 1676 he was presented to the rectory of Islip, Oxfordshire. As a stout royalist and one who had preached passive obedience, South, like others of his stamp, went through a difficult period of indecision following the Restoration. Though he ended by taking the oath, he is reported to have declined a bishopric relinquished by a non-juror, and it is certain that his hostility to the dissenters underwent no mollification. He made a final show of his Toryism during the Sacheverell uproar in 1710. Some three years before his death he was offered both the See of Rochester and the Deanery of Westminster, but these too he declined.

Whereas both Barrow and Tillotson wrote their sermons with great care, South was a brilliant extempore preacher, and in this respect was entirely in accord with Restoration fashion, which in reaction against both the written and the carefully memorized sermon—the latter being the type which had come into favor among dissenters—decreed that the preacher should enter the pulpit with at most only a set of notes, relying for elocutionary effect upon his readiness of wit and speech. South's method was thus quite modern. His style, on the other hand, is sometimes marked by an excess of wit and by passages in which he gave free rein to his so-called "graphic humour," and in these respects it did not fully reflect, as did the style of both Barrow and Tillotson, the new ideal of simplicity and conceptual lucidity. This is not to say that South failed to achieve a style acceptable to his generation. His theory of rhetoric was not precisely that expounded by various members of the Royal Society, but it was carefully meditated—there were few preachers of the time who dealt so fully with the subject in their sermons—and gave to his language a directness and bite that sometimes points in the direction of Swift.

South's general position as theologian, thinker, and commentator on the issues of his time, though consistent, is not easily described in brief terms. Like the rationalistic divines of his day, he frequently discussed natural religion and right reason; but like the more Calvinistic divines of an older period, he gave great emphasis to the insufficiency of fallen man's natural knowledge and to the need of Revelation. He made constant war against all those whom he regarded as enemies of the Church of England, including not only Hobbists, Arians, Socinians but—and chiefly—the Puritans and Dissenters on the one hand and Roman Catholicism on the other, and in this he takes his place as one of the militant defenders of the Anglican *via media.* On the ethical side he belongs to a substantially different tradition from the one represented by Barrow: he makes much of the role of the passions in human conduct, but mistrusts them; he bids his auditors to submit to the Divine Will, bids them to hope for salvation through conversion, Justification, and the Atonement.

John Tillotson (1630–1694)

Tillotson, who rose to be Dean of St. Paul's (1689) and then Archbishop of Canterbury (1691), was one of the most distinguished of that group of Anglican clergy known as the Latitudinarians. The term had first been applied to the Cambridge Platonists, but shortly came to designate a somewhat different, though in many ways cognate, group of Restoration divines—others being Stillingfleet, Patrick, Fowler, and Burnet—whose views concerning salvation had departed far from earlier Calvinistic doctrine and who laid great stress upon man's rational capacity, emphasized morality, deplored unnecessary differences of opinion, and hoped for a *rapprochement* with the Dissenters. The events of the Revolution of 1688 were such as to bring churchmen of this sort into places of importance, and Tillotson was only one of a very considerable number of Latitudinarian divines who were raised to the bishops' bench shortly after the accession of William and Mary.

Tillotson's career was a striking one. Born of Puritan parents in the parish of Halifax, Yorkshire, he was admitted as a pensioner at Clare Hall, Cambridge, in 1647. The master of Clare was then Ralph Cudworth, the Platonist, but Tillotson, still a pronounced Calvinist, is said to have been little influenced by him at this time. He proceeded B.A. in 1650, was elected a fellow in 1651, and received the M.A. in 1654. In the immediately ensuing years he went up to London to serve as tutor to a young man of wealth and position, found himself—under the influence of Chillingworth's famous book, *The Religion of Protestants* (1637)—moving steadily away from Calvinism, and received orders from the Bishop of Galloway, though he continued to identify himself with the Presbyterians until the Act of Uniformity. In 1663 he replaced the ejected rector of a small Suffolk church, but resigned shortly thereafter when it became apparent that his preaching was distasteful to his puritanical parishioners. Through his friendship with John Wilkins, formerly Master of Trinity College, Cambridge, and an old parliamentarian who had conformed at the Restoration and had been presented by King Charles to a London vicarage, Tillotson now became Tuesday lecturer at St. Lawrence Jewry. In 1666 he was elected preacher at Lincoln's Inn, granted the degree of D.D. and made one of the King's chaplains. At the time of the Revolution he and his fellow Latitudinarians played a not inconsiderable part in the national drama by insuring the acceptance on the part of the established church of a change in the person of the sovereign, a change which had seemed to many to be incompatible with the theory of passive obedience and non-resistance which had been preached so long from so many Anglican pulpits. Though it was as a result of the

Revolution that Tillotson succeeded to the Primacy, there were few who regarded him as a time-server. His deep sincerity, his sweetness of temper, and his generosity towards all manner of charitable causes were recognized by all.

It is to a combination of style and thought that we may attribute Tillotson's popularity as a London preacher and the great influence which he exerted not only over his immediate auditors but upon the entire spirit of Anglicanism as it sought to retain a moral and spiritual hold upon the educated classes of the metropolitan area. In homiletics he carried to its ultimate development the movement towards a plain, simple style of discourse, a style which sought to achieve its effect not through learned quotations but through common sense and reasonableness, not through the witty language of imagery and allusion but through unadorned statements which carried force by reason of conceptual clarity. Here was the triumph of the well-modulated style. It was accompanied, in Tillotson as in practically all his contemporaries who achieved recognition for this kind of preaching, by a rationalistic attitude in striking contrast with the Calvinism which had shaped the thought of so many Anglican thinkers of earlier decades. The modern commentator who is repelled by what he takes to be the coldness of Tillotson's sermons is perhaps expressing less distaste for his prose style than for the character of his intellectual-religious outlook. The precepts of Christianity, Tillotson declared, are reasonable and wise; they are according to the light of reason; they are useful and beneficial. In short, they direct us to nothing "but what is most reasonable and fit to be done by us, nothing but what if we were to consult our own interest and happiness, and did rightly understand our selves, we would choose for our selves. . . . " The essence of Tillotson's so-called rationalism is to be looked for in his complete confidence that God and man stand in an entirely harmonious relationship one to another, God being the sum and comprehension of all perfection, the author of this admirable frame of the universe, man being drawn to Him and to His precepts by natural instincts, natural reason, the general consent of all ages, external Revelation, and the motions of the spirit within the individual. Though Tillotson and Locke differ greatly in respect to their theories of knowledge—Tillotson invoking inborn instincts and inborn reason, Locke relying solely upon experience—they are not far apart in spirit. In both of them latter seventeenth-century English Protestantism speaks with emphasis—how great emphasis we are apt to forget as we lose sight of the day-to-day issues and struggles out of which this faith in reasonableness arose.

Of older books, no longer strictly up-to-date regarding many details but still helpful, two may be mentioned: John Tullock, *Rational Theology and Christian Philosophy in England in the Seventeenth Century* (1872), and John Hunt, *Religious Thought in England from the Reformation to the End of the Last Century* (3 vols., 1870–1873). The general history of this period is reviewed by William H. Hutton, *The English Church from the Accession of Charles I to the Death of Anne* (1913). Paul Elmer More and Frank L. Cross jointly edited *Anglicanism: The Thought and Practice of the Church of England, Illustrated from the Religious Literature of the Seventeenth Century* (1935), in which will be found, in addition to the selections given, an introduction and biographical notes on the chief Anglican figures of the century. The most recent treatment of post-Restoration Anglicanism is by G. R. Cragg, *From Puritanism to the Age of Reason. A Study of Changes in Religious Thought within the Church of England, 1660 to 1700* (1950). Barrow is the subject of a modern study by P. H. Osmond, *Isaac Barrow, His Life and Times* (1944). The sermon literature and pulpit oratory of the period are touched upon by Caroline F. Richardson, *English Preachers and Preaching, 1640–1670: A*

Secular Study (1928), and Charles Smyth, *The Art of Preaching. A Practical Survey of Preaching in the Church of England, 747–1939* (1940), the authoritative treatment being by W. Fraser Mitchell, *English Pulpit Oratory from Andrewes to Tillotson: A Study of Its Literary Aspects* (1932). Barrow, South, and Tillotson as preachers are discussed in detail by Smyth and Mitchell; Basil Willey has some interesting remarks in his *Seventeenth Century Background* (1934); and in several articles listed in the bibliography, R. F. Jones has shed light on some of the forces influencing the style of Restoration sermons. Bibliographies of both primary and important secondary materials are given by Mitchell and Cragg.

Isaac Barrow

THE PLEASANTNESS OF RELIGION[1]

Prov. iii.17.—Her ways are of pleasantness, and all her paths are peace.

The meaning of these words seems plain and obvious, and to need little explication. *Her ways,* that is, the ways of Wisedom. What this Wisedom is, I shall not undertake accurately to describe. Briefly, I understand by it, An habitual skill or faculty of judging aright about matters of practice, and chusing according to that right judgment, and conforming the actions to such good choice. *Ways* and *paths* in Scripture-dialect are the courses and manners of action. For *doing* there is commonly called *walking;* and the methods of doing are the *ways* in which we walk. By *pleasantness* may be meant the joy and delight accompanying, and by *peace* the content and satisfaction ensuing such a course of actions. So that, in short, the sense of these words seems simply to be this, That a course of life directed by wisedom and good judgment is delightfull in the practice, and brings content after it. The truth of which Proposition it shall be my endeavour at this time to confirm by divers Reasons, and illustrate by several instances.

I. Then, Wisedom of it self is delectable and satisfactory, as it implies a revelation of Truth, and a detection of Errour to us. 'Tis like Light, pleasant to behold,[2] casting a sprightly lustre, and diffusing a benign influence all about; presenting a goodly prospect of things to the eyes of our mind; displaying objects in their due shapes, postures, magnitudes, and colours; quickning our spirits with a comfortable warmth, and disposing our minds to a chearfull activity; dispelling the darkness of ignorance, scattering the mists of doubt, driving away the spectres of delusive fancy; mitigating the cold of sullen melancholy; discovering obstacles, securing progress, and making the passages of life clear, open, and pleasant. We are all naturally endowed with a strong appetite to know, to see, to pursue Truth; and with a bashfull abhorrency from being deceived, and entangled in mistake. And as success in enquiry after Truth affords matter of joy and triumph; so being conscious of Errour, and miscarriage therein, is attended with shame and sorrow. These desires Wisedom in the most perfect manner satisfies, not by entertaining us with dry, empty, fruitless theories, upon mean and vulgar subjects; but by enriching our minds with excellent and usefull knowledge, directed to the noblest objects, and serviceable to the highest ends. Nor in its own nature onely, but,

II. Much more in its worthy consequences is Wisedom exceedingly pleasant and peaceable: in general, by disposing us to acquire and to enjoy all the good, delight and happiness we are capable of; and by freeing us from all the inconveniences, mischiefs and infelicities our condition is subject to. For what-ever good from clear understanding, deliberate advice, sagacious

[1] Preached at St. Mary's, Oxford, June 30, 1661. Text: *Sermons Preached Upon Several Occasion, By Isaac Barrow, D.D., 1678*

[2] *Veritatis luce menti hominis nihil dulcius.* Cic. *Acad.* 2 [Barrow's note]

foresight, stable resolution, dexterous address, right intention and orderly proceeding doth naturally result, Wisedom conferrs: what-ever evil blind ignorance, false presumption, unwary credulity, precipitate rashness, unsteady purpose, ill contrivance, backwardness, inhability, unwieldiness and confusion of thought beget, Wisedom prevents. From a thousand snares and treacherous allurements, from innumerable rocks and dangerous surprises, from exceedingly many needless incumbrances and vexatious toils of fruitless endeavour, she redeems and secures us. More particularly,

III. Wisedom assures us we take the best course, and proceed as we ought. For by the same means we judge aright, and reflecting upon that judgment are assured we doe so: as the same arguments by which we demonstrate a theorem convince us we have demonstrated it, and the same light by which we see an object makes us know we see it. And this assurance in the progress of the action exceedingly pleases, and in the sequel of it infinitely contents us. He that judges amiss, not perceiving clearly the rectitude of his process, proceeds usually with a dubious solicitude, and at length, discovering his errour, condemns his own choice, and receives no other satisfaction but of repentance. Like a Traveller, who being uncertain whether he goes in the right way, wanders in continual perplexity, till he be informed, and then too late, understanding his mistake, with regret seeks to recover himself into it. But he that knows his way, and is satisfied that it is the true one, makes on merrily and carelessly, not doubting he shall in good time arrive to his designed journey's end. Two troublesome mischiefs therefore Wisedom free us from, the company of anxious doubt in our actions, and the consequence of bitter repentance. For no man can doubt of what he is sure, nor repent of what he knows good.

IV. Wisedom begets in us a hope of success in our actions, and is usually attended therewith. Now what is more delicious then hope? what more satisfactory then success? That is like the pursuit of a flying enemy, this like gathering the spoil; that like viewing the ripe corn, this like the joy of harvest it self. And he that aims at a good end, and knows he uses proper means to attain it, why should he despair of success, since effects naturally follow their causes, and the Divine providence is wont to afford its concourse to such proceedings? Beside that such well-grounded hope confirms resolution, and quickens activity, which mainly conduce to the prosperous issue of designs. Farther,

V. Wisedom prevents discouragement from the possibility of ill success, yea and makes disappointment it self tolerable. For if either the foresight of a possible miscarriage should discourage us from adventuring on action, or inculpable frustration were intolerable, we should with no heart apply our selves to any thing; there being no designs in this world, though founded upon the most sound advice, and prosecuted by the most diligent endeavour, which may not be defeated, as depending upon divers causes above our power, and circumstances beyond our prospect. The inconstant opinions, uncertain resolutions, mutable affections, and fallacious pretences of men, upon which the accomplishment of most projects rely, may easily deceive and disappoint us. The imperceptible course of nature exerting it self in sudden tempests, diseases, and unlucky casualties, may surprise us, and give an end to our businesses and lives together. However, the irresistible power of the Divine providence, guided by the unsearchable counsel of his will, we can never be assured that it will not interpose, and hinder the effects of our endeavours. Yet notwithstanding, when we act prudently, we have no reason to be disheartened; because, having good intentions, and using fit means, and having done our best, as no deserved blame, so no considerable dammage can arrive to us: and though we find Almighty God hath crossed us, yet we are sure he is not displeased with us. Which consideration, wherewith Wisedom furnishes us, will make the worst success not onely tolerable, but comfortable to us. For hence we have reason to hope, that the All-wise Goodness reserves a better reward for us, and will sometime recompense not onely the good purposes we unhappily pursued, but also the unexpected disappointment we patiently endured; and that however we shall be no losers in the end. Which discourse is mainly fortified by considering how the best and wisest attempts have oft miscarried. We see *Moses*, authorized by God's command, directed by his counsel, and conducted by his hand, intended to bring the *Israelites* into the land of *Canaan;* yet by the unreasonable incredulity and stubborn perverseness of that people he had his purpose frustrated. The holy Prophets afterward earnestly endeavoured to contain the same people within compass of obedience to the Divine commands, and to reduce them from their idolatrous and wicked courses; yet without correspondent effect. Our Saviour, by the example of his holy life, continual instruction, and vehement exhortations, assayed to procure a belief of and submission to his most excellent Doctrine; yet how few *believed his report*, and complied with his Discipline? Yea, Almighty God himself often complains, how in a manner his designs were defeated, his desires thwarted, his offers refused, his counsels rejected, his expectations deceived. *Wherefore*, (saith he concerning his Vineyard) *when I looked it should bring forth grapes, brought it forth wild grapes?*[3] And again, *I have spred out my hands all the day to a rebellious people.*[4] And again, *I have even sent unto you all my prophets daily, rising up early, and sending them; yet they hearkened not unto me.*[5] Wherefore there is no good cause we should be disheartned, or vexed, when success is wanting to well-advised purposes. 'Tis foolish and ill-grounded intentions, and practices unwarrantable by good reason, that make the undertakers solicitous of success, and being defeated leave them disconsolate. Yea farther,

VI. Wisedom makes all the troubles, griefs and pains incident to life, whether casual adversities, or natural afflictions, easie and supportable; by rightly valuing the importance, and moderating the influence of them. It suffers not busie fancy to alter the nature, amplifie the degree, or extend the duration of them, by representing them more sad, heavy and remediless then they truly are. It allows them no force beyond what naturally and necessarily they have, nor contributes nourishment to their increase. It keeps them at a due distance, not permitting them to encroach upon the Soul, or to propagate their influence beyond their proper sphere. It will not let external mischances, as poverty and disgrace, to produce an inward sense which is beyond their natural efficacy; nor corporeal affections of sickness and pain to disturb the mind, with which they have nothing to doe. The region of these malignant distempers being at most but the habit of the body, Wisedom by effectual antidotes repells them from the heart, and inward parts of the Soul. If any thing, sin, and our unworthy miscarriages toward God, should vex and discompose us; yet this trouble Wisedom, by representing the Divine Goodness, and his tender mercies in our ever-Blessed Redeemer, doth perfectly allay. And as for all other adversities, it abates their noxious power, by shewing us they are either meerly imaginary, or very short and temporary; that they admit of remedy, or at most do not exclude comfort, not wholly hindring the operations of the mind, nor extinguishing its joys; that they may have a profitable use, and pleasant end; and, however, neither imply bad Conscience, nor induce obligation to punishment. For,

VII. Wisedom hath always a good Conscience attending it, that purest delight and richest cordial of the Soul; that brazen wall, and impregnable fortress against both external assaults, and internal commotions; that *continual feast*, whereon the mind, destitute of all other repast, with a never-languishing appetite may entertain it self; that faithfull witness, and impartial judge, whoever accuses, always acquitting the innocent Soul; that certain friend, in no streight failing, in no adversity deserting; that sure refuge in all storms of fortune, and persecutions of disgrace. Which (as *Solomon* here notes) renders a man's *sleep sweet*, and undisturbed with fearfull phantasms, his heart light, and his steps secure; and, if any thing, can make the Stoical paradox good, and cause the Wise man to smile in extremity of torment; arming his mind with an invincible courage, and infusing a due confidence into it, whereby he bears up chearfully against malicious re-

[3] Isa. 5.4. [Barrow's note]
[4] Isa. 65.2. [Barrow's note]
[5] Jer. 7.25, 26. [Barrow's note]

proach, undauntedly sustains adversity, and triumphs over bad fortune. And this invaluable treasure the Wise man is onely capable of possessing; who certainly knows, and heartily approves the grounds upon which he proceeds; whenas the fool, building his choice upon blind chance, or violent passion, or giddy fancy, or uncertain example, not upon the steddy warrant of good reason, cannot avoid being perplexed with suspicion of mistake, and so necessarily is deprived of the comfort of a good Conscience.

VIII. Wisedom confers a facility, expert readiness, and dexterity in action; which is a very pleasant and commodious quality, and exceedingly sweetens activity. To doe things with difficulty, struggling, and immoderate contention, disheartens a man, quells his courage, blunts the edge of his resolution, renders him sluggish and averse from business, though apprehended never so necessary, and of great moment. These obstructions Wisedom removes, facilitating operations by directing the intention to ends possible and attainable, by suggesting fit means and instruments to work by, by contriving right methods and courses of process; the mind by it being stored with variety of good principles, sure rules, and happy expedients, reposed in the memory, and ready upon all occasions to be produced, and employed in practice.

IX. Wisedom begets a sound, healthfull and harmonious complexion of the Soul, disposing us with judgment to distinguish, and with pleasure to relish savoury and wholesome things, but to nauseate and reject such as are ingrateful and noxious to us; thereby capacifying us to enjoy pleasantly and innocently all those good things the Divine Goodness hath provided for, and consigned to us: whence to the Soul proceeds all that comfort, joy and vigour, which results to the Body from a good constitution, and perfect health.

X. Wisedom acquaints us with our selves, our own temper and constitution, our propensions and passions, our habitudes and capacities; a thing not onely of mighty advantage, but of infinite pleasure and content to us. No man in the world less knows a fool then himself; nay, he is more then ignorant, for he constantly errs in the point, taking himself for, and demeaning himself as toward another, a better, a wiser and abler man then he is. He hath wonderfull conceits of his own qualities and faculties; he affects commendations incompetent to him; he soars at employment surpassing his ability to manage. No Comedy can represent a mistake more odde, and ridiculous, then his: for he wanders, and stages, and hunts after, but never can find nor discern himself; but always encounters with a false shadow in stead thereof, which he passionately huggs and admires. But a Wise man, by constant observation, and impartial reflexion upon himself, grows very familiar with himself: he perceives his own inclinations, which if bad, he strives to alter and correct; if good, he cherishes and corroborates them: he apprehends the matters he is fitting for, and capable to manage, neither too mean and unworthy of him, nor too high and difficult for him; and those applying his care to, he transacts easily, chearfully, and successfully. So being neither puft up with vain and over-weening opinion, nor dejected with heartless diffidence of himself; neither admiring, nor despising; neither irksomely hating, nor fondly loving himself; he continues in good humour, maintains a sure friendship and fair correspondence with himself, and rejoyces in the retirement and private conversation with his own thoughts: whence flows a pleasure and satisfaction unexpressible.

XI. Wisedom procures and preserves a constant favour and fair respect of men, purchases a good name, and upholds reputation in the world: which things are naturally desirable, commodious for life, encouragements to good, and preventive of many inconveniences. The composed frame of mind, uniform and comely demeanour, compliant and inoffensive conversation, fair and punctual dealing, considerate motions and dexterous addresses of Wise men naturally beget esteem and affection in those that observe them. Neither then these things is there any thing more commendable to humane regard. As symmetry and harmony to the animal senses, so delectable is an even temper of Soul and orderly tenour of actions to rational apprehensions. Folly is freakish and humorous, impertinent and obstreperous, inconstant and inconsistent, peevish and exceptious; and consequently fastidious to society, and productive of aversation and disrespect. But the Wise man is stable in his ways, consonant to himself, suting his actions to his words, and those to his principles, and all to the rule of right reason; so that you may know where to find him, and how to deal with him, and may easily please him, which makes his acquaintance acceptable, and his person valuable: beside that real worth of it self commands respect, and extorts veneration from men, and usually prosperity waits upon his well-advised attempts, which exceedingly adorn, and advance the credit of the undertaker: however, if he fail sometime, his usual deportment salves his repute, and easily makes it credible it was no fault of his, but of his fortune. If a fool prosper, the honour is attributed to propitious chance; if he miscarry, to his own ill management: but the entire glory of happy undertakings crowns the head of Wisedom; while the disgrace of unlucky events falls otherwhere. His light, like that of the Sun, cannot totally be eclipsed; it may be dimmed, but never extinguished, and always maintains a day, though over-clouded with misfortune. Who less esteems the famous *African* Captain for being over-thrown in that last fatal battel, wherein he is said to have shewn the best skill, and yet endured the worst of success? Who contemns *Cato*, and other the grave Citizens of *Rome*, for embracing the just, but improsperous Cause of the Commonwealth? A Wise man's circumstances may vary and fluctuate like the flouds about a rock; but he persists unmovably the same, and his reputation unshaken: for he can always render a good accompt of his actions, and by reasonable apology elude the assaults of reproach.

XII. Wisedom instructs us to examin, compare, and rightly to value the objects that court our affections, and challenge our care; and thereby regulates our passions, and moderates our endeavours, which begets a pleasant serenity and peaceable tranquillity of mind. For when, being deluded with false shews, and relying upon ill-grounded presumptions, we highly esteem, passionately affect, and eagerly pursue things of little worth in themselves, or concernment to us, as we unhandsomely prostitute our affections, and prodigally miss-spend our time, and vainly lose our labour; so the event not answering our expectation, our minds thereby are confounded, disturb'd, and distempered. But when, guided by right reason, we conceive great esteem of, and zealously are enamoured with, and vigorously strive to attain things of excellent worth, and weighty consequence; the conscience of having well placed our affections, and well employed our pains, and the experience of fruits corresponding to our hopes ravishes our mind with unexpressible content. And so it is; Present appearance and vulgar conceit ordinarily impose upon our fancies, disguising things with a deceitfull varnish, and representing those that are vainest with the greatest advantage; whilst the noblest objects, being of a more subtile and spiritual nature, like fairest Jewels enclosed in a homely box, avoid the notice of gross sense, and pass undiscerned by us. But the light of Wisedom, as it unmasks specious imposture, and bereaves it of its false colours; so it penetrates into the retirements of true Excellency, and reveals its genuine lustre. For example, Corporeal Pleasure, which so powerfully allures and enchants us, Wisedom declares that it is but a present, momentary and transient satisfaction of brutish sense, dimming the light, sullying the beauty, impairing the vigour, and restraining the activity of the mind; diverting it from better operations, and indisposing it to enjoy purer delights; leaving no comfortable relish or gladsome memory behind it, but often followed with bitterness, regret and disgrace. That the Profit the World so greedily gapes after is but a possession of trifles, not valuable in themselves, nor rendering the Masters of them so; accidentally obtained, and promiscuously enjoyed by all sorts, but commonly by the worst of men; difficultly acquired, and easily lost; however, to be used but for a very short time, and then to be resigned into uncertain hands. That the Honour men so dote upon is, ordinarily, but the difference of a few petty circumstances, a peculiar name or title, a determinate place, a distinguishing ensign; things of onely imaginary excellence, derived from chance, and conferring no advantage, except from some little influence they have upon the arbitrary opinion and fickle humour of the people; complacence in which is vain, and reliance upon it dangerous. That Power and dominion, which men so impatiently struggle for, are but necessary evils introduced to restrain the bad tempers of men; most evil to them that enjoy them; requiring tedious attendance, distracting care, and vexatious toil; attended with frequent disappointment, opprobrious censure, and dangerous envy; having such reall burthens, and slavish encumbrances, sweetned onely by superficial pomps, strained obsequiousness, some petty privileges, and exemptions scarce worth mentioning. That Wit and parts, of which men make such ostentation, are but natural endowments, commendable onely in order to use, apt to engender pride and vanity, and hughly dangerous if abused or misemployed? What should I mention Beauty, that fading toy; or bodily Strength and activity, qualities so palpably inconsiderable? Upon these and such like flattering objects, so adored by vulgar opinion, Wisedom exercising severe and impartial judgment, and perceiving in them no intrinsick excellence, no solid content springing from them, no perfection thence accruing to the mind, no high reward allotted to them, no security to the future condition, or other durable advantages proceeding from them; it concludes they deserve not any high opinion of the mind, nor any vehement passion of the Soul, nor any laborious care to be employed on them, and moderates our affections toward them: it frees us from anxious desire of them; from being transported with excessive joy in the acquisition of them; from being overwhelmed with disconsolate sorrow at the missing of them, or parting with them; from repining and envying at those who have better success then our selves in the procuring them; from immoderate toil in getting, and care in preserving them: and so delivering us from all these unquiet anxieties of thought, tumultuous perturbations of passion, and tedious vexations of body, it maintains our minds in a chearfull calm, quiet indifferency, and comfortable liberty. On the other side, things of real worth and high concernment, that produce great satisfaction to the mind, and are mainly conducible to our happiness, such as are a right understanding and strong sense of our obligations to Almighty God, and relations to men, a sound temper and complexion of mind, a vertuous disposition, a capacity to discharge the duties of our places, a due qualification to enjoy the happiness of the other World; these and such like things, by discovering their nature, and the effects resulting from them, it engages us highly to esteem, ardently to affect, and industriously to pursue; so preventing the inconveniences that follow the want of them, and conveighing the benefits arising from the possession of them.

XIII. Wisedom distinguishes the circumstances, limits the measures, determines the modes, appoints the fit seasons of action; so preserving *decorum* and order, the parent of peace, and preventing confusion, the mother of iniquity, strife and disquiet. 'Tis in the business of humane life as in a building: a due proportion of bigness, a fit situation of place, a correspondency of shape, and sutableness of colour, is to be observed between the parts thereof: a defect in any of which requisites, though the materials hap to be choice and excellent, makes the whole fabrick deformed and ugly to judicious apprehension. The best actions, if they swell, and exceed their due measure, if they be unskilfully misplaced, if in uncouth manner performed, they lose their quality, and turn both to the disgrace and disadvantage of life. 'Tis commendable to pray; but they that would always be performing that duty, by their absurd devotion procured to themselves the title of Hereticks: and they that will stand praying in places of publick concourse, deserved our Saviour's reprehensions; and those men who, against the custom and ordinary use, would needs pray with their faces covered, you know S. *Paul* insinuates of them, that they were fond and contentious persons. Friendly admonition is very laudable, and of rare use; but being upon all occasions immoderately used, or in publick society so as to encroach upon modesty, or endammage reputation; or when the person admonished is otherwise employed, and attent upon his business; or being delivered in an imperiously-insulting way, or in harsh and opprobrious language;

it becomes unsavoury and odious, and both in shew and effect resembles a froward malicious exceptiousness. 'Twere infinite to compute in how many instances want of due order, measure and manner, do spoil and incommodate action. 'Tis Wisedom that applies remedy to these mischiefs. Things must be compared to, and arbitrated by, her standard, or else they will contain something of monstrous enormity; either strutting in unwieldy bulk, or sinking in defective scantness. If she do not fashion and model circumstances, they will fit ugly on the things that wear them; if she do not temper the colours, and describe the lineaments, the draught of practice will be rude and imperfect, and little resemble the true patterns of duty: but if she interpose, and perform her part, all things will appear conformable, neat and delicate.

XIV. Wisedom discovers our relations, duties and concernments, in respect of men, with the natural grounds of them; thereby both qualifying and inclining us to the discharge of them: whence exceeding convenience, pleasure and content ensues. By it we understand we are parts and members of the great Body, the Universe; and are therefore concerned in the good management of it, and are thereby obliged to procure its order and peace, and by no irregular undertaking to disturb or discompose it; which makes us honest and peaceable men: that we proceed from the same primitive stock, are children of the same father, and partake of the same bloud with all men; are endowed with like faculties of mind, passions of Soul, shape of body, and sense of things: that we have equally implanted in our original constitution inclinations to love, pity, gratitude, sociableness, quiet, joy, reputation: that we have an indispensable need and impatient desire of company, assistence, comfort, and relief: that therefore it is according to the design of nature, and agreeable to reason, that to those, to whom our natural condition by so many bands of cognation, similitude, and mutual necessitude, hath knit and conjoyned us, we should bear a kind respect and tender affection; should chearfully concurre in undergoing the common burthens; should heartily wish and industriously promote their good, assist them in accomplishing their reasonable desires, thankfully requite the courtesies received from them, congratulate and rejoyce with them in their prosperity, comfort them in their distresses, and, as we are able, relieve them; however, tenderly compassionate their disappointments, miseries and sorrows. This renders us kind and courteous neighbours; sweet and gratefull companions. It represents unto us the dreadfull effects and insupportable mischiefs arising from breach of faith, contravening the obligations of solemn pacts, infringing publick laws, deviating from the received rules of equity, violating promises, and interrupting good correspondence among men: by which considerations it engages us to be good citizens, obedient subjects, just dealers, and faithfull friends. It minds us of the blindness, impotence and levity, the proneness to mistake, and misbehaviour that humane nature necessarily is subject to; deserving rather our commiseration, then anger or hatred, which prompts us to bear the infirmities of our brethren, to be gentle in censure, to be insensible of petty affronts, to pardon injuries, to be patient, exorable, and reconcilable to those that give us greatest cause of offence. It teaches us, the good may, but the evil of our neighbour can in no wise advantage us; that from the suffering of any man, simply considered, no benefit can accrue, nor natural satisfaction arise to us; and that therefore 'tis a vain, base, brutish and unreasonable thing, for any cause whatsoever, to desire or delight in the grief, pain or misery of our neighbour, to hate or envy him, or insult over him, or devise mischief to him, or prosecute revenge upon him; which makes us civil, noble and placable enemies, or rather no enemies at all. So that Wisedom is in effect the genuine parent of all moral and political vertue, justice and honesty; as *Solomon* says in her person, *I lead in the way of righteousness*, and *in the midst of the paths of judgment.*[6] And how sweet these are in the practice, how comfortable in the consequences, the testimony of continual experience and the unanimous consent of all wise men sufficiently declare. But farther,

XV. The principal advantage of Wisedom is, its acquainting us with the Nature and reason of true Religion, and affording

[6] Prov. 8.20. [Barrow's note]

convictive arguments to persuade to the Practice of it; which is accompanied with the purest delight, and attended with the most solid content imaginable. I say, the Nature of Religion, wherein it consists, and what it requires; the mistake of which produceth daily so many mischiefs and inconveniences in the world, and exposes so good a name to so much reproach. It sheweth it consisteth not in fair professions and glorious pretences, but in real practice; not in a pertinacious adherence to any Sect or party, but in a sincere love of goodness, and dislike of naughtiness, where-ever discovering it self; not in vain ostentations and flourishes of outward performance, but in an inward good complexion of mind, exerting it self in works of true Devotion and Charity; not in a nice orthodoxie, or politick subjection of our judgments to the peremptory dictates of men, but in a sincere love of Truth, in a hearty approbation of and compliance with the Doctrines fundamentally good, and necessary to be believed; not in harsh censuring and virulently inveighing against others, but in carefull amending our own ways; not in a peevish crosness and obstinate repugnancy to received laws and customs, but in a quiet and peaceable submission to the express Laws of God, and lawfull commands of man; not in a furious zeal for or against trivial circumstances, but in a conscionable practising the substantial parts of Religion; not in a frequent talking or contentious disputing about it, but in a ready observance of the unquestionable rules and prescripts of it. In a word, that Religion consists in nothing else but doing what becomes our relation to God, in a conformity or similitude to his Nature, and in a willing obedience to his holy Will: to which by potent incentives it allures and persuades us; by representing to us his transcendently-glorious Attributes, conspicuously displayed in the frame, order and government of the World; that wonderfull Power, which erected this great and goodly fabrick; that incomprehensible Wisedom, which preserves it in a constant harmony; that immense Goodness, which hath so carefully provided for the various necessities, delights and comforts of its innumerable inhabitants. I say, by representing those infinitely-glorious Perfections, it engages us with highest respect to esteem, reverence and honour him. Also, by minding us of our manifold obligations to him, our receiving being, life, reason, sense, all the faculties, powers, excellencies, privileges and commodities of our natures from him; of his tender Care and loving Providence continually supporting and protecting us; of his liberal Beneficence, patient Indulgence, and earnest desire of our good and happiness by manifold expressions evidently manifested toward us; it inflames us with ardent love, and obliges us to officious gratitude toward him. Also, by declaring the necessary and irreconcilable contrariety of his Nature to all impurity and perverseness, his peerless Majesty, his irresistible Power, and his all-seeing Knowledge, it begets an awfull dread and a devout fear of him. By discovering him from his infinite Benignity willing, and from his unlimited Power onely able to supply our needs, relieve us in distresses, protect us from dangers, and confer any valuable benefit upon us, it engenders faith, and encourages us to rely upon him. By revealing to us his supereminent Sovereignty, uncontrollable Dominion, and unquestionable Authority over us; together with the admirable excellency, wisedom and equity of his Laws, so just and reasonable in themselves, so suitable to our nature, so conducible to our good, so easie and practicable, so sweet and comfortable; it powerfully inclines, and by a gentle force as it were constrains us to obedience. By such efficacious inducements Wisedom urges us to all duties of Religion, and withall surely directs us (as I before said) wherein it consists; teaching us to have right and worthy apprehensions of the Divine nature, to which our Devotion (if true and good) must be suited and conformed: and so it frees us, as from irreligion and profane neglect of God, so from fond superstitions, the sources of so much evil to mankind. For he that wisely hath considered the Wisedom, Goodness and Power of God, cannot imagine God can with a regardless eye overlook his presumptuous contempts of his Laws, or endure him to proceed in an outrageous defiance of Heaven, to continue hurting himself, or injuring his neighbour; nor can admit unreasonable terrours, or entertain suspicious conceits of God, as of an imperious Master, or implacable Tyrant over him, exacting impossible performances from, or delighting in the fatal miseries of his Creatures; nor can suppose him pleased with hypocritical shews, and greatly taken with superficial courtships of ceremonious address; or that he can in any wise favour our fiery zeals, fierce passions, or unjust partialities about matter of opinion and ceremony; or can doe otherwise then detest all factious, harsh, uncharitable and revengefull proceedings, of what nature, or upon what ground soever; or that he can be so inconsistent with himself, as to approve any thing but what is like himself, that is, Righteousness, Sincerity, and Beneficence.

Lastly, Wisedom attracts the Favour of God, purchaseth a glorious Reward, and secureth perpetual Felicity to us. *For God loveth none but him that dwelleth with wisedom.*[7] And, *glorious is the fruit of good labour: and the root of wisedom shall never fall away.*[8] And, *Happy is the man that findeth wisedom:*[9] and, *whoso findeth* her, *findeth life, and shall obtain favour of the Lord.*[10] These are the words of wise *Solomon*, in the Book of *Wisedom*, and in the *Proverbs*. God loveth her, as most agreeable to his nature; as resembling him; as an off-spring, beam and efflux of that Wisedom which founded the earth, and established the Heavens; as that which begetteth honour, love, and obedience to his Commands, and truly glorifies him; and as that which promotes the good of his Creatures, which he earnestly desires. And the paths she leads in are such as directly tend to the promised Inheritance of joy and bliss.

Thus have I simply and plainly presented you with part of what my meditation suggested upon this Subject: It remains that we endeavour to obtain this excellent endowment of Soul, by the faithfull exercise of our Reason, carefull observation of things, diligent study of the Divine Law, watchfull reflexion upon our selves, vertuous and religious practice; but especially, by imploring the Divine influence, the original spring of light, and the fountain of all true knowledge, following S. *James* his advice, *If any man lack wisedom, let him ask it of God, who giveth freely*. Therefore, O everlasting Wisedom, the Maker, Redeemer and Governour of all things, let some comfortable Beams from thy great Body of heavenly Light descend upon us, to illuminate our dark minds, and quicken our dead hearts; to enflame us with ardent love unto thee, and to direct our steps in obedience to thy Laws, through the gloomy shades of this world, into that region of eternal light and bliss, where thou reignest in perfect Glory and Majesty, one God ever-Blessed, world without end.

Amen.

Robert South

AN ACCOUNT OF THE NATURE AND MEASURES OF CONSCIENCE[11]

I John. iii.21.—Beloved, if our Heart condemn us not, we have Confidence toward God.

As nothing can be of more moment; so few things, *doubtless*, are of more difficulty, than for Men to be rationally satisfied about the estate of their Souls, with reference to God, and the great Concerns of Eternity. In their Judgment about which, if they err finally, it is like a man's missing his Cast when he throws *Dice* for *his Life;* His Being, his Happiness, and all that he does, or can enjoy in the World, is involved in the Error of one Throw. And therefore it may very well deserve our best Skill and Care, to enquire into those Rules, by which we may guide our *Judgment* in so weighty an Affair, both with safety and

[7] Wised. 7.28. [Barrow's note, the reference being to *The Wisdome of Solomon*, one of the books of the Apocrapha]

[8] 3.15. [Barrow's note]

[9] Prov. 3.13. [Barrow's note]

[10] 8.35. [Barrow's note]

[11] Part I. Preached before the University at Christ Church, Oxford, November 1, 1691. Text: South, *Twelve Sermons Preached Upon Several Occasions*, 1692

success. And this, I think, cannot be better done, than by separating the *false* and *fallacious*, from the *true* and *certain*. For, if the *Rule* we judge by, be *uncertain*, it is odds, but we shall judge wrong; and, if we should judge right; yet it is not properly *Skill*, but *Chance;* not a true Judgment, but a lucky Hit: Which certainly, the Eternal Interests of an Immortal Soul, are of much too high a Value to be left at the Mercy of.

First of all then: He who would pass such a Judgment *upon his Condition*, as shall be ratified in Heaven, and confirmed at that great Tribunal, from which there lies no Appeal, will find himself wofully deceived, if he judges of his *spiritual estate* by any of these Four following Measures: As,

1. The *general esteem of the World concerning him*. He, who owes his *Piety* to Fame and Hear-say, *and the Evidences of his Salvation* to popular Voice and Opinion, builds his House not only *upon the Sand*, but (which is worse) upon the *Wind;* and writes the *Deeds*, by which he holds his Estate, upon the face of a *River*. He makes a Bodily *Eye* the Judge of Things impossible to be *seen;* and Humour and Ignorance (which the generality of Men both think and speak by) the *great Proofs* of his Justification. But, surely, no man has the *Estate of his Soul* drawn upon *his Face*, nor the Decree of his *Election* wrote upon *his Forehead*. He who would know a man thoroughly, must follow him into the Closet of his Heart; the Door of which is kept shut to all the World besides, and the Inspection of which is only the Prerogative of Omniscience.

The favourable opinion, and good word of Men (to *some persons* especially) comes oftentimes at a very easy rate; and, by a few demure *Looks*, and affected *Whines*, set off with some odd, devotional Postures and Grimaces, and such other little Arts of Dissimulation, cunning Men will doe Wonders, and Commence presently Heroes for Sanctity, Self-denial, and Sincerity, while within perhaps they are as *Proud as Lucifer, as Covetous as Demas, as false as Judas;* and, in the whole Course of their Conversation, *Act*, and *are Acted* not by Devotion, but Design.

So that, for ought I see, though the *Mosaical* part of *Judaism* be abolished amongst Christians, the *Pharisaical* part of it never will. A grave, stanch, skilfully *managed Face*, set upon a grasping, aspiring Mind, having got many a sly Formalist the Reputation of a *Primitive and severe Piety* (forsooth) and made many such Mountebanks pass admired, even for *Saints upon Earth* (as the word is) who are like to be so no-where else.

But a man, who had never seen the stately outside of a *Tomb*, or *painted Sepulchre* before, may very well be excused, if he takes it rather for the *Repository of some rich Treasure*, than of a *noysome Corps;* but should he but once open and rake into it, though he could not *see*, he would quickly *smell out*, his mistake. The greatest part of the World is nothing but *Appearance*, nothing but *Shew* and *Surface;* and many make it their Business, their Study and Concern, that it should be so; who having for many years together deceived all about them, are at last willing to deceive themselves too; and, by a long, immemorial Practice, and (as it were) *Prescription* of an aged, thorough-paced *Hypocrisie*, come at length to believe that for a *Reality*, which, at the first Practice of it, they themselves knew to be a Cheat. But, if Men love to be deceived, and fooled about so great an Interest as that of their *spiritual Estate*, it must be confessed that they cannot take a surer, and more effectual Course to be so, than by taking their Neighbour's Word for that, which can be known to them only from their *own Hearts*. For, certainly, it is not more absurd to undertake to tell the *Name* of an *unknown person by his looks*, than to Vouch a man's *Saintship* from the *vogue* of the World, founded upon his *External Behaviour*.

2 *ly*. The judgment of any *Casuist* or *Learned Divine*, concerning the *Estate of a man's Soul*, is not sufficient to give him Confidence towards God. And the Reason is, because no Learning whatsoever can give a man the Knowledge of another's *Heart*. Besides, that it is more than possible that the most profound, and experienced *Casuist* in the World, may mistake in his Judgment of a man's spiritual Condition; and, if he does judge right, yet the Man cannot be sure that he will declare that

Judgment sincerely and impartially, (the *greatest Clerks* being not always the *honestest*, any more than the *wisest Men*,) but may purposely sooth a man up for Hope or Fear, or the Service of some sinister Interest; and so shew him the face of a foul Soul in a flattering Glass: Considering how much the raising in some Men a false Hope of *another* World, may, with others, serve a real Interest in *this*.

There is a Generation of Men, who have framed their Casuistical Divinity to a perfect Compliance with all the corrupt Affections of a Man's Nature; and by that new-invented Engine of the *Doctrine of Probability*, will undertake to warrant, and quiet the Sinner's Conscience in the Commission of any Sin whatsoever, provided there be but the *Opinion of one Learned Man* to vouch it. For this, they say, is a sufficient Ground for the Conscience of any unlearned Person to rely, and to act upon. So that if but *one Doctor* asserts, that I may lawfully kill a Man, to prevent a Box on the Ear, or a Calumny, by which he would otherwise asperse my good Name, I may, with a good Conscience, doe it; Nay, I may safely rest upon this one Casuist's Judgment, though thousands, as learned as himself; yea, and the express *Law of God* besides, affirm the quite contrary. But these Spiritual Engineers know well enough, how to deal with any Commandment, either by Taking, or Expounding it, *away*, at their pleasure.

Such an Ascendant have these Romish Casuists over *Scripture*, *Reason*, and *Morality;* much like what is said of the stupid, modern *Jews*, that they have subdued their *Sense* and *Reason* to such a sottish Servitude to their *Rabbies*, as to hold, That in case two *Rabbies* should happen to contradict one another, they were yet bound to believe the Contradictory Assertions of both to be equally certain, and equally the Word of God: Such an Iron-digesting Faith have they, and such pity it is, that there should be no such thing in *Judaism* as *Transubstantiation* to employ it upon.

But, as for these Casuists, whom I have been speaking of; if the Judgment of *one Doctor* may authorize the Practice of any Action, I believe, it will *be hard to find* any sort or degree of Villainy, which the Corruption of Man's Nature is capable of committing, which shall not meet with a *Defence*. And of this, I could give such an Instance from something wrote by a certain Prelate of theirs, Cardinal and Arch-Bishop of *Beneventum*, as were enough, not only to astonish all Pious Ears, but almost to unconsecrate the very Church I speak in.

But the Truth is, the Way, by which these *Romish Casuists* speak *Peace* to the Consciences of Men, is either by teaching them, that many Actions, *are not Sins*, which yet really are so; or, by suggesting something to them, which shall satisfy their Minds, notwithstanding a known, actual, avowed Continuance in their Sins: Such as are their *Pardons* and *Indulgences*, and giving Men a share in the *Saints Merits*, out of the Common Bank and Treasury of the Church, which the *Pope* has the sole custody and disposal of, and is never kept *shut* to such as come with an *open hand*. So that, according to these *New Evangelists*, well may we pronounce, *Blessed are the Rich, for theirs is the Kingdom of Heaven*. But God deliver the World from such *Guides*, or rather such *Hucksters* of Souls, the very shame of Religion, and the shameless Subverters of Morality. And, it is really matter both of Wonder and Indignation, that such *Impostors* should at all concern themselves about Rules or Directions of Conscience, who seem to have no Consciences to apply them to.

3 *ly*. The *Absolution* pronounced by a Priest, whether *Papist* or *Protestant*, is not a certain, infallible Ground, to give the person, so absolved, confidence towards God: and the Reason is, Because, if *Absolution*, as such, could of itself secure a Man, as to the Estate of his Soul, then it would follow, That every person, so absolved, should, by virtue thereof, be *ipso facto*, put into such a Condition of safety, which is not imaginable.

For the Absolution pronounced must be either *Conditional*, as running upon the Conditions of *Faith* and *Repentance;* and *then*, if those Conditions are not found in the person so absolved, it is but a Seal to a Blank, and so a mere Nullity to him. Or, the *Absolution* must be pronounced in Terms *absolute*, and *unconditional:* And if so, then the said *Absolution* becomes valid and effectual, either by virtue of the *State* of the Person, to whom it was pronounced, as being a *true Penitent*, or by virtue of the *Opus Operatum*, or bare Action it self of the Priest Absolving him. If it receives its *Validity* from the former; then it is clear, That although it runs in Forms *Absolute*, yet it is indeed *Conditional*, as depending upon the *Qualification* of the Person, to whom it is pronounced; Who therefore owes the Remission of his Sins, not properly to the *Priest's Absolution*, but to his own *Repentance*, which made that Absolution effectual, and would undoubtedly have saved him, though the Priest had never Absolved him.

But if it be *asserted* that the *very Action* of the *Priest absolving him* has of it self this Virtue; then we must grant also, that it is in the Priest's power to save a Man, who never repented, nor did one good *Work* in all his life; for-as-much as it is in his Power to perform this *Action* upon him in full Form, and will full Intention to *Absolve him*. But the horrible Absurdity, Blasphemy, and Impiety of this Assertion, sufficiently proclaims its Falsity without any farther Confutation.

In a word, if a man be a *Penitent*, his *Repentance* stamps his *Absolution* effectual. If not, let the Priest repeat the same *Absolution* to him Ten thousand times; yet for all his being *absolved* in his *World*, God will condemn him in the other. And consequently, he who places his Salvation upon this Ground, will find himself like an imprisoned and condemned Malefactor, who in the Night dreams, that he is released, but in the Morning finds himself led to the *Gallows*.

4 *ly*. and *Lastly*, No Advantages *from External Church-Membership, or Profession of the true Religion*, can of themselves give a Man Confidence towards God. And yet perhaps, there is hardly any one Thing in the World, which Men, in all Ages, have, generally, more cheated themselves with. The Jews were an Eminent Instance of this. Who, because they were the *Sons of Abraham*, as it is readily acknowledged by our Saviour, *John* 8. 37. *And because they were entrusted with the Oracles of God*, Rom. 3. 2 *Together with the Covenants, and the Promises, Rom.* 9. 4. That is, in other Words, Because they were the *True Church*, and Professors of the *True Religion* (while all the World, about them, lay wallowing in *Ignorance*, *Heathenism*, and *Idolatry*) they concluded from hence, that God was so fond of them, that notwithstanding all their Villainies, and Immoralities, they were still the Darlings of Heaven, and the only Heirs Apparent of Salvation. They thought (it seems) God and themselves linked together in so *fast*, but withal so *strange* a Covenant, that although they never performed their part of it, God was yet bound to make good every Tittle of his.

And this made *John* the *Baptist*, set himself with so much Acrimony, and Indignation, to baffle this Senseless, Arrogant Conceit of theirs, which made them huff at the Doctrine of Repentance, as a Thing below them, and not at all belonging to them; In *Matth*. 3. V. 9. *Think not* (says he) *to say within your selves, we have Abraham to our Father*. This he knew lay deep in their *Hearts*, and was still in their *Mouths*, and kept them Insolent, and Impenitent under Sins of the highest and most clamorous Guilt; *though* our Saviour himself also, not long after this, assured them that they were of a very different Stock, and Parentage from that, which they boasted of; and that whosoever was their *Father* upon the *Natural* Account, the Devil was certainly so upon a *Moral*.

In like manner, how vainly do the Romanists pride, and value themselves upon the Name of *Catholics*, of the *Catholic Religion*, and of the *Catholic Church?* though a Title no more applicable to the *Church of Rome*, than a Man's *Finger*, when it is swelled and putrified, can be called his *whole Body:* a Church which allows *Salvation* to none without it, nor awards *Damnation* to almost any within it. And therefore, as the former Empty *Plea* served the sottish *Jews;* so, no wonder, if this equally serves these, to put them into a *Fools Paradise*, by feeding their Hopes, without changing their Lives; and, as an Excellent Expedient, first to assure them of Heaven, and then to bring them easily to it; and so in a word, to save both *their Souls*, and *their Sins* too.

And to shew, how the same Cheat runs through all Professions, though not in the same Dress; none are more powerfully, and grossly under it, than another Sort of

Men, who, on the Contrary, place *their whole Acceptance with God*, and indeed, their whole *Religion*, upon a *Mighty Zeal* (or rather out-cry) against *Popery, and Superstition;* verbally, indeed, uttered *against the Church of Rome*, but really meant against the *Church of England.* To which Sort of Persons I shall say no more but this, (and that in the Spirit of Truth and Meekness) *namely;* That Zeal and Noise *against Popery*, and real Services *for it*, are no such inconsistent Things, as some may imagine; indeed no more than *Invectives against Papists, and solemn Addresses of Thanks to them*, for that very Thing, by which they would have brought in Popery upon us. And if those of the Separation do not yet know so much, (thanks to them for it) we of the Church of *England* do; and so may themselves too, in due time. I speak not this by way of *Sarcasm*, to reproach them, (I leave that to their own Consciences, which will do it more effectually) but by way of *Charity* to warn them: For let them be assured, that this whole Scene and Practice of theirs, is as really *Superstition*, and as false a Bottom to rest their Souls upon, as either *the Jews alledging Abraham for their Father*, while the *Devil* claimed them for his *Children;* or the Papists relying upon *their Indulgences*, their *Saints Merits*, and *Supererogations*, and such other Fopperies, as can never *settle*, nor indeed so much as *reach*, the Conscience; and much less recommend it *to that Judge*, who is not to be flamm'd off with Words and Phrases, and *Names*, though taken out of the Scripture itself.

Nay, and I shall proceed yet further. It is not a Man's being of the *Church of England* it self (though undoubtedly the purest and best reformed Church in the world; indeed so well reformed, that it will be found a much easier Work *to alter*, than to *better* its Constitution;) I say, it is not a Man's being even of this Excellent Church, which can of it self clear Accounts between God and his Conscience. Since bare Communion with a good Church, can never alone *make a good Man:* For, if it could, I am sure we should have no bad ones in ours; and much less such as would betray it.

So that we see here, that it is but too manifest, that Men of all Churches, Sects and Perswasions, are *strangely* apt to flatter, and deceive themselves with what they *believe*, and what they *profess;* and if we thoroughly consider the Matter, we shall find the Fallacy to lie in this. That those Religious Institutions, which God designed only for *Means, Helps*, and *Advantages*, to promote and further Men in the Practice of Holiness, they look upon rather, as a *Privilege* to serve them *instead of it*, and really to commute *for it.* This is the very Case, and a fatal Self-imposture it is certainly, and such an one as defeats the Design, and *destroys* the Force of all Religion.

And thus, I have shewn *four* several, uncertain, and deceitful *Rules*, which Men are prone to judge of their *Spiritual Estate* by.

But now, have we any better or more certain, to substitute, and recommend in the Room of them? Why, yes; if we believe the Apostle, a Man's own *Heart* or *Conscience* is that, which, above all other Things, is able to give him *Confidence towards God.* And the Reason is, because the Heart knows that by it self, which, nothing in the World besides, can give it any *knowledge* of; and without the Knowledge of which, it can have no Foundation to build any true Confidence upon. *Conscience*, under God, is the only competent Judge of what the Soul has done, and what it has not done; what Guilt it has contracted, and what it has not; as it is in I *Corinth. 2.11. What Man knoweth the Things of a Man, save the Spirit of Man which is in him?* Conscience is its own Counsellor, the sole Master of its own Secrets: And it is the Privilege of our Nature, that every Man should keep the Key of his own Breast.

Now for the farther Prosecution of the Words, I shall *do these four Things.*

1. I shall shew, how the *Heart* or *Conscience* ought to be informed, in order to its founding in us a rational Confidence towards God.

2. I shall shew, *how* and *by what means we may* get it thus informed, and afterwards preserve and keep it so.

3. I shall shew, *Whence it is* that the Testimony of Conscience thus informed

comes to be so Authentic, and so much to be relied upon: And,

4*ly. and Lastly*, I shall assign *some particular Cases or Instances*, in which the Confidence suggested by it, does most eminently shew, and exert it self.

1. And first for the First of these, *How the Heart or Conscience*, etc. It is certain, that no Man can have any such Confidence towards God, only because his Heart tells him *a Lye;* and that it may do so, is altogether as certain. For there is the Erroneous, as well as the rightly informed Conscience; and if the Conscience happens to be deluded, and thereupon to give *false Directions* to the Will, so that by Vertue of those *Directions*, it is betrayed into a Course of Sin: Sin does not therefore cease to be Sin, because a Man committed it *Conscientiously*. If Conscience comes to be perverted so far, as to bring a Man under a Perswasion, that it is either Lawfull, or his Duty, *to resist the Magistrate, to seize upon his Neighbours just Rights, or Estate, to worship Stocks and Stones, or to lye, equivocate*, and the like, this will not *absolve* him before God; since Errour, which is in it self, *Evil*, can never make another Thing *Good*. He who does an unwarrantable Action, through a false *Information*, which *Information* he ought not to have believed, cannot in Reason *make the Guilt of one Sin, the Excuse of another*.

Conscience therefore must be rightly informed, before the Testimony of it can be Authentick, in what it pronounces concerning the Estate of the Soul. It must proceed by the Two grand Rules of *Right Reason and Scripture;* these are the Compass which it must steer by. For Conscience comes *formally* to oblige, only as it is the Messenger of the Mind of God to the Soul of Man; which he has revealed to him, partly by the Impression of certain Notions, and Maxims upon the *Practical* Understanding, and partly by the declared Oracles of his Word. So far therefore as Conscience reports any Thing agreeable to, or deducible from these, it is to be hearkened to, as the Great Conveyer of Truth to the Soul; but when it reports any Thing dissonant to these, it obliges no more than the Falsehood reported by it.

But since there is none who follows an *Erroneous Conscience*, but does so, because he thinks it *true*, and moreover thinks it true, because he is perswaded, that it proceeds according to the Two forementioned Rules of *Scripture*, and *Right Reason;* how shall a Man be able to satisfie himself, when his Conscience is *rightly informed*, and when *possessed with an Errour?* For to affirm, that the Sentence passed by a *rightly informed Conscience*, gives a Man a rational Confidence towards God; but, in the mean time, not to assign any means possible, by which he may know, when his Conscience is thus *rightly informed*, and *when not*, it must equally bereave him of such a Confidence, as placing the Condition upon which it depends wholly out of his Knowledge.

Here therefore is the Knot, here the Difficulty, how to state some Rule of Certainty, by which Infallibly to distinguish, when the Conscience is *right, and to be relied upon; When erroneous, and to be distrusted*, in the Testimony it gives about the Sincerity, and Safety of a Man's spiritual Condition.

For the Resolution of which, I answer, That it is not necessary for a Man to be assured of the *Rightness* of his Conscience, by such an *infallible Certainty of Perswasion*, as amounts to the Clearness of a Demonstration; but it is sufficient, if he knows it upon Grounds of such a convincing Probability, as shall exclude all rational Grounds of doubting of it. For, I cannot think, that the *Confidence*, here spoken of, rises so high as to *Assurance*. And the Reason is, because it is manifestly such a *Confidence*, as is common to all sincere Christians. Which yet, *Assurance* (we all know) is not.

The Truth is, the Word in the Original, which is παῤῥησία, signifies properly *Freedom, or Boldness of Speech;* though *the Latin* Translation renders it by *Fiducia*, and so corresponds with *English*, which renders it *Confidence*. But whether *Fiducia*, or *Confidence* reaches the full Sense of παῤῥησία, may very well be disputed. However it is certain, that neither the Word in the *Original*, nor yet in the *Translation*, imports *Assurance*. For *Freedom*, or *Boldness of Speech*, I am sure, does not; and *Fiducia*, or *Confidence*, signifies only a

Man's being actually perswaded of a Thing, upon better Arguments for it, than any that he can see against it; which he may very well be, and yet not *be assured* of it.

From all which, I conclude; That the *Confidence* here mentioned in the Text, amounts to no more, than a *Rational well grounded Hope*. Such an one, as the Apostle tells us, in *Rom.* 5.5. *Maketh not ashamed*.

And upon these Terms, I affirm, *That such a Conscience*, as has imployed the Utmost of its Ability to give it self the best Information, and clearest Knowledge of its Duty, that it can, is a Rational Ground for a Man to build *such an Hope upon;* and, consequently, for him to confide in.

There is an *innate Light* in every Man, discovering to him the first Lines of Duty, in the common Notions of *Good and Evil;* which by Cultivation, and Improvement, may be advanced to higher, and brighter Discoveries. And from hence it is, that the Schoolmen, and Moralists, admit not of any *Ignorantia Juris*, speaking of *Natural Moral Right*, to give excuse to Sin. Since all such Ignorance is *voluntary*, and therefore culpable; for as much as it was in every Man's Power to have prevented it, by a due Improvement of the *Light of Nature*, and the Seeds of Moral Honesty sown in his Heart.

If it be here demanded, Whether a Man may not remain ignorant of his Duty, after he has used the *utmost means* to inform himself of it? I answer, that so much of Duty as is absolutely necessary to save him, he shall upon the use of such a Course come to know; and that which he continues ignorant of, having done the utmost lying in his Power, that he might not be ignorant of it, shall never damn him. Which Assertion is proved thus: The gospel damns no body for being ignorant of that which he is not obliged to know; but that, which upon the Improvement of a Man's utmost Power, he cannot know, he is not obliged to know; for that otherwise he would be obliged to an Impossibility; since that which is out of the Compass of any Man's Power, is to that man *Impossible*.

He therefore who exerts all the Powers, and Faculties of his Soul, and plies all Means and Opportunities in the Search of Truth, which God has vouchsafed him, may rest upon the Judgment of his Conscience so informed, as a Warrantable Guide of those Actions, which he must account to God for. And if by following such a Guide, he falls into the *Ditch*, the *Ditch* shall never drown him, or if it should, the Man perishes not by his *Sin*, but by his *Misfortune*. In a word, he who endeavours to know the utmost of his Duty, that he can, and practises the utmost that he knows, has the Equity and Goodness of the great God to stand as a mighty Wall, or Rampart between him, and Damnation, for any Errours or Infirmities, which the Frailty of his Condition has invincibly, and therefore *inculpably* exposed him to.

And if a Conscience thus qualified, and informed, be not the *Measure*, by which a Man may take a true Estimate of his Absolution, before the Tribunal of God, all the Understanding of humane Nature, cannot find out any Ground for the Sinner to pitch the Sole of his Foot upon, or rest his Conscience with any Assurance, but is left in the Plunge of Infinite Doubts, and Uncertainties, Suspicions, and Misgivings, both as to the Measures of his present Duty, and the final Issues of his future Reward.

Let this *Conclusion* therefore stand as the firm Result of the foregoing Discourse, and the Foundation of what is to follow; That such a Conscience, as has not been wanting to it self, in endeavouring to get the *utmost*, and clearest Information about the Will of God, that its Power, Advantages, and Opportunities could afford it, is that great *Internal Judge, whose Absolution is a Rational, and sure Ground of Confidence towards God:* And so I pass to the second Thing proposed. Which is to shew, *How, and by what Means, we may get our Heart or Conscience thus informed, and afterwards preserve and keep it so.*

In order to which amongst many Things, that might be alleaged as highly usefull, and conducing to this great Work. I shall insist upon these Four: As,

1. Let a Man carefully attend to the *Voice* of his *Reason*, and all the Dictates of Natural Morality; so as by no means, to doe any thing contrary to them. For though *Reason is not to be relied* upon, as

a Guide universally sufficient to direct us what to doe; yet it is generally *to be relied* upon, and obeyed, where it tells us, what we are *not to doe*. It is, indeed, but a weak, and diminutive *Light*, compared to *Revelation;* but it ought to be no disparagement to a *Star*, that it is not a *Sun*. Nevertheless, as weak, and as small as it is, it is a *Light always* at hand, and though enclosed (as it were) in a dark Lanthorn, may yet be of singular use to prevent many a *foul Step*, and to keep us from many a *dangerous Fall*. And every Man brings such a Degree of this Light into the World with him; that *though it cannot bring him to Heaven;* yet, if he be true to it, it will carry him a great way; indeed so far, that if follows it faithfully, I doubt not, but he shall meet with *another Light*, which shall carry him quite through.

How far it may be improved, is evident from that high and refined Morality, which shined forth both in the *Lives*, and *Writings* of some of the Ancient Heathens, who yet had no other *Light* but this, both to *live*, and to *write* by. . . .[12]

. . . . .

And then for their Writings; what admirable Things occur in the Remains of *Pythagoras*, and the Books of *Plato*, and of several other Philosophers? short, I confess, of the Rules of Christianity, but generally above the Lives of Christians.

Which being so, ought not the *Light of Reason* to be look'd upon by us as a Rich, and a Noble Talent, and such an one as we must account to God for? for it is certainly from him. It is a Ray of Divinity darted into the Soul. *It is the Candle of the Lord* (as *Solomon* calls it) and God never lights us up a *Candle* either *to put it out*, or to *sleep by*. If it be made conscious to a *Work of Darkness*, it will not fail to discover, and reprove it; and therefore the *checks* of it are to be revered, as the Echo of a *Voice from Heaven;* for, *whatsoever Conscience binds here on Earth*, will be certainly bound there too; and it were a great Vanity, to hope, or imagine, that either Law or Gospel will absolve, what Natural Conscience *condemns*. No Man ever yet offended his own *Conscience*, but first, or last, it was revenged upon him for it. So that it will concern a Man, to treat this great Principle awfully, and warily, by still observing what it commands, but especially what it *forbids;* And, if he would have it always a faithfull, and sincere Monitor to him, let him be sure never to turn a *deaf Ear to it;* for *not to hear* it, is the Way to *silence* it. Let him strictly observe the first Stirrings, and Intimations; the first hints, and Whispers of *Good and Evil*, that pass in his Heart; and this will keep Conscience so quick, and vigilant, and ready to give a Man true Alarms, upon the least Approach of his spiritual Enemy, that he shall be hardly capable of a great Surprise.

On the contrary, if a Man accustoms himself to Slight, or pass over these first Motions to Good, or Shrinkings of his Conscience from Evil, which Originally are as Natural to the Heart of Man, as the *Appetites of Hunger, and Thirst* are to the *Stomach;* Conscience will by Degrees grow dull, and unconcerned; and, from not *spying out Motes*, come at length to over-look *Beams;* from Carelessness it shall fall into a *Slumber*, and from a Slumber, it shall settle into a deep, and long *Sleep;* till, at last, perhaps it sleeps it self into a Lethargy, and that such an one, that nothing but *Hell*, and Judgment shall be able to awaken it. For long *disuse* of any thing made for Action, will in time take away the very *use* of it. As I have read of one, who having for a Disguise, kept one of his Eyes a long time covered; when he took off the Covering, found his Eye indeed where it was, but his Sight was gone. He who would keep his Conscience *awake*, must be careful to keep it stirring.

2. Let a Man be very *tender*, and regardful of every pious Motion, and Suggestion made by *the Spirit of God* to his Heart. I do not hereby go about to establish *Enthusiasm*, or such phantastick Pretences of Intercourse with God, as Papists, and Fanatics (who in most Things copy *from* one another, as well as rail *at* one another) do usually boast of. But certainly, if *the Evil Spirit* may, and often does suggest wicked, and vile Thoughts to the Minds of Men; as all do, and must grant, and is sufficiently proved from the *Devil's putting it*

[12] The present editor has here omitted a short passage from the original text.

into the Heart of Judas, to betray Christ, John 13.2. And his *filling the Heart of Ananias, to lye to the Holy Ghost*, Acts 5.3. It cannot after this, with any Colour of Reason be doubted, but that the *Holy Spirit of God*, whose Power, and Influence to do Good is much greater, than that of the *wicked Spirit* to Evil, does frequently inject into, and imprint upon the Soul many blessed Motions, and Impulses to Duty, and many powerfull Avocations from Sin. So that a Man shall not only (as the Prophet says) *hear a Voice behind him*, but also *a Voice within him*, telling him which way he ought to go.

For doubtless, there is something more in those Expressions of *being led by the Spirit, and being taught by the Spirit*, and the like, than mere *Tropes*, and Metaphors; and nothing less is, or can be imported by them, than that God sometimes *speaks* to, and *converses with* the Hearts of Men, *immediately by himself:* And, happy those, who by thus hearing him speak in a *still Voice*, shall prevent his speaking to them *in Thunder*.

But you will here ask, perhaps, how we shall distinguish in such Motions, which of them proceed immediately from the *Spirit of God*, and which from the Conscience? In answer to which, I must confess, that I know no certain Mark of Discrimination, to distinguish them by; save only in general, that such as proceed immediately from God, use to strike the Mind suddenly, and very powerfully. But then I add also, that as the Knowledge of this, in Point of Speculation, is so *nice and difficult*, so (thanks be to God) in Point of Practice it is not *necessary*. But let a Man universally observe, and obey every good Motion rising in his Heart, knowing that every such Motion proceeds from God, either *mediately*, or *immediately;* and that, whether God speaks *immediately* by himself to the Conscience, or *mediately* by the Conscience to the Soul, the Authority is the same in both, and the Contempt of either is Rebellion.

Now the Thing which I drive at, under this Head of Discourse, is to shew, *That as* God is sometimes pleased to address himself, in this Manner to the Hearts of Men; so, if the *Heart will receive*, and *answer* such Motions, by a ready, and obsequious Compliance with them, there is no doubt, but they will both return more frequently, and still more and more powerfully, till at length they produce such *a Degree of Light* in the Conscience, as shall give a Man, both a clear *Sight* of his Duty, and a certain *Judgment* of his Condition.

On the contrary, as all Resistance whatsoever of the Dictates of Conscience, even in the Way of Natural *Efficiency* brings a kind of Hardness, and *Stupefaction* upon it; So the *Resistance* of these *peculiar Suggestions of the Spirit*, will cause in it also a *Judicial Hardness*, which is yet worse than the other. So that God shall withdraw from such an Heart, and the *Spirit* being *grieved* shall depart, and these *blessed Motions* shall cease, and affect, and visit it no more. The Consequence of which is very terrible; as rendring a Man *past feeling*. And then the less he feels in this World, the more he shall *be sure* to feel in the next. But,

3. Because the *Light* of *Natural Conscience*, is in many Things defective, and dimn, and the *Internal Voice of God's Spirit*, not always distinguishable, above all, let a Man attend to the Mind of God, uttered in his *Revealed Word*. I say, his *Revealed Word*. By which, I do not mean, that Mysterious, Extraordinary, (and *of late*, so much studied) Book called the *Revelation*, and which perhaps the more it is studied, the less 'tis understood, as generally either finding a Man crack'd, or making him so; But I mean those other Writings of the *Prophets*, and *Apostles*, which exhibit to us a plain, *sure*, perfect, and intelligible Rule; a Rule that will neither fail, nor distract such as make use of it. A Rule to judge of the two former Rules by: For nothing that contradicts the *Revealed Word of God*, is either the Voice of *Right Reason*, or of the *Spirit of God;* nor is it possible, that it should be so, without God's contradicting himself.

And therefore we see, what high Elogies are given to the *Written Word*, by the inspired Pen-men of both *Testaments. It giveth Understanding to the simple* says *David*, in *Psalm* 119.130 And that, you will say, is no such easy Matter to doe.

It is able to *make the Man of God perfect*, (says St. *Paul*) 2 *Tim.* 3.17. *It is quick and powerfull, and sharper than any*

Two-edged Sword, piercing even to the dividing asunder of the Soul, and spirit; and is a Discerner of the Thoughts, and Intents of the Heart, Heb. 4.12. Now what a Force and Fulness, what a Vigour and Emphasis is there in all these Expressions! Enough (one would think) to recommend and endear the Scriptures, even to the Papists themselves. For if (as the Text says) *They give understanding to the simple;* I know none more concerned to read, and study them, than their Popes.

Wherefore since the *Light*, and Energy of the *Written Word* is so mighty, let a Man bring and hold his Conscience to this steady Rule: The unalterable Rectitude of which, will infallibly discover the *Rectitude*, or *Obliquity*, of whatsoever it is applied to. We shall find it a *Rule*, both to instruct us what *to doe*, and to assure us in what *we have done*. For though *Natural Conscience* ought to be listened to, yet it is *Revelation* alone, that is to be relied upon: *As we* may observe in the Works of Art, a Judicious Artist will indeed *use* his *Eye*, but he will *trust* only to his Rule.

There is not any one Action whatsoever, which a Man *ought to doe*, or to *forbear*, but the Scripture will give him a clear Precept, or Prohibition for it.

So that if a Man will commit such Rules to his Memory, and stock his Mind with Portions of Scripture answerable to all the Heads of Duty and Practice, his Conscience can never be at a Loss, either for a Direction of his Actions, or an Answer to a Temptation: It was the very Course which our Saviour himself took, when the Devil plied him with Temptation upon Temptation. Still he had a *suitable Scripture* ready to repell, and baffle them all, one after another: Every pertinent Text urged home, being a direct Stabb to a Temptation.

Let a Man therefore consider, and recount with himself the several Duties, and Vertues of a Christian. Such as, *Temperance, Meekness, Charity, Purity of Heart, Pardoning of Enemies, Patience*. (I had almost said, *Passive Obedience* too, but that such old fashioned Christianity, seems as much out of Date with some, *as Christ's Divinity, and Satisfaction.*) I say, let a Man consider these, and the like *Virtues*, together with the *contrary Sins and Vices*, that do oppose them; and then, as out of a full Armory, or Magazine, let him furnish his Conscience with Texts of Scripture, particularly enjoyning the one, and forbidding, or threatning the other. And yet I do not say, that he should stuff his Mind like the *Margent* of some Authors, with *Chapter* and *Verse* heaped together, at all Adventures; but only that he should fortifie it with some few Texts, which are home, and apposite to his Case. And a Conscience thus supplied, will be like a Man armed at all points; and always ready either to receive, or to attack his Enemy. Otherwise it is not a Man's *having Arms in his house;* no, nor yet his having Courage, and Skill to use them; but it is his having them still about him, which must both secure him from being set upon, and defend him when he is.

Accordingly, Men must know, that without taking the forementioned Course, all that they do in this Matter, is but lost Labour; and that they *read the Scriptures* to as little purpose, as *some use to quote them;* Much *Reading* being like much *Eating*, wholly useless without Digestion; and it is impossible for a Man to digest his Meat, without also retaining it.

Till Men get what they read into their *Minds*, and fix it in their *Memories*, they keep their Religion as they use to doe their Bibles, only in their Closet, or carry it in their Pocket; and that, you may imagine, must improve, and affect the Soul, just as much as a Man's having plenty of Provision only in his Stores, will nourish, and support his Body. When Men forget the Word heard, or read by them, the *Devil is said to steal it out of their Hearts*, Luke 8.12. And for this Cause, we do with as much *Reason*, as *propriety of Speech*, call the Committing of a Thing to memory, the *getting it by heart*. For it is the *Memory*, that must transmit it to the *Heart;* and it is vain to expect, that the Heart should keep its hold of any Truth, when the Memory has let it go.

4. The *Fourth* and *Last* way, that I shall mention, *for the getting of the Conscience rightly informed*, and afterwards *keeping* it so, is frequently and impartially to account with it. It is with a Man and his Conscience, as with one Man, and another; amongst whom we use to say, that *Even*

Reckoning makes lasting Friends; and the way to make Reckonings *even*, I am sure, is to make them *often*. Delays in Accompts are always suspicious; and bad enough in themselves, but commonly much worse in their Cause. For, to *deferr* an Accompt, is the ready way to *perplex* it; and, when it comes to be perplexed, and intricate, no Man, either as to his Temporal or Spiritual Estate, can know of himself *what he is, or what he has*, or upon what bottom he stands. But the amazing Difficulty, and greatness of his Account, will rather terrifie than inform him; and keep him from setting heartily about such a Task, as he despairs ever to go through with. For, no Man willingly begins, what he has no hope to finish.

But, let a Man apply to this Work, by frequent Returns, and short Intervals, while the Heap is small, and the Particulars few, and he will find it easie, and conquerable; And his Conscience, like a faithful Steward, shall give him in a plain, open, and entire Account of himself, and hide nothing from him. Whereas we know, if a Steward or Cashier be suffered to run on from year to year without bringing him to a Reckoning, it is odds but such sottish forbearance, will, in time, teach him to shuffle; and strongly tempt him to be a Cheat, if not also make him so: For, as the Accompt *runs on*, generally the Accomptant *goes backward*.

And for this Cause, some judge it adviseable for a Man to account with *his Heart* every day; and this, no doubt, is the best, and surest Course; for still the *oftener*, the *better*. And some prescribe Accompting once a Week; longer than which it is, by no means, safe to delay it: For, a Man shall find his Heart deceitfull, and Memory weak, and Nature extremely averse from seeking narrowly after That, which it is unwilling to find; and being found, will assuredly disturb it.

So that upon the whole matter it is infinitely absurd to think that *Conscience* can be kept in order without frequent Examination. If a man would have Conscience deal clearly with him, he must deal severely with That. Often *scouring* and cleansing it will make it *bright;* and, when it is so, he may see himself in it: And, if he sees any Thing amiss, let this satisfy him, That no man is, or can be, the *worse* for knowing the very *worst* of himself.

On the contrary; if *Conscience* by a long neglect of, and dis-acquaintance with it self, comes to contract an inveterate Rust or Soil, a man may as well expect to see his Face in a *Mud-wall*, as that such a Conscience should give him a true Report of his Condition; no, it leaves him wholly in the Dark, as to the greatest Concern he has in both Worlds. He can neither tell, whether God be his *Friend*, or his *Enemy*, or rather he has shrewd Cause to suspect him his *Enemy*, and cannot possibly know him to be his *Friend*. And this being his Case, he must live in Ignorance, and die in Ignorance; and it will be hard for a man to die *in it*, without dying *for it* too.

And now, what a *wretched* Condition must that man needs be in, whose Heart is in such a Confusion, such Darkness, and such a settled Blindness, that it shall not be able to tell him so much as one true Word of himself? *Flatter* him it may (I confess) (as those are generally good at *flattering*, who are good for nothing else) but, in the mean time, the poor Man is left under the fatal Necessity of a remediless Delusion: For, in judging of a man's Self, if *Conscience* either cannot or will not inform him, there is a certain Thing called *Self-love* that will be sure to deceive him. And thus I have shewn, in four several Particulars, *what is to be done*, both for the getting and keeping of the Conscience, so informed, as that it may be able to give us a Rational *Confidence towards God*. As,

1. That the *Voice* of Reason, in all the Dictates of *Natural Morality*, ought carefully to be attended to by a strict Observance of what it *commands*, but especially of what it *forbids*.

2. That every Pious Motion from *the Spirit of God* ought tenderly to be cherished, and by no means checked or *quenched* either by Resistance or Neglect.

3. That *conscience* is to be kept close to the Rule of the written Word.

4 *ly*. and *Lastly*, That it is frequently to be examined, and severely accounted with.

And, I doubt not, but a *Conscience* thus disciplined, shall give a man such a faithful Account of himself, as shall never shame, nor lurch the *Confidence*, which he shall take up from it.

Nevertheless, to prevent all mistakes in so critical a Case, and so high a Concern. I shall close up the foregoing Particulars with this *twofold Caution.*

First, Let no man *think*, that every *Doubting* or *Mis-giving* about the Safety of his Spiritual Estate, over-throws the *Confidence hitherto spoken of.* For (as I shew before) the *Confidence* mentioned in the Text, is not properly *Assurance*, but only a *Rational, well-grounded Hope;* And therefore may very well consist with some Returns of *Doubting.* For, we know, in that Pious and Excellent *Confession* and *Prayer*, made by the poor Man to our Saviour, in *Mark* 9.24. how, in the very same Breath, in which he says, *Lord, I believe;* He says also, *Lord, help my unbelief.* So that we see here, that the Sincerity of our *Faith* or *Confidence* will not secure us against all Vicissitudes of Wavering or Distrust; indeed, no more than a strong Athletick Constitution of Body will secure a man always against Heats, and Colds, and Rheums, and such-like *Indispositions.*

And one great Reason of this, is; Because such a *Faith* or *Confidence* as we have been treating of, resides in the Soul or Conscience, as *an Habit.* And *Habits*, we know, are by no means either inconsistent with, or destroyed by every contrary *Act.* But, especially, in the Case now before us, where the Truth and Strength of *our Confidence towards God* does not consist so much, *in the present Act*, by which it exerts it self, no, nor yet *in the Habit* producing this Act; as it does in the *Ground* or *Reason*, which this Confidence is *built upon;* which being the *standing sincerity of a man's Heart*, though the present *Act* be interrupted, (as, no doubt, through *Infirmity*, or *Temptation*, it may be very often,) yet, so long as *that sincerity*, upon which this *Confidence* was first founded, does continue, as soon as the *Temptation* is removed, and gone, the fore-mentioned *Faith*, or *Affiance*, will, by renewed, vigorous and fresh Acts, recover and exert it self, and with great comfort, and satisfaction of mind, give a man *confidence towards God.* Which, though it be, indeed, a lower, and a lesser thing than *Assurance*, yet, as to all the Purposes of a Pious Life, may, for ought I see, prove much more useful; as both affording a man *due comfort*, and yet leaving room for *due caution* too; which are Two of the principal Uses that Religion serves for, in this *World.*

2. The other *Caution*, with reference to the foregoing Discourse, is this: *Let no man*, from what has been said, reckon a *bare silence of Conscience* in not *accusing*, or *disturbing* him, a sufficient Argument for *Confidence towards God.* For, such a *Silence* is so far from being always so, that it is usually worse than the fiercest and loudest *Accusations;* since it may, and for the most part does proceed, from a kind of *numbness*, or stupidity of *Conscience;* and an absolute Dominion obtained by Sin over the Soul; so that it shall not so much as *dare to complain, or make a stir.* For, as our Saviour says, *Luke* 11.21. *while the strong Man armed keeps his Palace, his Goods are in peace.* So, while Sin rules and governs with a strong Hand, and has wholly subdued the Conscience to a slavish Subjection to its Tyrannical Yoke, the Soul *shall be at Peace*, such a false *Peace* as it is; but for that very Cause *worse* a great deal, and more destructive, than, when, by continual Alarms and Assaults, it gives a man neither Peace nor Truce, Quiet nor Intermission. And therefore it is very remarkable, that the Text expresses the sound Estate of the Heart or the Conscience, here spoken of, not barely by its *not accusing*, but by its not *condemning* us; which word imports properly an Acquitment, or Discharge of a man upon some precedent *Accusation*, and *a full Trial and Cognizance of his Cause* had thereupon. For as *Condemnation*, being a *Law Term*, and so relating to the Judicial Proceedings of *Law Courts*, must still presuppose an Hearing of the Cause, before any Sentence can pass; so likewise in the *Court of Conscience*, there must be a strict and impartial Enquiry into all a man's Actions, and a thorough hearing of all that can be pleaded for, and against him, before Conscience can rationally either *condemn*, or *discharge him:* And if, indeed, upon such a fair and full Trial he can come off, he is then *Rectus in curiâ*, clear and *innocent*, and consequently may reap all that satisfaction from himself, which it is Natural for *Innocence* to afford the person who has it. I do not here speak of a *Legal Innocence*, (none but Sots and Quakers

dream of such things;) For, as Saint *Paul* says, *Galat.* 2.16. *By the Works of the Law shall no flesh living be justified:* But I speak of an *Evangelical Innocence;* such an one as the Oeconomy of the Gospel accepts, whatsoever the Law enjoyns; and though mingled with several Infirmities, and Defects, yet amounts to such a pitch of Righteousness, as we call *Sincerity*. And whosoever has this, shall never be Damned for want of the other.

And now, how vastly does it concern all those, who shall think it worth their while to be in earnest with their Immortal Souls, not to abuse and delude themselves with a false Confidence? a thing so easily taken up, and so hardly laid down. Let no man conclude, because his Conscience *says nothing to him*, that therefore it *has nothing to say*. Possibly some never so much as doubted of the safety of their Spiritual Estate, in all their Lives; and if so, let them not flatter themselves, but rest assured, that they have so much the more reason a great deal to doubt of it now. For the Causes of such a profound *stillness*, are generally gross Ignorance, or long Custom of Sinning, or both; and these are very dreadful Symptoms indeed, to such as are not *Hell and Damnation-proof*. When a man's Wounds cease to *smart*, only because he has lost his *feeling*, they are never the less *mortal* for his not seeing his Need of a *Chirurgeon*. It is not meer, actual, present Ease, but Ease after Pain, which brings the most durable and solid Comfort. Acquitment before Trial can be no security. *Great* and *strange Calms* usually portend, and go before the most violent *Storms*. And therefore, since *Storms* and *Calms* (especially with reference to the State of the Soul) doe always follow one another; Certainly of the Two, it is much more Eligible, to have the *Storm first*, and the *Calm afterwards:* Since a Calm before a Storm is commonly a Peace of a man's own making: *but a Calm, after a Storm*, a Peace of God's.

To which God, who only can speak such Peace to us, as neither the World nor the Devil shall be able to take from us, be rendred and ascribed, as is most due, all Praise, Might, Majesty, and Dominion, both now, and for ever-more. Amen.

John Tillotson

THE ADVANTAGES OF RELIGION TO SOCIETIES[13]

Prov. xiv.34.—Righteousness exalteth a nation; but sin is the reproach of any people.

One of the first principles that is planted in the nature of man, and which lies at the very root and foundation of his being, is the desire of his own preservation and happiness. Hence is it that every man is led by interest, and does love or hate, choose or refuse things, according as he apprehends them to conduce to this end, or to contradict it. And because the happiness of this life is most present and sensible, therefore human nature (which in this degenerate state is extremely sunk down into sense) is most powerfully affected with sensible and temporal things. And consequently, there cannot be a greater prejudice raised against any thing than to have it represented as inconvenient and hurtful to our temporal interests.

Upon this account it is that Religion hath extremely suffer'd in the opinion of many, as if it were opposite to our present welfare, and did rob men of the greatest advantages and conveniences of life. So that he would do right to Religion, and make a ready way for the entertainment of it among men, cannot take a more effectual course than by reconciling it with the happiness of mankind, and by giving satisfaction to our reason, that it is so far from being an enemy that it is the greatest friend to our temporal interests; and that it doth not only tend to make every man happy consider'd singly and in a private capacity, but is excellently fitted for the benefit of human society.

How much Religion tends even to the temporal advantage of private persons I

[13] Text: *The Works of the Most Reverend Dr. John Tillotson . . . In Three Volumes . . . By Thomas Birch, M.A. . . . ,* 1752

shall not now consider, because my Text leads me to discourse of the other, namely, to shew how advantageous Religion and Virtue are to the publick prosperity of a Nation, which I take to be the meaning of this *Aphorism* of *Solomon*, *Righteousness exalteth a Nation, etc.*

And here I shall not restrain *righteousness* to the particular virtue of justice (tho' in this sense also this saying is most true) but enlarge it according to the *genius* and strain of this Book of the *Proverbs*, in which the words *wisdom* and *righteousness* are commonly used very comprehensively so as to signify all Religion and Virtue. And that this word is so to be taken in the Text may appear farther from the opposition of it to sin or vice in general; *Righteousness* exalteth a Nation, but *Sin* is the reproach of any People.

You see then what will be the subject of my present discourse; namely, That *Religion and Virtue are the great causes of publick happiness and prosperity.*

And though the truth of this hath been universally acknowledged and long enough experienced in the world, yet because the fashion of the age is to call every thing into question, it will be requisite to satisfy mens reason about it. To which end I shall do these two things.

1. Endeavour to give an account of this Truth.

2. To vindicate it from the pretences and insinuations of atheistical persons. I shall give you this twofold account of it.

1. From the justice of the Divine providence.

2. From the natural tendency of the thing.

1. From the justice of the Divine providence. Indeed, as to particular persons the providences of God are many times promiscuously administred in this world; so that no man can certainly conclude God's love or hatred to any person by any thing that befalls him in this life. But God does not deal thus with Nations. Because publick bodies and communities of men, as such, can only be rewarded and punished in this world. For in the next, all those publick societies and combinations wherein men are now link'd together under several Governments, shall be dissolved. God will not then reward or punish Nations, as Nations; But every man shall then give an account of himself to God, and receive his own reward, and bear his own burden. For although God account it no disparagement to his justice to let particular good men suffer in this world, and pass *through many tribulations into the kingdom of God*, because there is another day a coming which will be a more proper season of reward; yet in the usual course of his providence he recompenseth religious and virtuous Nations with temporal blessings and prosperity. For which reason St. *Austin* tells us that the mighty success and long prosperity of the *Romans* was a reward given them by God for their eminent justice and temperance, and other virtues. And on the other hand, God many times suffers the most grievous sins of particular persons to go unpunished in this world, because he knows that his justice will have another and better opportunity to meet and reckon with them. But the general and crying Sins of a Nation cannot hope to escape publick judgments, unless they be prevented by a general repentance. God may defer his judgments for a time, and give a People a longer space of repentance, he may stay 'till the iniquities of a Nation be full, but sooner or later they have reason to expect his vengeance. And usually the longer punishment is delay'd it is the heavier when it comes.

Now all this is very reasonable, because this world is the only season for National punishments. And indeed they are in a great degree necessary for the present vindication of the honour and majesty of the Divine Laws, and to give some check to the overflowing of wickedness. Publick judgments are the banks and shores upon which God breaks the insolency of sinners and stays their proud waves. And though among men the multitude of offenders be many times a cause of impunity, because of the weakness of human Governments which are glad to spare where they are not strong enough to punish, yet in the government of God things are quite otherwise. No combination of sinners is too hard for him, and the greater and more numerous the offenders are, the more his justice is concern'd to vindicate the affront. However God may pass by single sinners in this world, yet when a Nation combines against him, *when hand joins in hand the wicked shall not go unpunished.*

This the *Scripture* declares to be the settled course of God's providence; That a righteous Nation shall be happy; *The work of righteousness shall be peace; and the effects of righteousness, quietness and assurance for ever.* And on the other hand, that he useth to shower down his judgments upon a wicked people, *he turneth a fruitful land into barrenness for the wickedness of them that dwell therein.*

And the experience of all ages hath made this good. All along the History of the *Old Testament*, we find the interchangeable providences of God towards the People of *Israel* always suited to their manners. They were constantly prosperous or afflicted according as piety and virtue flourished or declined amongst them. And God did not only exercise this providence towards his own People, but he dealt thus also with other Nations. The *Roman Empire* whilst the virtue of that people remained firm was *strong as iron*, as 'tis represented in the Prophesy of *Daniel:* But upon the dissolution of their manners the *iron* began *to be mixt with miry clay*, and the *feet* upon which that Empire stood, *to be broken.* And tho' God in the administration of his justice be not tied to precedents, and we cannot argue from Scripture-examples that the providences of God towards other Nations shall in all circumstances be conformable to his dealings with the People of *Israel;* yet thus much may with great probability be collected from them, that as God always blessed that People while they were obedient to him, and followed them with his judgments when they rebelled against him, so he will also deal with other Nations. Because the reason of those dispensations as to the main and substance of them seems to be perpetual, and founded in that which can never change, the justice of the Divine providence.

2dly. The truth of this farther appears from the natural tendency of the thing. For Religion in general, and every particular virtue, doth in its own nature conduce to the publick Interest.

Religion, where-ever it is truly planted, is certainly the greatest obligation upon conscience to all civil offices and moral duties. Chastity and temperance and industry do in their own nature tend to health and plenty. Truth and fidelity in all our dealings do create mutual love and good-will and confidence among men, which are the great bands of peace. And on the contrary, wickedness doth in its own nature produce many publick mischiefs. For as sins are link'd together and draw on one another, so almost every vice hath some temporal inconvenience annexed to it and naturally following it. Intemperance and lust breed infirmities and diseases, which being propagated spoil the strain of a Nation. Idleness and luxury bring forth poverty and want; and this tempts men to injustice, and that causeth enmity and animosities, and these bring on *strife* and *confusion and every evil work.* This Philosophical account of publick troubles and confusions St. *James* gives us, *Whence come wars and fightings among you? are they not hence, even from your lusts that war in your members?*

But I shall shew more particularly, that Religion and Virtue do naturally tend to the good order and more easy government of human society, because they have a good influence both upon Magistrates and Subjects.

1. Upon Magistrates. Religion teacheth them to rule over men in the fear of God, because though they be Gods on earth yet they are subjects of Heaven, and accountable to Him who is higher than the highest in this world. Religion in a Magistrate strengthens his authority, because it procures veneration and gains a reputation to it. And in all the affairs of this world so much reputation is really so much power. We see that piety and virtue, where they are found among men of lower degree, will command some reverence and respect: But in persons of eminent place and dignity they are seated to a great advantage, so as to cast a lustre upon their very Place and by a strong reflexion to double the beams of Majesty. Whereas impiety and vice do strangely lessen greatness, and do secretly and unavoidably derive some weakness upon authority itself. Of this the *Scripture* gives up a remarkable instance in *David.* For among other things which made *the Sons of Zeruiah too hard for him* this probably was none of the least, that they were particularly conscious to his crimes.

2. Religion hath a good influence upon the People; to make them obedient to government, and peaceable one towards another.

1. To make them obedient to Government, and conformable to Laws; and that *not only for wrath* and out of fear of the Magistrate's power, which is but a weak and loose principle of obedience, and will cease, whenever men can rebel with safety, and to advantage; but out *of Conscience,* which is a firm and constant and lasting principle, and will hold a man fast when all other obligations will break. He that hath entertain'd the true principles of Christianity is not to be tempted from his obedience and subjection by any worldly considerations, because he believes that *whosoever resisteth authority resisteth the ordinance of God*, and that *they who resist shall receive to themselves damnation.*

2. Religion tends to make men peaceable one towards another. For it endeavours to plant all those qualities and dispositions in men which tend to peace and unity, and to fill men with a spirit of universal love and good-will. It endeavours likewise to secure every man's interest by commanding the observation of that great rule of equity, *Whatsoever ye would that men should do unto you, do ye even so to them;* by injoining that truth and fidelity be inviolably observed in all our words, promises and contracts. And in order hereunto it requires the extirpation of all those passions and vices which render men unsociable and troublesome to one another, as pride, covetousness and injustice, hatred and revenge and cruelty; and those likewise which are not so commonly reputed vices, as self-conceit and peremptoriness in a man's own opinions and all peevishness and incompliance of humour in things lawful and indifferent.

And that these are the proper effects of true piety the doctrine of our Saviour and his Apostles every where teacheth us. Now if this be the design of Religion to bring us to this temper, thus to heal the natures of men and to sweeten their spirits, to correct their passions and to mortify all those lusts which are the causes of enmity and division, then it is evident that in its own nature it tends to the peace and happiness of human society; and that if men would but live as Religion requires they should do, the world would be a quiet habitation, a most lovely and desirable place in comparison of what now it is. And indeed the true reason why the societies of men are so full of tumult and disorder, so troublesome and tempestuous, is because there is so little of true Religion among men; so that were it not for some small remainders of piety and virtue which are yet left scatter'd among mankind, human society would in a short space disband and run into confusion, the earth would grow wild and become a great forest, and mankind would become beasts of prey one towards another. And if this discourse hold true, surely then one would think that virtue should find itself a seat where-ever human societies are, and that Religion should be owned and encouraged in the world until men cease to be governed by reason.

II. I come to vindicate this truth from the insinuations and pretences of atheistical persons. I shall mention two.

1. That government may subsist well enough without the belief of a God and a state of rewards and punishments after this life.

2. That as for virtue and vice they are arbitrary things.

1. That government may subsist well enough without the belief of a God or a state of rewards and punishments after this life. And this the Atheist does and must assert, otherwise he is by his own confession a declared enemy to Government and unfit to live in human society.

For answer to this, I will not deny that though the generality of men did not believe any superior Being nor any rewards and punishments after this life, yet notwithstanding this there might be some kind of Government kept up in the world. For supposing men to have reason, the necessities of human nature and the mischiefs of confusion would probably compel them into some kind of order. But then I say withal, that if these principles were banished out of the world Government would be far more difficult than now it is, because it would want its firmest basis and foundation; there would be infinitely more disorders in the world if men were restrained from injustice and violence only by human laws, and not by principles of conscience and the dread of another world. Therefore Magistrates have always thought themselves concerned to cherish Religion, and to maintain in the minds of men the belief of a God and another life. Nay that common suggestion of atheistical persons, that Religion was at first a politick device and is still kept up in the world as a State-engine to awe men into obedience, is a clear acknowledgment of the usefulness of it to the ends of Government, and does as fully contradict that pretence of theirs which I am now confuting as any thing that can be said.

2. That virtue and vice are arbitrary things, founded only in the imaginations of men and in the constitutions and customs of the world, but not in the nature of the things themselves; and that *that* is virtue or vice, good or evil, which the Supreme Authority of a Nation declares to be so. And this is frequently and confidently asserted by the ingenious author of a very bad book, I mean the *Leviathan.*

Now the proper way of answering any thing that is confidently asserted is to shew the contrary, namely, That there are some things that have a natural evil and deformity in them, as perjury, perfidiousness, unrighteousness and ingratitude, which are things not only condemned by the positive laws and constitutions of particular Nations and Governments but by the general verdict of human nature: And that the virtues contrary to these have a natural goodness and comeliness in them, and are suitable to the common principles and sentiments of humanity.

And this will most evidently appear by putting this supposition. Suppose the reverse of all that which we now call virtue were solemnly enacted, and the practice of fraud and rapine, and perjury, and falseness to a man's word, and all manner of vice and wickedness were established by a Law: I ask now, if the case between virtue and vice were thus alter'd, would that which we now call vice in process of time gain the reputation of virtue, and that which we now call virtue grow odious and contemptible to human nature? If it would not, then is there something in the nature of good and evil, of virtue and vice, which does not depend upon the pleasure of authority, nor is subject to any arbitrary Constitution. But that it would not be thus I am very certain, because no Government could subsist upon these terms. For the very injoining of fraud and rapine and perjury and breach of trust doth apparently destroy the greatest end of Government, which is to preserve men in their rights against the incroachments of fraud and violence. And this end being destroyed human societies would presently fly in pieces, and men would necessarily fall into a state of war. Which plainly shews that virtue and vice are not arbitrary things, but that there is a natural and immutable and eternal reason for that which we call goodness and virtue, and against that which we call vice and wickedness.

Thus I have endeavoured to evidence and vindicate this truth. I shall only draw an Inference or two from this discourse, and so conclude.

1. If this discourse be true, then those who are in place of power and authority are peculiarly concerned to maintain the honour of Religion.

2. It concerns every one to live in the practice of it.

1. Magistrates are concerned to maintain the honour of Religion, which doth not only tend to every man's future happiness, but is the best instrument of Civil Government and of the temporal prosperity of a Nation. For the whole design of it is to procure the private and publick happiness of mankind, and to restrain men from all those things which would make them miserable and guilty to themselves, unpeaceable and troublesome to the world. Religion hath so great an influence upon the felicity of men that it ought to be upheld, and the veneration of it maintained, not only out of a just dread of the divine vengeance in another world, but out of regard to the temporal peace and prosperity of men. It will requite all the kindness and honour we can do it, by the advantages it will bring to Civil Government, and by the blessings it will draw down upon it. God hath promised that *those that honour him he will honour*, and in the common course of his providence he usually makes this good, so that the Civil Authority ought to be very tender of the honour of God and Religion, if for no other reason yet out of *reason of State.*

It were to be wished that all men were so piously disposed, that Religion by its own authority and the reasonable force of it might be sufficient to establish its Empire in the minds of men. But the corruptions of men will always make a strong opposition against it. And therefore at the first planting of the Christian Religion in the world God was pleased to accompany it with a miraulous power: But after it was planted this extraordinary power ceased, and God hath now left it to be maintained and supported by more ordinary and human ways, by the countenance of Authority, and the assistance of Laws; which were never more necessary than in this degenerate age, which is prodigiously sunk into Atheism and Profaneness, and is running headlong into an humour of scoffing at God and Religion and every thing that is sacred. For some ages before the Reformation Atheism was confined to *Italy*, and had its chief residence at *Rome*. All the mention that is of it in the History of those times the Papists themselves give us in the lives of their own Popes and Cardinals, excepting two or three small Philosophers that were retainers to that Court. So that this Atheistical humour among Christians was the spawn of the gross superstitions and corrupt manners of the *Romish* Church and Court. And indeed nothing is more natural than for extremes in Religion to beget one another, like the vibrations of a *pendulum* which the more violently you swing it one way the farther it will return the other. But in the last age, *Atheism* travell'd over the *Alps* and infected *France*, and now of late it hath crossed the Seas and invaded our Nation, and hath prevailed to amazement: For I do not think that there are any people in the World that are generally more indisposed to it and can worse brooke it; seriousness and zeal in Religion being almost the natural temper of the *English*. So that nothing is to me matter of greater wonder, than that in a grave and sober Nation profaneness should ever come to gain so much ground and the best and wisest Religion in the world to be made the scorn of fools. For besides the profane and atheistical discourses about God and Religion, and the bold and senseless abuses of this *sacred Book*, the great instruments of our salvation, which are so frequent in the publick places of resort, I say, besides these (I speak it knowingly) a man can hardly pass the streets without having his ears grated and pierced with such horrid and blasphemous oaths and curses as are enough, if we were guilty of no other sin, to sink a Nation. And this not only from the *Tribe* that wear Liveries, but from those that go before them and should give better example. Is it not then high time that the Laws should provide by the most prudent and effectual means to curb these bold and insolent defiers of Heaven, who take a pride in being monsters, and boast themselves in the follies and deformities of human nature? The Heathens would never suffer their Gods to be reviled, which yet were no Gods. And shall it among the professors of the true Religion be allowed to any man to make a mock of him that made Heaven and Earth, and to breathe out blasphemies against Him who gives us life and breath and all things? I doubt not but hypocrisy is a great wickedness and very odious to God, but by no means of so pernicious example as open profaneness. Hypocrisy is a more modest way of sinning, it shews some reverence to Religion, and does so far own the worth and excellency of it as to acknowledge that it deserves to be counterfeited: Whereas profaneness declares openly against it, and endeavours to make a party to drive it out of the world.

2. It concerns every one to live in the practice of Religion and Virtue; Because the publick happiness and prosperity depends upon it. It is most apparent that of late years Religion is very sensibly declin'd among us. The manners of men have almost been universally corrupted by a Civil War. We should therefore all jointly endeavour to retrieve the ancient virtue of the Nation, and to bring into fashion again that solid and substantial, that plain and unaffected piety, (free from the extremes both of superstition and enthusiasm) which flourish'd in the age of our immediate Forefathers. Which did not consist in idle talk but in real effects, in a sincere love of God and of our neighbour, in a pious devotion and reverence towards the Divine Majesty, and in the virtuous actions of a good life; in the denial of *ungodliness and worldly lusts*, and *in living soberly and*

righteously and godly in this present world. This were the true way to reconcile God to us, to stop the course of his judgments, and to bring down the blessings of Heaven upon us. God hath now been pleased to settle us again in peace both at home and abroad, and he hath put us once more into the hands of our own counsel. Life and Death, blessing and cursing, prosperity and destruction are before us. We may choose our own fortune, and if we be not wanting to ourselves we may under the influence of God's grace and assistance, which is never wanting to our sincere endeavours, become a happy and a prosperous People.

The good God make us all wise to know and to do the things that belong to the temporal peace and prosperity of the Nation, and to the eternal happiness and salvation of every one of our souls; which we humbly beg for the sake of Jesus Christ, to whom, etc.

John Dryden

NO OTHER major poet could suffer less than Dryden by having his life compressed into a very brief biography. We know little of Dryden the man. But Dryden is a poet of public themes and a bare sketch of dates and activities is enough to relate him to the social milieu whose life he celebrated, among whose intellectual problems he sought his way, and which did so much (as he never tired of saying) to direct the aims of his poetry and to explain its tone.

He was born on August 9, 1631, the eldest of fourteen children, in his maternal grandfather's parsonage at Aldwinckle All Saints, Northamptonshire, into a younger branch of the gentry. His family took the Parliamentary side in the Civil War, his cousin Sir Gilbert Pickering serving later on the Council and in the administration under Cromwell. Dryden went at an unknown date to Westminster School, under the great, stern (and royalist) head-master, Busby. The later years of his school education were signalized by the writing of his elegy on Hastings, a noble school fellow, for publication in a volume containing poems by Denham, Marvell, Herrick, and others. From Westminster he proceeded to Trinity College, Cambridge. He took his B.A. in 1654 and stayed on at the university, though without any further degree, until about 1657. In that year he probably came to London, held a small post under the Protectorate, as his detractors delighted to remember, and began some sort of journey-work for the publisher Herringman. In 1658, at the age of 27, he wrote his *Heroick Stanzas* on Cromwell's memory, published with the eulogies of Waller and Sprat. Except for several trifles, it is the first verse we have from him since the poem on Hastings. It was the first great occasion which offered itself to a young poet to make his mark. Davenant was then only beginning to re-open the theatre with entertainments under another guise. In 1654, on the death of Dryden's father, he had inherited a small estate or farm lying amid the land of the elder branch of his family at Canons-Ashby in Northamptonshire. This yielded him an income of about £40 a year (which he never tried to better by increasing the rent to his tenant). From his first coming to London he was a London man. His time was devoted to the very practical, strenuous, and unremitting literary labors by which he earned the major part of his income, at times large but latterly almost never adequate to his way of life. He counted, at least in later years, on spending a part of every summer in the country among kinsfolk or perhaps at the close of his life with great patrons. This was a time for refreshment, comparative relaxation, and quiet study. His *Essay of Dramatick Poesie* was written in one such period of retirement, early during the plague of 1665, at the home of the Earl of Berkshire, whose daughter Lady Elizabeth he had married in 1663, and whose son, Sir Robert, had been an early friend, and collaborator in his first play. The connection was not later significant in his life.

In 1660 he celebrated the return of Charles II with an elaborate poem, *Astræa Redux*, the return of Justice to earth. This involved a radical break with his tradition. But, as Dr. Johnson observed, he changed with the nation. It was a natural shift that led him to believe in and support a monarchy which promised once more enduring order, and an audience and patronage for the literature he planned to write. Dryden's work could not like Milton's, which represented man in his eternal aspect, be written on evil days though fallen and evil times. Dryden was a man of thirty dedicated by his own temperament and by his sense of the intellectual and social temper of his age to a literature which must be made by bringing its intellectual, ethical, and social vision to bear on the conflicts, the reconciliations, the adjustments of this world. The illusions it fostered—if the illusions of the heroic drama and the state poems were genuine—centered in a ceremonious and sentimental conception of a national monarchy.

From 1664 to about 1681 Dryden drew his excellent living, besides his pension, chiefly from the stage. These years saw the rise and decline of the heroic drama to which he made a major contribution (*The Indian Emperor*, 1667; *The Conquest of Granada* in two parts, 1672; *Aureng-zebe*, 1676.), and the rise of Restoration comedy, to which he contributed at this time five plays (*Marriage á la Mode*, 1672, being generally thought the finest). This period also saw a number of his tragicomedies and tragedies; an occasional play against the Dutch; his operatic version of *Paradise Lost*, *The State of Innocence;* his adaptations of Shakespeare's *Tempest* (his worst work), and *Troilus and Cressida;* and, in 1679, *All for Love*, the tragedy based on his study of *Antony and Cleopatra.* He wrote also a number of prologues and epilogues for the plays of others and for performances at Oxford. The plays were published soon after their performance, and the prologues and epilogues to them as well as songs often appeared in miscellanies also. Several of the special prologues and epilogues were printed only in broadsides, and one of his own for *The Rival Ladies* remained in manuscript till our day.

In 1666 he began, with *An Essay of Dramatick Poesie*, his great series of discussions of his dramatic work, probably immediately inspired by the discourses of Corneille and Racine. The *Essay* is the only one written separately, and the most general in its range of criticism, though still intimately bound up with the problems of his own writing. The others are prefaces to particular works, and though full of general critical ideas, are related to particular discussions and disputes with other writers. Their themes are tragedy, tragicomedy, and the opera. Dryden never regarded comedy as one of his major powers.

In 1670 he was appointed Poet-Laureate and Historiographer Royal, posts which were confirmed in 1685 by King James but which he lost at the Revolution of 1688, when he remained a Roman Catholic and refused to take the oath of allegiance to William and Mary. His duties as historiographer probably included such tasks as a defense of the papers of Anne, Duchess of York, and several controversial writings at least suggested by the position. (See a discussion by R. W. Ham *RES* XI (1935), 284–298.) His chief state poem after *Astræa Redux* was *Threnodia Augustalis*, on the death of Charles.

In 1678 he began his series of great satiric and didactic poems with *MacFlecknoe*, first published in 1682 but now generally considered to have been written in or near 1678 and circulated in manuscript. (For discussion see articles listed in Monk). Though, as the poem was printed (anonymously) in 1682, the title refers to Shadwell's politics, there is no reference to politics in the poem itself, and it actually dates before the political crisis. By raillery in a mock-heroic form it seeks to uphold the great tradition of comedy and character portrayal and of an ideal of reasonable, lucid, and significant style against the mass of dunces, the scribblers of the kingdom of dullness who seek in this as in previous ages to entrench themselves in public favor. It was the outcome of a long-standing literary quarrel with Thomas Shadwell (involving inevitably also jealousy about patronage), a quarrel in which Dryden seems to have shown considerable patience before he struck. Shadwell's numerous attacks on Dryden were only a few of the many bitter attacks on his art, his politics, his character and life, which reached their apogee in physical violence when he was set upon and brutally beaten as he returned home through Rose Alley one night in 1679.

With the rise of the threatening political hurricane of the last years of Charles's reign (see introduction), he wrote *Absalom and Achitophel* (1681), a half epic, half satiric poem on the conflict over the succession; *The Medal* (1682), a satire directed wholly against Shaftesbury; and some lines of *Absalom and Achitophel*, Part II (1682), satirizing the writers on the Whig side. 1682 brought forth also *Religio Laici*, the first fruits of his serious reflection on religion, and the only one of this group other than *MacFlecknoe* which may be considered wholly free and disinterested rather than brought forth or controlled by occasional considerations.

The Hind and the Panther was published in 1687, again an occasional poem, though it complements *Religio Laici* in defending his new religious position and contains in the first part a great and untrammelled realization of Dryden's view of the Catholic Church. But it is deeply involved in the politics of religion under James II (discussed in a preface), in part pleading with the Anglicans to return to Roman Catholicism, or at least to trust Catholicism and the King, and to unite with the Catholics in defense of order against the Dissenters; in part asking for mere toleration of the Catholics and forbearance towards them in their painful and dubious situation. Under the form of beast fable and allegory, it is partly narrative, partly direct argument; after the opening symbolic vision of the Church, suggesting a figure in medieval tapestry, it is largely satiric in tone. The third part contains a new type of writing for Dryden in the two brilliant fables by which he hoped with irony to mitigate the bitter tone of current controversy. But the poem succeeded only in calling forth some of those fierce attacks on Dryden and mockery of him long current and inspired now, no doubt, by the fright with which many saw the greatest pen of the age at the service of so dread an enemy.

One of the great preoccupations of the day was to translate the classics and to adapt them by "imitation"; for English was sorely lacking in complete versions of classical poetry or in ones suited to the matured taste and expression of a neoclassical age. Interest centered in the Latin poets, a little because Latin was best known and Latin translation most practised at school; more because Latin, especially lyric, elegy, and satire, reflected best the ideals of the age, and the forms favored in English literature.

In 1684 Dryden had given some attention to editing for Tonson the *First Miscellany*, which collected some of Dryden's own poems and translations, as well as translations and verses by various other hands. As Dryden's income from his pensions vanished, he devoted himself largely to translations, to the editing of the further series of miscellanies, accompanied by a series of his great essays in the form of prefaces. There are *Sylvae, or the Second Part of the Poetical Miscellanies, 1685; Examen Poeticum, Being the Third Part of Miscellany Poems, 1793; The Annual Miscellany for the Year 1694* (no preface); the satires of Juvenal translated by Dryden and others and of Persius translated by Dryden in 1693 with a preface on *The Original and Progress of Satire;* his translation of Virgil, 1697; *Fables Ancient and Modern*, 1700, a collection of translations and adaptations by him from Homer, Ovid, Boccaccio, and Chaucer, containing great narratives. Plays of the later years were *Don Sebastian;* 1690; (performed 1689); *Amphytrion*, 1690; *Cleomenes*, 1690 (finished by Southerne); *King Arthur*, a Dramatic Opera, 1691; *Love Triumphant*, 1694. Finally, these are the years of the odes and several of his greatest occasional pieces: the lines on Oldham for Oldham's *Remains*, 1684; the lines on Congreve's *Double Dealer*, 1694; the ode on Mrs. Killigrew for the volume of her poems, 1685; the *Song for St. Cecilia's Day*, 1687, and *Alexander's Feast*, 1697, both written at the request of the Musical Society for their annual celebrations. *Eleanora*, a religious memorial poem on the Countess of Abington, is a less successful type of occasional poem. *The Secular Masque* is another new form for Dryden, though akin to his operas. It was written in 1700 together with a prologue and epilogue on the occasion of a performance of Fletcher's *Pilgrim* for Dryden's benefit, to celebrate the turn of the century, very shortly before his death in that year. Much additional work, such as a translation of a life of Xavier and a character of Polybius prefixed to a translation by another need not be mentioned in detail.

Various collections of Dryden's works by Tonson culminated in the issue in 1701 of sets of complete works in four volumes containing poems and translations; plays in two volumes; and the Virgil. Other editions and issues followed. The standard modern edition of all of Dryden except several recently discovered prologues is that by Scott, revised by Saintsbury, full of Scott's masterly knowledge of the period and vigorous and happy comment on Dryden, though now in need of correction on many points (1882). Among complete editions of the poems are the distinguished one with full notes by G. R. Noyes (1908, revised with additional poems and notes, 1950) and that by John Sargeaunt (1910) which preserves the spelling and punctuation of the original editions. The essays (almost all the original prose) were edited by W. P. Ker, (London, 1900, first issue) with authoritative introduction and notes. The letters, by C. E. Ward (Durham, 1942). Montagu Summers's edition of the plays (London 1931–1932) gives all the plays but has not won the confidence of scholars either in its text or its notes. Selections of the plays are available in the Mermaid edition, edited by Saintsbury (London, 1904?) and in *Selected Dramas of Dryden* with *The Rehearsal* edited by G. R. Noyes (1910); *The Best of Dryden*, containing selections from the poems and the essays is valuable for the introduction and notes by the editor, Louis Bredvold (New York, 1933). G. R. Noyes and G. R. Potter have edited *Hymns Attributed to Dryden* but with an introduction demonstrating as conclusively as it can be shown that only *Veni Creator Spiritus* is by Dryden. *The Songs* have been edited by C. L. Day, with musical scores for some (1932), and *The Prologues and Epilogues* by W. B. Gardner (1952). Hugh MacDonald published *John Dryden: a Bibliography of Early Editions and of Drydeniana* (1939), which may be supplemented by Osborn's review and check-list, *MP* XXXIX (1941–1942), 69, 197, 313.

Dryden wished, as we have said, to celebrate the public and intellectual life of his day and to observe men in a realistic spirit. So much of his writing is didactic, occasional, and controversial that it calls for a word on his general intellectual outlook, his politics, and his religion. We shall best understand them if we conceive of him as possessed by a two-fold sense of life: the first residing in a sense of transcending order and tradition, but an order worked out only in time and through progressing civilization, and embodied in visible forms and institutions; the second being empirical and skeptical, distrustful of absolutes, determined to limit the reach of speculation, and very perceptive of how closely the individual is engaged in the condition of his age and place. He was early a member of the Royal Society, though never, so far as we know, active in it; he drew upon his sense of the rapid progress made within a hundred years of concentrated effort by science, to support his conviction that the English language and the artistic command of it were just coming into full maturity, and to defend the moderns in the drama. Distrusting the folly of the mass of men, he mocked the judgment of his dramatic audience and was aware of the limitations of the theatre in his day; yet he was serious in testing the theory of the drama by the actual response of his own public, as well as by his experience as a writer. His criticism moves between that empirical sensitiveness on the one hand and on the other a belief that literature idealizes and orders life, finding the norm of nature or reason or judgment and moving forward in the channels created by the great geniuses who have seen furthest into the universal in man and in the forms of art. His happy power of engaging himself in the merits of any author on whom he was working, his fresh spontaneous power to accept his own experience and taste are most delightfully illustrated in his *Preface* to *The Fables*.

In politics the cast and development of his mind are even clearer when once the events of 1678 and following have called forth his serious reflection on the subject. His heroic plays are filled with debate on the current theory of politics (and his version of *Paradise Lost* with the latest philosophical discussion) which can neither quite be identified with the characters nor drawn out to a statement of Dryden's own position until perhaps the lesson on kingship in *Aureng-Zebe*, which is ethical rather than political. What is clear is his love of balancing and contrasting the ideas which separately limit the views of particular men but which are all likely to contain some measure of truth. Even in defending the King's position against the exclusion bill in *Absalom* he did not take an absolute line on the issues then debated. He did not defend the extreme royalist position, then very popular, attributing divine right and absolute power to the King. On the other hand he brought forward the question of the theory of contract only to leave it unresolved. Rather he appealed to tradition and to the ideal of order, reason and good sense in men of character and experienced in the actual history of the century as opposed to the enthusiastic self-will and divisiveness he found in the populace and the sectarians. G. Davies has studied closely the relation of *Absalom* to the King's policy, *HLQ* X (1946). Dryden's very choice of a form for the poem is characteristic of his temper: he grouped the two opposing sets of characters around their leaders, Charles and Shaftesbury, with searching characterizations of each of them in which he blended moral ideas and the actuality of their lives, and left the men thus exposed to be judged by his readers. He might have summed up much of his view in saying with Butler a little earlier that states are not made by plan, as architects build houses, but grow as trees grow.

His religion is important as the subject of two of his great poems. Of his development, surely no better judgment will be made than his own in *The Hind and the Panther*, lines 68–77. He cannot have thought very seriously about religion and morality much before 1680. In *Absalom and Achitophel* his position on the politics of religion is boldly and frivolously anticlerical; his aim is to dispel religious fears as things set on by the interest of priests, and to concentrate on politics. Yet he asks us to judge Shaftesbury's character and action by the parallel constantly suggested to our minds of Satan and the temptation of Adam and Eve as Milton had depicted them. This ethical religious tradition is further closely interwoven with the literary and intellectual tradition of the warfare in the individual and in society between reason and unreason. This latter tradition is particularly manifest in the formal character portraits which make so large a part of the poem but religion is present too. These portraits use to the full the Biblical parallels chosen to represent each person, the portraits of Shimei and Corah showing with particular force his judgment of their religion, not by creed and form, but by the traditional humanist's measure of it, by its fruits in character and personality. In *MacFlecknoe* he ironically equates the mission of the dunces to darken the world of literature with the mission of Christ to bring light. In this passage, we cannot be certain of the full import of his tone. He had earlier been capable of a frivolously blasphemous image in praising the Duke of York. Pope, at any rate, would appear to have taken the allusion in *MacFlecknoe* seriously and perhaps drew from it the dominating image of *The Dunciad*, the warfare of Dulness against the works of light. The argument of *Religio Laici* has a strong anti-intellectual cast. Natural religion, Deism, he rejected because man's reason was insufficient to have arrived at so clear a notion of God and because the ethical order envisaged by Deism was too self-sufficient; it did not reckon with the essential humility of man's position before the judgment of God. He accepted the revelation of the Bible and on matters not clearly stated in it, the interpretation by reason and tradition as used in the *via media* of the English Church; but he was keenly aware of the uncertainty of the text of the Bible and of tradition. Presently, pushing a little further with this line of skeptical thought about the Bible (awakened in him by a translation of Père Simon's critical discussion of the problems of the Biblical text) he became a Roman Catholic.

The insufficiency of reason to fix and interpret the text led him to accept an authoritative and inspired church; and the purely skeptical view of the uncertainty of the senses, a point of radical distinction from the Latitudinarian divines, satisfied him on the doctrine of the Mass. And while it may be doubted whether he would have pushed his thought so far in a wholly unfavorable atmosphere, his reasons are clear, and consistent with his growth. The picture of the Church with which *The Hind and the Panther* opens, rich in its medieval symbol and in the classical and resonant echoes of its diction, expresses exactly that leap out of the skeptical and empirical into an acceptance of traditional order which is the classical ideal of all his poetry. At the same time, it is an objective, formal, neo-classical picture of a palpable order, contrasting with that conception of an immanent and metaphysical order diffused through the world and present in all its allegories which runs through the writing of the Elizabethans and Jacobeans. In that contrast it illustrates vividly the movement of Europe and England toward the Age of Reason.

It is characteristic of Dryden's temper and his place in history that he had to turn back from the august and serene figure with which the poem opens to the very actual world, to argue about the politics of religion in the first book and in the last to mock man's unreasonableness and uncharitableness to man. Finally, the brief masque written by the old man looking back over the century jeers at the illusion of life with a surer touch of raillery than he ever commanded in the comedy of his youth.

None of Dryden's greatest poems were written until he was in his late forties. Meanwhile he had thought and written much about the aim and method of poetry and the nature of poetic expression, as great poets have always done, and particularly in ages of transition when new conceptions of the imagination and reason are gaining force. He had put forth an immense energy in the designing of heroic plays and a new comedy. The splendid ordonnance, the lucid and flexible and easy firmness of definition of his prose had sprung forth like wisdom full grown in his *Essay of Dramatick Poesie* when he devoted himself in a moment of enforced leisure to discuss the dramatic problems which had been the subject of his concentrated work and thought. But the plays themselves are largely the failures of genius.

To the pattern of comedy he contributed important elements, without quite getting inside the spirit of the Court wits who were at once its heroes and its chief authors, or mastering their grace and sophistication of irresponsibility. And the ideals of love and honor, mingled with studies of absolute self-will which formed the stuff of the heroic play can not be considered even an ideal extension of any realities in the Court of Charles II; they remain in character and passion elaborate, formal ghosts of drama despite a skill in ordonnance. Even *All for Love*, despite the beauties of much of its poetry and all that Dryden drew of character, tone, and expression from his close study of Shakespeare, does not mediate successfully between that older drama and the new French study of typical character motives at which it aims. The major characters do not come alive in either a temporal or a moral order; the sense of great historic issues is, however, keen.

In poetry, too, except for slight pieces and for the intimate mockery, the broad musical comedy bawdry, and the serious critical definition of his prologues and epilogues, he had not found subjects which awakened his deepest insights or called forth his expression into organic life. But yet in poems like *Annus Mirabilis* and *Astræa* the sheer massive power of creating poems, of elaborating attitudes, of describing, of weaving a texture of ordered imagery and music—in a rhetoric more to the taste of his day than of ours—had made him easily the first poet of his age.

In the lines on Cromwell, in *Astræa Redux* and other compliments to royalty, even in *Annus Mirabilis*, his task had been to create a ceremonious poetry to replace the metaphysical reflections and symbolic mode of Donne or Marvell. The work of Denham and Waller was lucid and reasonable but very slight. There were no canvases equal to reflecting the amplitude and splendor of great personages and national events. These Dryden supplied, filling them more with the forms and appurtenances of ceremony than with ideas.

But when in 1678 he came to write of the world of actualities and of people with whom his imagination and life had been so long and so deeply engaged, in the form of satire and didactic poetry, he harvested what had been preparing in his experience of court and town, theatre and coffee house, in the debates and definitions of the heroic plays, the descriptions and reflections of *Antony and Cleopatra*, the criticism and the bawdy, railling, mockery or self-defense of the prologues and epilogues. All these poems celebrate order in this world. Even when he is most involved in the limitations of a particular issue or a special defense he brings to bear on the daily, the perennial follies, passions, blindnesses, and egotisms of his world, judgment, proportion, ethical tradition, the great and practical heritage of classical Roman literature. It is not merely the speed of his poems, their wonderful variation of tone, their rich play of life and range of reflection, their unflagging fertility and felicity of invention and of allusion (illustrated, to take one minor instance, in the ludicrous implied association of fat Shadwell in *Absalom* II, with Falstaff and his little page) that keep them alive, but the quality of their judgment of life, still fresh and searching to-day, while their particular injustices and limitations are buried in history.

In Dryden the purely neo-classical ideal which had been at work in poetry for over two hundred years, emerges into dominance. The older allegorical and metaphysical-symbolic poetry fails with the intellectual views on which it had depended. The conception of poetry as a form in which the ideal and the absolute receive simple expression through a particular subject in which they are at work, sensuously and passionately realized in the rich ornament of detail, had received its most perfect expression in Milton just as Dryden was beginning his career. But Milton's synthesis of Christian Platonism and literary classicism was also impossible to the younger generation of the age of skepticism and "reason." The older poetry had been, indeed, penetrated in varying degrees by the classical heritage of form, as Aristotle and later Scaliger, and as the ancient, medieval, and modern grammarians and rhetoricians had studied it. But by Dryden's time, it was chiefly through the study of forms or kinds or genres of poem, and of the modes of expression that one approached poetry. The great types which had been used to represent various aspects of life in classical and to some measure in French poetry were Dryden's constant study, a list of models expanded presently by the study also of the forms of earlier English poetry. His work was the remaking of the classical forms of didactic and satiric poetry and the ode to his own needs. If one knows the tradition of the elegy in the earlier seventeenth century, his poem on Hastings is a very miracle of selection, combination, and ordering, a poem which announces a great poet, however jejune itself as a poem. *Mrs. Killigrew* makes the death of a young poetess and artist the subject of a reflection upon death and the significance of art, not in the Renaissance form of the allegorized pastoral, but in Pindaric ode which perfects that form in English both in design of substance and in metrical structure; the lines on Oldham, more intimate, take their form from Catullus's elegy upon his brother, their style from Horace but just suggesting the high style in associations drawn from Catullus and from Virgil. *Religio Laici,* a quietly reasoned discussion of religion, makes Horace's epistles the model of its tone and expression. But it is particularly in bringing formal satire to maturity that he shows most brilliantly his power to reshape the heritage of the past. *MacFlecknoe* is pure mock-heroic and burlesque; *Absalom* triumphantly unites the epic and the satiric through the union of narrative and "character" controlled by its contrasting tones of scorn, raillery, and irony. *The Hind and the Panther*, despite its disordered mass of materials and variety of aims, retrieves out of medieval beast fable its opening lines, and out of the new passion for classical fable one of the greatest and freshest of English narrative poems.

Dryden's songs illustrate the same study of form in another way. Those which belong to his comedies celebrate the themes of the court wits (though others develop a far wider range). The earliest, as plain as theirs, do not quite achieve their lyric grace and power. They were, after all, only a superficial dramatic representation; under them did not lie the experience and disillusion from which Rochester or Sedley draw force. But he never failed to give this verse a neat life; and as he went on, working with musicians and studying, one surmises, Ben Jonson's lyrics from the masques and, at least once, an Italian art song, he learned how to give them, by intricate phrasal and stanzaic pattern and modulation of vowel and consonant, and select image, a formal life of their own.

Dryden's thought about expression moves between two poles. On the one hand he sought to create and triumphantly succeeded in creating what the best thought of his age was striving towards: a norm of diction, a norm of idiom or phrasing and sentence pattern which should represent with ideal lucidity and centrality the turn of thought, the insights, and the judgment of cultivated men of the world; and rhythms, whether in verse or in the other harmony of prose, which should concentrate this manner of speech and at the same time control it and elevate it into art. On the other hand, in keeping with his formal approach, he thought about the elements of expression, in addition to music, particularly related to emotion, and to awakening it in the reader: figure, range of allusion or associations to be brought into play, levels of diction, and in his lyrics, proportion of meaning to pure sound pattern. The two approaches are bound together by the idea of decorum, or the adapting of the elements of style objectively to subject and tone of treatment. Literature was an art representing life in serious or comic idealization to the imagination of an audience. In the earlier poems, where he has no theme that deeply engages him, we think he plays too much with the mere figures, the instruments of expression, in order to awaken admiration or other becoming attitudes in us. He is formalistic and frigid. Though Virgil be Dryden's professed model in detail, his figures do not, like Virgil's, body forth a living world. And we may doubt whether, even in happier times and with more freedom, he would have been capable of the sustained vision out of which the epic is written, and which has been given to so few. But in his own field and with his own insights how supremely great is his command of all the varieties of substance, of tone, and of the rhetoric and music which voice them. To the two-fold nature of his engagement in life and his sense of order and tradition, he owes much of the greatness of his style, its combination of immediacy with order and art, the wonderful individual cry of its music. As Gerard Manly Hopkins was to say, "What is there in Dryden? Much, but above all this: he is the most masculine of our poets; his style and his rhythms lay the strongest stress of all our literature on the naked thew and sinew of the English language." In an age which greatly feared all enthusiasm, he held firmly and alone to the grandeur of poetry.

In verse he wrought to the most perfect flexibility and artistic finish the couplet (called from the plays of this age, the heroic couplet) which he had inherited from Jonson, Waller, Denham, and others. He perfectly understood all its elements or, as we should say in speaking of a ballet, the positions it could use in constructing a dance. By control of the elements of stress, rhetoric, pause, monosyllabic, disyllabic, and pollysyllabic diction Dryden got the supple variation of his musical tone, answering to the varied temper of his import. By reducing the most formal elements almost below the surface and uniting them with familiar diction and phrase, he secured the middle manner of *Religio Laici*, the raillery of the portrait of Zimri. By developing them and elaborating them richly, in combination with sustained imagery and connotative, latinate diction, he could secure the thunder of his portrait of Shaftesbury, the splendor of the opening lines of *The Hind*.

Dryden's critical prose is intimately bound up with his creative writing. Below the surface, much more than appears in his numerous references, lies reading and reflection on a vast tissue of Renaissance and contemporary criticism with which his basic critical assumptions are inwoven. What gives it life is his relation of his views to the immediate problems of his own writing, and the energy of his particular judgments. *An Essay of Dramatick Poesie* is his masterpiece in the discussion of formal criticism, the rules, and the general aims of poetry, though it is also a very free discussion of the ideals and problems of his art; the *Preface to the Fables*, in taste and appreciation. His prose gave firmness, flexibility and imaginative amplitude, sureness and range of diction to the modern, lucid, reasonable prose which men had been working half a century to perfect. His sentences express at once the mind's discovery of its experiences and the succinct definition, balancing and contrasting, of its judgment upon them. He never gave up, as Ker observes, the witty imagery which recalls earlier prose, and which gives such reach and actuality to his observations. His paragraphs move forward from thought to thought with a common sense that subdues us insensibly to their wonderful ordonnance. In tone and music he moves from the magical homeliness of his observations on himself in *The Fables* to the spacious periods, the marching triads of the opening paragraph of the *Essay* and of many another piece.

Outstanding studies of Dryden's life and poetry and prose include Johnson's *Life* (1779); Malone's life in *Prose Works*, Volume I (1800); Saintsbury's *John Dryden*, (English Men of Letters, 1902; biography and criticism); J. M. Osborn, *John Dryden: Some Biographical Facts and Problems* (1940), a keen analysis of previous biographies with a group of collateral studies; H. Macdonald, "The Attacks on Dryden," *Essays and Studies*, XXI (1936); A. Beljame, *La Publique et les hommes de Lettres* (1897, tr. 1948); A. W. Verrall, *Lectures on Dryden* (1914); M. Van Doren, *The Poetry of John Dryden* (1920), revised as *John Dryden: A Study of His Poetry* (1946), a brilliant critical study; T. S. Eliot, *Homage to John Dryden*

(1924), and *John Dryden* (1932); David Nichol Smith, *John Dryden* (1950); L. Bredvold, *The Intellectual Milieu of John Dryden* (1934), the major study of his thought.

Shorter biographical, bibliographical, and critical studies are so numerous and of such varied value that the reader should consult S. H. Monk's invaluable *John Dryden: A List of Critical Studies* (1950) which stars important material. A few additions to this bibliography by Osborn will be found in *PQ* XXX (1951), p. 268.

So much of Dryden's work is topical, and he has fared so well with his earlier editors that your editors are inevitably greatly indebted to them, especially to Scott-Saintsbury, Noyes, and Ker, more than the brevity of their notes has allowed them to acknowledge, except in special cases. They are fully responsible, however, for all the decisions implied in their notes.

UPON THE DEATH OF THE LORD HASTINGS[1]

Must Noble *Hastings* Immaturely die,
(The Honour of his ancient Family?)
Beauty and Learning thus together meet,
To bring a *Winding* for a *Wedding-sheet?*[2]
Must *Vertue* prove *Death's* Harbinger? Must She,
With him expiring, feel Mortality?
Is *Death* (Sin's wages) Grace's now? shall Art
Make us more Learned, only to depart?
If Merit be Disease, if Vertue Death;
To be Good, Not to be, who'd then bequeath
Himself to Discipline? Who'd not esteem
Labour a Crime, Study self-murther deem?
Our *Noble Youth* now have pretence to be
Dunces securely, Ign'rant healthfully.
Rare Linguist! whose Worth speaks it self; whose Praise,
Though not his Own, all *Tongues* Besides do raise:
Then[3] Whom Great *Alexander* may seem less,
Who conquer'd Men, but not their Languages.
In his Mouth Nations speak; his Tongue might be
Interpreter to *Greece, France, Italy.*
His native Soyl was the four parts o' th' Earth;
All *Europe* was too narrow for his Birth.
A young Apostle; and (with rev'rence may
I speak 'it) inspir'd with gift of Tongues, as They.
Nature gave him, a Childe, what Men in vain
Oft strive, by Art though further'd, to obtain.
His body was an Orb, his sublime Soul
Did move on Vertue's and on Learning's pole:
Whose Reg'lar Motions better to our view,
Then *Archimedes* Sphere, the Heavens did shew.
Graces and Vertues, Languages and Arts,
Beauty and Learning, fill'd up all the parts.
Heav'ns Gifts, which do, like falling Stars, appear

[1] Text: *Lachrymæ Musarum*, Second Edition, 1650. Dryden was not quite 18 when Hastings died.

[2] Hastings died just before his expected marriage to a daughter of the physician, Sir Theodore de Mayerne.

[3] than

Scatter'd in Others; all, as in their Sphear,
Were fix'd and conglobate[4] in's Soul, and thence
Shone th'row his Body with sweet Influence;[5]
Letting their Glories so on each Limb fall,
The whole Frame render'd was Celestial.
Come, learned *Ptolomy*,[6] and tryal make,
If thou this Hero's Altitude canst take;
But that transcends thy skill; thrice happie all,
Could we but prove thus Astronomical.
Liv'd *Tycho*[7] now, struck with this Ray, (which shone
More bright i' th' Morn then others Beam at Noon)
He'd take his *Astrolabe*,[8] and seek out here
What new Star 't was did gild our Hemisphere.
Replenish'd then with such rare Gifts as these,
Where was room left for such a Foul Disease?
The Nations sin hath drawn that Veil which shrouds
Our Day-spring in so sad benighting Clouds.
Heaven would no longer trust its Pledge; but thus
Recall'd it; rapt its *Ganymede*[9] from us.
Was there no milder way but the Small Pox,
The very filth'ness of *Pandora's* Box?[10]
So many Spots, like *næves*,[11] our *Venus* soil?
One Jewel set off with so many a Foil?[12]
Blisters with pride swell'd, which th'row 's flesh did sprout
Like Rose-buds, stuck i' th' Lilly-skin about.
Each little Pimple had a Tear in it,
To wail the fault its rising did commit:
Who, Rebel-like, with their own Lord at strife,
Thus made an Insurrection 'gainst his Life.
Or were these Gems sent to adorn his Skin,
The Cab'net of a richer Soul within?
No Comet need foretel his Change drew on,
Whose Corps might seem a *Constellation.*
O had he di'd of old, how great a strife
Had been, who from his Death should draw their Life?[13]
Who should by one rich draught become whate'er
Seneca, Cato, Numa, Cæsar, were:
Learn'd, Vertuous, Pious, Great, and have by this
An Universal *Metempsuchosis.*
Must all these ag'd Sires in one Funeral

[4] united in one ball

[5] as that supposedly exerted by the stars upon the earth and earthly bodies, having in mind also that the soul forms or influences the body

[6] the great Greek astronomer

[7] Tycho Brahe, the famous Danish astronomer of the Renaissance, who had explained the famous "new star" of 1572

[8] instrument formerly used for taking the altitude of stars

[9] Zeus rapt or seized Ganymede from earth to be his cup-bearer in heaven.

[10] the worst of the ills which Epimetheus, in Greek legend, let loose among men when he was unable to resist opening the box given to his wife Pandora by Zeus, in anger that Prometheus had created man

[11] blemishes [12] sheet of metal placed under a jewel to enhance its shining

[13] through metempsychosis or transmigration of souls drawing forth from his soul the qualities of the philosophers Seneca or Cato, the law-giver, Numa, or the soldier, statesman, and writer, Caesar (all Roman)

Expire? All die in one so young, so small?
Who, had he liv'd his life out, his great Fame
Had swoln 'bove any *Greek* or *Romane* name?
But hasty Winter, with one blast, hath brought
The hopes of Autumn, Summer, Spring, to nought.
Thus fades the Oak i' th' sprig, i' th' blade the Corn;
Thus, without Young, this *Phœnix* dies,[14] new born.
Must then old three-legg'd gray-beards,[15] with their Gout,
Catarrhs, Rheums, Aches, live three Ages out?
Times Offal, onely fit for th' Hospital,
Or t' hang an Antiquaries room withal;
Must Drunkards, Lechers, spent with Sinning, live
With such helps as Broths, Possits,[16] Physick give?
None live but such as should die? Shall we meet
With none but Ghostly Fathers in the Street?
Grief makes me rail; Sorrow will force its way;
And Show'rs of Tears, Tempestuous Sighs best lay.
The Tongue may fail; but over-flowing Eyes
Will weep out lasting streams of *Elegies*.
 But thou, O *Virgin-widow*, left alone,
Now thy Beloved, Heaven-ravisht *Spouse* is gone,
(Whose skilful Sire in vain strove to apply
Med'cines, when thy Balm was no remedy)
With greater then *Platonick* love,[17] O wed
His Soul, tho' not his Body, to thy Bed:
Let that make thee a Mother; bring thou forth
Th' *Ideas* of his Vertue, Knowledge, Worth;
Transcribe th' Original in new Copies; give
Hastings o' th' better part: so shall he live
In's Nobler Half; and the great Grandsire be
Of an Heroick Divine Progenie:
An Issue which t' Eternity shall last,
Yet but th' Irradiations[18] which he cast.
Erect no *Mausolœums*:[19] for his best
Monument is his Spouses Marble brest.

[14] the perennial seventeenth-century reference to the supreme sole bird which did not mate but renewed itself by burning and arising from the ashes

[15] old men dependent on crutches, as in the riddle put to Oedipus by the Sphinx

[16] drink made of hot milk curdled with wine or ale, a frequent medicine

[17] perhaps having in mind that in Platonic love, as popularly conceived, though the basic union was of souls, bodies too were to be united in marriage, "else a great prince in prison lies"

[18] beams of light

[19] tombs, so called from the famous one of Mausolus, built in the fourth century B.C.

HEROIQUE STANZAS, CONSECRATED TO THE GLORIOUS MEMORY OF HIS MOST SERENE AND RENOWNED HIGHNESSE, OLIVER, LATE LORD PROTECTOR OF THIS COMMON-WEALTH, &c.

Written after the Celebration of his Funerall[1]

And now 'tis time; for their officious haste,
Who would before have born him to the sky,
Like eager *Romans*[2] ere all Rites were past
Did let too soon the sacred Eagle fly.

Though our best notes are treason to his fame,
Joyn'd with the loud applause of publique voice,
Since Heav'n, what praise we offer to his name,
Hath render'd too authentick by its choice.

Though in his praise no Arts can liberall[3] be,
Since they, whose muses have the highest flown,
Add not to his immortal Memorie;
But do an act of friendship to their own.

Yet 'tis our duty and our interest too,
Such Monuments as we can build, to raise;
Lest all the World prevent[4] what we should do,
And claim a *Title* in him by their praise.

How shall I then begin, or where conclude,
To draw a *Fame* so truly *Circular?*[5]
For in a round, what order can be shew'd,
Where all the parts so *equall perfect* are?

His *Grandeur* he derived from Heav'n alone,
For he was great e're Fortune made him so;
And Warr's, like mists that rise against the Sunne,
Made him but greater seem, not greater grow.

No borrow'd Bay's[6] his *Temples* did adorn,
But to our *Crown* he did fresh *Jewell's* bring,
Nor was his Vertue poyson'd, soon as born
With the too early thoughts of being King.

Fortune (that easie Mistresse of the young
But to her auncient servants coy and hard)
Him, at that age, her favorites rank'd among
When she her best-lov'd *Pompey*[7] did discard.

[1] Text: *Three Poems Upon the Death of His Highnesses Oliver*, etc., 1659

[2] The Romans let fly from the pyre of a dead emperor an eagle supposed to bear his soul to heaven, where it was deified. Dryden has properly waited till after the funeral for his glorification of Cromwell.

[3] play upon the two senses, *liberal* arts, or studies of a gentleman, and *generous*

[4] anticipate [5] rounded out

[6] wreaths worn by conquerors, here evidently, by monarchs who might inherit or borrow them

[7] the Roman general, fortunate until he broke with Caesar and was overcome and slain in Egypt at the age of forty

He, private, marked the Faults of others sway,
  And set as *Sea-mark's*[8] for himself to shun;
Not like rash *Monarchs*, who their Youth betray
  By Acts their Age too late would wish undone.

And yet *Dominion* was not his Designe,
  We owe that blessing not to him, but Heav'n,
Which to faire Acts unsought Rewards did joyn,
  Rewards that lesse to him, than us, were given.

Our former Cheifs, like sticklers[9] of the Warre
  First sought t' inflame the Parties, then to poise[10]
The quarrel lov'd, but did the cause abhorre,
  And did not strike to hurt but make a noise.

Warre our consumption, was their gainfull trade;
  We inward bled, whilst they prolong'd our pain;
He fought to end our fighting, and assaid
  To stanch[11] the blood by breathing[12] of the vein.

Swift and resistlesse through the Land he past,
  Like that bold *Greek*,[13] who did the East subdue;
And made to battails such Heroick haste
  As if on wings of victory he flew.

He fought secure of fortune, as of fame,
  Till by *new maps*, the Island might be shown,
Of Conquests which he strew'd where-e're he came
  Thick as the *Galaxy*[14] with starrs are sown.

His *Palmes* though under weights they did not stand,[15]
  Still thriv'd; no *Winter* could his Laurels fade;
Heav'n in his Portraict shew'd a Workman's hand
  And drew it perfect yet without a shade.

Peace was the Prize of all his toyles and care,
  Which Warre had banisht and did now restore;
Bolognia's walls thus mounted in the Ayre,
  To seat themselves more surely then before.[16]

[8] beacon, lighthouse, etc.

[9] means both *umpire* and *backer;* those who pushed on the quarrel only to stop it. The earlier chief generals of Parliament such as Essex, Manchester, Waller, sought to come to an agreement with Charles for a limitation of his power, rather than utterly to overthrow the monarchy; Cromwell threw in his lot with the army of Independents and prosecuted the second civil war to its ultimate close in Commonwealth and Protectorate, and in the trial and execution of the King.

[10] balance [11] stop the flow of

[12] open a vein to let blood flow, as medical aid; figure intentionally paradoxical

[13] Alexander of Macedon [14] the milky way

[15] The palm tree is supposed to grow more vigorously if weighted down. The allusion is to the portraits of Charles I in the *Eikon Basilike*, prepared by him during his confinement, in which palms holding weights with the motto *Crescit sub Pondere Virtus* (virtue grows beneath a weight) appear as symbols of the suffering king. The book was published in many editions and by royalists held almost or quite as the work of a martyr.

[16] Walls surmounted by a chapel to the Virgin were said to have been blown up in war and at once miraculously restored, 1512.

Her Safety, rescu'd *Ireland*, to him owes
And treacherous Scotland, to no int'rest true,
Yet blest that fate which did his Armes dispose,
Her Land to Civilize as to subdue.

Nor was he like those starr's which only shine,
When to pale *Mariners* they stormes portend.
He had his calmer influence, and his Mine[17]
Did Love and Majesty together blend.

'Tis true, his Count'nance did imprint an awe,
And naturally all Souls to his did bow;
As *Wands* of *Divination* downward draw,
And point to beds where Sov'raign Gold doth grow.

When, past all Off'rings to *Feretrian Jove*,[18]
He Mars[19] depos'd and Arms to Gowns made yield,
Successfull Councels did him soon approve
As fit for close *Intrigues*,[20] as open field.

To suppliant *Holland* he vouchsaf'd a peace,
Our once bold Rivall in the *British Main*,
Now tamely glad her unjust claime to cease,
And buy our Friendship with her Idoll Gaine.

Fame of th' asserted[21] Sea, through *Europe* blown,
Made *France* and *Spaine* ambitious of his Love;
Each knew that *Side* must conquer he would own
And for him fiercely as for Empire strove.

No sooner was the *French* man's cause embrac'd,
Than the light *Moonsire*[22] the grave *Don* out-waigh'd,
His fortune turn'd the Scale where it was cast,
Tho' *Indian* mines[23] were in the other layd.

When absent, yet we conquer'd in his right;
For though some meaner Artist's skill were shown
In mingling Colours, or in placing light,
Yet still the faire *Designment*[24] was his own.

For from all tempers he cou'd service draw
The worth of each, with its alloy he knew;
And, as the *Confident* of *Nature*, saw
How she Complexions did divide and brew.[25]

[17] mien, countenance, aspect, here as of a star, shedding influence
[18] Jove Feretrus, Jove as the God to whom the spoils of battle are dedicated, also as bringer of peace.
[19] Roman god of war [20] intricacy
[21] over which England had asserted her supremacy: a Latin construction
[22] monsieur [23] gold or diamond [24] design
[25] divide and mingle the elements of hot, cold, moist, and dry to make up the quality or complexion of particular things.

Or he their single vertues did survay
By intuition, in his own large brast,
Where all the rich *Idea's*[26] of them lay,
That were the rule and measure to the rest.

When such *Heroique Vertue* Heav'n sets out,
The Starrs like *Commons* sullenly obey;
Because it draines them when it comes about;[27]
And therefore is a taxe they seldom pay.

From this high-spring, our forraign Conquests flow
Which yet more glorious triumphs do portend;
Since their Commencement to his Armes they owe,
If Springs as high as Fountaines may ascend.

He made us *Free men* of the *Continent*[28]
Whom Nature did like Captives treat before,
To nobler preys the *English Lyon* sent,
And taught him first in *Belgian walks* to rore.

That old unquestion'd Pirate of the Land,
Proud *Rome*, with Dread, the Fate of *Dunkirk* har'd;
And trembling wish't behind more *Alps* to stand,
Although an *Alexander*[29] were her guard.

By his command we boldly crosst the Line
And bravely fought where *Southern Starrs*[30] arise;
We trac'd the farre-fetchd Gold unto the mine
And that which brib'd our fathers made our prize.

Such was our Prince, yet own'd a soul above
The highest acts it could produce to show:
Thus poor *Mechanique*[31] *Arts* in publique move,
Whilst the deep secrets beyond practice goe.

Nor dy'd he when his ebbing Fame went lesse,
But when fresh Laurells courted him to live;
He seem'd but to prevent[32] some new successe;
As if above what triumphs Earth could give.

His latest Victories still thickest came
As, near the *Center*, *Motion* does increase;
Till he, pres'd down by his own weighty name,
Did, like the *vestal*,[33] under spoyles decease.

[26] From the universal forms in his breast he understood the qualities of things.

[27] arrives in the course of its revolution

[28] As the price of her alliance, France yielded the English the port of Dunkirk, thus giving them a town of their own on the continent.

[29] Pope Alexander VII (suggesting Alexander the Great)

[30] alluding to an expedition against Santa Domingo, 1654, which actually took Jamaica

[31] craftsman's [32] anticipate

[33] Tarpeia, the Roman vestal who betrayed her country for "what the enemy bore on their arms," and whom they smothered under their shields instead of giving her the bracelets she had expected

But first the *Ocean*, as a tribute sent
  That Gyant *Prince* of all her Watery Herd;[34]
And th' Isle when her *Protecting Genius* went,
  Upon his *Obsequies* loud sighs[35] confer'd.

No Civil broyles have since his death arose,
  But *Faction* now, by *Habit*, does obey
And warrs have that respect for his repose,
  As *Winds* for *Halcyons*[36] when they breed at Sea.

His Ashes in a peacefull Urne shall rest,
  His Name a great example stands to show
How strangely high endeavours may be blest,
  Where *Piety* and *valour* joyntly goe.

TO MY FRIEND, DR. CHARLETON, ON HIS LEARNED AND USEFUL WORKS; AND MORE PARTICULARLY THIS OF STONE-HENG, BY HIM RESTORED TO THE TRUE FOUNDERS[1]

The longest Tyranny that ever sway'd,
Was that wherein our Ancestors betray'd
Their free-born *Reason* to the *Stagirite*,[2]
And made his Torch their universal Light.
So *Truth*, while onely one suppli'd the State,
Grew scarce, and dear, and yet sophisticate[3]
Until 'twas bought, like Emp'rique[4] Wares, or Charms,
Hard words seal'd up with *Aristotle*'s Armes.
Columbus was the first that shook his Throne;
And found a *Temp'rate* in a *Torrid* Zone;
The fevrish aire fann'd by a cooling breez;
The fruitful Vales set round with shady Trees;
And guiltless *Men*, who danc'd away their time,
Fresh as their *Groves* and *Happy* as their *Clime*.
Had we still paid that homage to a *Name*,
Which onely *God* and *Nature* justly claim;
The *Western* Seas had been our utmost bound,
Where *Poets* still might dream the *Sun* was drown'd:[5]
And all the *Starrs*, that shine in *Southern* Skies,
Had been admir'd by none but *Salvage* Eyes.
  Among th' *Assertors*[6] of free Reason's claim,

[34] a whale which came up the Thames as far as Greenwich, about six miles below London

[35] very heavy winds

[36] bird fabled by the Greeks to breed on a nest at sea in the winter solstice and to charm winds and waves into calm for her time

[1] printed in Charleton's *Chorea Gigantum*, 1663, a work on the great pre-Celtic remains of Stonehenge in England (now believed to be erected for observation of the seasonal movements of the sun. Before Charleton the ring of gigantic stones had been supposed a Roman temple; but he argued it to be of Danish structure and used for the coronation of kings. Text, *Chorea Gigantum*. But changes were made in Dryden's poem as the book went through the press, and as the text we had access to was in a middle state, we have altered lines 10, 50, 52, and 54 slightly to bring them into line with the final form as given by MacDonald.

[2] Aristotle. This was the conventional picture given, by the new science, of medieval thought.

[3] adulterate [4] quack [5] according to Greek and Roman myth

[6] one who asserts, champion

Th' *English* are not the least in Worth, or Fame.
The World to *Bacon*[7] does not onely owe
Its *present* Knowledge, but its *future* too.
Gilbert[8] shall live, till *Lode-stones* cease to draw,
Or *British* Fleets the boundless Ocean awe.
And noble *Boyle*,[9] not less in *Nature* seen,[10]
Than his great *Brother* read in *States* and *Men.*
The *Circling* streams, once thought but pools, of blood
(Whether Life's fewel or the Bodie's food)
From dark Oblivion *Harvey*'s[11] name shall save;
While *Ent*[12] keeps all the honour that he gave.
Nor are *You*, Learned Friend, the least renown'd;
Whose Fame, not circumscrib'd with *English* ground,
Flies like the nimble journeys of the Light;
And is, like that, unspent too in its flight.
Whatever *Truths* have been, by *Art*, or *Chance*,
Redeem'd from *Error*, or from *Ignorance*,
Thin in their *Authors*, (like rich veins of Ore)
Your Works unite, and still discover more.
Such is the healing virtue of Your Pen,
To perfect Cures on *Books*, as well as *Men.*
Nor is This Work the least: You well may give
To *Men* new vigour, who makes *Stones* to live.
Through You, the *DANES* (their short Dominion lost)[13]
A longer Conquest than the *Saxons* boast.
STONE-HENG, once thought a *Temple*, You have found
A *Throne*, where Kings, our Earthly Gods, were Crown'd.
Where by their wondring Subjects They were seen,
Joy'd with their Stature and their Princely meen.[14]
Our *Soveraign* here above the rest might stand;
And here be chose again to rule the Land.
These Ruines sheltered once *His* Sacred Head,
Then when from *Wor'sters*[15] fatal Field *He* fled;
Watch'd by the Genius of this Royal place,
And mighty Visions of the Danish Race.
His *Refuge* then was for a *Temple* shown:
But, *He* Restor'd, 'tis now become a *Throne.*

[7] Bacon, the great philosopher of the beginning of the century not only added to knowledge, but helped to found modern science and, Dryden implies, its method.

[8] William Gilbert (1540–1603) one of the first great experimenters with the magnet or lodestone

[9] Robert Boyle, the great chemist (1627–1691) and his brother, Roger, Earl of Orrery (1621–1679)

[10] accomplished, experienced

[11] William Harvey (1578–1657) demonstrated the circulation of the blood.

[12] George Ent (1604–1680) physician and scientist who defended Harvey's views

[13] The Danish kings ruled in England for about 50 years in the tenth and eleventh centuries.

[14] mien, bearing

[15] After the final total defeat of his forces at Worcester in 1651, Charles II in a series of hidings and runnings got to the coast and shipped for the continent.

OF DRAMATICK POESIE, AN ESSAY[1]

TO THE READER

The Drift of the ensuing Discourse was chiefly to vindicate the Honour of our English *Writers, from the Censure of those who unjustly prefer the* French *before them. This I intimate, lest any should think me so exceeding vain, as to teach others an Art, which they understand much better than my self. But if this incorrect Essay, written in the Countrey without the Help of Books, or Advice of Friends, shall find any Acceptance in the World, I promise to my self a better Success of the Second Part, wherein I shall more fully Treat of the Virtues and Faults of the* English *Poets, who have written either in this, the Epique, or the Lyrique way.*

ESSAY

It was that memorable day,[2] in the first Summer of the late War, when our Navy ingag'd the Dutch: A Day wherein the two most mighty and best appointed Fleets which any Age had ever seen, disputed the command of the greater half of the Globe, the commerce of Nations, and the riches of the Universe. While these vast floating Bodies, on either side, mov'd against each other in parallel Lines, and our Country-men, under the happy Conduct of his Royal Highness,[3] went breaking, by little and little, into the Line of the Enemies; the noise of the Cannon from both Navies reach'd our Ears about the City: so that all Men, being alarm'd with it, and in a dreadful suspence of the event, which they knew was then deciding, every one went following the sound as his fancy led him; and leaving the Town almost empty, some took towards the Park, some cross the River, others down it; all seeking the noise in the depth of silence.

Amongst the rest, it was the fortune of *Eugenius*,[4] *Crites*,[5] *Lisideius*[6] and *Neander*,[7] to be in company together: three of them persons whom their Wit and Quality have made known to all the Town: and whom I have chose to hide under these borrowed names, that they may not suffer by so ill a relation as I am going to make of their discourse.

Taking then a Barge which a Servant of *Lisideius* had provided for them, they made haste to shoot the Bridge,[8] and left behind them that great fall of waters which hindred them from hearing what they desir'd: after which, having disingag'd themselves from many Vessels which rode at Anchor in the *Thames*, and almost blockt up the passage towards *Greenwich*,[9] they ordered the Watermen to let fall their Oares more gently; and then every one favouring his own curiosity with a strict silence, it was not long ere they perceiv'd the Air to break about them like the noise of distant Thunder, or of Swallows in a Chimney: those little undulations of sound, though almost vanishing before they reach'd them, yet still seeming to retain somewhat of their first horrour which they had betwixt the Fleets: after they had attentively listened till such time as the Sound by little and little went from them; *Eugenius* lifting up his head, and taking notice of it, was the first who congratulated to the rest[10] that happy Omen of our Nations Victory: adding, that we had but this to desire in confirmation of it, that we might hear no more of that noise which was now leaving the *English* Coast. When the rest had concurr'd in the same Opinion,

[1] first published 1668; second edition with changes, chiefly in minor points of syntax, making it more formal, 1684; and again, 1693 (in the same text as 1684); dedicated to Lord Buckhurst. Ker gives the text of 1668 with the variant readings of 1684–1693.

[2] June 3, 1665

[3] James, Duke of York, the admiral

[4] Lord Buckhurst, later Earl of Dorset

[5] Traditionally taken as Sir Robert Howard. G. R. Noyes has suggested Roscommon.

[6] Sir Charles Sedley

[7] Dryden himself. The work must be regarded as a work of critical art, in which the views of the speakers, except those of Neander, do not represent literally or in all regards those of the actual men. G. Williamson, "The Occasion of Dryden's *Essay of Dramatic Poesy*," *MP* XLIV (1946) has discussed the immediate critical essays which preceded the essay.

[8] to shoot the water under London Bridge

[9] about six miles down the river

[10] expressed his joy to the rest at

Crites, a Person of a sharp Judgment, and somewhat too delicate a taste in Wit, which the World have mistaken in him for ill Nature, said, smiling to us, That if the concernment of this Battel had not been so exceeding great, he could scarce have wish'd the Victory at the price he knew he must pay for it, in being subject to the reading and hearing of so many ill Verses, as he was sure would be made on that Subject. Adding, That no Argument could scape some of those eternal Rhymers, who watch a Battel with more diligence than the Ravens and Birds of Prey; and the worst of them surest to be first in upon the Quarry, while the better able, either out of Modesty writ not at all, or set that due Value upon their Poems, as to let them be often desired, and long expected! There are some of those impertinent People of whom you speak, answer'd *Lisideius*, who, to my knowledge, are already so provided, either way, that they can produce not only a Panegyrick[11] upon the Victory, but if need be, a Funeral Elegy on the Duke: wherein, after they have crown'd his Valour with many Laurels, they will at last deplore the odds under which he fell, concluding that his courage deserv'd a better destiny. All the Company smil'd at the conceit[12] of *Lisideius;* but *Crites*, more eager than before, began to make particular exceptions against some Writers, and said the public Magistrate ought to send betimes to forbid them; and that it concern'd the Peace and Quiet of all honest People, that ill Poets should be as well silenc'd as seditious Preachers. In my Opinion, replied *Eugenius*, you pursue your Point too far; for as to my own particular,[13] I am so great a Lover of Poesie, that I could wish them all rewarded, who attempt but to do well; at least, I would not have them worse us'd than one of their Brethren was by *Sylla* the Dictator: *Quem in concione vidimus* (says *Tully*) *cum ei libellum malus poeta de populo subjecisset, quod epigramma in eum fecisset tantummodo alternis versibus longiusculis, statim ex iis rebus quas tunc vendebat jubere ei praemium tribui, sub ea conditione ne quid postea scriberet.*[14] I could wish, with all my heart, replied *Crites;* that many whom we know were as bountifully thank'd upon the same condition, that they would never trouble us again. For, amongst others, I have a mortal Apprehension of two Poets, whom this Victory with the help of both her wings, will never be able to escape; 'tis easie to guess whom you intend, said *Lisideius;* and without naming them, I ask you if one of them[15] does not perpetually pay us with clenches[16] upon words, and a certain clownish kind of Raillery? If now and then he does not offer at a *Catachresis* or *Clevelandism*,[17] wresting and torturing a word into another meaning: in fine, if he be not one of those whom the *French* would call *un mauvais buffon;*[18] one who is so much a well-willer to the Satyr,[19] that he intends, at least, to spare no Man; and though he cannot strike a blow to hurt any, yet he ought to be punish'd for the malice of the Action; as our Witches are justly hang'd because they think themselves to be such: and suffer deservedly for believing they did mischief, because they meant it. You have described him, said *Crites*, so exactly, that I am afraid to come after you with my other extremity of Poetry:[20] He is one of those, who having had some advantage of Education and Converse, knows better than the other what a Poet should be, but puts it into practice more unluckily than any Man; his Stile and Matter are every where alike; he is the most calm, peaceable

[11] poem or oration of praise

[12] thought

[13] personal interest, concern

[14] "Sulla, whom we ourselves saw in the public assembly, when a bad poet of the common people had submitted to him a little book, a poet who had recently made an epigram against him, with every other verse too long, straightway order this poet to be rewarded out of the things he was then offering for sale, on the condition that he should write nothing more hereafter." Cicero, *Oration for Archias*, 10, 25

[15] Ker identifies as Robert Wild, who celebrated General Monk.

[16] puns or plays

[17] extreme or violent figure of speech, called Clevelandism from a briefly popular "witty" poet (1613–1658)

[18] an awkward clown

[19] satire

[20] not identified

Writer you ever read: he never disquiets your Passions with the least concernment,[21] but still leaves you in as even a Temper as he found you; he is a very Leveller[22] in Poetry, he creeps along with ten little words in every line, and helps out his Numbers with *For to,* and *Unto,* and all the pretty Expletives he can find, till he drags them to the end of another line; while the Sense is left tir'd half way behind it: he doubly starves all his Verses, first, for want of Thought, and then of Expression; his Poetry neither has Wit it, nor seems to have it; like him in *Martial.*

Pauper videri Cinna vult et est pauper.[23]

He affects Plainness, to cover his want of Imagination: when he writes the serious way, the highest Flight of his Fancy is some miserable *Antithesis,* or seeming Contradiction; and in the Comick, he is still reaching at some thin Conceit,[24] the Ghost of a Jest, and that too flies before him, never to be caught; these Swallows which we see before us on the *Thames,* are the just resemblance of his Wit: you may observe how near the water they stoop, how many proffers they make to dip, and yet how seldom they touch it: and when they do, 'tis but the surface: they skim over it but to catch a gnat, and then mount into the Air and leave it. Well, Gentlemen, said *Eugenius,* you may speak your pleasure of these Authors; but though I and some few more about the Town may give you a peaceable hearing, yet assure your selves, there are multitudes who would think you malicious, and them injur'd: especially him whom you first described; he is the very *Withers*[25] of the City:[26] they have bought more editions of his Works than would serve to lay under their Pies[27] at the Lord Mayor's *Christmass.* When his famous Poem first came out in the year 1660, I have seen them reading it in the midst of Change-time;[28] nay, so vehement they were at it, that they lost their Bargain by the Candles ends:[29] but what will you say if he has been received amongst great Persons? I can assure you, this day, he is, the envy of one, who is Lord in the Art of Quibbling; and who does not take it well, that any man should intrude so far into his Province. All I would wish, replied *Crites,* is That they who love his Writings, may still admire him, and his Fellow Poet, *qui Bavium non odit, etc.*[30] is Curse sufficient. And farther, added *Lisideius,* I believe there is no Man who writes well, but would think he had hard measure, if their Admirers should praise any thing of his: *Nam quos contemnimus, eorum quoque laudes contemnimus.*[31] There are so few who write well in this Age, said *Crites,* that methinks any praises should be welcome; they neither rise to the Dignity of the last Age, nor to any of the Ancients: and we may cry out of the Writers of this time, with more reason than *Petronius* of his, *Pace vestrâ liceat dixisse, primi omnium eloquentiam perdidistis:*[32] you have debauched the true old Poetry so far, that Nature, which is the Soul of it, is not in any of your Writings.

If your quarrel (said *Eugenius*) to those who now write, be grounded only on your Reverence to Antiquity, there is no Man more ready to adore those great *Greeks* and *Romans* than I am: but on the other side, I cannot think so contemptibly of the Age in which I live, or so dishonourably of my own Countrey, as not to judge we equal the Ancients in most kinds of Poesie, and in some surpass them; neither know I any reason why I may not be as zealous for the Reputation of our Age, as we find the

[21] feeling of interest, anxiety

[22] alluding to the political group of the mid century, extreme republicans

[23] "Cinna wishes to appear poor; and he is poor." VIII, 19.

[24] thought, wittily put

[25] See Volume I.

[26] he writes for a popular audience, not the Court

[27] paper of old or unsold books used to line pie-plates

[28] hours when the exchange was open

[29] bids being accepted while the candle burns

[30] Virgil said of two bad poets (Eclogues III, 90), "He who hates not the verse of Baevius, may love thine, Maevius."

[31] "For we despise the praise of those we despise."

[32] "By your leave, one may say you first of all [you orators] destroyed Eloquence." Petronius, *Satyricon,* 2

Ancients themselves were in reference to those who lived before them. For you hear your *Horace* saying,

Indignor quidquam reprehendi, non quia crassè
Compositum, illepidéve putetur, sed quia nuper.

And after,

Si meliora dies, ut vina, poemata reddit,
Scire velim pretium chartis quotus arroget annus?[33]

But I see I am ingaging in a wide Dispute, where the Arguments are not like to reach close on either side; for Poesie is of so large an extent, and so many both of the Ancients and Moderns have done well in all kinds of it, that in citing one against the other, we shall take up more time this Evening, than each Man's occasions will allow him: therefore I would ask *Crites* to what part of Poesie he would confine his Arguments, and whether he would defend the general cause of the Ancients against the Moderns, or oppose any Age of the Moderns against this of ours.

Crites a little while considering upon this Demand, told *Eugenius* that if he pleased, he would limit their Dispute to *Dramatick Poesie;* in which he thought it not difficult to prove, either that the Ancients were superiour to the Moderns, or the last Age to this of ours.

Eugenius was somewhat surpriz'd, when he heard *Crites* make choice of that Subject; for ought I see, said he, I have undertaken a harder Province than I imagin'd; for though I never judg'd the Plays of the *Greek* or *Roman* Poets comparable to ours; yet on the other side, those we now see acted, come short of many which were written in the last Age: but my comfort is, if we are o'ercome, it will be only by our own Country-men: and if we yield to them in this one part of Poesie, we more surpass them in all the other; for in the Epique or Lyrick way it will be hard for them to shew us one such amongst them, as we have many now living, or who lately were. They can produce nothing so courtly writ, or which expresses so much the Conversation of a Gentleman, as Sir *John Suckling;* nothing so even, sweet, and flowing as Mr. *Waller:* nothing so Majestick, so correct, as Sir *John Denham;* nothing so elevated, so copious, and full of Spirit, as Mr. *Cowley:* as for the *Italian*, *French*, and *Spanish* Plays, I can make it evident, that those who now write, surpass them; and that the *Drama* is wholly ours.

All of them were thus far of *Eugenius* his Opinion, that the sweetness of *English* Verse was never understood or practis'd by our Fathers; even *Crites* himself did not much oppose it: and every one was willing to acknowledge how much our Poesie is improv'd, by the happiness of some Writers yet living;[34] who first taught us to mould our thoughts into easie and significant words; to retrench the superfluities of expression, and to make our Rhyme so properly a part of the Verse, that it should never mis-lead the sence, but it self be led and govern'd by it.

Eugenius was going to continue this Discourse, when *Lisideius* told him that it was necessary, before they proceeded further, to take a standing measure[35] of their Controversie; for how was it possible to be decided who writ the best Plays, before we know what a Play should be? but, this once agreed on by both Parties, each might have recourse to it, either to prove his own advantages, or to discover the failings of his Adversary.

He had no sooner said this, but all desir'd the favour of him to give the definition of a Play; and they were the more importunate, because neither *Aristotle*, nor *Horace*,[36] nor any other, who had writ of that Subject, had ever done it.

Lisideius, after some modest Denials, at last confess'd he had a rude Notion of it; indeed rather a Description than a Definition: but which serv'd to guide him in his private thoughts, when he was to make a Judgment of what others writ: That he

[33] "I am angry when any work is found fault with, not because it is stupidly or awkwardly written, but because it is modern." "If time makes poems, like wine, better, I should like to know what year gives writing a value." *Epistles*, II, i,76; and II, i,34

[34] Suckling had died in 1642; Cowley just before the *Essay* was published; the rest were living.

[35] standard

[36] reference to the *Poetics* of the Greek critic, the *Art of Poetry* of the Roman

conceiv'd a Play ought to be, *A just and lively Image of Humane Nature, representing its Passions and Humours,*[37] *and the Changes of Fortune to which it is subject; for the Delight and Instruction of Mankind.*

This Definition, though *Crites* rais'd a Logical Objection against it; that it was only *à genere et fine,*[38] and so not altogether perfect; was yet well received by the rest: and after they had given order to the Water-men to turn their Barge, and row softly, that they might take the cool of the Evening in their return; *Crites,* being desired by the Company to begin, spoke on behalf of the Ancients, in this manner.

If Confidence presage a Victory, *Eugenius,* in his own Opinion, has already triumphed over the Ancients; nothing seems more easie to him, than to overcome those whom it is our greatest Praise to have imitated well: for we do not only build upon their foundations; but by their Models. *Dramatique Poesie* had time enough reckoning from *Thespis* (who first invented it) to *Aristophanes,*[39] to be born, to grow up, and to flourish in Maturity. It has been observed of Arts and Sciences, that in one and the same Century they have arriv'd to great Perfection; and no wonder, since every Age has a kind of Universal Genius, which inclines those that live in it to some particular Studies: the Work then being push'd on by many hands, must of necessity go forward.

Is it not evident, in these last hundred years (when the Study of Philosophy[40] has been the business of all the *Virtuosi*[41] in *Christendome*) that almost a New Nature has been reveal'd to us? that more Errors of the School[42] have been detected, more useful Experiments in Philosophy have been made, more Noble Secrets in Opticks, Medicine, Anatomy, Astronomy, discover'd, than in all those credulous and doting Ages from *Aristotle*[43] to us? So true it is, that nothing spreads more fast than Science, when rightly and generally cultivated.

Add to this, the more than common Emulation that was in those times of writing well; which though it be found in all Ages and all Persons that pretend to the same Reputation; yet Poesie being then in more Esteem than now it is, had greater Honours decreed to the Professours of it; and consequently the Rival-ship was more high between them; they had Judges ordain'd to decide their Merit, and Prizes to reward it: and Historians have been diligent to record of *Eschylus, Euripides, Sophocles, Lycophron,*[44] and the rest of them, both who they were that vanquish'd in these Wars of the Theater, and how often they were crown'd: while the *Asian* Kings and *Grecian* Common-wealths scarce afforded them a Nobler Subject than the unmanly Luxuries of a Debauch'd Court, or giddy Intrigues of a Factious City. *Alit aemulatio ingenia* (saith *Paterculus*)[45] *et nunc invidia, nunc admiratio incitationem accendit:* Emulation is the Spur of Wit, and sometimes Envy, sometimes Admiration quickens our Endeavours.

But now since the Rewards of Honour are taken away, that vertuous Emulation is turn'd into direct Malice; yet so slothful, that it contents it self to condemn and cry down others, without attempting to do better: 'Tis a Reputation too unprofitable, to take the necessary pains for it; yet wishing they had it, that desire is incitement enough to hinder others from it. And this, in short, *Eugenius,* is the reason, why you have now so few good Poets; and so many severe Judges: Certainly, to imitate the Ancients well, much Labour and long Study is required: which pains, I have al-

[37] individual peculiarities of disposition

[38] according to its general class and its purpose, (not according to its particular character as drama)

[39] Thespis is little more than a name to us; Aristophanes, the comedian of the time of Socrates.

[40] natural philosophy; science

[41] connoiseurs, men of interest in arts or sciences, but not professionals

[42] medieval, scholastic philosophy, especially that based on Aristotle

[43] fourth century B.C.; ignoring among other things, the great Greek science after Aristotle

[44] the first three great Greek tragedians; Lycophron a late Greek tragedian of Alexandria

[45] a Roman soldier and historian of the first century A.D.

ready shewn, our Poets would want incouragement to take, if yet they had Ability to go through the Work. Those Ancients have been faithful Imitators, and wise Observers of that Nature which is so torn and ill represented in our Plays; they have handed down to us a perfect Resemblance of her; which we, like ill Copyers, neglecting to look on, have rendred monstrous, and disfigur'd. But, that you may know how much you are indebted to those your Masters, and be ashamed to have so ill requited them: I must remember[46] you, that all the Rules by which we practise the *Drama* at this day, (either such as relate to the Justness and Symmetry of the Plot; or the Episodical Ornaments, such as Descriptions, Narrations, and other Beauties, which are not essential to the Play;) were delivered to us from the Observations which *Aristotle* made, of those Poets, who either liv'd before him, or were his Contemporaries: we have added nothing of our own, except we have the Confidence to say our Wit is better; Of which none boast in this our Age, but such as understand not theirs. Of that Book which *Aristotle* has left us, περὶ τῆς Ποιητιχῆς *Horace* his Art of Poetry is an excellent Comment, and, I believe, restores to us that second Book of his concerning Comedy, which is wanting in him.[47]

Out of these two have been extracted the Famous Rules which the *French* call, *Des Trois Unitez*, or, The Three Unities, which ought to be observ'd in every regular Play; namely, of Time, Place, and Action.

· · · · ·

[Here we omit about four thousand words, from page 7 to the bottom of page 13, in which Crites praises the Greeks for having followed the three unities (actually the product of Renaissance criticism, for Aristotle discusses unity of action at length, but does not bind a play to one day or one place) and for their superior wit. Eugenius replies that they worked out only imperfectly the formal structure of a play, that they worked over the same old plots and thin characters, and that they did not, in fact, follow the unities. He continues:]

But as they have fail'd both in laying of their Plots, and in the management, swerving from the Rules of their own Art, by mis-representing Nature to us, in which they have ill satisfied one intention of a Play, which was delight, so in the instructive part they have err'd worse: instead of punishing Vice, and rewarding Vertue, they have often shewn a Prosperous Wickedness, and an Unhappy Piety: They have set before us a bloody image of revenge in *Medea*, and given her Dragons to convey her safe from punishment. A *Priam* and *Astyanax* murder'd, and *Cassandra* ravish'd, and the Lust and Murder ending in the victory of him who acted them:[48] In short, there is no indecorum[49] in any of our modern Plays, which if I would excuse, I could not shadow with some Authority from the Ancients.

And one farther Note of[50] them let me leave you: Tragedies and Comedies were not writ then as they are now, promiscuously, by the same person; but he who found his genius bending to the one, never attempted the other way. This is so plain, that I need not instance to you, that *Aristophanes*, *Plautus*, *Terence*, never any of them writ a Tragedy; *Aeschylus*, *Euripides*, *Sophocles* and *Seneca*, never medled with Comedy:[51] the Sock and Buskin[52] were not worn by the same Poet: having then so much care to excel in one kind, very little is to be pardon'd them if they miscarried in it; and this would lead me to the consideration of their Wit, had not *Crites* given me sufficient warning not to be too bold in my judgment of it; because the Languages being dead, and many of the Customs, and little accidents on which it depended, lost to us, we are not competent Judges of it. But tho' I grant, that here and there we may miss the application of a Proverb or a Custom, yet a thing well said will be Wit in all Languages; and tho' it

[46] remind

[47] That is, it has not come down to us; the book is the *Poetics*.

[48] represented in the *Medea* and the *Trojan Women* of Euripides

[49] unfitting element; here unsuited to the aims of tragedy, to teach

[50] observation on, or characteristic of

[51] He names the chief Greek and Roman dramatists whose work we have.

[52] foot-wear worn in comedy and tragedy respectively

may lose something in the Translation, yet to him who reads it in the Original, 'tis still the same; He has an Idea of its excellency, tho' it cannot pass from his mind into any other expression or words than those in which he finds it. When *Phaedria* in the Eunuch[53] had a command from his Mistress to be absent two days, and encouraging himself to go through with it, said, *Tandem ego non illâ caream, si opus sit, vel totum triduum?*[54] *Parmeno*, to mock the softness of his Master, lifting up his hands and eyes, cries out as it were in admiration, *Hui! universum triduum!*[55] the elegancy of which *universum*, tho' it cannot be rendred in our Language, yet leaves an impression on our Souls: but this happens seldom in him, in *Plautus* oftner; who is infinitely too bold in his Metaphors and coyning words; out of which many times his Wit is nothing, which questionless was one reason why *Horace* falls upon him so severely in those Verses:

Sed Proavi nostri Plautinos et numeros, et
Laudavere sales, nimium patienter utrumque,
Ne dicam stolidé.[56]

For *Horace* himself was cautious to obtrude a new word on his Readers, and makes custom and common use the best measure of receiving it into our Writings.

Multa renascentur quae nunc cecidere, cadentque,
Quae nunc sunt in honore vocabula, si volet usus,
Quem penes, arbitrium est, et jus, et norma loquendi.[57]

The not observing this Rule is that which the World has blam'd in our Satyrist *Cleveland;* to express a thing hard and unnaturally, is his new way of Elocution: 'Tis true, no Poet but may sometimes use a *Catachresis; Virgil* does it,

Mistaque ridenti Colocasia fundet Acantho.[58]

In his Eclogue of *Pollio*, and in his 7th *Aeneid*,

Mirantur et undae,
Miratur nemus, insuetum fulgentia longe,
Scuta virum fluvio, pictasque, innare carinas.[59]

And *Ovid* once so modestly, that he asks leave to do it,

Si verbo audacia detur,
Haud metuam summi dixisse Palatia coeli.[60]

Calling the Court of *Jupiter* by the name of *Augustus* his Pallace, tho' in another place he is more bold, where he says, *Et longas visent Capitolia pompas.*[61] But to do this always, and never be able to write a line without it, tho' it may be admir'd by some few Pedants, will not pass upon those who know that Wit is best convey'd to us in the most easie language; and is most to be admir'd when a great thought comes drest in words so commonly receiv'd, that it is understood by the meanest apprehensions, as the best Meat is the most easily digested: but we cannot read a Verse of *Cleveland's* without making a face at it, as if every word were a Pill to swallow: he gives us many times a hard Nut to break our Teeth, without a Kernel for our pains. So that there is this difference betwixt his *Satyrs* and Doctor *Donn's*, That the one gives us deep thoughts in common language, tho' rough cadence; the other gives us common thoughts in abstruse words: 'tis true, in some places his Wit is inde-

[53] by the Roman, Terence

[54] "Shall I not go without her, if I must, for a whole three days?"

[55] not, of course, translatable, but something like, "A-ah, that eternal three days!"

[56] "But our ancestors praised Plautus's verse and his witticisms [admiring] both too patiently, not to say dully." *The Art of Poetry*, 270

[57] "Many words shall be reborn which now have perished and shall perish which are now in honor if it is the will of usage, in whom resides the judgement and law and the norm of speaking." *The Art of Poetry*, 70

[58] "[The earth] shall pour forth Egyptian beans mixed with smiling acanthus." *Eclogues*, iv, 20

[59] "The waves are filled with wonder, the woods are filled with wonder, unaccustomed to the gleaming afar of the shields of men on the river, and the painted keels swimming." *Aeneid*, viii, 91

[60] "If a boldness of word may be allowed, I do not fear to say, the Palace of high heaven," *Metamorphoses* i, 175; (our word *palace* takes its meaning from the name of Augustus's palace).

[61] "And the Capitol sees the long ceremony." *ibid.* 561

pendent of his Words, as in that of the Rebel *Scot:*

Had Cain *been* Scot, *God would have chang'd his doom;*
Not forc'd him wander, but confin'd him home.

Si sic, omnia dixisset![62] This is wit in all Languages: 'tis like Mercury, never to be lost or kill'd: And so that other,

For Beauty, like White Powder, makes no noise,
And yet the silent Hypocrite destroys.[63]

You see the last line is highly Metaphorical, but it is so soft and gentle that it does not shock us as we read it.

But, to return from whence I have digress'd, to the consideration of the Ancients Writing and their Wit, (of which, by this time, you will grant us in some measure to be fit Judges,) Tho' I see many excellent thoughts in *Seneca*,[64] yet he, of them who had a Genius most proper for the Stage, was *Ovid;*[65] he had a way of writing so fit to stir up a pleasing admiration and concernment, which are the objects of a Tragedy, and to shew the various movements of a Soul combating betwixt two different Passions, that had he liv'd in our Age, or in his own, could have writ with our Advantages, no Man but must have yielded to him; and therefore I am confident the *Medea* is none of his; for though I esteem it for the Gravity and Sententiousness of it, which he himself concludes to be suitable to a Tragedy, *Omne genus scripti gravitate Tragoedia vincit*,[66] yet it moves not my Soul enough to judge that he, who in the Epique way wrote things so near the *Drama*, as the Story of *Myrrha*, of *Caunus* and *Biblis*, and the rest, should stir up no more concernment[67] where he most endeavour'd it. The Masterpiece of *Seneca* I hold to be that Scene in the *Troades*, where *Ulysses* is seeking for *Astyanax* to kill him; There you see the Tenderness of a Mother, so represented in *Andromache*, that it raises compassion to a high degree in the Reader, and bears the nearest resemblance of any thing in the Tragedies of the Ancients, to the excellent Scenes of Passion in *Shakespear*, or in *Fletcher:* for Love-Scenes you will find few among them, their Tragick Poets dealt not with that soft Passion, but with Lust, Cruelty, Revenge, Ambition, and those bloody Actions they produc'd; which were more capable of raising Horrour than Compassion in an Audience: leaving Love untouch'd, whose Gentleness would have temper'd them, which is the most frequent of all the Passions, and which being the private concernment of every Person, is sooth'd by viewing its own Image in a publick Entertainment.

[We omit a brief passage of transition, pp. 16–17, (in which Eugenius is allowed the better of the argument) leading to the question whether the French or the English are to be preferred.]

. . . . .

If the Question had been stated, replied *Lisideius*, who had writ best, the *French* or *English* forty years ago, I should have been of your Opinion, and adjudg'd the Honor to our own Nation; but since that time, (said he, turning towards *Neander*) we have been so long together bad *Englishmen*, that we had not leisure to be good Poets; *Beaumont*, *Fletcher*, and *Johnson* (who were only capable of bringing us to that degree of Perfection which we have) were just then leaving the World; as if in an Age of so much Horrour, Wit and those milder Studies of Humanity, had no farther business among us. But the Muses, who ever follow Peace, went to plant in another Countrey; it was then that the great Cardinal of *Richlieu*[68] began to take them into his protection; and that, by his encouragement, *Corneille* and some other French-men reform'd their Theatre, (which before was as much below ours as

[62] "If he had said everything that way!" Juvenal, *Satire* 10, 123

[63] *Cleveland*, "Rupertismus," 33–40

[64] Roman philosopher and writer of tragedies widely read, translated, and imitated in The Renaissance

[65] See also the *Preface to the Fables* on this widely read and imitated poet.

[66] "Tragedy surpasses every kind of writing in weight." *Tristia* II, 381. This *Medea* is his, despite Dryden's doubt.

[67] concern

[68] great statesman (chief minister) of France and founder of the French Academy

it now surpasses it and the rest of *Europe;*) but because *Crites*, in his Discourse for the Ancients, has prevented[69] me, by observing many Rules of the Stage, which the Moderns have borrow'd from them; I shall only, in short, demand of you, whether you are not convinc'd that of all Nations the French have best observ'd them? In the unity of time you find them so scrupulous, that it yet remains a dispute among their Poets, whether the artificial day of twelve hours, more or less, be not meant by *Aristotle*,[70] rather than the natural one of twenty four; and consequently whether all Plays ought not to be reduc'd into that compass? This I can testifie, that in all their *Drama's* writ within these last twenty Years and upwards, I have not observ'd any that have extended the time to thirty hours: in the unity of place they are full as scrupulous, for many of their Criticks limit it to that very spot of ground where the Play is suppos'd to begin; none of them exceed the compass of the same Town or City.

The unity of Action in all their Plays is yet more conspicuous, for they do not burden them with Under-plots, as the English do; which is the reason why many Scenes of our Tragi-comedies carry on a design that is nothing of kin to the main Plot; and that we see two distinct Webs in a Play, like those in ill-wrought Stuffs; and two Actions, that is, two Plays carried on together, to the confounding of the Audience; who, before they are warm in their concernments for one part, are diverted to another; and by that means espouse the interest of neither. From hence likewise it arises, that the one half of our Actors are not known to the other. They keep their distances as if they were *Mountagues* and *Capulets*, and seldom begin an acquaintance till the last Scene of the Fifth Act, when they are all to meet upon the Stage. There is no Theatre in the World has any thing so absurd as the English Tragicomedy, 'tis a *Drama* of our own invention, and the fashion of it is enough to proclaim it so; here a course of Mirth, there another of Sadness and passion, and a third of Honour and a Duel: Thus in two hours and a half we run through all the fits of *Bedlam*.[71] The French afford you as much variety on the same day, but they do it not so unseasonably, or *mal ù propos* as we: Our Poets present you the Play and the Farce together; and our Stages still retain somewhat of the original civility of the Red-Bull;[72]

Atque ursum et pugiles media inter carmina poscunt.[73]

The end of Tragedies or serious Plays, says *Aristotle*, is to beget admiration, compassion, or concernment; but are not mirth and compassion things incompatible? and is it not evident, that the Poet must of necessity destroy the former by intermingling of the latter? that is, he must ruin the sole end and object of his Tragedy to introduce somewhat that is forced in to it, and is not of the body of it: Would you not think that Physician mad, who having prescribed a Purge, should immediately order you to take Restringents?

But to leave our Plays, and return to theirs, I have noted one great advantage they have had in the Plotting of their Tragedies; that is, they are always grounded upon some known History; according to that of *Horace*, *Ex noto fictum carmen sequar;*[74] and in that they have so imitated the Ancients, that they have surpass'd them. For the Ancients, as was observ'd before, took for the foundation of their Plays some Poetical Fiction, such as under that consideration could move but little concernment in the Audience, because they already knew the event of it. But the French goes farther;

Atque ita mentitur; sic veris falsa remiscet,
Primo ne medium, medio ne discrepet imum.[75]

He so interweaves Truth with probable Fiction, that he puts a pleasing Fallacy

[69] anticipated

[70] who had merely observed that most Greek plays took place within a day

[71] Bethlehem Hospital for the insane

[72] an old theatre, chiefly given over to vaudeville and prize-fighting

[73] "They ask for bears and boxing among the plays." Horace, *Epistles*, II, 1.

[74] "I aim at poetry moulded from the familiar." *Art of Poetry*, 240

[75] "And so he feigns, so he mingles false things with true that the middle does not disagree with the beginning, the end with the middle." *ibid.*, 151

upon us; mends the intrigues of Fate, and dispenses with the severity of History, to reward that Vertue which has been rendred to us there unfortunate. Sometimes the story has left the success so doubtful, that the Writer is free, by the priviledge of a Poet, to take that which of two or more relations will best sute with his design: As for example, In the death of *Cyrus*, whom *Justin* and some others report to have perish'd in the *Scythian* War, but *Xenophon*[76] affirms to have died in his bed of extream old age. Nay more, when the event is past dispute, even then we are willing to be deceiv'd, and the Poet, if he contrives it with appearance of truth, has all the audience of his Party; at least during the time his Play is acting: so naturally we are kind to Vertue, when our own interest is not in question, that we take it up as the general concernment of Mankind. On the other side, if you consider the Historical Plays of *Shakespear*, they are rather so many Chronicles of Kings, or the business many times of thirty or forty Years, crampt into a representation of two hours and a half, which is not to imitate or paint Nature, but rather to draw her in miniature, to take her in little; to look upon her through the wrong end of a Perspective,[77] and receive her Images not only much less, but infinitely more imperfect than the life: this, instead of making a Play delightful, renders it ridiculous.

Quodcunque ostendis mihi sic, incredulus odi.[78]

For the Spirit of Man cannot be satisfied but with truth, or at least verisimility;[79] and a Poem is to contain, if not τὰ ἔτυμα, yet ἐτύμοισιν ὁμοια,[80] as one of the Greek Poets has express'd it.

[We omit a brief passage, pp. 20–23, which praises the French for concentrating on a single main figure and for relating certain elements that take place off stage, often in beautiful poetry.]

. . . . .

But I find I have been too long in this Discourse, since the French have many other excellencies not common to us; as that you never see any of their Plays end with a conversion, or simple change of will, which is the ordinary way which our Poets use to end theirs. It shews little art in the conclusion of a Dramatick Poem, when they who have hinder'd the felicity during the four Acts, desist from it in the fifth, without some powerful cause to take them off their design; and tho' I deny not but such reasons may be found, yet it is a path that it cautiously to be trod, and the Poet is to be sure he convinces the Audience, that the Motive is strong enough. As for example, The conversion of the Usurer in *The Scornful Lady*,[81] seems to me a little forc'd; for being an Usurer, which implies a lover of Money to the highest degree of covetousness, (and such the Poet has represented him) the account he gives for the sudden change is, that he has been dup'd by the wild young fellow, which in reason might render him more wary another time, and make him punish himself with harder fare and courser cloaths to get up again what he had lost: but that he should look on it as a Judgment, and so repent, we may expect to hear in a Sermon, but I should never indure it in a Play.

I pass by this; neither will I insist on the care they take, that no person after his first entrance shall ever appear, but the business which brings him upon the Stage shall be evident: which rule if observ'd, must needs render all the events in the Play more natural: for there you see the probability of every accident, in the cause that produc'd it; and that which appears chance in the Play, will seem so reasonable to you, that you will there find it almost necessary; so that in the exit of the Actor you have a clear account of his purpose and design in the next entrance: (tho', if the Scene be well wrought, the event will commonly deceive you) for there is nothing so absurd, says *Corneille*,[82] as for an Actor to

[76] in his *Cyropedia*

[77] telescope

[78] "Whatever you show me in this way, disbelieving in it, I dislike." *Art of Poetry*, 188, (but there said of violent action on the stage)

[79] This concept, widely discussed in the Renaissance, means in neo-classical criticism, that which is probable according to our sense of the general nature of men and things.

[80] "if not *the truth*, yet *things like the truth;*" (last phrase from Homer)

[81] by Beaumont and Fletcher

[82] The character of Dryden's writing on the drama owes much to P. Corneille's *Discourses*.

leave the Stage, only because he has no more to say.

I should now speak of the beauty of their Rhime, and the just reason I have to prefer that way of writing in Tragedies before ours in Blank-Verse; but because it is partly receiv'd[83] by us, and therefore not altogether peculiar to them, I will say no more of it in relation to their Plays. For our own, I doubt not but it will exceedingly beautifie them, and I can see but one reason why it should not generally obtain, that is, because our Poets write so ill in it. This indeed may prove a more prevailing argument than all others which are us'd to destroy it, and therefore I am only troubled when great and judicious Poets, and those who are acknowledg'd such, have writ or spoke against it; as for others, they are to be answer'd by that one Sentence of an ancient Author.

Sed ut primo ad consequendos eos quos priores ducimus accendimur, ita ubi aut praeteriri, aut aequari eos posse desperavimus, studium cum spe senescit: quod, scilicet, assequi non potest, sequi desinit; praeteritoque eo in quo eminere non possumus, aliquid in quo nitamur conquirimus.[84]

Lisideius concluded in this manner; and *Neander* after a little pause thus answer'd him.

I shall grant *Lisideius*, without much dispute, a great part of what he has urg'd against us; for I acknowledge, that the French contrive their Plots more regularly, and observe the Laws of Comedy, and decorum of the Stage (to speak generally) with more exactness than the English. Farther, I deny not but he has tax'd us justly in some irregularities of ours which he has mention'd; yet, after all, I am of opinion, that neither our Faults nor their Vertues are considerable enough to place them above us.

For the lively imitation of Nature being in the definition of a Play, those which best fulfil that Law ought to be esteem'd superiour to the others. 'Tis true, those beauties of the French-poesie are such as will raise perfection higher where it is, but are not sufficient to give it where it is not: they are indeed the Beauties of a Statue, but not of a Man, because not animated with the Soul of Poesie, which is Imitation of Humour[85] and Passions: and this *Lisideius* himself, or any other, however byassed to their Party, cannot but acknowledge, if he will either compare the Humours of our Comedies, or the Characters of our serious Plays with theirs. He who will look upon theirs which have been written till these last Ten years or thereabouts, will find it an hard matter to pick out two or three passable Humours amongst them. *Corneille* himself, their Arch-Poet, what has he produc'd, except *The Lier*,[86] and you know how it was cry'd up in *France;* but when it came upon the *English* Stage, though well translated, and that part of *Dorant* acted [sic] so much Advantage as I am confident it never receiv'd in its own Countrey, the most favourable to it would not put it in competition with many of *Fletcher's* or *Ben. Johnson's*. In the rest of *Corneille's* Comedies you have little Humour; he tells you himself his way is first to shew two Lovers in good Intelligence with each other; in the working up of the Play, to embroil them by some mistake, and in the latter end to clear it, and reconcile them.

[We omit about 2500 words, pp. 25–29, defending the complex English plot as giving a more varied view of life, and as more exciting, and maintaining that English audiences demand violent scenes.]

. . . I hope I have already prov'd in this Discourse, that though we are not altogether so punctual as the French, in observing the Laws of Comedy; yet our Errours are so few, and little, and those things wherein we excel them so considerable, that we ought of right to be preferr'd

[83] accepted.

[84] "But as at first we are enkindled to follow those whom we think greatest so when we give up hope that we can surpass them or even equal them, our eagerness wears out with our hope; what, in truth, it cannot overtake, it ceases to follow; [and as if leaving a place already occupied it seeks a new;] and passing over that in which we cannot excell, we look about for something in which we can shine." Velleius Paterculus, i, 17

[85] individual, peculiar trait of character resulting from a dominant humour or bodily fluid; so throughout

[86] 1644; translated into English as *The Mistaken Beauty* or, *The Lyar*

before them. But what will *Lisideius* say, if they themselves acknowledge they are too strictly bounded by those Laws, for breaking which he has blam'd the English? I will alledge *Corneille's* words, as I find them in the end of his Discourse of the three Unities; *Il est facile aux speculatifs d'estre severes*, etc. " 'Tis easie for speculative persons to judge severely; but if they would produce to publick view ten or twelve pieces of this nature, they would perhaps give more latitude to the Rules than I have done, when by experience they had known how much we are limited and constrain'd by them, and how many beauties of the Stage they banish'd from it." To illustrate a little what he has said: By their servile observations of the unities of time and place, and integrity[87] of Scenes, they have brought on themselves that dearth of Plot, and narrowness of Imagination, which may be observ'd in all their Plays. How many beautiful accidents might naturally happen in two or three days, which cannot arrive with any probability in the compass of 24 hours? There is time to be allowed also for maturity of design, which amongst great and prudent persons, such as are often represented in Tragedy, cannot, with any likelihood of truth, be brought to pass at so short a warning. Farther, By tying themselves strictly to the unity of place, and unbroken Scenes, they are forc'd many times to omit some beauties which cannot be shewn where the Act began; but might, if the Scene were interrupted, and the Stage clear'd for the persons to enter in another place; and therefore the French Poets are often forc'd upon absurdities: for if the Act begins in a Chamber, all the persons in the Play must have some business or other to come thither, or else they are not to be shewn that Act, and sometimes their characters are very unfitting to appear there: As, Suppose it were the King's Bed-chamber, yet the meanest Man in the Tragedy must come and dispatch his business there, rather than in the Lobby or Court-yard, (which is fitter for him) for fear the Stage should be clear'd, and the Scenes broken. Many times they fall by it into a greater inconvenience; for they keep their Scenes unbroken, and yet change the place; as in one of their newest Plays,[88] where the Act begins in the Street. There a Gentleman is to meet his Friend; he sees him with his Man, coming out from his Father's house; they talk together, and the first goes out: the second, who is a Lover, has made an appointment with his Mistress; she appears at the Window, and then we are to imagine the Scene lies under it. This Gentleman is call'd away, and leaves his Servant with his Mistress: presently her Father is heard from within; the young Lady is afraid the Serving-man should be discover'd and thrusts him into a place of safety, which is suppos'd to be her Closet.[89] After this, the Father enters to the Daughter, and now the Scene is in a House: for he is seeking from one Room to another for this poor *Philipin*, or French *Diego*,[90] who is heard from within, drolling and breaking many a miserable conceit[91] on the subject of his sad condition. In this ridiculous manner the Play goes forward, the Stage being never empty all the while: so that the Street, the Window, the two Houses, and the Closet, are made to walk about, and the Persons to stand still. Now what I beseech you is more easie than to write a regular French Play, or more difficult than to write an irregular English one, like those of *Fletcher*, or of *Shakespeare?*

If they content themselves as *Corneille* did, with some flat design, which like an ill Riddle, is found out e're it be half propos'd; such Plots we can make every way regular as easily as they: but when e're they endeavour to rise to any quick turns and counter-turns of Plot, as some of them have attempted, since *Corneille's* Plays have been less in vogue, you see they write as irregularly as we, though they cover it more speciously. Hence the reason is per-

[87] *liaison* or connection so that during any one act, the action never breaks off and the stage is empty

[88] Ker identifies this as Thomas Corneille's *L'Amour à la mode*, partly confused with a play by Quinnault.

[89] private room

[90] *Philipin:* a common name in French drama for the comic servant; *Diego:* the comic servant in Tuke's *The Adventures of Five Hours.*

[91] thought, dressed out in image or word play

spicuous, why no French Plays, when translated, have, or ever can succeed on the English Stage. For, if you consider the Plots, our own are fuller of variety; if the Writing, ours are more quick and fuller of spirit: and therefore 'tis a strange mistake in those who decry the way of writing Plays in Verse, as if the English therein imitated the French. We have borrowed nothing from them; our Plots are weav'd in English Looms: we endeavour therein to follow the variety and greatness of characters which are deriv'd to us from *Shakespeare* and *Fletcher:* the copiousness and well-knitting of the intrigues we have from *Johnson*, and for the Verse it self we have English Precedents of elder date than any of *Corneille's* Plays: (not to name our old Comedies before *Shakespeare*, which were all writ in Verse of six feet, or *Alexandrin's*, such as the French now use) I can shew in *Shakespeare*, many Scenes of rhyme together, and the like in *Ben. Johnson's* Tragedies: In *Cataline* and *Sejanus* sometimes thirty or forty lines; I mean, besides the Chorus, or the Monologues, which by the way, shew'd *Ben.* no enemy to this way of writing, especially if you read his *Sad Shepherd*, which goes sometimes on Rhyme, sometimes on blank Verse, like an Horse who eases himself on Trot and Amble. You find him likewise commending *Fletcher's* Pastoral of the Faithful Shepherdess; which is for the most part Rhyme, though not refin'd to that purity to which it hath since been brought: And these Examples are enough to clear us from a servile imitation of the French.

But to return whence I have disgress'd, I dare boldly affirm these two things of the English *Drama:* First, That we have many Plays of ours as regular as any of theirs; and which, besides, have more variety of Plot and Characters: And secondly, that in most of the irregular Plays of *Shakespeare* or *Fletcher*, (for *Ben. Johnson's* are for the most part regular) there is a more masculine Fancy and greater Spirit in the writing, than there is in any of the French. I could produce even in *Shakespeare's* and *Fletcher's* Works, some Plays which are almost exactly form'd; as *The Merry Wives of* Windsor, and *The Scornful Lady:* but because (generally speaking) *Shakespeare*, who writ first, did not perfectly observe the Laws of Comedy, and *Fletcher*, who came nearer to perfection, yet through carelessness made many faults; I will take the pattern of a perfect Play from *Ben. Johnson*, who was a careful and learned Observer of the Dramatique Laws, and from all his Comedies I shall select *The Silent Woman;* of which I will make a short Examen, according to those Rules which the French observe.

As *Neander* was beginning to examine *The Silent Woman, Eugenius*, earnestly regarding him; I beseech you, *Neander*, said he, gratifie the company and me in particular so far, as before you speak of the Play, to give us a Character of the Author; and tell us frankly your opinion, whether you do not think all Writers, both French and English, ought to give place to him?

I fear, replied *Neander*, That in obeying your Commands, I shall draw some envy on my self.[92] Besides, in performing them, it will be first necessary to speak somewhat of *Shakespeare* and *Fletcher*, his Rivals in Poesie; and one of them, in my opinion, at least his equal, perhaps his superiour.

To begin then with *Shakespeare;* he was the Man who of all Modern, and perhaps Ancient Poets, had the largest and most comprehensive Soul. All the Images of Nature were still present to him, and he drew them not laboriously, but luckily: when he describes any thing, you more than see it, you feel it too. Those who accuse him to have wanted learning, give him the greater commendation: he was naturally learn'd; he needed not the Spectacles of Books to read Nature; he look'd inwards, and found her there. I cannot say he is every where alike; were he so, I should do him injury to compare him with the greatest of Mankind. He is many times flat, insipid; his Comick Wit degenerating into Clenches,[93] his serious Swelling into Bombast. But he is always great, when some great occasion is presented to him: no Man can say he ever had a fit subject for his Wit, and did

[92] How to evaluate and imitate Jonson became a major subject of controversy between Dryden and Shadwell, who claimed to be h' heir.

[93] plays on word; puns

not then raise himself as high above the rest of Poets,

Quantum lenta solent inter Viburna Cupressi.[94]

The consideration of this made Mr. *Hales* of *Eaton*[95] say, That there was no Subject of which any Poet ever writ, but he would produce it much better done in *Shakespeare;* and however others are now generally preferr'd before him,[96] yet the Age wherein he liv'd, which had Contemporaries with him, *Fletcher* and *Johnson* never equall'd them to him in their esteem: And in the last King's Court, when *Ben's* reputation was at highest, Sir *John Suckling,* and with him the greater part of the Courtiers, set our *Shakespeare* far above him.

Beaumont and *Fletcher*, of whom I am next to speak, had, with the advantage of *Shakespeare's* Wit, which was their precedent, great natural gifts, improv'd by study. *Beaumont* especially being so accurate a Judge of Plays, that *Ben. Johnson* while he liv'd, submitted all his Writings to his Censure,[97] and, 'tis thought, us'd his Judgment in correcting, if not contriving all his Plots. What value he had for him, appears by the Verses he writ to him; and therefore I need speak no farther of it. The first Play that brought *Fletcher* and him in esteem was their *Philaster;* for before that, they had written two or three very unsuccessfully: as the like is reported of *Ben. Johnson,* before he writ *Every Man in his Humour*. Their Plots were generally more regularly than *Shakespeare's*, especially those which were made before *Beaumont's* death; and they understood and imitated the Conversation of Gentlemen much better; whose wild Debaucheries, and quickness of Wit in Reparties, no Poet before them, could paint as they have done. Humour, which *Ben. Johnson* deriv'd from particular persons, they made it not their business to describe: they represented all the Passions very lively, but above all, Love. I am apt to believe the English Language in them arriv'd to its highest perfection; what words have since been taken in, are rather superfluous than ornamental.[98] Their Plays are now the most pleasant and frequent entertainments of the Stage; two of theirs being acted through the Year for one of *Shakespeare's* or *Johnson's:* the reason is, because there is a certain gayety in their Comedies, and Pathos in their more serious Plays, which suits generally with all Mens humours. *Shakespeare's* Language is likewise a little obsolete, and *Ben. Johnson's* Wit comes short of theirs.

As for *Johnson,* to whose Character I am now arriv'd, if we look upon him while he was himself, (for his last Plays were but his Dotages[99]) I think him the most learned and judicious Writer which any Theater ever had. He was a most severe Judge of himself as well as others. One cannot say he wanted Wit, but rather that he was frugal of it. In his Works you find little to retrench or alter. Wit and Language, and Humour also in some measure we had before him; but something of Art was wanting to the *Drama* till he came. He manag'd his strength to more advantage than any who preceded him. You seldom find him making Love in any of his Scenes, or endeavouring to move the Passions; his Genius was too sullen and Saturnine to do it gracefully, especially when he knew he came after those who had performed both to such an height. Humour was his proper Sphere, and in that he delighted most to represent Mechanick People.[100] He was deeply conversant in the Ancients, both *Greek* and *Latine,* and he borrow'd boldly from them: there is scarce a Poet or Historian among the *Roman* Authours of those times whom he has not translated in *Sejanus* and *Cataline*. But he has done his Robberies so openly, that one may see he fears not to be taxed by any Law. He invades Authours like a Monarch, and what would be Theft in other Poets, is only

[94] "As cypresses oft do among the bending osiers." Virgil, *Eclogue* I, 25

[95] 1584–1656; Fellow of Eton, member of Falkland's circle of liberals who sought peace, "one of the least men in the kingdome, and one of the greatest schollers in Europe"

[96] See G. E. Bentley.

[97] judgment

[98] Note that this word does not mean merely *decorative* or *embellishing* but supplying detail or expression suited to develop substance properly.

[99] *The New Inn* and *The Tale of a Tub* were failures.

[100] people in the handicrafts and other laborers

Victory in him. With the spoils of these Writers he so represents old *Rome* to us, in its Rites, Ceremonies, and Customs, that if one of their Poets had written either of his Tragedies, we had seen less of it than in him. If there was any fault in his Language, 'twas, that he weav'd it too closely and laboriously, in his Comedies especially: perhaps too, he did a little too much Romanize our Tongue, leaving the words which he translated almost as much *Latine* as he found them: wherein though he learnedly followed their Language, he did not enough comply with the Idiom of ours. If I would compare him with *Shakespeare*, I must acknowledge him the more correct Poet, but *Shakespeare* the greater Wit. *Shakespeare* was the *Homer*, or Father of our Dramatick Poets; *Johnson* was the *Virgil*, the Pattern of elaborate Writing; I admire him, but I love *Shakespeare*. To conclude of him[101] as he has given us the most correct Plays, so in the Precepts which he has laid down in his Discoveries,[102] we have as many and profitable Rules for perfecting the Stage as any wherewith the *French* can furnish us.

Having thus spoken of the Authour, I proceed to the Examination of his Comedy, *The Silent Woman.*

Examen of the Silent Woman

To begin first with the Length of the Action; it is so far from exceeding the Compass of a Natural Day, that it takes not up an Artificial one.[103] 'Tis all included in the Limits of Three hours and an half, which is no more than is required for the Presentment[104] on the Stage. A Beauty perhaps not much observ'd; if it had, we should not have look'd on the *Spanish* Translation of Five hours[105] with so much Wonder. The Scene of it is laid in *London;* the Latitude of Place is almost as little as you can imagine: for it lies all within the Compass of two Houses, and after the first Act, in one. The Continuity of Scenes is observ'd more than in any of our Plays, except his own *Fox* and *Alchymist*. They are not broken above twice or thrice at most, in the whole Comedy, and in the two best of *Corneille's* Plays, the *Cid* and *Cinna,* they are interrupted once.[106] The Action of the Play is intirely one; the end or Aim of which is the settling *Morose's* Estate on *Dauphine*. The Intrigue of it is the greatest and most Noble of any pure unmix'd Comedy in any Language: you see in it many Persons of various Characters and Humours, and all delightful: As first, *Morose*, or an old Man, to whom all Noise, but his own talking, is offensive. Some, who would be thought Criticks, say this Humour of his is forc'd: but to remove that Objection, we may consider him, first, to be naturally of a delicate hearing, as many are to whom all sharp Sounds are unpleasant; and secondly, we may attribute much of it to the peevishness of his Age, or the wayward Authority of an old Man in his own House, where he may make himself obeyed; and to this the Poet seems to allude in his Name *Morose*. Beside this, I am assur'd from divers Persons, that *Ben. Johnson* was actually acquainted with such a Man, one altogether as ridiculous as he is here represented. Others say it is not enough to find one Man of such an Humour; it must be common to more, and the more common the more natural. To prove this, they instance in[107] the best of Comical Characters, *Falstaffe:* There are many Men resembling him; Old, Fat, Merry, Cowardly, Drunken, Amorous, Vain, and Lying: But to convince these people, I need but tell them, that Humour is the ridiculous extravagance of Conversation[108] wherein one Man differs from all others. If then it be common, or communicated to many, how differs it from other Mens? Or what indeed causes it to be ridiculous so much as the singularity of it? As for *Falstaffe*, he is not properly one Humour, but a Miscellany of Humours or Images, drawn from so many several Men; that wherein he is singular in his Wit, or those things he says, *praeter expectatum*, unexpected by the Audience; his quick evasions

[101] to make a decisive judgment on

[102] See Volume I.

[103] twenty-four hours (from sun-rise to sunrise); and twelve (day-light), it being much controverted which the unity of time allowed

[104] representation

[105] Tuke's play was a translation of a Spanish play.

[106] Ker lists numerous interruptions.

[107] cite as an instance or illustration

[108] behavior, mode of life

when you imagine him surpriz'd, which as they are extremely diverting of themselves, so receive a great addition from his Person; for the very sight of such an unweildy old debauch'd Fellow, is a Comedy alone. And here having a place so proper for it, I cannot but enlarge somewhat upon this Subject of Humour into which I am fallen. The Ancients have little of it in their Comedies; for the τὸ γελοῖον,[109] of the old Comedy, of which *Aristophanes* was chief, was not so much to imitate a Man, as to make the People laugh at some odd Conceit, which had commonly somewhat of unnatural or obscene in it. Thus when you see *Socrates* brought upon the Stage,[110] you are not to imagine him made ridiculous by the Imitation of his Actions, but rather by making him perform something very unlike himself: something so childish and absurd, as by comparing it with the Gravity of the true *Socrates*, makes a ridiculous Object for the Spectators. In their new Comedy[111] which succeeded, the Poets sought indeed to express the ἦθος, as in their Tragedies the πάθος[112] of Mankind. But this ἦθος contain'd only the general Characters of Men and Manners; as Old Men, Lovers, Serving-men, Courtizans, Parasites, and such other Persons as we see in their Comedies; all which they made alike: that is, one Old Man or Father; one Lover, one Courtizan so like another, as if the first of them had begot the rest of every sort: *Ex homine hunc natum dicas.*[113] The same Custom they observ'd likewise in the Tragedies. As for the *French*, though they have the word *humeur* among them, yet they have small use of it in their Comedies, or Farces; they being but ill Imitations of the *ridiculum*,[114] or that which stirr'd up Laughter in the old Comedy. But among the *English* 'tis otherwise: where, by Humour is meant some extravagant Habit, Passion, or Affection; particular (as I said before) to some one Person: by the oddness of which, he is immediately distinguish'd from the rest of Men; which being lively and naturally represented, most frequently begets that malicious pleasure in the Audience which is testified by Laughter: as all things which are Deviations from Customs are ever the aptest to produce it: though by the way this Laughter is only accidental,[115] as the Person represented is Fantastick[116] or Bizarre; but Pleasure is essential to it, as the Imitation of what is natural. The Description of these Humours, drawn from the Knowledge and Observation of particular Persons, was the peculiar Genius and Talent of *Ben. Johnson;* to whose Play I now return.

Besides *Morose*, there are at least, nine or ten different Characters and Humours in the *Silent Woman*, all which Persons have several Concernments of their own, yet all us'd by the Poet, to the conducting of the main Design to Perfection. I shall not waste time in commending the writing of this Play, but I will give you my Opinion, that there is more Wit and acuteness of Fancy in it than in any of *Ben. Johnson's*. Besides, that he has here describ'd the Conversation of Gentlemen in the persons of *True-Wit*, and his Friends, with more Gayety, Air, and Freedom, than in the rest of his Comedies. For the Contrivance of the Plot, 'tis extreme elaborate, and yet withal easie; for the λύσις, or untying of it, 'tis so admirable, that when it is done, no one of the Audience would think the Poet could have miss'd it; and yet it was conceal'd so much before the last Scene, that any other way would sooner have enter'd into your Thoughts. But I dare not take upon me to commend the Fabrick of it, because it is altogether so full of Art, that I must unravel every Scene in it to commend it as I ought. And this excellent Contrivance is still the more to be admir'd, because 'tis Comedy where the Persons are only of common Rank, and their business private, not elevated by Passions or high Concernments, as in serious Plays. Here every one is a proper Judge of all he sees;

[109] the laughable

[110] in *The Clouds*

[111] of the fourth century; the chief writer, Menander, known to us through Plautus and Terence only

[112] ethos, character, habit of mind; pathos, suffering, passion

[113] "You would say the one is the born image of the other." Terence, *Eunuchus*, III, i, i

[114] laughable

[115] incidental, a secondary quality, non-essential

[116] governed by his fancy

nothing is represented but that with which he daily converses:[117] so that by consequence all faults lie open to discovery, and few are pardonable. 'Tis this which *Horace* has judiciously observ'd:

Creditur ex medio quia res arcessit habere
Sudoris minimum, sed habet Comœdia tanto
Plus oneris, quanto veniæ minus.[118]

But our Poet, who was not ignorant of these difficulties, has made use of all Advantages; as he who designs a large leap, takes his rise from the highest ground. One of these advantages is that which *Corneille* has laid down as the greatest which can arrive to any Poem, and which he himself could never compass above thrice in all his Plays, *viz.* the making choice of some signal and long-expected day, whereon the Action of the Play is to depend. This day was that design'd by *Dauphine*, for the setling of his Uncle's Estate upon him; which to compass he contrives to marry him: That the Marriage had been plotted by him long beforehand, is made evident, by what he tells *True-Wit* in the second Act, that in one moment he had destroy'd what he had been raising many months.

There is another Artifice of the Poet, which I cannot here omit, because by the frequent practice of it in his Comedies, he has left it to us almost as a Rule, that is, when he has any Character or Humour wherein he would shew a *Coupe de Maistre*,[119] or his highest skill; he recommends it to your observation, by a pleasant description of it before the Person first appears. Thus, in Bartholomew-Fair, he gives you the Pictures of *Numps* and *Cokes*, and in this, those of *Daw*, *Lafoole*, *Morose*, and the *Collegiate Ladies;* all which you hear describ'd before you see them. So that before they come upon the Stage you have a longing expectation of them, which prepares you to receive them favourably; and when they are there, even from their first appearance you are so far acquainted with them, that nothing of their humour is lost to you.

I will observe yet one thing further of this admirable Plot; the business of it rises in every Act. The second is greater than the first; the third than the second, and so forward to the fifth. There too you see, till the very last Scene, new difficulties arising to obstruct the Action of the Play; and when the Audience is brought into despair, that the business can naturally be effected, then, and not before, the discovery[120] is made. But that the Poet might entertain you with more Variety all this while, he reserves some new Characters to show you, which he opens not till the second and third Act. In the second, *Morose*, *Daw*, the *Barber* and *Otter;* in the third, the *Collegiate Ladies:* All which he moves afterwards in by-walks,[121] or under-plots, as Diversions to the main design, lest it should grow tedious, though they are still naturally join'd with it, and somewhere or other subservient to it. Thus, like a skilful Chess-player, by little and little, he draws out his Men, and makes his Pawns of use to his greater Persons.

If this Comedy, and some others of his, were translated into French Prose (which would now be no wonder to them, since *Moliere* has lately given them Plays out of Verse, which have not displeas'd them) I believe the Controversie would soon be decided betwixt the two Nations, even making them the Judges. But we need not call our Heroes to our Aid; Be it spoken to the Honour of the *English*, our Nation can never want in any Age such who are able to dispute the Empire of Wit with any People in the Universe. And though the fury of a Civil War, and Power, for twenty Years together, abandon'd to a barbarous Race of Men, Enemies of all good Learning, had buried the Muses under the ruins of Monarchy; yet with the restoration of our Happiness, we see reviv'd Poesie lifting up its head, and already shaking off the rubbish which lay so heavy on it. We have seen since his Majesty's return, many Dramatick Poems which yield not to those of any foreign Nation, and which deserve all Laurels but the English. I will

[117] consort familiarly with

[118] "Because the matter of comedy comes from common life, it is thought to be less sweated over, but comedy is so much more difficult as it receives so much less indulgence." *Epistles*, II, i, 168

[119] master stroke

[120] unfolding or resolution of the plot

[121] walk running off to the side, byway

set aside Flattery and Envy: it cannot be deny'd but we have had some little blemish either in the Plot or Writing of all those Plays which have been made within these seven Years: (and perhaps there is no Nation in the World so quick to discern them, or so difficult to pardon them, as ours:) yet if we can perswade our selves to use the candour of that Poet, who (though the most severe of Criticks) has left us this caution by which to moderate our censures;

> . . . *Ubi plura nitent in carmine, non ego paucis offendar maculis.*[122]

If in consideration of their many and great Beauties, we can wink at some slight and little Imperfections; if we, I say, can be thus equal[123] to our selves, I ask no favour from the French. And if I do not venture upon any particular judgment of our late Plays, 'tis out of the consideration which an Ancient Writer gives me; *Virorum, ut magna admiratio, ita censura difficilis:*[124] betwixt the extreams of admiration and malice, 'tis hard to judge upright of the living. Only I think it may be permitted me to say, that as it is no less'ning to us to yield to some Plays, and those not many of our own Nation in the last Age, so can it be no addition to pronounce of our present Poets, that they have far surpass'd all the Ancients, and the Modern Writers of other Countries.

This was the substance of what was then spoke on that occasion; and *Lisideius*, I think he was going to reply, when he was prevented[125] thus by *Crites:* I am confident, said he, that the most material things that can be said, have been already urg'd on either side; if they have not, I must beg of *Lisideius* that he will defer his Answer till another time: for I confess I have a joynt Quarrel to you both, because you have concluded, without any reason given for it, that Rhyme is proper for the Stage. I will not dispute how ancient it hath been among us to write this way; perhaps our Ancestors knew no better till *Shakespeare's* time. I will grant it was not altogether left by him, and that *Fletcher* and *Ben. Johnson* us'd it frequently in their Pastorals, and sometimes in other Plays. Farther, I will not argue whether we receiv'd it originally from our own Countrymen, or from the French; for that is an inquiry of as little benefit as theirs, who in the midst of the late Plague were not so sollicitous to provide against it, as to know whether we had it from the malignity of our own Air, or by transportation from *Holland*. I have therefore only to affirm, That it is not allowable in serious Plays; for Comedies I find you already concluding with me. To prove this, I might satisfie my self to tell you, how much in vain it is for you to strive against the stream of the Peoples inclination; the greatest part of which are prepossess'd so much with those excellent Plays of *Shakespeare*, *Fletcher*, and *Ben. Johnson*, (which have been written out of Rhyme) that except you could bring them such as were written better in it, and those too by persons of equal reputation with them, it will be impossible for you to gain your cause with them, who will still be judges. This it is to which in fine all your reasons must submit. The unanimous consent of an Audience is so powerful, that even *Julius Caesar* (as *Macrobius* reports of him) when he was perpetual Dictator, was not able to balance it on the other side. But when *Laberius*, a Roman Knight, at his request contended in the *Mime*[126] with another Poet, he was forc'd to cry out, *Etiam favente me victus es Laberi.*[127] But I will not on this occasion, take the advantage of the greater number, but only urge such reasons against Rhyme, as I find in the Writings of those who have argu'd for the other way. First then, I am of opinion, that Rhyme is unnatural in a Play, because Dialogue there is presented as the effect of sudden thought. For a Play is the imitation of Nature; and since no Man, without premeditation, speaks in Rhyme, neither ought he to do it on the Stage; this hinders not but the Fancy may

[122] "Where the great part of a poem shines, I shall not be offended by a few blots." *Art of Poetry*, 351

[123] just

[124] "Of living authors, since our admiration is great, so a critical account is difficult." Velleuis Paterculus, II, 36

[125] anticipated

[126] a light, farcical drama

[127] "Even though I favored you, you were beaten, Laberius."

be there elevated to an higher pitch of thought than it is in ordinary discourse: for there is a probability that Men of excellent and quick parts may speak noble things *ex tempore:* but those thoughts are never fetter'd with the numbers or sound of Verse without study, and therefore it cannot be but unnatural to present the most free way of speaking, in that which is the most constrain'd. For this Reason, says *Aristotle*, 'Tis best to write Tragedy in that kind of Verse which is the least such, or which is nearest Prose:[128] and this amongst the Ancients was the Iambique, and with us is blank Verse, or the measure of Verse, kept exactly without Rhyme. These Numbers[129] therefore are fittest for a Play; the others for a Paper of Verses, or a Poem, blank Verse being as much below them, as Rhyme is improper for the *Drama*. And if it be objected, that neither are blank Verses made *ex tempore*, yet as nearest Nature, they are still to be preferr'd. But there are two particular Exceptions which many besides my self have had to Verse; by which it will appear yet more plainly, how improper it is in Plays. And the first of them is grounded on that very reason for which some have commended Rhyme: they say the quickness of Repartees in argumentative Scenes receives an ornament from Verse. Now what is more unreasonable than to imagine, that a Man should not only imagine the Wit, but the Rhyme too upon the sudden? This nicking[130] of him who spoke before both in sound and measure, is so great an happiness, that you must at least suppose the persons of your Play to be born Poets, *Arcades omnes et cantare pares et respondere, parati*,[131] they must have arriv'd to the degree of *quicquid conabar dicere:*[132] to make Verses almost whether they will or no: if they are any thing below this, it will look rather like the design of two, than the answer of one: it will appear that your Actors hold intelligence together, that they perform their tricks like Fortune-tellers, by confederacy. The hand of Art will be too visible in it against that Maxim of all Professions; *Ars est celare artem*, That it is the greatest perfection of Art to keep it self undiscover'd. Nor will it serve you to object, that however you manage it, 'tis still known to be a Play; and consequently the Dialogue of two persons understood to be the labour of one Poet. For a Play is still an imitation of Nature; we know we are to be deceiv'd, and we desire to be so; but no Man ever was deceiv'd but with a probability of truth, for who will suffer a gross lie to be fasten'd on him? Thus we sufficiently understand that the Scenes which represent Cities and Countries to us, are not really such, but only painted on Boards and Canvass: But shall that excuse the ill painture or designment[133] of them? Nay, rather, ought they not to be labour'd with so much the more diligence and exactness to help the imagination, since the mind of Man does naturally tend to truth? and therefore the nearer any thing comes to the imitation of it, the more it pleases.

Thus, you see, your Rhyme is uncapable of expressing the greatest thoughts naturally, and the lowest it cannot with any grace: for what is more unbefitting the Majesty of Verse, than to call a Servant, or bid a Door be shut in Rhyme? And yet you are often forc'd on this miserable necessity. But Verse, you say, circumscribes a quick and luxuriant fancy, which would extend it self too far on every subject, did not the labour which is requir'd to well turn'd and polish'd Rhyme, set bounds to it. Yet this Argument, if granted, would only prove, that we may write better in Verse, but not more naturally. Neither is it able to evince that; for he who wants judgment to confine his fancy in blank Verse, may want it as much in Rhyme; and he who has it will avoid errours in both kinds. Latine Verse was as great a confinement to the imagination of those Poets, as Rhyme to ours: and yet you find *Ovid* saying too much on every subject. *Nescivit* (says *Seneca*) *quod bene*

[128] *Poetics* 1449, a, 14
[129] meter [130] rallying with
[131] "Arcadians all ready in a match to sing as well as to make reply." Virgil, *Eclogue* VII, 4, 5
[132] "[poetry came of its own accord in apt numbers and] whatever I attempted [*temptabam*] to say [was verse]." Ovid, *Tristia.* IV, 10, 25
[133] painting or design

cessit relinquere:[134] of which he gives you one famous instance in his Description of the Deluge,

Omnia pontus erat, deerant quoque Litora Ponto.[135]

Now all was Sea, nor had that Sea a Shore. Thus *Ovid's* fancy was not limited by Verse, and *Virgil* needed not Verse to have bounded his.

In our own Language we see *Ben. Johnson* confining himself to what ought to be said, even in the liberty of blank Verse; and yet *Corneille*, the most judicious of the *French* Poets, is still varying the same sense an hundred ways, and dwelling eternally on the same Subject, though confin'd by Rhyme. Some other Exceptions I have to Verse, but since these I have nam'd are for the most part already publick; I conceive it reasonable they should first be answer'd.

It concerns me less than any, said *Neander*, (seeing he had ended) to reply to this Discourse; because when I should have prov'd, that Verse may be natural in Plays, yet I should always be ready to confess, that those which I have written in this kind come short of that perfection which is requir'd. Yet since you are pleas'd I should undertake this Province, I will do it, though with all imaginable respect and deference, both to that Person from whom you have borrow'd your strongest Arguments,[136] and to whose Judgment when I have said all, I finally submit. But before I proceed to answer your Objections, I must first remember[137] you, that I exclude all Comedy from my defence; and next, that I deny not but blank Verse may be also us'd, and content my self only to assert, that in serious Plays where the Subject and Characters are great, and the Plot unmix'd with Mirth, which might allay or divert these Concernments which are produc'd as Rhyme, is there as natural, and more effectual than blank Verse.

And now having laid down this as a Foundation, to begin with *Crites*, I must crave leave to tell him, that some of his Arguments against Rhyme reach no farther than from the faults or defects of ill Rhyme, to conclude[138] against the use of it in general. May not I conclude against blank Verse by the same reason? If the words of some Poets who write in it, are either ill chosen, or ill placed, (which makes not only Rhyme, but all kind of Verse in any Language unnatural;) Shall I, for their vicious affectation, condemn those excellent Lines of *Fletcher*, which are written in that kind? Is there any thing in Rhyme more constrain'd than this Line in blank Verse? *I Heav'n invoke, and strong resistance make;* where you see both the clauses are plac'd unnaturally; that is, contrary to the common way of speaking, and that without the excuse of a Rhyme to cause it: yet you would think me very ridiculous, if I should accuse the stubbornness of blank Verse for this, and not rather the stiffness of the Poet. Therefore, *Crites*, you must either prove that words, though well chosen, and duly plac'd, yet render not Rhyme natural in it self; or that however natural and easie the Rhyme may be, yet it is not proper for a Play. If you insist on the former part, I would ask you what other conditions are requir'd to make Rhyme natural in it self, besides an election[139] of apt words, and a right disposition of them? For the due choice of your words expresses your sense naturally, and the due placing them adapts the Rhyme to it. If you object, that one Verse may be made for the sake of another, though both the Words and Rhyme be apt: I answer, it cannot possibly so fall out; for either there is a dependance of sense betwixt the first line and the second, or there is none: if there be that connection, then in the natural position of the words, the latter line must of necessity flow from the former: if there be no dependance, yet still the due ordering of words makes the last line as natural in it self as the other: so that the necessity of a Rhyme never forces any but bad or lazy Writers to say what they would not otherwise. 'Tis true, there is both Care and Art requir'd to write in Verse; A good Poet

[134] "He did not know how to leave what had come to a good conclusion." L. Annaeus Seneca the Elder (father of the great philosopher) *Controversia* IX, 5

[135] "Everything was sea and the sea lacked a shore." *Metamorphoses* I, 292

[136] Williamson has identified him as Sprat.

[137] remind

[138] come to a decision

[139] choice

never establishes the first line, till he has sought out such a Rhyme as may fit the sense, already prepar'd to heighten the second: many times the close of the sense falls into the middle of the next Verse, or farther of, and he may often prevail[140] himself of the same advantages in English which *Virgil* had in Latine, he may break off in the *Hemystich*,[141] and begin another line: indeed, the not observing these two last things, makes Plays, which are writ in Verse, so tedious: for though, most commonly, the sense is to be confin'd to the Couplet, yet nothing that does *perpetuo tenore fluere*,[142] run in the same channel, can please always. 'Tis like the murmuring of a Stream, which not varying in the fall, causes at first attention, at last drowsiness. Variety of cadences is the best rule, the greatest help to the Actors, and refreshment to the Audience.

If then Verse may be made natural in it self, how becomes it unnatural in a Play? You say the Stage is the representation of Nature, and no Man in ordinary conversation speaks in Rhyme. But you foresaw, when you said this, that it might be answer'd; neither does any man speak in blank Verse, or in Measure without Rhyme. Therefore you concluded, that which is nearest Nature is still to be preferr'd. But you took no notice, that Rhyme might be made as natural as blank Verse, by the well placing of the words, *etc.* all the difference between them when they are both correct, is the sound in one, which the other wants; and if so, the sweetness of it, and all the advantage resulting from it, which are handled in the Preface to the *Rival Ladies*,[143] will yet stand good. As for that place of *Aristotle*, where he says Plays should be writ in that kind of Verse which is nearest Prose; it makes little for you, blank Verse being properly but measur'd Prose. Now Measure alone in any modern Language, does not constitute Verse; those of the Ancients in Greek and Latine, consisted in quantity of words, and a determinate number of feet. But when, by the inundation of the *Goths* and *Vandals* into *Italy* new Languages were introduced, and barbarously mingled with the Latine (of which the *Italian*, *Spanish*, *French*, and ours, (made out of them and the *Teutonick*) are Dialects:) a new way of Poesie was practis'd;[144] new, I say, in those Countries, for in all probability it was that of the Conquerours in their own Nations: at least we are able to prove, that the Eastern People have us'd it from all Antiquity, *Vid.* Dan. *his Defence of Rhyme*.[145] This new way consisted in Measure or Number of Feet and Rhyme. The sweetness of Rhyme, and observation of Accent, supplying the place of quantity in Words, which could neither exactly be observ'd by those *Barbarians* who knew not the Rules of it, neither was it suitable to their Tongues as it had been to the Greek and Latine. No Man is tied in Modern Poesie to observe any farther Rule in the Feet of his Verse, but that they be dissylables; whether *Spondee*, *Trochee*, or *Iambique*, it matters not;[146] only he is obliged to Rhyme: Neither do the *Spanish*, *French*, *Italian*, or *Germans*, acknowledge at all, or very rarely, any such kind of Poesie as blank Verse amongst them. Therefore, at most, 'tis but a Poetick Prose, a *Sermo pedestris*,[147] and, as such, most fit for Comedies, where I acknowledge Rhyme to be improper. Farther, As to that Quotation of *Aristotle*, our Couplet Verses may be rendred as near Prose as blank Verse it self by using those advantages I lately nam'd, as breaks in an Hemystick, or running the Sense into another line, thereby making Art and Order appear as loose and free as Nature; or not tying our selves to Couplets strictly, we may use the benefit

[140] avail [141] half-line

[142] Ker points out that Cicero uses the phrase of the middle style.

[143] in the *Epistle Dedicatory*, rather, to this his first play, where he praises the use of rhyme as European and lauds the beauty of the verse of Waller and Denham

[144] Dryden follows Renaissance thought in general in regarding rhyme and number of syllables together as a substitute for fixed length of syllables in classical verse.

[145] Samuel Daniel's important critical work, 1607. The reader may like to remember that Milton's attack on rhyme as the invention of a barbarous age appeared in 1667.

[146] i.e., whether of two accented syllables, or with first or last of the two accented

[147] "A style that keeps to the ground."

of the Pindarique way,[148] practis'd in the Siege of *Rhodes*;[149] where the Numbers vary and the Rhyme is dispos'd carelessly, and far from often chyming. Neither is that other advantage of the Ancients to be despis'd, of changing the kind of Verse when they please with the change of the Scene, or some new entrance: for they confine not themselves always to *Iambiques*, but extend their liberty to all *Lyrique* Numbers, and sometimes even to *Hexameter*.[150] But I need not go so far to prove that Rhyme, as it succeeds to all other Offices of Greek and Latine Verse, so especially to this of Plays, since the custom of Nations at this day confirms it, the *French*, *Italian* and *Spanish* Tragedies are generally writ in it, and sure the universal Consent of the most civiliz'd parts of the World, ought in this, as it doth in other Customs, to include the rest.

But perhaps you may tell me I have propos'd such a Way to make Rhyme natural, and consequently proper to Plays, as is unpracticable, and that I shall scarce find six or eight lines together in any Play, where the words are so plac'd and chosen as is requir'd to make it natural. I answer, No Poet need constrain himself at all times to it. It is enough he makes it his general Rule; for I deny not but sometimes there may be a greatness in placing the words otherwise; and sometimes they may sound better, sometimes also the variety it self is excuse enough. But if, for the most part, the words be plac'd as they are in the negligence of Prose, it is sufficient to denominate[151] the way practicable; for we esteem that to be such, which in the tryal oftner succeeds than misses. And thus far you may find the Practice made good in many Plays; where you do not, remember still, that if you cannot find six natural Rhymes together, it will be as hard for you to produce as many lines in blank Verse, even among the greatest of our Poets, against which I cannot make some reasonable exception.[152]

And this, Sir, calls to my remembrance the beginning of your Discourse, where you told us we should never find the Audience favourable to this kind of Writing, till we could produce as good Plays in Rhyme, as *Ben. Johnson*, *Fletcher*, and *Shakespeare*, had writ out of it. But it is to raise envy to the living, to compare them with the dead. They are honour'd, and almost ador'd by us, as they deserve; neither do I know any so presumptuous of themselves as to contend with them. Yet give me leave to say thus much, without injury to their Ashes, that not only we shall never equal them, but they could never equal themselves, were they to rise and write again. We acknowledge them our Fathers in Wit, but they have ruin'd their Estates themselves before they came to their Childrens hands. There is scarce an Humour, a Character, or any kind of Plot, which they have not us'd. All comes sullied or wasted to us: and were they to entertain this Age, they could not now make so plenteous treatments out of such decay'd Fortunes. This therefore will be a good Argument to us either not to write at all, or to attempt some other way. There is no Bays[153] to be expected in their Walks; *Tentanda via est quà me quoque possum tollere humo*.[154]

This way of writing in Verse, they have only left free to us; our Age is arriv'd to a perfection in it, which they never knew; and which (if we may guess by what of theirs we have seen in Verse (as the *Faithful Shepherdess*, and *Sad Shepherd*:) 'tis probable they never could have reach'd. For the Genius of every Age is different: and though ours excel in this, I deny not but that to imitate Nature in that perfection which they did in Prose, is a greater commendation than to write in Verse exactly. As for what you have added, that the People are not generally inclin'd to like this way; if it were true, it would be no wonder, that betwixt the shaking off an old habit, and the introducing of a new, there should be difficulty. Do we not see them stick to *Hopkins* and *Sternhold's*

[148] in stanzas of varied line length, as Dryden's own odes and with rhyme variously spaced

[149] Davenant's heroic play

[150] dactylics [151] indicate

[152] objection

[153] crown of bay-laurel

[154] "I must try a way by which I too may rise from the earth [and fly a victor on the lips of men]." Virgil, *Georgics* III,8

Psalms,[155] and forsake those of *David*, I mean *Sandys*[156] his Translation of them? If by the People, you understand the Multitude, the ὁι πολλοὶ, 'tis no matter what they think; they are sometimes in the right, sometimes in the wrong; their judgment is a meer Lottery. *Est ubi plebs rectè putat, est ubi peccat. Horace* says it of the Vulgar, judging Poesie.[157] But if you mean the mix'd Audience of the Populace, and the Nobless, I dare confidently affirm, that a great part of the latter sort, are already favourable to Verse; and that no serious Plays written since the King's return have been more kindly receiv'd by them, than the Siege of *Rhodes*, the *Mustapha*, the *Indian* Queen, and *Indian* Emperor.[158]

But I come now to the inference of your first Argument. You said, that the Dialogue of Plays is presented as the effect of sudden thought, but no Man speaks suddenly, or *ex tempore* in Rhyme: And you inferr'd from thence, that Rhyme, which you acknowledge to be proper to Epique Poesie cannot equally be proper to Dramatick, unless we could suppose all Men born so much more than Poets, that Verses should be made in them, not by them.

It has been formerly urg'd by you, and confess'd by me, that since no Man spoke any kind of Verse *ex tempore*, that which was nearest Nature was to be preferr'd. I answer you therefore, by distinguishing betwixt what is nearest to the nature of Comedy, which is the imitation of common persons and ordinary speaking, and what is nearest the nature of a serious Play: this last is indeed the representation of Nature, but 'tis Nature wrought up to an higher pitch. The Plot, the Characters, the Wit, the Passions, the Descriptions, are all exalted above the level of common converse, as high as the imagination of the Poet can carry them, with proportion to verisimility.[159] Tragedy we know is wont to image to us the Minds and Fortunes of Noble Persons, and to portray these exactly; Heroick Rhyme is nearest Nature, as being the noblest kind of modern Verse.

Indignatur enim privatis, et prope socco,
Dignis carminibus, narrari cœna Thyestae.
(Says *Horace*.)[160]

And in another place,

Effutire levis indigna tragœdia versus.[161]

Blank Verse is acknowledg'd to be too low for a Poem; nay more, for a Paper of Verses; but if too low for an ordinary Sonnet, how much more for Tragedy, which is by *Aristotle*, in the dispute betwixt the Epique Poesie and the Dramatick, for many reasons he there alledges, rank'd above it?

But setting this defence aside, your Argument is almost as strong against the use of Rhyme in Poems as in Plays; for the Epique was is every where interlac'd with Dialogue, or discoursive Scenes; and therefore you must either grant Rhyme to be improper there, which is contrary to your assertion, or admit it into Plays by the same title which you have given it to Poems. For though Tragedy be justly preferr'd above the other, yet there is a great affinity between them, as may easily be discover'd in that definition of a Play which *Lisideius* gave us. The Genus of them is the same, a just and lively Image of Humane Nature, in its Actions, Passions, and Traverses[162] of Fortune: so is the end, namely for the Delight and Benefit of Mankind. The Characters and Persons are still the same, *viz.* the greatest of both sorts, only the manner of acquainting us with those Actions, Passions and Fortunes is different. Tragedy performs it *viva voce*, or by action, in Dialogue, wherein it excels the Epique Poem, which does it chiefly by narration, and therefore is not so lively an Image of Humane Nature. However, the agreement betwixt them is such, that if Rhyme be proper for one, it must be for the other.

[155] a byword for poor poetry; see *Religio Laici*

[156] mid-seventeenth century poet, praised also in the *Preface to the Fables*

[157] "Sometimes the common man judges rightly. Sometimes errs." *Epistles* II, i, 63; very inaccurately quoted, for throughout Dryden appears to quote from memory

[158] heroic plays by Davenant, Roger Boyle, Dryden and Howard, and Dryden

[159] without losing their probability to nature

[160] "I am disgusted if the feast of Thyestes is told in measures worthy of a common matter and almost of comedy." *Art of Poetry*, 90

[161] "Tragedy scorning to babble trivial verses." *Art of Poetry*, 231

[162] thwartings

Verse, 'tis true, is not the effect of sudden thought; but this hinders not that sudden thought may be represented in Verse, since those thoughts are such as must be higher than Nature can raise them without premeditation, especially to a continuance of them even out of Verse, and consequently you cannot imagine them to have been sudden either in the Poet, or the Actors. A Play, as I have said, to be like Nature, is to be set above it; as Statues which are plac'd on high are made greater than the life, that they may descend to the sight in their just proportion.

Perhaps I have insisted too long on this Objection; but the clearing of it will make my stay shorter on the rest. You tell us, *Crites*, that Rhyme appears most unnatural in Repartees, or short Replies: when he who answers, (it being presum'd he knew not what the other would say, yet) makes up that part of the Verse which was left incompleat, and supplies both the sound and measure of it. This, you say, looks rather like the confederacy of two, than the answer of one.

This, I confess, is an Objection which is in every Man's mouth who loves not Rhyme: but suppose, I beseech you, the Repartee were made only in blank Verse, might not part of the same Argument be turn'd against you? for the measure is as often supply'd there as it is in Rhyme. The latter half of the Hemystich as commonly made up, or a second line subjoyn'd as a reply to the former; which any one leaf in *Johnson's* Plays will sufficiently clear to you. You will often find in the Greek Tragedians, and in *Seneca*, that when a Scene grows up into the warmth of repartees, (which is the close fighting of it) the latter part of the Trimeter[163] is supply'd by him who answers; and yet it was never observ'd as a fault in them by any of the Ancient or Modern Criticks. The case is the same in our Verse as it was in theirs; Rhyme to us being in lieu of quantity to them. But if no latitude is to be allow'd a Poet, you take from him not only his licence of *quidlibet audendi*,[164] but you tie him up in a straighter compass than you would a Philosopher. This is indeed *Musas colere severiores*:[165] You would have him follow Nature, but he must follow her on foot: you have dismounted him from his *Pegasus*.[166] But you tell us, this supplying the last half of a Verse, or adjoining a whole second to the former, looks more like the design of two, than the answer of one. Suppose we acknowledge it: how comes this confederacy to be more displeasing to you than in a Dance which is well contriv'd? You see there the united design of many persons to make up one Figure: after they have separated themselves in many petty divisions, they rejoyn one by one into a gross:[167] the confederacy is plain amongst them; for chance could never produce any thing so beautiful, and yet there is nothing in it, that shocks your sight. I acknowledge the hand of Art appears in Repartee, as of necessity it must in all kind of Verse. But there is also the quick and poynant brevity of it (which is an high imitation of Nature in those sudden gusts of Passion) to mingle with it: and this join'd with the cadency[168] and sweetness of the Rhyme, leaves nothing in the Soul of the Hearer to desire. 'Tis an Art which appears; but it appears only like the shadowings of Painture, which being to cause the rounding of it, cannot be absent; but while that is considered they are lost: so while we attend to the other Beauties of the matter, the Care and Labour of the Rhyme is carried from us, or at least drown'd in its own Sweetness, as Bees are sometimes buried in their Honey. When a Poet has found the Repartee, the last perfection he can add to iit [sic] is, to put it into Verse. However good the thought may be; however apt the words in which 'tis couch'd, yet he finds himself at a little unrest, while Rhyme is wanting: he cannot leave it till that comes naturally, and then is at ease, and sits down contented.

From Replies, which are the most elevated Thoughts of Verse, you pass to those which are most mean, and which are com-

[163] the standard line of three double measures

[164] "daring something," Horace, *Art of Poetry*, 9, 10

[165] "to worship a more difficult muse." Martial IX, 12

[166] the winged horse of the poets

[167] whole [168] rhythmic fall

mon with the lowest of houshold Conversation. In these, you say, the Majesty of Verse suffers. You instance in[169] the calling of a Servant, or commanding a Door to be shut in Rhyme. This, *Crites*, is a good Observation of yours, but no Argument: for it proves no more but that such thoughts should be wav'd, as often as may be, by the Address of the Poet. But suppose they are necessary in the places where he uses them, yet there is no need to put them into Rhyme. He may place them in the beginning of a Verse, and break it off, as unfit, when so debas'd for any other use: or granting the worst, that they require more Room than the Hemystick will allow; yet still there is a choice to be made of the best words, and least vulgar (provided they be apt) to express such thoughts. Many have blam'd Rhyme in general, for this fault, when the Poet, with a little Care, might have redress'd it. But they do it with no more Justice, than if *English* Poesie should be made ridiculous for the sake of the Water-Poets[170] Rhymes. Our Language is noble, full, and significant; and I know not why he who is Master of it may not cloath ordinary things in it as decently as the *Latine;* if he use the same diligence in his choice of words.

Delectus verborum Origo est Eloquentiae.[171]

It was the Saying of *Julius Caesar*, one so curious in his, that none of them can be chang'd but for a worse. One would think unlock the door was a thing as vulgar as could be spoken; and yet *Seneca* could make it sound high and lofty in his Latine.——

Reserate clusos Regii postes Laris.
Set wide the Palace Gates.[172]

But I turn from this Exception, both because it happens not above twice or thrice in any Play that those vulgar Thoughts are us'd; and then too (were there no other Apology to be made, yet) the necessity of them (which is alike in all kind of writing) may excuse them. For if they are little and mean in Rhyme, they are of consequence such in Blank Verse. Besides that the great eagerness and precipitation, with which they are spoken, makes us rather mind the Substance than the Dress; that for which they are spoken, rather than what is spoke. For they are always the effect of some hasty concernment, and something of consequence depends on them.

Thus, *Crites*, I have endeavour'd to answer your Objections; it remains only that I should vindicate an Argument for Verse, which you have gone about to overthrow. It had formerly been said, that the easiness of Blank Verse, renders the Poet too luxuriant; but that the labour of Rhyme bounds and circumscribes an over-fruitful Fancy. The Scene there being commonly confin'd to the Couplet, and the words so order'd that the Rhyme naturally follows them, not they the Rhyme. To this you answer'd, That it was no Argument to the Question in hand, for the Dispute was not which way a Man may write best; but which is most proper for the Subject on which he writes.

First, give me leave, Sir, to remember[173] you, that the Argument against which you rais'd this Objection, was only secondary: it was built on this *Hypothesis*, that to write in Verse was proper for serious Plays. Which supposition being granted (as it was briefly made out in that discourse, by shewing how Verse might be made natural) it asserted, that this way of writing was an help to the Poets Judgment, by putting bounds to a wild overflowing Fancy. I think therefore it will not be hard for me to make good what it was to prove on that supposition. But you add, that were this let pass, yet he who wants judgment in the liberty of his Fancy, may as well shew the defect of it when he is confin'd to Verse: for he who has Judgment will avoid Errors; and he who has it not, will commit them in all kinds of writing.

This Argument, as you have taken it from a most acute Person,[174] so, I confess, it carries much weight in it. But by using the word Judgement here indefinitely, you

[169] give as your illustration

[170] John Taylor, a writer of rough popular verses, contemporary of Jonson; see *Discoveries*.

[171] "The choice of words is the beginning of Eloquence." Reported, as Ker points out, by Cicero in his *Brutus*, 72, 253.

[172] *Phaedra*, 871; *clusos* for *clausos*

[173] remind

[174] See note 136.

seem to have put a Fallacy upon us: I grant he who has Judgment, that is, so profound, so strong, or rather so infallible a Judgment, that he needs no helps to keep it always pois'd and upright, will commit no faults either in Rhyme or out of it. And on the other extream, he who has a Judgment so weak and craz'd, that no helps can correct or amend it, shall write scurvily out of Rhyme, and worse in it. But the first of these Judgments is no where to be found, and the latter is not fit to write at all. To speak therefore of Judgment as it is in the best Poets: they who have the greatest proportion of it, want other helps than from it within. As for example, you would be loth to say, that he who is indued with a sound Judgement has no need of History, Geography, or Moral Philosophy, to write correctly. Judgment is indeed the Master-workman in a Play: but he requires many subordinate hands, many tools to his Assistance. And Verse I affirm to be one of these: 'Tis a Rule and Line by which he keeps his building compact and even, which otherwise lawless Imagination would raise either irregularly or loosly. At least if the Poet commits Errors with this help, he would make greater and more without it: 'tis (in short) a slow and painful, but the surest kind of working. *Ovid*, whom you accuse for luxuriancy in Verse, had perhaps been farther guilty of it, had he writ in Prose. And for your Instance of *Ben. Johnson*, who, you say, writ exactly without the help of Rhyme; you are to remember 'tis only an aid to a luxuriant Fancy, which his was not: As he did not want Imagination, so none ever said he had much to spare. Neither was Verse then refin'd so much, to be an help to that Age, as it is to ours. Thus then the second Thoughts being usually the best, as receiving the maturest digestion from Judgment, and the last and most mature product of those thoughts being artful and labour'd Verse, it may well be inferr'd, that Verse is a great help to a luxuriant Fancy; and this is what that Argument which you oppos'd was to evince.

Neander was pursuing this Discourse so eagerly, that *Eugenius* had call'd to him twice or thrice 'ere he took notice that the Barge stood still, and that they were at the Foot of *Somerset*-Stairs, where they had appointed it to land. The Company were all sorry to separate so soon, tho' a great part of the Evening was already spent; and stood a-while looking back on the Water, upon which the Moon-beams play'd, and made it appear like floating Quick-silver: at last they went up thro' a Crowd of *French* People, who were merrily dancing in the open Air, and nothing concern'd for the noise of Guns, which had allarm'd the Town that Afternoon. Walking thence together to the *Piazze*, they parted there; *Eugenius* and *Lisideius* to some pleasant Appointment they had made, and *Crites* and *Neander* to their several Lodgings.

PROLOGUE TO SECRET-LOVE; or, THE MAIDEN-QUEEN[1]

He who writ this, not without pains and thought
From *French* and *English* Theaters has brought
Th' exactest Rules by which a Play is wrought.

The Unities of Action, Place, and Time;
The Scenes unbroken; and a mingled chime
Of *Johnsons* humour, with *Corneilles* rhyme.[2]

But while dead colours he with care did lay,
He fears his Wit, or Plot he did not weigh,
Which are the living Beauties of a Play.

[1] Notes will be numbered continuously through the following group of prologues, epilogues, and songs. Play acted 1667, printed 1668; text, 1668.

[2] Jonson, the Elizabethan and Jacobean dramatist, was the model for the comedy of humours, or character governed by some dominant trait of temperament; from France, where French classical drama was being founded by Corneille, Charles II had brought the love of rhymed plays.

Plays are like Towns, which howe're fortifi'd
By Engineers, have still some weaker side
By the o'reseen[3] Defendant unespy'd.

And with that Art you make approaches now;
Such skilful fury in Assaults you show,
That every Poet without shame may bow.

Ours therefore humbly would attend your doom,
If Souldier-like, he may have termes to come
With flying colours, and with beat of Drum.[4]

The Prologue goes out, and stayes while a Tune is play'd, after which he returnes again.

Second Prologue

I had forgot one half I do protest,
And now am sent again to speak the rest.
He bowes to every great and noble Wit,
But to the little Hectors[5] of the Pit
Our Poet's sturdy, and will not submit.
He'll be before-hand with 'em, and not stay
To see each peevish Critick stab his Play:
Each Puny Censor,[6] who his skill to boast,
Is cheaply witty on the Poets cost.
No Criticks verdict, should, of right, stand good,
They are excepted all as men of blood:[7]
And the same Law should shield him from their fury
Which has exclud'd Butchers from a Jury.
You'd all be Wits . . .
But writing's tedious, and that way may fail;
The most compendious method is to rail:
Which you so like, you think your selves ill us'd
When in smart Prologues you are not abus'd.
A civil Prologue is approv'd by no man;
You hate it as you do a Civil woman:
Your Fancy's pall'd, and liberally you pay
To have it quicken'd, e're you see a Play.
Just as old Sinners worn from their delight,
Give money to be whip'd to appetite.
But what a Pox[8] keep I so much ado
To save our Poet? he is one of you;
A Brother Judgment, and as I hear say,
A cursed Critick as e're damn'd a Play.
Good salvage Gentlemen your own kind spare,
He is, like you, a very Wolf, or Bear;
Yet think not he'll your ancient rights invade,

[3] deluded
[4] recognition granted to gallant defenders, rather than unconditional surrender
[5] bullies seated on the floor of the auditorium rather than on the stage, like the court wits
[6] critic
[7] men who live by shedding blood; explained in the next lines
[8] a prissy oath or exclamation

Or stop the course of your free damning trade:
For he, (he vows) at no friends Play can sit
But he must needs find fault to shew his Wit:
Then, for his sake, ne're stint your own delight;
Throw[9] boldly, for he sets to all that write;
With such he ventures on an even lay,
For they bring ready money into Play.
Those who write not, and yet all Writers nick,[10]
Are Bankrupt Gamesters, for they damn on Tick.[11]

EPILOGUE TO TYRANNICK LOVE[12]

Spoken by Mrs. Ellen,[13] *When She was to Be Carried Off Dead by the Bearers*

To the Bearer. Hold, are you mad? you damn'd confounded Dog,
I am to rise, and speak the Epilogue.
To the Audience. I come, kind Gentlemen, strange news to tell ye,
I am the Ghost of poor departed *Nelly.*
Sweet Ladies, be not frighted, I'le be civil,
I'm what I was, a little harmless Devil.
For after death, we Sprights,[14] have just such Natures,
We had for all the World, when humane Creatures;
And therefore I that was an Actress here,
Play all my Tricks in Hell, a Goblin there.
Gallants, look to't, you say there are no Sprights;
But I'le come dance about your Beds at nights.
And faith you'l be in a sweet kind of taking,
When I surprise you between sleep and waking.
To tell you true, I walk because I dye[15]
Out of my Calling in a Tragedy.
O Poet, damn'd dull Poet, who could prove
So sensless! to make *Nelly* dye for Love,
Nay, what's yet worse, to kill me in the prime
Of *Easter*-Term, in Tart and Cheese-cake time!
I'le fit[16] the Fopp; for I'le not one word say
T'excuse his godly out of fashion Play.
A Play which if you dare but twice sit out,
You'l all be slander'd, and be thought devout.
But, farwel Gentlemen, make haste to me,
I'm sure e're long to have your company.
As for my Epitaph when I am gone,
I'le trust no Poet, but will write my own.

Here Nelly *lies, who, though she liv'd a Slater'n,*
Yet dy'd a Princess acting in S. Cathar'n.

[9] from dicing: throw boldly, he wagers (sets) on an equal stake (lay) [10] cheat
[11] credit [12] acted 1669; first printed 1670; text, second edition, 1672
[13] the famous Eleanor or Nell Gwynn, actress and mistress of Charles II. Her usual roles were comic, but in this she had been playing the part of a Christian martyr, St. Catherine of Alexandria.
[14] spirits
[15] one of innumerable puns on this word, which could mean to experience sexual consummation
[16] visit him with a fit penalty

SONG[17]

You charm'd me not with that fair face
  Though it was all Divine:
To be anothers is the Grace,
  That makes me wish you mine.
The God's and Fortune take their part
  Who like young Monarchs fight;
And boldly dare invade that Heart
  Which is anothers right.
First mad with hope we undertake
  To pull up every Bar;
But once possess'd, we faintly make
  A dull defensive War.
Now every friend is turn'd a foe
  In hope to get our store:
And passion makes us Cowards grow,
  Which made us brave before.

SONG[18]

Calm was the Even, and cleer was the Sky,
  And the new budding Flowers did spring
When all alone went *Amyntas* and I
  To hear the sweet Nightingal sing;
I sate, and he laid him down by me;
  But scarcely his breath he could draw;
For when with a fear, he began to draw near,
  He was dash'd with A ha ha ha ha!

He blush'd to himself, and lay still for a while,
  And his modesty curb'd his desire;
But streight I convinc'd all his fear with a smile,
  Which added new Flames to his Fire.
O *Sylvia*, said he, you are cruel,
  To keep your poor Lover in awe;
Then once more he prest with his hand to my breast,
  But was dash'd with A ha ha ha ha!

I knew 'twas his passion that caus'd all his fear;
  And therefore I pity'd his Case:
I whisper'd him softly, there's no Body near,
  And laid my Cheek close to his Face:
But as he grew bolder and bolder,
  A Shepherd came by us and saw;
And just as our bliss we began with a Kiss,
  He laugh'd out with A ha ha ha ha!

[17] from *An Evening's Love; or, The Mock-Astrologer*, 1668, Act II, sc.I. Text, first edition, 1671

[18] from the same, Act. IV, sc.I

THE ZAMBRA DANCE[19]

  Beneath a Myrtle Shade,
Which Love for none but happy Lovers made,
I slept, and straight my Love before me brought
Phillis, the Object of my waking thought:
Undress'd she came my flames to meet,
While Love strow'd flow'rs beneath her feet;
Flow'rs, which so press'd by her, became more sweet.

  From the bright Vision's Head
A careless Veil of Lawn was loosely spread:
From her white temples fell her shaded Hair,
Like cloudy sun-shine, not too brown nor fair.
Her Hands her lips did love inspire;
Her every Grace my heart did fire:
But most her eyes, which languish'd with desire.

  Ah, Charming fair, said I,
How long can you my bliss and yours deny?
By Nature and by love this lovely shade
Was for revenge of suffering Lovers made.
Silence and Shades with Love agree:
Both shelter you, and favour me;
You cannot blush, because I cannot see.

  No, let me die,[20] she said,
Rather than loose the spotless name of Maid:
Faintly methought she spoke, for all the while
She bid me not believe her, with a smile.
Then dye said I, she still deny'd:
And, is it thus, thus, thus she cry'd,
You use a harmless Maid! and so she dy'd.

  I wak'd, and straight I knew
I lov'd so well, it made my dream prove true:
Fancy, the kinder Mistriss of the two,
Fancy had done what *Phillis* wou'd not do.
Ah, Cruel Nymph! cease your disdain;
While I can dream, you scorn in vain:
Asleep or waking you must ease my pain.

[19] from *The Conquest of Granada*, Part I, Act III, sc.I. Text, 1672

[20] See note 15 for the point of this play on words.

EPILOGUE[21]

They, who have best succeeded on the Stage,
Have still conform'd their Genius to their Age.
Thus *Jonson* did Mechanique humour show,
When Men were dull, and Conversation low.
Then, Comedy was Faultless, but 'twas course:
Cobb's Tankard was a Jest, and *Otter's* Horse.[22]
And as their Comedy, their Love was mean;
Except, by chance, in some one labour'd Scene,
Which must attone for an ill-written Play.
They rose; but at their height could seldome stay.
Fame then was cheap, and the first comer sped;
And they have kept it since, by being dead.
But were they now to write, when Critiques weigh
Each Line, and ev'ry Word, throughout a Play,
None of 'em, no not *Jonson*, in his height,
Could pass, without allowing grains for weight.
Think it not envy that these truths are told;
Our Poet's not malicious, though he's bold.
'Tis not to brand 'em that their faults are shown,
But, by their errours, to excuse his own.
If Love and Honour now are higher rais'd,
'Tis not the Poet, but the Age is prais'd.
Wit's new ariv'd to a more high degree;
Our native Language more refin'd and free.
Our Ladies and our men now speak more wit
In conversation, than those Poets writ.
Then, one of these is, consequently, true;
That what this Poet writes comes short of you,
And imitates you ill, (which most he fears)
Or else his Writing is not worse than theirs.
Yet, though you judge, (as sure the Critiques will)
That some before him writ with greater skill:
In this one Praise he has their Fame surpast,
To please an Age more Gallant than the last.

SONG[23]

Why should a foolish Marriage Vow,
  Which long ago was made,
Oblige us to each other now
  When Passion is decay'd?
We lov'd, and we lov'd, as long as we cou'd,
  Till our Love was lov'd out in us both:
But our Marriage is dead, when the Pleasure is fled:
  'Twas Pleasure first made it an Oath.
If I have Pleasures for a Friend,
  And farther Love in store,

[21] for *The Conquest of Granada*, Part II, 1672. Text, 1672

[22] Cobb is a water-bearer from Jonson's *Everyman in His Humour;* Otter a "land and sea captain" from *The Silent Woman.* Dryden published with the play a defense of this epilogue or *An Essay on the Dramatique Poetry of the Last Age.*

[23] from *Marriage A -la Mode*, 1673, Act I, sc.1. Text of 1673

What Wrong has he whose Joys did end,
And who cou'd give no more?
'Tis a Madness that he should be jealous of me,
Or that I shou'd bar him of another:
For all we can gain, is to give our selves Pain,
When neither can hinder the other.

PROLOGUE[24]

Our Author by experience finds it true,
'Tis much more hard to please himself than you:
And out of no feign'd modesty, this day,
Damns his laborious Trifle of a Play:
Not that its worse than what before he writ,
But he has now another taste of Wit;
And to confess a truth, (though out of time)
Grows weary of his long-lov'd Mistris, Rhyme.[25]
Passion's too fierce to be in Fetters bound,
And Nature flies him like Enchanted Ground.
What Verse can do, he has perform'd in this,
Which he presumes the most correct of his.
But spite of all his pride, a secret shame
Invades his Breast at *Shakespear's* sacred name:
Aw'd when he hears his God-like *Romans* Rage,[26]
He, in a just despair, would quit the Stage.
And to an Age less polish'd, more unskill'd,
Does, with disdain, the foremost Honours yield,
As with the greater dead he dares not strive,
He would not match his Verse with those who live:
Let him retire, betwixt two Ages cast,
The first of this, and hindmost of the last.
A losing Gamester, let him sneak away;
He bears no ready Money from the Play.
The Fate which governs Poets, thought it fit,
He should not raise his Fortunes by his Wit.
The Clergy thrive, and the litigious Bar;
Dull Heroes fatten with the spoils of War;
All Southern Vices, Heav'n be prais'd, are here;
But Wit's a Luxury you think too dear.
When you to cultivate the Plant are loth,
'Tis a shrewd sign 'twas never of your growth:
And Wit in Northern Climates will not blow,
Except, like *Orange-Trees* 'tis Hous'd from Snow.
There needs no care to put a Play-House down,
'Tis the most desart place of all the Town.
We and our Neighbours,[27] to speak proudly, are
Like Monarchs, ruin'd with expensive War.
While, like wise *English*, unconcern'd, you sit,
And see us play the Tragedy of Wit.

[24] for *Aureng-Zebe: or. The Great mogul*, acted 1675. Text, first edition, 1676
[25] *All for Love*, his next tragedy, is in blank verse.
[26] Like Shakespeare's Roman plays, *Aureng-Zebe* deals with history remote in time and place.
[27] of the other play-house

EPILOGUE SPOKEN BY MRS. BOUTELL[28]

Oft has our Poet wisht, this happy Seat
Might prove his fading Muses last retreat.
I wonder'd at his wish, but now I find
He sought for quiet, and content of mind;
Which noiseful Towns, and Courts can never know,
And only in the shades like Laurels grow.
Youth, e'er it sees the World, here studies rest,
And Age returning thence concludes it best.
What wonder if we court that happiness
Yearly to share, which hourly you possess,
Teaching ev'n you, (while the vext World we show,)
Your Peace to value more, and better know?
'Tis all we can return for favours past,
Whose holy Memory shall ever last,
For Patronage from him whose care presides
O'er every noble Art, and every Science guides:
Bathurst,[29] a name the learn'd with reverence know,
And scarcely more to his own *Virgil* owe.
Whose Age enjoys but what his Youth deserv'd,
To rule those Muses whom before he serv'd:
His Learning, and untainted Manners too
We find (*Athenians*)[30] are deriv'd to you;
Such ancient hospitality there rests,
In yours, as dwelt in the first *Grecian* Breasts,
Whose kindness was Religion to their Guests.
Such Modesty did to our Sex appear,
As had there been no Laws we need not fear,
Since each of you was our Protector here.
Converse so chast, and so strict Virtue shown,
As might *Apollo* with the Muses own.
Till our return we must despair to find
Judges so just, so knowing, and so kind.

A SONG FROM THE ITALIAN[31]

By a dismal Cypress lying,
Damon cry'd, all pale and dying,
Kind is Death that ends my pain,
But cruel She I lov'd in vain.
The Mossy Fountains
Murmure my trouble,
And hollow Mountains
My groans redouble:
Every Nymph mourns me,
Thus while I languish;

[28] spoken in 1678; published in two slightly different forms in *Miscellanies*, 1684, one entitled "Spoken by Mrs. Marshall." Text, 1684, the version reprinted in 1701, but there titled "by Mrs. Marshall"

[29] President of Trinity College

[30] term commonly applied to members of the Universities, as devoted to culture and learning

[31] from *The Kind Keeper; or Mr. Limberham*, acted 1678, Act III, sc.I. Text, first edition, 1680. Day was unable to discover an original for this song.

She only scorns me,
Who caus'd my anguish.
No Love returning me, but all hope denying,
By a dismal Cypress lying,
Like a *Swan*, so sung he dying:
Kind is Death that ends my pain,
But cruel She I lov'd in vain.

PROLOGUE[32]

See my lov'd *Britons*, see your *Shakespeare* rise,
An awfull ghost confess'd to human eyes!
Nam'd, methinks, distinguish'd I had been,
From other shades, by this eternal Green,
About whose wreaths the vulgar Poets strive,
And with a touch their wither'd Bays[33] revive.
Untaught, unpractis'd in a barbarous Age,
I found not, but created first the Stage.
And, if I drain'd no *Greek* or *Latin* store,
'Twas, that my own abundance gave me more.
On Foreign Trade I needed not rely,
Like fruitfull *Britain*, rich without supply
In this my rough-drawn Play,[34] you shall behold
Some Master-strokes, so manly and so bold,
That he, who meant to alter, found 'em such,
He shook; and thought it Sacrilege to touch.
Now, where are the Successours to my Name?
What bring they to fill out a Poets Fame?
Weak, short-liv'd Issues of a feeble Age;
Scarce living to be Christen'd on the Stage!
For Humour Farce, for love, they rhyme dispence,
That tolls the knell for their departed sence.
Dulness might thrive in any Trade but this:
'T wou'd recommend to some fat Benefice.
Dulness, that in a Play house meets disgrace
Might meet with Reverence, in its proper place.
The fulsome clench that nauseats the Town
Wou'd from a Judge or Alderman go down!
Such virtue is there in a Robe and gown!
And that insipid stuff which here you hate
Might somewhere else be call'd a grave debate:
Dulness is decent in the Church and State.
But I forget that still 'tis understood,
Bad Plays are best decry'd by showing good:
Sit silent then, that my pleas'd Soul may see
A Judging Audience once, and worthy me:
My faithfull Scene from true Records shall tell
How *Trojan* Valour did the *Greek* excell;
Your great forefathers shall their fame regain,
And *Homer*'s angry Ghost repine in vain.

[32] for *Troilus and Cressida*, 1679. Text, first edition, 1679
[33] crowns of bay-leaves
[34] Dryden very much altered the structure as well as the characters.

SONG[35]

Can Life be a blessing,
Or worth the possessing,
Can life be a blessing if love were away?
Ah no! though our love all Night keep us waking,
And though he torment us with cares all the day,
Yet he sweetens, he sweetens our pains in the taking.
There's an hour at the last, there's an hour to repay.

In every possessing,
The ravishing blessing,
In every possessing the fruit of our pain,
Poor lovers forget long ages of anguish,
Whate're they have suffer'd and done to obtain;
'Tis a pleasure, a pleasure to sigh and to languish,
When we hope, when we hope to be happy again.

PROLOGUE[36]

If yet there be a few that take delight
In that which reasonable Men should write,
To them Alone we Dedicate this Night.
The Rest may satisfie their curious Itch
With City Gazets,[37] or some Factious Speech,
Or what-ere Libel, for the Publick Good,
Stirs up the Shrove-tide[38] Crew to Fire and Blood!
Remove your Benches, you apostate Pit,
And take Above, twelve penny-worth of Wit;
Go back to your dear Dancing on the Rope,
Or see what's worse, the Devil and the Pope![39]
The Plays that take on our Corrupted Stage,
Methinks, resemble the distracted Age;
Noise, Madness, all unreasonable Things,
That strike at Sense, as Rebels do at Kings!
The stile of Forty One our Poets write,
And you are grown to judge like Forty Eight.[40]
Such Censures our mistaking Audience make,
That 'tis almost grown Scandalous to Take!
They talk of Feavours that infect the Brains,
But Non-sence is the new Disease that reigns.
Weak Stomachs, with a long Disease opprest,
Cannot the Cordials of strong Wit digest;
Therefore thin Nourishment of Farce ye choose,
Decoctions of a Barly-water Muse:
A Meal of Tragedy wou'd make ye Sick,
Unless it were a very tender Chick.

[35] from the same play, same text, Act III, sc.1

[36] for Nahum Tate's *The Loyal General*, December 1679. Text: first edition, 1680

[37] gazette or bulletin; *City* would have reference to the political agitations centred there at this time

[38] the Sunday, Monday, and Tuesday before Ash Wednesday, times of popular merrymaking

[39] referring to the burnings in effigy of the Pope on November 5, in memory of the Gunpowder Plot, which were particularly fierce in this year

[40] Our poets write like the Parliament rebelling against Charles I in 1641, and the audience judges as fiercely and unreasonably as those who tried and condemned him in 1648.

Some Scenes in Sippets[41] wou'd be worth our time,
Those wou'd go down; some Love that's poach'd in Rime;
If these shou'd fail—
We must lie down, and, after all our cost,
Keep Holy-day, like Water-men[42] in Frost;
Whilst you turn Players on the Worlds great Stage,
And Act your selves the Farce of your own Age.

ABSALOM AND ACHITOPHEL. A POEM[1]

In pious Times, e'r Priest-Craft did begin,
Before *Polygamy* was made a Sin;
When Man, on many, multipli'd his kind,
E'r one to one was, cursedly, confin'd:
When Nature prompted and no Law deni'd
Promiscuous Use of Concubine and Bride;
Then, *Israel's* Monarch,[2] after Heavens own heart,
His vigorous warmth did, variously, impart
To Wives and Slaves: And, wide as his Command,
Scatter'd his Maker's Image through the Land.
Michal,[3] of Royal Blood, the Crown did wear,
A soil ungrateful to the Tiller's care:
Not so the rest; for several Mothers bore
To God-like *David* several sons before.
But since like Slaves his Bed they did ascend,
No True Succession could their Seed attend.
Of all this Numerous Progeny was none
So Beautiful so Brave as *Absalon:*[4]
Whether, inspir'd by some diviner Lust,
His father got him with a greater Gust,[5]
Or that his Conscious[6] Destiny made way,
By manly Beauty to Imperial Sway.
Early in Foreign Fields he won Renown
With Kings and States alli'd to *Israels* Crown:[7]
In Peace the thoughts of War he could remove
And seem'd as he were onely born for Love.
What e'r he did was done with so much ease,
In him alone, 'twas Natural to please;

[41] bits of toast or bread dipped in a liquid, or served as a garnish

[42] boatmen with boats for hire on the Thames

[1] Text: second edition, 1682.

[2] King Charles, allegorized as David. The poem treats the situation of the Exclusion Bill (see general introduction) allegorically in terms of the rebellion to which Achitophel, David's minister, persuaded David's favorite son Absalom. In that rebellion, Absalom perished while fleeing from the battle. Dryden uses the story, however, only to establish the general character of the rebellion; he treats it loosely, and calls in other stories and persons from the Bible for the same purpose of identifying actual men with recognized types of good and evil, wise or foolish, men. Dryden is not the first to draw the parallel, though the first to develop it fully. The main story is told in II Samuel, 13 and 18. The Biblical parallels would be well known to Dryden's readers and often form a very important part of his characterization.

[3] Queen Katherine, of the royal family of Portugal

[4] the Duke of Monmouth, Charles's eldest son and favorite

[5] zest

[6] aware of its purpose

[7] He had served in Louis XIV's campaigns against the Dutch in 1672 and 1673, and with the Dutch against the French in 1678.

His motions all accompanied with grace;
And *Paradise* was open'd in his face.
With secret Joy, indulgent *David* view'd
His Youthful Image in his Son renew'd;
To all his wishes Nothing he deni'd
And made the Charming *Annabel*[8] his Bride.
What faults he had (for who from faults is free?)
His father coud not or he would not see.
Some warm excesses, which the Law forbore,
Were constru'd Youth that purg'd by boiling o'r:
And *Amnon's*[9] Murther, by a specious Name,
Was call'd a Just Revenge for injur'd Fame.
Thus Prais'd and Lov'd, the Noble Youth remain'd,
While *David*, undisturb'd, in *Sion*[10] reign'd.
But Life can never be sincerely[11] blest:
Heav'n punishes the bad, and proves the best.
The *Jews*, a Headstrong, Moody, Murm'ring race
As ever tri'd th' extent and stretch of grace;
God's pamper'd People, whom, debauch'd with ease,
No King could govern nor no God could please;
(Gods they had tri'd of every shape and size
That God-smiths could produce or Priests devise:)
These *Adam*-wits,[12] too fortunately free,
Began to dream they wanted[13] liberty;
And when no rule, no president[14] was found
Of men, by Laws less circumscrib'd and bound;
They led their wild desires to Woods and Caves;
And thought that all but Savages were Slaves.
They who, when *Saul* was dead, without a blow
Made foolish *Ishbosheth*[15] the Crown forgo;
Who banisht *David* did from *Hebron*[16] bring,
And, with a General shout, proclaim'd him King:
Those very *Jews* who at their very best,
Their Humour[17] more than Loyalty exprest,
Now wondred why so long they had obey'd
An Idol-Monarch which their hands had made;
Thought they might ruine him they could create
Or melt him to that Golden Calf, a State.[18]
But these were random Bolts: No form'd Design
Nor Interest made the Factious Croud to join:
The sober part of *Israel*, free from stain,
Well knew the value of a peaceful reign;

[8] Anne Scott, Duchess of Buccleuch

[9] Generally taken as Sir John Coventry, who had been badly beaten and his nose slit by Monmouth's men in 1671. Possibly, as Verrall suggested, only the scriptural story is here alluded to.

[10] England, of course, and the Jews, the English [11] entirely, without mixture

[12] like Adam, who, through Eve was persuaded that he was not free until he had eaten of the forbidden tree

[13] lacked [14] precedent

[15] Saul and Ishbosheth; Oliver Cromwell and his son Richard, (II Sam. 2–4)

[16] Scotland. Charles had there been recognized as King in 1651.

[17] the prevailing one, that is, of the four humours; therefore, were irrational

[18] a commonwealth; so called because the Israelites made a golden calf to worship in their impatience while Moses was talking with God on the mountain

And, looking backward[19] with a wise afright,
Saw Seams of wounds, dishonest[20] to the sight:
In contemplation of whose ugly Scars,
They curst the memory of Civil Wars.
The moderate sort of Men, thus qualifi'd,[21]
Inclin'd the Ballance to the better side:
And *David's* mildness manag'd it so well,
The bad found no occasion to Rebel.
But, when to Sin our byast[22] Nature leans,
The careful Devil is still at hand with means;
And providently Pimps[23] for ill desires:
The Good Old Cause, reviv'd, a Plot requires,
Plots, true or false, are necessary things,
To raise up Common-wealths and ruine Kings.
  Th' Inhabitants of old *Jerusalem*,
Were *Jebusites*:[24] the Town so call'd from them;
And their's the Native right——
But when the chosen People grew more strong,
The rightful cause at length became the wrong;
And every loss the men of *Jebus* bore,
They still were thought God's enemies the more.
Thus, worn and weaken'd, well or ill content,
Submit they must to *David's* Government:
Impoverish't and depriv'd of all Command,
Their Taxes doubled as they lost their Land;
And, what was harder yet to flesh and blood,
Their Gods disgrac'd, and burnt like common Wood.[25]
This set the Heathen Priesthood in a flame,
For Priests of all Religions are the same:
Of whatsoe'er descent their Godhead be,
Stock, Stone, or other homely Pedigree,
In his defence his Servants are as bold,
As if he had been born of beaten Gold.
The *Jewish Rabbins*,[26] though their Enemies,
In this conclude them honest men and wise:
For 'twas their duty, all the Learned think,
T' espouse his Cause by whom they eat and drink.
From hence began that Plot,[27] the Nations Curse,
Bad in itself, but represented worse,
Rais'd in extremes, and in extremes decri'd,
With Oaths affirm'd, with dying Vows deni'd,
Not weigh'd or winnow'd by the Multitude,
But swallow'd in the Mass, unchew'd and crude.
Some Truth there was, but dash'd[28] and brew'd with Lies;
To please the Fools, and puzzle all the Wise.
Succeeding Times did equal Folly call
Believing nothing or believing all.
The *Egyptian*[29] Rites the *Jebusites* embrac'd,

[19] to the years of the civil war, about 1640–1660 [20] unseemly [21] calmed
[22] disposed (metaphor from game of bowls) [23] panders
[24] *Jerusalem:* London; *Jebusites:* Roman Catholics
[25] penalties imposed on Roman Catholics [26] clergy of the church of England
[27] the Popish Plot (See general introduction.)
[28] dilute, qualify [29] French

Where Gods were recommended by their taste.
Such sav'ry Deities must needs be good
As serv'd at once for Worship and for Food.
By force they could not Introduce these Gods,
For Ten to One in former days was odds.
So Fraud was us'd, (the Sacrificers Trade,)
Fools are more hard to Conquer than Persuade.
Their busie Teachers mingled with the *Jews;*
And rak'd, for Converts, even the Court and Stews:[30]
Which *Hebrew* Priests the more unkindly took,
Because the Fleece accompanies the Flock.
Some thought they God's Anointed meant to slay
By Guns, invented since full many a day:
Our Author swears it not; but who can know
How far the Devil and *Jebusites* may go?
This Plot, which fail'd for want of common Sense,
Had yet a deep and dangerous Consequence;
For as, when raging Fevers boil[31] the Blood
The standing Lake soon floats into a Floud;
And ev'ry hostile Humour which before
Slept quiet in its Channels bubbles o're:
So, several Factions from this first Ferment
Work up to Foam, and threat the Government.
Some by their Friends, more by themselves thought wise,
Oppos'd the Pow'r, to which they could not rise.
Some had in Courts been Great, and thrown from thence,
Like Fiends, were harden'd in Impenitence.
Some, by their Monarch's fatal mercy grown,
From Pardon'd Rebels, Kinsmen to the Throne
Were raised in Pow'r and Publick Office high;
Strong Bands,[32] if Bands ungrateful men coud tie.
Of these the false *Achitophel*[33] was first,
A Name to all succeeding Ages curst.
For close Designs and crooked Counsels fit,
Sagacious, Bold, and Turbulent of wit,
Restless, unfixt in Principles and Place,
In Pow'r unpleased, impatient of Disgrace;
A fiery Soul, which working out its way,
Fretted the Pigmy Body to decay:
And o'r inform'd the Tenement[34] of Clay
A daring Pilot in extremity;
Pleas'd with the Danger, when the Waves went high
He sought the Storms; but for a Calm unfit,
Would Steer too nigh the Sands to boast his Wit.
Great Wits are sure to Madness near alli'd
And thin Partitions do their Bounds divide;[35]
Else, why should he, with Wealth and Honour blest,
Refuse his Age the needful hours of Rest?
Punish a Body which he coud not please,

[30] brothels, alluding to the royal mistresses [31] make boil [32] bonds
[33] the Earl of Shaftesbury (see general introduction.) [34] dwelling
[35] an idea with a long history, originally derived from Aristotle, and probably intimating a prevalence in Shaftesbury's type of man of a dangerous melancholy humor which rendered him restless and ambitious

Bankrupt of Life, yet Prodigal of Ease?
And all to leave, what with his Toil he won
To that unfeather'd two-legg'd thing, a Son:
Got, while his Soul did huddled Notions[36] trie;
And born a shapeless Lump, like Anarchy.
In Friendship false, implacable in Hate,
Resolv'd to Ruine or to Rule the State:
To Compass this the Triple Bond he broke;
The Pillars of the Publick Safety shook,
And fitted *Israel* for a Foreign Yoke;
Then, seiz'd with Fear, yet still affecting Fame,
Usurp'd a Patriot's[37] All-attoning Name.
So easie still it proves in Factious Times,
With publick Zeal to cancel private Crimes:
How safe is Treason and how sacred ill,
Where none can sin against the Peoples Will,
Where Crouds can wink; and no offence be known,
Since in anothers guilt they find their own.
Yet, Fame deserv'd, no Enemy can grudge;[38]
The Statesman we abhor, but praise the Judge.
In *Israels* courts ne'er sat an *Abbethdin*[39]
With more discerning Eyes or Hands more clean,
Unbrib'd, unsought, the Wretched to redress;
Swift of Dispatch and easie of Access.
Oh, had he been content to serve the Crown
With Vertues onely proper to the Gown,
Or had the rankness of the Soil been freed
From Cockle that opprest the Noble Seed,
David, for him his tuneful Harp had strung,[40]
And Heav'n had wanted one Immortal Song.
But wild Ambition loves to slide, not stand,
And Fortunes Ice prefers to Vertues Land.
Achitophel, grown weary to possess[41]
A lawful Fame, and lazie Happiness,
Disdain'd the Golden Fruit to gather free[42]
And lent the Crowd his Arm to shake the Tree.
Now, manifest of Crimes,[43] contriv'd long since,
He stood at bold Defiance with his Prince:
Held up the Buckler of the Peoples Cause
Against the Crown; and sculk'd behind the Laws.
The wish'd occasion of the Plot he takes;
Some Circumstances finds, but more he makes.
By buzzing Emissaries, fills the ears
Of listening Crouds, with Jealousies[44] and Fears
Of Arbitrary Counsels brought to light,

[36] his conceptions were confused and this confusion derived through generation to his son

[37] a political name assumed by those who pressed the Exclusion Bill

[38] This and the following eleven lines did not appear in the first edition. The state of the first text suggests that these or kindred lines may have been in Dryden's original and then been removed while the book was in press (Noyes and MacDonald).

[39] an officer of the high court of the Jews; Shaftesbury was Lord Chancellor.

[40] probably no reference to King Charles: David might have sung a praise of Achitophel and would not have needed to sing a Psalm of lament, possibly Psalm 3 or his lament for Absalom.

[41] in possessing [42] freely; as it fell [43] made manifest in; a Latinate phrase

[44] over-anxious solicitude (for their rights)

And proves the King himself a *Jebusite*.[45]
Weak Arguments! which yet he knew full well,
Were strong with People easie to Rebel.[46]
For, govern'd by the *Moon*, the giddy *Jews*
Tread the same Track when she the Prime[47] renews:
And once in twenty Years, their Scribes record,
By natural Instinct they change their Lord.
Achitophel still wants a Chief, and none
Was found so fit as Warlike *Absalon:*
Not, that he wish'd his Greatness to create,
(For Politicians neither love nor hate:)
But, for[48] he knew, his Title not allow'd,
Would keep him still depending on the Croud,
That Kingly pow'r, thus ebbing out, might be
Drawn to the Dregs of a Democracie.
Him he attempts with studied Arts to please
And sheds his Venome in such words as these.
  Auspicious Prince! at whose Nativity
Some Royal Planet rul'd the Southern Sky;
Thy longing Countries Darling and Desire,
Their cloudy Pillar, and their guardian Fire,
Their second *Moses*, whose extended Wand
Divides the Seas and shows the promis'd Land,
Whose dawning Day, in every distant Age,
Has exercised the Sacred Prophets rage,
The Peoples Pray'r, the glad Diviners Theam,
The Young mens Vision and the Old mens Dream!
Thee, *Saviour*, Thee the Nations Vows[49] confess;
And, never satisfi'd with seeing, bless:
Swift, unbespoken Pomps, thy steps proclaim,
And stammering Babes are taught to lisp thy Name.
How long wilt thou the general Joy detain;
Starve, and defraud the People of thy Reign?
Content ingloriously to pass thy days,
Like one of Vertues Fools that Feeds on Praise;
Till thy fresh Glories, which now shine so bright,
Grow Stale and Tarnish with our dayly sight.
Believe me, Royal Youth, thy Fruit must be
Or[50] gather'd Ripe, or rot upon the Tree.
Heav'n, has to all allotted, soon or late,
Some lucky Revolution of their Fate:
Whose Motions, if we watch and guide with Skill,
(For humane Good depends on humane Will,)
Our Fortune rolls as from a smooth Descent
And, from the first impression, takes the Bent:
But, if unseiz'd, she glides away like wind;
And leaves repenting Folly far behind.
Now, now she meets you with a glorious prize
And spreads her Locks before her as she flies.
Had thus Old *David*, from whose Loins you spring,

[45] See general introduction. [46] at rebelling
[47] her return to the beginning of the cycle of years (actually 19) in which she was supposed to go through all phases of her relation to the sun
[48] because [49] declarations of loyalty or enthusiasm [50] either

Not dar'd, when Fortune call'd him, to be King,
At *Gath*[51] an Exile he might still remain;
And Heavens Anointing Oil had been in vain.
Let his successful Youth your hopes engage,
But shun th' example of Declining Age.
Behold him setting in his Western Skies,
The Shadows lengthening as the Vapours rise.
He is not now, as when, on *Jordan's*[52] Sand,
The Joyful People throng'd to see him Land,
Cov'ring the *Beach* and blackning all the *Strand:*
But like the Prince of Angels from his height,
Comes tumbling downward with diminish'd light:
Betray'd by one poor Plot to publick Scorn,
(Our onely blessing since his curst Return,)
Those heaps of People which one Sheaf did bind,
Blown off and scatter'd by a puff of Wind.
What strength can he to your Designs oppose,
Naked of Friends, and round beset with Foes?
If *Pharaoh's*[53] doubtful succour he should use,
A Foreign Aid woud more incense the *Jews:*
Proud *Egypt* woud dissembled Friendship bring;
Foment the War, but not support the King:
Nor woud the Royal Party e'r unite
With *Pharaoh's* arms, t' assist the *Jebusite;*
Or if they shoud, their Interest soon would break,
And, with such odious Aid, make *David* weak.
All sorts of men, by my successful Arts
Abhorring Kings, estrange their alter'd Hearts
From *David's* Rule: And 'tis the general Cry,
Religion, Common-wealth, and Liberty.
If you, as Champion of the Publique Good,
Add to their Arms a Chief of Royal Blood;
What may not *Israel* hope, and what Applause
Might such a General gain by such a Cause?
Not barren Praise alone, that Gaudy Flow'r,
Fair onely to the sight, but solid Pow'r:
And Nobler is a limited Command,
Giv'n by the Love of all your Native Land,
Than a Successive Title, Long, and Dark,
Drawn from the Mouldy Rolls of *Noah's* ark.
  What cannot Praise effect in Mighty Minds,
When Flattery Sooths and when Ambition Blinds!
Desire of Pow'r, on Earth a Vitious Weed,
Yet, sprung from High, is of Cœlestial Seed:
In God 'tis Glory: And when Men Aspire,
'Tis but a Spark too much of Heavenly Fire.
Th' Ambitious Youth, too Covetous of Fame,
Too full of Angels Metal[54] in his Frame,
Unwarily was led from Vertues ways,
Made Drunk with Honour, and debauch'd with Praise.
Half loath and half consenting to the Ill,

[51] Outside England; Charles was in Belgium when recalled.
[52] The waters surrounding England: Charles landed at Dover.
[53] Louis XIV, King of France [54] mettle; courage

(For Loyal Blood within him strugled still,)
He thus repli'd—And what Pretence have I
To take up Arms for Publick Liberty?
My Father Governs with unquestion'd Right;
The Faiths Defender[55] and Mankinds Delight,
Good, Gracious, Just, observant of the Laws;
And Heav'n by Wonders[56] has espous'd his Cause.
Whom has he Wrong'd in all his Peaceful Reign?
Who sues for Justice to his Throne in Vain?
What Millions has he pardoned of his Foes
Whom Just Revenge did to his Wrath expose?
Mild, Easie, Humble, Studious of our Good,
Enclin'd to Mercy, and averse from Blood.
If Mildness Ill with Stubborn *Israel* Suit,
His Crime is God's beloved Attribute.
What could he gain, his People to Betray[57]
Or change his Right, for Arbitrary Sway?
Let Haughty *Pharaoh* Curse with such a Reign
His Fruitful *Nile*, and Yoak a Servile Train.
If *David's* Rule *Jerusalem* Displease,
The *Dog-star* heats their Brains to this Disease.
Why then should I, Encouraging the Bad,
Turn Rebel and run Popularly Mad?
Were he a Tyrant who, by Lawless Might,
Opprest the *Jews* and rais'd the *Jebusite*,
Well might I Mourn; but Nature's holy Bands[58]
Would Curb my Spirits, and Restrain my Hands:
The People might assert their Liberty;
But what was Right in them, were Crime in me.
His Favour leaves me nothing to require;
Prevents my Wishes and out-runs Desire.
What more can I expect while *David* lives?
All but his Kingly Diadem he gives:
And that: But there he paus'd; then Sighing, said,
Is Justly destin'd for a Worthier head.
For when my Father from his Toyls shall Rest
And late Augment the Number of the Blest:
His Lawful Issue shall the Throne ascend,
Or the *Collat'ral*[59] Line, where that shall end.
His Brother, though Opprest with Vulgar Spight,
Yet Dauntless and Secure of Native Right,
Of every Royal Vertue stands possest;
Still Dear to all the Bravest and the Best.
His Courage Foes, his Friends his Truth Proclaim;
His Loyalty the King, the World his Fame.
His Mercy ev'n th' Offending Croud will find,
For sure he comes of a Forgiving Kind.
Why shoud I then Repine at Heavens Decree
Which gives me no Pretence to Royalty?
Yet oh that Fate, Propitiously Inclin'd,
Had rais'd my Birth, or had debas'd my Mind;

[55] one of the official titles of the kings of England [56] wonderful signs
[57] in betraying his people [58] bonds
[59] descended in parallel line from a common ancestor, in this case, Charles I

To my large Soul, not all her Treasure lent,
And then betrai'd it to a mean Descent.
I find, I find my mounting Spirits Bold,
And *David's* part disdains my Mothers Mold.
Why am I scanted by a Niggard Birth?
My soul Disclaims the Kindred of her Earth:
And, made for Empire, Whispers me within;
Desire of Greatness is a God-like Sin.
  Him Staggering so when Hells dire Agent found,
While fainting Vertue scarce maintain'd her Ground,
He pours fresh Forces in, and thus Replies:
  Th' eternal God, Supreamly Good and Wise,
Imparts not these Prodigious Gifts in vain;
What Wonders are Reserv'd to bless your Reign?
Against your will your Arguments have shown,
Such Vertue's only giv'n to guide a Throne.
Not that your Father's Mildness I contemn,
But manly Force becomes the Diadem.
'Tis true he grants the People all they crave;
And more perhaps than Subjects ought to have:
For Lavish Grants suppose a Monarch tame
And more his Goodness than his Wit proclaim.
But when should People strive their Bonds to break,
If not when Kings are Negligent or Weak?
Let him give on till he can give no more,
The thrifty Sanhedrin[60] shall keep him poor:
And every Sheckle[61] which he can receive
Shall cost a Limb of his Prerogative.[62]
To ply him with new Plots shall be my care;
Or plunge him deep in some Expensive War;
Which, when his Treasure can no more supply,
He must, with the Remains of Kingship, buy.
His faithful Friends, our Jealousies and Fears
Call *Jebusites;* and *Pharaoh's* Pensioners,
Whom, when our Fury from his Aid has torn,
He shall be naked left to publick Scorn.
The next Successor, whom I fear and hate,
My Arts have made obnoxious to the State;
Turn'd all his Vertues to his Overthrow,
And gain'd[63] our Elders to pronounce a Foe.
His Right, for Sums of necessary Gold,
Shall first be Pawn'd, and afterward be Sold;
Till time shall Ever-wanting *David* draw,
To pass your doubtful Title into Law.
If not; the People have a Right Supreme
To make their Kings; for Kings are made for them.
All Empire is no more than Pow'r in Trust,
Which, when resum'd, can be no longer Just.
Succession, for the general Good design'd,
In its own wrong a Nation cannot bind:

[60] high council of the Jews; allegorically, Parliament [61] Jewish coin
[62] constitutional rights of the sovereign, which Charles will be compelled to yield to secure every appropriation
[63] won

If altering that, the People can relieve,
Better one suffer, than a Nation grieve.
The *Jews* well know their pow'r: e'r *Saul*[64] they chose
God was their King, and God they durst Depose.
Urge now your Piety, your Filial Name,
A Father's Right and Fear of future Fame;
The Publick Good, that Universal Call,
To which even Heav'n submitted, answers all.
Nor let his Love enchant your generous Mind;
'Tis Natures trick to propagate her Kind.
Our fond Begetters, who would never die,
Love but themselves in their Posterity.
Or let his Kindness by th' Effects be tried
Or let him lay his vain Pretence aside.
God said he loved your Father; coud he bring
A better Proof than to anoint him King?
It surely shew'd, He lov'd the Shepherd well
Who gave so fair a Flock as *Israel*.
Would *David* have you thought his Darling Son?
What means he then, to Alienate[65] the Crown?
The name of Godly he may blush to bear:
'Tis after Gods own heart to Cheat his Heir.
He to his Brother gives Supreme Command;
To you a Legacie of Barren Land:
Perhaps th' old Harp on which he thrums his Lays:
Or some dull *Hebrew* Ballad in your Praise.
Then the next Heir, a Prince, Severe and Wise,
Already looks on you with Jealous Eyes,
Sees through the thin Disguises of your Arts,
And marks your Progress in the Peoples Hearts.
Though now his mighty Soul its Grief contains;
He meditates Revenge who least Complains.
And like a Lion, Slumb'ring in the way,
Or Sleep dissembling, while he waits his Prey,
His fearless Foes within his Distance draws,
Constrains his Roaring, and Contracts his Paws:
Till at the last, his time for Fury found,
He shoots with sudden Vengeance from the Ground:
The Prostrate Vulgar,[66] passes o'r and Spares;
But with a Lordly Rage, his Hunters tears;
Your Case no tame Expedients will afford;
Resolve on Death, or Conquest by the Sword,
Which for no less a Stake than Life, you Draw,
And Self-defence is Natures Eldest Law.
Leave the warm People no Considering time;
For then Rebellion may be thought a Crime.
Prevail[67] your self of what Occasion gives,
But trie your Title while your Father lives;
And that your Arms may have a fair Pretence,
Proclaim you take them in the King's Defence;
Whose Sacred Life each minute woud Expose,

[64] The Jews were governed by judges until God appointed Saul. The commonwealth which first emerged in the Civil War gave way to Cromwell's protectorate.
[65] transfer the ownership of [66] common men [67] avail

To Plots, from seeming Friends and secret Foes.
And who can sound the depth of *David's* Soul?
Perhaps his fear, his kindness may Controul.
He fears his Brother, though he loves his Son,
For plighted Vows too late to be undone.
If so, by Force he wishes to be gain'd,
Like Womens Leachery, to seem Constrain'd:
Doubt not; but when he most affects the Frown,
Commit a pleasing Rape upon the Crown.
Secure his Person to secure your Cause;
They who possess the Prince, possess the Laws.
He said, And this Advice above the rest
With *Absalom's* Mild Nature suited best;
Unblamed of Life[68] (Ambition set aside,)
Not stain'd with Cruelty, nor puft with pride.
How happy had he been, if Destiny
Had higher placed his Birth, or not so high!
His Kingly Vertues might have claim'd a Throne;
And blest all other Countries but his own:
But charming Greatness, since so few refuse:
'Tis Juster to Lament him, than Accuse.
Strong were his hopes a Rival to remove,
With Blandishments to gain the publick Love,
To Head the Faction while their Zeal was hot,
And Popularly Prosecute the Plot.
To farther this, *Achitophel* Unites
The Malecontents of all the *Israelites:*
Whose differing Parties he coud wisely Join
For several Ends, to serve the same Design.
The Best, and of the Princes some were such,
Who thought the pow'r of Monarchy too much:
Mistaken Men, and Patriots in their Hearts;
Not Wicked, but seduc'd by Impious Arts.
By these the Springs of Property[69] were bent,
And wound so high, they Crack'd the Government.
The next for Interest sought t' embroil the State,
To sell their Duty at a dearer rate;
And make their *Jewish* Markets of the Throne;
Pretending Publick Good, to serve their own
Others thought Kings an useless heavy Load,
Who Cost too much, and did too little Good.
These were for laying Honest *David* by
On Principles of pure good Husbandry.[70]
With them join'd all th' Haranguers of the Throng
That thought to get Preferment by the Tongue.
Who follow next, a double danger bring,
Not onely hating *David*, but the King;[71]
The *Solymæan* Rout;[72] well Vers'd of old
In Godly Faction, and in Treason bold;
Cowring and Quaking at a Conqu'ror's Sword,

[68] unblamed in life, of blameless life
[69] the theory that property was the basis of the state
[70] economy [71] i.e., the kingship
[72] the London crowd, Solyma being a name for Jerusalem

But Lofty[73] to a Lawful Prince Restor'd;
Saw with Disdain an *Ethnick*[74] Plot begun
And Scorned by *Jebusites* to be Out-done.
Hot *Levites*[75] Headed these; who pul'd[76] before
From th' *Ark*, which in the Judges days they bore,
Resum'd their Cant, and with a Zealous Crie
Pursu'd their old belov'd Theocracie.
Where Sanhedrin and Priest enslav'd the Nation
And justifi'd their Spoils by Inspiration:[77]
For who so fit for Reign as *Aaron's* Race,[78]
If once Dominion they could found in Grace?
These led the Pack; though not of surest scent,
Yet deepest mouth'd against the Government.
A numerous Host of dreaming Saints succeed;
Of the true old Enthusiastick Breed:
'Gainst Form and Order they their Pow'r imploy;
Nothing to Build, and all things to Destroy.
But far more numerous was the Herd of such,
Who think too little, and who talk too much.
These, out of meer instinct, they knew not why,
Adored their Fathers' God, and Property:
And, by the same blind Benefit of Fate,
The Devil and the *Jebusite* did hate:
Born to be sav'd, even in their own despight;
Because they could not help believing right.
Such were the Tools; but a whole Hydra[79] more
Remains, of sprouting heads too long to score.
Some of their Chiefs were Princes of the Land;
In the first Rank of these did *Zimri*[80] stand:
A man so various, that he seem'd to be
Not one, but all Mankind's Epitome.
Stiff in Opinions, always in the wrong;
Was Every thing by starts, and Nothing long:
But, in the course of one revolving Moon,
Was Chymist, Fidler, States-Man, and Buffoon:
Then all for Women, Painting, Rhiming, Drinking,
Besides ten thousand Freaks that dy'd in thinking.
Blest Madman, who coud every hour employ,
With something New to wish, or to enjoy!
Railing and praising were his usual Theams;
And both (to shew his Judgment) in Extreams:
So over Violent, or over Civil,
That every Man, with him, was God or Devil.
In squandring Wealth was his peculiar Art:
Nothing went unrewarded, but Desert.
Begger'd by fools, whom still he found[81] too late:

[73] haughty [74] outside the Jewish nation; that is, outsiders, Roman Catholics
[75] priests, clergymen (Presbyterian) [76] whine
[77] claiming inspiration from God: the enthusiastic sects really wanted no form of government but a theocracy or government through the church alone, which for them meant the few elected to receive God's grace.
[78] Levites, priests [79] fabulous snake whose many heads grew again as they were cut off
[80] the Duke of Buckingham (I Kings 16 and Num. 25), master of the horse to Charles II
[81] found out

He had his Jest, and they had his Estate.
He laugh'd himself from Court; then sought Relief
By forming Parties, but could ne'r be Chief:
For, spight of him, the weight of Business fell
On *Absolon* and wise *Achitophel:*
Thus wicked but in Will, of Means bereft,
He left not Faction, but of[82] that was left.
Titles and Names 'twere tedious to Reherse
Of Lords, below the Dignity of Verse.
Wits, Warriors, Commonwealths-men were the best:
Kind Husbands and meer Nobles all the rest
And, therefore in the name of Dulness, be
The well-hung *Balaam*[83] and cold *Caleb*[84] free;
And Canting *Nadab*[85] let Oblivion damn,
Who made new Porridge for the Paschal Lamb.
Let Friendships holy Band some Names assure,
Some their own Worth, and some let Scorn secure.
Nor shall the Rascal Rabble here have Place,
Whom Kings no Titles gave, and God no Grace:
Not Bull-fac'd *Jonas*,[86] who coud Statutes draw
To mean Rebellion, and make Treason Law.
But he, though bad, is follow'd by a worse,
The Wretch, who Heav'ns Anointed dar'd to Curse.
Shimei,[87] whose Youth did early Promise bring
Of Zeal to God, and Hatred to his King;
Did wisely from Expensive Sins refrain,
And never broke the Sabbath, but for Gain:
Nor ever was he known an Oath to vent,
Or Curse, unless against the Government.
Thus, heaping Wealth, by the most ready way
Among the *Jews*, which was to Cheat and Pray;
The City, to reward his pious Hate
Against his Master, chose him Magistrate:
His Hand a Vare[88] of Justice did uphold;
His Neck was loaded with a Chain of Gold.
During his Office, Treason was no Crime.
The Sons of *Belial*[89] had a Glorious Time:
For *Shimei*, though not prodigal of pelf,
Yet lov'd his wicked Neighbour as himself:
When two or three were gather'd to declaim
Against the Monarch of *Jerusalem*,
Shimei was always in the midst of them.
And, if they Curst the King when he was by,

[82] by

[83] the Earl of Huntington, or the Earl of Essex (Num. 23 and following); *well-hung* may mean voluble, or in contrast with *cold* may have a coarse meaning implying sexual energy

[84] Lord Gray, supposed to have been a complaisant husband (Num. 13, 30.)

[85] Lord Howard of Escrick, former preacher of the anabaptists. Canting applied to non-conformists in general; they called the services in the Prayer Book "porridge." (Lev., 10.1.)

[86] Sir William Jones, Attorney General, but afterwards against the Court (the prophet Jonas?)

[87] Slingsby Bethel, one of the sheriffs of London elected in 1680 and therefore required to call the grand jury (which refused to find a case against Shaftesbury); accused by Dryden of begrudging the usual great hospitality of the City, but a man who actually is known to have given at least one great gift to charity (II Sam. 16; I Kings 2.)

[88] wand or staff [89] applied to those who drew the Jews aside to false gods

Woud rather Curse, than break good Company.
If any durst his Factious Friends accuse,
He pact a jury of dissenting *Jews:*
Whose fellow-feeling, in the godly Cause,
Would free the suff'ring Saint[90] from Humane Laws.
For Laws are onely made to Punish those
Who serve the King, and to protect his Foes.
If any leisure time he had from Pow'r,
(Because 'tis Sin to mis-imploy an hour;)
His bus'ness was, by Writing, to persuade
That kings were Useless, and a Clog to Trade:
And, that his noble Stile he might refine,
No *Rechabite*[91] more shund the fumes of Wine.
Chaste were his Cellars; and his Shrieval[92] Board
The Grossness of a City Feast abhor'd:
His Cooks, with long disuse, their Trade forgot;
Cool was his Kitchin, though his Brains were hot.
Such frugal Vertue Malice may accuse;
But sure 'twas necessary to the *Jews:*
For Towns once burnt, such Magistrates require
As dare not tempt Gods Providence by Fire.
With Spiritual Food he fed his Servants well,
But free from Flesh that made the *Jews* rebel:
And *Moses's* Laws he held in more account,
For forty days of Fasting in the Mount.
To speak the rest, who better are forgot,
Would tire a well-breath'd Witness of the Plot:
Yet, *Corah*,[93] thou shalt from Oblivion pass;
Erect thy self thou Monumental Brass:
High as the Serpent of thy Metal made,
While Nations stand secure beneath thy shade.[94]
What though his Birth were base, yet Comets rise
From Earthy Vapours e'r they shine in Skies.
Prodigious Actions may as well be done
By Weaver's issue as by Prince's son.
This Arch-Attestor for the Publick Good
By that one Deed Enobles all his Bloud.
Who ever ask'd the Witnesses high race
Whose Oath with Martyrdom did *Stephen* grace?[95]
Ours was a *Levite*, and as times went then,
His tribe were God-almighties Gentlemen.
Sunk were his Eyes, his Voice was harsh and loud,
Sure signs he neither Cholerick was, nor Proud:
His long Chin prov'd his Wit; his Saint-like Grace
A Church Vermilion,[96] and a *Moses's* Face.
His Memory, miraculously great,
Coud Plots, exceeding mans belief, repeat;
Which, therefore cannot be accounted Lies,

[90] a title among the Dissenters for those who belonged to the true church, not a formally constituted group, but composed of the true believers, elected for salvation

[91] a sect who would drink no wine (Jer. 35.)

[92] pertaining to a sheriff [93] Titus Oates (See general introduction.)

[94] referring to the brazen serpent erected by Moses which saved the Israelites (Num. 21.6–9.)

[95] (Acts 6–8.) The witnesses are explicitly described as false.

[96] scarlet color (as if rouged and as ruddy as churchmen often are)

For humane Wit coud never such devise.
Some future Truths are mingled in his Book;
But where the Witness fail'd, the Prophet spoke:
Some things like Visionary flights appear;
The Spirit caught him up, the Lord knows where:
And gave him his *Rabinical* degree,
Unknown to Foreign University.
His Judgment yet his Mem'ry did excel,
Which piec'd his wondrous Evidence so well:
And suited to the temper of the Times;
Then groaning under *Jebusitick* Crimes.
Let *Israels* foes suspect his Heav'nly call,
And rashly judge his Writ Apocryphal;[97]
Our Laws for such affronts have Forfeits made:
He takes his Life, who takes away his Trade.
Were I myself in Witness *Corah's* place,
The Wretch who did me such a dire disgrace
Should whet my memory, though once forgot,
To make him an Appendix of my Plot.
His Zeal to Heav'n, made him his Prince despise,
And load his Person with indignities:
But Zeal peculiar priviledge[98] affords,
Indulging latitude to deeds and words:
And *Corah* might for *Agag's* murther[99] call,
In terms as course as *Samuel* us'd to *Saul*.
What others in his Evidence did join,
(The best that coud be had for love or coin,)
In *Corah's* own predicament will fall
For *Witness* is a Common Name to all.
Surrounded thus with Friends of every sort,
Deluded *Absolom* forsakes the Court:
Impatient of high hopes, urg'd with renown,
And Fir'd with near possession of a Crown.
The admiring Croud are dazled with surprize
And on his goodly person feed their eyes:
His joy conceal'd, he sets himself to show;
On each side bowing popularly low:
His looks, his gestures, and his words he frames,
And with familiar ease repeats their Names.
Thus, form'd by Nature, furnished out with Arts,
He glides unfelt into their secret hearts:
Then with a kind compassionating look,
And sighs, bespeaking pity e'r he spoke,
Few words he said, but easie those and fit,
More slow than Hybla[100] drops, and far more sweet.
I mourn, my Country-men, your lost Estate,
Though far unable to prevent your Fate:

[97] of doubtful authenticity; not in the received Protestant Canon of the Bible

[98] Some of the extreme sects claimed that being changed by the Divine Spirit, they were free of normal moral law.

[99] This is interpreted in the Key published by Tonson as referring to Godfrey, but it has been suggested by de Beer that it is the Lord Chief Justice, Scroggs, who instructed the jury to find Wakeman innocent and was attacked by Oates and Bedloe. (I Sam. 15.)

[100] famous for its honey

Behold a Banish'd man, for your dear cause
Expos'd a prey to Arbitrary Laws!
Yet oh! that I alone coud be undone,
Cut off from Empire, and no more a Son!
Now all your Liberties a spoil are made;
Egypt and *Tyrus*[101] intercept your Trade,
And *Jebusites* your Sacred Rites invade.
My Father, whom with reverence yet I name,
Charm'd into Ease, is careless of his Fame:
And, brib'd with petty sums of Foreign Gold,
Is grown in *Bathsheba's*[102] Embraces old:
Exalts his Enemies, his Friends destroys,
And all his pow'r against himself imploys.
He gives, and let him give my right away;
But why should he his own, and yours betray?
He onely, he can make the Nation bleed,
And he alone from my revenge is freed.
Take then my tears (with that he wip'd his Eyes)
'Tis all the Aid my present pow'r supplies:
No Court-Informer can these Arms accuse;
These Arms may Sons against their Fathers use;
And, 'tis my wish, the next Successor's Reign
May make no other *Israelite* complain.
  Youth, Beauty, Graceful Action seldom fail:
But Common Interest always will prevail:
And pity never Ceases to be shown
To him, who makes the Peoples wrongs his own.
The Croud, (that still believe their Kings oppress,)
With lifted hands their young *Messiah* bless:
Who now begins his Progress[103] to ordain;
With Chariots, Horsemen, and a num'rous train:
From East to West his Glories he displays:
And, like the Sun, the Promis'd Land surveys.
Fame runs before him, as the Morning-Star;
And shouts of Joy salute him from afar:
Each house receives him as a Guardian God;
And Consecrates the Place of his abode:
But hospitable Treats did most commend
Wise *Issachar*,[104] his wealthy Western Friend.
This moving Court, that caught the Peoples Eyes,
And seem'd but Pomp, did other Ends disguise:
Achitophel had form'd it, with intent
To sound the depths, and fathom where it went,
The Peoples hearts; distinguish Friends from Foes;
And trie their strength, before they came to Blows.
Yet all was colour'd with a smooth pretence
Of specious love, and duty to their Prince.
Religion, and Redress of Grievances,
Two names, that always cheat and always please,
Are often urg'd; and good King *David's* life
Endanger'd by a Brother and a Wife.

[101] France and Holland [102] the Duchess of Portsmouth, a chief mistress of the King
[103] state journey made by a sovereign, usually to honor his people and secure popularity
[104] Thomas Thynne, who entertained Monmouth on his Western trip (Gen. 49.)

Thus, in a Pageant Shew, a Plot is made;
And Peace it self is War in Masquerade.
Oh foolish *Israel!* never warn'd by Ill:
Still the same Bait, and circumvented still!
Did ever men forsake their present ease,
In midst of health imagine a Disease;
Take pains Contingent mischiefs to foresee,
Make Heirs for Monarchs, and for God decree?
What shall we think! Can People give away
Both for themselves and Sons their Native sway?
Then they are left Defenceless, to[105] the Sword
Of each unbounded Arbitrary Lord:
And Laws are vain, by which we Right enjoy,
If Kings unquestion'd can those Laws destroy.
Yet if the Croud be Judge of Fit and Just,
And Kings are onely Officers in Trust,
Then this resuming Cov'nant[106] was declar'd
When Kings were made, or is for ever bar'd:
If those who gave the Scepter, coud not tie
By their own Deed their own Posterity,
How then coud *Adam* bind his future Race?
How coud his Forfeit on Mankind take place?
Or how coud heavenly Justice damn us all
Who ne'r consented to our Fathers Fall?
Then Kings are Slaves to those whom they command,
And Tenants to their Peoples pleasure stand.
Add that the Pow'r, for Property allow'd,
Is mischievously seated in the Croud;
For who can be secure of private Right,
If Sovereign Sway may be dissolv'd by Might?
Nor is the Peoples Judgment always true:
The Most may err as grosly as the Few.
And faultless Kings run down, by Common Cry,
For Vice, Oppression and for Tyranny.
What Standard is there in a fickle rout,
Which, flowing to the Mark,[107] runs faster out?
Nor onely crouds, but Sanhedrins[108] may be
Infected with this publick Lunacy:
And Share the madness of Rebellious Times,
To Murther Monarchs for Imagin'd crimes.
If they may Give and Take when e'r they please,
Not Kings alone, (the Godheads Images,)
But Government it self at length must fall
To Natures state, where all have Right to all.[109]
Yet, grant our Lords the People Kings can make,
What prudent men a setled Throne woud shake?
For whatsoe'r their Sufferings were before,
That Change they Covet makes them suffer more.
All other Errors but disturb a State;

[105] against
[106] if government arose from a covenant among the people, and if the people retained the right to resume the power (which Hobbes had maintained could not be resumed)
[107] high-water mark or mark on a nautical measuring line
[108] parliaments
[109] before government has arisen (perhaps with Hobbes's view of the state of nature in mind)

But Innovation[110] is the Blow of Fate.
If ancient Fabricks nod, and threat to fall,
To Patch the Flaws, and Buttress up the Wall,
Thus far 'tis Duty; but here fix the Mark:
For all beyond it is to touch our Ark.[111]
To change Foundations, cast the Frame anew,
Is work for Rebels who base Ends pursue:
At once Divine and Humane Laws controul,
And mend the Parts by ruine of the Whole.
The tamp'ring World is subject to this Curse,
To Physick their Disease into a Worse.
  Now, what Relief can Righteous *David* bring?
How Fatal 'tis to be too good a King!
Friends he has few, so high the madness grows;
Who dare be such, must be the People's Foes:
Yet some there were, ev'n in the worst of days;
Some let me name, and Naming is to praise.
  In this short File *Barzillai*[112] first appears;
Barzillai crown'd with Honour and with Years:
Long since, the rising Rebels he withstood
In Regions Waste, beyond the *Jordans* Flood:[113]
Unfortunately Brave to buoy the State;
But sinking underneath his Master's Fate:
In Exile with his God-like Prince he Mourn'd,
For him he Suffer'd, and with him Return'd.
The Court he practis'd, not the Courtier's Art:
Large was his Wealth, but larger was his Heart:
Which, well the Noblest Objects knew to chuse,
The Fighting Warriour, and Recording Muse.
His Bed coud once a Fruitful Issue boast:
Now more than half a Father's Name is lost.
His Eldest Hope,[114] with every Grace adorn'd,
By me (so Heav'n will have it) always Mourn'd
And always honour'd, snatch'd in manhoods prime
B' unequal Fates and Providences crime:
Yet not before the Goal of Honour won,
All Parts fulfill'd of Subject and of Son;
Swift was the Race, but short the Time to run.
Oh Narrow Circle, but of Pow'r Divine,
Scanted in Space, but perfect in thy Line![115]
By Sea, by Land, thy Matchless Worth was known;
Arms thy Delight, and War was all thy Own:
Thy force, Infus'd, the fainting *Tyrians* prop'd;[116]
And haughty *Pharaoh* found his Fortune stop'd.
Oh Ancient Honour, Oh unconquered Hand,
Whom Foes unpunish'd never coud withstand!
But *Israel* was unworthy of thy Name:
Short is the date of all Immoderate Fame.

[110] alteration of the established order
[111] the ark of the covenant, a sacrilege to touch
[112] the Duke of Ormond (II Sam. 19.31–38.) [113] in Ireland [114] Thomas, Earl of Ossory
[115] The circle was a symbol of the divine; here a life short, but perfect; *line*, line of a drawing, form.
[116] He had fought with the Dutch under the Prince of Orange, against the French.

It looks as Heav'n our Ruine had design'd,
And durst not trust thy Fortune and thy Mind.
Now, free from Earth, thy disencumbred Soul
Mounts up, and leaves behind the Clouds and Starry Pole:
From thence thy kindred Legions maist thou bring,
To aid the Guardian Angel of thy King.
Here stop my Muse, here cease thy painful flight;
No pinions can pursue Immortal height:
Tell good *Barzillai* thou canst sing no more,
And tell thy Soul she should have fled before;
Or fled she with his life, and left this Verse
To hang on her departed Patron's Herse?[117]
Now take thy steepy flight from Heav'n, and see
If thou canst find on Earth another *He;*
Another he would be too hard to find;
See then whom thou canst see not far behind.
Zadoc[118] the priest, whom, shunning Pow'r and Place,
His lowly mind advanc'd to *David's* Grace:
With him the *Sagan* of *Jerusalem,*[119]
Of hospitable Soul and noble Stem;[120]
Him of the Western dome,[121] whose weighty sense
Flows in fit words and heavenly eloquence.
The Prophets Sons by such Example led,
To Learning and to Loyalty were bred:
For *Colleges* on bounteous Kings depend,
And never Rebel was to Arts a Friend.
To these succeed the Pillars of the Laws,
Who best coud plead, and best can judge a Cause.
Next them a train of Loyal Peers ascend:
Sharp judging *Adriel,*[122] the Muses Friend,
Himself a Muse:—In Sanhedrins debate
True to his Prince, but not a Slave of State.
Whom *David's* love with Honours did adorn,
That from his disobedient Son were torn.
Jotham[123] of piercing Wit and pregnant Thought,
Endew'd[124] by nature and by learning taught
To move Assemblies, who but onely tri'd
The worse a while, then chose the better side;
Nor chose alone, but turned the Balance too;
So much the weight of one brave man can do.
Hushai[125] the friend of *David* in distress,
In publick storms of manly stedfastness;

[117] Poems were sometimes hung over the hearse or framework set above a coffin.

[118] Sancroft, Archbishop of Canterbury (II Sam. 8.)

[119] the Bishop of London, as priest next in rank to the high priest

[120] line of ancestry, family line

[121] the Dean of Westminster Abbey, and therefore a pattern to the boys of Westminster School (of whom Dryden had once been one) who would hear his sermons

[122] the Earl of Mulgrave, perhaps the author of an *Essay on Satire*, containing characters some of whom are the same persons as Dryden here portrays; a friend and patron of Dryden (I Sam. 18.19; II Sam. 21.8.)

[123] the Earl of Halifax, who secured the vote against the Exclusion Bill in the House of Lords. See pp. 380–414.

[124] possessed of quality

[125] Laurence Hyde, Earl of Rochester (II Sam. 15–17.)

By Foreign Treaties he inform'd his Youth;
And join'd Experience to his Native Truth.
His frugal care suppli'd the wanting Throne;
Frugal for that, but bounteous of his own:
'Tis easie Conduct when Exchequers flow;
But hard the task to manage well the low:
For Sovereign Power is too deprest or high,
When Kings are forced to sell, or Crouds to buy.
Indulge one labour more, my weary Muse,
For *Amiel;*[126] who can *Amiel's* praise refuse?
Of ancient race by birth, but nobler yet
In his own worth, and without Title great:
The Sanhedrin long time as Chief he rul'd,
Their Reason guided, and their Passion cool'd;
So dextrous was he in the Crown's defence,
So form'd to speak a Loyal Nations Sense,
That, as their Band was *Israels* Tribes in small,
So fit was he to represent them all.
Now rasher Charioteers the Seat ascend,
Whose loose Carriers[127] his steady Skill commend:
They, like th' unequal Ruler of the Day,[128]
Misguide the Seasons, and mistake the Way;
While he withdrawn at their mad Labour smiles
And safe enjoys the Sabbath of his Toils.
These were the chief; a small but faithful Band
Of Worthies in the Breach who dar'd to stand
And tempt th' united Fury of the Land.
With grief they view'd such powerful Engines[129] bent
To batter down the lawful Government.
A numerous Faction with pretended frights,
In Sanhedrins to plume[130] the Regal Rights.
The true Successor from the Court remov'd:
The plot, by hireling Witnesses improv'd.
These Ills they saw, and, as their Duty bound,
They shew'd the King the danger of the Wound:
That no Concessions from the Throne woud please;
But Lenitives[131] fomented the Disease;
That *Absalom*, ambitious of the Crown,
Was made the Lure to draw the People down:
That false *Achitophel's* pernitious Hate
Had turn'd the Plot to ruine Church and State;
The Council violent, the Rabble worse:
That *Shimei* taught *Jerusalem* to Curse.
With all these loads of Injuries opprest,
And long revolving[132] in his careful Brest,
Th' event of things; at last his patience tir'd,
Thus from his Royal Throne, by Heav'n ispir'd,
The God-like *David* spoke; with awful fear

[126] Edward Seymour, speaker of the House of Commons, 1673–1679 (II Sam. 9 and 17.)

[127] career, rapid course

[128] Phaeton, who obtained from his father, Apollo, the sun, permission to drive his horses for a day, but was carried to disaster

[129] engines of war, artillery [130] strip out, (as feathers, hairs) [131] soothing drugs

[132] turning over; the phrase, like many in this passage, is Latinate, and based on Virgil

His Train[133] their Maker in their Master hear.
  Thus long have I by Native Mercy sway'd,
My Wrongs dissembl'd, my Revenge delay'd;
So willing to forgive th' Offending Age;
So much the Father did the King asswage.[134]
But now so far my Clemency they slight,
Th' Offenders question my Forgiving[135] Right.
That one was made for many, they contend;
But 'tis to Rule, for that's a Monarch's End.
They call my tenderness of Blood, my Fear,
Though Manly tempers can the longest bear.
Yet since they will divert my Native course,
'Tis time to show I am not Good by Force.
Those heap'd Affronts that haughty Subjects bring,
Are burdens for a Camel, not a King:
Kings are the publick Pillars of the State,
Born to sustain and prop the Nations weight:
If my young *Sampson* will pretend a Call
To shake the Column, let him share the Fall:[136]
But oh that yet he woud repent and live!
How easie 'tis for Parents to forgive!
With how few Tears a Pardon might be won
From Nature, pleading for a Darling Son!
Poor pitied youth, by my Paternal care,
Rais'd up to all the Height his Frame coud bear:
Had God ordain'd his Fate for Empire born,
He woud have giv'n his Soul another turn:
Gull'd with a Patriot's name,[137] whose Modern sense
Is one that woud by Law supplant his Prince:
The Peoples Brave,[138] the Politicians Tool;
Never was Patriot yet, but was a Fool.
Whence comes it that Religion and the Laws
Should more be *Absalon's* than *David's* Cause?
His old Instructor, e'r he lost his Place,
Was never thought indu'd with so much Grace.
Good heav'ns, how Faction can a Patriot Paint!
My Rebel ever proves my Peoples Saint:
Woud *They* impose an Heir upon the Throne?
Let Sanhedrins be taught to give their Own.
A king's at least a part of Government;
And mine as requisite as their Consent;
Without my leave a future King to choose,
Infers a Right the present to Depose:
True, they petition me t' approve their Choice:
But *Esau's* Hands suit ill with *Jacob's* Voice.[139]

[133] courtiers, followers, who hear the voice of God through him
[134] make mild
[135] right to forgive, or rather, right, which might punish, but is forgotten because it does forgive
[136] Sampson who, pulling down the pillars of the Temple to slay the Phillistines, was himself slain in the ruin (here, of course, an ironic reference). Lines 957–960 added in the second section
[137] See line 179.
[138] bravo, bully, brave soldier
[139] as Jacob stole Esau's birthright of the blessing from their father Isaac, by coming to the old blind man in gloves which made him appear to be hairy-handed Esau

My Pious Subjects for my Safety pray,
Which to Secure they take my Pow'r away.
From Plots and Treasons Heav'n preserve my Years,
But save me most from my Petitioners.
Unsatiate as the barren Womb or Grave;
God cannot Grant so much as they can Crave.
What then is left but with a Jealous Eye
To guard the Small remains of Royalty?
The Law shall still direct my peaceful Sway,
And the same Law teach Rebels to obey:
Votes shall no more Establish'd Pow'r controul,
Such Votes as make a Part exceed the Whole:
No groundless Clamours shall my Friends remove
Nor Crouds have pow'r to Punish e'r they Prove:
For Gods and God-like kings their Care express,
Still to defend their Servants in distress.
Oh that my Pow'r to Saving were confin'd:
Why am I forc'd, like Heav'n, against my mind,
To make Examples of another Kind?
Must I at length the Sword of Justice draw?
Oh curst Effects of necessary Law!
How ill my Fear they by my Mercy scan,
Beware the Fury of a Patient Man.
Law they require, let Law then shew her Face;
They could not be content to look on Grace,
Her hinder parts, but with a daring Eye
To tempt the terror of her Front, and die.[140]
By their own Arts 'tis Righteously decreed,
Those dire Artificers of Death shall bleed.
Against themselves their Witnesses will Swear,
Till Viper-like their Mother Plot they tear,
And such for Nutriment that bloudy gore
Which was their Principle of Life before.
Their *Belial* with their *Belzebub*[141] will fight;
Thus on my Foes, my Foes shall do me Right.
Nor doubt th' event: for Factious crouds engage
In their first Onset, all their Brutal Rage;
Then let 'em take an unresisted Course:
Retire and Traverse,[142] and Delude their Force:
But when they stand all Breathless, urge the fight,
And rise upon 'em with redoubled might:
For Lawful Pow'r is still Superiour found,
When long driv'n back, at length it stands the ground.
He said. Th' Almighty, nodding, gave Consent;
And peals of Thunder shook the Firmament.[143]
Henceforth a Series of new time began,
The mighty Years in long Procession ran:
Once more the God-like *David* was Restor'd,
And willing Nations knew their Lawful Lord.

[140] Moses (Exodus 33) was forbidden to see the Lord's face, which no man could see and live, but was allowed to see his hinder parts as he passed by.

[141] devils; witnesses to the Plot

[142] move from side to side in fencing or fighting

[143] The image is taken from the mode in which the Greek Zeus or Roman Jove signifies assent.

MacFLECKNOE. OR A SATYR UPON THE TRUE-BLEW PROTESTANT POET, T. S.[1]

All humane things are subject to decay,
And, when Fate summons, Monarchs must obey:
This *Fleckno*[2] found, who, like *Augustus*,[3] young
Was call'd to Empire and had govern'd long:
In Prose and Verse was own'd, without dispute
Through all the realms of Non-sense, absolute.
This aged Prince now flourishing in Peace,
And blest with issue of a large increase,
Worn out with business, did at length debate
To settle the Succession of the State;
And pond'ring which of all his Sons was fit
To Reign, and wage immortal War with Wit,
Cry'd, 'tis resolv'd; for Nature pleads that He
Should onely rule, who most resembles me:
Sh——[4] alone my perfect image bears,
Mature in dullness from his tender years;
Sh—— alone of all my Sons is he
Who stands confirm'd in full stupidity.
The rest to some faint meaning make pretence,
But *Sh*—— never deviates into sense.
Some Beams of Wit on other souls may fall,
Strike through and make a lucid intervall;
But *Sh*——'s genuine night admits no ray,
His risings Fogs prevail upon the Day:
Besides, his goodly Fabrick fills the eye
And seems design'd for thoughtless Majesty:
Thoughtless as Monarch Oakes, that shade the plain,
And, spread in solemn state, supinely reign.
Heywood and *Shirley*[5] were but Types of thee,
Thou last great Prophet of Tautology:[6]
Even I, a dunce of more renown than they,
Was sent before but to prepare thy way;
And coarsely clad in *Norwich* Drugget came
To teach the Nations in thy greater name.[7]
My warbling Lute, the Lute I whilom strung,

[1] very probably written in 1678, and circulated in manuscript; published in an unauthorized and poor text, 1682. Text, *Miscellany Poems,* 1684 (the second and authorized edition, though unsigned by Dryden)

[2] an Irish Catholic priest and minor poet (earlier pilloried by Marvell); died 1678

[3] who became emperor, after the end of the Triumvirate, as heir to Caesar, at the age of 32

[4] Shadwell, a rival dramatist, who claimed alone to understand how to follow Jonson in writing comedy of humors

[5] earlier dramatists, very popular with the city in their day, but not in the great line of dramatists as Dryden and the Court judged

[6] the repeating of the same thing in different words, pointlessly

[7] *Norwich* Drugget, a coarse woolen fabric, worn by poor men of letters (and incidentally said to have been worn by Dryden himself in his earlier days); but more importantly, Flecknoe is alluding to himself as only proclaiming the true prophet of dullness, as John the Baptist came to preach Christ

When to King *John* of *Portugal* I sung,[8]
Was but the prelude to that glorious day,
When thou on silver *Thames* did'st cut thy way,
With well tim'd oars before the Royal Barge,
Swelled with the Pride of thy Celestial charge;
And, big with Hymn, Commander of an Host,
The like was ne'er in *Epsom* blankets tost.[9]
Methinks I see the new *Arion* Sail,[10]
The Lute still trembling underneath thy nail.
At thy well sharpned thumb from Shore to Shore
The Treble squeaks for fear, the Bases roar:
Echoes from *Pissing-Ally, Sh*—— call,
And *Sh*—— they resound from *A*[*ston*] *Hall.*[11]
About thy boat the little Fishes throng,[12]
As at the Morning Toast,[13] that Floats along.
Sometimes, as Prince of thy Harmonious band,
Thou wield'st thy Papers in thy threshing hand.
St. *André*'s[14] feet ne'er kept more equal time,
Not ev'n the feet of thy own *Psyche*'s rhime:[15]
Though they in number as in sense excell,
So just, so like tautology they fell
That, pale with envy, *Singleton*[16] forswore
The Lute and Sword which he in Triumph bore,
And vow'd he ne'er would act *Villerius* more.
Here stopt the good old Syre; and wept for joy,
In silent raptures of the hopefull boy.
All Arguments, but most his Plays, perswade
That for anointed dulness he was made.
Close to the Walls which fair *Augusta*[17] bind,
(The fair *Augusta* much to fears inclin'd)
An ancient fabrick, raised t' inform the sight,
There stood of yore, and *Barbican*[18] it hight:
A watch Tower once, but now, so Fate ordains,
Of all the Pile an empty name remains.
From its old Ruins Brothel houses rise,
Scenes of lewd loves, and of polluted joys,
Where their vast Courts the Mother-Strumpets keep,
And, undisturbed by Watch, in silence sleep.[19]
Near these a Nursery erects its head,

[8] Flecknoe had visited Portugal. The lines recall (in parody) a scene in Waller's poem on Prince Charles's escape at St. Andrew's (in Spain) in which the prince entertained guests on the water (N. H. Oswald, *The Satires of John Dryden: a Critical Edition*, unpublished U. of California Thesis, 1946).

[9] Shadwell's *Sullen Lovers* has such a scene; and he wrote a play *Epsom Wells*.

[10] Arion, a Greek musician, jumping overboard to escape the jealousy of his fellow sailors was, for his music, carried safely by dolphins.

[11] Reference unknown.

[12] no specific incident is known [13] Offal floating on the river, like toast on wine.

[14] a famous dancing master [15] an opera by Shadwell

[16] Singleton, a noted musical performer, gives up the part of Villerius in Davenant's *Seige of Rhodes.*

[17] London, fearful of plots

[18] Barbican, in the city; Bun-Hill, Watling Street, outlying and very unfashionable parts of London

[19] These two lines parody a description of the infernal regions in Cowley's *Davideis. Watch,* officers of the law

Where Queens are formed, and future Hero's bred;
Where unfledged Actors learn to laugh and cry,
Where infant Punks their tender voices try,
And little *Maximins*[20] the Gods defy.
Great *Fletcher* never treads in Buskings here,
Nor greater *Johnson* dares in Socks appear.[21]
But gentle *Simkin* just reception finds
Amidst this Monument of vanisht minds;
Pure Clinches[22] the suburbian Muse affords;
And *Panton*[23] waging harmless war with words.
Here *Fleckno*, as a place to Fame well known,
Ambitiously design'd his *Sh*——'s throne.
For ancient *Decker*[24] prophesi'd long since,
That in this Pile should Reign a mighty Prince,
Born for a scourge of Wit, and flayle of Sense,
To whom true dulness should some *Psyches*[25] owe,
But Worlds of *Misers* from his pen should flow;
Humorists and Hypocrites it should produce,
Whole *Raymond* Families and Tribes of *Bruce*.
Now Empress Fame had publisht the renown,
Of *Sh*——'s Coronation through the Town.
Rows'd by report of Fame, the Nations meet,
From near *Bun-Hill* and distant *Watling-street*.
No *Persian* Carpets spread th' imperial way,
But scatter'd Limbs of mangled Poets lay:
From dusty shops neglected Authors come,
Martyrs of Pies and Reliques of the Bum.[26]
Much *Heywood*, *Shirly*, *Ogleby* there lay,[27]
But loads of *Sh*—— almost choakt the way.
Bilk't[28] *Stationers* for Yoemen stood prepar'd
And *H*[*erringman*][29] was Captain of the Guard.
The hoary Prince in Majesty appear'd,
High on a Throne of his own Labours rear'd.
At his right hand our young *Ascanius* sat
Rome's other hope and Pillar of the State.[30]
His Brows thick fogs, instead of glories, grace,
And lambent dullness plaid around his face.
As *Hannibal* did to the Altars come,
Swore by his *Syre* a mortal Foe to *Rome*;[31]

[20] a ranting, much-mocked character in Dryden's early play *Tyrannic Love*

[21] Fletcher, in tragic foot-gear, Jonson, in comic, the great Jacobean dramatists

[22] puns, plays on words [23] said to be a celebrated punster

[24] Thomas Dekker, Jacobean dramatist, popular in the city, a rival of Jonson

[25] This and the next two lines refer to plays, adaptations, characters by Shadwell.

[26] unsold plays, reduced to be used as paper, for these low needs. *Hypocrites* should be italicized as an unpublished play by Shadwell (Borgman, *Shadwell* 1928).

[27] See line 29; Ogleby, a prolific translator of Dryden's day, not very skillful

[28] Book-sellers whose bills or profit have not been paid them take the place of yeomen in a royal pageant.

[29] Dryden's early publisher up to 1678, as well as Shadwell's; Dryden perhaps when he first came to London did hack-work for him.

[30] Ascanius in Virgil described as here, is the son of Aeneas, who is destined to found the Roman state.

[31] Hannibal is said at the age of nine to have taken a solemn oath never to make peace with Rome, which later he almost conquered.

So *Sh*—— swore, nor should his Vow bee vain,
That he till Death true dullness would maintain;
And, in his father's Right, and Realms defence,
Ne'er to have Peace with Wit, nor truce with Sense.
The King himself the sacred Unction made,
As King by Office, and as Priest by Trade:
In his sinister[32] hand, instead of Ball,
He placed a mighty Mug of potent Ale;
Love's Kingdom[33] to his right he did convey,
At once his Sceptre and his rule of Sway;
Whose righteous Lore the Prince had practis'd young
And from whose Loyns recorded *Psyche* sprung.
His temples, last, with Poppies[34] were o'erspread,
That nodding seem'd to consecrate his head:
Just at that point of time, if Fame not lye,
On his left hand twelve reverend *Owls* did fly.
So *Romulus*,[35] tis sung, by *Tyber*'s *Brook*,
Presage of Sway from twice six Vultures took.
Th' admiring throng loud acclamations make
And Omens of his future Empire take.
The Syre then shook the honours of his head,
And from his brows damps of oblivion shed
Full on the filial dullness: long he stood,
Repelling from his Breast the raging God;
At length burst out in this prophetick mood:
  Heavens bless my Son, from *Ireland* let him reign
To far *Barbadoes* on the Western main;
Of his Dominion may no end be known,
And greater than his Father's be his Throne.
Beyond loves Kingdom let him stretch his Pen;
He paused, and all the people cry'd *Amen*.
Then thus continued he, my son, advance
Still in new Impudence, new Ignorance.
Success let others teach, learn thou from me
Pangs without birth, and fruitless Industry.
Let *Virtuoso*'s in five years be Writ;
Yet not one thought accuse thy toyl of Wit.
Let gentle *George*[36] in triumph tread the stage,
Make *Dorimant* betray, and *Loveit* rage;
Let *Cully*, *Cockwood*, *Fopling*, charm the Pit,
And in their folly show the Writers wit.
Yet still thy fools shall stand in thy defence
And justifie their Author's want of sense.
Let 'em be all by thy own model made
Of dulness and desire no foreign aid:
That they to future ages may be known,
Not Copies drawn, but Issue of thy own.
Nay let thy men of wit too be the same,

[32] left. The term would be used in heraldry, as befits a coronation and the pageantry of it burlesqued in this and the following lines.

[33] Flecknoe wrote a play called *Love's Kingdom.*

[34] symbols of drowsiness, as producing opium

[35] one of the twin founders of Rome

[36] Sir George Etherege, one of the court circle and a writer of the comedies in which the following characters appear

All full of thee, and differing but in name;
But let no alien *S-dl-y*[37] interpose
To lard with wit thy hungry *Epsom* prose.
And when false flowers of *Rhetorick*[38] thou would'st cull,
Trust Nature, do not labour to be dull;
But write thy best, and top; and in each line
Sir *Formal's*[39] oratory will be thine.
Sir *Formal*, though unsought, attends thy quill,
And does thy *Northern Dedications*[40] fill.
Nor let false friends seduce thy mind to fame,
By arrogating *Johnson*'s[41] Hostile name.
Let Father *Fleckno* fire thy mind with praise
And Uncle *Ogleby* thy envy raise.
Thou art my blood, where *Johnson* has no part:
What share have we in Nature or in Art?
Where did his wit on learning fix a brand
And rail at Arts he did not understand?
Where made he love in Prince *Nicander*'s[42] vein,
Or swept the dust in *Psyche*'s humble strain?
Where sold he Bargains, Whip stitch, kiss my Arse,[43]
Promis'd a Play and dwindled to a Farce?
When did his Muse from *Fletcher* scenes purloin,
As thou whole *Eth'ridg* dost transfuse to thine?
But so transfused as Oyls on Waters flow,
His always floats above, thine sinks below.
This is thy Province, this thy wondrous way,
New Humours[44] to invent for each new Play:
This is that boasted Byas[45] of thy mind,
By which one way, to dullness, 'tis inclin'd,
Which makes thy writings lean on oneside still,
And, in all changes that way bends thy will.
Nor let thy mountain belly make pretence
Of likeness; thine's a tympany[46] of sense.
A Tun[47] of Man in thy large Bulk is writ,
But sure thou 'rt but a Kilderkin[48] of wit.
Like mine thy gentle numbers feebly creep;
Thy Tragick Muse gives smiles, thy Comick sleep.
With whate'er gall thou settst thy self to write,
Thy inoffensive Satyrs[49] never bite.
In thy fellonious heart though Venom lies,

[37] Sir Charles Sedley, a patron of Shadwell, who had written a prologue for his *Epsom Wells*

[38] the term applied to the various figures of speech taught from the rhetoric books

[39] an orator in Shadwell's *Virtuoso*

[40] dedications to the Duke and Duchess of Newcastle

[41] Shadwell claimed to be the comedian who followed Ben Jonson in writing comedy of humors, but as Dryden held that he did not truly understand Jonson's comedy, and as Flecknoe held that it was his gift to be dull, Jonson is hostile.

[42] a character in *Psyche*

[43] vulgar language representative of Shadwell's attempts at the comic [44] See note 41.

[45] inclination: metaphor from the game of bowls

[46] morbid swelling, tumor; figuratively, bombast; Shadwell, like Jonson, being very large

[47] very large cask, holding 252 wine gallons

[48] small cask containing 16 or 18 gallons

[49] satire; the spelling recalls the then supposed connection of the word with a satyr, or goat-like creature of Greek folk-lore

It does but touch thy *Irish* pen, and dyes[50]
Thy Genius calls thee not to purchase fame
In keen Iambicks, but mild Anagram:
Leave writing Plays, and chuse for thy command
Some peacefull Province in Acrostick Land.
There thou maist wings display, and Altars raise,
And torture one poor word Ten thousand ways;[51]
Or, if thou would'st thy diff'rent talants suit,[52]
Set thy own Songs, and sing them to thy lute.
He said, but his last words were scarcely heard
For *Bruce* and *Longvil* had a *Trap* prepar'd,[53]
And down they sent the yet declaiming Bard.
Sinking he left his Drugget robe behind,
Borne upwards by A subterranean wind.
The Mantle fell to the young Prophet's part[54]
With double portion of his Father's Art.

from THE SECOND PART OF ABSALOM AND ACHITOPHEL[1]

Next these, a Troop of buisy Spirits press,
Of little Fortunes, and of Conscience Less;
With them the Tribe, whose Luxury had drain'd
Their Banks, in former Sequestrations[2] gain'd:
Who Rich and Great by past Rebellions grew,
And long to fish the troubled Waves anew.
Some future Hopes, some present Payment draws,
To Sell their Conscience and espouse the Cause,
Such Stipends those vile Hirelings best befit,
Priests without Grace, and Poets without wit,
Shall that false *Hebronite*[3] escape our Curse,
Judas[4] that keeps the Rebells Pension-Purse;
Judas that pays the Treason-writers Fee,
Judas that well deserves his Namesake's Tree;
Who at *Jerusalem's* own Gates Erects
His College for a Nursery of Sects.
Young Prophets with an early Care secures,
And with the Dung of his own Arts manures.
What have the Men of *Hebron* here to doe?
What part in *Israels* promis'd Land have you?
Here *Phaleg*[5] the Lay *Hebronite* is come,
'Cause like the rest he could not live at Home;

[50] Snakes cannot live in Ireland; Shadwell becomes Irish as the son of Flecknoe.

[51] George Herbert had written emblem poems the length of whose lines gave them these shapes on the page; but such emblems had passed with metaphysical poetry, and Dryden lumps them with anagrams and acrostics.

[52] bring into agreement

[53] Dryden takes this device from Shadwell's own *Virtuoso*.

[54] as Elijah's mantle fell on Elisha

[1] By Dryden and Tate. These are Dryden's lines. Text: second edition, 1682

[2] seizures of property by the State, referring to many sequestrations from the royalists in the Civil War, the proceeds of which were granted to Parliament men

[3] Scotchman

[4] Robert Ferguson, a non-conformist preacher, a pamphleteer for Shaftesbury at this time

[5] James Forbes, a Scottish dissenting clergyman, an unsuccessful tutor to the young Earl of Derby. I Chron. 1, 19.

Who from his own Possessions cou'd not drain
An *Omer*[6] even of *Hebronitish* Grain,
Here Struts it like a Patriot, and talks high
Of Injur'd Subjects, alter'd Property:
An Emblem of that buzzing Insect Just,
That mounts the Wheell, and thinks she raises Dust.
Can dry Bones Live? or *Skeletons* produce
The Vital Warmth of Cuckoldizing Juice?
Slim *Phaleg* cou'd, and at the Table fed,
Return'd the gratefull product to the Bed.
A Waiting-man to Trav'ling Nobles chose,
He, his own Laws wou'd Sawcily impose;
Till Bastinado'd[7] back again he went,
To Learn those Manners he to Teach was sent.
Chastiz'd, he ought to have retreated Home,
But He reads politicks to *Absalom.*
For never *Hebronite*, though Kickt and Scorn'd,
To his own Country willingly return'd.
—But leaving famish'd *Phaleg* to be fed
And to talk Treason for his daily Bread,
Let *Hebron*, nay let Hell produce a Man
So made for Mischief as *Ben Jochanan*[8]
A *Jew* of humble Parentage was He,
By Trade a Levite, though of low Degree:
His Pride no higher than the Desk aspir'd,
But for the Drudgery of Priests was hir'd
To Reade and Pray in Linen Ephod brave,
And pick up single Sheckles[9] from the Grave.
Married at last, and finding Charge come faster,
He cou'd not live by God, but chang'd his Master:
Inspir'd by Want, was made a Factious Tool,
They Got a Villain, and we lost a Fool.
Still Violent, whatever Cause he took,
But most against the Party he forsook,
For Renegadoes, who ne'er turn by halves,
Are bound in Conscience to be double Knaves.
So this Prose-Prophet took most monstrous Pains
To let his Masters see he earn'd his Gains.
But as the Dev'l ows all his Imps a Shame,
He chose th' *Apostate* for his proper Theme;
With little Pains he made the Picture true,
And from Reflexion took the Rogue he drew.
A wondrous Work, to prove the *Jewish* nation
In every Age a Murmuring Generation;
To trace 'em from their Infancy of Sinning,
And shew 'em Factious from their First Beginning;
To prove they cou'd Rebell, and Rail, and Mock,
Much to the Credit of the Chosen Flock;
A strong Authority which must Convince,
That Saints own no Allegiance to their Prince.

[6] a Biblical measure [7] beaten

[8] the Reverend Samuel Johnson, who wrote a pamphlet drawing a parallel for rebellion from the martyrs under Julian the Apostate

[9] Jewish coin

As 'tis a Leading-Card[10] to make a Whore,
To prove her Mother had turn'd up before.
But tell me, did the Drunken *Patriarch*[11] Bless
The Son that shewd his Father's Nakedness?[12]
Such Thanks the present Church thy Pen will give,
Which proves Rebellion was so Primitive.
Must Ancient Failings be Examples made,
Then Murtherers from *Cain* may learn their Trade?
As thou the Heathen and the Saint hast drawn,
Methinks th' Apostate was the better man:
And thy hot *Father* (waving my respect)
Not of a mother church but of a Sect.[13]
And Such he needs must be of thy Inditing,
This Comes of drinking Asses milk and writing.
If *Balack*[14] should be cal'd to leave his place,
(As Profit is the loudest call of Grace,)
His Temple, dispossessed of one, would be
Replenish'd with seven Devils more by thee.
Levi,[15] thou art a load, I'll lay thee down,
And shew Rebellion bare, without a Gown;
Poor Slaves in metre, dull and adle-pated,
Who Rhime below ev'n *David's* Psalms translated.[16]
Some in my Speedy pace I must outrun,
As lame *Mephibosheth*[17] the Wisard's Son;
To make quick way I'll Leap o'er heavy blocks,
Shun rotten *Uzza*[18] as I woud the Pox;
And hasten *Og* and *Doeg* to rehearse,
Two Fools that Crutch their Feeble sense on Verse,
Who by my Muse, to all succeeding times
Shall live in spight of their own Dogrell Rhimes.
Doeg,[19] though without knowing how or why,
Made still a blund'ring kind of Melody;
Spurd boldly on, and Dash'd through Thick and Thin,
Through Sense and Non-sense; never out nor in;
Free from all meaning, whether good or bad,
And in one word, Heroically mad:
He was too warm on Picking-work to dwell,
But Faggotted his Notions as they fell,
And, if they Rhim'd and Rattl'd, all was well.[20]
Spightfull he is not, though he wrote a Satyr,
For still there goes some *thinking* to ill-Nature:

[10] that is, the card which determines the suit to be followed

[11] text: *Patriot;* but *Patriarch* of the first edition is correct

[12] alluding to the story of the drunkenness of Noah (Gen. 9.18–27.)

[13] Johnson drew on a furious writing of Gregory Nazianzen against Julian.

[14] Gilbert Burnet (see *The Hind and the Panther*), whom Charles tried to have dismissed as Chaplain of the Rolls (Num. 22–24)

[15] i.e., the clergy

[16] by Sternhold and Hopkins (see *Religio Laici* and *Essay of Dramatic Poesy*.)

[17] Samuel Pordage, reputed author of several pamphlets in answer to Dryden (II Sam. 4–21.)

[18] listed in the Key as J. H. (I Chron. 13.)

[19] Elkenah Settle, a very minor writer, Tory, then Whig, then Tory; active in burning the Pope in effigy while a Whig, at this time; writer of answers to and attacks on Dryden (I Sam. 21–22.)

[20] These lines were suggested by a character of a schoolboy, written by Shadwell (Oswald).

He needs no more than Birds and Beasts to think,
All his occasions are to eat and drink.
If he call Rogue and Rascal from a Garrat,
He means you no more Mischief than a Parat:
The words for Friend and Foe alike were made,
To Fetter 'em in Verse is all his Trade.
For Almonds he'll cry Whore to his own Mother:
And call young *Absalom* King *David's* Brother.[21]
Let him be Gallows-Free by my consent,
And nothing suffer, since he nothing meant:
Hanging Supposes humane Soul and reason,
This Animal's below committing Treason:
Shall he be hang'd who never cou'd Rebell?
That's a preferment for *Achitophel.*
The Woman that Committed Buggary,
Was rightly Sentenc'd by the Law to die;
But 'twas hard Fate that to the Gallows led
The Dog that never heard the Statute read.
Railing in other Men may be a crime,
But ought to pass for mere instinct in him;
Instinct he follows and no farther knows,
For to write Verse with him is to *Transprose.*
'Twere pity treason at his Door to lay
Who *makes Heaven's gate a Lock to its own Key:*[22]
Let him rayl on, let his invective muse
Have four and Twenty letters to abuse,[23]
Which if he Jumbles to one line of Sense,
Indict him of a Capital Offence.
In Fire-works give him leave to vent his spight,
Those are the only Serpents[24] he can write;
The height of his ambition is we know
But to be Master of a Puppet-show;[25]
On that one Stage his works may yet appear,
And a months Harvest keeps him all the Year.
   Now stop your noses, Readers, all and some,
For here's a tun of Midnight work to come,
Og[26] from a Treason Tavern rowling home.
Round as a Globe, and Liquored ev'ry chink,
Goodly and Great he Sayls behind his Link;
With all this Bulk there's nothing lost in *Og,*
For ev'ry inch that is not Fool is Rogue:
A Monstrous mass of foul corrupted matter,
As all the Devils had spew'd to make the batter.
When wine has given him courage to Blaspheme,
He curses God, but God before Curst him;
And if man cou'd have reason, none has more,
That made his Paunch so rich and him so poor.
With wealth he was not trusted, for Heav'n knew
What 'twas of Old to pamper up a *Jew;*

[21] In his poem *Absalom Senior or Achetophel Tranpros'd,* Absalom represented Charles's brother, the Duke of York.

[22] a line from his poem [23] i and j u and v being regarded as one letter (Noyes)

[24] still a kind of fire-work

[25] He *was* finally connected with one. Puppet shows are especially given at Christmas time.

[26] Shadwell (Deut. 1 and 3.)

To what would he on Quail and Pheasant swell,
That ev'n on Tripe and Carrion cou'd rebell?
But though Heaven made him poor, (with rev'rence speaking,)
He never was a Poet of God's making;
The Midwife laid her hand on his Thick Skull,
With this Prophetick blessing—*Be thou Dull;*
Drink, Swear, and Roar, forbear no lew'd delight
Fit for thy Bulk, doe anything but write.
Thou art of lasting Make, like thoughtless men,
A strong Nativity—but for the Pen;
Eat Opium, mingle Arsenick in thy Drink,
Still thou mayst live, avoiding Pen and Ink.
I see, I see, 'tis Counsell given in vain,
For Treason botcht in Rhime will be thy bane;
Rhime is the Rock on which thou art to wreck,
'Tis fatal to thy Fame and to thy Neck.
Why should thy Metre good King *David* blast?
A Psalm of his will Surely be thy last.
Dar'st thou presume in verse to meet thy foes,
Thou whom the Penny Pamphlet foil'd in prose?
Doeg, whom God for Mankinds mirth has made,
O'er-tops thy tallent in thy very Trade;
Doeg to thee, thy paintings are so Course,
A Poet is, though he's the Poets Horse.
A Double Noose thou on thy Neck dost pull
For writing Treason and for Writing dull;
To die for Faction is a common Evil,
But to he hang'd for Non-sense is the Devil.
Hadst thou the Glories of thy King exprest,
Thy praises had been Satyr at the best;
But thou in Clumsy verse, unlickt, unpointed,
Hast Shamefully defi'd the Lord's Anointed:
I will not rake the Dunghill of thy Crimes,
For who would reade thy Life that reads thy rhimes?
But of King *David's* Foes be this the Doom,
May all be like the Young-man *Absalom;*
And for my Foes may this their Blessing be,
To talk like *Doeg* and to Write like Thee.

RELIGIO LAICI; OR, A LAYMAN'S FAITH. A POEM[1]

Dim, as the borrow'd beams of Moon and Stars
To *lonely*, *weary*, *wandring* Travellers,
Is *Reason* to the *Soul:* And as on high,
Those rowling Fires *discover* but the Sky
Not light us *here;* so *Reason's* glimmering Ray
Was lent, not to *assure* our *doubtfull* way,
But *guide* us upward to a *better Day*.
And as those nightly Tapers disappear
When Day's bright Lord ascends our Hemisphere;
So pale grows *Reason* at *Religions* sight;
So *dyes*, and so *dissolves* in *Supernatural Light*.

[1] first published, November 1682; Text: third edition, 1683

Some few, whose Lamp shone brighter,[2] have been led
From Cause to Cause, to *Natures* secret head;
And found that *one first principle* must be:
But *what*, or *who*, that *UNIVERSAL HE;*
Whether some *Soul* incompassing this Ball
Unmade, unmov'd; yet *making, moving All;*
Or various *Atom's*, interfering Dance
Leapt into *Form*, (the Noble work of *Chance;*)
Or this great *All* was from *Eternity;*
Not ev'n the *Stagirite* himself could see;
And *Epicurus guess'd* as well as He:
As *blindly* grop'd they for a *future* State;
As *rashly Judg'd* of *Providence* and *Fate:*
But least of all could their Endeavours find
What most concern'd the good of Humane kind:
For *Happiness* was never to be found;
But vanish'd from 'em, like Enchanted ground.
One thought *Content* the Good to be enjoy'd:
This, every little *Accident* destroy'd:
The *wiser Madmen* did for *Vertue* toyl:
A Thorny, or at best a barren Soil:
In *Pleasure* some their glutton Souls would steep;
But found their Line too short, the Well too deep;
And leaky Vessels which no *Bliss* cou'd keep.[3]
Thus, *anxious Thoughts* in *endless Circles* roul,
Without a *Centre* where to fix the *Soul:*
In this wilde Maze their vain Endeavours end.
How can the *less* the *Greater* comprehend?
Or *finite Reason* reach *Infinity?*
For what cou'd *Fathom GOD* were *more* than *He.*
The *Deist*[4] thinks he stands on firmer ground;
Cries ἑύρεκα[5] the mighty Secret's found:

[2] There follows a survey of important ancient attempts to explain the universe and to define the aim or end of human nature. The philosophers chiefly described are Aristotle (the Stagerite, i.e., citizen of Stagira), who argued from the motion of the cosmos back to the unmoved first mover; and Epicurus, who developed an atomic philosophy, which supposed the world to have arisen from the random movement of atoms ("the gods" living in a serene world above and unconcerned with ours). As to the end of life, Aristotle and others argued that it was virtue; the Cyrenaics, pleasure; Epicurus was often cited earlier as arguing for sensual pleasure; but by this time it was well known that the pleasure he argued for was not to be found in the senses, or in worldly activity, but in the content of a self-dependence, free from the world.

[3] the Christian (and the Stoic and Epicurean) argument that the pleasure of the senses is overbalanced by the ennui which it brings

[4] The great medieval tradition had held that man's reason, despite its partial corruption by original sin, could by its natural operation understand that there was a God, that he ought to be worshipped by prayer and praise, and that the perfect order of a future world would redress the imperfect justice of this, truths confirmed by the fact that they were held everywhere and by all, always. It held, however, that the truths given us in revelation, and the grace of God, were necessary to live this life well and to achieve that after-life. But in the seventeenth century, the idea of natural religion rather than an elaboration of theological dogma became attractive to some minds and was fully worked out in a body of thought called Deism, involving a purely impersonal relation to God, as opposed to Theism, which posits an immediate personal relationship. Dryden, contrary to the view of the medieval church and of the *via media* of the Anglican Church, holds the sceptical view that reason can tell man very little indeed.

[5] *I have found it*, a Greek phrase spoken by Archimedes when he thought of the theory of specific gravity and now applied to anyone who has found the answer to an intellectual search

God is that *Spring* of *Good; Supreme*, and *Best;*
We, made to *serve*, and in that Service *blest;*
If so, some *Rules* of Worship must be given,
Distributed alike to all by Heaven:
Else *God* were *partial*, and to *some* deny'd
The Means his Justice shou'd for *all* provide.
This *general Worship* is to *PRAISE*, and *PRAY:*
One part to *borrow* Blessings, one to *pay:*
And when frail Nature slides into *Offence*,
The *Sacrifice* for *Crimes* is *Penitence*.
Yet, since th' Effects of Providence, we find
Are variously dispens'd to Humane kind;
That *Vice Triumphs*, and *Vertue suffers* here,
(A Brand that Sovereign Justice cannot bear;)
Our Reason prompts us to a *future* State:
The *last Appeal* from *Fortune*, and from *Fate:*[6]
Where God's all-righteous ways will be declar'd;
The *Bad* meet *Punishment*, the *Good*, *Reward*.
  Thus Man by his own strength to Heaven wou'd soar:
And wou'd not be Oblig'd to God for more.
Vain, wretched Creature, how art thou misled
To think thy Wit these God-like Notions bred!
These Truths are not the product of thy Mind,
But dropt from Heaven, and of a Nobler kind.
Reveal'd Religion first inform'd thy Sight,
And *Reason* saw not, till *Faith* sprung[7] the Light.
Hence all thy *Natural Worship* takes the *Source:*
'Tis *Revelation* what thou thinkst *Discourse*.[8]
Else, how com'st *Thou* to see these truths so clear,
Which so obscure to *Heathens* did appear?
Not *Plato* these, nor *Aristotle* found:
Nor He whose Wisedom *Oracles* renown'd.[9]
Hast thou a Wit so deep, or so sublime,
Or canst thou lower dive, or higher climb?
Canst *Thou*, by *Reason*, more of *God-head* know
Than *Plutarch*, *Seneca*, or *Cicero?*
Those Gyant Wits, in happyer Ages born,
(When *Arms*, and *Arts* did *Greece* and *Rome* adorn)
Knew no such *Systeme:* no such Piles cou'd raise
Of *Natural Worship*, built on *Pray'r* and *Praise*,
To One sole GOD.
Nor did Remorse, to Expiate Sin, prescribe:
But slew their fellow Creatures for a Bribe:[10]
The guiltless *Victim* groan'd for their Offence;
And *Cruelty*, and *Blood* was *Penitence*.
If *Sheep* and *Oxen* cou'd Attone for Men
Ah! at how cheap a rate the *Rich* might Sin!
And great Oppressours might Heavens Wrath beguile
By offering his own Creatures for a Spoil!
  Dar'st thou, poor Worm, offend *Infinity?*
And must the Terms of Peace be given by *Thee?*

[6] from a blind distribution of events by fortune, or a deterministic one by fate
[7] roused (the game) from the covert [8] activity of the reason
[9] Socrates, called by the Delphic oracle the wisest of the Greeks
[10] in sacrifice of animals

Then *Thou* art *Justice* in the *last Appeal;*
Thy easie God instructs Thee to *rebell:*
And, like a King remote, and weak, must take
What Satisfaction *Thou* art pleas'd to make.
But if there be a *Pow'r* too *Just*, and *strong*
To wink at *Crimes*, and bear unpunish'd *Wrong;*
Look humbly upward, see his Will disclose
The *Forfeit* first, and then the *Fine* impose:
A *Mulct*[11] *thy* Poverty cou'd never pay
Had not *Eternal Wisedom* found the way:
And with Cœlestial Wealth supply'd thy Store:
His Justice makes the *Fine*, *his Mercy* quits the *Score.*
See God descending in thy Humane Frame;
Th' *offended*, suff'ring in th' *Offenders* Name:
All thy Misdeeds to him imputed see,
And all his Righteousness devolv'd on thee.
For granting we have Sin'd, and that th' offence
Of *Man*, is made against *Omnipotence*,
Some Price, that bears *proportion*, must be paid;
And *Infinite* with *Infinite* be weigh'd.
See then the *Deist lost: Remorse* for *Vice*,
Not paid, or *paid, inadequate* in price:
What farther means can *Reason* now direct,
Or what Relief from *humane Wit* expect?
That shews us *sick;* and sadly are we sure
Still to be *Sick*, till *Heav'n* reveal the *Cure:*
If then *Heaven's Will* must needs be understood,
(Which must, if we want *Cure*, and *Heaven*, be *Good*)
Let all Records of *Will reveal'd* be shown;
With *Scripture*, all in equal ballance thrown,
And *our one Sacred Book* will be *That one.*
Proof needs not here, for whether we compare
That Impious, Idle, Superstitious Ware
Of *Rites, Lustrations, Offerings*, (which before,
In various Ages, various Countries bore)
With *Christian Faith* and *Vertues*, we shall find
None answ'ring the great ends of humane kind
But *This one Rule of Life: That* shews us best
How *God* may be *appeas'd*, and *Mortals blest.*
Whether[12] from length of *Time* its worth we draw,
The *World* is scarce more *Ancient* than the *Law:*
Heav'ns early Care prescrib'd for every Age;
First, in the *Soul*, and after, in the *Page.*
Or, whether more abstractedly we look,
Or on the *Writers*, or the *written Book*,
Whence, but from *Heav'n*, cou'd men unskill'd in Arts,
In several Ages born, in several parts,
Weave such *agreeing Truths?* or *how*, or *why*
Shou'd *all* conspire to cheat us with a *Lye?*
Unask'd their *Pains*, *ungratefull* their *Advice*,
Starving their *Gain*, and *Martyrdom* their *Price.*
If on the Book it self we cast our view,

[11] fine imposed for offense
[12] Note that the construction here goes back to line 126.

Concurrent Heathens[13] prove the Story *True:*
The *Doctrine, Miracles;* which must convince,
For *Heav'n* in *Them* appeals to *humane Sense:*
And though they *prove* not, they *Confirm* the Cause,
When what is *Taught* agrees with *Natures Laws.*
Then for the *Style; Majestick* and *Divine,*
It speaks no less than God in every Line:
Commanding words; whose *Force* is still the same
As the first *Fiat*[14] that produc'd our Frame.[15]
All Faiths *beside,* or[16] did by *Arms* ascend;
Or *Sense* indulg'd has made *Mankind* their *Friend:*
This *onely* Doctrine does our *Lusts* oppose:
Unfed by Natures Soil, in which it grows;
Cross[17] to our *Interests,* curbing Sense, and Sin;
Oppress'd without, and undermin'd within,
It thrives through pain; its own Tormentours tires;
And with a stubborn patience still aspires.
To what can *Reason* such Effects assign
Transcending *Nature,* but to *Laws Divine?*
Which in that Sacred Volume are contain'd;
Sufficient, clear, and for that use ordain'd.
But stay: the *Deist* here will urge anew,
No *Supernatural Worship* can be *True:*
Because a *general Law* is that alone
Which must to *all,* and every *where* be known:
A Style so large as not *this* Book can claim
Nor ought that bears *reveal'd* Religions *Name.*
'Tis said the sound of a *Messiah's Birth*
Is gone through all the habitable Earth:
But still that Text must be confin'd alone
To what was *Then* inhabited, and known:
And what Provision cou'd from *thence* accrue
To *Indian* Souls, and Worlds discover'd *New?*
In other parts it helps, that Ages past,
The Scriptures there were *known,* and were *imbrac'd,*
Till Sin spread once again the Shades of Night:
What's that to these who never *saw* the Light?
Of all Objections this indeed is chief
To startle Reason, stagger frail Belief:
We grant, 'tis true, that Heav'n from humane Sense
Has hid the secret paths of *Providence:*
But *boundless Wisedom, boundless Mercy,* may
Find ev'n for those *be-wildred* Souls, a *way:*
If from his *Nature Foes* may Pity claim,
Much more may *Strangers* who ne'er heard his *Name.*
And though *no Name* be for[18] *Salvation* known,
But that of his *Eternal Sons* alone;
Who knows how far transcending Goodness can
Extend the *Merits* of *that Son* to *Man?*
Who knows what *Reasons* may his *Mercy* lead;

[13] heathen historians concurring or agreeing in their accounts of historical detail
[14] *fiat lux:* "and God said, *let there be light* and there was light."
[15] the world, the cosmos
[16] either [17] opposed [18] to serve for, to secure

Or *Ignorance invincible*[19] may plead?
Not onely *Charity* bids hope the *best*,
But *more* the great Apostle has exprest:[20]
That, if the Gentiles, (whom no Law[21] inspir'd,)
By Nature did what was by *Law requir'd;*
They, who the written Rule had never known,
Were to themselves both Rule and Law alone:
To Natures plain Indictment they shall plead;
And, by their Conscience, be condemn'd or freed.
Most righteous Doom! because a *Rule reveal'd*
Is *none* to *Those*, from whom it was *conceal'd*.
Then those who follow'd *Reasons* Dictates right;
Liv'd up, and lifted high their *Natural Light;*
With *Socrates* may see their Maker's Face,
While Thousand *Rubrick-Martyrs*[22] want a place.
  Nor does it baulk my *Charity*, to find
Th' *Egyptian* Bishop[23] of another mind:
For, though his *Creed Eternal Truth* contains,
'Tis hard for *Man* to doom to *endless pains*
All who believ'd not all, his Zeal requir'd;
Unless he first cou'd prove he was inspir'd.
Then let us either think he meant to say
This Faith, where *publish'd*, was the onely way;
Or else conclude that, *Arius* to confute,
The good old Man, too eager in dispute,
Flew high; and as his *Christian* Fury rose
Damn'd all for *Hereticks* who durst *oppose*.

  Thus far my Charity this path has try'd;
(A much unskilfull, but well meaning guide:)
Yet what they are, ev'n these crude thoughts were bred
By reading that, which better thou hast read.[24]
Thy Matchless Author's work: which thou, my Friend
By well translating better dost commend:
Those youthfull hours which, of thy Equals most
In *Toys*[25] have *squander'd*, or in *Vice* have *lost*,
Those hours hast thou to Nobler use employ'd;
And the severe Delights of Truth enjoy'd.
Witness this weighty Book, in which appears
The crabbed Toil of many thoughtfull years,

[19] the doctrine that some souls who are prevented by invincible ignorance from believing in Christ will yet be saved by God's mercy and grace

[20] St. Paul

[21] The Law is strictly, and as used here by St. Paul, that part of the Old Testament dealing with theology and rites (all, other than the Prophets), or loosely, the Old Testament dispensation; Dryden is applying the idea by a parallel to the whole of revelation; the Gentiles are those outside Israel, who have not the Law.

[22] those who bear witness (martyrs) to their religion by strictly following all the prescribed guides and instructions set down in red letters at the head of the passage

[23] Athanasius drew up one of the creeds held central in Christian theology, directed especially to declare the doctrine of the Trinity against the unitarian heresy of Arius.

[24] Henry Dickinson, the young friend to whom the poem is addressed, had just translated Fr. Richard Simon's *Critical History of the Old Testament*, a very learned work of scholarship discussing the text and the transmission of the Old Testament. His work involved a study of commentaries, including those of the rabbis.

[25] trifles

Spent by thy Authour, in the Sifting Care[26]
Of *Rabbins* old Sophisticated[27] Ware
From Gold Divine; which he who well can sort
May afterwards make *Algebra* a Sport.
A Treasure, which if *Country-Curates* buy,
They *Junius*, and *Tremellius*[28] may defy:
Save pains in various readings, and Translations;
And without *Hebrew* make most learn'd quotations.
A Work so full with various Learning fraught,
So nicely pondred, yet so strongly wrought,
As Natures height and Arts last hand requir'd:
As much as Man cou'd compass, uninspir'd.[29]
Where we may see what *Errours* have been made
Both in the *Copiers* and *Translaters Trade:*
How *Jewish, Popish,* Interests have prevail'd,
And where *Infallibility* has *fail'd.*
   For some, who have his secret meaning *guess'd*
Have found our Authour not too *much* a *Priest:*
For *Fashion-sake* he seems to have recourse
To *Pope*, and *Councils*, and *Traditions* force:
But he that *old* Traditions cou'd subdue,
Cou'd not but find the weakness of the *New:*
If *Scripture*, though deriv'd from *heav'nly birth*,
Has been but carelesly preserv'd on *Earth;*
If *God's own People*, who of *God* before
Knew what we know, and had been promis'd more,
In fuller Terms, of Heaven's assisting Care,
And who did neither *Time*, nor *Study* spare
To keep this Book *untainted*, *unperplext;*
Let in gross *Errours* to corrupt the *Text:*
Omitted *paragraphs*, embroyl'd the *Sense;*
With vain *Traditions* stopt the gaping Fence,
Which every common hand pull'd up with ease:
What Safety from such *brushwood-helps* as these?
If *written words* from time are not secur'd,
How can we think have *oral Sounds* endur'd?
Which *thus* transmitted, if *one* Mouth has fail'd,
Immortal Lyes on *Ages* are intail'd:[30]
And that some such have been, is prov'd too plain;
If we consider *Interest*, *Church*, and *Gain.*
   Oh but says one, *Tradition* set aside,
Where can we hope for an *unerring Guide?*
For since th' *original* Scripture has been lost,
All Copies *disagreeing*, *maim'd* the *most*,
Or *Christian Faith* can have no *certain* ground,
Or *Truth* in *Church Tradition* must be found.
   Such an *Omniscient* Church we wish indeed;

[26] care of sifting [27] adulterate, artificial; here, man-made

[28] Calvinists of the sixteenth century who had made a very widely used Latin translation of the Bible, with commentaries

[29] a work, that is, purely of reason and scholarship; Dryden implies in this and the following lines, that he holds man's natural reason to be the proper and sufficient instrument for such commentary. Later he came to believe that God gave continuing inspiration to the (Roman) Church and her Councils. See lines 276–305.

[30] entail; settle the succession (of a landed estate) so that it cannot be altered

'Twere worth *Both Testaments*, and cast in the *Creed:*
But if *this Mother* be a *Guide* so sure,
As can all *doubts resolve*, all *truth secure*,
Then her *Infallibility*, as well
Where Copies are *corrupt*, or *lame*, can tell;
Restore *lost Canon*[31] with as little pains,
As *truly explicate*[32] what still *remains:*
Which yet no *Council* dare *pretend* to doe;
Unless like *Esdras*,[33] they cou'd *write* it new:
Strange Confidence, still to *interpret* true,
Yet not be sure that all they have explain'd,
Is in the blest *Original* contain'd.
More Safe, and much more modest 'tis, to say
God wou'd not leave Mankind without a way:
And that the *Scriptures*, though not *every where*
Free from Corruption, or intire, or clear,
Are uncorrupt, sufficient, clear, intire,
In *all* things which our needfull[34] *Faith* require.
If *others* in the *same Glass better* see
'Tis for *Themselves* they look, but not for *me:*
For *MY* Salvation must its Doom[35] receive
Not from what *OTHERS*, but what *I* believe.
Must *all Tradition* then be set aside?
This to affirm were Ignorance, or Pride.
Are there not many points, some needfull sure
To saving Faith, that Scripture leaves obscure?
Which every Sect will wrest a several way
(For what *one* Sect Interprets, *all* Sects *may:*)
We hold, and say we prove from Scripture plain,
That *Christ* is *GOD;* the bold *Socinian*[36]
From the *same* Scripture urges he's but *MAN*.
Now what Appeal can end th' important Suit;
Both parts *talk* loudly, but the *Rule* is *mute?*
Shall I speak plain, and in a Nation free
Assume an honest *Layman's Liberty?*
I think (according to my little Skill,
To my own Mother-Church submitting still)
That many have been sav'd, and many may,
Who never heard this Question brought in play.
Th' *unletter'd* Christian, who believes in *gross*,[37]
Plods on to *Heaven;* and ne'er is at a loss:
For the strait-gate wou'd be made *streighter* yet,
Were *none* admitted there but men of *Wit*.
The few, by Nature form'd, with Learning fraught,
Born to instruct, as others to be taught,
Must Study well the Sacred Page; and see

[31] books which should form part of the recognized Bible
[32] interpret
[33] the reputed author of prophecies among the Apocryphal books of the Bible; see II Esdras 14.
[34] necessary (to salvation) [35] judgment
[36] a follower of the two brothers Socinus, who held that Christ was man only, though miraculously conceived
[37] in a general way, without scrutiny of detail

Which Doctrine, this, or that, does best agree
With the whole Tenour of the Work Divine:
And plainliest points to Heaven's reveal'd Design:
Which Exposition flows from *genuine Sense;*
And which is *forc'd* by *Wit* and *Eloquence.*
Not that Traditions parts are useless here:
When general, old, disinteress'd[38] and clear:
That Ancient Fathers[39] thus expound the Page,
Gives *Truth* the reverend Majesty of *Age:*
Confirms its force, by biding every *Test;*
For best *Authority's* next *Rules* are *best.*[40]
And still the nearer to the Spring we go
More limpid, more unsoyl'd the Waters flow.
Thus, *first Traditions* were a proof alone;
Cou'd we be *certain* such they *were*, so *known:*
But since some Flaws in long descent may be,
They make not *Truth* but *Probability.*
Even *Arius* and *Pelagius* durst provoke[41]
To what the *Centuries preceding* spoke.
Such difference is there in an oft-told Tale:
But Truth by its own Sinews will prevail.
Tradition written therefore more commends
Authority, than what from *Voice* descends:
And this, as perfect as its kind can be,
Rouls down to us the Sacred History:
Which, from the *Universal Church receiv'd*,
Is *try'd*, and *after*, for its *self* believ'd.
  The partial *Papists* wou'd infer from hence
Their Church, in last resort, shou'd Judge the *Sense.*
But first they wou'd assume, with wondrous Art,
Themselves to be the *whole*, who are but *part*
Of that vast Frame, the Church; yet grant they were
The handers down, can they from thence infer
A right t' interpret? or wou'd they alone
Who brought the Present, claim it for their own?
The *Book's* a *Common Largess*[42] to *Mankind;*
Not more for *them*, than *every* Man design'd:
The *welcome News* is in the *Letter* found;
The *Carrier's* not Commission'd to *expound.*
It *speaks* it *Self*, and what it does contain,
In all things *needfull* to be *known*, is *plain.*
  In times o'ergrown with Rust and Ignorance,
A gainfull Trade their Clergy did advance:
When want of Learning kept the *Laymen* low,
And none but *Priests* were *Authoriz'd* to *know:*
When what small Knowledge was, in them did dwell;
And he a *God* who cou'd but *Reade* or *Spell;*
Then *Mother Church* did mightily prevail:

[38] disinterested; without special interest to bias one's view
[39] early Christian writers, of the first five centuries
[40] for the nearest rules of the best authority are best; or possibly, for best authorities, next to rules, are the best (Noyes)
[41] heretics of the fourth and fifth centuries (who were the objects of stern controversies) dared to appeal to
[42] gift freely bestowed by a high personage

She parcel'd out the Bible by *retail:*
But still *expounded* what She *sold* or *gave;*
To keep it in *her Power* to *Damn* and *Save:*
Scripture was *scarce*, and as the Market went,
Poor *Laymen* took *Salvation* on *Content;*[43]
As needy men take Money, good or bad:
God's Word they had not, but the *Priests* they had.
Yet, whate'er *false Conveyances*[44] they made,
The *Lawyer* still was *certain* to be paid.
In those dark times they learn'd their knack so well,
That by long use they grew *Infallible:*
At last, a knowing Age began t' enquire
If *they* the *Book*, or *That* did *them* inspire:
And, making narrower search they found, thô late,
That what they thought the *Priest*'s was *Their* Estate:
Taught by the *Will produc'd*, (the written Word)
How long they had been *cheated* on *Record.*[45]
Then, every man who saw the Title fair,
Claim'd a Child's part, and put in for a Share:
Consulted Soberly his private good;
And sav'd himself as cheap as e'er he cou'd.
'Tis true, my Friend, (and far be flattery hence)
This good had full as bad a Consequence:
The Book thus put in every vulgar hand,
Which each presum'd he best cou'd understand,
The *Common Rule* was made the *common Prey;*
And at the mercy of the *Rabble* lay.
The tender Page with horney Fists was gaul'd;
And he was gifted most that loudest baul'd:
The *Spirit*[46] gave the *Doctoral Degree:*
And every member of a *Company*[47]
Was of *his Trade*, and of the *Bible free.*
Plain *Truths* enough for needfull *use* they found;
But men wou'd still be itching to *expound:*
Each was ambitious of th' obscurest place,
No measure ta'n from *Knowledge*, all from *GRACE.*
Study and *Pains* were now no more their Care;
Texts were explain'd by *Fasting*, and by *Prayer:*
This was the Fruit the *private Spirit* brought;
Occasion'd by *great Zeal*, and *little Thought.*
While Crouds unlearn'd, with rude Devotion warm,
About the Sacred Viands buz and swarm.
The *Fly-blown Text* creates a *crawling Brood;*
And turns to *Maggots* what was meant for *Food.*
A Thousand daily Sects rise up, and dye;
A Thousand more the perish'd Race supply:
So all we make of Heavens discover'd Will
Is, not to have it, or to use it ill.
The Danger's much the same; on several Shelves

[43] accept without question [44] transference of property
[45] by a (false) document formally recording the right or ownership
[46] The individualist or enthusiast believes that the divine spirit gives him power to interpret the Bible, without regard to his education or learning.
[47] guild, corporation of men of a trade or skill

If *others* wreck *us*, or *we* wreck our *selves*.
  What then remains, but, waving each Extreme,
The Tides of Ignorance, and Pride to stem?
Neither so rich a Treasure to forgo;
Nor proudly seek beyond our pow'r to know:
Faith is not built on disquisitions vain;
The things we *must* believe, are *few*, and *plain:*
But since men *will* believe more than they *need;*
And every man will make *himself* a Creed:
In doubtfull questions 'tis the safest way
To learn what unsuspected[48] Ancients say:
For 'tis not likely *we* shou'd higher Soar
In search of Heav'n, than *all the Church before:*
Nor can we be deceiv'd, unless we see
The *Scripture*, and the *Fathers disagree.*
If after all, they stand suspected still,
(For no man's Faith depends upon his Will;)
'Tis some Relief, that points not clearly known,
Without much hazard may be let alone:
And, after hearing what our Church can say,
If still our Reason runs another way,
That private Reason 'tis more Just to curb,
Than by Disputes the publick Peace disturb.
For points obscure are of small use to learn:
But *Common quiet* is *Mankind*'s *concern.*
  Thus have I made my own Opinions clear:
Yet neither Praise expect, nor Censure fear:
And this unpolish'd, rugged Verse, I chose;
As fittest for Discourse, and nearest Prose:
For, while from *Sacred Truth* I do not swerve,
***Tom Sternhold*'s,[49] or *Tom Sha—ll*'s[50] *Rhimes* will serve.**

A SONG[1]

Farewell ungratefull Traytor,
  Farewell my perjur'd Swain,
Let never injur'd Creature
  Believe a Man again.
The Pleasure of Possessing
Surpasses all Expressing,
But 'tis too short a Blessing,
  And Love too long a Pain.

'Tis easie to deceive us
  In pity of your Pain,
But when we love you leave us
  To rail at you in vain.
Before we have descry'd it
There is no Bliss beside it,
But she that once has try'd it
  Will never love again.

[48] whose texts are not suspected of corruption
[49] one of two famous and very prosaic translators of the Psalms into verse
[50] Shadwell
[1] from the *Spanish Fryar*, acted 1680, Act V, sc. 1; text 1681

The Passion you pretended
Was onely to obtain,
But when the Charm is ended
The Charmer you disdain.
Your Love by ours we measure
Till we have lost our Treasure,
But Dying[2] is a Pleasure,
When Living is a Pain.

TO THE MEMORY OF MR. OLDHAM[3]

Farewel, too little and too lately known,
Whom I began to think and call my own;
For sure our Souls were near ally'd, and thine
Cast in the same Poetick mould as mine.
One common Note on either Lyre did strike,
And Knaves and Fools we both abhorr'd alike:
To the same Goal did both our Studies drive,
The last set out the soonest did arrive.[4]
Thus *Nisus* fell upon the slippery place,
Whilst his young Friend perform'd and won the Race.
O early ripe! to thy abundant store
What could advancing Age have added more?
It might (what Nature never gives the young)
Have taught the numbers[5] of thy native Tongue.
But Satyr needs not those, and Wit will shine
Through the harsh cadence of a rugged line.
A noble Error, and but seldom made,
When Poets are by too much force betray'd.
Thy generous fruits, though gather'd ere their prime,
Still shew'd a quickness; and maturing time
But mellows what we write to the dull sweets of Rime.
Once more, hail, and farewel; farewel, thou young,
But ah too short, *Marcellus*[6] of our Tongue;
Thy Brows with Ivy, and with Laurels bound;[7]
But Fate and gloomy Night encompass thee around.

HORAT. ODE 29. BOOK 3. PARAPHRAS'D IN PINDARIQUE VERSE[8]

Descended of an ancient Line,
That long the *Tuscan* Scepter sway'd,
Make haste to meet the generous wine,
Whose piercing is for thee delay'd:
The rosie wreath is ready made;
And artful hands prepare
The fragrant *Syrian* Oyl, that shall perfume thy hair.

[2] double meaning [3] Text: *The Remains of Mr. Oldham*, 1684

[4] Oldham had begun to publish satire in 1678 (?) after Dryden had written, but before he had published, *MacFlecknoe*. The story referred to is the race in which Nisus and Euryalus took part in *Aeneid*, V, Nisus leading until he slipped.

[5] verse harmony

[6] the brilliant nephew and chief hope of Augustus Cæsar, who died in his twenties

[7] for poetry and for victory

[8] Text: first edition, *Sylvae*, 1685. "Pindarique" refers to the metrical structure, which unlike that of Horace, is an elaborately varied stanza. Cowley had set the pattern for such translation. We have thought it pointless to annotate the references to Roman life. Lines 40 and following are applied to London.

When the Wine sparkles from a far,
  And the well-natur'd Friend cries, come away;
Make haste, and leave thy business and thy care,
  No mortal int'rest can be worth thy stay.

Leave for a while thy costly Country Seat;
  And, to be Great indeed, forget
The nauseous pleasures of the Great:
  Make haste and come:
Come, and forsake thy cloying store;
  Thy Turret that surveys, from high,
The smoke, and wealth, and noise of *Rome;*
  And all the busie pageantry
That wise men scorn, and fools adore:
Come, give thy Soul a loose, and taste the pleasures of the poor.

Sometimes 'tis grateful to the Rich, to try
A short vicissitude, and fit of Poverty:
  A savoury Dish, a homely Treat,
  Where all is plain, where all is neat,
  Without the stately spacious Room,
The *Persian* Carpet, or the *Tyrian* Loom,
Clear up the cloudy foreheads of the Great.

The Sun is in the Lion mounted high;
      The *Syrian* Star
      Barks from afar;
  And with his sultry breath infects the Sky;
The ground below is parch'd, the heav'ns above us fry.
  The Shepherd drives his fainting Flock,
  Beneath the covert of a Rock;
  And seeks refreshing Rivulets nigh:
  The *Sylvans* to their shades retire,
Those very shades and streams new shades and streams require;
And want a cooling breeze of wind to fan the raging fire.

  Thou, what befits the new Lord May'r,
  And what the City Faction dare,
  And what the *Gallique*[9] Arms will do,
  And what the Quiver bearing Foe,
  Art anxiously inquisitive to know:
But God has, wisely, hid from humane sight
  The dark decrees of future fate;
  And sown their seeds in depth of night;
He laughs at all the giddy turns of State;
When Mortals search too soon, and fear too late.

    Enjoy the present smiling hour;
    And put it out of Fortunes pow'r:
  The tide of bus'ness, like the running stream,
    Is sometimes high, and sometimes low,
  A quiet ebb, or a tempestuous flow,
      And alwayes in extream.

[9] French

Now with a noiseless gentle course
It keeps within the middle Bed;
Anon it lifts aloft the head,
And bears down all before it, with impetuous force:
And trunks of Trees come rowling down,
Sheep and their Folds together drown:
Both House and Homested into Seas are borne,
And Rocks are from their old foundations torn,
And woods made thin with winds, their scatter'd honours mourn.

Happy the Man, and happy he alone,
He, who can call to day his own:
He, who, secure within, can say,
Tomorrow do thy worst, for I have liv'd today.
Be fair, or foul, or rain, or shine,
The joys I have possest, in spight of fate, are mine.
Not Heav'n it self upon the past has pow'r;
But what has been, has been, and I have had my hour.

Fortune, that with malicious joy,
Does Man her slave oppress,
Proud of her Office to destroy,
Is seldome pleas'd to bless.
Still various, and unconstant still;
But with an inclination to be ill;
Promotes, degrades, delights in strife,
And makes a Lottery of life.
I can enjoy her while she's kind;
But when she dances in the wind,
And shakes her wings, and will not stay,
I puff the Prostitute away:
The little or the much she gave, is quietly resign'd:
Content with poverty, my Soul, I arm;
And Vertue, tho' in rags, will keep me warm.

What is't to me,
Who never sail in her unfaithful Sea,
If Storms arise, and Clouds grow black;
If the Mast split and threaten wreck,
Then let the greedy Merchant fear
For his ill gotten gain;
And pray to Gods that will not hear,
While the debating winds and billows bear
His Wealth into the Main.
For me, secure from Fortunes blows,
(Secure of what I cannot lose,)
In my small Pinnace I can sail,
Contemning all the blustring roar;
And running with a merry gale,
With friendly Stars my safety seek
Within some little winding Creek;
And see the storm a shore.

TO THE PIOUS MEMORY OF THE ACCOMPLISHT YOUNG LADY MRS. ANNE KILLIGREW. EXCELLENT IN THE TWO SISTER-ARTS OF POESIE, AND PAINTING. AN ODE[10]

Thou youngest Virgin-Daughter of the Skies,
Made in the last Promotion of the *Blest;*
Whose Palmes, new pluckt from Paradise,
In spreading *Branches* more sublimely rise,
Rich with Immortal Green above the rest:
Whether, adopted to some Neighbouring Star,
Thou rol'st above us, in thy wand'ring Race,
Or, in Procession fixt and regular,
Mov'd with the Heav'ns Majestick Pace;
Or, call'd to more Superiour *Bliss,*
Thou tread'st, with Seraphims, the vast *Abyss.*
What ever happy Region be thy place,
Cease thy Celestial Song a little space;
(Thou wilt have time enough for Hymns Divine,
Since Heav'ns Eternal Year is thine.)
Here then a Mortal Muse thy Praise rehearse,
In no ignoble Verse:
But such as thy own voice did practise here,
When thy first Fruits of Poesie were giv'n;
To make thy self a welcome Inmate there:
While yet a young Probationer,
And Candidate of Heav'n.

If by Traduction[11] came thy Mind,
Our Wonder is the less to find
A Soul so charming from a Stock so good;
Thy Father[12] was transfus'd into thy *Blood:*
So wert thou born into a tuneful strain,
(An early, rich, and inexhausted Vein.)
But if thy Præexisting Soul
Was form'd, at first, with Myriads more,
It did through all the Mighty Poets roul,
Who *Greek* or *Latine* Laurels wore,
And was that *Sappho*[13] last, which once it was before.
If so, then cease thy flight, *O Heaven-born Mind!*
Thou hast no *Dross* to purge from thy Rich Ore:
Nor can thy Soul a fairer Mansion find,
Than was the *Beauteous* Frame she left behind:
Return, to fill or mend the Quire,[14] of thy Celestial kind.

May we presume to say, that at thy *Birth,*
New joy was sprung in *Heav'n,* as well as here on *Earth.*
For sure the Milder Planets did combine

[10] first published, in a slightly different form, in *Poems of Mrs. Anne Killigrew,* 1686; text, *Examen Poeticum,* 1693

[11] transmission by generation through her parents; Dryden follows this with the other of the two theories debated throughout the middle ages as to the origin of souls

[12] Dr. Henry Killigrew, who had written one tragedy

[13] the great Greek poetess [14] choir

On thy *Auspicious* Horoscope[15] to shine,
And ev'n the most Malicious were in Trine.[16]
Thy *Brother-Angels* at thy *Birth*
Strung each his Lyre, and tun'd it high,
That all the People of the Skie
Might know a Poetess was born on Earth.
And then if ever, Mortal Ears
Had heard the Musick of the Spheres!
And if no clust'ring Swarm of *Bees*[17]
On thy sweet Mouth distill'd their golden Dew,
'Twas that, such vulgar Miracles,
Heav'n had not Leasure to renew:
For all the *Blest* Fraternity of Love
Solemniz'd there thy *Birth*, and kept thy Holyday above.

O gracious God! How far have we
Prophan'd thy Heav'nly Gift of Poesy?
Made prostitute and profligate the Muse,
Debas'd to each obscene and impious use,
Whose Harmony was first ordain'd *Above*
For Tongues of *Angels*, and for *Hymns of Love?*
O wretched We! why were we hurry'd down
This lubrique[18] and adult'rate Age,
(Nay added fat Pollutions of our own)
T' increase the steaming Ordures[19] of the Stage?
What can we say t' excuse our *Second Fall?*
Let this thy *Vestal*, Heav'n, attone for all?
Her *Arethusian*[20] Stream remains unsoil'd,
Unmixt with Forreign Filth, and undefil'd,
Her Wit was more than Man, her Innocence a Child!

Art she had none, yet wanted none:
For Nature did that Want supply,
So rich in Treasures of her Own,
She might our boasted *Stores* defy:
Such Noble Vigour did her Verse adorn,
That it seem'd borrow'd, where 'twas only born.
Her Morals too were in her *Bosom* bred,
By great Examples daily fed,
What in the best of *Books*, her Father's Life, she read.
And to be read her self she need not fear,
Each Test, and ev'ry Light, her Muse will bear,
Though *Epictetus*[21] with his Lamp were there.
Ev'n Love (for Love sometimes her Muse exprest)

[15] scheme showing the position of the heavenly bodies at her birth, that position as Dryden supposed influencing her character and fate (judicial astrology)

[16] aspect of two planets 120° apart and therefore favorable

[17] such as swarmed about the mouth of Plato

[18] lubricious, lewd [19] dung; obscenity

[20] Arethusa, a chaste water nymph of Elis in Greece who, when she was pursued by the river god Alpheus, fled underground and after passing under the sea, emerged on the island of Ortygia, near Sicily

[21] famous Stoic philosopher who lived very simply in a small hut with only a bed and lamp for furniture; probably, however, as Noyes suggests, Dryden is thinking of Diogenes with his lantern searching for an honest man

Was but a *Lambent-flame*[22] which play'd about her *Breast:*
Light as the Vapours of a Morning Dream,
So cold her self, whilst she such Warmth exprest,
'Twas *Cupid* bathing in *Diana*'s[23] Stream.

Born to the Spacious Empire of the *Nine*,[24]
One wou'd have thought, she shoud have been content
To manage well that Mighty Government;
But what can young ambitious Souls confine?
To the next Realm she stretcht her Sway
For *Painture* near adjoyning lay,
A plenteous Province, and alluring Prey.
A Chamber of Dependences[25] was fram'd,
(As Conquerors will never want Pretence,
When arm'd, to justifie th' Offence)
And the whole Fief, in right of Poetry she claim'd.
The Country open lay without Defence:
For Poets frequent In-rodes there had made,
And perfectly cou'd represent
The Shape, the Face, with ev'ry Lineament;
And all the large Demains which the *Dumb-sister*[26] sway'd,
All bow'd beneath her Government,
Receiv'd in Triumph wheresoe're she went.
Her Pencil drew, what e're her Soul design'd,
And of the *happy Draught* surpass'd the *Image* in her *Mind.*
The *Sylvan* Scenes of Herds and Flocks,
And fruitful Plains and barren Rocks,
Of shallow *Brooks* that flow'd so clear,
The bottom did the top appear;
Of deeper too and ampler Floods,
Which as in Mirrors, shew'd the Woods;
Of lofty Trees, with Sacred Shades,
And Perspectives[27] of pleasant Glades,
Where Nymphs of brightest Form appear,
And shaggy Satyrs standing near,
Which them at once admire and fear.
The Ruines too of some Majestick Piece,
Boasting the Pow'r of ancient *Rome* or *Greece.*
Whose Statues, Freezes, Columns broken lie,
And tho' defac'd, the Wonder of the Eye,
What *Nature*, *Art*, bold *Fiction* e're durst frame,
Her forming Hand gave Feature to the Name.
So strange a Concourse ne're was seen before,
But when the peopl'd *Ark* the whole Creation bore.

[22] a flame that plays softly on a surface without burning it
[23] the god of love, the goddess of chastity
[24] the Muses
[25] government for dependencies(?)
[26] alluding to the parallel, frequent in this age, between poetry, a speaking picture, and painting, a silent poem
[27] scene drawn in perspective or offering a long vista; a type of landscape just becoming enormously popular

The Scene then chang'd, with bold Erected Look
Our Martial King the sight with Reverence strook:[28]
For not content t' express his Outward Part,
Her Hand call'd out the Image of his Heart,
His Warlike Mind, his Soul devoid of Fear,
His High-designing *Thoughts*, were figur'd there,
As when, by Magick, Ghosts are made appear.
Our Phenix[29] Queen was portrai'd too so bright,
Beauty alone cou'd *Beauty* take so right:
Her Dress, her Shape, her Matchless Grace,
Were all observ'd, as well as heavenly Face.
With such a Peerless Majesty she stands,
As in that Day she took the Crown from Sacred Hands:
Before a Train of Heroins was seen,
In *Beauty* foremost, as in Rank, the Queen!
Thus nothing to her *Genius* was deny'd,
But like a *Ball* of Fire the further thrown,
Still with a greater *Blaze* she shone,
And her bright Soul broke out on ev'ry side.
What next she had design'd, Heaven only knows,
To such Immod'rate Growth her Conquest rose,
That Fate alone its Progress cou'd oppose.

Now all those Charms, that blooming Grace,
The well-proportion'd Shape, and beauteous Face,
Shall never more be seen by Mortal Eyes;
In Earth the much lamented Virgin lies!
Not Wit, nor Piety cou'd Fate prevent;
Nor was the cruel *Destiny* content
To finish all the Murder at a blow,
To sweep at once her *Life*, and *Beauty* too;
But, like a hardn'd Fellon, took a pride
To work more Mischievously slow,
And plunder'd first, and then destroy'd.
O double Sacriledge on things Divine,
To rob the Relique, and deface the Shrine!
But thus *Orinda* dy'd:[30]
Heaven, by the same Disease, did both translate,
As equal were their Souls, so equal was their Fate.

Mean time her *Warlike Brother* on the Seas
His waving Streams[31] to the Winds displays,
And vows for his Return, with vain Devotion, pays,
Ah, Generous Youth, that Wish forbear,
The Winds too soon will waft thee here!
Slack all thy Sails, and fear to come,
Alas, thou know'st not, thou art wreck'd at home!
No more shalt thou behold thy Sister's Face,
Thou hast already had her last Embrace.

[28] struck; the King and Queen are James II and Mary of Modena, to whom Anne Killigrew had been a lady-in-waiting

[29] the famous bird of whom only one existed at a time

[30] the poetess, Katherine Philips. Both died of small-pox.

[31] streamers; he was a captain in the navy.

But look aloft, and if thou ken'st from far,
Among the *Pleiad*'s[32] a New-kindl'd Star,
If any Sparkles, than the rest, more bright,
'Tis she that shines in that propitious Light.

When in mid-Air, the Golden Trump shall sound,
To raise the Nations under Ground;
When in the Valley of *Jehosaphat*,[33]
The Judging God shall close the Book of Fate;
And there the last *Assizes* keep,
For those who Wake, and those who Sleep;
When ratling *Bones* together fly,
From the four Corners of the Skie,
When Sinews o're the Skeletons are spread,
Those cloath'd with Flesh, and Life inspires the Dead;
The Sacred Poets first shall hear the Sound,
And formost from the Tomb shall bound:
For they are cover'd with the lightest Ground,
And streight, with in-born Vigour, on the Wing,
Like mounting Larks, to the new Morning sing.
There *Thou*, sweet Saint, before the Quire[34] shalt go,
As Harbinger of Heav'n, the Way to show,
The Way which thou so well hast learn'd below.

THE HIND AND THE PANTHER[1]

A Poem in Three Parts

from THE PREFACE TO THE READER

I have but one word more to say concerning the Poem as such, and abstracting from the matters, either Religious or Civil which are handled in it. The *first Part*, consisting most in general Characters and Narration, I have endeavour'd to raise, and give it the Majestick Turn of Heroick Poesie. The *second*, being Matter of Dispute, and chiefly concerning Church Authority, I was oblig'd to make as plain and perspicuous as possibly I cou'd: yet not wholly neglecting the Numbers, tho' I had not frequent occasions for the Magnificence of Verse. The *third*, which has more of the nature of domestick Conversation, is, or ought to be more free and familiar than the two former.

There are in it two *Episodes* or *Fables*, which are interwoven with the main design; so that they are properly parts of it, tho' they are also distinct Stories of themselves. In both of these I have made use of the Common Places of Satyr, whether true or false, which are urg'd by the members of the one Church against the other: at which I hope no *Reader* of either *Party* will be scandaliz'd; because they are not of my invention; but as old, to my knowledge, as the times of *Boccace* and *Chawcer* on the one side, and as those of the Reformation on the other.

[32] the constellation of seven stars
[33] alluding to the valley of dry bones in Ezekiel 37
[34] choir
[1] published in the spring of 1687; text, second edition, 1687

THE FIRST PART

A milk white *Hind*,[2] immortal and unchang'd,
Fed on the lawns, and in the forest rang'd;
Without unspotted, innocent within,
She fear'd no danger, for she knew no sin.
Yet had she oft been chas'd with horns and hounds,
And Scythian[3] shafts; and many winged wounds
Aim'd at Her heart; was often forc'd to fly,
And doom'd[4] to death, though fated not to dy.
 Not so her young; for their unequal line
Was Heroe's make, half humane, half divine.
Their earthly mold obnoxious[5] was to fate,
Th' immortal part assum'd immortal state.
Of these a slaughtered army lay in bloud,
Extended o'er the *Caledonian*[6] wood,
Their native walk; whose vocal bloud arose,
And cry'd for pardon on their perjur'd foes;
Their fate was fruitful, and the sanguin seed
Endu'd with souls, encreas'd the sacred breed.
So Captive *Israel* multiply'd in chains,
A numerous Exile; and enjoy'd her pains.
With grief and gladness mixt, their mother view'd
Her martyr'd offspring, and their race renew'd;
Their corps to perish, but their kind to last,
So much the deathless plant the dying fruit surpass'd.
 Panting and pensive now she rang'd alone,
And wander'd in the kingdoms, once Her own.
The common Hunt, though from their rage restrain'd
By sov'reign pow'r, her company disdain'd:
Grin'd as They pass'd and with a glaring eye
Gave gloomy signs of secret enmity.
'Tis true, she bounded by, and trip'd so light
They had not time to take a steady sight.
For truth has such a face and such a meen
As to be lov'd needs only to be seen.
 The bloudy *Bear*[7] an *Independent* beast,
Unlick'd to form, in groans her hate express'd.
Among the timorous kind the *Quaking Hare*[8]
Profess'd neutrality; but would not swear.
Next her the *Buffoon Ape*,[9] as Atheists use,
Mimick'd all Sects, and had his own to chuse:
Still when the Lyon[10] look'd, his knees he bent,
And pay'd at Church a Courtier's Complement.

[2] the Roman Catholic Church

[3] The Scythians tipped their arrows with viper's poison and human blood, which brought death at a single touch.

[4] adjudged, condemned [5] open to injury by [6] (strictly Scottish, but here) British

[7] the Independents (precursors of our Congregationalists), chiefly responsible for the execution of Charles I

[8] the Quakers, who refused at that time to take oaths of any sort

[9] the Freethinkers, some of whom Dryden seems to have thought to have conformed to Catholicism for politic reasons only during James's reign

[10] King James II

The bristl'd *Baptist Boar*,[11] impure as He,
(But whitn'd with the foam of sanctity)
With fat pollutions fill'd the sacred place,
And mountains levell'd in his furious race,
So first rebellion founded was in grace.
But since the mighty ravage which he made
In *German* Forests, had his guilt betrayd,
With broken tusks, and with a borrow'd name
He shun'd the vengeance, and conceal'd the shame;
So lurk'd in Sects unseen. With greater guile
False *Reynard*[12] fed on consecrated spoil:
The graceless beast by *Athanasius* first
Was chas'd from *Nice;* then by *Socinus* nurs'd
His impious race their blasphemy renew'd,
And natures King through natures opticks[13] view'd.
Revers'd they view'd him lessen'd to their eye,
Nor in an Infant could a God descry:
New swarming Sects to this obliquely tend,
Hence they began, and here they all will end.[14]
What weight of antient witness can prevail
If private reason hold the publick scale?
But, gratious God, how well dost thou provide
For erring judgments an unerring Guide?
Thy throne is darkness in th' abyss of light,
A blaze of glory that forbids the sight;
O teach me to believe Thee thus conceal'd,
And search no farther than thy self reveal'd;
But her alone for my Directour take
Whom thou hast promis'd never to forsake!
My thoughtless youth was wing'd with vain desires,
My manhood, long misled by wandring fires,
Follow'd false lights; and when their glimps was gone,
My pride struck out new sparkles of her own.
Such was I, such by nature still I am,
Be thine the glory, and be mine the shame.
Good life be now my task: my doubts are done,
(What more could fright my faith, than Three in One?)
Can I believe eternal God could lye
Disguis'd in mortal mold and infancy?
That the great maker of the world could dye?
And after that, trust my imperfect sense
Which calls in question his omnipotence?
Can I my reason to my faith compell,
And shall my sight, and touch, and taste rebell?[15]
Superiour faculties are set aside,
Shall their subservient organs be my guide?

[11] the Anabaptists or Baptists still greatly feared because of their peasant's uprising in Germany, where they originated, in 1534–1535, though those of that sect in England at this time had no designs of political activity

[12] Unitarians, denying the divinity of Christ, a doctrine controverted by Athanasius at the council of Nice, and appearing in Dryden's day in the teaching of the two brothers Socinus

[13] glasses [14] The text has a comma here.

[15] This and the following couplets discuss the meaning of the communion service or the sacrament of the mass, from the point of view then most significant in Anglican discussion, whether in this sacrament the senses were to be depended on, or were transcended.

Then let the moon usurp the rule of day,
And winking tapers shew the sun his way;
For what my senses can themselves perceive
I need no revelation to believe.
Can they who say the Host should be descry'd
By sense, define a body glorify'd?
Impassible, and penetrating parts?
Let them declare by what mysterious arts
He shot that body through th' opposing might
Of bolts and barrs impervious to the light,
And stood before his train confess'd in open sight.
 For since thus wondrously he pass'd, 'tis plain
One single place two bodies did contain,
And sure the same Omnipotence as well
Can make one body in more places dwell.
Let reason then at Her own quarry fly,
But how can finite grasp Infinity?
 'Tis urg'd again that faith did first commence
By miracles, which are appeals to sense,
And thence concluded that our sense must be
The motive still of credibility.
For latter ages must on former wait,
And what began belief, must propagate.
 But winnow well this thought, and you shall find,
'Tis light as chaff that flies before the wind.
Were all those wonders wrought by pow'r divine
As means or ends of some more deep design?
Most sure as means, whose end was this alone,
To prove the god-head of th' eternal Son.
God thus asserted: man is to believe
Beyond what sense and reason can conceive.
And for mysterious things of faith rely
On the Proponent,[16] heav'ns authority.
If then our faith we for our guide admit,
Vain is the farther search of human wit,
As when the building gains a surer stay,
We take th' unuseful scaffolding away:
Reason by sense no more can understand,
The game is play'd into another hand.
Why chuse we then like *Bilanders*[17] to creep
Along the coast, and land in view to keep,
When safely we may launch into the deep?
In the same vessel which our Saviour bore
Himself the Pilot, let us leave the shoar,
And with a better guide a better world explore.
Could He his god-head veil with flesh and bloud
And not veil these again to be our food?
His grace in both is equal in extent,
The first affords us life, the second nourishment.
And if he can, why all this frantick pain
To construe what his clearest words contain,
And make a riddle what He made so plain?
To take up half on trust, and half to try,

[16] the one who proposes them to us [17] coasting vessels used in Holland (Christie)

Name it not faith, but bungling biggottry.
Both knave and fool the Merchant we may call
To pay great summs, and to compound[18] the small.
For who wou'd break with heav'n, and wou'd not break for all?
Rest then, my soul, from endless anguish freed;
Nor sciences thy guide, nor sense thy creed.
Faith is the best ensurer of thy bliss;
The Bank above must fail before the venture miss.
But heav'n and heav'n-born faith are far from Thee
Thou first Apostate to Divinity.
Unkennel'd range in thy *Polonian* Plains;
A fiercer foe th' insatiate *Wolf*[19] remains.
  Too boastful *Britain* please thy self no more,
That beasts of prey are banish'd from thy shoar:
The *Bear*, the *Boar*, and every salvage name,
Wild in effect, though in appearance tame,
Lay waste thy woods, destroy thy blissfull bow'r,
And muzl'd though they seem, the mutes devour.
More haughty than the rest the *wolfish* race,
Appear with belly Gaunt, and famish'd face:
Never was so deform'd a beast of Grace.
His ragged tail betwixt his leggs he wears
Close clap'd for shame, but his rough crest he rears,
And pricks up his predestinating ears.
His wild disorder'd walk, his hagger'd eyes,
Did all the bestial citizens surprize.
Though fear'd and hated, yet he rul'd awhile
As Captain or Companion of the spoil.
Full many a year his hatefull head had been
For tribute paid, nor since in *Cambria*[20] seen:
The last of all the Litter scap'd by chance,
And from *Geneva* first infested *France*.
Some Authors thus his Pedigree will trace,
But others write him of an upstart Race:
Because of *Wickliff*'s Brood no mark he brings
But his innate Antipathy to Kings.
These last deduce him from th' *Helvetian*[21] kind
Who near the *Leman lake* his Consort lin'd.[22]

[18] settle a debt by agreement for a portion of the sum due, when the debtor is "broken" and cannot pay the whole

[19] The Presbyterians, whom Dryden treats at such length because of their historical importance in England (see introduction) and on the continent. The tail between the legs refers to their use of the short Geneva gown, typical of their attitude on symbol, ritual, and so forth; the predestinating ears to the spiritual pride which others found in their doctrine of predestination and election.

[20] Wales. The reference may be to an ancient endeavor to exterminate the wolves from Wales, or, allegorically to the destruction in 603 of a large number of Welsh monks who refused to accept St. Augustine as their archbishop and thereby to accept Roman Christianity. The following lines, however, would show that Dryden is using the story only as an example; that Cambria really means Britain as a whole, and the hunted wolves are Wycliffe and his followers, the Lollards of the fourteenth century, from whom, then, Presbyterianism would be held to have spread to the continent. Wycliffe was by some accused of complicity in Wat Tyler's peasant rebellion.

[21] Swiss

[22] copulated with

That fi'ry *Zuynglius*[23] first th' Affection bred,
And meagre *Calvin* blest the Nuptial Bed.
In *Israel* some believe him whelp'd long since,
When the proud *Sanhedrim*[24] oppres'd the Prince,
Or, since he will be *Jew*, derive him high'r
When *Corah*[25] with his Brethren did conspire,
From *Moyses* Hand the Sov'reign sway to wrest,
And *Aaron* of his Ephod to devest:
Till opening Earth made way for all to pass,
And cou'd not bear the Burd'n of a *class*.
The *Fox* and he came shuffl'd in the Dark,
If ever they were stow'd in *Noah's* Ark:
Perhaps not made; for all their barking train
The Dog (a common species) will contain.
And some wild curs, who from their masters ran,
Abhorring the supremacy of man,
In woods and caves the rebel-race began.
O happy pair, how well have you encreas'd,
What ills in Church and State have you redress'd!
With Teeth untry'd, and rudiments of Claws
Your first essay was on your native Laws:
Those having torn with Ease, and trampl'd down,
Your Fangs you fasten'd on the miter'd Crown,[26]
And freed from God and Monarchy your Town.
What though your native kennel still be small
Bounded betwixt a Puddle and a Wall,
Yet your Victorious Colonies are sent
Where the North Ocean girds the Continent.
Quickned with fire below your Monsters Breed,
In Fenny *Holland* and in fruitful *Tweed*.[27]
And like the first the last effects to be
Drawn to the dreggs of a Democracy.
As, where in Fields the fairy rounds are seen,
A rank sow'r herbage rises on the Green;
So, springing where these mid-night Elves advance,
Rebellion Prints the Foot-steps of the Dance.
Such are their Doctrines, such contempt they show
To Heaven above, and to their Prince below,
As none but Traytors and Blasphemers know.
God, like the Tyrant of the Skies is plac'd,
And Kings, like slaves, beneath the Croud debas'd.
So fulsome is their food, that Flocks refuse
To bite; and only Dogs for Physick use.
As, where the Lightning runs along the Ground,
No husbandry can heal the blasting Wound,
Nor bladed Grass, nor bearded Corn succeeds,

[23] Zwingli, the first preacher of the reformed religion in Switzerland, and Calvin, who was the chief promulgator of Presbyterian doctrine, and the establisher of Presbyterian discipline, at Geneva, 1536–1564

[24] high court of justice and supreme council in the discipline set up by Moses, which Calvinism resembled in being a theocracy

[25] See *Absalom and Achitophel*, note 140.

[26] Before the Reformation, Geneva had been governed by her bishop.

[27] Scotland. Dryden believed that Presbyterianism, like Independency, looked to a Republican form of government, though in the Civil War the Scottish Presbyterians had not done so.

But Scales of Scurf, and Putrefaction breeds:
Such Warrs, such Waste, such fiery tracks of Dearth
Their Zeal has left, and such a teemless Earth.
But as the Poisons of the deadliest kind
Are to their own unhappy Coasts confin'd,
As only *Indian* Shades[28] of sight deprive
And Magick Plants will but in *Colchos*[29] thrive;
So Presby'try and Pestilential Zeal
Can only flourish in a Common-weal.
From *Celtique* Woods is chas'd the *wolfish* Crew,
But ah! some Pity e'en to Brutes is due,
Their native Walks, methinks, they might enjoy
Curb'd of their native Malice to destroy.
Of all the Tyrannies on humane kind
The worst is that which Persecutes the mind.
Let us but weigh at what offence we strike,
'Tis but because we cannot think alike.
In punishing of this, we overthrow
The Laws of Nations and of Nature too.
Beasts are the Subjects of Tyrannick sway,
Where still the stronger on the weaker Prey.
Man only of a softer mold is made;
Not for his Fellows ruine, but their Aid.
Created kind, beneficient and free,
The noble Image of the Deity.
[30]One Portion of informing Fire was giv'n
To Brutes, th' Inferiour Family of Heav'n:
The Smith Divine, as with a careless Beat,
Struck out the mute Creation at a Heat:
But when arriv'd at last to humane Race,
The Godhead took a deep consid'ring space:
And, to distinguish Man from all the rest,
Unlock'd the sacred Treasures of his Breast:
And Mercy mixt with reason did impart;
One to his Head, the other to his Heart:
Reason to Rule, but Mercy to forgive:
The first is Law, the last Prerogative.
And like his Mind his outward form appear'd:
When issuing Naked, to the wondring Herd,
He charm'd their Eyes, and for[31] they lov'd, they fear'd.
Not arm'd with horns of arbitrary might,
Or Claws to seize their furry spoils in Fight,
Or with increase of Feet, t'o'ertake 'em in their flight.
Of easie shape, and pliant ev'ry way;
Confessing still the softness of his Clay,
And kind as Kings upon their Coronation-Day:
With open Hands, and with extended space
Of Arms to satisfy a large embrace.
Thus kneaded up with Milk, the new made Man
His Kingdom o'er his Kindred world began:
Till Knowledge mis-apply'd, mis-understood,

[28] some form of nightshade (?)
[29] Medea of Cholcos restored her father to youth by boiling him in magic herbs.
[30] paragraph indentation passed over in the original [31] because

And pride of Empire sour'd his Balmy Blood.
Then, first rebelling, his own stamp he coins;
The Murth'rer *Cain*[32] was latent in his Loins;
And Blood began its first and loudest Cry
For diff'ring worship of the Deity.
Thus persecution rose, and farther Space
Produc'd the mighty hunter[33] of his Race.
Not so the blessed *Pan*[34] his flock encreas'd,
Content to fold 'em from the famish'd Beast:
Mild were his laws; the Sheep and harmless Hind
Were never of the persecuting kind.
Such pity now the pious Pastor shows,
Such mercy from the *British* Lyon flows,
That both provide protection for their foes.
   Oh happy Regions, *Italy* and *Spain*,
Which never did those monsters entertain!
The *Wolfe*, the *Bear*, the *Boar*, can there advance
No native claim of just inheritance.[35]
And self-preserving laws, severe in show,
May guard their fences from th' invading foe.
Where birth has plac'd 'em let 'em safely share
The common benefit of vital air.
Themselves unharmful, let them live unharm'd;
Their jaws disabl'd, and their claws disarm'd:
Here, only in nocturnal howlings bold,
They dare not seize the Hind nor leap the fold.
More pow'rful, and as vigilant as they,
The *Lyon* awfully forbids the prey.[36]
Their rage repress'd, though pinch'd with famine sore,
They stand aloof, and tremble at his roar;
Much is their hunger, but their fear is more.
   These are the chief; to number o'er the rest,
And stand, like *Adam*, naming ev'ry beast,
Were weary work; nor will the Muse describe
A slimy-born and sun-begotten Tribe:[37]
Who, far from steeples and their sacred sound,
In fields their sullen conventicles[38] found:
These gross, half animated lumps I leave;
Nor can I think what thoughts they can conceive.
But if they think at all, 'tis sure no high'r
Than matter, put in motion, may aspire.
Souls that can scarce ferment their mass of clay;
So drossy, so divisible are They,
As wou'd but serve pure bodies for allay:[39]
Such souls as *Shards*[40] produce, such beetle things,

[32] See Gen. 4. [33] Nimrod

[34] Christ; this allegory of Pan, the Greek god of shepherds, was common in the Renaissance.

[35] Dryden argued for toleration, as men's minds could not be compelled to belief; at the same time he argued that in Italy and Spain, where dissent from the Roman Church had not got a foothold, it should be kept rigidly out.

[36] James protects the Roman Catholics.

[37] alluding to the idea, which had not very long been finally discarded by science, that flies and reptiles were spontaneously generated by the sun from the slime of the Nile banks

[38] clandestine religious meeting

[39] alloy [40] dung (Noyes)

As only buz to heav'n with ev'ning wings;
Strike in the dark, offending but by chance,
Such are the blind-fold blows of ignorance.
They know not beings, and but hate a name,
To them the *Hind* and *Panther* are the same.
  The *Panther*[41] sure the noblest, next the *Hind*,
And fairest creature of the spotted kind;
Oh, could her in-born stains be wash'd away,
She were too good to be a beast of Prey!
How can I praise, or blame, and not offend,
Or how divide the frailty from the friend!
Her faults and vertues lye so mix'd, that she
Nor wholly stands condemn'd, nor wholly free.
Then, like her injur'd *Lyon*, let me speak,
He cannot bend her, and he would not break.
Unkind already, and estrang'd in part,
The *Wolfe* begins to share her wandring heart.
Though unpolluted yet with actual ill,
She half commits, who sins but in Her will.
If, as our dreaming *Platonists* report,
There could be spirits of a middle sort,
Too black for heav'n, and yet too white for hell,
Who just dropt half way down, nor lower fell;
So pois'd, so gently she descends from high,
It seems a soft dismission[42] from the skie.
Her house not ancient, whatsoe'er pretence
Her clergy Heraulds[43] make in her defence.
A second century not half-way run
Since the new honours of her blood begun.
A *Lyon*[44] old, obscene, and furious made
By lust, compress'd her mother in a shade.
Then, by a left-hand marr'age weds the Dame,
Cov'ring adult'ry with a specious name:
So schism begot; and sacrilege and she,
A well-match'd pair, got graceless heresie.
God's and Kings rebels have the same good cause,
To trample down divine and humane laws:
Both wou'd be call'd Reformers, and their hate,
Alike destructive both to Church and State:
The fruit proclaims the plant; a lawless Prince
By luxury reform'd incontinence,
By ruins, charity,[45] by riots, abstinence.
Confessions, fasts and penance set aside;
Oh with what ease we follow such a guide!
Where souls are starv'd, and senses gratify'd.
Where marr'age pleasures, midnight pray'r supply,
And mattin bells (a melancholly cry)
Are tun'd to merrier notes, *encrease* and *multiply*.

[41] the Church of England [42] dispersal, allowance to go

[43] Anglicans hold their church to be catholic, their priesthood to have apostolic succession from St. Peter

[44] Henry VIII, the first sovereign to become head of the church

[45] alluding to the dissolution of the abbeys and other religious houses and in the lines following to the marriage of the clergy

Religion shows a Rosie colour'd face;
Not hatter'd out[46] with drudging works of grace;
A down-hill Reformation rolls apace.
What flesh and blood wou'd croud the narrow gate
Or, till they waste their pamper'd paunches, wait?
All wou'd be happy at the cheapest rate.
Though our lean faith these rigid laws has giv'n,
The full fed *Musulman* goes fat to heav'n;
For his *Arabian*[47] Prophet with delights
Of sense, allur'd his eastern Proselytes.
The jolly *Luther*, reading him, began
T'interpret Scriptures by his *Alcoran;*
To grub the thorns beneath our tender feet,
And make the paths of *Paradise* more sweet:
Bethought him of a wife e'er half way gone.
(For 'twas uneasie travailing[48] alone,)
And in this masquerade of mirth and love,
Mistook the bliss of heav'n for *Bacchanals*[49] above.
Sure he presum'd of[50] praise, who came to stock
Th' etherial pastures with so fair a flock;
Burnish'd, and bat'ning[51] on their food, to show
The diligence of carefull herds below.
Our *Panther*, though like these she chang'd her head,
Yet, as the mistress of a monarch's bed,
Her front erect with majesty she bore,
The Crozier weilded, and the Miter[52] wore.
Her upper part of decent discipline
Shew'd affectation of an ancient line:
And fathers, councils, church and churches head,
Were on her reverend *Phylacteries*[53] read.
But what disgrac'd and disavow'd the rest,
Was *Calvin's* brand, that stigmatiz'd the beast.
Thus, like a creature of a double kind,
In her own labyrinth she lives confin'd.[54]
To foreign lands no sound of Her is come,
Humbly content to be despis'd at home.
Such is her faith, where good cannot be had,
At least she leaves the refuse of the bad.
Nice in her choice of ill, though not of best,
And least deform'd, because reform'd the least;
In doubtful points betwixt her diff'ring friends,[55]
Where one for substance, one for sign contends,
Their contradicting terms she strives to joyn.
Sign shall be substance, substance shall be sign.

[46] harrass, wear out [47] Mohamed
[48] either laboring or travelling, or, here, both
[49] celebrations of Bacchus, god of wine
[50] relied on [51] feeding greedily
[52] staff and headdress of a bishop, signifying the episcopal form of church government
[53] religious observances (from the name for the parchment inscribed with a portion of the law worn in leather cases by Jews to remind them of the whole Law)
[54] like the minotaur, half man and half bull, in the labyrinth of King Minos of Crete
[55] The following lines allude to the Anglican interpretation of the communion service, and particularly to the statement of it in the catechism.

A real presence all her sons allow,
And yet 'tis flat Idolatry to bow,
Because the God-head's there they know not how.
Her Novices are taught that bread and wine
Are but the visible and outward sign
Receiv'd by those who in communion joyn.
But th' inward grace, or the thing signify'd,
His blood and body, who to save us dy'd;
The faithful this thing signify'd receive.
What is't those faithful then partake or leave?
For what is signify'd and understood,
Is, by her own confession, flesh and blood.
Then, by the same acknowledgement, we know
They take the sign, and take the substance too.
The lit'ral sense is hard to flesh and blood,
But nonsense never can be understood.
Her wild belief on ev'ry wave is tost,
But sure no Church can better morals boast.
True to her King her principles are found;
Oh that her practice were but half so sound!
Stedfast in various turns of state she stood,
And seal'd her vow'd affection with her blood;
Nor will I meanly tax her constancy,
That int'rest or obligement[56] made the tye,
(Bound to the fate of murdr'd Monarchy:)
(Before the sounding Ax so falls the Vine,
Whose tender branches round the Poplar twine.)
She chose her ruin, and resign'd her life,
In death undaunted as an *Indian* wife:
A rare example: But some souls we see
Grow hard, and stiffen with adversity:
Yet these by fortunes favours are undone,
Resolv'd into a baser form they run,
And bore the wind, but cannot bear the sun.
Let this be natures frailty or her fate,
Or *Isgrim's*[57] counsel, her new chosen mate;
Still she's the fairest of the fallen Crew,
No mother more indulgent but the true.
Fierce to her foes, yet fears her force to try,
Because she wants innate[58] auctority;
For how can she constrain them to obey
Who has her self cast off the lawful sway?
Rebellion equals all, and those who toil
In common theft, will share the common spoil.
Let her produce the title and the right
Against her old superiours first to fight;
If she reform by Text, ev'n that's as plain
For her own Rebels to reform again.
As long as words a diff'rent sense will bear,
And each may be his own Interpreter,

[56] obligation, when she was bound to the fate of ruined monarchy (murdered Charles I)

[57] original note: the Wolfe; (i.e., the Presbyterians, the name deriving from the medieval beast fable of Reynard)

[58] inborn authority (as the inspired Church)

Our ai'ry faith will no foundation find:
The word's[59] a weathercock for ev'ry wind:
The *Bear*, the *Fox*, the *Wolfe*, by turns prevail,
The most in pow'r supplies the present gale.
The wretched *Panther* crys aloud for aid
To church and councils, whom she first betray'd;
No help from Fathers or traditions train,[60]
Those ancient guides she taught us to disdain.
And by that scripture which she once abus'd
To Reformation, stands her self accus'd.
What bills for breach of laws can she prefer,
Expounding which she owns her self may err?
And, after all her winding ways are try'd,
If doubts arise she slips herself aside,
And leaves the private conscience for the guide.
If then that conscience set th' offender free,
It bars her claim to church auctority.
How can she censure, or what crime pretend,
But Scripture may be constru'd to defend?
Ev'n those whom for rebellion she transmits
To civil pow'r, her doctrine first acquits;
Because no disobedience can ensue,
Where no submission to a Judge is due.
Each judging for himself, by her consent,
Whom thus absolv'd she sends to punishment.
Suppose the Magistrate revenge her cause,
'Tis only for transgressing humane laws.
How answ'ring to its end a church is made,
Whose pow'r is but to counsel and perswade?
O solid rock, on which secure she stands!
Eternal house, not built with mortal hands![61]
O sure defence against th' infernal gate,
A patent during pleasure of the state!
  Thus is the *Panther* neither lov'd nor fear'd,
A meer mock Queen of a divided Herd;
Whom soon by lawful pow'r she might controll,
Her self a part submitted to the whole.
Then, as the Moon who first receives the light
By which she makes our nether regions bright,
So might she shine, reflecting from afar
The rays she borrow'd from a better Star:
Big with the beams which from her mother flow
And reigning o'er the rising tides below:
Now, mixing with a salvage croud, she goes
And meanly flatters her invet'rate foes,
Rul'd while she rules, and losing ev'ry hour
Her wretched remnants of precarious pow'r.
  One evening while the cooler shade she sought,
Revolving many a melancholy thought,

[59] the Bible, the interpretation of the Bible

[60] band of followers, line of the church fathers and of tradition (to which the Anglicans appeal in the interpretation of Scripture)

[61] alluding to Christ's description of Peter as the rock on which he will build, Paul's reference to Christ as dwelling in the temple not built with hands (in contrast to the Greek gods)

Alone she walk'd, and look'd around in vain,
With ruful visage for her vanish'd train:[62]
None of her sylvan subjects made their court;
Leveés and coucheés pass'd without resort.[63]
So hardly can Usurpers manage well
Those, whom they first instructed to rebel:
More liberty begets desire of more,
The hunger still encreases with the store.
Without respect they brush'd along the wood
Each in his clan, and filled with loathsome food;
Ask'd no permission to the neighb'ring flood,
The *Panther*, full of inward discontent,
Since they wou'd goe, before 'em wisely went:
Supplying want of pow'r by drinking first,
As if she gave 'em leave to quench their thirst.
Among the rest, the *Hind*, with fearful face
Beheld from far the common wat'ring place,
Nor durst approach; till with an awful roar
The sovereign *Lyon* bad her fear no more.
Encourag'd thus she brought her younglings nigh,
Watching the motions of her Patron's eye,
And drank a sober draught; the rest amaz'd
Stood mutely still, and on the stranger gaz'd:
Survey'd her part by part, and sought to find
The ten-horn'd monster[64] in the harmless *Hind*,
Such as the *Wolfe* and *Panther* had design'd.
They thought at first they dream'd, for 'twas offence
With them, to question certitude of sense,
Their guide in faith; but nearer when they drew,
And had the faultless object full in view,
Lord, how they all admir'd her heav'nly hiew![65]
Some, who before her fellowship disdain'd,
Scarce, and but scarce, from in-born rage restrain'd,
Now frisk'd about her, and old kindred feign'd.
Whether for love or int'rest, ev'ry sect
Of all the salvage nation shew'd respect:
The Vice-roy *Panther* could not awe the herd,
The more the company the less they fear'd.
The surly *Wolfe* with secret envy burst,
Yet cou'd not howl, the *Hind* had seen him first:[66]
But what he durst not speak, the *Panther* durst.
  For when the herd suffis'd, did late repair
To ferney heath, and to their forest lare,
She made a mannerly excuse to stay,
Proff'ring the *Hind* to wait[67] her half the way:
That since the Skie was clear, an hour of talk
Might help her to beguile the tedious walk.
With much good-will the motion was embrac'd,

[62] band of followers [63] public audiences at rising or retiring passed without attendance

[64] The Church of Rome was identified by the reformers with the ten-horned monster referred to in Revelation 17.

[65] hue

[66] According to a classical superstition, a man who was seen by a wolf before he saw the wolf lost his voice. Dryden gives the hind this power over the wolf himself.

[67] attend upon

To chat awhile on their adventures pass'd:
Nor had the grateful *Hind* so soon forgot
Her friend and fellow-suff'rer in the plot[68]
Yet wondring how of late she grew estrang'd,
Her forehead cloudy, and her count'nance chang'd,
She thought this hour th' occasion would present
To learn her secret cause of discontent,
Which, well she hop'd, might be with ease redress'd,
Consid'ring Her a well-bred civil beast,
And more a Gentlewoman than the rest.
After some common talk what rumours ran.
The Lady of the spotted-muff began.

from THE THIRD PART

[In the Second Part the hind and the panther, alone, argue their positions, the hind urging the panther that she is really going contrary to her own interests and indeed to her life, in protecting and keeping close to the other beasts rather than aiding the lion to protect the hind. In the Third Part they pass to acrimonious reflection upon each other, concluding with the two fables of which Dryden spoke in the preface. We give the first of these, the panther's account of the situation of the hind. The Roman Catholics were in a situation of the utmost doubtfulness and frustration. King James, by a power for which he claimed prerogative as king, was suspending the laws against them and advancing them to posts in the state and the army, and required Dryden in part to defend his action in the introduction to this poem. But the old established Catholics, and Dryden with them, saw that this support would end with the monarchy of James (he had not yet a son), and was likely to bring a severe reaction and greater stringency against them. During this crisis a meeting of the leading Roman Catholics was held at the Savoy with a Jesuit, Father Petre, in the chair. Many wished to ask the King to limit himself to getting the possession of their estates secured to them by act of Parliament; others, to getting permission for them to sell their estates and to emigrate with the funds thus gained. Father Petre wished them to press their advantage under the King. This conference and this painful situation seem to be covered by Dryden in his fable of the swallows, as Scott surmised. Dryden sympathizes with the group most moderate in their wishes to remain quiet under such toleration as they already had. But it must be remembered that the story is told, with malice, by the panther; nor is her point of view only given; Dryden's own irony prevails. It is not certain that Dryden intended the martin as Father Petre (though the portrait would accord with an Anglican view of him) nor who were the swifts and the cuckoo. For our interests, this does not greatly matter, though if we had the identification it would make us surer judges of Dryden's skill in occasional allegory. But the fable stands in its full narrative power without this knowledge.]

To this the Panther, with a scornfull smile:
Yet still you travail[69] with unwearied toil,
And range around the realm without controll,
Among my sons for Proselytes to prole,
And here and there you snap some silly soul.
You hinted fears of future change in state;
Pray Heav'n you do not prophesie your fate;
Perhaps you think your time of triumph near,
But may mistake the season of the year;
The *Swallows* fortune gives you cause to fear.
For charity (reply'd the matron) tell
What sad mischance those pretty birds befell.
Nay, no mischance (the salvage dame reply'd)
But want of wit in their unerring guide,
And eager haste, and gaudy hopes, and giddy pride.

[68] the Popish Plot
[69] both labor and journey

Yet, wishing timely warning may prevail,
Make you the moral, and I'll tell the tale.
The *Swallow*, priveleg'd above the rest
Of all the birds, as man's familiar Guest,
Pursues the Sun in summer brisk and bold,
But wisely shuns the persecuting cold:
Is well to chancells and to chimnies known,
Though 'tis not thought she feeds on smoak alone.
From hence she has been held of heav'nly line,
Endu'd with particles of soul divine.
This merry chorister had long possess'd
Her summer seat, and feather'd well her nest:
Till frowning skys began to change their chear,
And time turn'd up the wrong side of the year:
The shedding trees began the ground to strow
With yellow leaves, and bitter blasts to blow.
Sad auguries of winter thence she drew,
Which by instinct, or Prophecy, she knew:
When prudence warned her to depart betimes[70]
And seek a better heav'n and warmer clymes.
Her sons were summon'd on a steeples height,
And, call'd in common council, vote a flight;
The day was nam'd, the next that shou'd be fair,
All to the gen'ral rendezvous repair:
They try their flutt'ring wings, and trust themselves in air,
But whether upward to the moon they go,
Or dream the winter out in caves below,
Or hawk at flies elsewhere, concerns not us to know.
Southwards, you may be sure, they bent their flight,
And harbour'd in a hollow rock at night:
Next morn they rose, and set up ev'ry sail;
The wind was fair but blew a *mackrel*[71] gale:
The sickly young sat shiv'ring on the shoar,
Abhorr'd salt-water never seen before,
And pray'd their tender mothers to delay
The passage, and expect[72] a fairer day.
With these the Martyn readily concurr'd,
A church-begot, and church-believing bird;
Of little body, but of lofty mind,
Round-bellied, for a dignity design'd,
And much a dunce, as Martyns are by kind.[73]
Yet often quoted canon-laws and code
And Fathers[74] which he never understood;
But little learning need in noble blood.
For, sooth to say, the Swallow brought him in,
Her houshold chaplain, and her next of kin;
In Superstition silly to excess,
And casting Schemes, by planetary guess:[75]
In fine, shortwing'd, unfit himself to fly,
His fear foretold foul weather in the sky.
Besides, a *Raven* from a wither'd oak

[70] in good time [71] such as brings mackerels in [72] wait for [73] nature
[74] church laws, church statutes and older church writers
[75] working schemes of the positions of the planets to prophesy by

Left[76] of their lodging, was observ'd to croke.
That omen lik'd him not, so his advice
Was present safety, bought at any price;
(A seeming pious care that cover'd cowardise.)
To strengthen this, he told a boding[77] dream
Of rising waters and a troubled stream,
Sure signs of anguish, dangers, and distress,
With something more, not lawful to express,
By which he slily seem'd to intimate
Some secret revelation of their fate.
For, he concluded, once upon a time,
He found a leaf inscrib'd with sacred rime,
Whose antique characters did well denote
The *Sibyl's* hand of the *Cumaean* grot:[78]
The mad Divineress had plainly writ,
A time should come (but many ages yet,)
In which sinister[79] destinies ordain
A dame should drown with all her feather'd train,
And seas from thence be call'd the *Chelidonian* main.[80]
At this, some shook for fear; the more devout
Arose, and bless'd[81] themselves from head to foot.
'Tis true, some stagers[82] of the wiser sort
Made all these idle wonderments their sport:
They said, their onely danger was delay,
And he who heard what ev'ry fool coud say,
Woud never fix his thoughts, but trim his time away.
The passage yet was good, the wind, 't is true,
Was somewhat high, but that was nothing new,
Nor more than usual *Equinoxes* blew.
The sun (already from the Scales[83] declin'd)
Gave little hopes of better days behind,
But change from bad to worse of weather and of wind.
Nor need they fear the dampness of the sky
Should flag their wings, and hinder them to fly,[84]
'Twas onely water thrown on sails too dry.
But, least of all *Philosophy* presumes
Of truth in dreams, from melancholy fumes:[85]
Perhaps the *Martyn*, hous'd in holy ground,
Might think of Ghosts that walk their midnight round,
Till grosser atoms, tumbling in the stream
Of fancy, madly met, and clubb'd[86] into a dream.
As little weight his vain presages bear
Of ill effect to such alone who fear.
Most prophecies are of a piece with these;

[76] Omens from the left hand were unpropitious. [77] ominous

[78] The Cumaean Sibyl was supposed to have left a group of prophecies, treasured in Rome in historic times.

[79] unfavorable; *sinister*, deriving from the Latin word for *left*

[80] from the Greek word for swallow, *chelidon*, imitating the fact that the Icarian Sea was supposedly named for the fall of Icarus into it

[81] crossed themselves to secure blessing [82] old hands

[83] the sign of the zodiac in which the sun is from September—October

[84] make droop and hinder them from flying

[85] They have evidently been reading Hobbes, whose theory of dreams this is.

[86] gathered together

Each *Nostradamus*[87] can foretell with ease:
Not naming persons, and confounding times,
One casual truth supports a thousand lying rimes.
Th' advice was true; but fear had seiz'd the most,
And all good counsel is on cowards lost.
The question crudely put, to shun delay,
'T was carried by the *major* part to stay.
His point thus gain'd, Sir Martyn dated thence
His pow'r, and from a priest became a prince.
He order'd all things with a busie care,
And cells and refectories did prepare.
And large provisions laid of winter fare.
But now and then let fall a word or two
Of hope that heav'n some miracle might show,
And, for their sakes, the sun shoud backward go;
Against the laws of nature upward climb,
And, mounted on the *Ram*,[88] renew the prime:
For which two proofs in Sacred story lay,
Of *Ahaz* dial,[89] and of *Joshuah's*[90] day.
In expectation of such times as these,
A chapel hous'd 'em, truly call'd of ease:[91]
For *Martyn* much devotion did not ask;
They pray'd sometimes, and that was all their task.
It happen'd (as beyond the reach of wit
Blind prophecies may have a lucky hit)
That this accomplish'd, or at least in part,
Gave great repute to their new *Merlin's* art.
Some Swifts,[92] the giants of the swallow kind,
Large-limbed, stout-hearted, but of stupid mind,
(For *Swisses*,[93] or for *Gibeonites*[94] design'd,)
These Lubbers,[95] peeping through a broken pane,
To suck fresh air, survey'd the neighboring plain,
And saw (but scarcely could believe their eyes)
New blossoms flourish, and new flow'rs arise;
As God had been abroad, and, walking there
Had left his foot-steps, and reform'd the year:
The sunny hills from far were seen to glow
With glittering beams, and in the meads below
The burnish'd brooks appear'd with liquid gold to flow.
At last they heard the foolish *Cuckow* sing,
Whose note proclaim'd the holy-day of spring.
No longer doubting, all prepare to fly,
And repossess their patrimonial sky.
The *Priest* before 'em did his wings display;
And that good omens might attend their way,
As luck would have it, 't was St. *Martyn's* day.[96]

[87] French astrologer of the sixteenth century
[88] the sign of the zodiac in which the sun is in late March and early April
[89] As a sign to Hezekiah God turned the sun back ten degrees on the dial.
[90] The sun and the moon stood still at Joshua's command that a victory might be completed.
[91] A chapel of ease is a subsidiary chapel for those dwelling at some distance from a church.
[92] otherwise called Martlets (original note); not certainly identified; possibly Irish Catholics
[93] members of the Pope's Swiss Guard
[94] condemned to be hewers of wood and drawers of water [95] clumsy fellows
[96] November 11; St. Martin's Summer is equivalent to Indian Summer

Who but the *Swallow* now triumphs alone?
The canopy of heaven is all her own,
Her youthful offspring to their haunts repair;
And glide along in glades, and skim in air,
And dip for insects in the purling springs,
And stoop on rivers to refresh their wings.
Their mothers think a fair provision made,
That ev'ry son can live upon his trade,
And now the carefull charge is off their hands,
Look out for husbands, and new nuptial bands.
The youthful widow longs to be supplyed;
But first the lover is by Lawyers ty'd
To settle jointure[97]-chimneys on the bride.
So thick they couple, in so short a space,
That Martyn's marr'age-offrings[98] rise apace;
Their ancient houses, running to decay,
Are furbish'd up, and cemented with clay:
They teem already; store of eggs are laid,
And brooding mothers call *Lucina's*[99] aid.
Fame spreads the news, and foreign fowls appear
In flocks to greet the new returning year,
To bless the founder, and partake the cheer.
And now 't was time (so fast their numbers rise)
To plant abroad, and people colonies;
The youth drawn forth, as *Martyn* had desir'd,
(For so their cruel destiny requir'd,)
Were sent far off on an ill-fated day;
The rest wou'd needs[100] conduct 'em on their way,
And Martyn went, because he fear'd alone to stay.
So long they flew with inconsiderate haste
That now their afternoon began to waste;
And, what was ominous, that very morn
The sun was enter'd into *Capricorn;*[101]
Which, by their bad astronomer's account,
That week the virgin balance[102] shoud remount;
An infant moon eclips'd him in his way,
And hid the small remainders of his day.
The crowd, amaz'd, pursu'd no certain mark;
But birds met birds, and justled in the dark;
Few mind the publick in a Panick fright;
And fear increas'd the horror of the night.
Night came, but unattended with repose,
Alone she came, no sleep their eyes to close:
Alone, and black she came; no friendly stars arose.
What should they doe, beset with dangers round,
No neighb'ring Dorp,[103] no lodging to be found,
But bleaky plains, and bare unhospitable ground?
The latter brood, who just began to fly,

[97] estate arranged in a marriage
[98] fees paid for marriage settlement for the support of a wife after her husband shall have died
[99] Roman goddess of childbirth
[100] were determined to [101] sign of the zodiac for December–January
[102] signs of the zodiac for August–September, September–October
[103] village

Sick-feather'd, and unpractis'd in the sky,
For succour to their helpless mother call;
She spread her wings; some few beneath 'em craul;
She spread 'em wider yet, but cou'd not cover all.
T'augment their woes, the winds began to move
Debate in air, for empty fields above,
Till *Boreas*[104] got the skyes, and pour'd amain
His rattling hail-stones mix'd with snow and rain.
The joyless morning late arose, and found
A dreadful desolation reign a-round,
Some buried in the Snow, some frozen to the ground:
The rest were strugling still with death, and lay
The *Crows* and *Ravens* rights, an undefended prey;
Excepting *Martyn's* race; for they and he
Had gain'd the shelter of a hollow tree:
But, soon discover'd by a sturdy clown,
He headed all the rabble of a town,
And finish'd 'em with bats, or poll'd[105] 'em down.
Martyn himself was caught a-live, and tryed
For treas'nous crimes, because the laws provide
No *Martyn* there in winter shall abide.[106]
High on an Oak, which never leaf shall bear,
He breath'd his last, expos'd to open air,
And there his corps, unbless'd, are hanging still,
To show the change of winds with his prophetic bill.[107]

A SONG FOR ST. CECILIA'S DAY, 1687[1]

From Harmony, from Heav'nly Harmony
This Universal Frame began.
When Nature underneath a heap
Of jarring Atoms lay,
And cou'd not heave her Head,
The tuneful Voice was heard from high,
Arise ye more than dead.

Then cold, and hot, and moist, and dry,
In order to their stations leap,
And MUSICK's Pow'r obey.
From Harmony, from Heav'nly Harmony
This Universal Frame began:
From Harmony to Harmony
Through all the compass of the Notes it ran,
The Diapason[2] closing full in Man.

What Passion cannot MUSICK raise and quell!
When *Jubal*[3] struck the corded Shell,
His list'ning Brethren stood around
And wondring, on their Faces fell
To worship that Celestial Sound.
Less than a God they thought there cou'd not dwell
Within the hollow of that Shell
That spoke so sweetly and so well.
What Passion cannot MUSICK raise and quell!

The TRUMPETS loud Clangor,
Excites us to Arms
With shrill Notes of Anger
And mortal Alarms,

[104] the North Wind, in Roman myth

[105] clip or strip as in pruning trees (Noyes)

[106] Catholic priests were forbidden by law to be in England.

[107] A dried bird hung up was supposed by the pointing of its bill to indicate which way the wind would change (Scott).

[1] Text: *Examen Poeticum*, 1693; originally printed in a broadside, 1687, from which our text varies only in spelling and typography, and but little. Sung to music by G. B. Draghi on Nov. 22, 1687, feast of St. Cecilia (patron saint of music and traditionally the inventor of the organ). Later set by Händel.

[2] notes combined into a harmony

[3] Gen. 4.21: "the father of all such as handle the harp and organ"

The double double double beat
Of the thundring DRUM
Cries, heark the Foes come;
Char[g]e, Charge, 'tis too late to retreat.

The soft complaining FLUTE
In dying Notes discovers
The Woes of hopeless Lovers,
Whose Dirge is whisper'd by the warbling LUTE.

Sharp VIOLINS proclaim
Their jealous Pangs, and Desperation,
Fury, frantick Indignation,
Depth of Pains, and height of Passion,
For the fair, disdainful Dame.

But oh! what Art can teach
What human Voice can reach
The sacred ORGANS praise?
Notes inspiring holy Love,
Notes that wing their Heav'nly ways
To mend the Choires above.

Orpheus[4] cou'd lead the savage race;
And Trees unrooted left their place;
Sequacious of[5] the Lyre:
But bright *CECILIA* rais'd the wonder high'r;
When to her ORGAN, vocal Breath was giv'n
An Angel heard, and straight appear'd
Mistaking Earth for Heav'n.

GRAND CHORUS

As from the pow'r of Sacred Lays
The Spheres began to Move,
And sung the great Creator's praise
To all the bless'd above;
So when the last and dreadful hour
This crumbling Pageant shall devour,
The TRUMPET *shall be heard on high,*
The Dead shall live, the Living die,
And MUSICK *shall untune the Sky.*

LINES PRINTED UNDER THE ENGRAVED PORTRAIT OF MILTON, IN TONSON'S FOLIO OF THE "PARADISE LOST," 1688[6]

Three Poets,[7] in three distant Ages born,
Greece, *Italy*, and *England* did adorn.
The First in loftiness of thought surpass'd,
The Next in Majesty; in both the Last.
The force of Nature could no farther goe;
To make a Third she joynd the former two.

MERCURY'S SONG TO PHÆDRA[8]

Fair *Iris* I love, and hourly I dye,
But not for a Lip, nor a languishing Eye:
She's fickle and false, and there we agree;
For I am as false and as fickle as she:
We neither believe what either can say;
And, neither believing, we neither betray.
'Tis civil to swear, and say things of course;
We mean not the taking for better for worse.
When present, we love; when absent, agree:
I think not of *Iris*, nor *Iris* of me:
The Legend of Love no Couple can find
So easie to part, or so equally join'd.

[4] Greek demi-god who brought civilization by music and whom even the trees followed
[5] following
[6] Text, Milton, 1688
[7] Homer, Virgil, Milton
[8] from *Amphitryon*, 1690, Act IV, sc.1. Text, first edition, 1690

SONG[9]

Enter *Comus* with three Peasants, who sing the following Song in Parts.

Com. Your Hay it is Mow'd and your Corn is Reap'd;
Your Barns will be full, and your Hovels heap'd:
Come, my Boys, Come;
Come, my Boys, Come;
And merrily Roar out Harvest Home;
Harvest Home,
Harvest Home;
And merrily Roar out Harvest Home.
Chorus. Come, my Boys, come, &c.

1 Man. We ha' cheated the Parson, we'll cheat him agen;
For why shou'd a Blockhead ha' One in Ten?[10]
One in Ten,
One in Ten;
For why shou'd a Blockhead ha' One in Ten?
Chorus. One in Ten,
One in Ten;
For why shou'd a Blockhead ha' One in Ten?

2. For Prating so long like a Book-learn'd Sot,
Till Pudding and Dumplin burn to Pot;
Burn to Pot,
Burn to Pot;
Till Pudding and Dumplin burn to Pot.
Chorus. Burn to Pot, &c.

3. We'll toss off our Ale till we canno' stand,
And Hoigh for the Honour of Old *England:*
Old *England,*
Old *England;*
And Hoigh for the Honour of Old *England.*
Chorus. Old *England,* &c.

The Dance vary'd into a round Country-Dance.

Enter *Venus.*[11]

Venus. Fairest Isle, all Isles Excelling,
Seat of Pleasures, and of Loves;
Venus, here, will chuse her Dwelling,
And forsake her *Cyprian* Groves.

Cupid[12] from his Fav'rite Nation,
Care and Envy will Remove;
Jealousie, that poysons Passion,
And Despair that dies for Love.

[9] from *King Arthur:* or *The British Worthy,* acted 1691, Act V, sc.1. Text, first edition, 1691. Music by Purcell and available in editions of his work.

[10] tithe, or one part in ten of the harvest, taken for the support of the church and clergy

[11] goddess of beauty in Roman myth (Greek Aphrodite), who loved to haunt the groves of Cyprus

[12] her son, god of love

Gentle Murmurs, sweet Complaining,
  Sighs that blow the Fire of Love;
Soft Repulses, kind Disdaining,
  Shall be all the Pains you prove.

Every Swain[13] shall pay his Duty,
  Grateful every Nymph shall prove;
And as these Excel in Beauty,
  Those shall be Renown'd for Love.

SONG[14]

No, no, poor suff'ring Heart no Change endeavour,
Choose to sustain the smart, rather than leave her;
My ravish'd Eyes behold such Charms about her,
I can dye with her, but not live without her.
One tender Sigh of hers to see me Languish,
Will more than pay the price of my past Anguish:
Beware, O cruel Fair, how you smile on me,
'Twas a kind Look of yours that has undone me.

Love has in store for me one happy Minute,
And She will end my pain who did begin it;
Then no day void of Bliss, or Pleasure leaving,
Ages shall slide away without perceiving:
Cupid shall guard the Door the more to please us,
And keep out Time and Death when they would seize us:
Time and Death shall depart, and say in flying,
Love has found out a way to Live by Dying.

VENI CREATOR SPIRITUS, TRANSLATED IN PARAPHRASE[15]

Creator Spirit, by whose aid
The World's Foundations first were laid,
Come visit ev'ry pious Mind;
Come pour thy Joys on Human Kind:
From Sin, and Sorrow set us free;
And make thy Temples worthy Thee.
  O, Source of uncreated Light,
The Father's promis'd *Paraclite!*[16]
Thrice Holy Fount, thrice Holy Fire,
Our Hearts with Heav'nly Love inspire;
Come, and thy Sacred Unction bring
To Sanctifie us, while we sing!
  Plenteous of Grace, descend from high,
Rich in thy sev'n-fold Energy!
Thou strength of his Almighty Hand,
Whose Pow'r does Heaven and Earth command:
Proceeding Spirit, our Defence,
Who do'st the Gift of Tongues dispence,
And crown'st thy Gift, with Eloquence!
  Refine and purge our Earthy Parts;
But, oh, inflame and fire our Hearts!
Our Frailties help, our Vice controul;
Submit the Senses to the Soul;

[13] young rustic, but commonly used in the poetry of this period for youth, as "nymph" for young girl

[14] from *Cleomenes*, acted 1692, Act II, sc.2. Text, first edition, 1692; music available in editions of Purcell

[15] Text: *Examen Poeticum*, 1693; original, a Latin hymn of the ninth century by Hrabanus Maurus, for Pentecost, when the disciples were given the gift of tongues

[16] The Holy Ghost, the advocate and aiding spirit; translated *Comforter* in the authorized version of the Bible.

And when Rebellious they are grown,
Then, lay thy hand, and hold 'em down.
  Chace from our Minds the infernal Foe;
And Peace, the fruit of Love, bestow:
And, lest our Feet shou'd step astray,
Protect, and guide us in the way.
  Make us Eternal Truths receive,
And practise, all that we believe:
Give us thy self, that we may see
The Father and the Son, by thee.
  Immortal Honour, endless Fame
Attend th' Almighty Father's Name:
The Saviour Son, be glorify'd,
Who for lost Man's Redemption dy'd:
And equal Adoration be
Eternal *Paraclete*, to thee.

from THE SIXTH BOOK OF THE ÆNEIS[17]

[The shade of Anchises in the underworld is showing Æneas some of the heroes of the Roman race who will be descended from him.]

Let others better mold the running Mass
Of Mettals, and inform the breathing Brass;
And soften into Flesh a Marble Face:
Plead better at the Bar; describe the Skies,
And when the Stars descend, and when they rise.
But, *Rome*, 'tis thine alone, with awful sway,
To rule Mankind; and make the World obey;
Disposing Peace, and War, thy own Majestick Way.
To tame the Proud, the fetter'd Slave to free;
These are Imperial Arts, and worthy thee.
He paus'd: And while with wond'ring Eyes they view'd
The passing Spirits, thus his Speech renew'd.
See great *Marcellus!*[18] how, untir'd in Toils,
He moves with Manly grace, how rich with Regal Spoils!
He, when his Country, (threaten'd with Alarms,)
Requires his Courage, and his Conqu'ring Arms,
Shall more than once the *Punic* Bands affright:
Shall kill the *Gaulish* King in single Fight:
Then, to the Capitol in Triumph move,
And the third Spoils shall grace *Feretrian Jove.*[19]
Æneas, here, beheld of Form Divine
A Godlike Youth,[20] in glitt'ring Armour shine:
With great *Marcellus* keeping equal pace;
But gloomy were his Eyes, dejected was his Face:
He saw, and, wond'ring, ask'd his airy Guide,
What, and of whence was he, who press'd the Hero's side?
His Son, or one of his Illustrious Name,
How like the former, and almost the same:
Observe the Crowds that compass him around;
All gaze, and all admire, and raise a shouting sound:
But hov'ring Mists around his Brows are spread,
And night, with sable Shades, involves[21] his Head.
Seek not to know (the Ghost reply'd with Tears)
The Sorrows of thy Sons, in future Years.

[17] Text of 1697. Book VI, lines 1169–1227

[18] a great Roman statesman and soldier who as consul defeated the Isumbres and slew their leader and who later played a leading part against Hannibal in the Punic wars

[19] He was allowed the honor of presenting in the temple of Feretrian Jove the *spolia opima* of the third order, the armor of the opposing general slain by him in single combat.

[20] the young Marcellus, descended of the other, who was the nephew and son-in-law of Augustus, and his presumed heir, but who died at the age of 19

[21] wraps its folds about

This Youth (the blissful Vision of a day)
Shall just be shown on Earth, and snatch'd away.
The Gods too high had rais'd the *Roman* State;
Were but their Gifts as permanent as great.
What groans of Men shall fill the *Martian* Field![22]
How fierce a Blaze his flaming Pile shall yield!
What Fun'ral Pomp shall floating *Tiber* see,
When, rising from his Bed, he views the sad Solemnity!
No Youth shall equal hopes of Glory give:
No Youth afford so great a Cause to grieve.
The *Trojan* Honour,[23] and the *Roman* Boast;
Admir'd when living, and Ador'd when lost!
Mirror of ancient Faith in early Youth!
Undaunted Worth, Inviolable Truth!
No Foe unpunish'd in the fighting Field,
Shall dare thee Foot to Foot, with Sword and Shield.
Much less, in Arms oppose thy matchless Force,
When thy sharp Spurs shall urge thy foaming Horse.
Ah, cou'dst thou break through Fates severe Decree,
A new *Marcellus* shall arise in thee!
Full Canisters[24] of Fragrant Lillies bring,
Mix'd with the Purple Roses of the Spring:
Let me with Fun'ral Flow'rs his body strow;
This Gift which Parents to their Children owe,
This unavailing Gift, at least I may bestow!

TO MY DEAR FRIEND MR. CONGREVE, ON HIS COMEDY, CALL'D, THE DOUBLE-DEALER[25]

Well then; the promis'd hour is come at last;
The present Age of Wit obscures the past:
Strong were our Syres; and as they Fought they Writ,
Conqu'ring with force of Arms, and dint of Wit;
Theirs was the Gyant Race, before the Flood;
And thus, when *Charles* Return'd, our Empire stood.
Like *Janus*[26] he the stubborn Soil manur'd,
With Rules of Husbandry the rankness cur'd:
Tam'd us to manners, when the Stage was rude;
And boistrous *English* Wit, with Art indu'd.
Our Age was cultivated thus at length;
But what we gain'd in skill we lost in strength.
Our Builders were, with want of Genius, curst;
The second Temple was not like the first:[27]
Till you, the best *Vitruvius*,[28] come at length;

[22] the Campus Martius, the great open space for public games or assemblies or ceremonies in Rome

[23] since the Trojans were the founders of Rome [24] baskets

[25] Text, Congreve: *The Double-Dealer*, 1694. Dryden says in a letter to Walsh that he wrote the poem before the play was acted, 1693

[26] Actually Saturn taught the Romans the rules of husbandry, in gratitude to Janus who was ruler of Rome and received him as joint ruler.

[27] The temple built in Jerusalem after the return from exile was less beautiful than Solomon's earlier temple.

[28] Great Roman writer on architecture, widely read in the Renaissance and after. Doric, of the three types of pillar developed in Greek architecture, is the plainest and largest in circumference, Corinthian the lighter one with acanthus leaves on the capital.

Our Beauties equal; but excel our strength.
Firm *Dorique* Pillars found Your solid Base:
The Fair *Corinthian* Crowns the higher Space;
Thus all below is Strength, and all above is Grace.
In easie Dialogue is *Fletcher's* Praise:
He mov'd the mind, but had not power to raise.
Great *Johnson*[29] did by strength of Judgment please:
Yet doubling *Fletcher's* Force, he wants his Ease.
In differing Tallents both adorn'd their Age;
One for the Study, t' other for the Stage.
But both to *Congreve* justly shall submit,
One match'd in Judgment, both o'er-match'd in Wit.
In him all Beauties of this Age we see;
Etherege[30] his Courtship, *Southern's*[31] Purity;
The Satire, Wit, and Strength of Manly *Witcherly*.[32]
All this in blooming Youth[33] you have Atchiev'd;
Now[34] are your foil'd Contemporaries griev'd;
So much the sweetness of your manners move,
We cannot envy you because we Love.
Fabius might joy in *Scipio*, when he saw
A Beardless Consul made against the Law,
And joyn his Suffrage to the Votes of *Rome;*
Though He with *Hannibal* was overcome.[35]
Thus old *Romano* bow'd to *Raphel's* Fame;[36]
And Scholar to the Youth he taught, became.
Oh that your Brows my Lawrel[37] had sustain'd,
Well had I been Depos'd, if you had reign'd!
The Father had descended for the Son;
For only You are lineal to the Throne.
Thus when the State one *Edward* did depose;
A Greater *Edward* in his room arose.[38]
But now, not I, but Poetry is curs'd;
For *Tom* the second reigns like *Tom* the first.[39]
But let 'em not mistake my Patron's part;[40]
Nor call his Charity their own desert.
Yet this I Prophecy; Thou shalt be seen,
(Tho' with some short Parenthesis between:)
High on the Throne of Wit; and seated there,

[29] the great Jacobean dramatists of the "Gyant Race"
[30] one of the founders of Restoration comedy
[31] a contemporary who colaborated with Dryden on *Cleomenes*
[32] See p. 442. [33] Congreve was 23
[34] as Noyes points out, an obvious misprint for *nor* (as in ed. 1710)
[35] Fabius. General during Hannibal's incursion into Italy, opposed young Scipio's plan of carrying the war into Africa. Scipio after his victory and return was made consul under the legal age. Fabius might, like Dryden, have rejoiced in the youth's victory had Scipio been as sweet as Congreve.
[36] Dryden appears to be thinking of Perugino, Raphael's master, for Julio Romano was his pupil.
[37] the Poet Laureateship
[38] Edward II was deposed and the great Edward III succeeded.
[39] Thomas Shadwell, Poet Laureate and Historiographer, 1688 to 1692; Thomas Rhymer, Historiographer after 1692
[40] Dorset, as Lord Chamberlain, had secured the Laureateship for Shadwell, when Dryden was no longer, as a Catholic, capable of holding it.

Not mine (that's little) but thy Lawrel wear.
Thy first attempt[41] an early promise made;
That early promise this has more than paid.
So bold, yet so judiciously you dare,
That Your least Praise, is to be Regular.
Time, Place, and Action, may with pains be wrought,
But Genius must be born; and never can be taught.
This is your Portion; this Your Native Store;
Heav'n that but once was Prodigal before,
To *Shakespeare* gave as much; she cou'd not give him more.
Maintain your Post: That's all the Fame You need;
For 'tis impossible you shou'd proceed.[42]
Already I am worn with Cares and Age;
And just abandoning th' Ungrateful Stage:
Unprofitably kept at Heav'ns expence,
I live a Rent-charge[43] on his Providence:
But You, whom ev'ry Muse and Grace adorn,
Whom I foresee to better Fortune born,
Be kind to my Remains; and oh defend,
Against Your Judgment Your departed Friend![44]
Let not the Insulting Foe my Fame pursue;
But shade those Lawrels which descend to You:
And take for Tribute what these Lines express:
You merit more; nor cou'd my Love do less.

ALEXANDER'S FEAST; OR, THE POWER OF MUSIQUE. AN ODE, IN HONOUR OF ST. CECILIA'S DAY[1]

Twas at the Royal Feast, for *Persia* won,
By *Philip's* Warlike Son:[2]
Aloft in awful State
The God-like Heroe sate
On his Imperial Throne:
His valiant Peers were plac'd around;
Their Brows with Roses and with Myrtles bound.
(So shou'd Desert in Arms be Crown'd:)
The Lovely *Thais*[3] by his side,
Sate like a blooming *Eastern* Bride
In Flow'r of Youth and Beauty's Pride.
Happy, happy, happy Pair!
None but the Brave
None but the Brave
None but the Brave deserves the Fair.

[41] *The Old Batchelour;* produced 1693

[42] go further

[43] periodical charge on land, reserved for one who is not owner

[44] fulfilled in Congreve's preface to Dryden's plays, 1717

[1] First sung, November 22, 1697, to music by Jeremiah Clarke; later set by Händel. The story, going back to early sources,—Plutarch is one—was retold in various Renaissance works. Text: *Fables,* 1700

[2] Alexander the Great was the son of Philip of Macedon.

[3] a famous Athenian courtesan

CHORUS

Happy, happy, happy Pair!
None but the Brave,
None but the Brave
None but the Brave deserves the Fair.

Timotheus[4] plac'd on high
Amid the tuneful Quire,
With flying Fingers touch'd the Lyre:
The trembling Notes ascend the Sky,
And Heav'nly Joys inspire.
The Song began from *Jove*;[5]
Who left his blissful Seats above,
(Such is the Pow'r of mighty Love.)
A Dragon's fiery Form bely'd the God:
Sublime on Radiant Spires He rode,
When He to fair *Olympia* press'd:
And while He sought her snowy Breast:
Then, round her slender Waist he curl'd,
And stamp'd an Image of himself, a Sov'raign of the World.
The list'ning Crowd admire the lofty Sound,
A present Deity, they shout around:
A present Deity the vaulted Roofs rebound.
With ravish'd Ears
The Monarch hears,
Assumes the God,
Affects to nod,[6]
And seems to shake the Spheres.

CHORUS

With ravish'd Ears
The Monarch hears,
Assumes the God,
Affects to nod,
And seems to shake the Spheres.

The Praise of *Bacchus*[7] then, the sweet Musician sung;
Of *Bacchus* ever Fair, and ever Young:
The jolly God in Triumph comes;
Sound the Trumpets; beat the Drums;
Flush'd with a purple Grace
He shews his honest Face,
Now gives[8] the Hautboys[9] breath; He comes, He comes.
Bacchus ever Fair and Young,
Drinking Joys did first ordain:
Bacchus Blessings are a Treasure;
Drinking is the Soldiers[10] Pleasure;
Rich the Treasure;
Sweet the Pleasure;
Sweet is Pleasure after Pain.

[4] known only in connection with this story
[5] Equivalent of Greek Zeus, King of the gods. The legendary Alexander of the romances claimed descent from this union with Olympia[s], in some versions.
[6] that is, to rule things by his nod, which was the declaration of his will
[7] god of wine [8] *give* in first edition, probably correct
[9] oboe [10] Noyes points out that this is equivalent to *soldier's*, not *soldiers'*.

CHORUS

Bacchus *Blessings are a Treasure;*
Drinking is the Soldier's Pleasure;
Rich the Treasure,
Sweet the Pleasure;
Sweet is Pleasure after Pain.

Sooth'd with the Sound the King grew vain;
Fought all his Battails o'er again;
And thrice He routed all his Foes; and thrice he slew the slain.
The Master saw the Madness rise;
His glowing Cheeks, his ardent Eyes;
And while He Heav'n and Earth defy'd,
Chang'd his Hand, and check'd his Pride.
He chose a Mournful Muse
Soft Pity to infuse:
He sung *Darius*[11] Great and Good,
By too severe a Fate,
Fallen, fallen, fallen, fallen,
Fallen from his high Estate
And weltring in his Blood:
Deserted at his utmost Need,
By those his former Bounty fed:
On the bare Earth expos'd He lies,
With not a Friend to close his Eyes.
With down-cast Looks the joyless Victor sate,
Revolving in his alter'd Soul
The various Turns of Chance below;
And, now and then, a Sigh he stole;
And Tears began to flow.

CHORUS

Revolving in his alter'd Soul
The various Turns of Chance below;
And, now and then, a Sigh he stole;
And Tears began to flow.

The Mighty Master smil'd to see
That Love was in the next Degree:[12]
'Twas but a Kindred-Sound to move;
For Pity melts the Mind to Love.
Softly sweet in *Lydian*[13] Measures,
Soon he sooth'd his Soul to Pleasures.
War, he sung, is Toil and Trouble;
Honour but an empty Bubble.
Never ending, still beginning,
Fighting still, and still destroying,
If the World be worth thy Winning,
Think, O think, it worth Enjoying.

[11] Darius III, the last of the old line of Persian Kings, defeated by Alexander at Arbela (331 B.C.) and slain the next year

[12] order (of things in related rank)

[13] In the Greek view of music, the Lydian mode stirred the soft emotions.

Lovely *Thais* sits beside thee,
Take the Good the Gods provide thee.
The Many rend the Skies, with loud Applause;
So Love was Crown'd, but Musique won the Cause.
The Prince, unable to conceal his Pain,
Gaz'd on the Fair
Who caus'd his Care,
And sigh'd and look'd, sigh'd and look'd,
Sigh'd and look'd, and sigh'd again:
At length, with Love and Wine at once oppress'd,
The vanquish'd Victor sunk upon her Breast.

CHORUS

The Prince, unable to conceal his Pain,
Gaz'd on the Fair
Who caus'd his Care,
And sigh'd and look'd, sigh'd and look'd,
Sigh'd and look'd, and sigh'd again:
At length, with Love and Wine at once oppress'd,
The vanquish'd Victor sunk upon her Breast.

Now strike the Golden Lyre again;
A lowder yet, and yet a lowder Strain.
Break his Bands of Sleep asunder,
And rouze him, like a rattling Peal of Thunder.
Hark, hark, the horrid Sound
Has rais'd up his Head,
As awak'd from the Dead,
And amaz'd, he stares around.
Revenge, Revenge, *Timotheus* cries,
See the Furies[14] arise!
See the Snakes that they rear,
How they hiss in their Hair,
And the Sparkles that flash from their Eyes!
Behold a ghastly Band,
Each a Torch in his Hand!
Those are *Grecian* Ghosts, that in Battail were slain,
And unbury'd remain
Inglorious on the Plain.
Give the Vengeance due
To the Valiant Crew.
Behold how they toss their Torches on high,
How they point to the *Persian* Abodes,
And glitt'ring Temples of their Hostile Gods![15]
The Princes applaud, with a furious Joy;
And the King seiz'd a Flambeau,[16] with Zeal to destroy;
Thais led the Way,
To light him to his Prey,
And, like another *Hellen,* fir'd[17] another *Troy.*

[14] snake-haired goddesses of Greek myth, sent to punish crimes
[15] hostile, that is, to the Greek conquerors
[16] torch
[17] Helen of Troy "fired" Troy in that the Greeks burned Troy at the close of the war they had begun after she fled with the Trojan Paris from her husband Menelaus of Sparta.

CHORUS

And the King seiz'd a Flambeau, with Zeal to destroy;
Thais *led the Way,*
To light him to his Prey,
And, like another Hellen, *fir'd another* Troy.

Thus, long ago
'Ere heaving Bellows learn'd to blow,
While Organs yet were mute;
Timotheus, to his breathing Flute,
And sounding Lyre,
Cou'd swell the Soul to rage, or kindle soft Desire.
At last Divine *Cecilia* came,
Inventress of the Vocal Frame;[18]
The sweet Enthusiast[19] from her Sacred Store,
Enlarg'd the former narrow Bounds,
And added Length to solemn Sounds,
With Nature's Mother-Wit, and Arts unknown before,
Let old *Timotheus* yield the Prize,
Or both divide the Crown;
He rais'd a Mortal to the Skies;
She drew an Angel down.[20]

GRAND CHORUS

At last, Divine Cecilia *came,*
Inventress of the Vocal Frame;
The sweet Enthusiast, from her Sacred Store,
Enlarg'd the former narrow Bounds,
And added Length to solemn Sounds,
With Nature's Mother-Wit, and Arts unknown before.
Let old Timotheus *yield the Prize,*
Or both divide the Crown;
He rais'd a Mortal to the Skies;
She drew an Angel down.

PREFACE TO FABLES ANCIENT AND MODERN[1]

'Tis with a Poet, as with a Man who designs to build, and is very exact, as he supposes, in casting up the Cost beforehand: But, generally speaking, he is mistaken in his Account, and reckons short of the Expence he first intended: He alters his Mind as the Work proceeds, and will have this or that Convenience more, of which he had not thought when he began. So has it hapned to me; I have built a House, where I intended but a Lodge: Yet with better Success than a certain Nobleman, who beginning with a Dogkennil, never liv'd to finish the Palace he had contriv'd.

From translating the First of *Homer's Iliads*, (which I intended as an Essay[2] to the whole Work) I proceeded to the Translation of the Twelfth Book of *Ovid's Metamorphoses*, because it contains, among other Things, the Causes, the Beginning, and Ending, of the *Trojan* War: Here I ought in reason to have stopp'd; but the Speeches of *Ajax* and *Ulysses* lying next in my way, I could not balk[3] 'em. When I had compass'd[4] them, I was so taken with the former Part of the Fifteenth Book, (which is the Master-piece of the whole *Metamorphoses*) that I enjoyn'd my self the pleas-

[18] the organ
[19] one specially inspired by God
[20] See the first *Song for Saint Cecilia's Day*.

[1] Text: *Fables* Ancient *and* Modern, 1700
[2] trial, preliminary attempt
[3] shirk [4] accomplished

ing Task of rendring it into *English*. And now I found, by the Number of my Verses, that they began to swell into a little Volume; which gave me an Occasion of looking backward on some Beauties of my Author, in his former Books: There occur'd to me the Hunting of the Boar, *Cinyras* and *Myrrha*, the good-natur'd Story of *Baucis* and *Philemon*, with the rest, which I hope I have translated closely enough, and given them the same Turn of Verse, which they had in the Original; and this, I may say without vanity, is not the Talent of every Poet: He who has arriv'd the nearest to it, is the Ingenious and Learned *Sandys*,[5] the best Versifier of the former Age; if I may properly call it by that Name, which was the former Part of this concluding Century. For *Spencer* and *Fairfax* both flourish'd in the Reign of Queen *Elizabeth:* Great Masters in our Language; and who saw much farther into the Beauties of our Numbers, than those who immediately followed them. *Milton* was the Poetical Son of *Spencer*, and Mr. *Waller* of *Fairfax;* for we have our Lineal Descents and Clans, as well as other Families: *Spencer* more than once insinuates, that the Soul of *Chaucer* was transfus'd into his Body; and that he was begotten by him Two hundred years after his Decease. *Milton* has acknowledg'd to me, that *Spencer* was his Original; and many besides my self have heard our famous *Waller* own, that he deriv'd the Harmony of his Numbers from the *Godfrey of Bulloign*, which was turn'd into *English* by Mr. Fairfax.[6] But to return: Having done with *Ovid* for this time, it came into my mind, that our old *English* Poet *Chaucer* in many Things resembled him, and that with no disadvantage on the Side of the Modern Author, as I shall endeavour to prove when I compare them: And as I am, and always have been studious to promote the Honour of my Native Country, so I soon resolv'd to put their Merits to the Trial, by turning some of the *Canterbury* Tales into our Language, as it is now refin'd: For by this Means both the Poets being set in the same Light, and dress'd in the same *English* Habit, Story to be compar'd with Story, a certain Judgement may be made betwixt them, by the Reader, without obtruding my Opinion on him: Or if I seem partial to my Country-man, and Predecessor in the Laurel, the Friends of Antiquity are not few: And besides many of the Learn'd, *Ovid* has almost all the *Beaux*, and the whole Fair Sex his declar'd Patrons. Perhaps I have assum'd somewhat more to my self than they allow me; because I have adventur'd to sum up the Evidence: But the Readers are the Jury; and their Privilege remains entire to decide according to the Merits of the Cause: Or, if they please to bring it to another Hearing, before some other Court. In the mean time, to follow the Thrid of my Discourse, (as Thoughts, according to Mr. *Hobbs*, have always some Connexion[7]) so from *Chaucer* I was led to think on *Boccace*, who was not only his Contempory, but also pursu'd the same Studies; wrote Novels in Prose, and many Works in Verse; particularly is said to have invented the Octave Rhyme, or *Stanza* of Eight Lines, which ever since has been maintain'd by the Practice of all *Italian* Writers, who are, or at least assume the Title of *Heroick Poets:* He and *Chaucer*, among other Things, had this in common, that they refin'd their Mother-Tongues; but with this difference, that *Dante* had begun to file their Language, at least in Verse, before the time of *Boccace*, who likewise receiv'd no little Help from his Master *Petrarch:* But the Reformation of their Prose was wholly owing to *Boccace* himself; who is yet the Standard of Purity in the *Italian* Tongue; though many of his Phrases are become obsolete, as in process of Time it must needs happen. *Chaucer* (as you have formerly been told by our learn'd Mr. *Rhymer*)[8] first adorn'd and amplified our barren Tongue from the *Provencall*,[9] which was then the most polish'd of all the Modern Languages: But this Subject has been

[5] Sandys translated Ovid into pentameter couplets, largely end-stopped.

[6] in *ottava rima* or octave rhyme but with end-stopped, balanced lines, and the final couplet very distinct

[7] i.e., by association

[8] in his *Short View of Tragedy*

[9] not, of course, an accurate view

copiously treated by that great Critick, who deserves no little Commendation from us his Countrymen. For these Reasons of Time, and Resemblance of Genius, in *Chaucer* and *Boccace,* I resolv'd to join them in my present Work; to which I have added some Original Papers of my own; which whether they are equal or inferiour to my other Poems, an Author is the most improper Judge; and therefore I leave them wholly to the Mercy of the Reader: I will hope the best, that they will not be condemn'd; but if they should, I have the Excuse of an old Gentleman, who mounting on Horseback before some Ladies, when I was present, got up somewhat heavily, but desir'd of the Fair Spectators, that they would count Fourscore and eight before they judg'd him. By the Mercy of God, I am already come within Twenty Years of his Number, a Cripple in my Limbs, but what Decays are in my Mind, the Reader must determine. I think my self as vigorous as ever in the Faculties of my Soul, excepting only my Memory, which is not impair'd to any great degree; and if I lose not more of it, I have no great reason to complain. What Judgement I had, increases rather than diminishes; and Thoughts, such as they are, come crowding in so fast upon me, that my only Difficulty is to chuse or to reject; to run them into Verse, or to give them the other Harmony of Prose, I have so long studied and practis'd both that they are grown into a Habit, and become familiar to me. In short, though I may lawfully plead some part of the old Gentleman's Excuse; yet I will reserve it till I think I have greater need, and ask no Grains of Allowance for the Faults of this my present Work, but those which are given of course to Humane Frailty. I will not trouble my Reader with the shortness of Time in which I writ it; or the several Intervals of Sickness: They who think too well of their own Performances, are apt to boast in their Prefaces how little Time their Works have cost them; and what other Business of more importance interfer'd: But the Reader will be as apt to ask the Question, Why they allow'd not a longer Time to make their Works more perfect? and why they had so despicable an Opinion of their Judges, as to thrust their indigested Stuff upon them, as if they deserv'd not better?

With this Account of my present Undertaking, I conclude the first Part of this Discourse: In the second Part, as at a second Sitting, though I alter not the Draught, I must touch the same Features over again, and change the Dead-colouring of the Whole. In general I will only say, that I have written nothing which savours of Immorality or Profaneness; at least, I am not conscious to my self of any such Intention. If there happen to be found an irreverent Expression, or a Thought too wanton, they are crept into my Verses through my Inadvertency: If the Searchers find any in the Cargo, let them be stav'd[10] or forfeited, like Counterbanded[11] Goods; at least, let their Authors be answerable for them, as being but imported Merchandise, and not of my own Manufacture. On the other Side, I have endeavour'd to chuse such Fables, both Ancient and Modern, as contain in each of them some instructive Moral, which I could prove by Induction, but the Way is tedious; and they leap foremost into sight, without the Reader's Trouble of looking after them. I wish I could affirm with a safe Conscience, that I had taken the same Care in all my former Writings; for it must be own'd, that supposing Verses are never so beautiful or pleasing, yet if they contain any thing which shocks Religion, or Good Manners, they are at best, what *Horace* says of good Numbers without good Sense, *Versus inopes rerum, nugaeque canorae:*[12] Thus far, I hope, I am Right in Court,[13] without renouncing to my other Right of Self-defence, where I have been wrongfully accus'd, and my Sense wire-drawn into Blasphemy or Bawdry as it has often been by a Religious Lawyer,[14] in a late Pleading against the Stage; in which he mixes Truth with Falshood, and has not forgotten the old Rule, of calumniating strongly, that something may remain.

[10] be broken, as a barrel

[11] declared contraband

[12] "verses empty of matter, sounding trifles," *Art of Poetry,* 322

[13] have pleaded justly

[14] reference is to the Reverend Jeremy Collier in his famous *A Short View of the Immorality and Profaneness of the English Stage,* 1698

I resume the Thrid of my Discourse with the first of my Translations, which was the First *Iliad* of *Homer*. If it shall please God to give me longer Life, and moderate Health, my Intentions are to translate the whole *Ilias;* provided still, that I meet with those Encouragements from the Publick, which may enable me to proceed in my Undertaking with some Chearfulness. And this I dare assure the World before-hand, that I have found by Trial, *Homer* a more pleasing Task than *Virgil*, (though I say not the Translation will be less laborious.) For the *Grecian* is more according to my Genius, than the *Latin* Poet. In the Works of the two Authors we may read their Manners, and natural Inclinations, which are wholly different. *Virgil* was of a quiet, sedate Temper; *Homer* was violent, impetuous, and full of Fire. The chief Talent of Virgil was Propriety of Thoughts, and Ornament of Words:[15] *Homer* was rapid in his Thoughts, and took all the Liberties both of Numbers,[16] and of Expressions, which his Language, and the Age in which he liv'd allow'd him: *Homer's* Invention[17] was more copious, *Virgil's* more confin'd: So that if *Homer* had not led the Way, it was not in *Virgil* to have begun Heroick Poetry: For, nothing can be more evident, than that the *Roman* Poem is but the second Part of the *Ilias;* a Continuation of the same Story: And the Persons already form'd: The Manners of *Æneas*, are those of *Hector* superadded to those which *Homer* gave him. The Adventures of *Ulysses* in the *Odysseis*, are imitated in the first Six Books of *Virgil's Æneis:* And though the Accidents[18] are not the same, (which would have argu'd him of a servile, copying, and total Barrenness of Invention) yet the Seas were the same, in which both the *Heroes* wander'd; and *Dido* cannot be deny'd to be the Poetical Daughter of *Calypso*. The Six latter Books of *Virgil*'s Poem, are the Four and twenty *Iliads* contracted: A Quarrel occasion'd by a Lady, a Single Combate, Battels fought, and a Town besieg'd. I say not this in derogation to *Virgil*, neither do I contradict any thing which I have formerly said in his just Praise: For his *Episodes*[19] are almost wholly of his own Invention; and the Form which he has given to the Telling, makes the Tale his own, even though the Original Story had been the same. But this proves, however, that *Homer* taught *Virgil* to design: And if Invention be the first Vertue of an Epick Poet, then the *Latin* Poem can only be allow'd the second Place. Mr. *Hobbs*, in the Preface to his own bald Translation of the *Ilias*, (studying Poetry as he did Mathematicks, when it was too late) Mr. *Hobbs*, I say, begins the Praise of *Homer* where he should have ended it. He tells us, that the first Beauty of an Epick Poem consists in Diction, that is, in the Choice of Words, and Harmony of Numbers: Now, the Words are the Colouring[20] of the Work, which in the Order of Nature[21] is last to be consider'd. The Design, the Disposition, the Manners, and the Thoughts, are all before it: Where any of those are wanting or imperfect, so much wants or is imperfect in the Imitation of Humane Life; which is in the very Definition of a Poem. Words indeed, like glaring Colours, are the first Beauties that arise, and strike the Sight; but if the Draught[22] be false or lame, the Figures ill dispos'd, the Manners obscure or inconsistent, or the Thoughts unnatural, then the finest Colours are but Dawbing, and the Piece is a beautiful Monster at the best. Neither *Virgil* nor *Homer* were deficient in any of the former Beauties; but in this last, which is Expression, the *Roman* Poet is at least equal to the *Grecian*, as I have said elsewhere; supplying the Poverty of his Language, by his Musical Ear, and by his Diligence. But to return: Our two Great Poets, being so different in their Tempers, one Cholerick and Sanguin, the other Phlegmatick and Mel-

[15] Suitability of thoughts to character, (and theme, and tone); beauty of words, "apt, sounding, and significant."

[16] versification

[17] power of designing and developing the story

[18] particulars

[19] the lesser incidents or scenes which fill out the story

[20] See the common comparison of poetry to painting.

[21] explained by what follows: in the order of significance for aesthetic effect (also, of composition)

[22] drawing

ancholick;[23] that which makes them excel in their several Ways, is, that each of them has follow'd his own natural Inclination, as well in Forming the Design, as in the Execution of it. The very *Heroes* shew their Authors: *Achilles* is hot, impatient, revengeful, *Impiger, iracundus, inexorabilis, acer*[24] *etc. Ænaeas* patient, considerate, careful of his People, and merciful to his Enemies; ever submissive to the Will of Heaven, *quo fata trahunt retrahuntque, sequamur.*[25] I could please my self with enlarging on this Subject, but am forc'd to defer it to a fitter Time. From all I have said, I will only draw this Inference, That the Action of *Homer* being more full of Vigour than that of *Virgil*, according to the Temper of the Writer, is of consequence more pleasing to the Reader. One warms you by Degrees; the other sets you on fire all at once, and never intermits his Heat. 'Tis the same Difference which *Longinus*[26] makes betwixt the Effects of Eloquence in *Demosthenes*, and *Tully*.[27] One persuades; the other commands. You never cool while you read *Homer*, even not in the Second Book, (a graceful Flattery to his Countrymen;) but he hastens from the Ships,[28] and concludes not that Book till he has made you an Amends by the violent playing of a new Machine.[29] From thence he hurries on his Action with Variety of Events, and ends it in less Compass than Two Months. This Vehemence of his, I confess, is more suitable to my Temper: and therefore I have translated his First Book with greater Pleasure than any Part of *Virgil:* But it was not a Pleasure without Pains: The continual Agitations of the Spirits, must needs be a Weakning of any Constitution, especially in Age: and many Pauses are required for Refreshment betwixt the Heats; the *Iliad* of its self being a third part longer than all *Virgil*'s Works together.

This is what I thought needful in this Place to say of *Homer*. I proceed to *Ovid*, and *Chaucer;* considering the former only in relation to the latter. With *Ovid* ended the Golden Age of the *Roman* Tongue: From *Chaucer* the Purity of the *English* Tongue began. The Manners of the Poets were not unlike: Both of them were well-bred, well-natur'd,[30] amorous, and Libertine,[31] at least in their Writings, it may be also in their Lives. Their Studies were the same, Philosophy, and Philology.[32] Both of them were knowing in Astronomy,[33] of which *Ovid*'s Books of the *Roman* Feasts, and *Chaucer*'s Treatise of the *Astrolabe*, are sufficient Witnesses. But *Chaucer* was likewise an Astrologer, as were *Virgil, Horace, Persius*, and *Manilius*. Both writ with wonderful Facility and Clearness; neither were great Inventors: For *Ovid* only copied the *Grecian* Fables; and most of *Chaucer*'s Stories were taken from his *Italian* Contemporaries, or their Predecessors: *Boccace* his *Decameron* was first publish'd; and from thence our *Englishman* has borrow'd many of his *Canterbury* Tales: Yet that of *Palamon* and *Arcite* was written in all probability by some *Italian* Wit, in a former Age; as I shall prove hereafter: The Tale of *Grizild* was the Invention of *Petrarch;* by him sent to *Boccace;* from whom it came to *Chaucer: Troilus* and *Cressida* was also written by a Lombard Author; but much amplified by our *English* Translatour, as well as beautified; The Genius of our Countrymen in general being rather to improve an Invention, than to invent themselves; as is evident not only in our Poetry, but in many of our Manu-

[23] different in their temperament, according to the prevailing ones of the four humors or fluids of the body

[24] "courageous, wrathful, ruthless, furious." Horace, *Art of Poetry*, 121

[25] "where our fates draw us hither and yon, we follow."

[26] author of the famous rhetorical and critical treatise, *On the Sublime*, just within the preceding half century becoming influential

[27] Demosthenes, the great Greek orator; Cicero, the Roman

[28] A large part of Book II is devoted to a catalogue of the ships and whom they bore.

[29] literary device, element in a work of literature; but Dryden has reversed Homer's order

[30] Endowed with good parts and temperament. Dryden has in mind the *euphues* or well-natured man of Plato.

[31] following their impulses, or licentious

[32] the study of literature in all its aspects, including grammar, etc.

[33] This and the following references sufficiently explain themselves.

factures. I find I have anticipated already, and taken up from *Boccace* before I come to him: But there is so much less behind; and I am of the Temper of most Kings, *who love to be in Debt*, are all for present Money, no matter how they pay it afterwards: Besides, the Nature of a Preface is rambling; never wholly out of the Way, nor in it. This I have learn'd from the Practice of honest *Montaign*,[34] and return at my pleasure to *Ovid* and *Chaucer*, of whom I have little more to say. Both of them build on the Inventions of other Men; yet since *Chaucer* had something of his own, as *The Wife of Baths Tale*, *The Cock and the Fox*, which I have translated, and some others, I may justly give our Countryman the Precedence in that Part; since I can remember nothing of *Ovid* which was wholly his. Both of them understood the Manners; under which Name I comprehend the Passions, and, in a larger Sense, the Descriptions of Persons, and their very Habits: For an Example, I see *Baucis* and *Philemon* as perfectly before me, as if some ancient Painter had drawn them; and all the Pilgrims in the *Canterbury* Tales, their Humours,[35] their Features, and the very Dress, as distinctly as if I had supp'd with them at the *Tabard* in *Southwark*:[36] Yet even there too the Figures of *Chaucer* are much more lively, and set in a better Light: Which though I have not time to prove; yet I appeal to the Reader, and am sure he will clear me from Partiality. The Thoughts and Words remain to be consider'd, in the Comparison of the Two Poets; and I have sav'd my self one half of that Labour, by owning that *Ovid* liv'd when the *Roman* Tongue was in its Meridian; *Chaucer*, in the Dawning of our Language: Therefore that Part of the Comparison stands not on an equal Foot, any more than the Diction of *Ennius* and *Ovid*;[37] or of *Chaucer*, and our present *English*. The Words are given up as a Post not to be defended in our Poet, because he wanted the Modern Art of Fortifying.[38] The Thoughts remain to be consider'd: And they are to be measur'd only by their Propriety; that is, as they flow more or less naturally from the Persons describ'd, on such and such Occasions. The Vulgar[39] Judges, which are Nine Parts in Ten of all Nations, who call Conceits and Jingles Wit, who see *Ovid* full of them, and *Chaucer* altogether without them, will think me little less than mad, for preferring the *Englishman* to the *Roman*: Yet, with their leave, I must presume to say, that the Things they admire are only glittering Trifles, and so far from being Witty, that in a serious Poem they are nauseous, because they are unnatural. Wou'd any Man who is ready to die for Love, describe his Passion like *Narcissus?* Wou'd he think of *inopem me copia fecit*,[40] and a Dozen more of such Expressions, pour'd on the Neck of one another, and signifying all the same Thing? If this were Wit, was this a Time to be witty, when the poor Wretch was in the Agony of Death? This is just *John Littlewit* in *Bartholomew Fair*,[41] who had a Conceit (as he tells you) left him in his Misery; a miserable Conceit. On these Occasions the Poet shou'd endeavour to raise Pity: But instead of this, *Ovid* is tickling you to laugh. *Virgil* never made use of such Machines,[42] when he was moving you to commiserate the Death of *Dido:* He would not destroy what he was building. *Chaucer* makes *Arcite* violent in his Love, and unjust in the Pursuit of it: Yet when he came to die, he made him think more reasonably: He repents not of his Love, for that had[43] alter'd his Character; but acknowledges the Injustice of his Proceedings, and resigns *Emilia* to *Palamon*. What would *Ovid* have done on this Occasion? He would certainly have made *Arcite*

[34] the great French sceptical essayist of the Renaissance

[35] fluids that determined temperament; here, dominant traits

[36] where they met on the eve of the pilgrimage

[37] Ennius was the first major Latin poet; Ovid wrote at the height of Roman poetry.

[38] From the early Renaissance, poets had sought to enrich the language of poetry by bringing back words going out of use or foreign words for which there was no good or elegant English equivalent. Dryden brought in Latin, French and a few older English words.

[39] belonging to the mass of men or crowd

[40] "my abundance makes me poor"

[41] By Ben Jonson; *a conceit* is a thought, notion.

[42] devices [43] would have

witty on his Death-bed. He had complain'd he was farther off from Possession, by being so near, and a thousand such Boyisms, which *Chaucer* rejected as below the Dignity of the Subject. They who think otherwise, would by the same Reason prefer *Lucan* and *Ovid* to *Homer* and *Virgil*, and *Martial* to all Four of them. As for the Turn of Words,[44] in which *Ovid* particularly excels all Poets; they are sometimes a Fault, and sometimes a Beauty, as they are us'd properly or improperly; but in strong Passions always to be shunn'd, because Passions are serious, and will admit no Playing. The *French* have a high Value for them; and I confess, they are often what they call Delicate, when they are introduc'd with Judgement; but *Chaucer* writ with more Simplicity, and follow'd Nature more closely, than to use them. I have thus far, to the best of my Knowledge, been an upright Judge betwixt the Parties in Competition, not medling with the Design nor the Disposition of it; because the Design was not their own; and in the disposing of it they were equal. It remains that I say somewhat of *Chaucer* in particular.

In the first place, As he is the Father of *English* Poetry, so I hold him in the same Degree of Veneration as the *Grecians* held *Homer*, or the *Romans Virgil:* He is a perpetual Fountain of good Sense; learn'd in all Sciences;[45] and therefore speaks properly on all Subjects: As he knew what to say, so he knows also when to leave off; a Continence which is practis'd by few Writers, and scarcely by any of the Ancients, excepting *Virgil* and *Horace*. One of our late great Poets[46] is sunk in his Reputation, because he cou'd never forgive any Conceit which came in his way; but swept like a Drag-net, great and small. There was plenty enough, but the Dishes were ill sorted; whole Pyramids of Sweet-meats, for Boys and Women; but little of solid Meat, for Men: All this proceeded not from any want of Knowledge, but of Judgment; neither did he want that in discerning the Beauties and Faults of other Poets; but only indulg'd himself in the Luxury of Writing; and perhaps knew it was a Fault, but hop'd the Reader would not find it. For this Reason, though he must always be thought a great Poet, he is no longer esteem'd a good Writer: And for Ten Impressions, which his Works have had in so many successive Years, yet at present a hundred Books are scarcely purchas'd once a Twelvemonth: For, as my last Lord *Rochester*[47] said, though somewhat profanely, *Not being of God, he could not stand.*

Chaucer follow'd Nature every where; but was never so bold to go beyond her: And there is a great Difference of being *Poeta* and *nimis Poeta*,[48] if we may believe *Catullus*, as much as betwixt a modest Behaviour and Affectation. The Verse of *Chaucer*, I confess, is not Harmonious to us; but 'tis like the Eloquence of one whom *Tacitus* commends, it was *auribus istius temporis accommodata:*[49] They who liv'd with him, and some time after him, thought it Musical; and it continues so even in our Judgment, if compar'd with the Numbers of *Lidgate* and *Gower*[50] his Contemporaries: There is the rude Sweetness of a *Scotch* Tune in it, which is natural and pleasing, though not perfect. 'Tis true, I cannot go so far as he who publish'd the last Edition of him;[51] for he would make us believe the Fault is in our Ears, and that there were really Ten Syllables in a Verse where we find but Nine: But this Opinion is not worth confuting; 'tis so gross and obvious an Errour, that common Sense (which is a Rule in every thing but Matters of Faith and Revelation) must[52] convince the Reader, that Equality of Numbers in every Verse which we call

[44] a beauty of style consisting in the repetition of words, the second introducing a new phrase or clause and turning the thought; much studied by Dryden in his later years

[45] organized body of knowledge; "subject," as we should say

[46] Cowley [47] our second earl

[48] "too much a poet"; Catullus, Roman poet; but as Ker points out, really Martial III, 44

[49] "suited to the ears of that time"; Tacitus, greatest Roman historian

[50] more even, but far less responsive to speech rhythms than Chaucer

[51] Speght, editions of 1597 and 1602, pointed out that most of the lines do contain ten syllables; and we today recognize the great beauty of some nine syllable lines.

[52] misprinted *mnst* in the original

Heroick,[53] was either not known, or not always practis'd in *Chaucer*'s Age. It were an easie Matter to produce some thousands of his Verses, which are lame for want of half a Foot, and sometimes a whole one, and which no Pronunciation can make otherwise. We can only say, that he liv'd in the Infancy of our Poetry, and that nothing is brought to Perfection at the first. We must be Children before we grow Men. There was an *Ennius*, and in process of Time a *Lucilius*, and a *Lucretius*, before *Virgil* and *Horace;* even after *Chaucer* there was a *Spencer*, a *Harrington*, a *Fairfax*,[54] before *Waller* and *Denham* were in being: And our Numbers were in their Nonage[55] till these last appear'd. I need say little of his Parentage, Life, and Fortunes: They are to be found at large in all the Editions of his Works. He was employ'd abroad, and favour'd by *Edward* the Third, *Richard* the Second, and *Henry* the Fourth, and was Poet, as I suppose, to all Three of them. In *Richard*'s Time, I doubt, he was a little dipt in the Rebellion of the Commons; and being Brother-in-Law to John of Ghant,[56] it was no wonder if he follow'd the Fortunes of that Family; and was well with *Henry* the Fourth when he had depos'd his Predecessor. Neither is it to be admir'd, that *Henry*, who was a wise as well as a valiant Prince, who claim'd by Succession, and was sensible that his Title was not sound, but was rightfully in *Mortimer*, who had married the Heir of *York;* it was not to be admir'd, I say, if that great Politician should be pleas'd to have the greatest Wit of those Times in his Interests, and to be the Trumpet of his Praises. *Augustus* had given him the Example, by the Advice of *Mecænas*,[57] who recommended *Virgil* and *Horace* to him; whose Praises help'd to make him Popular while he was alive, and after his Death have made him Precious to Posterity. As for the Religion of our Poet, he seems to have some little Byas towards the Opinions of *Wickliff*,[58] after *John of Gaunt* his Patron; somewhat of which appears in the Tale of *Piers Plowman:*[59] Yet I cannot blame him for inveighing so sharply against the Vices of the Clergy in his Age: Their Pride, their Ambition, their Pomp, their Avarice, their Worldly Interest, deserv'd the Lashes which he gave them, both in that, and in most of his *Canterbury Tales:* Neither has his Contemporary *Boccace*, spar'd them. Yet both those Poets liv'd in much esteem, with good and holy Men in Orders: For the Scandal which is given by particular Priests, reflects not on the Sacred Function.[60] *Chaucer*'s *Monk*, his *Chanon*, and his *Fryar*, took not from the Character of his *Good Parson*. A Satyrical Poet is the Check of the Laymen, on bad Priests. We are only to take care, that we involve not the Innocent with the Guilty in the same Condemnation. The Good cannot be too much honour'd, nor the Bad too coursly us'd: For the Corruption of the Best, becomes the Worst. When a Clergy-man is whipp'd his Gown is first taken off, by which the Dignity of his Order is secur'd: If he be wrongfully accus'd he has his Action of Slander; and 'tis at the Poet's Peril, if he transgress the Law. But they will tell us, that all kind of Satire, though never so well deserv'd by particular Priests, yet brings the whole Order into Contempt. Is then the Peerage of *England* any thing dishonour'd, when a Peer suffers for his Treason? If he be libell'd, or any way defam'd, he has his *Scandalum Magnatum*[61] to punish the Offender. They who use this kind of Argument, seem to be conscious to themselves of somewhat which has deserv'd the Poet's Lash; and are less concern'd for their Publick Capacity, than for

[53] iambic pentameter

[54] Harrington, translator of *Orlando Furiosos*, 1591; Fairfax, translator of Ariosto, and Waller's model for verse

[55] under legal age

[56] John of Gaunt, uncle of Richard II was believed to have favored popular movements such as Wat Tyler's rebellion. He became Chaucer's brother-in-law by a late marriage.

[57] counsellor of the Emperor Augustus; patron of Virgil and Horace, so that his name became a byword for patron

[58] the early reformer and translator of the Bible; a view of Chaucer not held to-day

[59] Dryden has in mind not Langland's poem, but the *Ploughman's Tale*, printed with the *Canterbury Tales* and then ascribed to Chaucer.

[60] misprinted *Fuuction* in the original text

[61] charge of libel against authorities or magistrates

their Private: At least, there is Pride at the bottom of their Reasoning. If the Faults of Men in Orders are only to be judg'd among themselves, they are all in some sort Parties: For, since they say the Honour of their Order is concern'd in every Member of it, how can we be sure, that they will be impartial Judges? How far I may be allow'd to speak my Opinion in this Case, I know not: But I am sure a Dispute of this Nature caus'd Mischief in abundance betwixt a King of *England* and an Archbishop of *Canterbury;* one standing up for the Laws of his Land, and the other for the Honour (as he call'd it) of God's Church; which ended in the Murther of the Prelate, and in the whipping of his Majesty from Post to Pillar for his Penance.[62] The Learn'd and Ingenious Dr. *Drake*[63] has sav'd me the Labour on inquiring into the Esteem and Reverence which the Priests have had of old; and I would rather extend than diminish any part of it: Yet I must needs say, that when a Priest provokes me without any Occasion given him, I have no Reason, unless it be the Charity of a *Christian,* to forgive him: *Prior laesit*[64] is Justification sufficient in the Civil Law. If I answer him in his own Language, Self-defence, I am sure, must be allow'd me; and if I carry it farther, even to a sharp Recrimination, somewhat may be indulg'd to Humane Frailty. Yet my Resentment has not wrought so far, but that I have follow'd *Chaucer* in his Character of a Holy Man,[65] and have enlarg'd on that Subject with some Pleasure, reserving to my self the Right, if I shall think fit hereafter, to describe another sort of Priests, such as are more easily to be found than the Good Parson; such as have given the last Blow to Christianity in this Age, by a Practice so contrary to their Doctrine. But this will keep cold till another time. In the mean while, I take up *Chaucer* where I left him. He must have been a Man of a most wonderful comprehensive Nature, because, as it has been truly observ'd of him, he has taken into the Compass of his *Canterbury Tales* the various Manners and Humours (as we now call them) of the whole *English* Nation, in his Age. Not a single Character has escap'd him. All his Pilgrims are severally distinguish'd from each other; and not only in their Inclinations, but in their very Phisiogomies and Persons. *Baptista Porta*[66] could not have describ'd their Natures better, than by the Marks which the Poet gives them. The Matter and Manner of their Tales, and of their Telling, are so suited to their different Educations, Humours, and Callings, that each of them would be improper in any other Mouth. Even the grave and serious Characters are distinguish'd by their several sorts of Gravity: Their Discourses are such as belong to their Age, their Calling, and their Breeding; such as are becoming of[67] them and of them only. Some of his Persons are Vicious, and some Vertuous; some are unlearn'd, or (as *Chaucer* calls them) Lewd, and some are Learn'd. Even the Ribaldry of the Low Characters is different: The *Reeve,* the *Miller,* and the *Cook,* are several Men, and distinguish'd from each other, as much as the mincing Lady Prioress, and the broad-speaking gap-tooth'd Wife of *Bathe.* But enough of this: There is such a Variety of Game springing up before me, that I am distracted in my Choice, and know not which to follow. 'Tis sufficient to say according to the Proverb, that here is God's Plenty. We have our Forefathers and Great Grand-dames all before us, as they were in *Chaucer*'s Days; their general Characters are still remaining in Mankind, and even in *England,* though they are call'd by other Names than those of *Moncks,* and *Fryars,* and *Chanons,* and *Lady Abbesses,* and *Nuns:* For Mankind is ever the same, and nothing lost out of Nature, though every thing is alter'd. May I have leave to do my

[62] Henry II and Thomas à Becket, murdered by some of Henry's knights after a rash word of the King's

[63] James Drake, author of an answer to Collier, 1699

[64] "He injured me first"; a legal term used by Terence in the prologue to his *Eunuchus,* as Ker points out

[65] Dryden made a moralized translation of the character of the parson

[66] Giambattista Della Porta, Italian scientist of the sixteenth century, author of a work on physiognomy, *De humana physiognomia,* 1586

[67] fitting to

self the Justice, (since my Enemies will do me none, and are so far from granting me to be a good Poet, that they will not allow me so much as to be a Christian, or a Moral Man) may I have leave, I say, to inform my Reader, that I have confin'd my Choice to such Tales of *Chaucer*, as favour nothing of Immodesty. If I had desir'd more to please than to instruct, the *Reve*, the *Miller*, the *Shipman*, the *Merchant*, the *Sumner*, and above all, the *Wife of Bathe*, in the Town. But I will no more offend procur'd me as many Friends and Readers, as there are *Beaux* and Ladies of Pleasure in the Town. But I will no more offend against Good Manners: I am sensible as I ought to be of the Scandal I have given by my loose Writings; and make what Reparation I am able, by this Publick Acknowledgment. If any thing of this Nature, or of Profaneness, be crept into these Poems, I am so far from defending it, that I disown it. *Totum hoc indictum volo.*[68] *Chaucer* makes another manner of Apologie for his broad-speaking, and *Boccace* makes the like; but I will follow neither of them. Our Country-man, in the end of his Characters,[69] before the *Canterbury Tales*, thus excuses Ribaldry, which is very gross, in many of his Novels.

> But first, I pray you, of your courtesy,
> That ye ne arrete it nought my villany,
> Though that I plainly speak in this mattere
> To tellen you her words, and eke her chere:
> Ne though I speak her words properly,
> For this ye knowen as well as I,
> Who shall tellen a tale after a man
> He mote rehearse as nye, as ever He can:
> Everich word of it been in his charge,
> *All speke he, never so rudely, ne large.*
> Or else he mote tellen his tale untrue,
> Or feine things, or find words new:
> He may not spare, altho he were his brother,
> He mote as well say o word as another.
> *Christ* spake himself full broad in holy Writ,
> And well I wrote no Villany is it.
> Eke *Plato* saith, who so can him rede,
> The words mote been Cousin to the dede.

Yet if a Man should have enquir'd of *Boccace* or of *Chaucer*, what need they had of introducing such Characters, where obscene Words were proper in their Mouths, but very undecent to be heard; I know not what Answer they could have made: For that Reason, such Tales shall be left untold by me. You have here a *Specimen* of *Chaucer*'s Language, which is so obsolete, that his Sense is scarce to be understood; and you have likewise more than one Example of his unequal Numbers,[70] which were mention'd before. Yet many of his Verses consist of Ten Syllables, and the Words not much behind our present *English:* As for Example, these two Lines, in the Description of the Carpenter's Young Wife:

> Wincing she was, as is a jolly Colt,
> Long as a Mast, and upright as a Bolt.

I have almost done with *Chaucer*, when I have answer'd some Objections relating to my present Work. I find some People are offended that I have turn'd these Tales into modern *English;* because they think them unworthy of my Pains, and look on *Chaucer* as a dry, old-fashion'd Wit, not worth receiving. I have often heard the late Earl of *Leicester*[71] say, that Mr. *Cowley* himself was of that opinion; who having read him over at my Lord's Request, declar'd he had no Taste of him. I dare not advance my Opinion against the Judgment of so great an Author: But I think it fair, however, to leave the Decision to the Publick: Mr. *Cowley* was too modest to set up for a Dictatour; and being shock'd perhaps with his old Style, never examin'd into the depths of his good Sense. *Chaucer*, I confess, is a rough Diamond, and must first be polish'd e'er he shines. I deny not likewise, that living in our early Days of Poetry, he writes not always of a piece; but sometimes mingles trivial Things, with those of greater Moment. Sometimes also, though not often, he runs riot, like *Ovid*, and knows not when he has said enough. But there are more great Wits, beside *Chaucer*, whose Fault is their Excess of Conceits, and those ill sorted.[72] An Author is not to write all he can, but only all he ought. Having observ'd this Redundancy in

[68] "I wish all this unsaid."
[69] i.e., at the end of the Prologue
[70] uneven verses
[71] the third earl, to whom Dryden dedicated *Don Sebastian*
[72] ill-matched, ill-agreeing

Chaucer, (as it is an easie Matter for a Man of ordinary Parts to find a Fault in one of greater) I have not ty'd my self to a Literal Translation; but have often omitted what I judg'd unnecessary, or not of Dignity enough to appear in the Company of better Thoughts. I have presum'd farther in some Places, and added somewhat of my own where I thought my Author was deficient, and had not given his Thoughts their true Lustre, for want of Words in the Beginning of our Language. And to this I was the more embolden'd, because (if I may be permitted to say it of my self) I found I had a Soul congenial to his, and that I had been conversant in the same Studies. Another Poet, in another Age, may take the same Liberty with my Writings; if at least they live long enough to deserve Correction. It was also necessary sometimes to restore the Sense of *Chaucer*, which was lost or mangled in the Errors of the Press: Let this Example suffice at present in the Story of *Palamon* and *Arcite*, where the Temple of *Diana* is describ'd, you find these Verses, in all the Editions of our Author:

There saw I *Danè* turned unto a Tree,
I mean not the Goddess *Diane*,
But *Venus* Daughter, which that hight *Danè*.

Which after a little Consideration I knew was to be reform'd into this Sense, that *Daphne* the Daughter of *Peneus* was turn'd into a Tree. I durst not make thus bold with *Ovid*, lest some future *Milbourn*[73] should arise, and say, I varied from my Author, because I understood him not.

But there are other Judges who think I ought not to have translated *Chaucer* into *English*, out of a quite contrary Notion: They suppose there is a certain Veneration due to his old Language; and that it is little less than Profanation and Sacrilege to alter it. They are farther of opinion, that somewhat of his good Sense will suffer in this Transfusion, and much of the Beauty of his Thoughts will infallibly be lost, which appear with more Grace in their old Habit. Of this Opinion was that excellent Person, whom I mention'd, the late Earl of *Leicester*, who valu'd *Chaucer* as much as Mr. *Cowley* despis'd him. My Lord dissuaded me from this Attempt, (for I was thinking of it some Years before his Death) and his Authority prevail'd so far with me, as to defer my Understanding while he liv'd, in deference to him: Yet my Reason was not convinc'd with what he urg'd against it. If the first End of a Writer be to be understood, then as his Language grows obsolete, his Thoughts must grow obscure, *multa renascuntur quæ nunc cecidere; cadentque quæ nunc sunt in honore vocabula, si volet usus, quem penes arbitrium est et jus et norma loquendi.*[74] When an ancient Word for its Sound and Significancy deserves to be reviv'd, I have that reasonable Veneration for Antiquity, to restore it. All beyond this is Superstition. Words are not like Land-marks, so sacred as never to be remov'd: Customs are chang'd, and even Statutes are silently repeal'd, when the Reason ceases for which they were enacted. As for the other Part of the Argument, that his Thoughts will lose of their original Beauty, by the innovation of Words; in the first place, not only their Beauty, but their Being is lost, where they are no longer understood, which is the present Case. I grant, that something must be lost in all Transfusion, that is, in all Translations; but the Sense will remain, which would otherwise be lost, or at least be maim'd, when it is scarce intelligible; and that but to a few. How few are there who can read *Chaucer*, so as to understand him perfectly? And if imperfectly, then with less Profit, and no Pleasure. 'Tis not for the Use of some old *Saxon* Friends,[75] that I have taken these Pains with him: Let them neglect my Version, because they have no need of it. I made it for their sakes who understand Sense and Poetry, as well as they; when that Poetry and Sense is put into Words which they understand. I will go farther, and dare to add, that what Beauties I lose in some Places, I give to others which had them not originally: But in this I may be

[73] a scurrilous and stupid critic of Dryden's Virgil, a translator himself

[74] "Many words which now have died shall be born again, and many which are now honored shall fall, if it pleases usage, with whom resides the judgment, the law, and the norm of speaking." Horace, *The Art of Poetry*, 70–73

[75] Modern studies of Old English or Anglo-Saxon were beginning at this time.

partial to my self; let the Reader judge, and I submit to his Decision. Yet I think I have just Occasion to complain of them, who because they understand *Chaucer*, would deprive the greater part of their Countrymen of the same Advantage, and hoord him up, as Misers do their Grandam[76] Gold, only to look on it themselves, and hinder others from making use of it. In sum, I seriously protest, that no Man ever had, or can have, a greater Veneration for *Chaucer*, than my self. I have translated some part of his Works, only that I might perpetuate his Memory, or a least refresh it, amongst my Countrymen. If I have alter'd him any where for the better, I must at the same time acknowledge, that I could have done nothing without him: *Facile est inventis addere*,[77] is no great Commendation; and I am not so vain to think I have deserv'd a greater. I will conclude what I have to say of him singly, with this one Remark: A Lady of my Acquaintance, who keeps a kind of Correspondence with some Authors of the Fair Sex in *France*, has been inform'd by them, that *Mademoiselle de Scudery*, who is as old as *Sibyl*,[78] and inspir'd like her by the same God of Poetry, is at this time translating *Chaucer* into modern *French*. From which I gather, that he has been formerly translated into the old *Provencall*,[79] (for, how she should come to understand Old *English*, I know not.) But the Matter of Fact being true, it makes me think, that there is something in it like Fatality; that after certain Periods of Time, the Fame and Memory of Great Wits should be renew'd, as *Chaucer* is both in *France* and *England*. If this be wholly Chance, 'tis extraordinary; and I dare not call it more, for fear of being tax'd with Superstition.

Boccace comes last to be consider'd, who living in the same Age with *Chaucer*, had the same Genius, and follow'd the same Studies: Both writ Novels, and each of them cultivated his Mother-Tongue: But the greatest Resemblance of our two Modern Authors being in their familiar Style, and pleasing way of relating Comical Adventures, I may pass it over, because I have translated nothing from *Boccace* of that Nature. In the serious Part of Poetry, the Advantage is wholly on Chaucer's Side; for though the *Englishman* has borrow'd many Tales from the *Italian*, yet it appears, that those of *Boccace* were not generally of his own making, but taken from Authors of former Ages, and by him only modell'd: So that what there was of Invention in either of them, may be judg'd equal. But *Chaucer* has refin'd on *Boccace*, and has mended the Stories which he has borrow'd, in his way of telling; though Prose allows more Liberty of Thought, and the Expression is more easie, when unconfin'd by Numbers. Our Countryman carries Weight, and yet wins the Race at disadvantage. I desire not the Reader should take my Word; and therefore I will set two of their Discourses on the same Subject, in the same Light, for every Man to judge betwixt them. I translated *Chaucer* first, and amongst the rest, pitch'd on the Wife of *Bath*'s Tale; not daring as I have said, to adventure on her Prologue; because 'tis too licentious: There *Chaucer* introduced an old Woman of mean Parentage, whom a youthful Knight of Noble Blood was forc'd to marry, and consequently loath'd her: The Crone being in bed with him on the wedding Night, and finding his Aversion, endeavours to win his Affection by Reason, and speaks a good Word for her self, (as who could blame her?) in hope to mollifie the sullen Bridegroom. She takes her Topiques from the Benefits of Poverty, the Advantages of old Age and Ugliness, the Vanity of Youth, and the silly Pride of Ancestry and Titles without inherent Vertue, which is the true Nobility. When I had clos'd *Chaucer*, I return'd to *Ovid*, and translated some more of his Fables; and by this time had so far forgotten the Wife of *Bath*'s Tale, that when I took up *Boccace*, unawares I fell on the same Argument of preferring Virtue to Nobility of Blood, and Titles, in the Story of *Sigismonda;* which I had certainly avoided for the Resemblance of the two

[76] a genealogy of obvious comic origin. Ker cites Dryden's own *Wild Gallant*.

[77] "It is easy to add to what has already been discovered."

[78] very ancient woman who acted as prophetess of the god who inspired her, in Roman belief, particularly Apollo, as she uttered her prophecies in verse. Mlle. de Scudéry was the famous author of long heroic romances.

[79] Dryden confused Provençal and French.

Discourses, if my Memory had not fail'd me. Let the Reader weigh them both; and if he thinks me partial to *Chaucer*, 'tis in him to right *Boccace*.

I prefer in our Countryman, far above all his other Stories, the Noble Poem of *Palamon* and *Arcite*, which is of the *Epique* kind, and perhaps not much inferiour to the *Ilias* or the *Æneis:* the Story is more pleasing than either of them, the Manners as perfect, the Diction as poetical, the Learning as deep and various; and the Disposition[80] full as artful: only it includes a greater length of time; as taking up seven years at least; but *Aristotle* has left undecided the Duration of the Action; which yet is easily reduc'd into the Compass of a year, by a Narration of what preceded the Return of *Palamon* to *Athens*. I had thought for the Honour of our Nation, and more particularly for his, whose Laurel, tho' unworthy, I have worn after him,[81] that this Story was of *English* Growth, and *Chaucer*'s own: But I was undeceiv'd by *Boccace;* for casually looking on the End of his seventh *Giornata*,[82] I found *Dioneo* (under which name he shadows himself) and *Fiametta* (who represents his Mistress, the natural Daughter of *Robert* King of *Naples*) of whom these Words are spoken. *Dioneo e Fiametta gran pezza eantarono insieme d' Arcita, e di Palamone:*[83] by which it appears that this Story was written before the time of *Boccace;* but the Name of its Author being wholly lost, *Chaucer* is now become an Original; and I question not but the Poem has receiv'd many Beauties by passing through his Noble Hands. Besides this Tale, there is another of his own Invention, after the manner of the *Provencalls*, call'd *The Flower and the Leaf;*[84] with which I was so particularly pleas'd, both for the Invention and the Moral; that I cannot hinder my self from recommending it to the Reader.

As a Corollary to this Preface, in which I have done Justice to others, I owe somewhat to my self: not that I think it worth my time to enter the Lists with one M———, or one B———,[85] but barely to take notice, that such Men there are who have written scurrilously against me without any Provocation. M———, who is in Orders,[86] pretends amongst the rest this Quarrel to me, that I have fallen foul on Priesthood: If I have, I am only to ask Pardon of good Priests, and am afraid his part of the Reparation will come to little. Let him be satisfied that he shall not be able to force himself upon me for an Adversary. I contemn him too much to enter into Competition with him. His own Translations of *Virgil* have answer'd his Criticisms on mine. If (as they say, he has declar'd in Print) he prefers the Version of *Ogilby*[87] to mine, the World has made him the same Compliment: For 'tis agreed on all hands, that he writes even below *Ogilby:* That, you will say, is not easily to be done; but what cannot M——— bring about? I am satisfy'd however, that while he and I live together, I shall not be thought the worst Poet of the Age. It looks as if I had desir'd him underhand to write so ill against me: But upon my honest Word I have not brib'd him to do me this Service, and am wholly guiltless of his Pamphlet. 'Tis true I should be glad, if I could persuade him to continue his good Offices, and write such another Critique on any thing of mine: For I find by Experience he has a great Stroke[88] with the Reader, when he condemns any of my Poems to make the World have a better Opinion of them. He has taken some Pains with my Poetry; but no body will be persuaded to take the same with his. If I had taken to the Church (as he affirms, but which was never in my Thoughts) I should have more Sense, if not more Grace, than to have turn'd my self out of

[80] arrangement of parts

[81] Chaucer was regarded as having been poet laureate.

[82] Boccaccio's *Decameron* was arranged in groups of tales told on successive days.

[83] "D. and F. sang together a long piece about Arcite and Palamon"; *eantorono* is in the original.

[84] not by Chaucer, though once ascribed to him

[85] Milbourne and Sir Richard Blackmore, critics of Dryden, the second, author of an epic

[86] an ordained clergyman

[87] a contemporary author of a literal translation

[88] The metaphor is taken from games, as tennis.

my Benefice by writing Libels on my Parishioners. But his Account of my Manners and my Principles, are of a Piece with his Cavils[89] and his Poetry: And so I have done with him for ever.

As for the City Bard,[90] or Knight Physician, I hear his Quarrel to me is, that I was the Author of *Absalom* and *Architophel*, which he thinks is a little hard on his Fanatique Patrons in *London*.

But I will deal the more civilly with his two Poems, because nothing ill is to be spoken of the Dead: And therefore Peace be to the *Manes*[91] of his *Arthurs*. I will only say that it was not for this Noble Knight that I drew the Plan of an Epick Poem on King *Arthur* in my Preface to the Translation of *Juvenal*.[92] The Guardian Angels of Kingdoms were Machines too ponderous for him to manage; and therefore he rejected them as *Dares* did the Whirl-bats of *Eryx* when they were thrown before him by *Entellus*:[93] Yet from that Preface he plainly took his Hint: For he began immediately upon the Story; though he had the Baseness not to acknowledge his Benefactor; but in stead of it, to traduce me in a Libel.

I shall say the less of Mr. *Collier*,[94] because in many Things he has tax'd me justly; and I have pleaded Guilty to all Thoughts and Expressions of mine, which can be truly argu'd of[95] Obscenity, Profaneness, or Immorality; and retract them. If he be my Enemy, let him triumph; if he be my Friend, as I have given him no Personal Occasion to be otherwise, he will be glad of my Repentance. It becomes me not to draw my Pen in the Defence of a bad Cause, when I have so often drawn it for a good one. Yet it were not difficult to prove, that in many Places he has perverted my Meaning by his Glosses;[96] and interpreted my Words into Blasphemy and Baudry, of which they were not guilty. Besides that, he is too much given to Horse-play in his Raillery; and comes to Battel, like a Dictatour from the Plough. I will not say, *The Zeal of Gods House has eaten him up;* but I am sure it has devour'd some Part of his Good Manners and Civility. It might also be doubted, whether it were altogether Zeal, which prompted him to this rough manner of Proceeding; perhaps it became not one of his Function to rake into the Rubbish of Ancient and Modern Plays; a Divine might have employ'd his Pains to better purpose, than in the Nastiness of *Plautus* and *Aristophanes;* whose Examples, as they excuse not me, so it might be possibly suppos'd, that he read them not without some Pleasure. They who have written Commentaries on those Poets, or on *Horace*, *Juvenal*, and *Martial*, have explain'd some Vices, which without their Interpretation had been unknown to Modern Times. Neither has he judg'd impartially betwixt the former Age and us.

There is more Baudry in one Play of *Fletcher*'s, call'd *The Custom of the Country*, than in all ours together. Yet this has been often acted on the Stage in my remembrance. Are the Times so much more reform'd now, than they were Five and twenty Years ago? If they are, I congratulate the Amendment of our Morals. But I am not to prejudice the Cause of my Fellow-Poets, though I abandon my own Defence: They have some of them answer'd for themselves,[97] and neither they nor I can think Mr. *Collier* so formidable an Enemy, that we should shun him. He has lost Ground at the latter end of the Day, by pursuing his Point too far, like the Prince of *Condé* at the Battel of *Senneph*:[98] From

[89] captious objection [90] Blackmore

[91] shades of the dead: *Prince Arthur* (1695) and *King Arthur* (1697)

[92] Writing on the much discussed problem of the proper subject and treatment for a modern epic, Dryden had proposed King Arthur as a fitting English subject and the guardian angels of nations as the proper substitute for the supernatural persons of the ancient epics.

[93] The story is told in Virgil's *Aneid*, V, 400. Dares, an insolent young man, is carrying off the prize in a boxing match, for want of a competitor, when Entellus, who had hesitated to enter because of old age, throws into the ring the metal-weighted hand bindings of his famous teacher Eryx, which Dares dared not try to use.

[94] Jeremy Collier; see previous note.

[95] convicted of [96] interpretations of words

[97] There were several pamphlets in answer, including one by Congreve and another by Van Brugh.

[98] 1674; the great French general was opposed by Prince William, now King William.

Immoral Plays, to No Plays; *ab abusu ad usum, non valet consequentia.*[99] But being a Party, I am not to erect my self into a Judge. As for the rest of those who have written against me, they are such Scoundrels, that they deserve not the least Notice to be taken of them. B——— and M——— are only distinguish'd from the Crowd, by being remember'd to their Infamy.

. . . Demetri, Teque Tigelli
Discipularum inter jubeo plorare cathedras.[100]

THE SECULAR MASQUE[1]

Enter Janus.[2]

Janus.

Chronos, Chronos,[3] mend thy Pace,
An hundred times the rowling Sun
Around the Radiant Belt[4] has run
In his revolving Race.
Behold, behold, the Goal in sight,
Spread thy Fans,[5] and wing thy flight.

Enter Chronos, *with a Scythe in his hand, and a great Globe on his Back, which he sets down at his entrance.*

Chronos.

Weary, weary of my weight,
Let me, let me drop my Freight,
And leave the World behind.
I could not bear
Another Year
The Load of Human-kind.

Enter Momus[6] *Laughing.*

Momus.

Ha! ha! ha! Ha! ha! ha! well hast thou done,
To lay down thy Pack,
And lighten thy Back,
The world was a Fool, e'er since it begun,
And since neither *Janus*, nor *Chronos*, nor I,
Can hinder the Crimes,
Or mend the Bad Times,
'Tis better to Laugh than to Cry.

Cho. of all 3.

'Tis better to Laugh than to Cry.

Janus.

Since *Momus* comes to laugh below,
Old Time begin the Show,
That he may see, in every Scene,
What Changes in this Age have been,

Chronos.

Then Goddess of the Silver Bow begin.

[99] "It is invalid to argue from the abuse of a thing to the use."
[100] Horace bade Demetrius, a trainer of choruses, and Tigellius, a singer and would-be poet, to "go cry among the chairs of your lady pupils."
[1] Masque of the century (Latin *saecula*, era of time). Text, Fletcher's *The Pilgrim*, 1700
[2] god of the opening year [3] time [4] the zodiac [5] vans, wings
[6] spirit of uncontrolled mirth or mockery

Horns, or Hunting-Musique within.

Enter Diana.[7]

Diana. With Horns and with Hounds I waken the Day.
And hye to my Woodland walks away;
I tuck up my Robe, and am buskin'd[8] soon,
And tye to my Forehead a wexing Moon.
I course the fleet Stagg, unkennel the Fox,
And chase the wild Goats or'e summets of Rocks,
With shouting and hooting we pierce thro' the Sky;
And Eccho turns Hunter, and doubles the Cry.

Cho. of all. *With shouting and hooting, we pierce through the Skie,*
And Eccho turns Hunter, and doubles the Cry.

Janus. Then our Age was in it's Prime,

Chronos. Free from Rage.

Diana. — — And free from Crime.

Momus. A very Merry, Dancing, Drinking,
Laughing, Quaffing, and unthinking Time.

Cho. of all. *Then our Age was in it's Prime,*
Free from Rage, and free from Crime,
A very Merry, Dancing, Drinking,
Laughing, Quaffing, and unthinking Time.

Dance of Diana's *Attendants.*

Enter Mars.[9]

Mars. Inspire[10] the Vocal Brass, Inspire;
The World is past its Infant Age:
Arms and Honour,
Arms and Honour,
Set the Martial Mind on Fire,
And kindle Manly Rage.
Mars has lookt the Sky to Red;
And Peace, the Lazy Good, is fled.
Plenty, Peace, and Pleasure fly;
The Sprightly Green
In *Woodland*-Walks, no more is seen;
The Sprightly Green, has drunk the *Tyrian* Dye.[11]

Cho. of all. *Plenty, Peace, &c.*

Mars. Sound the Trumpet, Beat the Drum,
Through all the World around;
Sound a Reveille, Sound, Sound,
The Warrior God is come.

Cho. of all. *Sound the Trumpet, &c.*

[7] goddess of the moon and of chastity, huntress [8] clad in high-lace hunting shoes
[9] god of war [10] breathe into [11] purple

Momus. Thy Sword within the Scabbard keep,
And let Mankind agree;
Better the World were fast asleep,
Than kept awake by Thee.
The Fools are only thinner,
With all our Cost and Care;
But neither side a winner,
For Things are as they were.

Cho. of all. *The Fools are only, &c.*

Enter Venus.[12]

Venus. Calms appear, when Storms are past;
Love will have his Hour at last:
Nature is my kindly[13] Care;
Mars destroys, and I repair;
Take me, take me, while you may,
Venus comes not ev'ry Day.

Cho. of all. *Take her, take her, &c.*

Chronos. The World was then so light,
I scarcely felt the Weight;
Joy rul'd the Day, and Love the Night.
But since the Queen of Pleasure left the Ground,
I faint, I lag,
And feebly drag
The pond'rous Orb around.

Momus. All all, of a piece throughout;
Pointing to *Diana.* Thy Chase had a Beast in View;
to *Mars.* Thy Wars brought nothing about;
to *Venus.* Thy Lovers were all untrue.

Janus. 'Tis well an Old Age is out,

Chro. And time to begin a New.

Cho. of all. *All, all, of a piece throughout;*
Thy Chase had a Beast in View;
Thy Wars brought nothing about;
Thy Lovers were all untrue.
'Tis well an Old Age is out,
And time to begin a New.
Dance of Huntsmen, Nymphs,
Warriours and Lovers.

[12] goddess of love and procreative nature
[13] looking out for the kinds or generations of creatures

John Locke

JOHN LOCKE was born in 1632 in a Somerset village not far from Bristol, the son of a county attorney of strong Puritan convictions who fought for Parliament in 1642. The family fortune suffered badly in consequence of the father's active part in the Civil War, but Locke was in turn elected to Westminster School, then under Parliament's control, and six years later to a junior studentship at Christ Church, the Dean of which was the distinguished Independent divine, John Owen. His association with Oxford, begun in 1652, was to be maintained for some thirty-two years. He proceeded to the B.A. in 1655, to the M.A. in 1658, and was appointed thereafter to a senior studentship at Christ Church and to several lectureships. Though he accepted the Restoration, he chose to disregard the advice of those friends who urged him to take Holy Orders, preferring instead to train himself in medicine (though he never sought a professional career, he did eventually take his M.B. at Oxford). It was during these earlier years at Oxford—down to 1667, that is, when a new chapter in his life was to begin—that he came to a full realization of the diversity and scope of the problems of the age in religion, politics, ethics, and science, and it is clear from his notes dating from this period that as yet his concern was with these broad questions rather than any philosophical technicalities. A friendship with Lord Ashley, begun at Oxford in 1666, brought about a great change in Locke's manner of life. Ashley, to become Earl of Shaftesbury in 1672 and eventually the leader of the opposition at the time of the Exclusion Bill, was already a man of great influence and affairs. In 1667 Locke went to live with Ashley in London in the capacity of family adviser and physician. He was made a Fellow of the Royal Society in 1668. For some months he served as secretary to the Council of Trade and Plantations, of which Ashley—now Shaftesbury—was president. It was in 1670–1671 that a small group of friends, meeting in Locke's rooms, fell into a discussion which proved to be the starting point of the *Essay Concerning Human Understanding*, the two earliest drafts of which were written in 1671. From 1675 to the spring of 1679 Locke was in France for reasons of health, studying Cartesianism and post-Cartesian French thought at first hand. He returned to London and to Shaftesbury's service at a critical moment, for Shaftesbury, now heading the Opposition, was arrested, tried, and acquitted in 1681, and thereafter fled to the Continent where he died early in 1683. Locke, though he retired to Oxford a good many months before, felt that he was in danger by reason of his association with Shaftesbury, and accordingly in September, 1683, he fled to Holland, where he lived for the next five years (in 1684 he was deprived of his studentship at Christ Church at Charles's order). Locke's residence in Holland proved to be the most fruitful period of his intellectual life. It was here that he composed the *Essay Concerning Human Understanding*, the *Treatises of Civil Government*, and the *Epistola de Tolerantia.* Locke probably played some part in shaping up the plans which resulted in the Restoration of 1688. He returned to England early in 1689. The closing period of his life

—1689 to his death in 1704—saw him established in the post-Restoration world as a commanding figure. For some years he served as a Commissioner to the new Board of Trade and Plantations. It was during this period, too, that most of his writings saw publication. He spent his final years at Oates in Essex, where he resided with Sir Francis and Lady Masham, the latter being the daughter of Ralph Cudworth, the Cambridge Platonist.

In 1689 appeared the *Epistola de Tolerantia* and its English version, *A Letter Concerning Toleration.* In 1690 were published *An Essay Concerning Human Understanding* (2nd ed., 1694; 3rd ed., 1695; 4th ed., 1700) and *Two Treatises of Government.* There followed *Some Thoughts Concerning Education* (1693) and *The Reasonableness of Christianity* (1695). In defense of the *Letter Concerning Toleration* Locke published a *Second Letter* in 1690, a *Third* in 1692, and left a fourth unfinished. Attacks upon the *Reasonableness of Christianity* drew from him two *Vindications* (1695, 1697), and in his final years he was drawn into controversy with Stillingfleet, Bishop of Worcester, issuing a *Letter* (1697) and two *Replies* (1697, 1699) to Stillingfleet. The collected *Works* are available in a ten-volume edition (London, 1801). Most of the major works are available in modern editions, the *Essay* having been edited by A. C. Fraser (2 vols., 1894), the second *Treatise of Civil Government* and the *Letter Concerning Toleration* by J. W. Gough (1947), the first two *Treatises of Government* by T. I. Cook (1947), and the *Thoughts Concerning Education* by H. R. Penniman in his book of selections entitled *John Locke On Politics and Education* (1947).

It matters a great deal whether we approach Locke by way of the eighteenth century, during the course of which he dominated English thinking in so many ways, or through the seventeenth, the dramatic events of which constituted the background of his intellectual development. So remarkably did Locke anticipate many essential features of the eighteenth-century attitude that it is often difficult not to read him in terms of his followers, and thus to find in him a complacency and in the end a shallowness which have sometimes been taken as characteristic of that entire age falling between the English and the French Revolutions. But if there are many who now feel that too much has been made of eighteenth-century complacency, at least so far as the English scene is concerned, so most qualified students of Locke would insist that he can be rightly understood only in connection with the many conflicts—religious, political, intellectual—that marked the years between his birth and the Revolution of 1688.

Long before he established any claim to the title of philosopher in the special and professional sense, he was a philosopher of the everyday, lay variety, keenly aware of the events of his time and seeking an interpretation of them in the disclosure of fundamental principles. He began life as a Puritan; at Cambridge he observed intellectual toleration in action; at the Restoration he was ready to conform, hoping for a new religious unity through a recognition of differences, and when disappointed in these hopes he began his long study of the problem of toleration. In regard to political theory, he had been educated from boyhood to believe in the rights of Parliament; his association with Shaftesbury confirmed him in Whig principles. Rejecting with equal vehemence the theory of Divine Right, as expounded by Filmer, and the theory of the all-powerful state, as set forth by Hobbes, he set himself the task of redefining man and the state and their relationship in terms of the time-honored tradition of Reason and Nature. At Oxford he had become interested in the new science, and particularly in the experimental approach as practiced by Robert Boyle, who was in residence at Oxford from 1654 to 1668 and whom Locke knew intimately and greatly admired; and the new science was raising numerous questions concerning God's relation to the cosmos, man's place in the scheme of creation, and the powers of the human intellect.

It is notable that the earlier papers of Locke reveal no concern with those narrower philosophic problems which were to occupy him in the *Essay;* they show, instead, that his interests were coextensive with the broad problems of his period as they arose in matters of a religious, political, and moral nature. The *Essay* itself had its origin, we are told, in a discussion concerning the principles of revealed religion and morality. Nor should it be forgotten that much of what we now think of as characteristic of Locke's writings—the clear ordering of the thought, the firm statement of first principles, the atmosphere of calm assurance—was by way of reaction against a disordered time —a reasoned pattern of thought which, until stability was assured by the Revolution, found little correspondence in the outward affairs of the nation. In him we find the essence of seventeenth-century Protestantism, and at the same time a mind conditioned by the steadfast assumption that man's place in the chain is one of strictly limited powers. Locke must search for God through "reason," spurning anything and everything associated either with "inspiration" or sheer faith. He is convinced at the same time that what we can know of God's will is limited, just as our knowledge of the ultimate objects in nature, of physical entities and qualities, is limited. He would have us rest in the assurance, however, that God and reason are not essentially different, that the reason within us is sufficient to enable us to live in obedience to God's will, and that if we will but acknowledge our limited powers of mind, thus foregoing divisive opinions, we shall discover how far these powers will carry us towards peace and happiness. Locke's voice may now sound thin, but in the latter years of the seventeenth century, when it was still touch and go between the forces that were struggling for dominance, there was much to give it resonance.

Thomas Fowler's *Locke* (English Men of Letters Series, 1880) and A. C. Fraser's *Locke* (Philosophical Classics, 1890) are generally available and still serve as useful introductions. The most helpful general study is that by R. I. Aaron, *John Locke* (1937). H. J. Laski's *Political Thought In England from Locke to Bentham* (1920) is well known. There is a suggestive article by H. C. Driver, "John Locke," in Hearnshaw's *Social and Political Ideas of Some English Thinkers of the Augustan Age* (1928). J. W. Gough has an authoritative discussion of Locke's political ideas and theory of toleration in the "Introduction" of his edition of *The Second Treatise of Civil Government* and *A Letter Concerning Toleration* (1947). D. G. James's *The Life of Reason* (1949) contains a lengthy essay on Locke. J. W. Gough has a collection of eight short studies in the volume entitled *John Locke's Political Philosophy* (1950).

from AN ESSAY CONCERNING HUMAN UNDERSTANDING[1]

[In "The Epistle To The Reader," which serves as a forward to the *Essay*, Locke tells of the origin of his book and of the purpose it is designed to serve. "Were it fit to trouble thee with the history of this *Essay*," he writes, addressing the reader, "I should tell thee, that five or six friends meeting at my chamber, and discussing on a subject very remote from this, found themselves quickly at a stand, by the difficulties that rose on every side. After we had awhile puzzled ourselves, without coming any nearer a resolution of those doubts which perplexed us, it came into my thoughts that we took a wrong course; and that before we set ourselves upon inquiries of that nature, it was necessary to examine our own abilities, and see what *objects* our understandings were, or were not, fitted to deal with." As for the completed

[1] Text: 1690

work, it is not intended for "masters of knowledge," being spun out of the author's own coarse thoughts and fitted to men of his own size. Master-builders there are—Boyle, Sydenham, Huggenius, "the incomparable Mr. Newton"—but Locke will not consider himself one of these. He is no more than an under-laborer, "clearing the ground a little, and removing some of the rubbish that lies in the way of knowledge."

[The short "Introduction," the full text of which is given below, follows the "Epistle."]

INTRODUCTION

§. 1. Since it is the *Understanding* that sets Man above the rest of sensible Beings, and gives him all the Advantage and Dominion, which he has over them; it is certainly a Subject, even for its Nobleness, worth our Labour to enquire into. The Understanding, like the Eye, whilst it makes us see, and perceive all other Things, takes no notice of it self: And it requires Art and Pains to set it at a distance, and make it its own Object: But whatever be the Difficulties, that lie in the way of this Enquiry; whatever it be, that keeps us so much in the Dark to our selves; sure I am, that all the Light we can let in upon our own Minds; all the Acquaintance we can make with our own Understandings, will not only be very pleasant; but bring us great Advantage, in directing our Thoughts in the search of other Things.

§. 2. This, therefore, being my *Purpose* to enquire into the Original, Certainty, and Extent of humane Knowledge; together, with the Grounds and Degrees of Belief, Opinion, and Assent; I shall not at present meddle with the Physical Consideration of the Mind; or trouble my self to examine, wherein its Essence consists, or by what Motions of our Spirits, or Alterations of our Bodies, we come to have any Sensation by our Organs, or any *Idea's* in our Understandings; and whether those *Idea's* do in their Formation, any, or all of them, depend on Matter, or no. These are Speculations, which, however curious and entertaining, I shall decline, as lying out of my Way, in the Design I am now upon. It shall suffice to my present Purpose, to consider the discerning Faculties of a Man, as they are employ'd about the Objects, which they have to do with: and I shall imagine I have not wholly misimploy'd my self in the Thoughts I shall have on this Occasion, if, in this Historical plain Method, I can give any Account of the Ways, whereby our Understandings come to attain those Notions of Things we have, and can set down any Measures of the Certainty of our Knowledge, or the Grounds of those Persuasions, which are to be found amongst Men, so various, different, and wholly contradictory; and yet asserted some where or other with such Assurance, and Confidence, that he that shall take a view of the Opinions of Mankind, observe their Opposition, and at the same time, consider the Fondness, and Devotion wherewith they are embrac'd; the Resolution, and Eagerness, wherewith they are maintain'd, may perhaps have Reason to suspect, That either there is no such thing as Truth at all; or that Mankind hath no sufficient Means to attain a certain Knowledge of it.

§. 3. It is therefore worth while, to search out the *Bounds* between Opinion and Knowledge; and examine by what Measures, in things whereof we have no certain Knowledge, we ought to regulate our Assent, and moderate our Persuasions. In Order whereunto, I shall pursue this following Method.

First, I shall enquire into the *Original* of those *Idea's*, Notions, or whatever else you please to call them, which a Man observes, and is conscious to himself he has in his Mind; and the ways whereby the Understanding comes to be furnished with them.

Secondly, I shall endeavour to shew, what *Knowledge* the Understanding hath by those *Idea's;* and the Certainty, Evidence, and Extent of it.

Thirdly, I shall make some Enquiry into the Nature and Grounds of *Faith*, or *Opinion:* whereby I mean that Assent, which we give to any Proposition as true, of whose Truth yet we have no certain Knowledge: And here we shall have Occasion to examine the Reasons and Degrees of *Assent*.

§. 4. If by this Enquiry into the Nature of the Understanding, I can discover the Powers thereof; at *how far* they reach; to which things they are in any Degree proportionate; and where they fail us, I suppose it may be of use, to prevail with the busie Mind of Man, to be more cautious in meddling with things exceeding its Comprehension; to stop, when it is at the utmost Extent of its Tether; and to sit down in a quiet Ignorance of those Things, which, upon Examination, are found to be beyond the reach of our Capacities. We should not then perhaps be so forward, out of an Affectation of an universal Knowledge, to raise Questions, and perplex our selves and others with Disputes about Things, to which our Understandings are not suited; and of which we cannot frame in our Minds any clear or distinct Perceptions, or whereof (as it has perhaps too often happen'd) we have not any Notions at all. If we can find out, how far the Understanding can extend its view; how far it has Faculties to attain Certainty; and in what Cases it can only judge and guess, we may learn to content our selves with what is attainable by us in this State.

§. 5. For though the *Comprehension* of our Understandings, comes exceeding short of the vast Extent of Things; yet, we shall have Cause enough to magnifie the bountiful Author of our Being, for that Portion, and Degree of Knowledge, he has bestowed on us, so far above all the rest of the Inhabitants of this our Mansion. Men have Reason to be well satisfied with what God hath thought fit for them, since he has given them (as St. Peter says, πάντα πρὸς ζωὴν καὶ εὐσέβειαν), Whatsoever is necessary for the Conveniences of Life, and Information of Vertue; and has put within the reach of their Discovery the Provisions, that may support, or sweeten this Life, and the Way that leads to a better. How short soever their Knowledge may come of an universal, or perfect Comprehension of whatsoever is, it yet secures their great Concernments, that they have Light enough to lead them to the Knowledge of their Maker, and the Discovery of their own Duties. Men may find Matter sufficient to busie their Heads, and employ their Hands with Variety, Delight, and Satisfaction; if they will not boldly quarrel with their own Constitution, and throw away the Blessings their Hands are fill'd with, because they are not big enough to grasp every thing. We shall not have much Reason to complain of the narrowness of our Minds, if we will but employ them about what may be of use to us; for of that they are very capable: And it will be an unpardonable, as well as Childish Peevishness, if we undervalue the Advantages of our Knowledge, and neglect to improve it to the ends for which is was given us, because there are some Things that are set out of the reach of it. It will be no Excuse to an idle and untoward Servant, who would not attend his Business by Candle-light, to plead that he had not broad Sunshine. The Candle, that is set up in us, shines bright enough for all our Purposes. The Discoveries we can make with this, ought to satisfie us: And we shall then use our Understandings right, when we entertain all Objects in that Way and Proportion, that they are suited to our Faculties; and upon those Grounds, they are capable of being propos'd to us, and not peremptorily, or intemperately require Demonstration, and demand Certainty, where Probability only is to be had, and which is sufficient to govern all our Concernments. If we will disbelieve every thing, because we cannot certainly know all things; we shall do much-what as wisely as he, who would not use his Legs, but sit still and perish, because he had no Wings to fly.

§. 6. When we know our own *Strength*, we shall the better know what to undertake with hopes of Success: And when we have well survey'd the *Powers* of our own Minds, and made some Estimate what we may expect from them, we shall not be inclined either to sit still, and not set our Thoughts on work at all in Despair of knowing any thing; nor on the other side question every thing, and disclaim all Knowledge, because some Things are not to be understood. 'Tis of great use to the Sailor to know the length of his Line, though he cannot with it fathom all the depths of the Ocean. 'Tis well he knows, that it is long enough to reach the bottom at such Places, as are necessary to direct his Voyage, and caution him against running upon Shoals, that may ruine him. Our Business here is not to know all things, but those which concern our Conduct. If we can find out those Measures, whereby a rational Creature put in that State, which Man is in, in this World, may, and ought to govern his Opinions and Actions depending thereon, we need not be troubled, that some other things scape our Knowledge.

§. 7. This was that which gave the first Rise to this Essay concerning the Understanding. For I thought that the first Step towards satisfying several Enquiries, the Mind of Man was very apt to run into, was, To take a Survey of our own Understandings, examine our own Powers, and see to what things they were adapted. Till that was done, I suspected we began at the wrong end, and in vain sought for Satisfaction in a quiet and secure Possession of Truths, that most concern'd us, whilst we let loose our Thoughts into the vast Ocean of *Being*, as if all that boundless Extent, were the natural, and undoubted Possession of our Understandings, wherein there was nothing exempt from its Decisions, or that escaped its Comprehension. Thus Men, extending their Enquiries beyond their Capacities, and letting their Thoughts wander into those depths, where they can find no sure Footing; 'tis no Wonder, that they raise Questions, and multiply Disputes, which never coming to any clear Resolution, are proper only to continue and increase their Doubts, and to confirm them at last in perfect Scepticism. Whereas were the Capacities of our Understandings well considered, the Extent of our Knowledge once discovered, and the Horizon found, which sets the Bounds between the enlightned and dark Parts of Things; between what is, and what is not comprehensible by us, Men would perhaps with less scruple acquiesce in the avow'd Ignorance of the one, and imploy their Thoughts and Discourse, with more Advantage and Satisfaction in the other.

§. 8. Thus much I thought necessary to say concerning the Occasion of this Enquiry into humane Understanding. But, before I proceed on to what I have thought on this Subject, I must here in the Entrance beg Pardon of my Reader, for the frequent use of the Word *Idea*, which he will find in the following Treatise. It being that Term, which, I think, serves best to stand for whatsoever is the Object of the Understanding when a Man thinks, I have used it to express whatever is meant by *Phantasm, Notion, Species*, or whatever it is, which the Mind can be employ'd about in thinking; and I could not avoid frequently using it.

I presume it will be easily granted me, that there are such *Idea's* in Men's Minds; every one is conscious of them in himself, and a Man's Words and Actions will satisfie him, that they are in others.

Our first Enquiry then shall be how they come into the Mind.

[The general pattern of the *Essay* is suggested, however inadequately, in the rough summary given in the third paragraph of the above "Introduction." The origin of ideas and notions, and "the ways whereby the understanding comes to be furnished with them" are dealt with in Book II. The discussion concerning "the certainty, evidence, and extent" of knowledge—the second head in the summary—and the "inquiry into the nature and grounds of faith or opinion"—the third head—are the subjects of Book IV. Book I, showing how our ideas and notions do *not* originate, and consisting of Locke's famous attack upon innate ideas or principles, is to be regarded as an introduction to Book II. Book III, "Of Words," was an afterthought on Locke's part. It is, among other things, one of the earliest of modern semantic studies. But the heart of the *Essay* lies in Books II and IV. In Book II we have the substance of Locke's empiricism, his "new way of ideas": the mind is originally a white paper (there are, i.e., no innate ideas); its ideas are furnished by experience; and it is out of these ideas that we acquire our knowledge. Man is so constituted that only through sensation and through reflection upon the ideas furnished by experience can he come by knowledge: "Thus the first capacity of human intellect is,—that the mind is fitted to receive the impressions made on it; either through the senses by outward objects, or by its own operations when it reflects on them. This is the first step a man makes towards the discovery of anything, and the groundwork whereon to build all those notions which ever he shall have naturally in this world. All those sublime thoughts which tower above the clouds, and reach as high as heaven itself, take their rise and footing here: in all that great extent wherein the mind wanders, in those remote speculations it may seem to be elevated with, it stirs not one jot beyond those ideas which *sense* or *reflection* have offered for its contemplation." (Book II, I.24.) It is, finally, in Book IV, and specifically in the last twenty-three chapters thereof (Chapters 9–21), that Locke's course brings him back at last to those more general matters whose discussion had originally set him forth upon his long inquiry—the nature and extent of human knowledge, the grounds and degrees of belief, opinion, and assent. Locke answers that we have knowledge of ourselves by intuition, of God by demonstration, of other things by sensation; that the extent of our certain knowledge being so slight, we must in most things be ruled by probability; that reason is natural revelation, revelation "*natural reason* enlarged by a new set of discoveries communicated by God immediately; which reason vouches the truth of, by the testimony and proofs it gives that they come from God." (Book IV, XIX.4)]

from THE SECOND TREATISE OF CIVIL GOVERNMENT[2]

[The *First Treatise of Civil Government* is a discussion and vigorous rejection of the theory of Divine Right as set forth by Sir Robert Filmer in his *Patriarcha,* which was written in the time of Charles I but not published until 1680. Locke begins his *Second Treatise* with the following summary of the *First.*]

OF CIVIL-GOVERNMENT

BOOK II

CHAP. I. §. 1. It having been shewn in the foregoing discourse,

1. That *Adam* had not, either by natural right of fatherhood, or by positive donation from God, any such authority over his children, or dominion over the world, as is pretended:

2. That if he had, his heirs, yet, had no right to it:

3. That if his heirs had, there being no law of nature nor positive law of God that determines which is the right heir in all cases that may arise, the right of succession, and consequently of bearing rule, could not have been certainly determined:

4. That if even that had been determined, yet the knowledge of which is the eldest line of *Adam's* posterity, being so long since utterly lost, that in the races of mankind and families of the world, there remains not to one above another, the least pretence to be the eldest house, and to have the right of inheritance:

All these premises having, as I think, been clearly made out, it is impossible that the rulers now on earth should make any benefit, or derive any the least shadow of authority from that, which is held to be the fountain of all power, *Adam's private dominion and paternal jurisdiction;* so that he that will not give just occasion to think that all government in the world is the product only of force and violence, and that men live together by no other rules but that of beasts, where the strongest carries it, and so lay a foundation for perpetual disorder and mischief, tumult, sedition and rebellion, (things that the followers of that hypothesis so loudly cry out against) must of necessity find out another rise of government, another original of political power, and another way of designing and knowing the persons that have it, than what Sir *Robert Filmer* hath taught us.

§. 2. To this purpose, I think it may not be amiss, to set down what I take to be political power; that the power of a *magistrate* over a subject may be distinguished from that of a *father* over his children, a *master* over his servant, a *husband* over his wife, and a *lord* over his slave. All which distinct powers happening sometimes together in the same man, if he be considered under these different relations, it may help us to distinguish these powers one from another, and shew the difference betwixt a ruler of a common-wealth, a father of a family, and a captain of a galley.

§. 3. *Political power,* then, I take to be a *right* of making laws with penalties of death, and consequently all less penalties, for the regulating and preserving of property, and of employing the force of the community, in the execution of such laws, and in the defence of the common-wealth from foreign injury; and all this only for the publick good.

[After this opening chapter Filmer drops from view, and in so far as Locke has an opponent in the subsequent pages of the *Second Treatise* it is Hobbes, though Hobbes is not mentioned by name. The description in Chapter II of the state of nature, the law of nature existing therein, and civil government, which though a remedy for the inconvenience of the state of nature is not the absolute thing that

[2] Text: 1764

some have held it to be, is by way of contrast with Hobbe's theories in the *Leviathan.*]

CHAP. II

Of the State of Nature

§. 4. To understand political power right, and derive it from its original, we must consider, what state all men are naturally in, and that is, a *state of perfect freedom* to order their actions, and dispose of their possessions and persons, as they think fit, within the bounds of the law of nature, without asking leave, or depending upon the will of any other man.

A *state* also *of equality,* wherein all the power and jurisdiction is reciprocal, no one having more than another; there being nothing more evident, than that creatures of the same species and rank, promiscuously born to all the same advantages of nature, and the use of the same faculties, should also be equal one amongst another without subordination or subjection, unless the lord and master of them all should, by any manifest declaration of his will, set one above another, and confer on him, by an evident and clear appointment, an undoubted right to dominion and sovereignty.

§. 5. This *equality* of men by nature, the judicious *Hooker* looks upon as so evident in itself, and beyond all question, that he makes it the foundation of that obligation to mutual love amongst men, on which he builds the duties they owe one another, and from whence he derives the great maxims of *justice* and *charity.*

. . . . . .

§. 6. But though this be *a state of liberty,* yet *it is not a state of licence:* though man in that state have an uncontroulable liberty to dispose of his person or possessions, yet he has not liberty to destroy himself, or so much as any creature in his possession, but where some nobler use than its base preservation calls for it. The *state of nature* has a law of nature to govern it, which obliges every one: and reason, which is that law, teaches all mankind, who will but consult it, that being all *equal and independent,* no one ought to harm another in his life, health, liberty, or possessions: for men being all the workmanship of one omnipotent, and infinitely wise maker; all the servants of one sovereign master, sent into the world by his order, and about his business; they are his property, whose workmanship they are, made to last during his, not one another's pleasure: and being furnished with like faculties, sharing all in one community of nature, there cannot be supposed any such *subordination* among us, that may authorize us to destroy one another, as if we were made for one another's uses, as the inferior ranks of creatures are for our's. Every one, as he is *bound to preserve himself,* and not to quit his station wilfully, so by the like reason, when his own preservation comes not in competition, ought he, as much as he can, *to preserve the rest of mankind,* and may not, unless it be to do justice on an offender, take away, or impair the life, or what tends to the preservation of the life, the liberty, health, limb, or goods of another.

§. 7. And that all men may be restrained from invading others rights, and from doing hurt to one another, and the law of nature be observed, which willeth the peace and *preservation of all mankind,* the *execution* of the law of nature is, in that state, put into every man's hands, whereby every one has a right to punish the transgressors of that law to such a degree, as may hinder its violation: for the *law of nature* would, as all other laws that concern men in this world, be in vain, if there were no body that in the state of nature had a *power to execute* that law, and thereby preserve the innocent and restrain offenders. And if any one in the state of nature may punish another for any evil he has done, every one may do so: for in that *state of perfect equality,* where naturally there is no superiority or jurisdiction of one over another, what any may do in prosecution of that law, every one must needs have a right to do.

§. 8. And thus, in the state of nature, *one man comes by a power over another;* but yet no absolute or arbitrary power, to use a criminal, when he has got him in his hands, according to the passionate heats, or boundless extravagancy of his own will; but only to retribute to him, so far as calm reason and conscience dictate, what is proportionate to his transgression, which is so much as may serve for *reparation* and *restraint:* for these two are the only reasons, why one man may lawfully do harm to another, which is that we call *punishment.* In transgressing the law of nature, the offender declares himself to live by another rule than that of reason and common equity, which is that measure God has set to the actions of men, for their mutual security; and so he becomes dangerous to mankind, the tye, which is to secure them from injury and violence, being slighted and broken by him. Which being a trespass against the whole species, and the peace and safety of it, provided for by the law of nature, every man upon this score, by the right he hath to preserve mankind in general, may restrain, or where it is necessary, destroy things noxious to them, and so may bring such evil on any one who hath transgressed that law, as may make him repent the doing of it, and thereby deter him, and by his example others, from doing the like mischief. And in this case, and upon this ground, every man hath a right to punish the offender, and be executioner of the law of nature.

. . . . .

§. 13. To this strange doctrine, *viz.* That *in the state of nature every one has the executive power* of the law of nature, I doubt not but it will be objected, that is unreasonable for men to be judges in their own cases, that self-love will make men partial to themselves and their friends: and on the other side, that ill nature, passion and revenge will carry them too far in punishing others; and hence nothing but confusion and disorder will follow, and that therefore God hath certainly appointed government to restrain the partiality and violence of men. I easily grant, that *civil government* is the proper remedy for the inconveniences of the state of nature, which must certainly be great, where men may be judges in their own case, since it is easy to be imagined, that he who was so unjust as to do his brother an injury, will scarce be so just as to condemn himself for it: but I shall desire those who make this objection, to remember, that *absolute monarchs* are but men; and if government is to be the remedy of those evils, which necessarily follow from men's being judges in their own cases, and the state of nature is therefore not be endured, I desire to know what kind of government that is, and how much better it is than the state of nature, where one man, commanding a multitude, has the liberty to be judge in his own case, and may do to all his subjects whatever he pleases, without the least liberty to any one to question or controul those who execute his pleasure? and in whatosever he doth, whether led by reason, mistake or passion, must be submitted to? much better it is in the state of nature, wherein men are not bound to submit to the unjust will of another: and if he that judges, judges amiss in his own, or any other case, he is answerable for it to the rest of mankind.

§. 14. It is often asked as a mighty objection, *where are*, or ever were there any *men in such a state of nature?* To which it may suffice as an answer at present, that since all princes and rulers of *independent* governments all through the world, are in a state of nature, it is plain the world never was, nor ever will be, without numbers of men in that state. I have named all governors of *independent communities*, whether they are, or are not, in league with others: for it is not every compact that puts an end to the state of nature between men, but only this one of agreeing together mutually to enter into one community, and make one body politic; other promises, and compacts, men may make with another, and yet still be in the state of nature. The promises and bargains for truck, *etc.* between the two men in the desert island, mentioned by *Garcilasso de la Vega*, in his history of *Peru;* or between a *Swiss* and an *Indian*, in the woods of *America*, are binding to them, though they are perfectly in a state of nature, in reference to one another: for truth and keeping of faith belongs to men, as men, and not as members of society.

§. 15. To those that say, there were never any men in the state of nature, I will not only oppose the authority of the judicious *Hooker*, *Eccl. Pol. lib.* i. *sect.* 10. where he says, *The laws which have been hitherto mentioned*, i.e. the laws of nature, *to bind men absolutely*, *even as they are men*, *al-*

though they have never any settled fellowship, never any solemn agreement amongst themselves what to do, or not to do: but forasmuch as we are by ourselves sufficient to furnish ourselves with competent store of things, needful for such a life as our nature doth desire, a life fit for the dignity of man; therefore to supply those defects and imperfections which are in us, as living singly and solely by ourselves, we are naturally induced to seek communion and fellowship with others: this was the cause of men's uniting themselves at first in politick societies. But I moreover affirm, that all men are naturally in that state, and remain so, till by their own consents they make themselves members of some politic society; and I doubt not in the sequel of this discourse, to make it very clear.

[Chapter III is entitled "Of the State of War." Whereas Hobbes had held that the state of war and the state of nature are the same, Locke insists upon distinguishing between them: men are in a state of nature when they live together "according to nature, without a common superior on earth with authority to judge between them;" war is force upon another person "where there is no common superior on earth to appeal to for relief." Thus, though the state of nature is not inevitably one of war, wars will in all probability arise. It is, in fact, the desire to avoid the state of war that is "one great reason of men's putting themselves into society and quitting the state of nature." Chapters VII and VIII describe this civil society which men put themselves into when they quit the state of nature.]

CHAP. VII

Of Political or Civil Society

. . . . . .

§. 87. Man being born, as has been proved, with a title to perfect freedom, and an uncontrouled enjoyment of all the rights and priviledges of the law of nature, equally with any other man, or number of men in the world, hath by nature a power, not only to preserve his property, that is, his life, liberty and estate, against the injuries and attempts of other men; but to judge of, and punish the breaches of that law in others, as he is persuaded the offence deserves, even with death itself, in crimes where the heinousness of the fact, in his opinion, requires it. But because no *political society* can be, nor subsist, without having in itself the power to preserve the property, and in order thereunto, punish the offences of all those of that society; there, and there only is *political society*, where every one of the members hath quitted this natural power, resigned it up into the hands of the community in all cases that exclude him not from appealing for protection to the law established by it. And thus all private judgment of every particular member being excluded, the community comes to be umpire, by settled standing rules, indifferent, and the same to all parties; and by men having authority from the community, for the execution of those rules, decides all the differences that may happen between any members of that society concerning any matter of right; and punishes those offences which any member hath committed against the society, with such penalties as the law has established: whereby it is easy to discern, who are, and who are not, in *political society* together. Those who are untied into one body, and have a common established law and judicature to appeal to, with authority to decide controversies between them, and punish offenders, are in *civil society* one with another: but those who have no such common people, I mean on earth, are still in the state of nature, each being, where there is no other, judge for himself, and executioner; which is, as I have before shewed it, the perfect *state of nature*.

§. 88. And thus the common-wealth comes by a power to set down what punishment shall belong to the several transgressions which they think worthy of it, committed amongst the members of that society, (which is the *power of making laws*) as well as it has the power to punish any injury done unto any of its members, by any one that is not of it, (which is the *power of war and peace;*) and all this for the preservation of the property of all the members of that society, as far as is possible. But though every man who has entered into civil society, and is become a member of any common-wealth, has thereby quitted his power to punish offences, against the law of *nature*, in prosecution of his own private judgment, yet with the judgment of offences, which he has given up to the legislative in all cases, where he can appeal to the magistrate, he has given up a right to the common-wealth to employ his force, for the execution of the judgments of the common-wealth, whenever he shall be called to it; which indeed are his own judgments, they being made by himself, or his representative. And herein we have the original of the *legislative* and *executive power* of civil society, which is to judge by standing laws, how far offences are to be punished, when committed within the common-wealth; and also to determine, by occasional judgments founded on the present circumstances of the fact, how far injuries from without are to be vindicated; and in both these to employ all the force of all the members, when there shall be need.

§. 89. Where-ever therefore any number of men are so united into one society, as to quit every one his executive power of the law of nature, and to resign it to the public, there and there only is a *political, or civil society*. And this is done, where-ever any number of men, in the state of nature, enter into society to make one people, one body politic, under one supreme government; or else when any one joins himself to, and incorporates with any government already made: for hereby he authorizes the society, or which is all one, the legislative thereof, to make laws for him, as the public good of the society shall require; to the execution whereof, his own assistance (as to his own decrees) is due. And this *puts men* out of a state of nature *into* that of a *common-wealth*, by setting up a judge on earth, with authority to determine all the controversies, and redress the injuries that may happen to any member of the common-wealth; which judge is the legislative, or magistrates appointed by it. And where-ever there are any number of men, however associated, that have no such decisive power to appeal to, there they are still in *the state of nature*.

§. 90. Hence it is evident, that *absolute monarchy*, which by some men is counted for the only government in the world, is indeed *inconsistent with civil society*, and so can be no form of civil-government at all: for the *end of civil society*, being to avoid, and remedy those inconveniencies of the state of nature, which necessarily follow from every man's being judge in his own case, by setting up a known authority, to which every one of that society may appeal upon any injury received, or controversy that may arise, and which every one of the[3] society ought to obey; where-ever any persons are, who have not such an authority to appeal to, for the decision of any difference between them, there those persons are still *in the state of nature;* and so is every *absolute prince*, in respect of those who are under his *dominion.*

§. 91. For he being supposed to have all, both legislative and executive power in himself alone, there is no judge to be found, no appeal lies open to any one, who may fairly, and indifferently, and with authority decide, and from whose decision relief and redress may be expected of any injury or inconveniency, that may be suffered from the prince, or by his order: so that such a man, however intitled, *Czar*, or *Grand Seignior*, or how you please, is as much *in the state of nature*, with all under his dominion, as he is with the rest of mankind: for where-ever any two men are, who have no standing rule, and common judge to appeal to on earth, for the determination of controversies of right betwixt them, there they are still *in the state of*[4] *nature*, and under all the inconveniencies of it, with only this woful difference

[3] The public power of all society is above every soul contained in the same society; and the principal use of that power is, to give laws unto all that are under it, which laws in such cases we must obey, unless there be reason shewed which may necessarily inforce, that the law of reason, or of God, doth enjoyn the contrary, *Hook. Eccl. Pol. l.* i. *sect.* 16. [Locke's note]

[4] To take away all such mutual grievances, injuries and wrongs, *i.e.* such as attend men in the state of nature, there was no way but only by growing into composition and agreement amongst themselves, by ordaining some kind of government public, and by yielding themselves subject thereunto, that unto whom they granted authority to rule and govern, by them the peace, tranquillity and happy estate of the rest might be procured. Men always knew that where force and injury was offered, they might be defenders of themselves; they knew that however men may seek their own commodity,

to the subject, or rather slave of an absolute prince: that whereas, in the ordinary state of nature, he has a liberty to judge of his right, and according to the best of his power, to maintain it; now, whenever his property is invaded by the will and order of his monarch, he has not only no appeal, as those in society ought to have, but as if he were degraded from the common state of rational creatures, is denied a liberty to judge of, or to defend his right; and so is exposed to all the misery and inconveniencies, that a man can fear from one, who being in the unrestrained state of nature, is yet corrupted with flattery, and armed with power.

§. 92. For he that thinks *absolute power purifies men's blood*, and corrects the baseness of human nature, need read but the history of this, or any other age, to be convinced of the contrary. He that would have been insolent and injurious in the woods of *America*, would not probably be much better in a throne; where perhaps learning and religion shall be found out to justify all that he shall do to his subjects, and the sword presently silence all those that dare question it: for what the *protection of absolute monarchy* is, what kind of fathers of their countries it makes princes to be, and to what a degree of happiness and security it carries civil society, where this sort of government is grown to perfection, he that will look into the late relation of *Ceylon*,[5] may easily see.

§. 93. In *absolute monarchies* indeed, as well as other governments of the world, the subjects have an appeal to the law, and judges to decide any controversies, and restrain any violence that may happen betwixt the subjects themselves, one amongst another. This every one thinks necessary, and believes he deserves to be thought a declared enemy to society and mankind, who should go about to take it away. But whether this be from a true love of mankind and society, and such a charity as we owe all one to another, there is reason to doubt: for this is no more than what every man, who loves his own power, profit, or greatness, may and naturally must do, keep those animals from hurting, or destroying one another, who labour and drudge only for his pleasure and advantage; and so are taken care of, not out of any love the master has for them, but love of himself, and the profit they bring him: for if it be asked, what security, *what fence* is there, in such a state, *against the violence and oppression of this absolute ruler?* the very question can scarce be borne. They are ready to tell you, that it deserves death only to ask after safety. Betwixt subject and subject, they will grant, there must be measures, laws and judges, for their mutual peace and security: but as for the *ruler*, he ought to be *absolute*, and is above all such circumstances; because he has a power to do more hurt and wrong, it is right when he does it. To ask how you may be guarded from harm, or injury, on that side where the strongest hand is to do it, is presently the voice of faction and rebellion: as if when men quitting the state of nature entered into society, they agreed that all of them but one, should be under the restraint of laws, but that he should still retain all the liberty of the state of nature, increased with power, and made licentious by impunity. This is to think, that men are so foolish, that they take care to avoid what mischiefs may be done them by *pole-cats*, or *foxes;* but are content, nay, think it safety, to be devoured by *lions*.

§. 94. But whatever flatterers may talk to amuze people's understandings, it hin-

yet if this were done with injury unto others, it was not to be suffered, but by all men, and all good means to be withstood. Finally, they knew that no man might in reason take upon him to determine his own right, and according to his own determination proceed in maintenance thereof, in as much as every man is towards himself, and them whom he greatly affects, partial; and therefore that strifes and troubles would be endless, except they gave their common consent, all to be ordered by some, whom they should agree upon, without which consent there would be no reason that one man should take upon him to be lord or judge over another, *Hooker's Eccl. Pol. l.* i. *sect.* 10. [Locke's note]

[5] *An Historical Relation of the Island Ceylon* (1681). The author, Robert Knox, who was held a captive in Ceylon for twenty years, describes the tyrannical rule of the island king in Part II, Chap. III. A modern edition of Knox's *Historical Relation* was printed in Glasgow in 1911.

ders not men from feeling; and when they perceive, that any man, in what station soever, is out of the bounds of the civil society which they are of, and that they have no appeal on earth against any harm, they may receive from him, they are apt to think themselves in the state of nature, in respect of him whom they find to be so; and to take care, as soon as they can, to have that *safety and security in civil society*, for which it was first instituted, and for which only they entered into it. And therefore, though perhaps at first, (as shall be shewed more at large hereafter in the following part of this discourse) some one good and excellent man having got a pre-eminency amongst the rest, had this deference paid to his goodness and virtue, as to a kind of natural authority, that the chief rule, with arbitration of their differences, by a tacit consent devolved into his hands, without any other caution, but the assurance they had of his uprightness and wisdom; yet when time, giving authority, and (as some men would persuade us) sacredness of customs, which the negligent, and unforeseeing innocence of the first ages began, had brought in successors of another stamp, the people finding their properties not secure under the government, as then it was, (wheras government has no other end but the preservation of[6] property) could never be safe nor at rest, *nor think themselves in civil society*, till the legislature was placed in collective bodies of men, call them senate, parliament, or what you please. By which means every single person became subject, equally with other the meanest men, to those laws, which he himself, as part of the legislative, had established; nor could any one, by his own authority, avoid the force of the law, when once made; nor by any pretence of superiority plead exemption, thereby to license his own, or the miscarriages of any of his dependants.[7] *No man in civil society can be exempted from the laws of it:* for if any man may do what he thinks fit, and there be no appeal on earth, for redress or security against any harm he shall do; I ask, whether he be not perfectly still in the state of nature, and so can be *no part or member of that civil society;* unless any one will say, the state of nature and civil society are one and the same thing, which I have never yet found any one so great a patron of anarchy as to affirm.

CHAP. VIII

Of the Beginning of Political Societies

§. 95. Men being, as has been said, by nature, all free, equal and independent, no one can be put out of his estate, and subjected to the political power of another, without his own consent. The only way whereby any one divests himself of his natural liberty, and puts on the *bonds of civil society*, is by agreeing with other men to join and unite into a community, for their comfortable, safe, and peaceable living one amongst another, in a secure enjoyment of their properties, and a greater security against any, that are not of it. This any number of men may do, because it injures not the freedom of the rest; they are left as they were in the liberty of the state of nature. When any number of men have so *consented to make one community or government*, they are thereby presently incorporated, and make *one body politic*, wherein the *majority* have a right to act and conclude the rest.

§. 96. For when any number of men have, by the consent of every individual, made a *community*, they have thereby made that *community* one body, with a power to act as one body, which is only by the will and determination of the *majority:*

[6] At the first, when some certain kind of regiment was once appointed, it may be that nothing was then farther thought upon for the manner of governing, but all permitted unto their wisdom and discretion, which were to rule, till by experience they found this for all parts very inconvenient, so as the thing which they had devised for a remedy, did indeed but increase the sore, which it should have cured. They saw, that *to live by one man's will, became the cause of all mens misery*. This constrained them to come unto laws, wherein all men might see their duty beforehand, and know the penalties of transgressing them. *Hooker's Eccl. Pol. l.* i. *sect.* 10. [Locke's note]

[7] Civil law being the act of the whole body politic, doth therefore over-rule each several part of the same body. *Hooker, ibid.* [Locke's note]

for that which acts any community, being only the consent of the individuals of it, and it being necessary to that which is one body to move one way; it is necessary the body should move that way whither the greater force carries it, which is the *consent of the majority:* or else it is impossible it should act or continue one body, *one community*, which the consent of every individual that united into it, agreed that it should; and so every one is bound by that consent to be concluded by the *majority*. And therefore we see, that in assemblies, impowered to act by positive laws, where no number is set by that positive law which impowers them, the *act of the majority* passes for the act of the whole, and of course determines, as having, by the law of nature and reason, the power of the whole.

§. 97. And thus every man, by consenting with others to make one body politic under one government, puts himself under an obligation, to every one of that society, to submit to the determination of the *majority*, and to be concluded by it; or else this *original compact*, whereby he with others incorporates into *one society*, would signifie nothing, and be no compact, if he be left free, and under no other ties than he was in before in the state of nature. For what appearance would there be of any compact? What new engagement if he were no farther tied by any decrees of the society, than he himself thought fit, and did actually consent to? This would be still as great a liberty, as he himself had before his compact, or any one else in the state of nature hath, who may submit himself, and consent to any acts of it if he thinks fit.

§. 98. For if *the consent of the majority* shall not, in reason, be received as *the act of the whole*, and conclude every individual; nothing but the consent of every individual can make any thing to be the act of the whole: but such a consent is next to impossible ever to be had, if we consider the infirmities of health, and avocations of business, which in a number, though much less than that of a common-wealth, will necessarily keep many away from the public assembly. To which if we add the variety of opinions, and contrariety of interests, which unavoidably happen in all collections of men, the coming into society upon such terms would be only like *Cato's* coming into the theatre,[8] only to go out again. Such a constitution as this would make the mighty *Leviathan* of a shorter duration, than the feeblest creatures, and not let it outlast the day it was born in: which cannot be supposed, till we can think, that rational creatures should desire and constitute societies only to be dissolved: for where the *majority* cannot conclude the rest, there they cannot act as one body, and consequently will be immediately dissolved again.

§. 99. Whosoever therefore out of a state of nature unite into a *community*, must be understood to give up all the power, necessary to the ends for which they unite into society, to the *majority* of the community, unless they expressly agreed in any number greater than the majority. And this is done by barely agreeing to *unite into one political society*, which is *all the compact* that is, or needs be, between the individuals, that enter into, or make up a *common-wealth*. And thus that, which begins and actually *constitutes any political society*, is nothing but the consent of any number of freemen capable of a majority to unite and incorporate into such a society. And this is that, and that only, which did, or could give beginning to any *lawful government* in the world.

[8] as much as to say that the only reason that Cato the Censor (234–149 B.C.) would deign to enter the theatre would be the opportunity thereby afforded him of expressing his moral distaste for it by leaving

Samuel Pepys

SAMUEL PEPYS was born in London on February 23, 1633, the son of a humble but enterprising tailor and his wife, who before her marriage had been a washmaid. Pepys' parents were convinced Puritans, and Pepys' conscience was always to bear the impress of his early training. But from his father Pepys also received a delight in music that was to prove no less lasting, and an encouragement to education that was to carry him through St. Paul's school with its Latin, Greek, and Hebrew. The still Puritan schoolboy exulted in the execution of Charles I, and won a scholarship to Cambridge, enrolling at Trinity but soon transferring to Magdalene. In spite of the trouble with the stone that was to haunt him all his life Pepys did well, taking his degree in 1653. But he married quite rashly for love the pretty daughter of a poor Huguenot exile. The rise of a cousin to the Admiralty Commission at that time gave Pepys his first opening as his cousin's servant, and he set up housekeeping in a turret of Whitehall. Modest as it was, his position gave him a chance to meet important people, a chance which Pepys, with his warm and outgoing personal charm, proceeded to improve to the utmost. In 1658 he became a clerk in the Exchequer and set up modest housekeeping in his own house.

Meanwhile like a great many of the children of the Puritans of his generation Pepys had come to have an attachment to the forms of the Established Church, and like a majority of the nation, to look to the King as a way out of the prevailing confusion and corruption. Indeed, Pepys would seem to have played some modest part in establishing connections between his powerful cousin Montagu and the King. The Restoration brought Pepys his first considerable appointment, the post of Clerk of the Acts for the Navy, and the beginning of the career of public service which was to lay not only the foundation of the greatness of the British Navy but to make the service of the Admiralty the prototype of the British Civil Service.

In the year of the Restoration Pepys also began in shorthand the great *Diary* upon which his fame in later days has chiefly rested. It has been suggested that the traditional motive of the Puritan diary may have contributed to the inspiration of Pepys' undertaking, and this hypothesis is confirmed by the many passages in which Pepys takes stock of the progress of his business affairs, sets down with candor his various lapses from grace, and records his resolution to forego pleasure, particularly the pleasure of pretty women and the theater, and devote himself more assiduously to his work. The *Diary* makes clear how very real were the temptations of pleasure to the young Puritan and how ambitious he was to win place and reputation and the means of satisfying his love of having everything handsome about him. To a young man who seemingly could not forbear trying to win about every pretty woman who came in his way, and who seems to have felt no scruple about trying the virtue of the maids in his household or the wives of men in the naval service who came to solicit his patronage of their husbands, growing prosperity and power did not lessen temptation.

But whatever the motives which made Pepys begin the *Diary*, he clearly came to take great pleasure in the opportunity to live over and take possession of his busy and fruitful days. Clearly he took increasing satisfaction in watching his personal estate grow from the fees which were the perquisites of office and the presents which were apparently an ubiquitous feature of that patronage-seeking age. Pepys had his standards in such matters. He always bridled at any suggestion that his interest was to be bought or his judgment of the King's interest bribed. But he quite frankly rejoiced in the generous present tactfully given for favor received or the general tribute to influence, gracefully invested for unspecified good will. And not without reason priding himself on his integrity and the modesty of his exactions in that fee-ridden age, he watched his private fortune grow to a competence that if never to be described as wealth certainly made it possible for Pepys to live with not a little of the splendor which position demanded in those days, the elegance which his own love of beauty craved, and the open-handed hospitality which his own sociable love of cultivated company inspired.

But it is more than the triumphs of "thriving" and of professional recognition that makes the *Diary* such delightful reading. Its author had a breadth of interest and a range of curiosity that make it one of the best abstracts and records of the time, both in its greater and its lesser moments. He loved a bit of court gossip, disapproving perhaps (he was to become very severe on other men's indulgences), but avidly interested; he was enchanted to be admitted behind the scenes of the theater and watch the human beings emerge from the stage costumes; on the other hand, he followed the experiments and the reports of experiments of the Royal Society with enthusiasm, and he cultivated the society of musicians, artists, scholars, and divines with delight. But rewarding as is his report of all these things, the real treasure of the *Diary* is not here. It is in the magic of Pepys' record of the endless delight of the little things of life; of good food and wine, in the beginning spiced with hunger and later sauced with pride of service and company, but always savored with full acuteness of sense; of music, heard and made alike, the most constant source of release and refreshment in all Pepys' busy life and perhaps the purest satisfaction of his yearning for beauty; of feminine grace and charm, caught in a roving glance at sermon time as well as at theater and Court; of the excitement of strange objects from old time or far place, redolent of adventure and wonder; and of all the moving accidents of the thronging streets and the busy river of the city-world of Pepys' everyday love. And not least of all it is in the satisfaction which Pepys discovered in the putting of all these things into words, the sheer delight of literary creation.

The threat of blindness in 1669 ended the great *Diary*. There were to be other journals and records of travel and tours of inspection, but they were in the nature of things, public or semi-public. While Pepys' eyes continued to give him trouble, the feared blindness did not materialize, and the career of public service expanded beyond the young diarist's most optimistic dreams. As early as 1662 Pepys had become interested in the history of the Navy, and a real devotion to his work was beginning to reënforce a young man's ambition. He became aware of the merchants' cheating in naval supplies and exposed a flagrant example, and so winning the confidence of his superiors, began to discover the excitements of the reformer. By 1664 as the preparations for the Dutch War accelerated, Pepys had set himself to thwart as best he could the immemorial profiteering of military preparation for war. He began to grapple with the chronic financial problem of the Navy, one facet, though a critical one, of the outmoded public financial arrangements of the time. Neither plague, nor his own pleasure-loving truancies, nor grief over the death of his deceived but loved wife in 1669 could turn him from the path to which he had set himself. And the fact that the Duke, the Lord High Admiral of the Navy, and the King came to notice and to appreciate his work with intelligent interest spurred him on. He met the challenge of Parliamentary appearances, and as early as 1669 in rebutting a political attack on the Navy Office discovered the power of experience and knowledge to hold their own in the defense of standards of public service. When the Duke of York because of his faith was driven from his post as Lord High Admiral in 1673, and a Commission was appointed to execute the greater part of the office, leaving the patronage to the crown, Pepys became Secretary to the Office of the Lord High Admiral and as the virtual head of the office proceeded to push the reforms that were to give England her modern Navy and the base of power for the building of her empire. In his setting up of rules of procedure, in his enforcement of standards of selection and conduct of officers, in his provision for professional training, in his appeal to experts for specialized advice, above all in his promotion of systematic inquiry and research for a factual basis of decision on matters like naval supply and construction, Pepys may well be said to have laid the foundations of the modern British Civil Service as well.

He had the satisfaction not only of seeing the work of his brain prosper but of seeing it recognized by royal favor and public acclaim. As early as 1665 he had become a Fellew of the Royal Society. In 1673 he became a member of Parliament, Master of Trinity House in 1677, and in 1676 a Governor of Christ's Hospital. So he came to give his attention and patronage to a wide variety of projects concerned with his interests in naval matters, in discovery, etc. In an age in which birth and family connections were prerequisites to public service and wealth was indispensable to the maintenance of position, the poor tailor's son by his own exertions had become a great man.

But the very nature of Pepys' success had inevitably made him enemies, and the intimacy of his relations to his patron, James, Duke of York, laid him open, if not to suspicion, certainly to attack in the resurgent no-Popery of the Titus Oates period. An attempt of Shaftesbury and his party to prove Pepys a papist and a traitor not only forced him to resign his office, but actually brought him to the Tower in 1679, and only the loyalty of Pepys' friends and servants and his experienced resourcefulness in gathering evidence on the character and history of his immediate accusers saved him. But though with the King's favor he was presently able to restore his personal fortunes, he had to see much of his work undone as the King's ships rotted at their wharves and the old corruption returned to sap the service he had built up.

The return of the exiled Duke to his post under the nominal direction of the King restored the actual administrative control of the Navy to Pepys, and he set himself to undo the damage that had been done. He was cheered in his labors by still further evidences of the esteem in which he was held by his friends, especially by his election to the presidency of the Royal Society in 1684. In 1685 the death of Charles brought his patron, James, to the throne, and Pepys was able to organize the Naval Commission according to his own ideas, and to rebuild the Navy on his own lines. He was now at the height of his power and prestige, able to indulge to the full his tastes in collecting books and rarities, giving distinguished concerts at Admiralty House, receiving the dedications of grateful authors, etc. He accomplished the restoration of the Navy, but the King's weakness and folly, and his Admiral's timidity failed to make effective use of it, and William of Orange eluded its watch and landed in the west on November 5, 1688. In the new regime there would clearly be no place for one so intimately associated with James and known for his loyalty to him in good weather and bad. Pepys resigned his office in 1689. In the middle of 1690 he was actually imprisoned on suspicion of continuing loyalty to James, but he was soon released for reasons of health, and in October the proceedings were dropped.

Until 1700, when ill health forced him to retire permanently to Clapham, Pepys busied himself with his books, his various interests like the Royal Society and Christ's Hospital, living the life of a virtuoso and a patron of learning in friendly intercourse with various others of the leading virtuosi of the time. And with the help of his friend Evelyn he collected materials for the writing of the memoirs of the Royal Navy and made plans for the great history that was still unwritten when he died in 1703.

The *Diary* was not published until 1825 when Lord Braybrooke edited John Smith's deciphered transcription of the shorthand original and published it with a selection from Pepys' correspondence. In that edition only about half of the original was published. In the editions that followed, Lord Braybrooke made some additions but clearly saw no need of attempting to complete the reprinting of the *Diary*. In 1875–1879 the Reverend Mynors Bright who had made a fresh transcription of the whole diary published about four-fifths of it. In 1893–1899 Henry B. Wheatley published the entire transcription of Bright, except for a few passages that he judged unprintable, and published it with the addition of Lord Braybrooke's notes. Wheatley's still remains the standard version of the great *Diary*, but a new and unabridged transcript by F. McD. C. Turner is in progress.

Important publications of other works of Pepys are the following: *Memoires Relating to the State of the Royal Navy* (1690), ed. J. R. Tanner (1906); *Private Correspondence and Miscellaneous Papers*, ed. J. R. Tanner (1926); *Further Correspondence*, ed. J. R. Tanner (1929); *Letters and Second Diary*, ed. R. G. Howarth (1932); *Shorthand Letters*, ed. E. Chappell (1933); *The Tangier Papers of Samuel Pepys*, ed. E. Chappell (1935).

The fullest account of Pepys' life is Arthur Bryant, *Samuel Pepys* (1933–1938). The naval aspect is stressed in J. R. Tanner, *Samuel Pepys and the Royal Navy* (1920); and E. Chappell, *Samuel Pepys as a Naval Administrator* (1933). Pepys' friendship with John Evelyn and the comparable areas of their lives and experience are studied in C. Marburg, *Mr. Pepys and Mr. Evelyn* (1935), with thirty-seven letters not published before and finding lists for the letters exchanged between the two friends. For the *Diary* itself there is J. R. Tanner, *Mr. Pepys: An Introduction to the Diary, Together with a Sketch of his Later Life* (1925). Useful special articles are: W. Matthews, "Samuel Pepys: Tachygraphist," *MLR* XXIX (1933); and H. Alexander, "The Language of Pepys's Diary," *Queen's Quarterly* LIII (1946).

from DIARY OF SAMUEL PEPYS[1]

[May] 23rd [1660].[2] The Doctor[3] and I waked very merry, only my eye was very red and ill in the morning from yesterday's hurt. In the morning came infinity of people on board from the King to go along with him. My Lord,[4] Mr. Crew,[5] and

[1] Text: Wheatley, 8 vols., 1893–1899, reprinted by permission of G. Bell and Sons, Ltd.

[2] on board the *Naseby* off the Dutch coast

[3] Dr. Timothy Clarke, one of the original Fellows of the Royal Society, and later physician-in-ordinary to Charles II. (The indebtedness of this and the ensuing notes to the Wheatley-Braybrooke notes is obvious.)

[4] Sir Edward Montagu, afterward Earl of Sandwich; Commissioner of the Admiralty (1655), and Joint-Commander with Blake of the English battle fleet (1656); Pepy's cousin and first patron

[5] John (later Lord) Crewe, father of Lady Montagu

others, go on shore to meet the King as he comes off from shore, where Sir R. Stayner[6] bringing His Majesty into the boat, I hear that His Majesty did with a great deal of affection kiss my Lord upon his first meeting. The King, with the two Dukes[7] and Queen of Bohemia,[8] Princess Royal,[9] and Prince of Orange,[10] came on board, where I in their coming in kissed the King's, Queen's, and Princess's hands, having done the other before. Infinite shooting off of the guns, and that in a disorder on purpose, which was better than if it had been otherwise. All day nothing but Lords and persons of honour on board, that we were exceeding full. Dined in a great deal of state, the Royall company by themselves in the coach,[11] which was a blessed sight to see. I dined with Dr. Clerke, Dr. Quarterman,[12] and Mr. Darcy[13] in my cabin. This morning Mr. Lucy[14] came on board, to whom and his company of the King's Guard in another ship my Lord did give three dozen of bottles of wine. He made friends between Mr. Pierce[15] and me. After dinner the King and Duke[16] altered the name of some of the ships, viz. the Nazeby into Charles;[17] the Richard, James; the Speaker, Mary; the Dunbar (which was not in company with us), the Henry; Winsly, Happy Return; Wakefield, Richmond; Lambert, the Henrietta; Cheriton, the Speedwell; Bradford, the Success. That done, the Queen, Princess Royal, and Prince of Orange, took leave of the King, and the Duke of York went on board the London, and the Duke of Gloucester, the Swiftsure. Which done, we weighed anchor, and with a fresh gale and most happy weather we set sail for England. All the afternoon the King walked here and there, up and down (quite contrary to what I thought him to have been), very active and stirring. Upon the quarter-deck he fell into discourse of his escape from Worcester,[18] where it made me ready to weep to hear the stories that he told of his difficulties that he had passed through, as his travelling four days and three nights on foot, every step up to his knees in dirt, with nothing but a green coat and a pair of country breeches on, and a pair of country shoes that made him so sore all over his feet, that he could scarce stir. . . .

[May] 24th [1660]. Up, and make myself as fine as I could, with the linning[19] stockings on and wide canons[20] that I bought the other day at Hague. Extraordinary press of noble company, and great mirth all the day. There dined with me in my cabin (that is, the carpenter's) Dr. Earle[21] and Mr. Hollis,[22] the King's Chaplins, Dr. Scarborough,[23] Dr. Quarterman, and Dr. Clerke, Physicians, Mr. Darcy, and Mr. Fox[24] (both very fine gentlemen), the

[6] Sir Richard Stayner, the Vice-Admiral

[7] James, Duke of York, and Henry, Duke of Gloucester

[8] Elizabeth, daughter of James I and widow of Frederick, Elector Palatine

[9] Mary, Princess Dowager of Orange

[10] son of William of Orange and Mary, eldest daughter of Charles II, later William III

[11] captain's cabin

[12] William Quartermain, physician-in-ordinary to Charles II

[13] Marmaduke Darcy, one of Charles II's companions in exile

[14] an early social acquaintance of Pepys

[15] Dr. James Pierce, surgeon to the Duke of York

[16] quite certainly the Duke of York

[17] Here as throughout the list, the King and Duke changed the names commemorating the Parliamentary and Cromwellian victories and leaders to honor the royal family and the triumph of the Restoration.

[18] The defeat at Worcester in 1651 not only ended the Royalist resistance, but in the Prince's escape gave the Royalists one of their most romantic legends.

[19] linen

[20] rolls worn for decoration around the lower ends of the legs of breeches

[21] John Earle, the author of *Microcosmographie*, Bishop of Worcester (1662) and Salisbury (1663)

[22] Denzil Holles, one of the five members of the House of Commons whom Charles I charged with high treason in 1641 and one of the Parliamentary Commissioners sent to Charles II at the Hague, Baron Holles (1661)

[23] Charles Scarburgh, physician to Charles II, James II, and William III, knighted in 1669

[24] Stephen Fox, who announced the death of Cromwell to Charles II; afterwards Paymaster of the Forces, knighted (1665)

King's servants, where we had brave[25] discourse. Walking upon the decks, where persons of honour all the afternoon, among others, Thomas Killigrew[26] (a merry droll, but a gentleman of great esteem with the King), who told us many merry stories. . . .

[May] 25th [1660]. By the morning we were come close to the land, and every body made ready to get on shore. The King and the two Dukes did eat their breakfast before they went, and there being set some ship's diet before them, only to show them the manner of the ship's diet, they eat of nothing else but pease and pork, and boiled beef. I had Mr. Darcy in my cabin and Dr. Clerke, who eat with me, told me how the King had given £50 to Mr. Sheply[27] for my Lord's servants, and £500 among the officers and common men of the ship. I spoke with the Duke of York about business, who called me Pepys by name, and upon my desire did promise me his future favour. Great expectation of the King's making some Knights, but there was none. About noon (though the brigantine[28] that Beale made was there ready to carry him) yet he would go in my Lord's barge with the two Dukes. Our Captain steered, and my Lord went along bare with him. I went, and Mr. Mansell,[29] and one of the King's footmen, with a dog that the King loved, (which [dirted] the boat, which made us laugh, and methink that a King and all that belong to him are but just as others are), (in a boat by ourselves, and so got on shore when the King did, who was received by General Monk[30] with all imaginable love and respect at his entrance upon the land of Dover. Infinite the crowd of people and the horsemen, citizens, and noblemen of all sorts. The Mayor of the town came and gave him his white staff, the badge of his place, which the King did give him again. The Mayor also presented him from the town a very rich Bible, which he took and said it was the thing that he loved above all things in the world. A canopy was provided for him to stand under, which he did, and talked awhile with General Monk and others, and so into a stately coach there set[31] for him, and so away through the town towards Canterbury, without making any stay at Dover. The shouting and joy expressed by all is past imagination. . . .

Feb[ruary] 15th [1664/1665]. Up and to my office, where busy all the morning. At noon with Creed[32] to dinner to Trinity-house,[33] where a very good dinner among the old sokers,[34] where an extraordinary discourse of the manner of the loss of the "Royall Oake" coming home from Bantam, upon the rocks of Scilly, many passages therein very extraordinary, and if I can I will get it in writing. Thence with Creed to Gresham College,[35] where I had been by Mr. Povy[36] the last week proposed to be admitted a member; and was this day admitted, by signing a book and being taken by the hand by the President, my Lord Brunkard,[37] and some words of admittance said to me. But it is a most acceptable thing to hear their discourse, and see their experiments; which were this day upon the nature of fire, and how it goes out in a place where the ayre is not free, and sooner out where the ayre is exhausted, which they showed by an engine[38] on purpose. After this being done, they to the Crowne Taverne, behind the 'Change, and

[25] fine

[26] a royal favorite and author of several plays

[27] W. Shepley, servant of Sir Edward Montagu, steward at Hinchingbrooke

[28] light, swift vessel

[29] a Reformado or volunteer with officer's rank

[30] who occupied London and in March, 1660, declared for a "free Parliament," which, when elected, called back Charles II

[31] placed in readiness

[32] John Creed, Pepys' predecessor as secretary to Montagu, Deputy Treasurer of the Fleet

[33] Trinity House Corporation was chartered by Henry VIII for the encouragement of commerce and navigation.

[34] topers

[35] where the Royal Society met

[36] Thomas Povy, who resigned the office of First Treasurer for Tangier to Pepys

[37] William, Viscount Brouncker, Naval Commissioner and President of the Royal Society

[38] contrivance

there my Lord and most of the company to a club supper; Sir P. Neale,[39] Sir R. Murrey,[40] Dr. Clerke, Dr. Whistler,[41] Dr. Goddard,[42] and others of most eminent worth. Above all, Mr. Boyle[43] to-day was at the meeting, and above him Mr. Hooke,[44] who is the most, and promises the least, of any man in the world that ever I saw. Here excellent discourse till ten at night, and then home, and to Sir W. Batten's,[45] where I hear that Sir Thos. Harvy[46] intends to put Mr. Turner[47] out of his house and come in himself, which will be very hard to them, and though I love him not, yet for his family's sake I pity him. So home and to bed.

[May] 28th [1665]. (Lord's day). By water to the Duke of Albemarle,[48] where I hear that Nixon[49] is condemned to be shot to death for his cowardice, by a Council of War. Went to chapel and heard a little musique, and there met with Creed, and with him a little while walking, and to Wilkinson's[50] for me to drink, being troubled with winde, and at noon to Sir Philip Warwicke's[51] to dinner, where abundance of company come in unexpectedly; and here I saw one pretty piece of household stuff, as the company increaseth, to put a larger leaf upon an ovall table. After dinner much good discourse with Sir Philip, who I find, I think, a most pious, good man, and a professor of a philosophicall manner of life and principles like Epictetus,[52] whom he cites in many things. Thence to my Lady Sandwich's,[53] where, to my shame, I had not been a great while before. Here, upon my telling her a story of my Lord Rochester's[54] running away on Friday night last with Mrs. Mallett, the great beauty and fortune of the North, who had supped at White Hall with Mrs. Stewart,[55] and was going home to her lodgings with her grandfather, my Lord Haly, by coach; and was at Charing Cross seized on by both horse and foot men, and forcibly taken from him, and put into a coach with six horses, and two women provided to receive her, and carried away. Upon immediate pursuit, my Lord of Rochester (for whom the King had spoke to the lady often, but with no successe) was taken at Uxbridge; but the lady is not yet heard of, and the King mighty angry, and the Lord sent to the Tower. Hereupon my Lady did confess to me, as a great secret, her being concerned in this story. For if this match breaks between my Lord Rochester and her, then, by the consent of all her friends, my Lord Hinchingbroke[56] stands fair,[57] and is invited for her. She is worth, and will be at her mother's death (who keeps but a little from her), £2,500 per annum. Pray God give a good success to it! But my poor Lady, who is afeard of the sickness,[58] and resolved to be gone into the country, is forced to stay in towne a day or two, or

[39] Sir Paul Neile, son of the Archbishop of York, and a member of the first council of the Royal Society

[40] Sir Robert Moray, president at first founding of the Royal Society

[41] Dr. Daniel Whistler, Gresham Professor of Geometry (1648–1657), President of the College of Physicians (1683), one of the original Fellows of the Royal Society

[42] Jonathan Goddard, physician to Cromwell, Gresham College Professor of Physic, and member of the first council of the Royal Society

[43] Robert Boyle, famous Irish scientist and philosopher

[44] Robert Hooke, Professor of Geometry at Gresham College, and Curator of Experiments to the Royal Society

[45] Sir William Batten, after a somewhat checkered career in the Navy, a Commissioner of the Navy after the Restoration

[46] Extra Commissioner of the Navy (1665)

[47] Thomas Turner, Chief Clerk in the Navy Office

[48] General Monk

[49] Captain Edward Nixon, accused of running away from an engagement with Dutch ships

[50] "Wilkinson's the cook's in King Street"

[51] Sir Philip Warwick, Secretary of the Treasury

[52] Roman Stoic philosopher, originally a slave

[53] wife of Pepys' first patron, Montagu, now Earl of Sandwich

[54] John Wilmot, second Earl of Rochester; see pp. 449–462.

[55] Frances Theresa Stuart, later Duchess of Richmond, famous Court beauty

[56] Edward Montagu, son of the Earl and Countess of Sandwich

[57] has a fair chance

[58] plague

three about it, to see the event of it. Thence home and to see my Lady Pen,[59] where my wife and I were shown a fine rarity: of fishes kept in a glass of water, that will live so for ever; and finely marked they are, being foreign.[60] So to supper at home and to bed, after many people being with me about business, among others the two Bellamys about their old debt due to them from the King for their victualling business, out of which I hope to get some money.

[June] 7th [1665]. This morning my wife and mother rose about two o'clock; and with Mercer,[61] Mary,[62] the boy,[63] and W. Hewer,[64] as they had designed, took boat and down to refresh themselves on the water to Gravesend. Lay till 7 o'clock, then up and to the office upon Sir. G. Carteret's[65] accounts again, where very busy; thence abroad and to the 'Change, no news of certainty being yet come from the fleete. Thence to the Dolphin Taverne, where Sir J. Minnes,[66] Lord Brunkard, Sir Thomas Harvy, and myself dined, upon Sir G. Carteret's charge, and very merry we were, Sir Thomas Harvy being a very drolle.[67] Thence to the office, and meeting Creed away with him to my Lord Treasurer's, there thinking to have met the goldsmiths, at White Hall,[68] but did not, and so appointed another time for my Lord to speak to them to advance us some money. Thence, it being the hottest day that ever I felt in my life, and it is confessed so by all other people the hottest they ever knew in England in the beginning of June, we to the New Exchange,[69] and there drunk whey, with much entreaty getting it for our money, and [they] would not be entreated to let us have one glasse more. So took water and to Fox Hall,[70] to the Spring garden, and there walked an houre or two with great pleasure, saving our minds ill at ease concerning the fleete and my Lord Sandwich, that we have no newes of them, and ill reports run up and down of his being killed, but without ground. Here staid pleasantly walking and spending but *6d.* till nine at night, and then by water to White Hall, and there I stopped to hear news of the fleete, but none come, which is strange, and so by water home, where weary with walking and with the mighty heat of the weather, and for my wife's not coming home, I staying walking in the garden till twelve at night, when it begun to lighten exceedingly, through the greatness of the heat. Then despairing of her coming home, I to bed. This day, much against my will, I did in Drury Lane see two or three houses marked with a red cross upon the doors, and "Lord have mercy upon us" writ there;[71] which was a sad sight to me, being the first of the kind that, to my remembrance, I ever saw. It put me into an ill conception of myself and my smell, so that I was forced to buy some roll-tobacco to smell to and chaw,[72] which took away my apprehension.

[August] 31st [1665]. Up; and, after putting several things in order to my removal, to Woolwich;[73] the plague having a great encrease this week, beyond all expectation of almost 2,000, making the general Bill[74] 7,000, odd 100; and the plague above 6,000. I down by appointment to Greenwich, to our office,[75] where I did some business, and there dined with our company and Sir W. Boreman,[76] and Sir

[59] Margaret, wife of Sir William Penn, Admiral and Commissioner of the Navy

[60] goldfish (?)

[61] Mary Mercer, companion to Mrs. Pepys

[62] the Pepys' cook

[63] Tom Edwards, a boy from the choir of the Chapel Royal

[64] Will Hewer, Pepys' personal servant and clerk

[65] Sir George Carteret, Treasurer of the Navy

[66] Sir John Minnes, Vice-Admiral and Comptroller of the Navy

[67] wag

[68] famous old royal palace, containing among other offices, the Treasurer's

[69] popular place of resort after the Restoration

[70] another popular haunt of pleasure-seekers, better known as Vauxhall

[71] a sign of plague within the house

[72] as a disinfectant and preventive of infection

[73] famous dockyard and naval station

[74] bill of mortality, a periodical report of the number of deaths in a given district

[75] Navy office

[76] Sir William Boreman, Clerk to the Board of Green Cloth

The. Biddulph,[77] at Mr. Boreman's,[78] where a good venison pasty, and after a good merry dinner I to my office, and there late writing letters, and then to Woolwich by water, where pleasant with my wife and people, and after supper to bed. Thus this month ends with great sadness upon the publick, through the greatness of the plague every where through the kingdom almost. Every day sadder and sadder news of its encrease. In the City died this week 7,496, and of them 6,102 of the plague. But it is feared that the true number of the dead this week is near 10,000; partly from the poor that cannot be taken notice of, through the greatness of the number, and partly from the Quakers and others that will not have any bell ring for them. . . .

[September] 3rd (Lord's day) [1665]. . . . Church being done, my Lord Bruncker, Sir J. Minnes, and I up to the Vestry[79] at the desire of the Justices of the Peace, Sir Theo. Biddulph and Sir W. Boreman and Alderman Hooker,[80] in order to the doing something for the keeping of the plague from growing; but Lord! to consider the madness of the people of the town, who will (because they are forbid) come in crowds along with the dead corps to see them buried; but we agreed on some orders for the prevention thereof. Among other stories, one was very passionate,[81] methought, of a complaint brought against a man in the towne for taking a child from London from an infected house. Alderman Hooker told us it was the child of a very able[82] citizen in Gracious Street, a saddler, who had buried all the rest of his children of the plague, and himself and wife now being shut up and in despair of escaping, did desire only to save the life of this little child; and so prevailed to have it received stark-naked into the arms of a friend, who brought it (having put it into new fresh clothes) to Greenwich; where upon hearing the story, we did agree it should be permitted to be received and kept in the towne. Thence with my Lord Bruncker to Captain Cocke's,[83] where we mighty merry and supped, and very late I by water to Woolwich, in great apprehensions of an ague. Here was my Lord Bruncker's lady of pleasure,[84] who I perceive, goes every where with him; and he, I find, is obliged to carry her, and make all the courtship to her that can be.

[September] 4th [1665]. Writing letters all the morning, among others to my Lady Carteret,[85] the first I have wrote to her, telling her the state of the city as to health and other sorrowfull stories, and thence after dinner to Greenwich, to Sir J. Minnes, where I found my Lord Bruncker, and having staid our hour for the Justices by agreement, the time being past we to walk in the Park with Mr. Hammond[86] and Turner, and there eat some fruit out of the King's garden[87] and walked in the Parke, and so back to Sir. J. Minnes, and thence walked home, my Lord Bruncker giving me a very neat cane to walk with; but it troubled me to pass by Coome farme[88] where about twenty-one people have died of the plague, and three or four days since I saw a dead corps in a coffin lie in the Close[89] unburied, and a watch is constantly kept there night and day to keep the people in, the plague making us cruel, as doggs, one to another.

[November] 5th (Lord's day) [1665]. Up, and after being trimmed,[90] by boat to the Cockpitt,[91] where I heard the Duke of Albemarle's chaplin make a simple sermon: among other things, reproaching the imperfection of humane learning, he cried: "All our physicians cannot tell what an

[77] Sir Theophilus Biddulph, member of Parliament for Lichfield

[78] obscure acquaintance of Pepys, mentioned several times in the *Diary*

[79] the body charged with the administration of the temporal affairs of the parish

[80] later Sir William Hooker, Lord Mayor (1673)

[81] pitiful [82] prosperous

[83] Captain George Cocke, a wealthy hemp merchant, Navy paymaster

[84] mistress

[85] daughter of the Earl of Sandwich, wife of Sir Philip Carteret

[86] unidentified

[87] Charles II attempted the restoration of the royal palace at Greenwich.

[88] Combe Farm, near Greenwich

[89] farmyard

[90] dressed

[91] Duke of Albemarle's lodging

ague is, and all our arithmetique is not able to number the days of a man;" which, God knows, is not the fault of arithmetique, but that our understandings reach not the thing. To dinner, where a great deale of silly discourse, but the worst is I hear that the plague increases much at Lambeth, St. Martin's and Westminster, and fear it will all over the city. Thence I to the Swan, thinking to have seen Sarah[92] but she was at church, and so I by water to Deptford, and there made a visit to Mr. Evelyn,[93] who, among other things, showed me most excellent painting in little; in distemper, Indian incke, water colours: graveing; and, above all, the whole secret of mezzo-tinto, and the manner of it, which is very pretty,[94] and good things done with it. He read to me very much also of his discourse, he hath been many years and now is about, about Guardenage; which will be a most noble and pleasant piece. He read me part of a play or two of his making, very good, but not as he conceits[95] them, I think, to be. He showed me his Hortus Hyemalis;[96] leaves laid up in a book of several plants kept dry, which preserve colour, however, and look very finely, better than any Herball. In fine, a most excellent person he is, and must be allowed a little for the conceitedness; but he may well be so, being a man so much above others. . . .

[March] 9th [1665/1666]. Up, and being ready, to the Cockpitt to make a visit to the Duke of Albemarle, and to my great joy find him the same man to me that [he has been] heretofore, which I was in great doubt of, through my negligence in not visiting of him a great while; and having now set all to rights there, I am in mighty ease in my mind and I think shall never suffer matters to run so far backward again as I have done of late, with reference to my neglecting him and Sir W. Coventry.[97] Thence by water down to Deptford, where I met my Lord Bruncker and Sir W. Batten by agreement, and to measuring Mr. Castle's[98] new third-rate ship, which is to be called the Defyance. And here I had my end in saving the King some money and getting myself some experience in knowing how they do measure ships. Thence I left them and walked to Redriffe, and there taking water was overtaken by them in their boat, and so they would have me in with them to Castle's house, where my Lady Batten and Madam Williams[99] were, and there dined and a deale of doings. I had a good dinner and counterfeit mirthe and pleasure with them, but had but little thinking how I neglected my business. Anon, all home to Sir W. Batten's and there Mrs. Knipp[100] coming we did spend the evening together very merry. She and I singing, and, God forgive me! I do still see that my nature is not to be quite conquered, but will esteem pleasure above all things, though yet in the middle of it, it has reluctances after[101] my business, which is neglected by my following my pleasure. However musique and women I cannot but give way to, whatever my business is. They being gone I to the office a while and so home to supper and to bed.

[September] 2nd (Lord's Day) [1666]. Some of our mayds sitting up late last night to get things ready against our feast to-day, Jane called us up about three in the morning, to tell us of a great fire they saw in the City. So I rose and slipped on my night-gowne,[102] and went to her window, and thought it to be on the back-side of Marke-lane at the farthest; but, being unused to such fires as followed, I thought it far enough off; and so went to bed again and to sleep. About seven rose again to dress myself, and there looked out at the window, and saw the fire not so much as it was and further off. So to my closett[103] to set things to rights after yesterday's cleaning. By and by Jane comes and tells me that she hears that above 300 houses have

[92] maid at the Swan Tavern (Herbert's) of whom Pepys was for a considerable period enamored

[93] the famous diarist. See pp. 103–114.

[94] ingeniously contrived [95] thinks

[96] literally *winter garden*

[97] Sir William Coventry, secretary to James, Duke of York

[98] timber merchant

[99] Lord Brouncker's "lady of pleasure"

[100] Mrs. Knepp, charming little actress, who quite enchanted Pepys with her singing

[101] qualms about

[102] dressing gown

[103] private room, study

been burned down to-night by the fire we saw, and that it is now burning down all Fish-street, by London Bridge. So I made myself ready presently, and walked to the Tower, and there got up upon one of the high places, Sir J. Robinson's[104] little son going up with me; and there I did see the houses at that end of the bridge all on fire, and an infinite great fire on this and the other side the end of the bridge; which, among other people, did trouble me for poor little Michell[105] and our Sarah[106] on the bridge. So down, with my heart full of trouble, to the Lieutenant of the Tower, who tells me that it begun this morning in the King's baker's house in Pudding-lane, and that it hath burned St. Magnus's Church and most part of Fish-street already. So I down to the water-side, and there got a boat and through bridge, and there saw a lamentable fire. Poor Michell's house, as far as the Old Swan, already burned that way, and the fire running further, that in a very little time it got as far as the Steele-yard, while I was there. Everybody endeavouring to remove their goods, and flinging into the river or bringing them into lighters that lay off; poor people staying in their houses as long as till the very fire touched them, and then running into boats, or clambering from one pair of stairs by the water-side to another. And among other things, the poor pigeons, I perceive, were loth to leave their houses, but hovered about the windows and balconys till they were, some of them burned, their wings, and fell down. Having staid, and in an hour's time seen the fire rage every way, and nobody, to my sight, endeavouring to quench it, but to remove their goods, and leave all to the fire, and having seen it get as far as the Steele-yard, and the wind mighty high and driving it into the City; and every thing, after so long a drought, proving combustible, even the very stones of churches, and among other things the poor steeple by which pretty Mrs.——— lives, and whereof my old schoolfellow Elborough[107] is parson, taken fire in the very top, and there burned till it fell down: I to White Hall (with a gentleman with me who desired to go off from the Tower, to see the fire, in my boat); to White Hall, and there up to the King's closett[108] in the Chappell, where people come about me, and I did give them an account dismayed them all, and word was carried in to the King. So I was called for, and did tell the King and Duke of Yorke what I saw, and that unless his Majesty did command houses to be pulled down nothing could stop the fire. . . . Good hopes there was of stopping it at the Three Cranes above, and at Buttolph's Wharf below bridge, if care be used; but the wind carries it into the City, so as we know not by the water-side what it do there. River full of lighters and boats taking in goods, and good goods swimming in the water, and only I observed that hardly one lighter or boat in three that had the goods of a house in, but there was a pair of Virginalls[109] in it. Having seen as much as I could now, I away to White Hall by appointment, and there walked to St. James's Parke, and there met my wife and Creed and Wood[110] and his wife, and walked to my boat; and there upon the water again, and to the fire up and down, it still encreasing, and the wind great. So near the fire as we could for smoke; and all over the Thames, with one's face in the wind, you were almost burned with a shower of fire drops. This is very true; so as houses were burned by these drops and flakes of fire, three or four, nay, five or six houses, one from another. When we could endure no more upon the water, we to a little ale house on the Bankside, over against the Three Cranes, and there staid till it was dark almost, and saw the fire grow; and, as it grew darker, appeared more and more, and in corners and upon steeples, and between churches and houses, as far as we could see up the hill of the City, in a most horrid malicious bloody flame, not like the

[104] Sir John Robinson, Lieutenant of the Tower

[105] young friend of Pepys whose wife had caught Pepys' eye before her marriage (she told him she was engaged)

[106] a former maid of the Pepys, dismissed at Mrs. Pepys' insistence

[107] Thomas Elborough

[108] private chamber for devotions

[109] a small rectangular spinet without legs

[110] a mast-maker

fine flame of an ordinary fire. Barbary[111] and her husband away before us. We staid till, it being darkish, we saw the fire as only one entire arch of fire from this to the other side the bridge, and in a bow up the hill for an arch of above a mile long: it made me weep to see it. The churches, houses, and all on fire and flaming at once; and a horrid noise the flames made, and the cracking of houses at their ruine. So home with a sad heart. . . .

[September] 5th [1666]. . . . I walked into the town, and find Fanchurch-streete, Gracious-street, and Lumbard-street all in dust. The Exchange a sad sight, nothing standing there, of all the statues or pillars, but Sir Thomas Gresham's[112] picture in the corner. Walked into Moorefields (our feet ready to burn, walking through the towne among the hot coles), and find that full of people, and poor wretches carrying their goods there, and every body keeping his goods together by themselves (and a great blessing it is to them that it is fair weather for them to keep abroad night and day); drank there, and paid twopence for a plain penny loaf. Thence homeward, having passed through Cheapside and Newgate Market, all burned, and seen Anthony Joyce's[113] house in fire. And took up (which I keep by me) a piece of glasse of Mercer's Chappell in the streete, where much more was, so melted and buckled with the heat of the fire like parchment. I also did see a poor cat taken out of a hole in the chimney, joyning to the wall of the Exchange, with the hair all burned off the body, and yet alive. . . .

[December] 28th [1667]. Up, and to the office, where busy all the morning, at noon home, and there to dinner with my clerks and Mr. Pelling,[114] and had a very good dinner, among others a haunch of venison boiled, and merry we were, and I rose soon from dinner, and with my wife and girle to the King's house,[115] and there saw "The Mad Couple,"[116] which is but an ordinary play; but only Nell's[117] and Hart's[118] mad parts are most excellently done, but especially her's: which makes it a miracle to me to think how ill she do any serious part, as, the other day, just like a fool or changeling; and, in a mad part, do beyond all imitation almost. [It pleased us mightily to see the natural affection of a poor woman, the mother of one of the children brought on the stage: the child crying, she by force got upon the stage, and took up her child and carried it away off the stage from Hart.] Many fine faces here to-day. Thence home, and there to the office late, and then home to supper and to bed. I am told to-day, which troubles me, that great complaint is made upon the 'Change,[119] among our merchants, that the very Ostend[120] little pickaroon[121] men-of-war do offer violence to our merchant-men, and search them, beat our masters, and plunder them, upon pretence of carrying Frenchmen's goods. Lord! what a condition are we come to, and that so soon after a war![122]

[March] 18th [1667/1668]. . . . Then there was another great business about our signing of certificates to the Exchequer for [prize] goods, upon the £1,250,000 Act,[123] which the Commissioners of the Treasury did all oppose, and to the laying fault upon us. But I did then speak to the justifying what we had done, even to the angering of Duncomb[124] and Clifford,[125] which I was vexed at: but, for all that, I did set the Office and myself right, and went away with the victory, my Lord Keeper saying

[111] Barbara Sheldon, wife of the son of Mr. Wood, the mast-maker

[112] the founder of the Royal Exchange

[113] the husband of one of Pepys' cousins, a man whom Pepys disliked but whose widow he befriended

[114] an apothecary [115] the King's Theatre

[116] a comedy by James Howard

[117] Nell Gwynn, the famous actress and mistress of Charles II

[118] Charles Hart, the actor

[119] the Exchange

[120] apparently the port of departure for a good many pirates and privateers at this time

[121] pirate or privateer

[122] the Dutch War (1664–1667)

[123] a hearing before the Council on the handling of prize money, which had attracted Parliamentary attention after the Dutch ships prize scandal of 1665

[124] Sir John Duncombe, a Commissioner of the Treasury

[125] Sir Thomas Clifford, another Commissioner of the Treasury

that he would not advise the Council to order us to sign no more certificates. But, before I began to say anything in this matter, the King and the Duke of York talking at the Council-table, before all the Lords, of the Committee of Miscarriages, how this entering of men before the ships could be ready would be reckoned a miscarriage; "Why," says the King, "it is then but Mr. Pepys making of another speech to them;"[126] which made all the Lords, and there were by also the Atturney[127] and Sollicitor-Generall,[128] look upon me. Thence Sir W. Coventry, W. Pen[129] and I, by hackney-coach[130] to take a little ayre in Hyde Park, the first time I have been there this year; and we did meet many coaches going and coming, it being mighty pleasant weather; and so, coming back again, I 'light in the Pell Mell; and there went to see Sir H. Cholmly,[131] who continues very ill of his cold. And there come in Sir H. Yelverton,[132] whom Sir H. Chomly commended me to his acquaintance, which the other received, but without remembering to me, or I him, of our being school-fellows together;[133] and I said nothing of it. But he took notice of my speech the other day at the bar of the House; and indeed I perceive he is a wise man by his manner of discourse, and here he do say that the town is full of it, that now the Parliament hath resolved upon £300,000, the King, instead of fifty, will set out but twenty-five ships, and the Dutch as many; and that Smith[134] is to command them, who is allowed to have the better of Holmes[135] in the late dispute, and is in good esteem in the Parliament, above the other. Thence home, and there, in favour to my eyes, stayed at home, reading the ridiculous History of my Lord Newcastle,[136] wrote by his wife,[137] which shews her to be a mad, conceited, ridiculous woman,[138] and he an asse to suffer her to write what she writes to him and of him. Betty Turner[139] sent my wife the book to read, and it being a fair print, to ease my eyes, which would be reading, I read that. Anon comes Mrs. Turner and sat and talked with us, and most about the business of Ackworth,[140] which comes before us tomorrow, that I would favour it, but I do not think, notwithstanding all the friendship I can shew him, that he can escape, and therefore it had been better that he had followed the advice I sent him the other day by Mrs. Turner, to make up the business. So parted, and I to bed, my eyes being very bad; and I know not how in the world to abstain from reading.

[April] 2nd [1668]. . . . Thence with Lord Brouncker to the Royall Society, where they were just done; but there I was forced to subscribe to the building of a college, and did give £40; and several others did subscribe, some greater and some less sums; but several I saw hang off: and I doubt it will spoil the Society, for it breeds faction[141] and ill-will, and becomes burdensome to some that cannot, or would not, do it. Here, to my great content, I did try the use of the Otacousticon,[142] which was only a great glass bottle, broke at the bottom putting the neck to my eare, and

[126] a reference to Pepys' recent successful defense of the Admiralty before Parliament

[127] Sir Geoffrey Palmer

[128] Sir Heneage Finch

[129] Admiral Sir William Penn, Commissioner of the Navy and intimate of Pepys

[130] coach standing for hire

[131] Sir Hugh Cholmely, member of the Tangier Commission

[132] Sir Henry Yelverton, member of Parliament for Northamptonshire

[133] at St. Paul's

[134] Captain Sir Jeremy Smith, later Comptroller of Victualling for the Navy

[135] Captain Sir Robert Holmes, who had brought charges of serious professional misconduct against Smith

[136] William Cavendish, First Duke of Newcastle, one of the most generous supporters of Charles I and Charles II, author of a book on horsemanship, and a dabbler in playwriting

[137] Margaret Cavendish, Duchess of Newcastle, author of poems, plays, an historically important autobiography, and *The Life of William Cavendish, Duke of Newcastle* (1667)

[138] For Evelyn's opinion of the same lady, see above, p. 110.

[139] according to Wheatley, daughter of Sergeant John Turner and Pepys' cousin, Jane Turner

[140] William Ackworth, accused of embezzling Navy stores but according to Pepys acquitted

[141] dissension

[142] ear-trumpet

there I did plainly hear the dashing of the oares of the boats in the Thames to Arundell[143] gallery window, which, without it, I could not in the least do, and may, I believe, be improved to a great height, which I am mighty glad of. Thence with Lord Brouncker and several of them to the King's Head Taverne by Chancery Lane, and there did drink and eat and talk, and, above the rest, I did hear of Mr. Hooke and my Lord an account of the reason of concords and discords in musique, which they say is from the equality of vibrations; but I am not satisfied in it, but will at my leisure think of it more, and see how far that do go to explain it. So late at night home with Mr. Colwell,[144] and parted, and I to the office, and then to Sir W. Pen to confer with him, and Sir R. Ford[145] and Young,[146] about our St. John Baptist prize, and so home, without more supper to bed, my family being now little by the departure of my wife and two maids.

[April] 7th [1668]. Up, and at the office all the morning, where great hurry to be made in the fitting forth of this present little fleet, but so many rubs by reason of want of money, and people's not believing us in cases where we had money unless (which in several cases, as in hiring of vessels, cannot be) they be paid beforehand, that every thing goes backward instead of forward. At noon comes Mr. Clerke, my solicitor, and the Auditor's men with my account drawn up in the Exchequer way with their queries, which are neither many nor great, or hard to answer upon it, and so dined with me, and then I by coach to the King's playhouse, and there saw "The English Monsieur;"[147] sitting for privacy sake in an upper box: the play hath much mirth in it as to that particular humour. After the play done, I down to Knipp, and did stay her undressing herself; and there saw the several players, men and women go by; and pretty to see how strange they are all, one to another, after the play is done. Here I saw a wonderful pretty maid of her own, that come to undress her, and one so pretty that she says she intends not to keep her, for fear of her being undone in her service, by coming to the playhouse. Here I hear Sir W. Davenant[148] is just now dead; and so who will succeed him in the mastership of the house is not yet known. The eldest Davenport[149] is, it seems, gone from this house to be kept by somebody; which I am glad of, she being a very bad actor. I took her then up into a coach and away to the Park, which is now very fine after some rain, but the company was going away most, and so I took her to the Lodge, and there treated her and had a deal of good talk, and now and then I did baiser la, and that was all, and that as much or more than I had much mind to because of her paint. She tells me mighty news, that my Lady Castlemayne[150] is mightily in love with Hart of their house: and he is much with her in private, and she goes to him, and do give him many presents; and that the thing is most certain, and Becke Marshall[151] only privy to[152] it, and the means of bringing them together, which is a very odd thing; and by this means she is even with the King's love to Mrs. Davis.[153] This done, I carried her and set her down at Mrs. Manuel's,[154] but stayed not there myself, nor went in; but straight home, and there to my letters, and so home to bed.

[143] Arundell House in the Strand where the Royal Society was meeting

[144] Daniel Colwall, treasurer of the Royal Society

[145] Sir Richard Ford, member of the Tangier Commission

[146] Mr. Young, the flag-maker in Cornhill

[147] comedy by James Howard

[148] Sir William Davenant, the distinguished playwright and manager

[149] Frances Davenport, the eldest sister of Elizabeth Davenport, famous as Roxalana in Davenant's *Siege of Rhodes*

[150] Barbara Villiers, wife of Roger Palmer (Earl of Castlemaine, 1661), mistress to Charles II, Duchess of Cleveland (1670)

[151] younger sister of the celebrated actress, Anne Marshall

[152] secretly cognizant of

[153] Mary Davis, comedian and dancer, who charmed Charles II with her singing and became his mistress

[154] "the Jew's wife," formerly an actress, whose singing Pepys admired, and whose home was apparently a gathering-place for music-lovers

George Savile, First Marquis of Halifax

GEORGE SAVILE (raised to the peerage as Baron Savile of Eland and Viscount Halifax in 1668, and created first Marquis of Halifax in 1682) was born in 1633, the eldest son of a wealthy and influential Yorkshire family, which during the Civil Wars managed to hold on to its property despite its declared Royalism. After the death of his father in 1644 Savile was sent abroad to be educated. On his return he settled down, an accomplished country gentleman, at his estate of Rufford Abbey, Nottinghamshire. Gradually, however, he was drawn into public life. During the earlier years of the Restoration his association with Buckingham identified him with the anti-Clarendon opposition, but it was not until he took his place in the House of Lords in 1668—having been raised to the peerage—that his active political career can be said to have begun.

From the first Halifax had deemed it necessary that France's disproportionate political power be held in check; and from such a point of view he had looked askance at that series of events which included Charles's Treaty of Dover (1670) and the royal Declaration of Indulgence (1672). With the collapse of Charles's policy and the breakup of the Cabal, the King sought to allay discontent by admitting Halifax and a few other new ministers to the Privy Council. In the period immediately following, Halifax came to be associated with Shaftesbury, his uncle by marriage, in the opposition party which was now beginning to take shape, and in consequence was expelled from the Privy Council. He was, however, again admitted into the administration when in 1679 Temple persuaded the King to adopt the scheme of an enlarged council. This marked the beginning of a crucial period in English political and constitutional history, and the part played therein by Halifax was of great importance. Shaftesbury had now emerged as the leader of the extreme opposition—the Whigs, as they were now called—who sought the exclusion of James from the succession. Halifax, in the past fully identified with the opposition party, now broke with Shaftesbury, sponsored "limitation" as against "exclusion," and came forward as spokesman for a moderate policy which would alleviate the violence of extreme factions and save the country from being again plunged into civil war. It was in the second Whig Parliament, which sat from October, 1680, to the following January, that there took place in the Lords the great debate between Shaftesbury and Halifax, with the latter triumphing when the Exclusion Bill was defeated. Halifax, now regarded by the Whigs as a renegade, attained great influence in the period directly after the dismissal (March, 1681) of Charles's last Parliament, and in 1682 was created Marquis and appointed to the office of Lord Privy Seal. As the political reaction gathered force—a reaction which some historians have gone so far as to call the reëstablishment of Stuart despotism—Halifax sought to moderate the spirit of the movement and to check the growing power of the Duke of York. With the accession of James, Halifax lost all influence, being first kicked upstairs to the post of Lord President of the Council and then dismissed from office.

From retirement Halifax issued two anonymous pamphlets of far-reaching effect, *A Letter to a Dissenter* (1687) and *The Anatomy of an Equivalent* (1688), in which he sought to rally the Dissenters against the offers of toleration made by James. But Halifax did not participate in the negotiations now under way with William of Orange; indeed, following William's arrival in England in November, 1688, he undertook to advise James at this juncture. In the end, however, he went over to William, and was speaker of the Lords in the Convention which met early in 1689 and offered the throne to William and Mary. Under William, Halifax again held office briefly as Lord Privy Seal, but he was hated by the more extreme Whigs. He shortly resigned his office, and during his last years was once more in opposition. He was in attendance in Parliament—having sat in the House of Lords for twenty-eight years—to within a few days of his death, which ocurred in April, 1695.

An anonymous political pamphlet issued in 1681, *Observations upon a late Libel,* is thought to be Halifax's first published work. It has reference to the dissolution of the third or Oxford Parliament early in 1681, and is a defence of the royal policy, for which Halifax as a minister bore some responsibility. All of the other writings of Halifax to receive publication during his lifetime appeared in a similarly anonymous form, most of them being—again like the *Observations*—political and occasional in nature: *The Character of a Trimmer,* aptly described by Raleigh as "a complete handbook to the politics of the closing years of Charles the Second's reign," was circulating in manuscript early in 1685, but was not printed until 1688; *A Letter to a Dissenter* was issued in 1687, the year of James's first Declaration of Indulgence; *Advice to a Daughter* and *The Anatomy of an Equivalent,* the former being one of Halifax's few non-political pieces, the latter a continuation in effect of the *Letter to a Dissenter,* appeared in 1688. These and other pieces were reprinted in the *Miscellanies,* the first edition of which appeared in 1700. The brilliant *Character of King Charles the Second* and the *Political, Moral and Miscellaneous Thoughts and Reflections* were not published until 1750. H. C. Foxcroft edited the works for her two-volume *Life and Letters of Sir George Savile, Bart. First Marquis of Halifax* (1898). *The Complete Works,* edited by Walter Raleigh, appeared in 1912. *The Observations upon a late Libel* has been edited (1940), with an introduction, by Hugh Macdonald.

It is scarcely necessary to dwell on Halifax's vital role in English political history throughout that crucial quarter of a century from 1668 to 1695 during which, as a member of the House of Lords, he was constantly at the service of his country. Both while holding office and when in opposition he sought to keep the nation on a reasonable course, a course which would assure unity and freedom from French influence at home, and—through counterbalancing the power of Louis XIV—safety from abroad. Accordingly he pitted all his powers against the immoderate Shaftesbury and won, but in the anti-Whig reaction which ensued he stood out against the policies of the extreme Tories, thus earning for himself their contemptuous epithet of "trimmer." He opposed James II, was dismissed from office, appealed effectively to the Dissenters—in two notable pamphlets—to stand out against the Royal Indulgences, yet went to James as an adviser after William had landed. He played a prominent part in the Convention which in

February, 1689, proclaimed William and Mary, again held office briefly as Lord Privy Seal, and then, the extreme Whigs still hating him and now seeking his impeachment, went over to the Parliamentary opposition. Despite the lucid statement of his political position given in *The Character of a Trimmer*, his conduct in the face of the mighty issues of his time was often misunderstood by his contemporaries. "He went backwards and forwards and changed sides so often that in conclusion no side trusted him." So wrote Bishop Burnet. But the true nature of Halifax's integrity, political intelligence, and grasp upon the human realities has long since become apparent. It is to be remembered that there was as yet no well-defined party system. For Halifax the terms *Whig* and *Tory*, coined during the struggle over exclusion, meant the violent extremities of factionalism. He thought instead in terms of long-range administrative policies, consistently exerting his influence so as to offset the passions of the moment. Such an attitude looked both backwards and forwards: backwards towards an older concept of national unity and an aristocratic sense of service to the country; forwards to the modern conviction that the sane society is one in which divergencies of policy are to be resolved gradually and by continued mediation.

Halifax's political writings, of which *The Character of a Trimmer* and *A Letter to a Dissenter* have been best remembered, may all be read with two somewhat different points of reference in mind. On the one hand they are occasional pieces, written each for a particular purpose and set deeply into the complexities of a given moment. But they are, at the same time, remarkably cool and disengaged generalizations. Halifax's admirable style—witty, ironic, epigrammatic, almost bare of literary allusions, and always hard and matter-of-fact where any opportunity offered to be emotionally grandiloquent—seems to give us the precise quality of his mind and of his experience. In a class somewhat apart, in that they were not called forth by the exigencies of public events but are solely in the nature of intellectual analyses, are the brilliant *Character of King Charles the Second* and the political section of the *Thoughts and Reflections*. The famous *Advice to a Daughter*, the best known of all Halifax's writings, is of course completely non-political. It was first published early in 1688, and though anonymous seems to have been generally ascribed to Halifax. As the numerous editions and the translations into French and Italian testify, it quickly achieved a very wide popularity. Elizabeth, to whom it was addressed, Halifax's only surviving daughter, had been born in 1675, and as the wife of Lord Stanhope was to become the mother of the famous fourth Earl of Chesterfield, author of the *Letters to his Son*. Nowhere does Halifax's style show to better advantage. We know that he had a deep love for Montaigne, but what he learned from the great Frenchman was not so much the loose or *libertine* style, which can be traced through seventeenth-century French letters and occasionally into English, as the happy use of everyday language and the common terms of expression. In content the *Advice* deserves to rank high if for no other reason than its importance in the way of social documentation. When Halifax hastens to characterize his "visions" of happiness to be enjoyed by his daughter as things "better suited to my partial *Wishes*, than to my reasonable *Hopes* for you," he is expressing something that comes close to being a fundamental attitude on the part of the educated man of this era. The complement of this is to be found in the witty depictions of the comic, as in the portrait given in the second section ("Home, Family, and Children") of the proud, careless wife; and in the definitions of vanity and affection which enliven the latter sections. The spirit here is for all the world that of the contemporary Restoration comedy of manners.

For a close study of Halifax, H. C. Foxcroft's *Life and Letters of Sir George*

Savile, Bart., First Marquis of Halifax, With a New Edition of His Works (1898) is indispensible. Some of the biographical material therein has, however, been revised in a later work by the same author: *A "Character" of The Trimmer: Being a Short Life of the First Marquis of Halifax* (1946). Walter Raleigh's Introduction to his edition of *The Complete Works of George Savile* (1912) is deservedly well-known. Hugh Macdonald's edition (1940) of the *Observations Upon a late Libel* contains a useful Introduction and an admirable bibliography of Halifax's works. G. P. Gooch's chapter on Halifax in his *Political Thought in England from Bacon to Halifax* (1914), A. W. Reed's discussion of Halifax in *The Social and Political Ideas of Some English Thinkers of The Augustan Age* (ed. F. J. C. Hearnshaw, 1928), and Bonamy Dobrée's essay in his *Variety of Ways* (1932) are all interesting.

from THE LADY'S NEW-YEAR'S-GIFT: OR, ADVICE TO A DAUGHTER[1]

Dear Daughter,

I Find, that even our most pleasing Thoughts *will* be unquiet; they *will* be in motion; and the *Mind* can have no rest whilst it is possess'd by a daring Passion. *You* are at present the chief Object of my *Care*, as well as of my *Kindness*, which sometimes throweth me into *Visions* of your being happy in the World, that are better suited to my partial *Wishes*, than to my reasonable *Hopes* for you. At other times, when my *Fears* prevail, I shrink as if I was struck, at the Prospect of *Danger*, to which a young Woman must be expos'd. By how much the more *Lively*, so much the more *Liable* you are to be hurt; as the finest Plants are the soonest nipped by the *Frost*. Whilst you are playing full of Innocence, the spitefull World will bite, except you are guarded by your *Caution.* Want of *Care* therefore, my dear Child, is never to be excus'd; since, as to *this* World, it hath the same effect as want of *Vertue*. Such an early sprouting Wit requireth so much the more to be sheltered by some *Rules*, like something strew'd on tender Flowers to preserve them from being blasted. You must take it well to be prun'd by so kind a Hand as that of a *Father*. There may be some bitterness in meer Obedience: The natural Love of *Liberty* may help to make the Commands of a Parent harder to go down: Some inward resistance there will be, where *Power* and not *Choice* maketh us move. But when a *Father* layeth aside his Authority, and persuadeth only by his Kindness, you will never answer it to Good Nature, if it hath not weight with you.

A great part of what is said in the following *Discourse* may be above the present growth of your Understanding; but that becoming every day taller, will in a little time reach up to it, so as to make it easie to you. I am willing to begin with you before your *Mind* is quite form'd, that being the time in which it is most capable of receiving a *Colour* that will last when it is mix'd with it. Few things are well learnt, but by early *Precepts:* Those well infus'd, make them *Natural;* and we are never sure of retaining what is valuable, till by a continued *Habit* we have made it a Piece of us.

Whether my skill can draw the Picture of a fine Woman, may be a question: but it can be none, That I have drawn that of a kind *Father:* If you will take an exact Copy, I will so far presume upon my workmanship, as to undertake you shall not make an ill *Figure*. Give me so much Credit as to try, and I am sure that neither your Wishes nor mine shall be disappointed by it.

RELIGION

The first thing to be considered, is *Religion*. It must be the chief Object of your Thoughts, since it would be a vain thing to direct your *Behaviour* in the World, and forget that which you are to have towards him who made it.

In a strict sense, it is the only thing

[1] Text: *Miscellanies,* 1700

necessary: you must take it into your *Mind*, and from thence throw it into your *Heart*, where you are to embrace it so close as never to lose the *Possession* of it. But then it is necessary to distinguish between the *Reality* and the *Pretence*.

Religion doth not consist in believing the Legend of the *Nursery*, where Children with their *Milk* are fed with the Tales of Witches, Hobgoblings, Prophecies, and Miracles. We suck in so greedily these early *Mistakes*, that our riper *Understanding* hath much ado to cleanse our *Minds* from this kind of *Trash:* The Stories are so entertaining, that we do not only believe them, but relate them: which makes the discovery of the *Truth* somewhat grievous, when it makes us lose such a Field of Impertinence, where we might have diverted our selves, besides the throwing some shame upon us for having ever received them. This is making the *World* a *Jest*, and imputing to God Almighty, That the Province he assigneth to the Devil, is to play at Blindmans-buff, and shew Tricks with Mankind; and is so far from being *Religion*, that it is not *Sense*, and hath right only to be call'd that kind of Devotion, of which *Ignorance* is the undouted *Mother*, without competition or dispute. These Mistakes are therefore to be left off with your Hanging sleeves; and you ought to be as much out of countenance to be found with them about you, as to be seen playing with Babies at an *Age* when other things are expected from you.

The next thing to be observ'd to you, is, That *Religion* doth as little consist in loud Answers and devout Convulsions at Church, or Praying in an extraordinary manner. Some Ladies are so extreme stirring at *Church*, that one would swear the *Worm* in their *Conscience* made them so unquiet. Others will have such a Divided Face between a *Devout Goggle* and an *Inviting Glance*, that the unnatural Mixture maketh even the *best Looks* to be at that time *ridiculous*. These affected *Appearances* are ever suspected, like very strong Perfumes, which are generally thought no very good Symptoms in those that make use of them. Let your earnestness therefore be reserv'd for your *Closet*, where you may have God Almighty to your self: In *Publick* be still and calm, neither undecently *Careless*, nor *Affected* in the other Extream.

It is not true Devotion, to put on an angry *Zeal* against those who may be of a differing Persuasion. *Partiality* to our selves makes us often mistake it for a *Duty*, to fall hard upon others in that case; and being push'd on by *Self-conceit*, we strike without mercy, believing that the *Wounds* we give are *Meritorious*, and that we are fighting God Almighty's Quarrel; when the truth is, we are only setting out our selves. Our *Devotion* too often breaketh out into that *Shape* which most agreeth with our particular *Temper*. The *Cholerick* grow into a hardned Severity against all who dissent from them; snatch at all the Texts of Scripture that suit with their *Complexion;* and because God's Wrath was some time kindled, they conclude, That *Anger* is a Divine Vertue; and are so far from imagining their ill natur'd *Zeal* requireth an *Apology*, that they value themselves upon it, and triumph in it. *Others*, whose Nature is more Credulous than ordinary, admit no Bounds or Measure to it; they grow as proud of extending their *Faith*, as Princes are of enlarging their *Dominions;* not considering that our *Faith*, like our Stomach, is capable of being over-charg'd; and that as the last is destroy'd by taking in more than it can digest, so our *Reason* may be extinguish'd by oppressing it with the weight of too many strange things; especially if we are forbidden to chew what we are commanded to swallow. The *Melancholy* and the *Sullen* are apt to place a great part of their *Religion* in dejected or ill-humor'd *Looks*, putting on an unsociable Face, and declaiming against the Innocent Entertainments of *Life*, with as much sharpness as they could bestow upon the greatest *Crimes*. This generally is only a *Vizard*, there is seldom any thing real in it. No other thing is the better for being *Sowre;* and it would be hard that *Religion* should be so, which is the best of things. In the mean time it may be said with truth, That this *surly* kind of *Devotion* hath perhaps done little less hurt in the World, by frighting, than the most scandalous *Examples* have done by infecting it.

Having told you, in these few Instances, to which many more might be added, what is not true *Religion;* it is time to describe to you, what is so. The ordinary *Definitions* of it are no more like it, than the common Sign-posts are like the Princes they would represent. The unskilful *Dawbers* in all Ages have generally laid on such ill *Colours*, and drawn such harsh *Lines*, that the Beauty of it is not easily to be discerned: They have put in all the forbidding Features that can be thought of; and in the first place, have made it an irreconcilable Enemy to *Nature;* when, in reality, they are not only *Friends*, but *Twins*, born together at the same time; and it is doing violence to them both, to go about to have them separated. Nothing is so kind and so inviting as true and *unsophisticated Religion:* Instead of imposing unnecessary Burdens upon our *Nature*, it easeth us of the greater weight of our *Passions* and *Mistakes:* Instead of subduing us with *Rigour*, it redeemeth us from the *Slavery* we are in to our selves, who are the most severe Masters, whilst we are under the Usurpation of our *Appetites* let loose and not restrain'd.

Religion is a chearful thing, so far from being always at *Cuffs* with *Good Humour*, that it is inseparably united to it. Nothing unpleasant belongs to it, though the *Spiritual Cooks* have done their unskilful part to give an ill *Relish* to it. A wise *Epicure* would be *Religious* for the sake of *Pleasure;* Good Sense is the Foundation of both; and he is a *Bungler* who aimeth at true *Luxury*, but where they are join'd.

Religion is exalted *Reason*, refin'd and sifted from the grosser parts of it: It dwelleth in the upper Region of the *Mind*, where there are fewest *Clouds* or *Mists* to darken or offend it: It is both the Foundation and the Crown of all Vertues: It is *Morality* improv'd and rais'd to its height, by being carried nearer *Heaven*, the only place where *Perfection* resideth. It cleanseth the *Understanding*, and brusheth off the Earth that hangeth about our *Souls*. It doth not want the *Hopes* and the *Terrors* which are made use of to support it; neither ought it to descend to the borrowing any Argument out of it self, since there we may find every thing that should invite us. If we were to be hired to *Religion*, it is able to out-bid the corrupted World, with all it can offer to us, being so much the *Richer* of the two, in every thing where *Reason* is admitted to be a Judge of the Value.

Since this is so, it is worth your pains to make *Religion* your choice, and not make use of it only as a *Refuge*. There are Ladies, who finding by the too visible decay of their good Looks, that they can shine no more by that *Light*, put on the *Varnish* of an affected Devotion, to keep up some kind of Figure in the World. They take Sanctuary in the *Church*, when they are pursued by growing *Contempt* which will not be stopt, but followeth them to the *Altar*. Such late penitence is only a disguise for the tormenting grief of being no more handsome. That is the killing thought which draweth the sighs and tears, that appear outwardly to be applied to a better end.

There are many who have an *Aguish Devotion*, Hot and Cold Fits, long Intermissions, and violent Raptures. This unevenness is by all means to be avoided. Let your method be a steady course of good *Life*, that may run like a smooth Stream, and be a perpetual Spring to furnish to the continued *Exercise* of *Vertue*. Your *Devotion* may be earnest, but it must be unconstrained; and like other Duties, you must make it your *Pleasure* too, or else it will have very little efficacy. By this *Rule* you may best judge of your own Heart. Whilst those *Duties* are *Joys*, it is an Evidence of their being sincere; but when they are a *Penance*, it is a sign that your *Nature* maketh some resistance; and whilst that lasteth, you can never be entirely secure of your self.

If you are often unquiet, and too nearly touch'd by the cross Accidents of *Life*, your *Devotion* is not of the right *Standard* there is too much *Allay* in it. That which is right and unmixt, taketh away the *Sting* of every thing that would trouble you: It is like a healing *Balm*, that extinguisheth the sharpness of the Blood; so this softeneth and dissolveth the *Anguish* of the *Mind*. A devout *Mind* hath the Privilege of being free from *Passions*, as some Climates are from all venomous kind of Creatures. It will raise you above the little *Vexations* to which others for want of it, will be expos'd, and bring you to a *Temper*, not of stupid *Indifference*, but of such a wise *Resignation*, that you may live in the

World, so as it may hang about you like a loose Garment, and not tied too close to you.

Take heed of running into that common *Error*, of applying God's Judgments upon particular Occasions. Our Weights and Measures are not competent to make the Distribution either of his *Mercy* or his *Justice:* He hath thrown a Veil over these things, which makes it not only an *Impertinence*, but a kind of *Sacrilege* for us to give Sentence in them without his *Commission.*

As to your particular *Faith*, keep to the *Religion* that is grown up with you, both as it is the best in it self, and that the reason of staying in it upon that Ground is somewhat stronger for your *Sex*, than it will perhaps be allow'd to be for ours; in respect that the Voluminous enquiries into the *Truth*, by Reading, are less expected from you. The *Best* of *Books* will be direction enough to you not to change; and whilst you are fix'd and sufficiently confirm'd in your own *Mind*, you will do best to keep vain *Doubts* and *Scruples* at such a distance that they may give you no disquiet.

Let me recommend you to a Method of being rightly inform'd, which can never fail: It is in short this. Get *Understanding*, and practice *Vertue* And if you are so *Blessed* as to have those for your *Share*, it is not surer that there is a *God*, than it is, that by him all *Necessary Truths* will be revealed to you.

HUSBAND

That which challengeth the place in your Thoughts, is how to live with a *Husband*. And though that is so large a Word, that few *Rules* can be fix'd to it which are unchangeable, the *Methods* being as various as the several *Tempers* of *Men* to which they must be suited; yet I cannot omit some *General Observations*, which, with the help of your own may the better direct you in the part of your Life upon which your *Happiness* most dependeth.

It is one of the *Disadvantages* belonging to your *Sex*, that young Women are seldom permitted to make their own *Choice;* their Friends Care and Experience are thought safer Guides to them, than their own *Fancies;* and their *Modesty* often forbiddeth them to refuse when their Parents recommend, though their *inward Consent* may not entirely go along with it. In this case there remaineth nothing for them to do, but to endeavour to make that easie which falleth to their *Lot*, and by a wise use of every thing they may dislike in a *Husband*, turn that by degrees to be very supportable, which, if neglected, might in time beget an *Aversion.*

You must first lay it down for a Foundation in general, That there is *Inequality* in the *Sexes*, and that for better Oeconomy of the World, the *Men*, who were to be the Law-givers, had the larger share of *Reason* bestow'd upon them; by which means your Sex is the better prepar'd for the *Compliance* that is necessary for the better performance of those *Duties* which seem to be most properly assign'd to it. This looks a little uncourtly at the first appearance; but upon Examination it will be found, that *Nature* is so far from being unjust to you, that she is partial on our side. She hath made you such large *Amends* by other Advantages, for the seeming *Injustice* of the first Distribution, that the Right of Complaining is come over to our Sex. You have it in your power not only to free your selves, but to subdue your Masters, and without violence throw both their *Natural* and *Legal Authority* at your Feet. We are made of differing *Tempers*, that our *Defects* may the better be mutually supplied: Your *Sex* wanteth our *Reason* for your *Conduct*, and our *Strength* for your *Protection: Ours* wanteth your *Gentleness* to soften, and to entertain us. The first part of our Life is a good deal subjected to you in the *Nursery*, where you Reign without Competition, and by that means have the advantage of giving the first *Impressions*. Afterwards you have stronger Influences, which, well manag'd, have more force in your behalf, than all our *Privileges* and *Jurisdictions* can pretend to have against you. You have more strength in your *Looks*, than we have in our *Laws*, and more power by your *Tears*, than we have by our *Arguments*.

It is true, that the *Laws* of *Marriage*, run in a harsher stile towards your *Sex*. *Obey* is an ungenteel word, and less easie to be digested, by making such an unkind distinction in the Words of the Contract, and so very unsuitable to the excess of *Good Manners,* which generally goes before it. Besides, the *universality* of the Rule seemeth to be a *Grievance,* and it appeareth reasonable, that there might be an *Exemption* for extraordinary Women, from ordinary Rules, to take away the just Exception that Lieth against the false measure of *general Equality.*

It may be alledged by the *Counsel* retained by your Sex, that as there is in all other Laws, an Appeal from the *Letter* to the *Equity,* in Cases that require it: It is as reasonable, that some *Court* of a larger *Jurisdiction* might be erected, where some *Wives* might resort and plead *specially.* And in such instances where Nature is so kind, as to raise them above the *level* of their own *Sex,* they might have *Relief,* and obtain a *Mitigation* in their own particular, of a *Sentence* which was given generally against *Woman kind.* The causes of *Separation* are now so very course, that few are *confident* enough to buy their *Liberty* at the price of having their Modesty so exposed. And for *disparity of Minds,* which above all other things requireth a *Remedy,* the *Laws* have made no *provision;* so little refin'd are numbers of Men, by whom they are compil'd. This and a great deal more might be said to give a colour to the Complaint.

But the Answer to it, in short is, That the *Institution* of *Marriage* is too sacred to admit a *Liberty* of *objecting* to it; That the supposition of yours being the weaker *Sex,* having without all doubt a good Foundation, maketh it reasonable to subject it to the *Masculine Dominion;* That no *Rule* can be so *perfect,* as not to admit some *Exceptions;* But the Law presumeth there would be so few found in this Case, who would have a sufficient Right to such a Privilege, that it is safer some *Injustice* should be *conniv'd* at in a very few Instances, than to break into an Establishment, upon which the Order of Humane Society doth so much depend.

You are therefore to make your best of what is *settled* by *Law* and *Custom,* and not vainly imagine, that it will be *changed* for your sake. But that you may not be discouraged, as if you lay under the weight of an *incurable Grievance,* you are to know, that by a *wise* and *dexterous* Conduct, it will be in your power to *relieve* your self from any thing that looketh like a disadvantage in it. For your better direction, I will give a hint of the most ordinary *Causes* of *Dissatisfaction* between Man and Wife, that you may be able by such a *Warning* to live so upon your *Guard,* that when you shall be married, you may know how to *cure* your Husband's *Mistakes,* and to *prevent* your own.

First then, you are to consider, you live in a time which hath rendred some kind of Frailties so habitual, that they lay claim to large *Grains* of *Allowance.* The World in this is somewhat unequal, and our Sex seemeth to play the *Tyrant* in distinguishing *partially* for our selves, by making that in the utmost degree *Criminal* in the *Woman,* which in a *Man* passeth under a much *gentler Censure.* The Root and the Excuse of this Injustice is the *Preservation* of Families from any *Mixture* which may bring a Blemish to them: And whilst the *Point* of *Honour* continues to be so plac'd, it seems unavoidable to give your *Sex,* the greater share of the Penalty. But if in this it lieth under any *Disadvantage,* you are more than recompens'd, by having the *Honour* of *Families* in your keeping. The Consideration so great a Trust must give you, maketh full amends; and this Power the World hath lodged in you, can hardly fail to restrain the Severity of an *ill* Husband, and to improve the Kindness and Esteem of a *good* one. This being so, remember, That next to the danger of *committing* the Fault your self, the greatest is that of *seeing* it in your *Husband.* Do not seem to look or hear that way: If he is a Man of Sense, he will reclaim himself; the Folly of it, is of it self sufficient to cure him: if he is not so, he will be provok'd, but not reform'd. To expostulate in these Cases, looketh like declaring War, and preparing Reprisals; which to a *thinking Husband* would be a dangerous Reflection. Besides, it is so course a Reason which will be assign'd for a Lady's too great Warmth upon such an occasion, that Modesty no less than Prudence ought to restrain her; since such an undecent Complaint makes a Wife much more ridiculous, than the Injury that provoketh her to it. But it is yet worse, and more unskilful, to *blaze it* in the World, expecting it should rise up in Arms to take her part: Whereas she will find, it can have no other Effect, than that she will be served up in all Companies, as the *reigning Jest* at that time; and will continue to be the common Entertainment, till she is rescu'd by some *newer Folly* that cometh upon the Stage, and driveth her away from it. The Impertinence of such Methods is so plain, that it doth not deserve the pains of being laid open. Be assur'd, that in these Cases your *Discretion* and *Silence* will be the most *prevailing Reproof*. An *affected Ignorance*, which is seldom a *Vertue*, is a great one here: And when your *Husband* seeth how unwilling you are to be uneasie, there is no stronger Argument to perswade him not to be unjust to you. Besides, it will naturally make him more *yielding* in other things: And whether it be to *cover* or redeem his *Offence*, you may have the good Effects of it whilst it lasteth, and all that while have the most reasonable Ground that can be, of presuming, such a Behaviour will at last entirely convert him. There is nothing so glorious to a *Wife*, as a Victory so gain'd: A Man so reclaim'd, is for ever after subjected to her *Vertue;* and her *bearing* for a time, is more than rewarded by a Triumph that will continue as long as her life.

The next thing I will suppose, is, That your *Husband* may love *Wine* more than is convenient. It will be granted, That though there are Vices of a deeper dye, there are none that have greater *Deformity* than this, when it is not restrain'd: But with all this, the same Custom which is the more to be lamented for its being so general, should make it less uneasie to every one in particular who is to suffer by the Effects of it: So that in the first place, it will be no new thing if you should have a *Drunkard* for your *Husband;* and there is by too frequent Examples evidence enough, that such a thing may happen, and yet a *Wife* may live too without being miserable. *Self-love* dictateth aggravating words to every thing we feel; *Ruine* and *Misery* are the Terms we apply to whatever we do not like, forgetting the Mixture allotted to us by the Condition of Human Life, by which it is not intended we should be quite exempt from trouble. It is fair, if we can escape such a degree of it as would oppress us, and enjoy so much of the pleasant part as may lessen the ill taste of such things as are unwelcome to us. Every thing hath two Sides, and for our own ease we ought to direct our Thoughts to that which may be least liable to exception. To fall upon the *worst side* of a *Drunkard*, giveth so unpleasant a prospect, that it is not possible to dwell upon it. Let us pass then to the more *favourable part*, as far as a *Wife* is concern'd in it.

I am tempted to say (if the Irregularity of the Expression could in strictness be justified) That a *Wife* is to thank God her *Husband* hath *Faults*. Mark the seeming paradox my Dear, for your own Instruction, it being intended no further. A *Husband* without *Faults* is a dangerous Observer; he hath an Eye so piercing, and seeth every thing so plain, that it is expos'd to his full Censure. And though I will not doubt but that your *Vertue* will disappoint the sharpest Enquiries; yet few Women can bear the having all they say or do *represented* in the clear Glass of an Understanding without *Faults*. Nothing softneth the *Arrogance* of our *Nature*, like a Mixture of some *Frailties*. It is by them we are best told, that we must not strike too hard upon others, because we our selves do so often deserve Blows: They pull our Rage by the Sleeve, and whisper Gentleness to us in our Censures, even when they are rightly applied. The *Faults* and *Passions* of *Husbands* bring them down to you, and make them content to live upon less unequal Terms, than Faultless Men would be willing to stoop to; so haughty is Mankind till humbled by common Weaknesses and Defects, which in our corrupted State contribute more towards the reconciling us one to another, than all the *Precepts* of the *Philosophers* and *Divines*. So that where the *Errors* of our *Nature* make amends for the *Disadvantages* of yours it is more your part to make use of the *Benefit*, than to quarrel at the *Fault*.

Thus in case a *Drunken Husband* should all to your share, if you will be *wise* and *patient*, his *Wine* shall be of your side; it will throw a *Veil* over your Mistakes, and will set out and improve every thing you do, that he is pleased with. Others will like him less, and by that means he may perhaps like you the more. When after having dined too well, he is received at home without a *Storm*, or so much as a *reproaching Look*, the *Wine* will naturally work out all in Kindness, which a *Wife* must encourage, let it be wrapped up in never so much Impertinence. On the other side it would boil up into *Rage*, if the mistaken *Wife* should treat him roughly, like a certain thing called a *kind Shrew*, than which the World, with all its Plenty, cannot shew a more Senseless, ill-bred, forbidding Creature. Consider, that where the Man will give such frequent Intermissions of the use of his *Reason*, the *Wife* insensibly getteth a Right of *Governing* in the Vacancy, and that raiseth her *Character* and *Credit* in the Family, to a higher pitch than perhaps could be done under a *sober Husband*, who never putteth himself into an Incapacity of holding the *Reins*. If these are not intire *Consolations*, at least they are *Remedies* to some Degree. They cannot make *Drunkenness* a *Vertue*, nor a *Husband* given to it a *Felicity;* but you will do your self no ill office in the endeavouring, by these means, to make the best of such a *Lot*, in case it should happen to be yours, and by the help of a wise Observation, to make that very supportable, which would otherwise be a *Load* that would oppress you.

The next Case I will put is that your *Husband* may be *Cholerick* or *Ill-humour'd*. To this it may be said, That *passionate* Men generally make amends at the Foot of the Account. Such a Man, if he is angry one day without any *Sense*, will the next day be as kind without any *Reason*. So that by marking how the *Wheels* of such a Man's Head are used to move, you may easily bring over all his *Passion* to your Party. Instead of being struck down by his Thunder, you shall direct it where and upon whom you shall think it best applied. Thus are the *strongest Poisons* turn'd to the *best Remedies;* but then there must be *Art* in it, and a *skilful Hand*, else the least *bungling* maketh it mortal. There is a great deal of nice Care requisite to deal with a Man of this Complexion. *Choler* proceedeth from *Pride*, and maketh a Man so partial to himself that he swelleth against Contradiction; and thinketh he is lessened if he is opposed. You must in this Case take heed of *increasing the Storm* by an *unwary Word*, or *kindling the Fire* whilst the Wind is in a Corner which may blow it in your Face: You are dextrously to yield every thing till he beginneth to cool, and then by slow degrees you may rise and gain upon him: Your *Gentleness* well timed, will, like a Charm, dispel his Anger ill placed; a *kind Smile* will *reclaim*, when a *shrill pettish Answer* would *provoke* him; rather than fail upon such occasions, when other *Remedies* are too weak, a little *Flattery* may be admitted, which by being necessary, will cease to be Criminal.

If *Ill-Humour* and *Sullenness*, and not open and sudden Heat is his Disease, there is a way of treating that too, so as to make it a Grievance to be endured. In order to it, you are first to know, that naturally *good Sense* hath a mixture of *surly* in it: and there being so much *Folly* in the World, and for the most part so triumphant, it giveth frequent Temptations to raise the *Spleen* of Men who think right. Therefore that which may generally be call'd *Ill-Humour*, is not always a Fault; it becometh one when either it is wrong applied, or that it is continued too long, when it is not so: For this Reason you must not too hastily fix an ill name upon that which may perhaps not deserve it; and though the Case should be, that your *Husband* might too sowerly resent any thing he disliketh, it may so happen, that more Blame shall belong to your *Mistake*, than to his *Ill-Humour*. If a *Husband* behaveth himself sometimes with an *Indifference* that a *Wife* may think offensive, she is in the wrong to put the worst sence upon it, if by any Means it will admit a better. Some *Wives* will call it *Ill-Humour* if their Husbands change their *Style* from that which they used whilst they made their first Addresses to them: Others will allow no *intermission* or *Abatement* in the Expressions of Kindness to them, not enough distinguishing Times, and forgetting that it is impossible for Men to keep themselves up all their Lives to the height of some *extravagant Moments*. A Man may at some times be less careful in little things, without any cold or disobliging Reason for it; as a *Wife* may be too expecting in smaller matters, without drawing upon her-self the inference of being *unkind*.

And if your *Husband* should be really sullen, and have such frequent Fits, as might take away the excuse of it, it concerneth you to have an Eye prepared to discern the first Appearances of Cloudy Weather, and to watch when the Fit goeth off, which seldom lasteth long if it is let alone. But whilst the Mind is fore, every thing galleth it, and that maketh it necessary to let the *Black Humour* begin to spend it self, before you come in and venture to undertake it.

If in the Lottery of the World you should draw a *Covetous Husband*, I confess it will not make you proud of your *good Luck;* yet even such a one may be endured too, though there are few Passions more untractable than that of *Avarice*. You must first take care that your *Definition* of *Avarice* may be a Mistake. You are to examine every Circumstance of your *Husband's* Fortune, and weigh the Reason of every thing you expect from him before you have right to pronounce that sentence. The Complaint is now so general against all *Husbands*, that it giveth great suspicion of its being often ill-grounded; it is impossible they should all deserve that Censure, and therefore it is certain, that it is many times misapplied. He that *spareth* in every thing is an *inexcusable Niggard;* he that *spareth* in nothing is as *inexcusable a Madman*. The *mean* is, to spare in what is least necessary, to lay out more liberally in what is most required in our several circumstances. Yet this will not always satisfie. There are *Wives* who are impatient of the Rules of Oeconomy, and are apt to call their *Husband*'s Kindness in question, if any other measure is put to their expence than that of their own Fancy. Be sure to avoid this dangerous Error, such a partiality to your Self, which is so offensive to an understanding Man, that he will very ill bear a *Wife*'s giving her self such an injurious *preference* to all the *Family*, and whatever belongeth to it.

But to admit the worst, and that your *Husband* is really a *Close-handed Wretch*, you must in this, as in other Cases, endeavour to make it less afflicting to you; and first you must observe *seasonable hours* of speaking. When you offer any thing in opposition to this reigning Humour, a *third hand* and a *wise Friend*, may often prevail more than you will be allowed to do in your own Cause. Sometimes you are dexterously to go along with him in things, where you see that the niggardly part of his Mind is most predominant, by which you will have the better opportunity of perswading him in things where he may be more indifferent. Our *Passions* are very unequal, and are apt to be raised or lessened, according as they work upon different Objects; they are not to be *stopped* or *restrained* in those things where our Mind is more particularly engaged. In other matters they are more tractable, and will sometimes give Reason a hearing, and admit a fair dispute. More than that, there are few Men, even in this instance of *Avarice*, so intirely abandoned to it, that at some hours, and upon some occasions, will not forget their natures, and for that time turn Prodigal. The same Man who will *grudge* himself what is *necessary*, let his *Pride* be raised and he shall be *profuse;* at another time his *Anger* shall have the same effect; a fit of *Vanity*, *Ambition*, and sometimes of *Kindness*, shall open and inlarge his *narrow Mind;* a Dose of Wine will work upon this tough humour, and for the time dissolve it. Your business must be, if this Case happeneth, to watch these *critical moments*, and not let one of them slip without making your advantage of it; and a *Wife* may be said to want *skill*, if by this means she is not able to secure her self in a good measure against the Inconveniences this scurvy quality in a *Husband* might bring upon her, except he should be such an incurable *Monster*, as I hope will never fall to your share.

The last supposition I will make, is, That your *Husband* should be *weak* and *incompetent* to make use of the Privileges that belong to him. It will be yielded, that such a one leaveth room for a great many Objections. But God Almighty seldom sendeth a *Grievance* without a *Remedy*, or at least such a Mitigation as taketh away a great part of the sting, and the smart of it. To make such a *Misfortune* less heavy, you are first to bring to your Observation, That a *Wife* very often maketh better Figure, for her *Husband*'s making no great one: And there seemeth to be little reason, why the same *Lady* that chuseth a *Waiting-Woman* with *worse Looks*, may not be content with a *Husband* with *less Wit;* the Argument being equal from the advantage of the Comparison. If you will be more ashamed in some Cases, of such a *Husband*, you will be less afraid than you would perhaps be of a wise one. His *Unseasonable Weakness* may no doubt sometimes grieve you, but then set against this, that it giveth you the *Dominion,* if you will make the right use of it. It is next to his being dead, in which Case the *Wife* hath right to Administer; therefore be sure, if you have such an Idiot, that none, except your self, may have the benefit of the forfeiture; Such a Fool is a dangerous Beast, if others have the keeping of him; and you must be very undexterous if when your *Husband* shall resolve to be an *Ass*, you do not take care he may be *your Ass*. But you must go skilfully about it and above all things, take heed of distinguishing in publick, what kind of *Husband* he is: Your inward thoughts must not hinder the outward payment of the consideration that is due to him: Your *slighting* him in *Company*, besides that it would, to a discerning By-stander, give too great encouragement for the making nearer applications to you, is in it self such an undecent way of assuming, that it may provoke the tame Creature to break loose, and to shew his *Dominion* for his Credit, which he was content to forget for his Ease. In short, the surest and the most approved method will be to do like a wise *Minister* to an easie *Prince;* first give him the Orders you afterwards receive from him.

With all this, that which you are to pray for, is a *Wise Husband*, one that by knowing how to be a *Master*, for that very reason will not let you feel the weight of it; one whose Authority is so soften'd by his Kindness, that it giveth you ease without abridging your *Liberty;* one that will return so much tenderness for your *Just Esteem* of him, that you will never want *power*, though you will seldom care to use it. Such a *Husband* is as much above all the other Kinds of them, as a *rational subjection* to a Prince, great in himself, is to be preferr'd before the disquiet and uneasiness of *Unlimited Liberty*

Before I leave this Head, I must add a little concerning your *Behaviour* to your *Husband's Friends*, which requireth the most refined part of your Understanding to acquit your self well of it. You are to study how to live with them with more care than you are to apply to any other part of your Life; especially at first, that you may not stumble at the first setting out. The *Family* into which you are grafted will generally be apt to expect, that like a Stranger in a Foreign Country, you should conform to their Methods, and not bring in a new Model by your own Authority. The *Friends* in such a Case are tempted to rise up in Arms as against an unlawful Invasion, so that you are with the utmost Caution to avoid the least appearances of any thing of this Kind. And that you may with less difficulty afterwards give your Directions, be sure at first to receive them from your *Husband*'s Friends. Gain them to you by early applying to them, and they will be so satisfied, that as nothing is more thankful than Pride, when it is complied with, they will strive which of them shall most recommend you; and when they have helped you to take Root in your *Husband*'s good Opinion, you will have less dependence upon theirs, though you must not neglect any reasonable means of preserving it. You are to consider, that a Man govern'd by his *Friends,* is very easily inflamed by them; and that one who is not so, will yet for his own sake expect to have them consider'd. It is easily improved to a point of Honour in a *Husband*, not to have his *Relations* neglected; and nothing is more dangerous, than to raise an Objection, which is grounded upon *Pride:* It is the most stubborn and lasting Passion we are subject to, and where it is the first cause of the *War*, it is very hard to make a secure *Peace*. Your *Caution* in this is of the last importance to you.

And that you may the better succeed in it, carry a strict Eye upon the *Impertinence* of your *Servants;* take heed that their *Ill-humour* may not engage you to take Exceptions, or their too much assuming in small matters, raise Consequences which may bring you under great Disadvantage. Remember that in the case of a *Royal Bride*, those about her are generally so far suspected to bring in a Foreign Interest, that in most Countries they are insensibly reduced to a very small number, and those of so low a Figure, that it doth not admit the being *Jealous* of them. In little and in the Proportion, this may be the Case of every *New married Woman*, and therefore it may be more adviseable for you, to gain the *Servants* you find in a Family, than to tie your self too fast to those you carry into it.

You are not to overlook these small Reflections, because they may appear low and inconsiderable; for it may be said, that as the *greatest streams* are made up of the *small drops* at the head of the Springs from whence they are derived, so the *greater circumstances* of your Life, will be in some degree directed by these seeming *trifles*, which having the advantage of being the first acts of it, have a greater effect than singly in their own nature they could pretend to.

I will conclude this Article with my Advice, That you would, as much as Nature will give you leave, endeavour to forget the great *Indulgence* you have found at home. After such a gentle Discipline as you have been under, every thing you dislike will seem the harsher to you. The tenderness we have had for you, *My Dear*, is of another nature, peculiar to kind Parents, and differing from that which you will meet with first in any Family into which you shall be transplanted; and yet they may be very kind too, and afford no justifiable reason to you to complain. You must not be frighted with the first Appearances of a *differing Scene;* for when you are used to it, you may like the House you go to, better than that you left; and your *Husband's* Kindness will have so much advantage of ours, that we shall yield up all *Competition*, and as well as we love you, be very well contented to Surrender to such a *Rival.*

HOUSE, FAMILY, AND CHILDREN

You must lay before you, *my Dear*, there are degrees of Care to recommend your self to the World in the several parts of your Life. In many things, though the doing them well may raise your *Credit* and *Esteem*, yet the omission of them would draw no immediate reproach upon you: In others, where your duty is more particularly applyed, the *neglect* of them is amongst those Faults which are not forgiven, and will bring you under a *Censure*, which will be much a heavier thing than the trouble you would avoid. Of this kind is the *Government* of your *House*, *Family*, and *Children*, which since it is the Province allotted to your Sex, and that the *discharging it well*, will for that reason be expected from you, if you either desert it out of *Laziness*, or manage it ill for *want of skill*, instead of a *Help* you will be an *Incumbrance* to the *Family* where you are placed.

I must tell you, that no *respect* is lasting, but that which is produced by our being in some degree useful to those that pay it. Where that faileth, the Homage and the Reverence go along with it, and fly to others where something may be expected in exchange for them. And upon this principle the *respects* even of the *Children* and the *Servants* will not stay with one that doth not think them worth their Care, and the old *House-keeper* shall make a better Figure in the Family, than the *Lady* with all her fine Cloaths, if she wilfully relinquishes her Title to the *Government.* Therefore take heed of carrying your *good Breeding* to such a height, as to be good for nothing, and to be proud of it. Some think it hath a great Air to be above troubling their thoughts with such ordinary things as their *House* and *Family;* others dare not admit *Cares* for fear they should hasten *Wrinkles?* mistaken *Pride* maketh some think they must keep themselves up, and descend not to these Duties, which do not seem enough refined for great *Ladies* to be imploy'd in; forgetting all this while, that it is more than the greatest *Princes* can do, at once to preserve respect, and to neglect their Business. No *Age* ever erected *Altars* to *insignificant Gods;* they had all some quality applied to them to draw *worship* from *Mankind;* this maketh it the more unreasonable for a *Lady* to expect to be consider'd, and at the same time resolve not to deserve it. *Good looks* alone will not do; they are not such a lasting *Tenure*, as to be relied upon; and if they should stay longer than they usually do, it will by no means be safe to depend upon them: For when time hath abated the violence of the first liking, and that the *Napp* is a little worn off, though still a good degree of kindness may remain, Men recover their sight which before might be dazell'd, and allow themselves to object as well as to admire.

In such a Case, when a *Husband* seeth an empty airy thing sail up and down the House to no kind of purpose, and look as if she came thither only to make a Visit. When he findeth that after her *Emptiness* hath been extreme busie about some very senseless thing, she eats her Breakfast half an hour before Dinner, to be at greater liberty to afflict the Company with her Discourse; then calleth for her Coach, that she may trouble her Acquaintance, who are already cloy'd with her: And having some *proper Dialogues* ready to display her *Foolish Eloquence* at the top of the Stairs, she setteth out like a Ship out of the Harbour, laden with trifles and cometh back with them: at her return she repeateth to her faithful waiting Woman, the *Triumphs* of that day's *Impertinence;* then wrap'd up in Flattery and clean Linen, goeth to Bed so satisfied, that it throweth her into pleasant Dreams of her own Felicity. Such a one is seldom serious but with her *Taylor;* her *Children* and Family may now and then have a random thought, but she never taketh aim but at something very Impertinent. I say, when a *Husband*, whose Province is without Doors, and to whom the Oeconomy of the House would be in some degree Indecent, findeth no *Order* nor *Quiet* in his *Family*, meeteth with *Complaints* of all kinds springing from this Root; The *Mistaken Lady*, who thinketh to make *amends* for all this, by having a well-chosen *Petty-Coat*, will at last be convinced of her *Error*, and with grief be forced to undergo the Penalties that belong to those who are willfully *Insignificant*. When this scurvy hour cometh upon her, she first groweth *Angry;* then when the time of it is past, would perhaps grow *wiser*, not remembring that we can no more have *Wisdom* than *Grace*, whenever we think fit to call for it. There are Times and Periods fix'd for both; and when they are too long neglected, the Punishment is, that they are *Irrecoverable*, and nothing remaineth but an useless *Grief* for the Folly of having thrown them out of our power. You are to think what a mean Figure a Woman maketh, when she is so degraded by her own Fault; whereas there is nothing in those Duties which are expected from you, that can be a lessening to you, except your want of *Conduct* makes it so. You may love your *Children* without living in the *Nursery*, and you may have a *competent* and *discreet care* of them, with out letting it break out upon the Company, or exposing your self by turning your Discourse that way, which is a kind of *Laying Children* to the *Parish*, and it can hardly be done any where, that those who hear it will be so forgiving, as not to think they are overcharged with them. A Woman's *tenderness* to her *Children* is one of the least deceitful Evidences of the Vertue; but yet the way of expressing it, must be subject to the Rules of *good Breeding:* And though a *Woman* of *Quality* ought not to be less kind to them, than *Mothers* of the *Meanest Rank* are to theirs, yet she may distinguish her self in the *manner*, and avoid the course Methods, which in Women of a lower size might be more excusable. You must begin early to make them *love* you, that they may *obey* you. This Mixture is no where more necessary than in Children. And I must tell you, that you are not to expect Returns of Kindness from yours, if ever you have any, without Grains of Allowance; and yet it is not so much a *defect* in their *good Nature*, as a *shortness of Thought* in them. Their first *Insufficiency* maketh them lean so entirely upon their *Parents* for what is *necessary*, that the *habit* of it maketh them continue the same *Expectations* for what is *unreasonable;* and as often as they are *denied*, so often they think they are *injured:* and whilst their *Desires* are strong, and their *Reasons* yet in the Cradle, their *Anger* looketh no farther than the thing they long for and cannot have; And to be *displeased* for their *own good*, is a *Maxim* they are very slow to understand: So that you may conclude, the first Thoughts of your *Children* will have no small Mixture of Mutiny; which being so natural, you must not be angry, except you would increase it. You must deny them as seldom as you can, and when there is no avoiding it, you must do it *gently;* you must flatter away their ill Humour, and take the next Opportunity of pleasing them in some other thing, before they either ask or look for it: This will strengthen your *Authority*, by making it soft to them; and confirm their *Obedience*, by making it their Interest. You are to have as strict a Guard upon your self amongst your *Children*, as if you were amongst your *Enemies*. They are apt to make wrong Inferences, to take Encouragement from half Words, and misapply what you may say or do, so as either to lessen their *Duty*, or to extend their *Liberty* farther than is convenient. Let them be more in awe of your *Kindness* than of your *Power*. And above all, take heed of supporting a *Favorite Child* in its Impertinence, which will give Right to the rest of claiming the same Privilege. If you have a divided Number, leave the *Boys* to the *Father*'s more peculiar Care, that you may with greater Justice pretend to a more immediate Jurisdiction over those of your own *Sex*. You are to live so with them, that they may never chuse to avoid you, except when they have *offended;* and then let them tremble, that they may distinguish: But their Penance must not continue so long as to grow too *sowre* upon their *Stomachs*, that it may not *harden* in stead of *correcting* them: The kind and severe Part must have their several *turns* seasonably applied; but your *Indulgence* is to have the broader mixture, that *Love*, rather than *Fear*, may be the Root of their *Obedience*.

Your *Servants* are in the next place to be considered; and you must remember not to fall in the mistake of thinking, that because they receive Wages, and are so much *Inferiour* to you, therefore they are *below* your Care to know how to manage them. It would be as good Reason for a *Master Workman* to despise the *Wheels* of his *Engines*, because they are made of *Wood*. These are the *Wheels* of your *Family;* and let your Directions be never so faultless, yet if these *Engines* stop or move wrong, the whole Order of your *House* is either at a stand, or discomposed. Besides, the *Inequality* which is between you, must not make you forget, that *Nature* maketh no such distinction, but that *Servants* may be looked upon as *humble Friends*, and that *Returns* of *Kindness* and *good Usage* are as much due to such of them as deserve it, as their *Service* is due to *us* when we require it. *A foolish haughtiness* in the Style of *speaking*, or in the manner of *commanding* them, is in it self very undecent; besides that it begetteth an *Aversion* in them, of which the least ill Effect to be expected, is, that they will be *slow* and *careless* in all that is injoyned them: And you will find it true by your Experience, that you will be so much the more *obeyed* as you are less *Imperious*. Be not *too hasty* in giving your *Orders*, nor *too angry* when they are not altogether *observed;* much less are you to be loud, and too much disturbed: An *evenness* in distinguishing when they do well or *ill*, is that which will make your *Family* move by a Rule, and without Noise, and will the better set out your Skill in conducting it with Ease and Silence, that it may be like a well disciplin'd Army; which knoweth how to anticipate the *Orders* that are fit to be given them. You are never to neglect the Duty of the *present Hour*, to do another thing, which though it may be better in it self, is not to be unseasonably preferred. Allot well chosen Hours for the Inspection of your *Family*, which may be so distinguished from the rest of your Time, that the *necessary Cares* may come in their proper Place, without any Influence upon your good Humour, or Interruption to other things. By these Methods you will put your self in possession of being valued by your Servants, and then their *Obedience* will naturally follow.

I must not forget one of the greatest *Articles* belonging to a *Family*, which is the *Expence*. It must not be such, as by failing either in the Time or measure of it, may rather draw *Censure* than gain *Applause*. If it was well examined, there is more Money given to be laughed at, than for any one thing in the World, though the Parchasers do not think so. A well-stated Rule is like the *Line*, when that is once pass'd we are under another *Pole;* so the first *straying* from a *Rule*, is a step towards making that which was before a *Vertue*, to change its Nature, and to grow either into a *Vice*, or at least an *Impertinence*. The Art of laying out Money wisely, is not attained to without a great deal of thought; and it is yet more difficult in the Case of a *Wife*, who is accountable to her *Husband* for her mistakes in it. It is not only his *Money*, his *Credit* too is at Stake, if what lyeth under the *Wife*'s Care is managed, either with undecent *Thrift*, or too loose *Profusion.* You are therefore to keep the *Mean* between these two *Extremes*, and it being hardly possible to hold the Balance exactly even, let it rather incline towards the *Liberal* side as more suitable to your *Quality*, and less subject to *Reproach.* Of the two a little *Money* misspent is sooner *recovered*, than the *Credit* which is lost by having it unhandsomely *saved;* and a Wise *Husband* will less forgive a shameful piece of *Parcimony*, than a little *Extravagance*, if it be not too often repeated. His *Mind* in this must be your chief *Direction;* and his *Temper*, when once known, will in great measure justifie your part in the management, if he is pleased with it.

In your *Clothes* avoid too much Gaudy; do not value your self upon an *Imbroidered Gown;* and remember, that a *reasonable Word*, or an *obliging Look*, will gain you more respect, than all your *fine Trappings.* This is not said to restrain you from a *decent Compliance* with the World, provided you take the wiser, and not the foolisher part of your Sex for your Pattern. Some *distinctions* are to be allowed, whilst they are well suited to your *Quality* and *Fortune*, and in the distribution of the Expence, it seemeth to me that a *full Attendance*, and *well chosen Ornaments* for your House, will make you a better Figure, than *too much glittering* in what you wear, which may with more ease be imitated by those that are below you. Yet this must not tempt you to starve every thing but your own Appartment; or in order to more abundance there, give just cause to the least Servant you have, to complain of the Want of what is necessary. Above all, fix it in your thoughts, as an unchangeable *Maxim*, That nothing is *truly fine* but what is *fit*, and that just so much as is proper for your *Circumstances* of their several kinds, is much finer than all you can add to it. When you once break through these bounds, you launch into a wide Sea of *Extravagance.* Every thing will become necessary, because you have a mind to it; and you have a mind to it, not because it is *fit* for you, but because some body else *hath it.* This *Lady's Logick* setteth *Reason* upon its Head, by carrying the *Rule from* things to *Persons*, and appealing from what is *right* to every Fool that is in the *wrong.* The word *necessary* is miserably applyed, it disordereth *Families*, and overturneth *Governments* by being so abused. Remember that *Children* and *Fools* want every thing because they want Wit to distinguish: and therefore there is no stronger Evidence of a *Crazy Understanding*, than the making too large a Catalogue of things necessary, when in truth there are so very few things that have a right to be placed in it. Try every thing first in your *Judgment*, before you allow it a place in your *Desire;* else your *Husband* may think it as necessary for him to deny, as it is for you to *have* whatever is unreasonable; and if you shall too often give him that advantage, the habit of *refusing* may perhaps reach to things that are not unfit for you.

There are unthinking *Ladies*, who do not enough consider, how little their own Figure agreeth with the *fine things* they are so proud of. Others when they have them will hardly allow them to be *visible;* they cannot be seen without *Light*, and that is many times so sawcy and so prying, that like a too forward *Gallant* it is to be forbid the *Chamber*. Some, when you are ushered into their *Dark Ruelle*,[2] it is with such solemnity, that a Man would swear there was something in it, till the *Unskillful Lady* breaketh silence, and beginneth a Chat, which discovereth it is a Puppet-play with Magnificent Scenes. Many esteem things rather as they are hard to be gotten, than that they are worth getting: This looketh as if they had an Interest to pursue that Maxim, because a great part of their own *value* dependeth upon it. Truth in these Cases would be often *unmannerly*, and might derogate from the *Prerogative*, great *Ladies* would assume to them selves, of being distinct Creatures from those of their Sex, which are inferiour, and of less difficult access.

In other things too, your Condition must give the rule to you, and therefore it is not a Wife's part to aim at more than a bounded

[2] A ruelle was the term in use during the seventeenth and eighteenth centuries for the bedroom where fashionable ladies held their morning reception.

Liberality; the farther extent of that *Quality* (otherwise to be commended) belongeth to the *Husband*, who hath better means for it. *Generosity* wrong placed becometh a *Vice*. It is no more a *Vertue* when it groweth into an *Inconvenience*, *Vertues* must be inlarged or restrained according to differing Circumstances. A *Princely Mind* will undo a *private Family:* Therefore things must be suited, or else they will not deserve to be Commended, let them in themselves be never so valuable: And the Expectations of the World are best answered when we acquit our selves in that manner which seemeth to be prescribed to our several Conditions, without usurping upon those Duties, which do not so particularly belong to us.

I will close the consideration of this *Article* of *Expence*, with this short word. Do not *fetter* your self with such a *Restraint* in it as may make you *Remarkable;* but remember that *Vertue* is the greatest *Ornament*, and good *Sence* the *best Equipage.*

[Three sections entitled "Behaviour and Conversation," "Friendships," and "Censure" are here omitted.]

VANITY AND AFFECTATION

I must with more than ordinary *earnestness* give you Caution against *Vanity*, it being the Fault to which your Sex seemeth to be the most *inclined;* and since *Affectation* for the most part attendeth it, I do not know how to divide them. I will not call them *Twins*, because more properly *Vanity* is the *Mother*, and *Affectation* is the Darling Daughter; *Vanity* is the Sin, and *Affectation* is the Punishment; the first may be called the Root of *Self-Love*, the other the *Fruit*. *Vanity* is never at its full growth till it spreadeth into *Affectation*, and then it is compleat.

Not to dwell any longer upon the definition of them, I will pass to the means and motives to avoid them. In order to it, you are to consider, that the World challengeth the right of distributing Esteem and Applause; so that where any assume by their single Authority to be their own *Carvers*, it groweth angry, and never faileth to seek *Revenge*. And if we may measure a Fault by the greatness of the *Penalty*, there are few of a higher size than *Vanity*, as there is scarce a Punishment which can be heavier than that of being laughed at.

Vanity maketh a Woman tainted with it, so top full of her self, that she spilleth it upon the *Company*. And because her own thoughts are intirely imployed in *Self-Contemplation;* she endeavoureth, by a cruel Mistake, to confine her *Acquaintance* to the same narrow Circle of that which only concerneth her Ladiship, forgetting that she is not of half that *Importance* to the World, that she is to her self, so mistaken she is in her Value, by being her own Appraiser. She will fetch such a Compass in Discourse to bring in her beloved *Self*, and rather than fail, her fine Petty-Coat, that there can hardly be a better Scene than such a Tryal of ridiculous Ingenuity. It is a Pleasure to see her Angle for *Commendations*, and rise so dissatisfied with Ill-bread *Company*, if they will not *bite*. To observe her throwing her *Eyes* about to fetch in Prisoners, and go about Cruizing like a Privateer, and so out of *Countenance*, if she return without *Booty*, is no ill piece of Comedy. She is so eager to draw respect, that she always misseth it, yet thinketh it so much her due, that when she faileth she groweth *waspish*, not considering, that it is impossible to commit a Rape upon the will; that it must be fairly gained, and will not be taken by *Storm;* and that in this Case, the Tax ever riseth highest by a *Benevolence*. If the World instead of admiring her *Imaginary Excellencies*, taketh the Liberty to laugh at them, she *appealeth* from it to her self, for whom she giveth *Sentence*, and proclaimeth it in all *Companies*. On the other side, if incouraged by a *Civil Word*, she is so obliging, that she will give thanks for being laughed at in good Language. She taketh a *Compliment* for a Demonstration, and setteth it up as an *Evidence*, even against her Looking-Glass. But the good *Lady* being all this while in a most profound *Ignorance* of her self, forgetteth that Men would not let her talk upon them, and throw so many *senseless words* at their head, if they did not intend to put her Person to Fine and Ransom, for her *Impertinence*. Good words of any other Lady, are so many Stones thrown at her, she can by no means bear them, they make her so uneasie, that she cannot keep her *Seat*, but up she riseth and goeth home half burst with *Anger* and *Strait-Lacing*. If by great chance she saith any thing that hath sense in it, she expecteth such an Excessive rate of *Commendations*, that to her thinking the Company ever riseth in her *Debt*. She looketh upon *Rules* as things made for the common People, and not for Persons of her *Rank;* and this Opinion sometimes tempteth her to Extend her Prerogative to the dispencing with the commandments. If by great *Fortune* she happeneth, in spite of her Vanity, to be honest, she is so troublesome with it, that as far as in her lieth, she maketh a *scurvy* thing of it. Her bragging of her *Vertue*, looketh as if it cost her so much pains to get the better of her Self, that the *Inferences* are very ridiculous. Her *good Humour* is generally applied to the laughing at *good Sense*. It would do one good to see how heartily she despiseth any thing that is fit for her to do. The greatest part of her *Fancy* is laid out in chusing her *Gown*, as her *Discretion* is chiefly imploy'd in *not paying* for it. She is faithful to the *Fashion*, to which not only her *Opinion*, but her *Senses* are wholly resigned: so obsequious she is to it, that she would be ready to be reconciled even to *Vertue* with all its *Faults*, if she had her Dancing Master's Word that it was practis'd at Court.

To a Woman so compos'd when *Affectation* cometh in to improve her *Character*, it is then raised to the highest *Perfection*. She first setteth up for a *Fine thing*, and for that Reason will distinguish her self, right or wrong, in every thing she doth. She would have it thought that she is made of so much the *finer Clay*, and so much more *sifted* than ordinary, that she hath no *common Earth* about her. To this end she must neither move nor speak like other Women, because it would be *vulgar;* and therefore must have a Language of her *own*, since *ordinary English* is too course for her. The *Looking-glass* in the Morning dictateth to her all the *Motions* of the Day, which by how much the more *studied*, are so much the more *mistaken*. She cometh into a Room as if her Limbs were set on with ill-made Screws, which maketh the Company fear the pretty thing should leave some of its *artificial Person* upon the Floor. She doth not like her self as *God Almighty* made her, but will have some of *her own* Workmanship; which is so far from making her a better thing than a *Woman*, that it turneth her into a worse Creature than a *Monkey*. She falleth out with *Nature*, against which she maketh War without admitting a *Truce*, those Moments excepted in which her *Gallant* may reconcile her to it. When she hath a mind to be *soft* and *languishing*, there is something so unnatural in that *affected Easiness*, that her *Frowns* could not be by many degrees so forbidden. When she would appear unreasonably *humble*, one may see she is so excessively *proud*, that there is no enduring it. There is such an *impertinent Smile*, such a *satisfied Simper*, when she faintly disowneth some fulsom Commendation a Man hapneth to bestow upon her against his Conscience, that her *Thanks* for it are more visible under such a thin *Disguise*, than they could be if she should *print* them. If a *handsomer Woman* taketh any liberty of *Dressing* out of the ordinary Rules the mistaken Lady followeth, without distinguishing the *unequal Pattern*, and maketh her self *uglier* by an example misplaced; either forgetting the Privilege of *good Looks* in *another*, or presuming, without sufficient reason upon *her own*. Her *Discourse* is a *senseless Chime* of *empty Words*, a heap of *Compliments* so equally applied to differing *Persons*, that they are neither valu'd nor believ'd. Her *Eyes* keep pace with her *Tongue*, and are therefore always in *motion*. One may discern that they generally incline to the *compassionate* side, and that, notwithstanding her pretence to *Vertue*, she is gentle to *distressed Lovers*, and *Ladies* that are *merciful*. She will repeat the tender part of a *Play* so feelingly, that the Company may guess, without Injustice, she was not altogether a *disinteressed Spectator*. She thinketh that *Paint* and *Sin* are concealed by railing at them. Upon the latter she is less hard, and being divided between the two opposite Prides of her *Beauty* and her *Vertue*, she is often tempted to give broad Hints that some body is dying for her; and of the two she is less unwilling to let the World think she may be sometimes *profan'd*, than that she is never *worshipped*.

Very great *Beauty* may perhaps so dazle for a time, that Men may not so clearly see the *Deformity* of these *Affectations;* But when the *Brightness* goeth off, and that the *Lover's Eyes* are by that means set at liberty to see things as they are, he will naturally return to his Senses, and recover the Mistake into which the Lady's *good Looks* had at first engaged him. And being once undeceived, ceaseth to worship that as a *Goddess*, which he seeth is only an *artificial Shrine* moved by *Wheels* and *Springs*, to delude him. Such Women please only like the *first Opening* of a *Scene*, that hath nothing to recommend it but that being *new*. They may be compared to *Flies*, that have pretty shining *Wings* for two or three hot Months, but the first cold Weather maketh an end of them; so the *latter Season* of these *fluttering Creatures* is dismal: From their nearest Friends they receive a very faint Respect; from the rest of the World, the utmost degree of contempt.

Let this *Picture* supply the place of any other *Rules* which might be given to prevent your *resemblance* to it, The *Deformity* of it, well considered, is *Instruction* enough; from the same reason, that the sight of a *Drunkard* is a better *Sermon* against that *Vice*, than the best that was ever preach'd upon that *Subject*.

PRIDE

After having said this against *Vanity*, I do not intend to apply the same *Censure* to *Pride*, well placed, and rightly defined. It is an *ambiguous Word;* one kind of it is as much a *Vertue*, as the other is a *Vice:* But we are naturally so apt to chuse the *worst*, that it is become dangerous to commend the *best* side of it.

A Woman is not to be proud of her fine Gown; nor when she hath less Wit than her Neighbours, to comfort her self that she hath more Lace. Some Ladies put so much weight upon *Ornaments*, that if one could see into their Hearts, it would be found, that even the Thought of *Death* is made less heavy to them by the contemplation of their being *laid out* in *State*, and *honourably attended* to the *Grave*. One may come a good deal short of such an *Extream*, and yet still be sufficiently *Impertinent*, by setting a wrong Value upon things, which ought to be used with more indifference. A Lady must not appear sollicitous to ingross *Respect* to her self, but be content with a reasonable *Distribution*, and allow it to others, that she may have it returned to her. She is not to be troublesomly *nice*, nor distinguish her self by being too *delicate*, as if ordinary things were too *course* for her; this is an *unmannerly* and an *offensive* Pride, and where it is practised, deserveth to be mortified, of which it seldom faileth. She is not to lean too much upon her Quality, much less to despise those who are below it. Some make *Quality* an *Idol*, and then their *Reason* must fall down and Worship it. They would have the World think, that no amends can ever be made for the want of a *great Title*, or an ancient *Coat of Arms:* They imagine, that with these *advantages* they stand upon the *higher Ground*, which maketh them look down upon *Merit* and *Vertue*, as things inferiour to them. This mistake is not only *senseless*, but *criminal* too, in putting a greater Price upon that which is a piece of *good luck*, than upon things which are valuable in themselves. *Laughing* is not enough for such a *Folly;* it must be severely *whipped*, as it justly deserves. It will be confessed, there are frequent *Temptations* given by *pert Upstarts* to be angry, and by that to have our Judgments corrupted in these Cases: But they are to be resisted; and the utmost that is to be allowed, is, when those of a *new Edition* will forget themselves, so as either to brag of their *weak side*, or to endeavour to hide their *Meanness* by their *Insolence*, to cure them by a little seasonable *Raillery*, a little *Sharpness* well placed, without dwelling too long upon it.

These and many other kinds of *Pride* are to be avoided.

That which is to be recommended to you, is an *Emulation* to raise your self to a *Character*, by which you may be distinguished; an Eagerness for precedence in *Virtue*, and all such other things as may gain you a greater share of the good opinion of the World. *Esteem* to *Vertue* is like a *cherishing Air* to *Plants* and *Flowers*, which maketh them blow and prosper; and for that reason it may be allowed to be in some degree the *Cause* as well as the

Reward of it. That *Pride* which leadeth to a *good End,* cannot be a *Vice,* since it is the beginning of a *Vertue;* and to be pleased with just *Applause*, is so far from a *Fault,* that it would be an *ill Symptom* in a Woman, who should not place the greatest part of her *Satisfaction* in it. *Humility* is no doubt a great *Vertue;* but it ceaseth to be so, when it is afraid to scorn an *ill thing.* Against *Vice* and *Folly* it is becoming your *Sex* to be *haughty;* but you must not carry the *Contempt* of *things* to *Arrogance* towards *Persons*, and it must be done with fitting *Distinctions*, else it may be *Inconvenient* by being unseasonable. A *Pride* that raiseth a little *Anger* to be out-done in any thing that is good, will have so good an *Effect*, that it is very hard to allow it to be a Fault.

It is no easie matter to carry even between these differing kinds so described; but remember that it is safer for a *Woman* to be thought too *proud*, than too familiar.

DIVERSIONS

The last thing I shall recommend to you, is a wise and safe method of using *Diversions.* To be too eager in the pursuit of Pleasure whilst you are *Young*, is dangerous; to catch at it in riper *Years*, is grasping a shadow; it will not be held. Besides that by being less natural it groweth to be indecent. *Diversions* are the most properly applied, to ease and relieve those who are *Oppressed*, by being to much imployed. Those that are *Idle* have no need of them, and yet they, above all others, give themselves up to them. To unbend our *Thoughts,* when they are too much stretched by our Cares, is not more natural than it is necessary, but to turn our whole Life into a *Holy day*, is not only ridiculous, but destroyeth Pleasure instead of *promoting* it. The *Mind* like the *Body* is tired by being always in one Posture, too serious breaketh, and too diverting looseneth it: It is *Variety* that giveth the Relish; so that *Diversions* too frequently repeated, grow first to be indifferent, and at last tedious. Whilst they are well chosen and well timed, they are never to be blamed; but when they are used to an Excess, though very *Innocent* at first, they often grow to be *Criminal*, and never fail to be *Impertinent.*

Some Ladies are bespoken for Merry Meetings, as *Bessus*[3] was for Duels. They are ingaged in a Circle of *Idleness,* where they turn round for the whole Year, without the *Interruption* of a serious Hour. They know all the Players Names, and are *Intimately* acquainted with all the Booths in *Bartholomew-Fair.* No Soldier is more *Obedient* to the sound of his Captain's *Trumpet*, than they are to that which summoneth them to a *Puppet-Play* or a *Monster.* The Spring that bringeth out *Flies,* and *Fools,* maketh them Inhabitants in *Hide-Park;* in the Winter they are an Incumbrance to the *Play House*, and the Ballast of the *Drawing-Room.* The Streets all this while are so weary of these daily Faces, that *Men's Eyes* are over-laid with them. The *Sight* is glutted with fine things, as the *Stomach* with sweet ones; and when a fair *Lady* will give too much of her self to the *World*, she groweth luscious, and oppresseth instead of pleasing. These *Jolly Ladies* do so continually seek *Diversion,* that in a little time they grow into a *Jest,* yet are unwilling to remember, that if they were seldomer seen they would not be so often *laughed at.* Besides they make themselves *Cheap,* than which there cannot be an *unkinder word* bestowed upon your *Sex.*

To play sometimes, to entertain *Company*, or to *divert* your self, is not to be disallowed, but to do it so often as to be called a *Gamester,* is to be avoided, next to the things that are most *Criminal.* It hath Consequences of *several kinds* not to be endured; it will ingage you into a habit of *Idleness* and *ill hours,* draw you into ill mixed *Company*, make you neglect your *Civilities* abroad, and your *Business* at home, and impose into your *Acquaintance* such as will do you no Credit.

To deep *Play* there will be yet greater *Objections.* It will give *Occasion* to the World to ask *spiteful Questions.* How you dare venture to *lose*, and what means you

[3] a character in Beaumont and Fletcher's *King and No King* who, by pretending to be booked solidly for a vast number of duels, succeeded in putting off his challengers

have to *pay* such great *summs?* If you pay *exactly*, it will be enquired from whence the *Money* cometh? If you owe, and especially to a Man, you must be so very *Civil* to him for his forbearance, that it layeth a ground of having it farther improved, if the *Gentleman* is so disposed; who will be thought no unfair *Creditor*, if where the *Estate* faileth he seizeth upon the Person. Besides if a *Lady* could see her own Face upon an *ill Game*, at a deep Stake, she would certainly forswear any thing that could put her looks under such a *Disadvantage*.

To *Dance* sometimes will not be imputed to you as a fault; but remember that the end of your *Learning* it, was, that you might the better know how to move *gracefully*. It is only an *advantage* so far. When it goeth beyond it, one may call it *excelling* in a Mistake, which is no very great Commendation. It is better for a *Woman* never to *Dance*, because she hath no skill in it, than to do it too often, because she doth it well. The easiest as well as the safest *Method* of doing it, is in *private Companies*, amongst *particular Friends*, and then carelesly, like a *Diversion*, rather than with *Solemnity*, as if it was a business, or had any thing in it to deserve a *Month's preparation* by serious Conference with a *Dancing-Master*.

Much more might be said to all these Heads, and many more might be added to them. But I must restrain my Thoughts, which are full of my Dear Child, and would overflow into a Volume, which would not be fit for a *New-Years-Gift*. I will conclude with my warmest Wishes for all that is good to you. That you may live so as to be an Ornament to your Family, and a Pattern to your Sex. That you may be blessed with a Husband that may value, and with Children that may inherit your Vertue; That you may shine in the World by a true Light, and silence Envy by deserving to be esteemed; That Wit and Vertue may both conspire to make you a great Figure. When they are separated, the first is so empty, and the other so faint, that they scarce have right to be commended. May they therefore meet and never part; let them be your Guardian Angels, and be sure never to stray out of the distance of their joint protection. May you so raise your Character, that you may help to make the next Age a better thing, and leave Posterity in your Debt for the advantage it shall receive by your Example

Let me conjure you, *My Dearest*, to comply with this kind Ambition of a Father, whose Thoughts are so ingaged in your behalf, that he reckoneth your Happiness to be the greatest part of his own.

from THE CHARACTER OF A TRIMMER[4]

[*The Character of a Trimmer* bears, preëminently, that double aspect which, as was pointed out above, is characteristic of Halifax's political writings. It is brilliant generalization. At the same time and at almost every point it is an occasional pamphlet, packed with references to the political situation as it stood between 1681, when Charles dissolved the Oxford Parliament, and the end of 1684, when the *Character* was written. Halifax had been increasingly under attack from the extreme Tories, who characterized his moderate position and his resistance to the reactionary policies of the Duke of York as that of a "trimmer." L'Estrange, in the Tory *Observator*, had been harping on the term for months. On the third and fourth of December, 1684, *The Observator* had given at full length the "Character and Humour" of a Trimmer. Though Halifax had never been referred to personally, he now responded to these attacks, acknowledged himself to be indeed a "trimmer"—after redefining the term—and went on to plot the course which he hoped

[4] The text is that of the *Miscellanies*, 1700. In his edition of Halifax's *Works* (Oxford, 1912), Raleigh based his text on the 1700 *Miscellanies* but followed H. C. Foxcroft in changing the *-es* or *-s* of the third person singular of the present tense to *-eth* or *-th*. Raleigh was confident that this change merely restored the forms which had been used by Halifax, which were present in manuscript versions, but had been altered without authorization by the printers of the *Miscellanies*. The present text abides in this instance by the *Miscellanies*, though Raleigh has been followed in the adoption—noted below—of two of Miss Foxcroft's emended readings.

the King would now be wise enough to take. In the first section ("Of the Laws and Government") Halifax is answering the charge that a trimmer is one who does not hold the law in due respect. He venerates the law, and regards the unworthy judge as a discredit to the King. Similarly, the trimmer looks to the English form of government as a mean between monarchy (or no liberty) and commonwealth (or no quiet). The latter part of this section contains an attack on the Duke of York and a vigorous appeal to Charles to summon a Parliament for consultation.]

THE PREFACE

It must be more than an ordinary provocation that can tempt a Man to write in an Age over-run with Scribblers, as EGYPT *was with Flies and Locusts: That worst Vermin of small Authors has given the World such a Surfeit, that instead of desiring to Write, a Man would be more inclin'd to wish, for his own ease, that he could not Read; but there are some things which do so raise our passions, that our Reason can make no Resistance; and when Madmen, in two Extreams, shall agree to make common sense Treason, and joyn to fix an ill Character upon the only Men in the Nation who deserve a good one; I am no longer Master of my better Resolution to let the World alone, and must break loose from my more reasonable Thoughts, to expose these false Coyners, who would make their Copper Wares pass upon us for good Payment.*

Amongst all the Engines of Dissention, there has been none more powerful in all Times, than the fixing Names upon one another of Contumely and Reproach, and the reason is plain, in respect of the People, who tho' generally they are uncapable of making a Syllogism or forming an Argument, yet they can pronounce a word; and that serves their turn to throw it with their dull malice at the Head of those they do not like; such things ever begin in Jest, and end in Blood, and the same word which at first makes the Company merry, grows in time to a Military Signal to cut one anothers Throats.

These Mistakes are to be lamented, tho' not easily cured, being suitable enough to the corrupted Nature of Mankind; but 'tis hard, that Men will not only invent ill Names, but they will wrest and misinterpret good ones; so afraid some are even of a reconciling sound, that they raise another noise to keep it from being heard, lest it should set up and encourage a dangerous sort of Men, who prefer Peace and Agreement, before Violence and Confusion.

Were it not for this, why, after we have played the Fool with throwing Whig *and* Tory *at one another, as Boys do Snow-Balls, do we grow angry at a new Name, which by its true signification might do as much to put us into our Wits, as the other has done to put us out of them?*

This innocent word Trimmer *signifies no more than this, That if Men are together in a Boat, and one part of the Company would weigh it down on one side, another would make it lean as much to the contrary; it happens there is a third Opinion of those, who conceive it would do as well, if the Boat went even, without endangering the Passengers; now 'tis hard to imagin by what Figure in Language, or by what Rule in Sense this comes to be a Fault, and it is much more a wonder it should be thought a Heresy.*

But so it happens, that the poor Trimmer *has now all the Powder spent upon him alone, while the* Whig *is a forgotten, or at least a neglected Enemy; there is no danger now to the State (if some Men may be believed) but from the Beast called a* Trimmer, *take heed of him, he is the Instrument that must destroy Church and State; a new kind of Monster, whose deformity is so expos'd, that, were it a true Picture that is made of him, it would be enough to fright Children, and make Women miscarry at the sight of it.*

But it may be worth the examining, whether he is such a Beast as he is Painted. I am not of that Opinion, and am so far from thinking him an Infidel either in Church or State, that I am neither afraid to expose the Articles of his Faith in Relation to Government, nor to say that I prefer them before any other Political Creed, that either our angry Divines, or our refined States-men would impose upon us.

I have therefore in the following Discourse endeavour'd to explain the Trimmer's *Principles and Opinions, and then leave it to all discerning and impartial Judges, whether he can with Justice be so*

Arraign'd, and whether those who deliberately pervert a good Name, do not very justly deserve the worst that can be put upon themselves.

THE TRIMMER'S OPINION OF THE LAWS AND GOVERNMENT

Our Trimmer, as he has a great Veneration for Laws in general, so he has more particular for our own, he looks upon them as the Chains that tye up our unruly Passions, which else, like wild Beasts let loose, would reduce the world into its first State of Barbarism and Hostility; the good things we enjoy, we owe to them; and all the ill things we are freed from is by their Protection.

God himself thought it not enough to be a Creator, without being a Lawgiver, and his goodness had been defective towards mankind in making them, if he had not prescribed Rules to make them happy too.

All Laws flow from that of Nature, and where that is not the Foundation, they may be legally impos'd, but they will be lamely obeyed: By this Nature is not meant that which Fools and Madmen misquote to justifie their Excesses; it is innocent and uncorrupted Nature, that which disposes Men to chuse Vertue, without its being prescribed, and which is so far from inspiring ill thoughts into us, that we take pains to suppress the good ones it infuses.

The Civilized World has ever paid a willing subjection to Laws, even Conquerors have done homage to them; as the *Romans*, who took Patterns of good Laws, even from those they had subdued; and at the same time that they Triumph'd over an enslav'd People, the very Laws of that place did not only remain safe, but became Victorious; their new Masters, instead of suppressing them, paid them more respect than they had from those who first made them: and by this wise method they arrived to such an admirable Constitution of Laws, that to this day they Reign by them; this Excellency of them Triumphs still, and the World pays now an acknowledgment of their obedience to that Mighty Empire, though so many Ages after it is dissolved; and by a later instance, the Kings of *France*, who, in practice use their Laws pretty familiarly, yet think their Picture is drawn with most advantage upon their Seals, when they are placed in the Seat of Justice; and tho' the Hieroglyphick is not there of so much use to the People as they would wish, yet it shews that no Prince is so Great, as not to think fit, for his own Credit at least, to give an outward, when he refuses a real worship to the Laws.

They are to mankind that which the Sun is to Plants, whilst it cherishes and preserves 'em. Where they have their force and are not clouded or suppress, every thing smiles and flourishes; but where they are darkened and not suffered to shine out, it makes every thing to wither and decay.

They secure Men not only against one another, but against themselves too; they are a Sanctuary to which the Crown has occasion to resort as often as the People, so that it is an Interest as well as a Duty to preserve them.

There would be no end of making a Panegyrick of Laws; let it be enough to add, that without Laws the World would become a Wilderness, and Men little less than Beasts; but with all this, the best things may come to be the worst, if they are not in good hands; and if it be true that the wisest Men generally make the Laws, it is as true, that the strongest do often Interpret them: and as Rivers belong as much to the Channel where they run, as to the Spring from whence they first rise, so the Laws depend as much upon the Pipes thro' which they are to pass, as upon the Fountain from whence they flow.

The Authority of a King who is Head of the Law, as well as the Dignity of Publick Justice, is debased, when the clear stream of the Law is puddled and disturbed by Bunglers, or convey'd by unclean Instruments to the People.

Our *Trimmer* would have them appear in their full lustre, and would be grieved to see the day, when, instead of speaking with Authority from the Seats of Justice, they should speak out of a Grate, with a lamenting voice like Prisoners that desire to be rescu'd.

He wishes that the Bench may have a Natural as well as a Legal Superiority to the Bar; he thinks Mens abilities very much misplac'd, when the Reason of him that pleads is visibly too strong for those who Judge and give Sentence.

When those from the Bar seem to dictate to their Superiours upon the Bench, their Furrs will look scurvily about them, and the respect of the World will leave the bare Character of a Judge, to follow the Essential knowledge of a Lawyer, who may be greater in himself, than the other can be with all his Trappings.

An uncontested Superiority in any Calling, will have the better of any discountenance[5] that Authority can put upon it, and therefore if ever such an unnatural Method should be introduc'd, it is then that *Westminster-Hall* might be said to stand upon its Head, and though Justice it self can never be so, yet the Administration of it would be rendred ridiculous.

A Judge has such power lodg'd in him, that the King will never be thought to have chosen well, where the voice of Mankind has not before-hand recommended the Man to his Station; when Men are made Judges of what they do not understand, the World censures such a Choice, not out of ill will to the Men, but fear to themselves.

If the King had the sole power of chusing Physicians, Men would tremble to see Bunglers preferred, yet the necessity of taking Physick from a Doctor, is generally not so great as that of receiving Justice from a Judge; and yet the Inferences will be very severe in such cases, for either it will be thought that such Men bought what they were able to deserve, or which is as bad, that Obedience shall be look'd upon as a better Qualification in a Judge, than Skill or Integrity, when such sacred things as the Laws are not only touch'd, but guided by prophane hands; Men will fear that out of the Tree of the Law, from whence we expect Shade and Shelter, such Workmen will make Cudgels to beat us with, or rather that they will turn the Canon upon our Properties, that were intrusted with them for their Defence.

To see the Laws Mangled, Disguised, Speak quite another Language than their own, to see them thrown from the Dignity of protecting Mankind, to the disgraceful Office of destroying them; and notwithstanding their Innocence in themselves, to be made the worst Instruments that the most refined Villany can make use of, will raise Mens Anger above the power of laying it down again, and tempt them to follow the Evil Examples given them of Judging without Hearing, when so provoked by their desire of Revenge. Our *Trimmer* therefore, as he thinks the Laws are Jewels, so he believes they are no better set, than in the constitution of our *English* Government, if rightly understood, and carefully preserved.

It would be too great Partiality to say they are perfect or liable to no Objection; such things are not of this world; but if they have more Excellencies and fewer Faults than any other we know, it is enough to recommend them to our Esteem.

The Dispute, which is a greater Beauty, a Monarchy or a Common-wealth, has lasted long between their contending Lovers, and (they have behav'd themselves so like Lovers, who in good Manners must be out of their Wits,) who used such Figures to exalt their own Idols on either side, and such angry Aggravations, to reproach one another in the Contest, that moderate men have in all times smil'd upon this eagerness, and thought it differ'd very little from a downright Frenzy: we in *England*, by a happy use of the Controversie, conclude them both in the wrong, and reject them from being our Pattern, not taking the words in the utmost extent, which is a thing, that Monarchy, leaves men no Liberty, and a Common-wealth such a one, as allows them no Quiet.

We think that a wise Mean, between these barbarous Extreams, is that which self-Preservation ought to dictate to our Wishes; and we may say we have attained to this Mean in a greater measure, than any Nation now in being, or perhaps any we have read of; tho never so much Celebrated for the Wisdom or Felicity of their Constitutions: We take from one the too great power of doing hurt, and yet leave enough to govern and protect us; we take from the other, the Confusion, the Parity, the Animosities, and the License, and yet reserve a due care of such a Liberty, as may consist with Mens Allegiance; but it being hard, if not impossible, to be exactly even, our Government has much the stronger Bias towards Monarchy, which

[5] The 1700 text gives *distinct Name. Discountenance* is H. C. Foxcroft's emended reading.

by the general Consent and Practice of Mankind, seems to have the Advantage in dispute against a Common-wealth; The Rules of a Common-wealth are too hard for the Bulk of Mankind to come up to; that Form of Government requires such a spirit to carry it on, as do's not dwell in great Numbers, but is restrained to so very few, especially in this Age, that let the Methods appear never so much reasonably in Paper, they must fail in Practice, which will ever be suited more to Mens Nature as it is, than as it should be.

Monarchy is lik'd by the People, for the Bells and the Tinsel, the outward Pomp and Gilding, and there must be milk for Babes, since the greatest part of Mankind are, and ever will be included in that List; and it is approv'd by wise and thinking Men, (all Circumstances and Objections impartially consider'd) that it has so great an advantage above all other Forms, when the Administration of that Power falls in good hands; that all other Governments look out of Countenance, when they are set in Competition with it. *Lycurgus*[6] might have sav'd himself the trouble of making Laws, if either he had been Immortal, or that he could have secur'd to Posterity, a succeeding Race of Princes like himself; his own Example was a better Law, than he could with all his skill tell how to make; such a Prince is a Living Law, that dictates to his Subjects, whose thoughts in that case never rise above their Obedience, the Confidence they have in the Vertue and Knowledge of the master, preventing the Scruples and Apprehensions to which Men are naturally inclin'd, in relation to those that govern them; such a Magistrate is the Life and Soul of Justice, whereas the Law is but a Body and a dead one too, without his Influence to give it warmth and vigour, and by the irresistible Power of his Vertue, he do's so reconcile Dominion and Allegiance, that all disputes between them are silenced and subdued, and indeed no Monarchy can be Perfect and Absolute without exception, but where the Prince is Superior by his Vertue, as well as by his Character and his Power; so that to screw out Precedents and unlimited Power, is a plain diminution to a Prince that Nature has made Great, and who had better make himself a glorious Example to Posterity, than borrow an Authority from Dark Records, raised out of the Grave, which besides their Non-usage, have always in them matter of Controversie and Debate, and it may be affirmed, that the instances are very rare of Princes having the worst in the dispute with their People, if they were Eminent for Justice in time of Peace, or Conduct in time of War, such advantage the Crown giveth to those who adorn it by their own Personal Vertues.

But since for the greater Honour of Good and wise Princes, and the better to set off their Character by the Comparison, Heaven has decreed there must be a mixture, and that such as are perverse and insufficient, or at least both, are perhaps to have their equal turns in the Government of the World, and besides, that the Will of Man is so various, and so unbounded a thing, and so fatal too when joined with Power misapply'd; it is no wonder if those who are to be govern'd, are unwilling to have so dangerous as well as so uncertain a Standard of their Obedience.

There must be therefore Rules and Laws: for want of which, or at least the Observation of them, it was a Capital for a Man to say that *Nero*[7] did not play well upon the Lute, as to commit Treason, or Blaspheme the Gods. And even *Vespasian*[8] himself had like to have lost his Life, for sleeping whilst he should have attended and admir'd that Emperours Impertinence upon the Stage. There is a wantonness in great Power that Men are generally too apt to be corrupted with, and for that Reason, a Wise Prince, to prevent the temptation arising from common frailty, would choose to Govern by Rules for his own Sake, as well as for his Peoples, since it only secures him from Errors, and does not lessen the real Authority, that a good

[6] said to have lived in the ninth century B.C., and to have given Sparta its laws

[7] Roman Emperor, 54–68 A.D.; Tacitus (*Annals*, XVI.5) and Suetonius (*History of Nero*, 25) set forth the matters here referred to.

[8] Roman Emperor, 69–79; the incident cited here is recounted by Suetonius (*History of Flavius Vespasianus Augustus*, 4).

Magistrate would care to be possess'd of; for if the Will of a Prince is contrary either to Reason it self, or to the universal Opinion of his Subjects, the Law by a kind restraint rescues him from a disease that would undo him; if his will on the other side is reasonable or well directed, that Will immediately becomes a Law, and he is arbitrary by an easie and natural Consequence, without taking pains, or overturning the World for it.

If Princes consider Laws as things impos'd on them, they have the appearance of Fetters of Iron, but to such as would make them their choise as well as their practice, they are Chains of Gold; and in that respect are Ornaments, as in others they are a defence to them, and by a Comparison, not improper for God's Vicegerents upon Earth; as our Maker never Commands our obedience to any thing, that as reasonable Creatures we ought not to make our own Election; so a good and wise Governour, tho' all Laws were abolish'd, would by the voluntary direction of his own Reason, do without restraint the very same things that they would have enjoyned.

Our *Trimmer* thinks that the King and Kingdom ought to be one Creature, not to be separated in their Political Capacity; and when either of them undertake to act a-part, it is like the crawling of Worms after they are cut in pieces, which cannot be a lasting motion, the whole Creature not stirring at a time. If the Body has a dead Palsie, the Head cannot make it move; and God hath not yet delegated such a healing power to Princes, as that they can in a moment say to a Languishing People oppress'd and in despair, take up your Beds and walk.

The Figure of a King, is so comprehensive and exalted a thing, that it is a kind of degrading him to lodge that power separately in his own Natural Person, which can never be safely or naturally great, but where the People are so united to him as to be Flesh of his Flesh, and Bone of his Bone; for when he is reduc'd to the single definition of a man, he sinks into so low a Character, that it is a temptation upon Mens Allegiance, and an impairing that veneration which is necessary to preserve their Duty to him; whereas a Prince who is so joined to his people that they seem to be his Limbs, rather than his Subjects, Cloathed with Mercy and Justice rightly apply'd in their several places, his Throne supported by Love as well as by Power, and the warm wishes of his devoted Subjects, like never-failing Incense, still ascending towards him, looks so like the best Image we can frame to our selves of God Almighty, that men would have much ado not to fall down and worship him, and would be much more tempted to the Sin of Idolatry, than to that of Disobedience.

Our *Trimmer* is of Opinion, that there must be so much Dignity inseparably annexed to the Royal Function, as may be sufficient to secure it from insolence and contempt; and there must be Condescensions from the Throne, like kind showers from Heaven, that the Prince may look so much the more like God Almighty's Deputy upon Earth; for power without love hath a terrifying aspect, and the Worship which is paid to it is like that which the *Indians* give out of fear to Wild Beasts and Devils: he that fears God only because there is an Hell, must wish there were no God; and he who fears the King, only because he can punish, must wish there were no King; so that without a principle of Love, there can be no true Allegiance, and there must remain perpetual Seeds of Resistance against a power that is built upon such an unnatural Foundation, as that of fear and terrour. All force is a kind of foul-Play, and whosoever aims at it himself, does by implication allow it to those he plays with; so that there will be ever Matter prepared in the minds of People when they are provoked, and the Prince, to secure himself must live in the midst of his own Subjects, as if he were in a Conquer'd Country, raise Arms as if he were immediately to meet or resist an Invasion, and all this while sleep as unquietly from the fear of the Remedies, as he did before from that of the Disease; it being hard for him to forget, that more Princes have been destroyed by their Guards than by their People; and that even at the time when the Rule was *Quod Principi placuit Lex esto:*[9]

[9] "Let that be the law which is pleasing to the prince."

the Armies and *Praetorian*[10] Bands which were the Instruments of that unruly Power, were frequently the means made use of to destroy them who had it. There will ever be this difference between God and his Vicegerents, that God is still above the Instruments he uses, and out of the danger of receiving hurt from them; But Princes can never lodge Power in any hands, which may not at some time turn it back upon them; for tho' it is possible enough for a King to have power to satisfie his Ambition; yet no Kingdom has Money enough to satisfie the avarice of under-Workmen, who learn from that Prince who will exact more than belongs to him, to expect from him much more than they deserve, and growing angry upon the first disappointment, they are the Devils which grow terrible to the Conjurers themselves who brought them up, and can't send them down again; And besides that there can be no lasting Radical Security, but where the Governed are satisfied with the Governours. It must be a Dominion very unpleasant to a Prince of an elevated Mind, to impose an abject and sordid servility, instead of receiving the willing Sacrifice of Duty and Obedience. The bravest Princes in all times, who were uncapable of any other kind of fear, have fear'd to grieve their own People; such a fear is a glory, and in this sense 'tis an infamy not to be a Coward: So that the mistaken Heroes who are void of this generous kind of fear, need no other aggravation to compleat their ill Characters.

When a Despotick Prince has bruised all his Subjects with a slavish Obedience, all the force he can use cannot subdue his own fears; Enemies of his own Creation, to which he can never be reconciled, it being impossible to do injustice and not to fear Revenge: there is no cure for this fear, but the not deserving to be hurt, and therefore a Prince who does not allow his thoughts to stray beyond the Rules of Justice, has always the blessing of an inward quiet and assurance, as a natural effect of his good Meaning to his People, and tho he will not neglect due precautions to secure himself in all Events, yet he is uncapable of entertaining vain and remote suspicions of those, of whom he resolves never to deserve ill.

It is very hard for a Prince to fear Rebellion, who neither does, nor intends to do any thing to provoke it; therefore too great a diligence in the Governours, to raise and improve dangers and fears from the People, is no very good Symptom, and naturally begets an inference that they have thoughts of putting their Subjects Allegiance to a Tryal; and therefore not without some Reason fear before hand, that the Irregularities they intend, may raise Men to a Resistance.

Our *Trimmer* thinks it no advantage to a Government, to endeavour the suppressing all kind of Right which may remain in the Body of the People, or to employ small Authors in it, whose Officiousness or want of Money may encourage them to write, tho' it is not very easie to have Abilities equal to such a Subject; they forget that in their too high strained Arguments for the Rights of Princes, they very often plead against humane Nature, which will always give a Bias to those Reasons which seem of her side; it is the People that Reads those Books, and it is the People that must judge of them; and therefore no Maxims should be laid down for the Right of Government, to which there can be any Reasonable Objection; for the World has an Interest, and for that Reason is more than ordinary discerning to find out the weak sides of such Arguments as are intended to do them hurt; and it is a diminution to a Government, to Promote or Countenance such well affected mistakes which are turned upon it with disadvantage, whenever they are detected and expos'd; and Naturally the too earnest Endeavours to take from Men the Right they have, tempt them, by the Example to Claim that which they have not.

In Power, as in most other things, the way for Princes to keep it, is not to grasp more than their Arms can well hold; the nice and unnecessary enquiring into these things, or the Licensing some Books, and suppressing some others without sufficient Reason to Justifie the doing either, is so far from being an Advantage to a Government, that it exposes it to the Censure of

[10] the bodyguard of the Roman emperors

being Partial and to the suspicion, of having some hidden designs to be carried on by these unusual methods.

When all is said, there is a Natural Reason of State, and undefinable thing, grounded upon the Common Good of Mankind, which is immortal, and in all Changes and Revolutions, still preserves its Original Right of saving a Nation, when the Letter of the Law perhaps would destroy it; and by whatsoever means it moves, carrieth a Power with it, that admits of no opposition, being supported by Nature, which inspires an immediate consent at some Critical times into every individual Member, to that which visibly tendeth to preservation of the whole; and this being so, a Wise Prince instead of Controverting the right of this Reason of State, will by all means endeavour it may be of his side, and then he will be secure.

Our *Trimmer* cannot conceive that the Power of any Prince can be lasting, but where 'tis built upon the foundation of his own unborrowed vertue, he must not only be the first Mover and the Fountain, from whence the great Acts of State originally flow, but he must be thought so to his People that they may preserve their veneration for him; he must be jealous of his Power, and not impart so much of it to any about him, as that he may suffer an Eclipse by it.

He cannot take too much care to keep himself up, for when a Prince is thought to be led by those, with whom he should onely advise, and that the Commands he gives are transmitted through him, and are not of his own growth; the World will look upon him as a Bird adorned with Feathers that are not his own, or consider him rather as an Engine than a living Creature; besides, 'twould be a Contradiction for a Prince to fear a Commonwealth, and at the same time create one himself, by delegating such a Power to any Number of Men near him, as is inconsistent with the Figure of a Monarch: it is the worst kind of Co-ordination the Crown can submit to; for it is the exercise of Power that draws the respect along with it, and when that is parted with, the bare Character of a King is not sufficient to keep it up; but tho' it is a diminution to a Prince, to parcel out so liberally his Power amongst his Favourites, it's worse to divide with any other Man,[11] and to bring himself in Competition with a single Rival; a Partner in Government is so unnatural a thing, that it is a squint-ey'd Allegiance that must be paid to such a double bottom'd Monarchy. The two Czars of *Muscovy*[12] are an Example that the more civiliz'd part of the World will not be proud to follow, whatsoever Gloss may be put upon this method, by those to whom it may be of some use, the Prince will do well to remember, and reflect upon the Story of certain Men who had set up a Statue in Honour of Sun, yet in a very little time they turned their backs to the Sun, and their Faces to the Statue.

These Mystical Unions are better plac'd in the other World, than they are in this, and we shall have much ado to find, that in a Monarchy Gods Vicegerency is delegated to more Heads than that which is anointed.

Princes may lend some of their Light to make another shine, but they must still preserve the superiority of being the brighter Planet, and when it happens that the Reversion is in Mens Eyes, there is more care necessary to keep up the Dignity of Possessions, that Men may not forget who is King, either out of their hopes or fears who shall be. If the Sun shou'd part with all his Light to any of the Stars, the *Indians* would not know where to find their God, after he had so desposed himself, and would make the Light (whereever it went) the Object of their Worship.

All Usurpation is alike upon Soveraignty, its no matter from what hand it comes; and Crowned Heads are to be the more Circumspect, in respect Mens thoughts are naturally apt to ramble beyond what is present, they love to work at a distance, and in their greedy Expectations; which their minds may be fill'd with of a new Master, the old one may be left to look a little out of Countenance.

Our *Trimmer* owns a Passion for lib-

[11] What follows has reference to the growing power of the Duke of York.

[12] Peter I of Russia (1672–1725) reigned jointly with his half brother, Ivan, from 1682 to 1689.

erty, yet so restrained, that it does not in the least impair or taint his Allegiance, he thinks it hard fcr a Soul that does not love Liberty, ever to raise its self to another World he takes it to be the foundation of all vertue, and the only seasoning that gives a relish to life, and tho' the laziness of a slavish subjection, has its Charms for the more gross and earthly part of Mankind, yet to men made of a better sort of Clay, all that the World can give without Liberty has no taste; it is true, nothing is sold so cheap by unthinking men, but that does no more lessen the real value of it, than a Country Fellows Ignorance does that of a Diamond, in selling it for a Pot of Ale. Liberty is the Mistress of Mankind, she has powerful Charms which do so dazzle us, that we find Beauties in her which perhaps are not there, as we do in other Mistresses; yet if she was not a Beauty, the World would not run mad for her; therefore since the reasonable desire of it ought not to be restrain'd, and that even the unreasonable desire of it cannot be entirely suppress'd, those who would take it away from a People possessed of it, are likely to fail in the attempting, or be very unquiet in the keeping of it.

Our *Trimmer* admires our blessed Constitution, in which Dominion and Liberty are so well reconciled; it gives to the Prince the glorious Power of commanding Freemen, and to the Subject, the satisfaction of seeing the Power so lodged, as that their Liberties are secure; it do's not allow the Crown such a Ruining Power, as that no grass can grow where e're it treads, but a Cherishing and Protecting Power; such a one as hath a grim Aspect only to the offending Subjects, but is the joy and the Pride of all the good ones; their own interest being so bound up in it, as to engage them to defend and support it; and tho in some instances the King is restrain'd yet nothing in the Government can move without him: our Laws make a distinction between Vassalage and Obedience; between devouring Perogatives, and a licentious ungovernable Freedom: and as of all the Orders of Building, the Composite is the best, so ours by a happy mixture and a wise choice of what is best in others, is brought into a Form that is our Felicity who live under it, and the envy of our Neighbour that cannot imitate it.

The Crown has power sufficient to protect our Liberties. The People have so much Liberty as is necessary to make them useful to the Crown.

Our Government is in a just proportion, no Tympany, no unnatural swelling either of Power or Liberty; and whereas in all overgrown Monarchies, Reason, Learning, and Enquiry are hang'd in Effigy for Mutineers; here they are encouraged and cherished as the surest Friends to a Government establish'd upon the Foundation of Law and Justice. When all is done, those who look for Perfection in this World, may look as the *Jews* have for their *Messias*, And therefore our *Trimmer* is not so unreasonably Partial as to free our Government; and from all objections, no doubt there have been fatal Instances of its Sickness, and more than that, of its Mortality, for sometime, tho' by a Miracle, it hath been reviv'd again: but till we have another race of Mankind, in all Constitutions that are bounded, there will ever be some matter of Strife, and Contention, and rather than want pretensions, Mens Passions and Interests will raise them from the most inconsiderable Causes.

Our Government is like our Climate, there are Winds which are sometimes loud and unquiet, and yet with all the Trouble they give us, we owe, great part of our Health unto them, they clear the Air, which else would be like a standing Pool, and in stead of Refreshment would be a Disease unto us.

There may be fresh Gales of asserting Liberty, without turning into such storms of Hurricane, as that the State should run any hazard of being Cast away by them; these strugglings which are natural to all mixed Governments, while they are kept from growing into Convulsions, do by a mutual agitation from the several parts, rather support and strengthen, than weaken or maim the Constitution; and the whole frame, instead of being torn or disjointed, comes to be the better and closer knit by being thus exercised; but what ever faults our Government may have, or a discerning Critick may find in it, when he looks upon it alone; let any other be set against it, and then it shews its Comparative Beauty; let us look upon the most glittering outside of unbounded Authority, and upon a nearer enquiry, we shall find nothing but poor and miserable deformity within; let us imagine a Prince living in his Kingdom, as if in a great Gally, his Subjects tugging at the Oar, laden with Chains, and reduced to real Rags, that they may gain him imaginary Lawrels; let us Represent him gazing among his Flatterers, and receiving their false Worship, like a Child never Contradicted, and therefore always Cozen'd: or like a Lady complemented only to be abused, condemned never to hear Truth, and Consequently never to do Justice, wallowing in the soft Bed of wanton and unbridled Greatness, not less odious to the Instruments themselves, than to the Objects of his Tyranny; blown up into an Ambitious Dropsy, never to be satisfied by the Conquest of other People, or by the Oppression of his own; by aiming to be more than a Man, he falls lower than the meanest of 'em, a mistaken Creature, swelled with Panegyricks, and flattered out of his Senses, and not only an Incumbrance, but a Nuisance to Mankind, a hardened and unrelenting Soul, and like some Creatures that grow fat with Poisons, he grows great by other Mens Miseries; an Ambitious Ape of the Divine Greatness, an unruly Gyant that would storm even Heaven it self, but that his scaling Ladders are not long enough; in short, a Wild and devouring Creature in rich Trappings, and with all his Pride no more than a Whip in God Almighty's hand, to be thrown into the Fire when the World has been sufficiently scourged with it: This Picture laid in right Colours would not incite Men to wish for such a Government, but rather to acknowledge the happiness of our own, under which we enjoy all the Priviledges Reasonable Men can desire, and avoid all the Miseries many others are subject to; so that our *Trimmer* would keep it with all its faults, and does as little forgive those who give the occasion of breaking it, as he does those that take it.

Our *Trimmer* is a Friend to Parliaments, notwithstanding all their faults, and excesses, which of late have given such matter of Objection to them; he thinks that tho' they may at sometimes be troublesome to Authority, yet they add the greatest strength to it under a wise Administration; he believes no Government is perfect except a kind of Omnipotence reside in it, to exercise upon great Occasions: Now this cannot be obtained by force alone upon People, let it be never so great, there must be their consent too, or else a Nation moves only by being driven, a sluggish and constrained Motion, void of that Life and Vigour which is necessary to produce great things, whereas the virtual Consent of the whole being included in their Representatives, and the King giving the sanction to the united sense of the People, every Act done by such an Authority, seems to be an effect of their choice as well as a part of their Duty; and they do with an eagerness, of which Men are uncapable whilst under a force, execute whatsoever is so enjoyned as their own Wills, better explained by Parliament, rather than from the terrour of incurring the Penalty of the Law for omitting it, and by means of this Political Omnipotence, what ever Sap or Juice there is in a Nation, may be to the last drop produc'd, whilst it rises naturally from the Root; whereas all power exercis'd without consent, is like the giving Wounds and Gashes, and tapping a Tree at unseasonable Times, for the present occasion, which in a very little time must needs destroy it.

Our *Trimmer* believes, that by the advantage of our Situation, there can hardly any such sudden Disease come upon us, but that the King may have time enough left to consult with his Physicians in Parliament; pretences indeed may be made, but a real necessity so pressing, that no delay is to be admitted, is hardly to be imagin'd, and it will be neither easie to give an instance of any such thing for the time past, or reasonable to Presume it will ever happen for the time to come: but if that strange thing should fall out, our *Trimmer* is not so streight-lac'd, as to let a Nation die, or be stiffled, rather than it should be help'd by any but the proper Officers. The Cases themselves will bring the Remedies along with them; and he is not afraid to allow that in order to its preservation, there is a hidden Power in Government, which would be lost if it was designed, a certain Mystery, by virtue of which a Nation may at some Critical times be secur'd from Ruine, but then it must be kept as a Mystery; it is rendred useless when touch'd by unskilful hands: and no Government ever had, or deserv'd to have that Power, which was so unwary as to anticipate their claim to it: Our *Trimmer* cannot help thinking it had been better, if the Triennial Act[13] had been observ'd; because 'tis the Law, and he would not have the Crown, by such an Example, teach the Nation to break it; all irregularity is catching, it has a Contagion in it, especially in an Age, so much enclin'd to follow ill Patterns than good ones.

He would have a Parliament, because 'tis an Essential part of the Constitution, even without the Law,[14] it being the only Provision in extraordinary Cases, in which there would be otherwise no Remedy, and there can be no greater Solecism in Government, than a failure of Justice.

He would have had one, because nothing else can unite and heal us, all other Means are meer Shifts and Projects, Houses of Cards, to be blown down with the least Breath, and cannot resist the Difficulties which are ever presum'd in things of this kind; and he would have had one, because it might have done the King good, and could not possibly have done him hurt, without his consent, which in that Case is not to be supposed, and therefore for him to fear it, is so strange and so little to be comprehended, that the Reasons can never be presum'd to grow in our Soyl, or to thrive in it when Transplanted from any other Country; and no doubt there are such irresistible Arguments for calling a Parliament, and tho it might be deny'd to the unmannerly mutinous Petitions of men, that are malicious and disaffected, it will be granted to the soft and obsequious Murmurs of his Majesty's best Subjects, and there will be such Retorick in their silent Grief, that it will at last prevail against the Artifices of those, who either out of Guilt or Interest, are afraid to throw themselves upon their Country, knowing how scurvily they have used it; that day of Judgment will come, tho we know neither the day nor the hour. And our *Trimmer* would live so as to be prepared for it, with full assurance in the mean time, that the lamenting Voice of a Nation cannot long be resisted, and that a Prince who could so easily forgive his People when they had been in the wrong,[15] cannot fail to hear them when they are in the right.

[In the next two sections Halifax discusses the religious situation in England as it involves the Church of England, the Dissenters, and the Roman Catholics. His position here, as always, is the middle one: loyalty to the Church of England, leniency for Dissenters, and virtual toleration for Roman Catholics provided they be excluded from office. The fourth section, entitled "The Trimmer's Opinion in Relation to things abroad," sets forth the writer's favorite thesis concerning the necessity of maintaining a balance of power in Europe. Since the Restoration, however, England has been a mere dependent on France, and certain "refined statesmen" are willing to set forth France and all she stands for in a favorable light. Halifax proceeds as follows:]

Our *Trimmer* cannot easily be converted out of his senses by these State Sophisters, and yet he has no such peevish Obstinacy as to reject all Correspondence with *France*, because we ought to be apprehensive of the too great power of it; he would not have the king's Friendship to the Confederates, extended to the involving him in any unreasonable or dangerous Engagements, neither would he have him lay aside the consideration of his better establishment at home, out of his excessive Zeal to secure his Allies abroad; but sure there might be a Mean between these two opposite Extreams, and it may be wish'd, that our Friendship with *France*, should at least be so bounded, that it may consist with the humour as well as the Interest of *England*. There is no Woman but has the fears of

[13] This Act provided that not more than three years should pass without a Parliament. Since the last Parliament—the Oxford Parliament—had been dissolved in March, 1681, the terms of the Act had been disregarded since March, 1684.

[14] i.e., without the Triennial Act

[15] The reference is to Charles's Act of Oblivion, 1660.

contracting too near an intimacy with a much greater Beauty, because it exposes her too often to a Comparison that is not advantageous to her; and sure it may become a Prince to be as jealous of his Dignity, as a Lady can be of her good Looks, and to be as much out of Countenance, to be thought an humble Companion to so much a greater Power; to be always seen in an ill Light, to be so darkned by the brightness of a greater Star, is somewhat mortifying; and when *England* might ride Admiral[16] at the head of the Confederates, to look like the Kitching-Yatch[17] to the Grand *Louis*, is but a scurvy Figure for us to make in the Map of *Christendom;* it would rise up in our *Trimmer's* stomach, if ever (which God forbid) the power of calling and intermitting Parliaments here, should be transferred to the Crown of *France*, and that all the opportunities of our own settlements at home should give way to their Projects abroad; and that our Interests should be so far sacrific'd to our Compliance, that all the Omnipotence of *France* can never make us full amends for it. In the mean time, he shrinks at the dismal prospect he can by no means drive away from his thoughts, that when *France* has gather'd all the fruit arising from our Mistakes, and that we can bear no more with them, they will cut down the Tree and throw it into the fire; for all this while, some Superfine States-Men, to comfort us, would fain parswade the World, that this or that accident may save us, and for all that, is or ought to be dear to us, would have us to rely wholly upon Chance, not considering that Fortune is Wisdoms Creature, and that God Almighty loves to be on the Wisest as well as the Strongest side; therefore this is such a miserable shift, such a shameful Evasion, that they would be laught to death for it, if the ruining Consequence of this Mistake did not more dispose Men to rage, and a detestation of it.

Our *Trimmer* is far from Idolatary in other things, in one thing only he comes near it, his Country is in some degree his Idol; he does not Worship the Sun, because 'tis not peculiar to us, it rambles about the World, and is less kind to us than others; but for the Earth of *England*, tho perhaps inferior to that of many places abroad, to him there is Divinity in it, and he would rather dye, than see a spire of *English* Grass[18] trampled down by a Foreign Trespasser: He thinks there are a great many of his mind, for all plants are apt to taste of the Soyl in which they grow, and we that grow here, have a Root that produces in us a Stalk of English Juice, which is not to be changed by grafting or foreign infusion; and I do not know whether any thing less will prevail, than the Modern Experiment, by which the Blood of one Creature is transmitted into another; according to which, before the *French* can be let into our Bodies, every drop of our own must be drawn out of them.

Our *Trimmer* cannot but lament, that by a Sacrifice too great for one Nation to another, we should be like a rich Mine, made useless only for want of being wrought, and that the Life and Vigour which should move us against our Enemies, is miserably other apply'd to tear our own Bowels; that being made by our happy situation, not only safer, but if we please greater too, than other Countries which far exceed us in extent; that having Courage by Nature, Learning by Industry, and Riches by Trade, we should corrupt all these Advantages, so as to make them insignificant, and by a fatality which seems peculiar to us, misplace our active rage one against another, whilst we are turn'd into Statues on that side where lies our greatest danger; to be unconcern'd not only at our Neighbours ruin but our own, and let our Island lie like a great Hulk in the Sea, without Rudder or Sail, all the Men cast away in her, or as if we were all Children in a great Cradle, and rockt asleep to a foreign Tune.

I say when our *Trimmer* representeth to his Mind, our Roses blasted and discolour'd, whilst the Lillies Triumph and grow Insolent, upon the Comparison; when he considers our own once flourish-

[16] *Admiral*, the admiral's ship

[17] The royal yacht was named *Kitchen.*

[18] The 1700 text gives "a piece of *English* glass"; "a spire of *English* grass" is H. C. Foxcroft's emended reading.

ing Lawrel, now withered and dying, and nothing left us but a remembrance of a better part in History than we shall make in the next Age; which will be no more to us than an Escutcheon hung upon our Door when we are Dead; when he foresees from hence, growing Infamy from abroad, confusion at home, and all this without the possibility of a Cure, in respect of the voluntary fetters good Men put upon themselves by their Allegiance without a good measure of preventing Grace, he would be tempted to go out of the World like a *Roman* Philosopher, rather than endure the burthen of Life under such a discouraging Prospect. But Mistakes, as all other things, have their Periods, and many times the nearest way to Cure, is not to oppose them, but stay till they are crusht with their own weight: for Nature will not allow any thing to continue long that is violent; violence is a wound, and as a wound, must be curable in a little time, or else 'tis Mortal; but a Nation comes near to be Immortal, therefore the wound will one time or another be cured, tho perhaps by such rough Methods, if too long forborn, as may even make the best Remedies we can prepare, to be at the same time a Melancholy Contemplation to us; there is but one thing (God Almighties Providence excepted) to support a Man from sinking under these afflicting thoughts, and that is the hopes we draw singly from the King himself, without the mixture of any other consideration.

Tho the Nation was lavish of their Kindness to him at his first coming, yet there remains still a stock of Warmth in Mens Hearts for him.

Besides the good Influences of his happy Planet are not yet all spent, and tho the Stars of Men past their youth are generally declining, and have less Force like the Eyes of decaying Beauties, yet by a Blessing peculiar to himself, we may yet hope to be sav'd by his Autumnal Fortune; He has something about him that will draw down a healing Miracle for his and our Deliverance; a Prince which seems fitted for such an offending Age, in which Mens Crimes have been so general, that the not forgiving his People has been the destroying of them, whose Gentleness gives him a natural Dominion that hath no bounds, with such a noble mixture of Greatness and Condescention, an engaging Look, that disarms Men of their ill Humours, and their Resentments; something in him that wanteth a Name, and can be no more defined than it can be resisted; a Gift of Heaven, of its last finishing, where it will be peculiarly kind; the only Prince in the World that dares be familiar, or that has right to triumph over those forms which were first invented to give awe to those who could not judge, and to hide Defects from those that could; a Prince that has exhausted himself by his Liberality, and endanger'd himself by his Mercy; who outshines by his own Light and natural Virtues all the varnish of studied Acquisitions; his Faults are like Shades to a good Picture, or like Allay to Gold, to make it the more useful, he may have some, but for any Man to see them through so many reconciling Virtues, is a Sacrilegious piece of ill nature, of which no generous Mind can be guilty; a Prince that deserves to be lov'd for his own sake, even without the help of a Comparison; our Love, our Duty, and our Danger, all join to cement our Obedience to him; in short whatever, he can do, it is no more possible for us to be angry with him, than with a Bank that secures us from the raging Sea, the kind Shade that hides us from the scorching Sun, the welcome Hand that reaches us a Reprieve, or with the Guardian Angel, that rescues our Souls from the devouring Jaws of wretched Eternity.

CONCLUSION

To Conclude, our *Trimmer* is so fully satisfy'd of the Truth of these Principles, by which he is directed, in reference to the Publick, that he will neither be Hectored and Threatned, Laught, nor Drunk out of them; and instead of being converted by the Arguments of his Adversaries to their Opinions, he is very much confirmed in his own by them; he professes solemnly that were it in his Power to chuse, he would rather have his Ambition bounded by the Commands of a Great and Wise Master, than let it range with a Popular License, tho' crown'd with success; yet he cannot commit such a Sin against the glorious thing call'd Liberty, nor let his Soul stoop so much below it self, as to be content without repining to have his Reason wholly subdu'd, or the Priviledge of Acting like a sensible Creature, torn from him by the imperious Dictates of unlimited Authority, in what hand soever it happens to be plac'd. What is there in this that is so Criminal, as to deserve the Penalty of that most singular Apophthegn, *A* Trimmer *is worse than a Rebel?* What do angry men ail to rail so against Moderation, do's it not look as if they were going to some very scurvy Extreme, that is too strong to be digested by the more considering part of Mankind? These Arbitrary Methods, besides the injustice of them, are (God be thanked) very unskilful too, for they fright the Birds, by talking so loud, from coming into the Nets that are laid for them; and when Men agree to rifle a House, they seldom give warning, or blow a Trumpet; but there are some small States-Men, who are so full charg'd with their own Expectations, that they cannot contain.

And kind Heaven by sending such a seasonable Curse upon their undertakings, has made their Ignorance an Antidote against their Malice; some of these cannot treat peaceably, yielding will not satisfy them, they will have men by storm; there are others, that must have Plots, to make their Service more necessary, and have an Interest to keep them alive, since they are to live upon them; and perswade the King to retrench his own Greatness, so as to shrink into the head of a Party, which is the betraying him into such an Unprincely mistake, and to such a wilful diminution of himself, that they are the last Enemies he ought to allow himself to forgive; such Men, if they could, would prevail with the Sun to shine only upon them and their Friends, and to leave all the rest of the World in the dark; this is a very unusual Monopoly, and may come within the Equity of the Law, which makes it Treason to Imprison the King, when such unfitting bounds are put to his Favour, and he confin'd to the narrow limits of a particular set of Men, that would inclose him; these Honest and only Loyal Gentlemen, if they may be allow'd to bear Witness for themselves, make a King their Engine, and degrade him into a property at the very time that their Flattery would make him believe they paid Divine Worship to him; besides these there is a flying Squadron on both sides, that are afraid the World should agree, small dabblers in Conjuring, that raise angry Apparitions to keep Men from being reconcil'd, like Wasps that fly up and down, buz and sting to keep Men unquiet; but these Insects are commonly short liv'd Creatures, and no doubt in a little time Mankind will be rid of them; they were Gyants at least who fought once against Heaven, but for such Pigmies as these to contend against it, is such a provoking Folly, that the insolent Bunglers ought to be laught and hist out of the World for it; they should consider there is a Soul in that great body of the People, which may for a time be drowzy and unactive, but when the Leviathan is rouz'd, it moves like an angry Creature, and will neither be convinc'd nor resisted: the People can never agree to shew their united Powers, till they are extremely tempted and provoked to it, so that to apply Cupping-Glasses to a great Beast naturally dispos'd to sleep, and to force the Tame thing whether it will or no to be Valiant, must be learnt out of some other Book than *Machiavil*,[19] who would never have prescrib'd such a preposterous Method. It is to be remembred, that if Princes have Law and Authority on their sides, the People on theirs may have Nature, which is a formidable Adversary; Duty, Justice, Religion, nay, even Humane Prudence too, bids the People suffer any thing rather than resist; but uncorrected Nature, where e're it feels the smart will run to the nearest Remedy, Mens Passions in this Case are to be consider'd as well as their Duty, let it be never so strongly enforc'd, for if their Passions are provok'd, they being as much a part of us as our Limbs, they lead Men into a short way of Arguing, that admits no distinction, and from the foundation of Self-Defence, they will draw Inferences, that will have miserable effects upon the quiet of a Government.

Our *Trimmer* therefore dreads a general discontent, because he thinks it differs, from a Rebellion, only as a Spotted Fever

[19] *The Prince* by Machiavelli (1469–1527)

does from the Plague, the same Species under a lower degree of Malignity; it works several ways; sometimes like a slow Poyson that has its Effects at a great distance from the time it was given, sometimes like a dry Flax prepared to catch at the first Fire, or like Seed in the ground ready to sprout upon the first Shower; in every shape 'tis fatal, and our *Trimmer* thinks no pains or precaution can be so great as to prevent it.

In short he thinks himself in the right, grounding his Opinion upon that Truth, which equally hates to be under the Oppressions of wrangling Sophistry of the one hand, or the short dictates of mistaken Authority on the other.

Our *Trimmer* adores the Goddess Truth, tho' in all Ages she has been scurvily used, as well as those that Worshipped her; 'tis of late become such a ruining Virtue, that Mankind seems to be agreed to commend and avoid it; yet the want of Practice which Repeals the other Laws, has no influence upon the Law of Truth, because it has root in Heaven, and an intrinsick value in it self, that can never be impaired; she shews her Greatness in this, that her Enemies even when they are successful are asham'd to own it; nothing but Power full of Truth has the prerogative of Triumphing, not only after Victories, but in spite of them, and to put Conquest her self out of Countenance; she may be kept under and supprest, but her Dignity still remains with her, even when she is in Chains; Falshood with all her Impudence, has not enough to speak ill of her before her Face, such Majesty she carries about her, that her most prosperous Enemies are fain to whisper their Treason; all the Power upon Earth can never extinguish her; she has liv'd in all Ages; and let the Mistaken Zeal of prevailing Authority, Christen any opposition to it, with what Name they please, she makes it not only an ugly and unmannerly, but a dangerous thing to persist; she has lived very retired indeed, nay sometimes so buried, that only some few of the discerning part of Mankind could have a Glimpse of her; with all that she has Eternity in her, she knows how to die, and from the darkest Clouds that shade and cover her, she breaks from time to time with Triumph for her Friends, and Terrour to her Enemies.

Our *Trimmer* therefore inspired by this Divine Virtue, thinks fit to conclude with these Assertions, That our Climate is a *Trimmer*, between that part of the World where Men are Roasted, and the other where they are Frozen; That our Church is a *Trimmer* between the Phrenzy of Platonick Visions, and the Lethargick Ignorance of Popish Dreams; That our Laws are *Trimmers*, between the Excess of unbounded Power, and the Extravagance of Liberty not enough restrained; That true Virtue has ever been thought a *Trimmer*, and to have its dwelling in the middle between the two Extreams; That even God Almighty himself is divided between his two great Attributes, his Mercy and his Justice.

In such Company, our *Trimmer* is not asham'd of his Name, and willingly leaves to the bold Champions of either Extream, the Honour of contending with no less Adversaries, than Nature, Religion, Liberty, Prudence, Humanity and Common Sense.

Thomas Traherne

OF THE life of Thomas Traherne very little is known for certain. Anthony à Wood reports in his *Athenae Oxonienses* that his father was a shoemaker of Hereford, and that he was entered as a commoner of Brasenose College, Oxford, on the first of March, 1652. The Register of that college confirms Wood's statement but gives Traherne's age as fifteen, which means that he must have been born between March 1, 1637, and February 28, 1639.

Of his family little more is known. There is evidence in the parish registers and other records of Hereford that would seem to confirm Wood's report, but there is also the possibility of distinguished and influential connections. What is certain is that Traherne completed his college course and received his B.A. in 1656. In December of 1657, having taken orders, he received the living of Credenhill from the Dowager Countess of Kent. In spite of an enthusiastic account of his entrance into his country cure, Traherne seems to have spent a good portion of the ten years during which he kept that parish as an absentee studying at Oxford, receiving the degree of M.A. in 1661 and of B.D. in 1669. During these years he would seem to have made a number of notable friendships, and some time before 1667 he was appointed chaplain to Sir Orlando Bridgeman, who in that year became Keeper of the Seals. Traherne's conversancy with the central issues of the political and religious life of London in the years that followed is apparent in *Roman Forgeries*, published in November of 1673. When Bridgeman was dismissed from office in 1672, he retired to the country, and Traherne would seem to have followed him, for he is found at his patron's deathbed early in 1674. He was himself buried in the parish church at Teddington on October 10, 1674. And in 1675 the second of his works to be published, the *Christian Ethicks*, appeared. A third, *A Serious and Pathetical Contemplation of the Mercies of God*, was published anonymously in 1699, and was identified as Traherne's by Bertram Dobell. The only one of these works that enjoyed any popularity in its own day was the least distinctive and characteristic, the *Roman Forgeries*. In spite of very considerable merits the other two works seem to have made little or no impression, and Traherne was pretty much forgotten.

It was only by accident that the manuscripts of the meditations and poems on which Traherne's modern reputation rests fell into the sympathetic hands of Bertram Dobell, who printed the poems in 1903, and the *Centuries of Meditations* in 1908. Further prose work of Traherne is known to exist in manuscript, the most important being a collection of private devotions which clarify Traherne's religious position as a quite orthodox member of the Church of England in the church-mystical tradition of Herbert, whom Traherne obviously admired and even imitated. Some early verse has been found, but it is doubtful if any further discoveries would change the impression of his poetry, so remarkably homogeneous in its substance and its effect.

For however obscure the external record of his life, Traherne's work is always most fully and directly and immediately personal. He is a prophet, a man with a message, indeed with a revelation, and the text of that revelation is his own spiritual history. It is the inspiration of the *Christian Ethicks,* and of *A Serious and Pathetical Contemplation,* but he tells the story directly in his poems and in the *Centuries of Meditations.* Most of the spiritual histories of the seventeenth century are conversion stories. Traherne's is, rather, the story of an illumination, an illumination of joy and wonder. Symbolically, the story opens with the embryonic mind's first glimmer of a consciousness of the members of its own body. In more literal biographical terms it began with a very remarkable four-year-old's sudden awareness of the meanness of the environment in which he found himself, a sharp sense of personal neglect, and a consequent incapacity to believe that one so neglected and so poverty-stricken could be in the hands of a good God. Then something happened to change the situation completely. Twice at least Traherne told the story directly, and scores of times he told it in hints and implications. It was simply that all at once the child perceived that he was not poor but rich, that, indeed, all the supposed riches of the world were insignificant beside what he already possessed in full, his own body and mind, the magnificence of the natural world, and the beauty and vitality of the human beings he beheld about him. Verily, he was the son of God, and the heir to all Creation.

The confidence and joy which this revelation brought to Traherne, the never-failing delight with which he recurred to it are remarkable for any age, and not least for his own. For this became the foundation of all his later experience: the never-ending speculation about eternity and infinity, the disillusioning experience of the adult world's corruption of the child's innocence with false values, the seeker's search for the hidden truth that will make all things clear. Yet for all his glorification of primal innocence Traherne was an educated and even, as his more impersonal prose writings make abundantly clear, a learned man, and while he might believe that man in his unfallen state would have no need of the labors of learning and would possess their fruits and more in the effortless vision of perfect felicity, in the world as he found it and with men as they were, learning was to be prized as one of the surest ways to the full discovery of the Universe which man had received as his inheritance.

As a poet the rediscovered Traherne made a deep impression on a time that was seeking greater freedom and naturalness in verse, and the charm of the freshness and directness and simplicity of his verse at its best is still potent. But Traherne is more a man of his time than was at first apppreciated. This is in part due to the fact that his brother, Philip Traherne, "corrected" his poetry, apparently in preparation for a publication that never came off, but only in part. For all Thomas Traherne's prophetic light, there is a certain didacticism in his treatment of his revelation, while the growing conceptualism of the period deprives his imagery, rich as it often is in its implications, of the warmth and color that come from more specific appeal to the senses. His symbolism obviously evoked lofty and intense feeling in his own consciousness, but it lacks the vitalizing power of sense appeal. And he has very little in the way of sound effect to compensate. His verse is often heavy and aimless in its movement and, for all its enthusiasm, curiously flat in pitch. The remarkable thing is that in spite of these limitations his poetry does convey a sense of conviction and of reality of feeling.

There is no such wonder about his prose. The *Centuries of Meditations* reveals both his competence with structure and his power of sustained execution. And every so often it breaks into passages of such breath-taking splendor that whatever one's prejudices about the confusion of the genres, it is clear that here is that rare thing, really poetic prose.

In an age of prophets Traherne stands out as a very original and distinctive one. By virtue of his subject matter and his mood he has been frequently associated with the metaphysical poets, but that may do him an injustice. In a good many ways he belongs to a later generation, a later generation even than Vaughan who outlived him, and in that context he might profitably be restudied particularly as a poet.

The terms in which Traherne's rediscoverer, Bertram Dobell, first presented him took too little account of Traherne's relations to his own time and too much of the predilections of the time to which the discovery was being presented, but Dobell's discernment and sympathetic insight into his subject's temper and point of view have put all later students of Traherne in his debt. And his remains the basic work on the text. That work has been carried on most notably by H. I. Bell who first published the poems from the Burney manuscript in the British Museum in 1910, and by Miss Gladys Wade, whose revised edition of 1932 is the standard edition. Miss Wade has also performed notable service in searching out all available records of Traherne and his family and friends and has made that investigation the basis of an imaginative reconstruction of his life and environment in *Thomas Traherne: a Critical Biography*, 1944. Some of Miss Wade's conclusions from the evidence are pretty speculative, but hers is a helpful and stimulating book, presenting a good deal of valuable material for further study. Miss Wade's biography is accompanied by a selective bibliography of criticism of Traherne by Mr. R. A. Parker.

Valuable discussions of Traherne's ideas are to be found in E. N. S. Thompson, "The Philosophy of Thomas Traherne," *PQ* VIII, 97–112 (1929); and T. O. Beachcroft, "Thomas Traherne and the Doctrine of Felicity," *Criterion* IX, 291–307 (1929–1930), and "Traherne and the Cambridge Platonists," *Dublin Review* CLXXXVI, 278–290 (1930). There are also chapters on Traherne in the books on the metaphysical poets by J. B. Leishman (1934), H. C. White (1936), I. Husain (1948); and in M. M. Mahood, *Poetry and Humanism* (1950).

from THE POETICAL WORKS[1]

The Salutation

These little Limmes,
These Eys and Hands which here I find,
These rosie Cheeks wherwith my Life begins,
Where have ye been? Behind
What Curtain were ye from me hid so long!
Where was? in what Abyss,[2] my Speaking Tongue?

When silent I,
So many thousand, thousand yeers,
Beneath the Dust did in a Chaos[3] lie,
How could I Smiles or Tears,
Or Lips or Hands or Eys or Ears perceiv?
Welcom ye Treasures which I now receiv.

I that so long
Was Nothing from Eternitie,
Did little think such Joys as Ear or Tongue,
To Celebrat[4] or See:
Such Sounds to hear, such Hands to feel, such Feet,
Beneath the Skies, on such a Ground[5] to meet.

[1] Text: Wade, 1932, reprinted by permission of P. J. and A. E. Dobell.
[2] primal chaos
[3] formless void of primordial matter
[4] proclaim
[5] an earth

New Burnisht Joys!
Which yellow Gold and Pearl excell!
Such Sacred Treasures are the Lims in Boys,
In which a Soul doth Dwell;
Their Organized Joynts, and Azure Veins
More Wealth include, then[6] all the World contains.

From Dust I rise,
And out of Nothing now awake,
These Brighter Regions which salute mine Eys,
A Gift from GOD I take.
The Earth, the Seas, the Light, the Day, the Skies,
The Sun and Stars are mine; if those I prize.[7]

Long time before
I in my Mother's Womb was born,
A GOD preparing did this Glorious Store,[8]
The World for me adorne,
Into this Eden[9] so Divine and fair,
So Wide and Bright, I com his Son and Heir.

A Stranger here
Strange Things doth meet, Strange Glories See;
Strange Treasures lodg'd[10] in this fair World appear,
Strange all, and New to me.
But that they mine should be, who nothing was,
That Strangest is of all, yet brought to pass.

Wonder

How like an Angel came I down!
How Bright are all Things here!
When first among his[11] Works I did appear
O how their GLORY me did Crown?
The World resembled his *Eternitie*,
In which my Soul did Walk;[12]
And evry Thing that I did see,
Did with me talk.[13]

The Skies in their Magnificence,
The Lively,[14] Lovely Air;
Oh how Divine, how Soft, how Sweet, how fair!
The Stars did entertain[15] my Sence,[16]
And all the Works of GOD so Bright and pure,
So Rich and Great did seem,
As if they ever must endure,[17]
In my Esteem.[18]

A Native[19] Health and Innocence
Within my Bones did grow,
And while my GOD did all his Glories shew,
I felt a Vigour[20] in my Sence
That was all SPIRIT. I within did flow
With Seas of Life, like Wine;
I nothing in the World did know,
But 'twas Divine.

Harsh ragged[21] Objects were conceald,
Oppressions Tears and Cries,
Sins, Griefs, Complaints, Dissentions, Weeping Eys,
Were hid: and only Things reveald,
Which Heav'nly Spirits, and the Angels prize.
The State of Innocence[22]
And Bliss,[23] not Trades and Poverties,[24]
Did fill my Sence.

The Streets were pavd with Golden[25] Stones,
The Boys and Girles were mine,[26]
Oh how did all their Lovly faces shine!
The Sons of Men[27] were Holy Ones.[28]
In Joy, and Beauty, then appear'd to me,
And evry Thing which here I found,

[6] than
[7] estimate the relative value of
[8] treasure
[9] Paradise of fresh and innocent joy from the Garden of Eden, the abode of the newly-created Adam and Eve
[10] as in a temporary shelter
[11] God's [12] move [13] exchange ideas(?)
[14] invigorating [15] engage the attention of
[16] senses (viewed as single faculty)
[17] continue in existence [18] estimation
[19] innate [20] energy [21] irregular
[22] of being unacquainted with evil
[23] blessedness, perfect felicity
[24] formerly used in the plural
[25] like the Heavenly City
[26] belonged to me [27] mortals
[28] persons consecrated by God

While like an Angel I did See,[29]
Adornd[30] the Ground.

Rich Diamond and Pearl and Gold
In Evry Place was seen;
Rare Splendors, Yellow, Blew, Red, White and Green,
Mine Eys did evry where behold.
Great Wonders clothd with Glory did appear,
Amazement[31] was my Bliss.
That and my Wealth was evry where:
No Joy to[32] this!

Cursd and Devisd[33] Proprieties,[34]
With Envy, Avarice
And Fraud, those Feinds that Spoyl even Paradice,
Fled from the Splendor of mine Eys.
And so did Hedges, Ditches,[35] Limits, Bounds,
I dreamd not ought[36] of those,
But wanderd[37] over all mens Grounds,
And found Repose.[38]

Proprieties themselvs were mine,
And Hedges Ornaments;
Walls, Boxes, Coffers, and their rich Contents
Did not Divide my Joys, but all combine,
Clothes, Ribbans, Jewels, Laces, I esteemd
My Joys by others worn;
For me they all to wear them seemd
When I was born.

Eden

A learned[39] and a Happy Ignorance
Divided me,[40]
From all the Vanitie,
From all the Sloth Care Pain and Sorrow that advance,
The Madness and the Miserie
Of Men. No Error,[41] no Distraction[42] I
Saw soil the Earth, or overcloud the Skie.

I knew not that there was a Serpents Sting,
Whose Poyson shed
On Men, did overspread
The World: not did I dream of such a Thing
As Sin; in which Mankind lay Dead.
They all were Brisk[43] and Living Weights[44] to me,
Yea[45] Pure, and full of Immortalitie.

Joy, Pleasure, Beauty, Kindness, Glory, Lov,
Sleep, Day, Life, Light,
Peace, Melody, my Sight,
My Ears and Heart did fill, and freely[46] mov.[47]
All that I saw did me Delight.
The *Universe* was then a World of Treasure,
To me an Universal[48] World of Pleasure.

Unwelcom Penitence was then unknown
Vain[49] Costly Toys,[50]
Swearing and Roaring Boys,[51]
Shops, Markets, Taverns, Coaches[52] were unshewn;[53]
So all things were that Drownd my Joys.
No Thorns choakt up my Path, nor hid the face
Of Bliss and Beauty, nor Ecclypst[54] the place.

Only what Adam in his first Estate,[55]
Did I behold;
Hard[56] Silver and Drie[57] Gold
As yet lay under Ground; my Blessed Fate
Was more acquainted with the Old
And Innocent Delights, which he did see
In his Original Simplicitie.[58]

[29] behold [30] made beautiful
[31] overwhelming wonder
[32] to be compared with this [33] assigned
[34] rights of possession, proprietorships
[35] on the borders of fields serving as fences
[36] did not think of them in the remotest way
[37] moved freely [38] peace of mind
[39] manifesting a profound knowledge
[40] cut me off [41] false beliefs
[42] dissension [43] lively [44] creatures
[45] indeed [46] abundantly
[47] affect the emotions
[48] existing in all things
[49] foolish [50] trifles
[51] riotous fellows of the reigns of Queen Elizabeth and James I
[52] symbol of wealth
[53] unshown, unexhibited [54] cast a shadow
[55] i.e., before he fell [56] harsh [57] barren
[58] naturalness or artlessness

Those Things which first his Eden did adorn,
My Infancy
Did crown. Simplicitie
Was my Protection when I first was born.
Mine Eys those Treasures first did see,
Which God first made. The first Effects[59] of Lov
My first Enjoyments upon Earth did prov;
And were so Great, and so Divine, so Pure;
So fair and Sweet,
So True; when I did meet
Them here at first, they did my Soul allure,
And drew away my Infant feet
Quite from the Works of Men; that I might see
The Glorious Wonders of the DEITIE.[60]

My Spirit

My Naked Simple Life was I.
That Act[61] so Strongly Shind
Upon the Earth, the Sea, the Skie,
It was the Substance[62] of My Mind.
The Sence it self was I.
I felt no Dross[63] nor Matter in my Soul,
No Brims nor Borders, such as in a Bowl
We see, My Essence[64] was Capacitie.[65]
That felt all Things,
The Thought that Springs
Therfrom's it self. It hath no other Wings
To Spread abroad, nor Eys to see,
Nor Hands Distinct to feel,
Nor Knees to Kneel:
But being Simple[66] like the Deitie
In its own Centre[67] is a Sphere[68]
Not shut up here, but every Where.

It Acts not from a Centre to
Its Object as remote,
But present is, when it doth view,[69]
Being with the Being it doth note.[70]
Whatever it doth do,
It doth not by another Engine[71] work,
But by it self; which in the Act doth lurk.[72]
Its Essence is Transformed into a true
And perfect Act.
And so Exact
Hath God appeared in this Mysterious Fact,
That tis all Ey, all Act, all Sight,
And what it pleas can be,
Not only see,
Or do; for tis more Voluble[73] then Light:
Which can put on ten thousand Forms,
Being clothd with what it self adorns.

This made me present evermore
With whatsoere I saw.
An Object, if it were before
My Ey, was by Dame[74] Natures Law,
Within my Soul. Her Store
Was all at once within me; all her Treasures
Were my Immediat and Internal Pleasures,
Substantial Joys, which did inform[75] my Mind.
With all she wrought,
My Soul was fraught,[76]
And evry Object in my Heart a Thought
Begot, or was; I could not tell,
Whether the Things did there
Themselvs appear,
Which in my Spirit *truly* seemd to dwell;
Or whether my conforming[77] Mind
Were not even all that therin shind.

But yet of this I was most sure,
That at the utmost Length,[78]
(So Worthy was it to endure)
My Soul could best Express its Strength.
It was so Quick and Pure,

[59] results
[60] Creator of the universe
[61] state of accomplished fact
[62] essential nature
[63] no foreign matter
[64] absolute being, essential nature
[65] ability to receive or contain
[66] uncompounded
[67] the middle point of a sphere, the point from which influences emanate
[68] in the old astronomy a concentric, transparent, hollow globe surrounding the earth
[69] observe closely [70] take notice of
[71] instrument [72] hide itself
[73] fluent [74] Mother
[75] give form to my mind, instruct
[76] equipped with, stored
[77] acting in conformity [78] distance

That all my Mind was wholy Evry where
What ere it saw, twas ever wholy there;
The Sun ten thousand Legions off, was nigh:
The utmost Star,
Tho seen from far,
Was present in the Apple[79] of my Eye.
There was my Sight, my Life, my Sence,
My Substance and my Mind
My Spirit Shind
Even there, not by a Transeunt[80] Influence.
The Act was Immanent,[81] yet there.
The Thing remote, yet felt even here.

O Joy! O Wonder, and Delight!
O Sacred Mysterie!
My Soul a Spirit infinit!
An Image of the Deitie!
A pure Substantiall[82] Light!
That Being Greatest which doth Nothing seem!
Why twas my All,[83] I nothing did esteem
But that alone. A Strange Mysterious Sphere!
A Deep Abyss
That sees and is
The only Proper[84] Place of Heavenly Bliss.
To its Creator tis so near[85]
In Lov and Excellence
In Life and Sence,
In Greatness Worth and Nature; And so Dear;
In it, without Hyperbole,
The Son and friend of God we see.

A Strange Extended Orb of Joy,
Proceeding from within,
Which did on evry side convey
It self, and being nigh of Kin
To God did evry Way
Dilate[86] it self even in an Instant, and
Like an Indivisible Centre Stand
At once Surrounding[87] all Eternitie.
Twas not a Sphere
Yet did appear
One infinit. Twas somwhat[88] evry where.
And tho it had a Power to see
Far more, yet still it shind
And was a Mind
Exerted[89] for it saw Infinitie
Twas not a Sphere,[90] but twas a Might[91]
Invisible, and gave Light.

O Wondrous Self![92] O Sphere of Light,
O Sphere of Joy most fair;
O Act, O Power infinit;
O Subtile, and unbounded Air![93]
O Living Orb of Sight!
Thou which within me art, yet Me! Thou Ey,
And Temple of his Whole Infinitie!
O what a World art Thou! a World within!
All Things appear,
All Objects are
Alive in thee! Supersubstancial,[94] Rare,[95]
Abov them selvs, and nigh of Kin
To those pure Things[96] we find
In his Great Mind
Who made the World! tho now Ecclypsd by Sin.
There[97] they are Useful and Divine,
Exalted there they ought to Shine.

Amendment[98]

That all things should be mine;
This makes his Bounty most Divine.
But that they all more Rich should be,
And far more Brightly shine,
As usd by Me:
It ravisheth my Soul to see the End,[99]
To which this Work so Wonderfull doth tend.

[79] pupil
[80] transient, passing from one thing to another
[81] performed wholly within the mind of the subject (in contrast to a transient act)
[82] subsisting by itself
[83] everything
[84] to which the name accurately belongs
[85] closely related by kinship
[86] expand [87] with its emanations
[88] in a certain degree [89] thrust forth
[90] star [91] power
[92] that which in a person is really he
[93] breath
[94] transcending all material substance, spiritual
[95] of uncommon excellence
[96] entities [97] in that place where
[98] general improvement
[99] purpose

That we should make the Skies
More Glorious far before thine Eys,
Then Thou didst make them, and even Thee
Far more thy Works to prize,
As usd they be,
Then as they're made; is a Stupendious[100] Work,
Wherin thy Wisdom Mightily doth lurk.

Thy Greatness, and thy Love,
Thy Power, in this, my Joy doth move,
Thy Goodness and Felicitie,
In this Exprest abov
All Praise, I see:
While thy Great Godhead over all doth reign,
And such an End in such a sort[101] attain.

What Bound may we Assign
O God to any Work of thine!
Their Endlessness discovers Thee
In all to be Divine;
A DEITIE.
That wilt for evermore Exceed the End
Of all that Creatures Wit[102] can comprehend.

Am I a Glorious Spring[103]
Of Joys and Riches to my King?
Are Men made Gods! And may they see
So Wonderfull a Thing
As GOD in me!
And is my Soul a Mirror that must Shine
Even like the Sun, and be far more Divine?

Thy Soul, O GOD, doth prize
The Seas, the Earth, our Souls, the Skies,
As we return the same to Thee;
They more delight thine Eys,
And Sweeter be,
As unto Thee we Offer up the same,
Then as to us, from Thee at first they came.

O how doth Sacred Lov
His Gifts refine, Exalt, Improve!
Our Love to Creatures makes them be
In thine Esteem above
Themselvs to Thee!
O here his Goodness evermore admire[104]
He made our Souls to make his Creatures Higher.

Love

O Nectar![105] O Delicious Stream!
O ravishing[106] and only Pleasure! Where
Shall such another Theme
Inspire my Tongue with Joys, or pleas mine Ear!
Abridgement[107] of Delights!
And Queen of Sights![108]
O Mine of Rarities! O Kingdom Wide!
O more! O Caus of all! O Glorious Bride[109]
O God! O Bride of God! O King!
O Soul and Crown of evry Thing!

Did not I covet to behold
Som Endless Monarch, that did always live
In Palaces of Gold
Willing all Kingdoms Realms and Crowns to give
Unto my Soul! Whose Lov
A Spring might prov
Of Endless Glories, Honors, friendships, Pleasures,
Joys, Praises, Beauties and Celestial Treasures!
Lo, now I see there's such a King,
The fountain Head of evry Thing!

Did my Ambition ever Dream
Of such a Lord, of such a Love! Did I
Expect so Sweet a Stream
As this at any time! Could any Ey
Believ it? Why all Power
Is used here
Joys down from Heaven on my Head to shower

[100] stupendous [101] way
[102] understanding
[103] source [104] marvel at
[105] from the drink of the gods in classical mythology, any delicious draught
[106] exciting ecstasy
[107] epitome
[108] visions
[109] probably an echo of the bride of Canticles (Song of Solomon), as mystically interpreted

And Jove[110] beyond the Fiction doth appear
Once more in Golden Rain to come
To Danae's[111] Pleasing Fruitfull Womb.

His Ganimede![112] His Life! His Joy!
Or he comes down to me, or takes me up
That I might be his Boy,
And fill, and taste, and give, and Drink the Cup.
But these (tho great) are all
Too short and small,
Too Weak and feeble Pictures[113] to Express
The true Mysterious Depths of Blessedness.
I am his Image, and his Friend.
His Son, Bride, Glory, Temple, End.[114]

News

News from a forein Country came,
As if my Treasures and my Joys lay there;
So much it did my Heart enflame,
'Twas wont to call my Soul into mine Ear;
Which thither went to meet
Th' approaching Sweet,[115]
And on the Threshold stood
To entertain the secret[116] Good;
It hover'd there
As if 'twould leav mine Ear,
And was so eager to embrace
Th' expected Tidings, as they came,
That it could change its dwelling-place
To meet the voice of Fame.[117]

As if new Tidings were the Things
Which did comprise my wished unknown Treasure,
Or els did bear them on their wings,
With so much Joy they came, with so much Pleasure,
My Soul stood at the Gate
To recreäte
It self with Bliss, and woo
Its speedier Approach; a fuller view
It fain[118] would take,
Yet Journeys back would make
Unto my Heart, as if 'twould fain
Go out to meet, yet stay within,
Fitting[119] a place to entertain
And bring the Tidings in.

What Sacred Instinct did inspire
My Soul in Childhood with an hope so strong?
What secret Force mov'd my Desire
T' expect[120] my Joys beyond the Seas, so yong?
Felicity I knew
Was out of view;
And being left alone,
I thought all Happiness was gon
From Earth: for this
I long'd-for absent Bliss,
Deeming that sure beyond the Seas,
Or els in somthing near at hand
Which I knew not, since nought did pleas
I knew, my Bliss did stand.

But little did the Infant dream
That all the Treasures of the World were by,[121]
And that himself was so the Cream
And Crown of all which round about did ly.
Yet thus it was! The Gem,
The Diadem,
The Ring enclosing all
That stood upon this Earthen Ball;[122]
The hev'nly Ey,
Much wider than the Sky,
Wherin they All included were;
The Lov, the Soul, that was the King
Made to possess them, did appear
A very little Thing.

[110] chief deity of the Romans, counterpart of the Greek Zeus

[111] mother of Perseus, to whom, in the Greek myth, Zeus came in the form of a shower of gold

[112] a beautiful boy who was carried by Zeus' eagle to Olympus to be the cupbearer of the gods

[113] symbols, figures

[114] the purpose for which God made the creation

[115] sweet sound [116] unseen

[117] report [118] gladly

[119] making ready [120] look for

[121] close at hand

[122] ball of the earth

On Leaping over the Moon

I saw new Worlds beneath the Water ly,
New Peeple; yea, another Sky,
And Sun, which seen by Day
Might things more clear display.
Just such another
Of late my Brother
Did in his Travel[123] see, and saw by Night,
A much more strange and wondrous Sight:
Nor could the World exhibit such another,
So Great a Sight, but in a Brother.

Adventure strange! No such in Story we
New or old, tru or feigned, see.
On Earth he seem'd to mov
Yet Heven went abov;
Up in the Skies
His Body flies
In open, visible, yet Magick, sort:[124]
As he along the Way did sport
Over the Flood[125] he takes his nimble Course
Without the help of feigned[126] Horse.

As he went tripping o'r the King's highway,
A little pearly River lay
O'r which, without a Wing
Or Oar, he dar'd to swim,
Swim throu the Air
On Body fair;
He would not use nor trust *Icarian*[127] Wings
Lest they should prov deceitful things;
For had he faln, it had been wondrous high,
Not from, but from abov, the Sky:

He might hav dropt throu that thin Element[128]
Into a fathomless[129] Descent;
Unto the nether[130] Sky
That did beneath him ly,
And there might tell
What Wonders dwell
On Earth abov. Yet doth he briskly run,
And bold the Danger overcom;
Who, as he leapt, with Joy related soon
How *happy he* o'r-leapt the Moon.

What wondrous things upon the Earth are don
Beneath, and yet abov, the Sun?
Deeds[131] all appear again
In higher Spheres; remain
In Clouds as yet:
But there they get
Another Light, and in another way
Themselvs to us *abov* display.
The Skies themselvs this earthly Globe surround;
W'are even here[132] within them found.

On hev'nly Ground within the Skies we walk,
And in this middle Center Talk:
Did we but wisely mov,
On Earth in Hev'n abov,
Then soon should we
Exalted be
Abov the Sky: from whence whoever falls,
Through a long dismall Precipice,[133]
Sinks to the deep Abyss[134] where *Satan*[135] crawls[136]
Where horrid Death and Despair lies.

As much as others thought themselvs to ly
Beneath the Moon, so much more high
Himself he thought to fly
Above the starry Sky,
As *that* he spy'd
Below the Tide.
Thus did he yield me in the shady[137] Night
A wondrous and instructiv Light,
Which taught me that under our Feet there is,
As o'r our Heads, a Place of Bliss.

[123] Miss Wade suggests that since Philip Traherne was in Smyrna 1670–1675, this dream experience must have been reported to the poet in a letter.

[124] manner [125] water as opposed to land

[126] fabled horse like Pegasus

[127] In Greek mythology Icarus was fabled to have flown so high in his flight from Crete that the sun melted the wax which fastened on his wings and he fell into the sea.

[128] air [129] measureless

[130] lower, under the earth

[131] feats, or things done [132] on this earth

[133] headlong fall [134] infernal pit

[135] the leader of the fallen angels

[136] a reference to his assuming the form of the serpent to tempt Eve

[137] shadowy

[To the Same Purpos]

To the same purpos; he, not long before
Brought home from Nurse,[138] going to the door
To do som little thing
He must not do within,
With Wonder cries,
As in the Skies
He saw the Moon, *O yonder is the Moon*
Newly com after me to Town,
That shin'd at Lugwardin[139] *but yester-night,*[140]
Where I enjoy'd the self-same Light.
As if it had ev'n twenty thousand faces,
It shines at once in many places;
To all the Earth so wide
God doth the Stars divide[141]
With so much Art
The Moon impart,[142]
They serv us all; serv wholy ev'ry One
As if they served him alone.
While evry single Person hath such Store,
'Tis want of Sense that makes us poor.

Consummation

The Thoughts of Men appear
Freely to mov within a Sphere
Of endless Reach; and run,
Tho in the Soul, beyond the Sun.
The Ground on which they acted[143] be
Is unobserv'd Infinity.

Traversing throu the Sky,
Tho here, beyond it far they fly:
Abiding in the Mind
An endless Liberty they find:
Throu-out all Spaces can extend,
Nor ever meet or know an End.

They, in their native Sphere,
At boundless Distances appear:
Eternity can measure;
Its no Beginning see with Pleasure.
Thus in the Mind an endless Space
Doth nat'rally display its face.

Wherin becaus we no
Object distinctly find or know;
We sundry Things invent,
That may our Fancy giv content;[144]
See Points of Space beyond the Sky,
And in those Points see Creatures ly.

Spy Fishes in the Seas,
Conceit them swimming there with Eas;
The Dolphins and the Whales,
Their very Finns, their very Scales,
As there within the briny Deep
Their Tails the flowing Waters sweep.

Can see the very Skies,
As if the same were in our Eys;
The Sun, tho in the Night,
As if it mov'd within our Sight;
One Space beyond another still
Discovered; think while[145] ye will.

Which, tho we don't descry,
(Much like by night an useless Ey,
Not shaded with a Lid,
But in a darksom Dungeon hid)
At last shall in a glorious Day
Be made its Objects to display

And then shall Ages be
Within its wide Eternity;
All Kingdoms stand,
Howe're remote, yet nigh at hand;
The Skies, and what beyond them ly,
Exposed unto evry Ey.

Nor shall we then invent
Nor alter Things; but with content
All in their places see,
As doth the Glorious Deity;
Within the Scope of whose Great Mind,
We all in their tru Nature find.

[138] from living with a nurse
[139] a little town about nine miles from Hereford
[140] last night
[141] dispense
[142] bestow
[143] carried out in action
[144] satisfaction
[145] as long as

Hosanna

No more shall Walls, no more shall Walls confine
That glorious Soul which in my Flesh doth shine:
No more shall Walls of Clay or Mud
Nor Ceilings made of Wood,
Nor Crystal Windows, bound my Sight,
But rather shall admit Delight.
The Skies that seem to bound
My Joys and Treasures,
Of more endearing Pleasures
Themselvs becom a Ground:[146]
While from the Center to the utmost Sphere
My Goods[147] are multiplied evry where.

The Deity, the Deity to me
Doth All things giv, and make me clearly see
The Moon and Stars, the Air and Sun
Into my Chamber[148] com:
The Seas and Rivers hither flow,
Yea, here the Trees of Eden grow,
The Fowls and Fishes stand,
Kings and their Thrones,
As 'twere, at my Command;
God's Wealth, His Holy Ones,
The Ages too, and Angels all conspire:
While I, that I the Center am, admire.

No more, No more shall Clouds eclyps my Treasures,
Nor viler Shades obscure my highest Pleasures;
No more shall earthen Husks confine
My Blessings which do shine
Within the Skies, or els *abov:*
Both Worlds one Heven made by Lov,
In common happy I
With Angels walk
And there my Joys espy;
With God himself I talk;
Wondring with Ravishment all Things to see
Such *Reall* Joys, so truly *Mine*, to be.

No more shall Trunks and Dishes be my Store,
Nor Ropes of Pearl, nor Chains of Golden Ore;
As if such Beings yet were not,
They all shall be forgot.
No such in Eden did appear,
No such in Heven: Heven here
Would be, were those remov'd;
The Sons of Men
Liv in Jerusalem,[149]
Had they not Baubles lov'd.
These Clouds dispers'd, the Hevens clear I see.
Wealth new-invented, *mine* shall never be.

Transcendent Objects doth my God provide,
In such convenient[150] Order all contriv'd,
That All things in their proper place
My Soul doth best embrace,
Extends its Arms beyond the Seas,
Abov the Hevens its self can pleas,
With God enthron'd may reign:
Like sprightly[151] Streams
My Thoughts on Things remain;
Ev'n as som vital[152] Beams
They reach to, shine on, quicken[153] Things, and make 59
Them truly Usefull; while I *All* partake.[154]

For Me the World created was by Lov;
For Me the Skies, the Seas, the Sun, do mov;
The Earth for Me doth stable[155] stand;
For Me each fruitful Land
For Me the very Angels God made *His*
And *my* Companions in Bliss:
His Laws command all Men
That they lov Me,
Under a Penalty
Severe, in case they miss:
His Laws require His Creatures all to prais
His Name, and when they do't be most my Joys.

[146] earth
[147] possessions
[148] private room
[149] the holy city
[150] appropriate

[151] lively, full of animation
[152] endowed with life
[153] animate, make alive
[154] share in
[155] firm

from CENTURIES OF MEDITATIONS[1]

THE FIRST CENTURY

8

What is more easy and sweet than meditation? Yet in this hath God commended[2] His Love, that by meditation it is enjoyed. As nothing is more easy than to think, so nothing is more difficult than to think well. The easiness of thinking we received from God, the difficulty of thinking well proceeded from ourselves. Yet in truth, it is far more easy to think well than ill, because good thoughts be sweet and delightful: Evil thoughts are full of discontent and trouble. So that an evil habit and custom have made it difficult to think well, not Nature. For by nature nothing is so difficult as to think amiss.

9

Is it not easy to conceive the World in your Mind? To think the Heavens Fair? The Sun Glorious? The Earth Fruitful? The Air Pleasant? The Sea Profitable? And the Giver Bountiful? Yet these are the things which it is difficult to retain. For could we always be sensible[3] of their use and value, we should be always delighted with their wealth and glory.

10

To think well is to serve God in the interior[4] court: To have a mind composed of Divine Thoughts, and set in frame,[5] to be like Him within. To conceive aright and to enjoy the world, is to conceive[6] the Holy Ghost,[7] and to see His Love: which is the Mind of the Father. And this more pleaseth Him than many Worlds, could we create as far and great as this. For when you are once acquainted with the world, you will find the goodness and wisdom of God so manifest therein, that it was impossible another, or better should be made. Which being made to be enjoyed, nothing can please or serve Him more, than the Soul that enjoys it. For that Soul doth accomplish the end[8] of His desire in Creating it.

11

Love is deeper than at first it can be thought. It never ceaseth but in endless things. It ever multiplies. Its benefits and its designs are always infinite. Were you not Holy, Divine, and Blessed in enjoying the World, I should not care so much to bestow it. But now in this you accomplish the end of your creation, and serve God best, and please Him most: I rejoice in giving it. For to enable you to please GOD, is the highest service a man can do you. It is to make you pleasing to the King of Heaven, that you may be the Darling[9] of His bosom.

12

Can you be Holy without accomplishing the end for which you are created? Can you be Divine unless you be Holy? Can you accomplish the end for which you were created, unless you be Righteous? Can you then be Righteous, unless you be just in rendering to Things their due esteem? All things were made to be yours, and you were made to prize them according to their value: which is your office and duty, the end for which you were created, and the means whereby you enjoy. The end for which you were created, is that by prizing all that God hath done, you may enjoy yourself and Him in Blessedness.

13

To be Holy is so zealously to desire, so vastly to esteem, and so earnestly to endeavour it, that we would not for millions of gold and silver, decline, nor fail, nor mistake in a tittle.[10] For then we please God when we are most like Him. We are like Him when our minds are in frame. Our minds are in frame when our thoughts are like His. And our thoughts are then

[1] Text: Dobell, 1927, reprinted by permission of P. J. and A. E. Dobell.
[2] entrusted [3] aware
[4] as of the Temple in Jerusalem
[5] order
[6] understand
[7] the Holy Spirit, the Third Person of the Trinity
[8] intended result
[9] favorite [10] the smallest part

like His when we have such conceptions of all objects as God hath, and prize all things according to their value. For God doth prize all things rightly, which is a Key that opens into the very thoughts of His bosom. It seemeth arrogance to pretend to the knowledge of His secret thoughts. But how shall we have the Mind of God, unless we know His thoughts? Or how shall we be led by His divine spirit, till we have His Mind? His thoughts are hidden: but He hath revealed unto us the hidden Things of Darkness. By His works and by His attributes we know His Thoughts: and by thinking the same, are Divine and Blessed.

14

When things are ours in their proper places, nothing is needful but prizing[11] to enjoy them. God therefore hath made it infinitely easy to enjoy, by making everything ours, and us able so easily to prize them. Everything is ours that serves us in its place. The Sun serves us as much as is possible, and more than we could imagine. The Clouds and Stars minister unto us, the World surrounds us with beauty, the Air refresheth us, the Sea revives the earth and us. The Earth itself is better than gold because it produceth fruits and flowers. And therefore in the beginning, was it made manifest to be mine, because Adam[12] alone was made to enjoy it. By making one, and not a multitude, God evidently shewed one alone to be the end of the World and every one its enjoyer. For every one may enjoy it as much as He.

15

Such endless depths lie in the Divinity, and in the wisdom of God, that as He maketh one, so He maketh every one the end of the World: and the supernumerary[13] persons being enrichers of his inheritance. Adam and the World are both mine. And the posterity of Adam enrich it infinitely. Souls are God's jewels, every one of which is worth many worlds. They are His riches because His image, and mine for that reason. So that I alone am the end of the World: Angels and men being all mine. And if others are so, they are made to enjoy it for my further advancement. God only being the Giver and I the Receiver. So that Seneca[14] philosophized rightly when he said "*Deus me dedit solum toti Mundo, et totum Mundum mihi soli*":[15] God gave me alone to all the World, and all the World to me alone.

16

That all the World is yours, your very senses and the inclinations of your mind declare. The Works of God manifest, His laws testify, and His word doth prove it. His attributes most sweetly make it evident. The powers of your soul confirm it. So that in the midst of such rich demonstrations, you may infinitely delight in God as your Father, Friend and Benefactor, in yourself as His Heir, Child and Bride,[16] in the whole World, as the Gift and Token of His love; neither can anything but Ignorance destroy your joys. For if you know yourself, or God, or the World, you must of necessity enjoy it.

17

To know GOD is Life Eternal. There must therefore some exceeding Great Thing be always attained in the Knowledge of Him. To know God is to know Goodness. It is to see the beauty of infinite Love: To see it attended with Almighty Power and Eternal Wisdom; and using both those in the magnifying of its object. It is to see the King of Heaven and Earth take infinite delight in *Giving*. Whatever knowledge else you have of God, it is but Superstition. Which Plutarch[17] rightly defineth, to be an *Ignorant Dread of His Divine Power, without any joy in His goodness*. He is not an Object of Terror, but Delight. To know Him therefore as He is, is to frame[18] the most beautiful idea

[11] proper valuing of them

[12] the first man

[13] extra

[14] Lucius Annaeus Seneca, Roman Stoic philosopher and moral writer (4? B.C.–65 A.D.)

[15] translated in the following sentence

[16] from Solomon's Song, the soul as the bride of God

[17] Greek historian, biographer, and moralist (46?–120?)

[18] give shape to, form

in all Worlds. He delighteth in our happiness more than we: and is of all other the most Lovely Object. An infinite Lord, who having all Riches, Honors, and Pleasures in His own hand, is infinitely willing to give them unto me. Which is the fairest idea that can be devised.

18

The WORLD is not this little Cottage of Heaven and Earth. Though this be fair, it is too small a Gift. When God made the World He made the Heavens, and the Heavens of Heavens,[19] and the Angels, and the Celestial Powers. These also are parts of the World: So are all those infinite and eternal Treasures that are to abide for ever, after the Day of Judgment.[20] Neither are these, some here, and some there, but all everywhere, and at once to be enjoyed. The WORLD is unknown, till the Value and Glory of it is seen: till the Beauty and the Serviceableness of its parts is considered. When you enter into it, it is an illimited[21] field of Variety and Beauty: where you may lose yourself in the multitude of Wonders and Delights. But it is an happy loss to lose oneself in admiration[22] at one's own Felicity: and to find GOD in exchange for oneself. Which we then do when we see Him in His Gifts, and adore His Glory.

THE THIRD CENTURY

1

Will you see the infancy of this sublime and celestial greatness? Those pure and virgin apprehensions I had from the womb, and that divine light wherewith I was born are the best unto this day, wherein I can see the Universe. By the Gift of God they attended me into the world, and by His special favour I remember them till[23] now. Verily they seem the greatest gifts His wisdom could bestow, for without them all other gifts had been dead and vain.[24] They are unattainable by book, and therefore I will teach them by experience. Pray for them earnestly: for they will make you angelical, and wholly celestial. Certainly Adam in Paradise had not more sweet and curious[25] apprehensions[26] of the world, than I when I was a child.

2

All appeared new, and strange at first, inexpressibly rare and delightful and beautiful. I was a little stranger, which at my entrance into the world was saluted and surrounded with innumerable joys. My knowledge was Divine. I knew by intuition those things which since my Apostasy,[27] I collected again by the highest reason. My very ignorance was advantageous. I seemed as one brought into the Estate of Innocence. All things were spotless and pure and glorious: yea, and infinitely mine, and joyful and precious. I knew not that there were any sins, or complaints[28] or laws. I dreamed not of poverties,[29] contentions or vices. All tears and quarrels were hidden from mine eyes. Everything was at rest,[30] free and immortal. I knew nothing of sickness or death or rents or exaction, either for tribute[31] or bread. In the absence of these I was entertained like an Angel with the works of God in their splendour and glory, I saw all in the peace of Eden; Heaven and Earth did sing my Creator's praises, and could not make more melody to Adam, than to me. All time was Eternity, and a perpetual Sabbath.[32] Is it not strange, that an infant should be heir of the whole World, and see those mysteries which the books of the learned never unfold?

3

The corn was orient[33] and immortal wheat, which never should be reaped, nor was ever sown. I thought it had stood from everlasting to everlasting. The dust and stones of the street were as precious as

[19] the highest of the seven heavens of the Jews, being the abode of God
[20] when all things are revealed, and the good and the bad forever separated
[21] unbounded
[22] wonder [23] up till

[24] devoid of real worth [25] attentive
[26] sympathetic perceptions
[27] fall from that first innocence
[28] lamentations [29] used in plural then
[30] in repose [31] price of security
[32] day of rest [33] brilliant, resplendent

gold: the gates[34] were at first the end of the world. The green trees when I saw them first through one of the gates transported and ravished me, their sweetness and unusual beauty made my heart to leap, and almost mad with ecstasy, they were such strange and wonderful things. The Men! O what venerable and reverend creatures did the aged seem! Immortal Cherubims![35] And young men glittering and sparkling Angels, and maids strange seraphic[36] pieces of life and beauty! Boys and girls tumbling in the street, and playing, were moving jewels. I knew not that they were born or should die; But all things abided eternally as they were in their proper places. Eternity was manifest in the Light of the Day, and something infinite behind everything appeared: which talked[37] with my expectation and moved my desire. The city seemed to stand in Eden, or to be built in Heaven. The streets were mine, the temple was mine, the people were mine, their clothes and gold and silver were mine, as much as their sparkling eyes, fair skins and ruddy faces. The skies were mine, and so were the sun and moon and stars, and all the World was mine; and I the only spectator and enjoyer of it. I knew no churlish proprieties,[38] nor bounds, nor divisions: but all proprieties and divisions were mine: all treasures and the possessors of them. So that with much ado[39] I was corrupted, and made to learn the dirty devices of this world. Which now I unlearn, and become, as it were, a little child again that I may enter into the Kingdom of God.[40]

7

The first Light which shined in my Infancy in its primitive[41] and innocent clarity was totally eclipsed: insomuch that I was fain[42] to learn all again. If you ask me how it was eclipsed? Truly by the customs and manners of men, which like contrary winds blew it out: by an innumerable company of other objects, rude, vulgar, and worthless things, that like so many loads of earth and dung did overwhelm and bury it: by the impetuous torrent of wrong desires in all others whom I saw or knew that carried me away and alienated me from it: by a whole sea of other matters and concernments[43] that covered and drowned it: finally by the evil influence of a bad education that did not foster and cherish it. All men's thoughts and words were about other matters. They all prized new things which I did not dream of. I was a stranger and unacquainted with them; I was little and reverenced their authority; I was weak, and easily guided by their example: ambitious also, and desirous to approve[44] myself unto them. And finding no one syllable in any man's mouth of those things, by degrees they vanished, my thoughts (as indeed what is more fleeting than a thought?) were blotted out; and at last all the celestial, great, and stable[45] treasures to which I was born, as wholly forgotten, as if they had never been.

8

Had any man spoken of it, it had been the most easy thing in the world, to have taught me, and to have made me believe that Heaven and Earth was God's House, and that He gave it me. That the Sun was mine, and that men were mine, and that cities and kingdoms were mine also: that Earth was better than gold, and that water, every drop of it was a precious jewel. And that these were great and living treasures: and that all riches whatsoever else was dross in comparison. From whence I clearly find how docible[46] our Nature is in natural things, were it rightly entreated.[47] And that our misery proceedeth ten thousand times more from the outward bondage of opinion and custom, than from any inward corruption or deprava-

[34] of the garden(?) of the city(?)
[35] the second order of angels of the Dionysian hierarchy, excelling in knowledge
[36] from seraphim, another order of heavenly beings, these excelling in love
[37] conferred
[38] proprietorships
[39] much trouble
[40] See Mark 10.15.
[41] belonging to the first age
[42] glad
[43] interests
[44] exhibit to advantage
[45] permanent
[46] teachable
[47] handled

tion[48] of Nature: And that it is not our parents' loins, so much as our parents' lives, that enthrals and blinds us. Yet is all our corruption derived from Adam: inasmuch as all the evil examples and inclinations of the world arise from his sin.[49] But I speak it in the presence of God and of our Lord Jesus Christ, in my pure primitive virgin Light, while my apprehensions were natural, and unmixed, I cannot remember but that I was ten thousand times more prone to good and excellent things than evil. But I was quickly tainted and fell by[50] others.

9

It was a difficult matter to persuade me that the tinselled ware upon a hobby-horse[51] was a fine thing. They did impose upon me, and obtrude[52] their gifts that made me believe a ribbon or a feather curious.[53] I could not see where was the curiousness or fineness: And to teach me that a purse of gold was of any value seemed impossible, the art[54] by which it becomes so, and the reasons for which it is accounted so, were so deep and hidden to my inexperience. So that Nature is still nearest to natural things, and farthest off from preternatural;[55] and to esteem that the reproach of Nature, is an error in them only who are unacquainted with it. Natural things are glorious, and to know them glorious: but to call things preternatural, natural, monstrous. Yet all they do it, who esteem gold, silver, houses, lands, clothes, etc., the riches of Nature, which are indeed the riches of invention. Nature knows no such riches: but art and error makes them. Not the God of Nature, but Sin only was the parent of them. The riches of Nature are our Souls and Bodies, with all their faculties, senses, and endowments. And it had been the easiest thing in the whole world [to teach me] that all felicity consisted in the enjoyment of all the world, that it was prepared for me before I was born, and that nothing was more divine and beautiful.

10

Thoughts are the most present things to thoughts, and of the most powerful influence. My soul was only apt[56] and disposed to great things; but souls to souls are like apples to apples, one being rotten rots another. When I began to speak and go, nothing began to be present to me, but what was present to me in their thoughts. Nor was anything present to me any other way, than it was so to them. The glass of imagination was the only mirror, wherein anything was represented or appeared to me. All things were absent which they talked not of. So I began among my playfellows to prize a drum, a fine coat, a penny, a gilded book, etc., who before never dreamed of such wealth. Goodly objects to drown all the knowledge of Heaven and Earth! As for the Heavens and the Sun and Stars they disappeared, and were no more unto me than the bare walls. So that the strange riches of man's invention overcame the riches of Nature, being learned more laboriously and in the second place.

11

By this let nurses, and those parents that desire Holy Children learn to make them possessors of Heaven and Earth betimes,[57] to remove silly objects from before them, to magnify nothing but what is great indeed, and to talk of God to them, and of His works and ways before they can either speak or go. For nothing is so easy as to teach the truth because the nature of the thing confirms the doctrine:[58] As when we say the sun is glorious, a man is a beautiful creature, sovereign over beasts and fowls and fishes, the stars minister unto us, the world was made for you, etc. But to say this house is yours, and these lands are

[48] corruption
[49] disobedience
[50] through the agency of others
[51] a stick with the head of a horse on which boys pretended to ride
[52] thrust forcibly
[53] skilfully wrought
[54] artifice
[55] unnatural
[56] suited
[57] early
[58] instruction

another man's, and this bauble is a jewel and this gew-gaw a fine thing, this rattle makes music, etc., is deadly barbarous[59] and uncouth[60] to a little child; and makes him suspect[61] all you say, because the nature of the thing contradicts your words. Yet doth that blot out all noble and divine ideas, dissettle his foundation, render him uncertain in all things, and divide him from God. To teach him those objects are little vanities, and that though God made them, by the ministry of man, yet better and more glorious things are more to be esteemed, is natural and easy.

[59] uncivilized [60] strange [61] distrust

Charles Sackville, Earl of Dorset

CHARLES SACKVILLE, Lord Buckhurst, and presently third Earl of Middlesex (1675) and sixth Earl of Dorset (1677), stands in age as about the middle of the younger group of famous wits and rakes of the household of Charles II (see Rochester). He was born in January, 1643. His education was private except for a short period under Busby at Westminster and included the usual period of travel on the continent. His grandmother had been governess to Charles I's children and it is likely that Charles II held grateful recollections of her and her husband's care. In 1661 Dorset first entered Parliament. He was out twice at least with the gentlemen who served at sea against the Dutch. In 1668 he became Groom and in 1669, Gentleman of the Bedchamber to the King, with whom he was a great personal favorite. From 1670 on, except for a brief period in 1688–1689, he was Lord Lieutenant of Sussex—where lie the Sackville family estates—a post of importance as well as dignity in the troubled times around the Revolution of 1688. He was several times a member of missions to France. Under James he lived in retirement. Under William and Mary he became Lord Chamberlain (chief administrator of the Court) and was several times one of the regents who advised the Queen in William's absence. His first marriage was late (1674) and was ended by his wife's death in five years. A second marriage in 1685 led to his "settling down." After years of second widowerhood he married again, unsuitably, a year before his own death in 1706.

Like Sedley and Rochester, Dorset wrote for private circulation, and apart from what got into miscellanies, he was not published until *The Works of the Earls of Rochester, Roscommon, Dorset, etc.* (1714 and again 1718, etc.); and *The Works of the Most Celebrated Minor Poets* (1749). The canon of his poems has been considered by Helen A. Bagley, "A Checklist of the Poems of Charles Sackville," *MLN* XLVII (1932) and R. G. Howarth, "Some Additions to the Poems of Lord Dorset," *MLN* L (1935); and several poems not hitherto printed as his are tentatively assigned to him by Brice Harris in his *Charles Sackville, Sixth Earl of Dorset*. This is a full study of his life and work but reserves final discussion of text and canon until a proposed edition is ready. Meanwhile, his poems as listed by Johnson may be found in Anderson or Chalmers. Johnson did a brief life. For further criticisms see the general bibliography.

Dorset's position, and even more his generosity, make us discount things that were said of his gifts and influence by his contemporaries. There is very little of his work and it is slight. But it has the casual ease, the frankness, and the grace, of the speech of an experienced man of the world of assured place. His two satires (against Edward Howard, a minor one of the mob of gentlemen who wrote with ease) written about 1669, are really, as Pope observed, no more than epigrams. They give pungent expression, however, to the myth so well used by Dryden and Pope, of the writer who is deliberately dull, a considered practitioner of the art of sinking in poetry. His lyrics are direct, at best, terse; at least, phlegmatic. In the ironic or critical lyric with which the wits defended or derided their own sophistication, he directs his aim against the harsh or superannuated beauty, an object also of his loved Horace. His directness attracts one's attention to his fondness for old ballads.

To the drama he contributed only Act IV of a translation of P. Corneille's *Pompey*. But his interest in the drama and his influence on it are represented in Dryden's *Essay of Dramatick Poesie*, in which, as Eugenius, he defends the moderns. That defense was amply born out by patronage, and willingness to read and comment on manuscripts of writers at large. Out of the great fortunes he inherited and amassed by eager solicitation and exploitation of posts and grants and privileges under two sovereigns, he was a very generous patron to very many writers, Dryden one of the chief, particularly after he had lost the laureateship and was in opposition to Dorset. The evidence suggests that with the ablest among them his intercourse was genial and on terms of intellectual equality. He, with his assured position and long tradition, rather than Rochester, affords us the pattern of the great governing aristocracy of the eighteenth century and their patronage of the arts.

SONG

Written at Sea, in the First Dutch War, 1665, The Night before an Engagement[1]

To all you ladies now at land
 We men at sea indite;
But first wou'd have you understand
 How hard it is to write;
The Muses now, and Neptune[2] too,
We must implore to write to you,
 With a fa, la, la, la, la.

For tho' the Muses should prove kind,
 And fill our empty brain;
Yet if rough Neptune rouze the wind,
 To wave the azure main,
Our paper, pen, and ink, and we,
Roll up and down our ships at sea,
 With a fa, &c.

Then, if we write not by each post,
 Think not we are unkind;
Nor yet conclude our ships are lost
 By Dutchmen, or by wind:
Our tears we'll send a speedier way,
The tide shall bring 'em twice a day.
 With a fa, &c.

The king with wonder, and surprize,
 Will swear the seas grow bold;
Because the tides will higher rise,
 Than e'er they us'd of old:
But let him know it is our tears
Bring floods of grief to Whitehall stairs.
 With a fa, &c.

Should foggy Opdam[3] chance to know
 Our sad and dismal story;
The Dutch wou'd scorn too weak a foe,
 And quit their fort at Goree:
For what resistance can they find
From men who've left their hearts behind!
 With a fa, &c.

Let wind and weather do its worst,
 Be you to us but kind;
Let Dutchmen vapour, Spaniards curse,
 No sorrow we shall find:
'Tis then no matter how things go,
Or who's our friend, or who's our foe.
 With a fa, &c.

[1] Text for all poems: *Works of the Most Celebrated Minor Poets*. The poem was almost certainly written at sea during the first campaign in 1664, and not a year later. Ault prints a version slightly less smooth and with a different order of stanzas from a manuscript of the reign of Charles. It is to the ballad tune of Shackley-hay. Ault gives an earlier ms. version.

[2] Roman god of the sea

[3] the Dutch admiral, who actually did not venture out to an engagement that year but remained under the guns of the island fort of Goree

To pass our tedious hours away,
  We throw a merry main;[4]
Or else at serious ombre[5] play;
  But, why should we in vain
Each others ruin thus pursue?
We were undone when we left you.
  With a fa, &c.

But now our fears tempestuous grow,
  And cast our hopes away;
Whilst you, regardless of our woe,
  Sit careless at a play:
Perhaps permit some happier man
To kiss your hand, or flirt your fan.
  With a fa, &c.

When any mournful tune you hear,
  That dies in ev'ry note;
As if it sigh'd with each man's care,
  For being so remote;
Think then how often love we've made
To you, when all those tunes were play'd.
  With a fa, &c.

In justice you cannot refuse,
  To think of our distress;
When we for hopes of honour lose
  Our certain happiness;
All those designs are but to prove
Ourselves more worthy of your love.
  With a fa, &c.

And now we've told you all our loves,
  And likewise all our fears;
In hopes this declaration moves
  Some pity from your tears:
Let's hear of no inconstancy,
We have too much of that at sea.
  With a fa, la, la, la, la.

SONG[6]

Phillis, for shame let us improve
  A thousand diff'rent ways,
Those few short moments snatch'd by love,
  From many tedious days.

If you want courage to despise
  The censure of the grave,
Though love's a tyrant in your eyes,
  Your heart is but a slave.

My love is full of noble pride,
  Nor can it e'er submit,
To let that fop, discretion, ride
  In triumph over it.

False friends I have, as well as you,
  Who daily counsel me
Fame and ambition to pursue,
  And leave off loving thee.

But when the least regard I shew
  To fools, who thus advise,
May I be dull enough to grow
  Most miserably wise.

SONG[7]

Dorinda's[8] sparkling wit, and eyes,
  United, cast too fierce a light,
Which blazes high, but quickly dies,
  Pains not the heart, but hurts the sight.

Love is a calmer, gentler joy,
  Smooth are his looks, and soft his pace;
Her Cupid is a black-guard[9] boy,
  That runs his link full in your face.

[4] at dice

[5] a card game popular as the bridge of our day

[6] Ault prints a version from *Westminster Drollery*, I, 1671.

[7] Ault gives an identical version of 1701.

[8] Katherine Sedley, daughter of Sir Charles, who was attached to the Court by 1676 and became a witty, termagant mistress of James, Duke of York.

[9] The word derives from a group of idle, dirty boys that haunted the Horse-Guards and stables and rode horses to water (Pinto, *Sir Charles Sedley*).

SONG[10]

Methinks the poor town has been troubled too long,
With Phillis and Chloris in every song;
By fools, who at once can both love and despair,
And will never leave calling 'em cruel and fair;
Which justly provokes me in rhime to express
The truth that I know of bonny black Bess.[11]

This Bess of my heart, this Bess of my soul,
Has a skin white as milk, and hair black as a coal;
She's plump, yet with ease you may span her round waist,
But her round swelling thighs can scarce be embrac'd:
Her belly is soft, not a word of the rest;
But I know what I think, when I drink to the best.

The plowman and 'squire, the arranter clown,
At home she subdu'd in her paragon-gown;
But now she adorns both the boxes and pit,
And the proudest town-gallants are forc'd to submit;
All hearts fall a leaping wherever she comes,
And beat day and night, like my lord Craven's Drums.[12]

I dare not permit her to come to Whitehall,
For she'd out-shine the ladies, paint, jewels, and all:
If a lord shou'd but whisper his love in a crowd,
She'd sell him a bargain,[13] and laugh out aloud:
Then the queen over-hearing what Betty did say,
Would send Mr. Roper[14] to take her away.

But to those that have had my dear Bess in their arms,
She's gentle, and knows how to soften her charms;
And to every beauty can add a new grace,
Having learn'd how to lisp, and to trip in her pace;
And with head on one side, and a languishing eye,
To kill us by looking as if she would die.

[10] published as a broadside, 1673, and numerous times in Playford's *Songs*

[11] one Bess Barnes (Ault)

[12] Lord Craven commanded a troop called out on March 24, 1668, to supress a mob of apprentices pulling down bawdy-houses on a holiday. (Ault)

[13] make a fool of him (by a bawdy rejoinder)

[14] a page of honor to the queen (Ault)

Sir Charles Sedley

SEDLEY was born in March, 1639, a posthumous child. As a child, he spent several years abroad with his mother. In 1656, at the age of seventeen, he went for a period to Wadham College, Oxford; and in the same year, on the death of his older brother, he inherited the baronetcy and very large estates, which he did not leave large. From 1656 until the Restoration, he and the young wife he had married in 1657 lived to amuse themselves, without serious responsibilities or prospects of responsibility. After the Restoration, he attached himself to the Court, becoming with his particular friend Buckhurst one of the earliest of the famous court wits, notable during the reign of Charles for wild escapades and casual pleasures, for light lyrics and ballads, asserting the triumph of youth and celebrating or mocking those pleasures, and for that interest in the drama, as writers and patrons, which created Restoration comedy. Sedley was Shadwell's patron and is Lisideus of Dryden's *Essay of Dramatick Poesie*, which gives us our chief account of Sedley's critical views. (For a further account of his position at Court, see Rochester.) From 1668 on, Sedley sat almost continuously in Parliament, with a steadily developing sense of responsibility. In 1670 he was a member of a diplomatic mission to France, and was in France at least one other time. Toward 1680 he moved to a "whig" position. He accepted cordially the Revolution of 1688. In 1672, he had arranged for his then insane wife (of a Roman Catholic family) to withdraw to a convent in France and after going through a form of marriage entered into an enduring union with Ann Ayscough. He died in 1701.

Sedley's verse, very little in all, was chiefly written for his intimates at Court during the Restoration, though a few pieces were penned much later. It began to be published in miscellanies—together with verses erroneously ascribed to him—by 1671 or 1672. In 1702 was published by Captain Ayloffe (a nephew of Anne Ayscough) *The Miscellaneous Works*, very probably from a manuscript prepared by Sedley himself. Several of the lyrics were in this edition considerably altered from early versions. This collection was followed by a number of editions all purporting to be more complete, but filled with poems rejected by his modern editor, V. de Sola Pinto, *The Poetical and Dramatic Works of Sir Charles Sedley* (1928). This edition contains a discussion of the canon, full textual notes, and a bibliography, and at the end, doubtful ascriptions. The 1702 volume contains lyrics, a few translations, including some epigrams of Martial and the fourth Georgic of Virgil, a partial version of his *Antony and Cleopatra* (here called *Beauty the Conqueror*), and some brief speeches delivered in Parliament. His plays include part of a translation of P. Corneille's *Pompey*, 1664; *The Mulberry Garden*, 1675; *Antony and Cleopatra*, 1677; *Bellamira* (an adaptation of Terence), 1687; and possibly *The Grumbler* (a translation from the French), published 1719. V. de Sola Pinto published a critical and biographical study, *Sir Charles Sedley*, in 1927. A definitive study of his milieu was made by Wilson, and a fine critical essay by Whibley in The *Cambridge History*, Vol. VIII, Chap. 8.

Rochester said of Sedley that he had

that prevailing gentle Art,
That can with a resistless Charm impart,
The loosest Wishes to the Chastest Heart.

In his verse we find easy simplicity rather than intensity, penetration, or finality. He does not strike the note of passion, (though his most famous lyric opens with a figure that resounds with the echo of a long tradition) nor of irony, but of carefree grace or light mockery. The logic or witty debate of his lyric reminds one of Carew, though it is apt to run on after his point is made; but the frank rendering of immediate feelings and confusions is of the Restoration. His translation of Virgil's georgic, despite a proneness to generality characteristic of the age, is a thing of remarkable grace. It contributes to the development of the couplet a number of sweet melodies which Pope was later to weave into his own rich and subtle variety.

SONG[1]

Phillis, let's shun the common Fate,
And let our Love ne'r turn to Hate;
I'll dote no longer then I can,
Without being call'd a faithless Man.
When we begin to want Discourse,
And Kindness seems to taste of Force,
As freely as we met, we'll part,
Each one possest of their own Heart.
Thus whilst rash Fools themselves undo;
We'll Game, and give off Savers too;[2]
So equally the Match we'll make,
Both shall be glad to draw the Stake!
A Smile of thine shall make my Bliss,
I will enjoy thee in a Kiss;
If from this Height our Kindness fall,
We'll bravely scorn to Love at all:
If thy Affection first decay,
I will the Blame on Nature lay.
Alas, what cordial can remove
The hasty Fate of dying Love?
Thus we will all the World excel
In Loving, and in Parting well.

SONG

Love still has something of the Sea,
From whence his Mother[3] rose;
No time his Slaves from Doubt can free,
Nor give their Thoughts repose:

They are becalm'd in clearest Days,
And in rough Weather tost;
They wither under cold Delays,
Or are in Tempests lost.

One while they seem to touch the Port,
Then straight into the Main,
Some angry Wind in cruel sport
The Vessel drives again.

At first Disdain and Pride they fear,
Which if they chance to 'scape,
Rivals and Falshood soon appear
In a more dreadful shape.

By such Degrees to Joy they come,
And are so long withstood,
So slowly they receive the Sum,
It hardly does them good.

'Tis cruel to prolong a Pain,
And to defer a Joy;[4]
Believe me, gentle *Celemene*
Offends the winged Boy.

An hundred thousand Oaths your Fears
Perhaps would not remove;
And if I gaz'd a thousand Years
I could no deeper love.

[1] Text for all poems: *Miscellaneous Works*, 1702

[2] We'll play (at dice or cards) and give over without loss or gain. (Pinto)

[3] Venus, goddess of love

[4] The semi-colon should probably come after line 21, *Pain;*.

THE INDIFFERENCE

Thanks, fair *Urania;* to your Scorn
I now am free, as I was born,
Of all the Pain that I endur'd
By your late Coldness I am cur'd.

In losing me, proud Nymph, you lose
The humblest Slave your Beauty Knows;
In losing you, I but throw down
A cruel Tyrant from her Throne.

My ranging Love did never find
Such Charms of Person and of Mind;
Y'ave Beauty, Wit, and all things know,
But where you shou'd your Love bestow.

I unawares my Freedom gave,
And to those Tyrants grew a Slave;
Would you have kept what you had won,
You should have more Compassion shewn.

Love is a Burthen, which two Hearts,
When equally they bear their Parts,
With Pleasure carry; but no one,
Alas, can bear it long alone.

I'm not of those who court their Pain,
And make an Idol of Disdain;
My Hope in Love does ne'er expire,
But it extinguishes Desire.

Nor yet of those who ill receiv'd,
Wou'd have it otherwise believ'd
And, where their Love cou'd not prevail,
Take the vain Liberty to rail.

Whoe'er wou'd make his Victor less,
Must his own weak Defence confess,
And while her Power he does defame,
He poorly doubles his own Shame.

Even that Malice does betray,
And speak Concern another way;
And all such Scorn in Men is but
The Smoke of Fires ill put out.

He's still in Torment, whom the Rage
To Detraction does engage;
In Love Indifference is sure
The only sign of perfect Cure.

SONG[5]

Hears not my *Phillis,* how the Birds
  Their feather'd Mates salute?
They tell their Passion in their Words;
  Must I alone be mute?
Phillis, *without Frown or Smile,*
Sat and knotted[6] *all the while.*

The God of Love in thy bright Eyes
  Does like a Tyrant reign;
But in thy Heart a Child he lyes,
  Without his Dart or Flame.
Phillis *without,* etc.

So many Months in Silence past,
  And yet in raging Love,
Might well deserve one Word at last
  My Passion shou'd approve.
Phillis *without,* etc.

Must then your faithful Swain expire,
  And not one Look obtain,
Which he to sooth his fond Desire,
  Might pleasingly explain?
Phillis *without,* etc.

ADVICE TO THE OLD BEAUX

Scrape no more your harmless Chins,
  Old Beaux, in hope to please;
You shou'd repent your former Sins,
  Not study their Increase;
Young awkard Fops, may shock our Sight,
But you offend by Day and Night.

In vain the Coachman turns about,
  And whips the dappl'd Greys;
When the old Ogler looks out,
  We turn away our Face.
True Love and Youth will ever charm,
But both affected, cannot warm.

[5] Pinto in his edition gives Purcell's music for this song.

[6] netting, a handicraft akin to crocheting, recently popular

Summer-fruits we highly prise,
They kindly cool the Blood;
But Winter berries we despise,
And leave 'em in the Wood;
On the Bush they may look well,
But gather'd, lose both taste and smell.

That you languish, that you dye,
Alas, is but too true;
Yet tax not us with Cruelty,
Who daily pity you.
Nature henceforth alone accuse,
In vain we grant, if she refuse.

SONG

Smooth was the Water, calm the Air,
The Evening-Sun deprest,
Lawyers dismist the noisie Bar,
The Labourer at rest,

When *Strephon*, with his charming Fair,
Cross'd the proud River *Thames*,
And to a Garden did repair,
To quench their mutual Flames.

The crafty Waiter soon espy'd
Youth sparkling in her Eyes;
He brought no Ham, nor Neats-tongues dry'd,
But Cream and Strawberries.

The amorous *Strephon* ask'd the Maid,
What's whiter than this Cream?
She blush'd, and could not tell, she said:
Thy Teeth, my pretty Lamb.

What's redder, than these Berries are?
I know not, she reply'd:
Those lips, which I'll no longer spare,
The burning Shepherd cry'd.

And strait began to hug her:
This Kiss, my Dear,
Is sweeter far
Than Strawberries, Cream and Sugar.

SONG

Phillis is my only Joy,
Faithless as the Winds or Seas;
Sometimes coming, sometimes coy,
Yet she never fails to please;
If with a Frown
I am cast down,
Phillis smiling,
And beguiling,
Makes me happier than before.

Tho', alas, too late I find,
Nothing can her Fancy fix;
Yet the Moment she is kind,
I forgive her all her Tricks;
Which, tho' I see,
I can't get free;
She deceiving,
I believing;
What need Lovers wish for more?

SONG (from *The Mulberry-Garden*, III, ii)[7]

Ah Cloris! that I now could sit
As unconcern'd, as when
Your Infant Beauty cou'd beget
No pleasure, nor no pain.

When I the dawn us'd to admire,
And prais'd the coming day;
I little thought the growing fire
Must take my Rest away.

Your Charms in harmless Childhood lay,
Like metals in the mine,
Age from no face took more away,
Than Youth conceal'd in thine.

But as your Charms insensibly
To their perfection prest,
Fond Love as unperceiv'd did flye,
And in my Bosom rest.

[7] Text, 1668

My passion with your Beauty grew,
And *Cupid* at my heart,
Still as his mother favour'd you,
Threw a new flaming Dart.

Each glori'd in their wanton part,
To make a Lover he
Employ'd the utmost of his Art,
To make a Beauty she.

Though now I slowly bend to love
Uncertain of my Fate,
If your fair self my Chains approve,
I shall my freedom hate.

Lovers, like dying men, may well
At first disorder'd be,
Since none alive can truly tell
What Fortune they must see.

William Wycherly

WYCHERLY was born in 1614. At about the age of fifteen he was sent to France, where he was educated in a cultured circle in the provinces. In 1660 he went for a brief period to Oxford and then was for a while a law student at the Inner Temple. Shortly he became a member of the group of court wits (see Rochester). Following his first play, *Love in a Wood*, 1617, he became intimate with the Duchess of Cleveland, one of the chief mistresses of the King. Three other plays succeeded: *The Gentleman Dancing Master*, 1673; *The Country Wife*, 1675; *The Plain Dealer*, 1677, probably the third play to be written. In 1679 or 1680 he married the Countess of Drogheda. He was several times in prison for debt. On his death-bed he married a second time. He died in 1716.

Besides his plays, his *Miscellany Poems* were published in 1704, and his *Posthumous Works*, Volume I, (ed. Theobald) in 1728, and Volume II, (ed. Pope) in 1729. Minor pieces were: *Hero and Leander in Burlesque*, (anonymously) 1669; *Epistles to the King and Duke*, 1683; *The Idleness of Business, a Satyr*, 1705; *On his Grace the Duke of Marlborough*, 1707. This volume contains his maxims as well as poems. W. C. Ward edited his plays in 1888; Montague Summers, his *Complete Works* in four volumes, in 1924. Two studies are Charles Perromat, *William Wycherly, sa vie—son oeuvre*, 1921, and Willard Connely, *Brawny Wycherly*, 1930. For his general setting see Wilson (general bibliography).

We do not know the date of Wycherly's poems; but the themes, including a large number on drinking, suggest that many of them were written in the period when he was a court wit of the Restoration. The drinking songs bear out to the full Rochester's observation to Savile on the disillusion that underlay the drinking, as the thought, of the wits. Early poems have been revised before publication in 1704. We do know that later poems were revised by young Pope, who made Wycherly's acquaintance in 1704.

Wycherly's reputation, higher now than at any time since the Restoration, rests upon his plays, by far the greatest of their period. In poetry he lacks concentration, vividness, lucidity, control of rhetoric, and music. Nonetheless he has a point of view to express, and where he gives it reign, experience of men. Whether most of his poems were written some time near his plays or a good bit later, their deeply sardonic note rounds out our impression of the Court of Charles and sustains us in a serious interpretation of the group. Wycherly's view of the world is skeptical in thought, acutely pessimistic in tone, troubled by gross or coarse images, without free play of imagination. What man can know is immediately clear to him; more subtle reason either by its dialectic deprives him of religion and hope (whether these promise realities or whether to possess them is only to be well-deceived, one cannot in different poems be sure), or it is the instrument of his passions. Ambition is but selfishness leading to enslavement, and

if one have innocence or honesty of purpose in the world, detraction will not let it live. His habit of writing is integral to his view; a series of paradoxes that hammer home his disillusioning point and end by giving it after all a weight which his lack of poetry would seem to deny.

UPON THE MOST USEFUL KNOWLEDGE, CRAFT OR CUNNING, WHICH IS MORE WISDOM, AS 'TIS LESS WIT[1]

Cunning, Wise, Cautious, Folly is, by which,
(Whilst Wit does beggar Man) they grow more Rich;
Wise Folly, on which Weak Men most rely,
And the most honourable Knavery,
Term'd by the Wise and Great, Sage Policy.
Wise Folly, and most honourable Fear,
Does most, in hiding of itself, appear:
Whence they, who seem of Wit and Wisdom too,
More shy, as more they seek themselves to show;
(Since Cunning hides it self,) distrust not it,
Which better Sense most often does out-wit,
And speaks itself, by Taciturnity,
Which ev'n in Fools, were Sense and Policy;
So, by its subtil Silence, still thinks fit,
To prove more Wisdom, as it shows less Wit;
Which minds its Int'rest most, as Honour least,
Then, as most useful Wisdom, 'tis the best,
Whilst Wit seeks Fame more than its Interest;
When Craft prefers its Int'rest to its Fame,
Thinks nought, that's its Advantage, is its Shame,
Whose Prudence, 'tis its Wisdom's to conceal,
Whilst Wisdom, is its Knowledge to reveal;
By which it is incapable to do
The safe, wise, great Things, which by Craft (we know)
Are done, since Wisdom's open to its Foe;
Will him, to his opposing it, defie,
Whilst Cunning for her's does in Ambush lie;
Wisdom does lose its End, for being known,
Gives Foes Suspicion, by its being shown;
Whilst its Design, wise Cunning cannot miss,
Since it by true Sense least suspected is;
Which since half Sense, half Policy, half Wit,
Puzzles true Sense, the more to deal with it;
In spight of Wit, it plays Discretion's part,
Since the best Skill is, to conceal one's Art;
And the Head's Prudence, not to show the Heart:
He's most Wise then, who seems to be so least.
Who hides his Wit, his Sense to manifest;
So Cunning proves the truest Wisdom then,
Which has no vain Aim ever to be seen;
True Wisdom, if sage Prudence, subtil Wit
It be, to be most shy of showing it;

[1] Text: *Miscellany Poems*, 1704

And that is the sole Reason, Cunning can
Its Credit more i'th' world than Wit maintain;
More in the World, than wit or Wisdom do,
Who seem so bold, so bold, so busie, forward too,
To show themselves; that they by their Pretence
To more Sense, show more their Impertinence;
'Till they their Folly, by their Sense proclaim,
Seek Praise, before their Profit, (to their Shame)
Whilst Profit before Praise, is Cunning's Aim:
When vainer Wisdom gives it self the Lie,
From ostentatious Self-sufficiency,
Becomes the greatest Folly, Vanity;
Whilst Craft proves Wisdom by its shunning Pride,
True Prudence, which itself to show, must hide,
Since ineffectual 'tis, when once 'tis spy'd;
If the true Politician's wisest Aim,
Be, not to keep from Guilt, but Guilt from Shame;
And since the greatest Aim now Wise Men have,
Is less their Virtue than their Fame to save,
They Credit keep, safely to play the Knave;
Stand on their Honour, tho' dishon'rably,
But by their false pretended Honesty,
To cheat those most, who most on it rely:
But by their Knavery, their Honour gain,
Since without Wealth, none Honour can maintain;
Whilst foolish Wits, more to their Reason's blame,
Will to their Profit still prefer their Fame,
To make sought Praise, by Vanity, their Shame:
When Craft its Sense, concealing it, has shown,
Since better thought of, but as less 'tis known;
So does, because itself it wou'd not show,
Too hard for Pow'r, Wealth, Wit, or Wisdom grow;
Then shou'd go for true Policy, nay Wit,
Since Men, undone by that, are made by it;
Whilst down-right Honesty, Wit, Wisdom are
Foes to their Friends, whom they keep Poor, and Bare,
To keep Men in more Want, more Fear, or Care.
Then, dull Plain-dealing, which by Truth seeks Fame,
By Man's pretence to Honour, grows his Shame;
And Wit preferring still, to Profit Praise,
Shou'd of[2] the Proof of Sense, turn its Disgrace.
But Cunning's Wit, nay Wisdom, Honour too;
Which can for all Three, without either go,
And can more than all Three together do,
To make Knaves gain Trusts, Int'rest, Credit, Fame,
To merit Censure, yet to bear no Blame,
To make their Fraud their Praise, though others Shame:
Then Cunning shou'd for the best Science go,
Which without Learning, does best Knowledge show;
Does Wit, Pow'r, Art, by Nature Best out-do;
Strange Science! since all Wisdom, Courage, Wit,
Must to it universally submit:

[2] out of, from

It rules the World, in spight of True Wit, so,
(Tho' but its Bastard-Brother) ought to go,
Like Bastards, for the Wiser of the Two;
Which (whilst the other makes Man less to thrive;)
Does help her Man the better still to live:
Which, tho' tis often call'd Sinister-Sense,[3]
Against Right Reason, makes the best Defence;
Which gives it, of its Foes, most Diffidence:[4]
Whilst where to have it, Right Sense never knows;
Since it ne'er by right Rules of Reason goes;
A Slight i'th' Brain 'tis, like a Slight in Strength,
The better Side makes of the worse, (at length;)
As Cheats by Tricks at Cards will cozen still
Those, who have in the true Play better Skill;
So Cunning then is Wisdom's highest Pitch;
'Tis, as at Cards, a Trick in Shuffling, which,
More than good Play, bold Pushers will enrich:
It is a Trick, which seems an Art, 'till known;
But shames the skilful Shuffler, and proves none,
When once it comes above-board to be shown;
'Tis Bastard-Sense, and like all Bastards so,
Does in the World but more successful grow,
Than the True, which does True Wits most undo.

A DRINKING-SONG, AGAINST ALL SORTS OF DISPUTES IN DRINKING; TO ONE, WHO ALWAYS BAWL'D TO HAVE REASON DONE HIM, AND WAS NOISIE, AND QUARRELSOM IN HIS CUPS

Come, Sons of *Mars*,[5] who thirst for Blood,
Here is that, of the Ruddy Grape,
To show, your Courage still is good,
A Bottle let no Head escape;

By drinking prove, both Strong, and Stout,
And bate[6] no Man, in Drink, an Ace,
But make your Man set Foot to Foot,
The Quarrelsom up with his Glass;

Be like Brave Men of Courage still,
Ne'r leave the Noble Work undone,
Till you your Bold Defyers kill,
Them thro' the Guts with Claret run;

Make Cowards kneel, with held-up Hands,
Braves[7] swallow, with their Wine, your Lie,
Knock him down, who your Health withstands,
To do you Reason, dares deny;

Shock Man, and Glass, make Gallons bounce,
To your Man's Nose, present the Glass,
So fire your Pipes, and Blood, at once,
Till dead-drunk, all fall on the Place;

Yet, without Noise in Drink, be Brave,
All true stout Drinkers, silent are;
But they, who Loud still, Reason crave,[8]
Will soonest beg you, them to spare;

Reason our Foe, let us destroy,
Which still disturbs us, when we drink;
Which lets us not our selves enjoy,
But puts us to the pains to think;

[3] *Sinister*, Latin for *left*, here means both *left*, *of evil import* (as left-hand omens are), *bastard*, (as bastards are children of the left hand)

[4] distrust

[5] Roman god of War

[6] diminish, be less than no man by a jot but make your man enter into equal combat

[7] bullies

[8] demand reasons

Which, more Disputes begins, than ends,
  Since it makes squabling Enemies,
Instead of kind, agreeing Friends,
  So Men, for Talking, much less Wise;

There's no Philosophy like Wine,
  Which does our Reason elevate;
It has a Quality Divine,
  Raising us above Human State:

Makes Man contemn Pow'r, Gold, and Love,
  Scorn Plagues, and Poverty, to bear;
And makes him think himself above,
  All Worldly Care, or Human Fear;

Poor Poets! then drink, and be Rich;
  Poor Spirits! drink till you grow Brave;
Proud Men! drink to the Highest Pitch;
  Drink Misers, till enough you have:

Soldiers, Slaves, Men of Bus'ness, take
  Your Glass off, if you'd active be;
For as the Head is made more weak,
  Man is more busie, bold, and free.

TO A WITTY MAN OF WEALTH AND QUALITY; WHO, AFTER HIS DISMISSAL FROM COURT, SAID, HE MIGHT JUSTLY COMPLAIN OF IT

You cannot justly of the Court complain,
Who, by Loss of your Place, your Freedom gain;
Who love your Liberty (as you say,) more,
Than either Titles, Honours, Wealth, or Pow'r;
Then are you Honour'd, by your Court-Disgrace,
Which turn'd you but out of a Servile Place;
Where you a Bond-slave to your Passions were,
Your Pride, Revenge, Lust, Avarice, or Fear,
There favour'd most, since no more Suffer'd there;
Since the best Grace a Good Man there can have,
Is to be made a Free-Man of a Slave;
Pow'r o'er himself, not others there to gain,
By being made more Great still, as less Vain;
Since Titles, Honours, grow his Infamy,
Who them must buy, with Guilt, or Slavery,
And gain Commands, by Loss of Liberty;
So more his Shame, must dear-bought Honour grow,
But as he more does for it, give, or ow;
And for it, he can give no Prize so high,
As are his Virtue, Faith, or Liberty;
Nor for Court-Grants, can give so great a Rate,
As he, who for 'em, leaves a good Estate,
Leaves great Commands, on others but to wait;
The best Command that any Man can have,
Over his Passions, to be less a Slave,
The less he does, of Wealth, Pow'r, Honour, crave;
To which Command, the Great, with Wealth, or Pow'r,
Attain but less, as they of both have more;
Which is, the Greater Pow'r, and Nobler yet,
As harder for the Rich, and Great, to get;
Is more, as Man with less is satisfied,
Since our own Satisfactions are deny'd,
More by our selves, as more's our Lust, or Pride;
If Av'rice, Pride, increase with Wealth or Pow'r,
Great Minds, by their Increase, are lessen'd more;

Whence, to be truly Great, or Rich, and Wise,
Fame, Wealth, Pow'r, none shou'd covet, but despise;
Wherefore 'tis said, a Man from Court shou'd go,
To go for Wise, Just, Honourable too;
Whose Scorn of Honours, Honour to him does,
Till his Humility his Glory grows,
Whilst his Vain-Glory wou'd True Honour lose;
Since all Court-Honours, which, with Titles raise
Men to more Pride, their Virtue more debase,
To make Court-Favour grow their worst Disgrace;
Whilst Love of Liberty, Contempt of Pow'r,
Less'ning Pride, Av'rice, make Man's Honour more,
Above the World, raising the Humble Mind,
Make Man more Free, as more his Aims confin'd
By Reason are; which curbs his Passions still,
And makes him, to his Fate, subject his Will,
Spight of his Fate, his Pleasure to fulfil;
To make him, by his Patience, and Content,
Sure of his Good Chance, and his Bad prevent;[9]
To disapoint all Envy, and Disgrace,
More to his Honour, to scorn Wealth, Pow'r, Praise;
Since Men deserve less Fortune, Pow'r, or Fame,
But as more vainly, they to more lay Claim;
Then, he deserves them most, who scorns them most,
Which most, but by Mens seeking them, are lost;
A Court-Disgrace, is no Man's Loss or Shame,
Till 'tis, for his ill bearing it, his Blame;
Till it his Trouble, or Resentment grows,
And he, for it, his Loss of Temper shows;
Court-Banishment, is but our Change of Place,
Which oft we do, for Pleasure, Choice, or Ease;
'Tis Change of Air, of Life, of Company,
Which pleases more, as done more willingly,
And out of our Love of Variety;
So that a Court-Dismissal to your Ease,
Is less your Banishment, than your Release;
With you shou'd, as with Honest Wise Men, pass,
But rather for your Honour, than Disgrace,
Since Crimes must gain, and keep at Court a Place;
And still, the Honestest, as Wisest sort
Of Men, chuse to dismiss themselves from Court;
The Court has then, more gracious to you been,
Putting you out, than when it took you in;
Since sure, the greatest Obligation still,
Is that, that's done a Man against his Will;
Which spares the Lazy, Proud, yet Bashful Wit,
The Trouble, Pains, or Shame of asking it.

[9] anticipate

A SONG: IN THE NAME OF A LOVER, TO HIS MISTRESS; WHO SAID, SHE HATED HIM FOR HIS GREY HAIRS, WHICH HE HAD AT THIRTY

O hate me not for my Gray Hair,
  Since you love still[10] Variety,
The Black, the Red, the Brown, the Fair,
  All in their Turns, delight your Eye;

Knots[11] of two Colours, nay of three,
  Can please you better than of one;
My Party-colours[12] then shou'd be,
  Better than all White, or all Brown;

You, when a Garland, you wou'd make,
  Not Flowers of the same Colour chuse;
But Various-coloured ones wou'd take,
  Change, but[13] in me, you wou'd refuse;

Wou'd you a Bracelet weave, or brede,[14]
  You'd different-colour'd Ribbons take;
To set off your Hair of your Head,
  With Powder Grey you make of[15] Black;

You the Grey Morning us'd to love,
  Which promis'd you Good Days and Bright;
Why then a Grey Head disapprove?
  Promising you a Pleasant Night;

Then hate me not for my Grey Hairs,
  Which are not so much mine, as thine;
Since caused but by the Grief and Cares,
  Thy Love gave me, so thine, not mine.

[10] always [11] rosettes [12] various colors [13] only [14] braid [15] from

John Wilmot, Second Earl of Rochester

JOHN WILMOT, second Earl of Rochester, was born in 1647. Before he entered his teens, he had inherited from his father the earldom and a debt of gratitude from King Charles for the first Earl's service in exile and for his securing of the King's escape after Worcester. In January, 1660, he went up to Wadham College, Oxford, and there in September 1661 he had the degree of M.A. conferred upon him. In 1661 he went abroad for several years with an able tutor supplied by the King. In the winter of 1664–1665 he came to Court, then seventeen, handsome, magnetic, gay, well-educated but of restless tastes. In 1666 he became a Gentleman of the Bedchamber to the King, in 1668, Gamekeeper for the County of Oxford, and in 1674, Ranger and Keeper of Woodstock Park. In 1665 and again in 1666 he served with notable courage among the gentlemen who went to sea with the fleet in the engagements against the Dutch. In 1667 he married an heiress of considerable fortune (though not enough to make him independent of his employments) whom he had tried to abduct two years earlier. From his first entry into the Court, he served there except for periods in the country to look after his estates, to recuperate his health from the excesses of his London life, or to wear out a disgrace because of an escapade, a quarrel with a royal mistress, or a too violent lampoon of the King. Lesser banishments were spent with friends in escapades, and at least one period in France. After a prolonged struggle with ill health, he died in 1680, worn down by exhaustion, syphilis and the mercury taken to cure it, and drink. During the last year of his life, he entered into serious conversations on religion with Gilbert, afterward Bishop, Burnett, and some weeks before his death he was converted under the ministrations of the family chaplain. The lesson of his life and repentance was spread abroad in Burnett's account of the conversations, which give a very illuminating view of the intellectual currents of the time. Recent studies of Rochester are the introduction to *The Collected Works*, ed. John Hayward (1926); Johannes Prinz, *John Wilmot, Earl of Rochester*, *Palestra* Vol. CLIV (1927); V. de Sola Pinto, *Rochester, Portrait of a Poet*, containing some manuscript versions of his poems, (1935); Charles Williams, *Rochester* (1935), an interpretation of his character; and Kenneth Murdock's briefer study of Rochester's place as a personality in the changing thought of the age, in *The Sun at Noon* (1939). Detail in all these works needs to be checked with the most recent studies of him by J. H. Wilson in his definitive edition of *The Rochester-Savile Letters* (1941) and his general study of *The Restoration Court Wits* (1948).

When Rochester entered the Court and the King's household, he became one of a band of wits living in and near the cluster of buildings known as the palace of Whitehall, the Gentlemen and Grooms of the Bedchamber to the King. His poetry arises from his life here, and it was for each other that the group of wits wrote their verses, to be passed around among them, or, if it were satire or lampoon, to be vented anonymously through the coffee-house, or "dropped" in Court, and perhaps reach the public in a broadside. A brief view of the situation and philosophy of these court wits is therefore the best commentary on Rochester's poetry. A group of brilliant young men was thrown together, to form some deep friendships and some grating enmities; a group small enough to feel quarrels and jealousies with peculiar bitterness, but large enough to feel to the full the sense of privilege which their inherited social position, their service about the King's person, their intelligence, and their common sophistication gave them, and to make their tastes and their judgment felt as patrons and arbiters of drama and poetry. Two of them, Etherege and Wycherly, described their lives or those akin to them in the most distinguished comedy of the Restoration proper and Rochester contributed to the drama only a version of Beaumont and Fletcher's *Valentinian,* two comic scenes, and possibly a lascivious closet play, *Sodom;* but he was an interested patron and arbiter. The not very clear story of his shifting and scornful patronage is reflected in his lively *Allusion to Horace.*

Those of the group in whom ambition and the tradition of public service were strong found employment of increasing importance on embassies and in administration of the Court. Rochester's interest did not lie there, and he was already dead at the age when Sedley and Dorset were settling into harness. It was the common philosophy of the group to devote to the immediate pleasures of wine, sex, and intrigue their abundant energies unemployed in business or writing. In this, they never lacked companionship; and the morality of the Court and the King's liking for them gave them absolute countenance and support in their pursuits, short of acts which the King felt to infringe upon his essential dignity, such as acts of violence in the presence, duels, extreme lampoons. On the other hand, their sense of superiority as wits was only partial compensation for a position bitterly galling to a man of penetration and sensibility, or of pride like Rochester's. They were expected to serve the King's interest unquestioningly in Parliament, of which many of them were members; they lived in the midst of flattery, treachery, self-seeking—more or less lived by it themselves. They had no power to advise the King, unless it were on literary matters. They themselves depended on the good-will of the King's mistresses, and they saw how the King's leading advisers used the mistresses, successfully as it appeared to them, to manage the King, while England drifted into weakness abroad and confusion at home. The consciousness of their slavery, which the reading of Epicurus might infuse in them, intensified the bitterness of their position. We are told, in the account of Rochester's repentance, that his friends plied him constantly with wine for the sake of the wit it evoked in him; but we reach a deeper truth in his own words that only in the third bottle did he and his intimates get below the tissue of their environment to dare words of honesty to each other. At the same time, Rochester's reported conversations with Burnett, as well as his verses, show the dry rationalism, the materialistic habit of imagination, the dread of enthusiasm binding him within the world which undeniably released certain powers in him, but which he scorned.

Rochester's poetry reflects his experience and his philosophy with the penetrating intelligence and the artistic detachment which his genius made possible. He, like his companions and like his prototype the *libertin* Suckling, felt that man had only the passing moment with its sensations and intuitions, and that his aim must be to secure immediate pleasures "short of injury to one's neighbor or the state." The anti-romantic philosophy of the *libertins* or Epicurus or Hobbes (rather as depicted by his opponents than in his wholeness) sharpened and gave confidence to a way of life that arose from situation and temperament, even while edging the hardness and irony that experience brought him. For the outcome did not answer to the philosophy, and the picture given in his verse is of men committed to live in the moment which is all they have, yet persistently conscious of time past and time to come, and shadowed by the threat of impotence that derides the life of sensation, as sensation had derided reason; to find that jealousy and pain are the necessary salt to sensation; to glimpse what enduring love might give and know one's fall from it; to see a kingdom betrayed by sensualities gross and dishonest. In his lampoons against the King, he stands with Marvell as one of the founders of satire against a kingdom in bankruptcy. His *Satyr Against Mankind* expresses a more general, cold, if somewhat turgid, contempt of life as he had found and made it. The design of it owes much to Boileau's eighth satire; and he begins like Boileau and other skeptics with a picture of the contempt of the beasts for man and his supposed reason. But from the ironic, traditional implication in Boileau's calm and deliberate picture that man has grown thus evil by abuse of reason as it is commonly understood, Rochester turns at first with hardness and then with fury to express his own philosophy: reason properly understood is only an instrument of sense and power, most useful when it achieves most commandingly the knavery and hypocrisy which, even if we had it not, is all the world would allow us. The most famous portrait of Rochester shows him crowning with laurels a favorite monkey, a deliberate symbol replacing the death's head so ubiquitous in earlier seventeenth-century art. His real range is represented in *A Letter from Artemisa.*

To his satire, Rochester brings a command of ironic situation, telling detail, a gift for epithet, and a scornful energy of line hardly to be met again till it is surpassed in certain passages of Pope's *Dunciad.* His lyrics are marked by lucidity, polished familiar ease, and a music which controls their tone firmly.

There was no good edition of Rochester before our time. A few pieces were published in broadsides during his life. Untrustworthy collections appeared for nearly a century after his death. The best of these is that edited by Rhymer for Tonson (1691 and 1696). Prinz's volume includes a bibliography and all of Rochester's letters, though subject to correction. The best edition, containing the poems, *Valentinian,* and the letters, is that by Hayward, with critical introduction and textual and explanatory notes (1926). It contains, however, some poems not by Rochester. A selection by H. Levin (1942) uses some manuscripts in making the text and contains a short critical introduction. That by Johns (1933) offers some alternative texts. Thorpe's facsimile (1950) of a copy of the earliest of the editions (1680 and following) dated Antwerp but probably actually printed in London (with a full *apparatus criticus* of variations in that edition) makes available the indecencies which were in some at least of the poems as Rochester wrote and circulated them, and which were removed from the 1691 edition. Among essays may be mentioned Johnson's *Life.* R. Ham in his study of *Otway and Lee* (1943) considers Rochester as a patron and the influence of Hobbes on his circle. Elton has an essay in his *The English Muse* (1933), and Whibley a criticism in the *Cambridge History,* Volume VIII, Chapter 8.

A DIALOGUE BETWEEN STREPHON AND DAPHNE[1]

STREPHON

Prithee now, fond[2] Fool, give o'er;
Since my Heart is gone before,
To what purpose shou'd I stay?
Love commands another way.

DAPHNE

Perjur'd Swain, I knew the time
When Dissembling was your Crime.
In pity now employ that Art
Which first betray'd, to ease my Heart.

STREPHON

Women can with pleasure feign:
Men dissemble still with pain.
What advantage will it prove
If I lye, who cannot love?

DAPHNE

Tell me then the reason why,
Love from Hearts in Love does fly?
Why the Bird will build a Nest,
Where he ne'er intends to rest?

STREPHON

Love, like other little Boys,
Cries for Hearts, as they for Toys:
Which, when gain'd, in Childish Play,
Wantonly are thrown away.

DAPHNE

Still on Wing, or on his Knees,
Love does nothing by degrees:
Basely flying when most priz'd,
Meanly fawning when despis'd:
Flatt'ring or insulting ever,
Generous and grateful never:
All his joys are fleeting Dreams,
All his Woes severe Extreams.

STREPHON

Nymph, unjustly you inveigh;
Love, like us, must Fate obey.
Since 'tis Nature's Law to Change,
Constancy alone is strange.
See the Heav'ns in Lightnings break,
Next in Storms of Thunder speak;
'Till a kind Rain from above
Makes a Calm,—so 'tis in Love.
Flames begin our first Address,
Like meeting Thunder we embrace:
Then you know the Show'rs that fall
Quench the fire, and quiet all.

DAPHNE

How shou'd I these Show'rs forget,
'Twas so pleasant to be wet?
They kill'd Love, I knew it well,
I dy'd[3] all the while they fell.
Say at least what *Nymph* it is
Robs my Breast of so much Bliss?
If she is fair, I shall be eas'd,
Thro' my Ruin you'll be pleas'd.

STREPHON

Daphne never was so fair:
Strephon, scarcely, so sincere.
Gentle, Innocent, and Free,
Ever pleas'd with only me.
Many Charms my Heart enthral,
But there's one above 'em all:
With aversion she does fly
Tedious, trading, Constancy.

DAPHNE

Cruel Shepherd! I submit;
Do what Love and you think fit:
Change is Fate, and not Design;
Say you wou'd have still been mine.

STREPHON

Nymph, I cannot: 'Tis too true,
Change has greater Charms than you:
Be, by my Example, wise,
Faith to Pleasure sacrifice.

DAPHNE

Silly Swain, I'll have you know,
'Twas my practice long ago:
Whilst you vainly thought me true,
I was false in scorn of you.
By my Tears, my Heart's disguise,
I thy Love and thee despise
Womankind more Joy discovers
Making Fools, than keeping Lovers.

[1] Text: the second Rhymer edition, Tonson 1694

[2] silly

[3] punning upon the use of *die* for the experiencing of sexual consummation

A SONG

Absent from thee I languish still;
Then ask me not, When I return?
The Straying Fool 'twill plainly kill,
To wish all Day, all Night to mourn.

Dear; from thine Arms then let me flie,
That my fantastick[4] Mind may prove,
The Torments it deserves to try,
That tears my fixt Heart from my Love.

When wearied with a world of Woe,
To thy safe Bosom I retire,
Where Love and Peace and Truth does flow,
May I contented there expire.

Lest once more wandring from that Heav'n,
I fall on some base Heart unblest;
Faithless to thee, false, unforgiven,
And lose my everlasting Rest.

LOVE AND LIFE. A SONG

All my past Life is mine no more,
The flying Hours are gone:
Like transitory Dreams giv'n o'er,
Whose Images are kept in store,
By Memory alone.

The Time that is to come is not;
How can it then be mine?
The present Moment's all my Lot;
And that, as fast as it is got,
Phillis, is only thine.

Then talk not of Inconstancy,
False Hearts, and broken Vows;
If I, by Miracle, can be
This live-long Minute true to thee,
'Tis all that Heav'n allows.

UPON DRINKING IN A BOWL

Vulcan[5] contrive me such a Cup
As *Nestor*[6] us'd of old:
Shew all thy Skill to trim it up;
Damask[7] it round with Gold.

Make it so large that, fill'd with Sack[8]
Up to the swelling Brim,
Vast Toasts, on the delicious Lake,
Like Ships at Sea, may swim.

Engrave not Battel on his Cheek;
With War I've nought to do:
I'm none of those that took *Mastrick,*
Nor *Yarmouth* Leaguer knew.[9]

Let it no Name of Planets tell,
Fixt Stars, or Constellations;
For I am no Sir *Sindrophel,*[10]
Nor none of his Relations.

But carve thereon a spreading Vine;
Then add two lovely Boys;
Their Limbs in amorous Folds intwine,
The Type of future Joys.

Cupid and *Bacchus*[11] my Saints are;
May Drink and Love still reign:
With Wine I wash away my Cares,
And then to Love again.

[4] given to fancy and therefore, in the conception of the day, shifting
[5] smith of the gods, who also made works for favored heroes
[6] the hero of the older generation in Homer's *Iliad*
[7] inlay a pattern
[8] a famous dry wine
[9] referring to the seige of Maestricht in Holland by the French and the gathering of English troops at Yarmouth (both 1673)
[10] an allusion to Samuel Butler's satire on the scientists
[11] the gods of love and wine

A SONG

My dear Mistress has a Heart
Soft as those kind Looks she gave me;
When with Love's resistless Art,
And her Eyes, she did enslave me.
But her Constancy's so weak,
She's so wild, and apt to wander;
That my jealous Heart wou'd break,
Should we live one Day asunder.

Melting Joys about her move,
Killing Pleasures, wounding Blisses;
She can dress her Eyes in Love,
And her Lips can arm with Kisses.
Angels listen when she speakes,
She's my Delight, all Mankinds Wonder:
But my jealous Heart would break,
Should we live one Day asunder.

A LETTER FROM ARTEMISA IN THE TOWN, TO CLOE, IN THE COUNTRY

Cloe, by your Command, in Verse I write:
Shortly you'll bid me ride astride, and fight:
Such Talents better with our Sex agree,
Than lofty Flights of dangerous Poetry.
Among the men, I mean the Men of Wit,
(At least they past for such before they writ)
How many bold Advent'rers for the Bays,
Proudly designing large Returns of Praise,
Who durst that stormy, pathless World explore,
Were soon dasht back, and wreckt on the dull Shore,
Broke of that little Stock they had before.
How wou'd a Womans tott'ring Barque[12] be tost,
Where stoutest Ships (the Men of Wit) are lost?
When I reflect on this, I straight grow wise;
And my own self I gravely thus advise:

Dear *Artemisa!* Poetry's a Snare:
Bedlam[13] has many Mansions; have a care:
Your Muse diverts you, makes the Reader sad:
You think your self inspir'd; he thinks you mad.
Consider too, 'twill be discreetly done,
To make your self the Fiddle of the Town.
To find the ill-humour'd Pleasure at their heed:
Curst when you fail, and scorn'd when you succeed.
Thus, like an arrant[14] Woman, as I am,
No sooner well convinc'd Writing's a shame;
That *Whore* is scarce a more reproachful Name
Than Poetess——
Like Men that marry, or like Maids that woo,
Because 'tis th' very worst thing they can do:
Pleas'd with the Contradiction, and the Sin,
Methinks I stand on Thorns till I begin.

Y' expect to hear, at least, what Love has past
In this lewd Town, since you and I saw last;
What change has happen'd of Intrigues, and whether
The old ones last, and who and who's together.

[12] (small) three-masted vessel [13] Bethlehem Hospital for the insane [14] downright

But how, my dearest *Cloe*, shou'd I set
My Pen to write, what I wou'd fain forget?
Or name that lost thing *Love*, without a Tear,
Since so debauch'd by ill-bred Customs here?
Love, the most gen'rous Passion of the Mind;
The softest Refuge Innocence can find;
The safe Director of unguided Youth:
Fraught with kind Wishes, and secur'd by Truth:
That Cordial-drop Heav'n in our Cup has thrown,
To make the nauseous Draught of Life go down:
On which one only Blessing God might raise,
In Lands of Atheists, Subsidies of Praise:
For none did e'er so dull, and stupid, prove,
But felt a God, and blest his Pow'r in Love:
This only Joy, for which poor we are made,
Is grown, like Play,[15] to be an arrant Trade:
The Rooks[16] creep in, and it has got, of late,
As many little Cheats, and Tricks, as that.
But, what yet more a Womans Heart wou'd vex,
'Tis chiefly carry'd on by our own Sex:
Our silly Sex, who, born like Monarchs, free,
Turn Gipsies for a meaner Liberty;
And hate Restraint, tho' but from Infamy:
They call whatever is not common Nice,
And, deaf to Nature's Rule, or Love's advice,
Forsake the Pleasure to pursue the Vice.
To an exact Perfection they have brought
The action Love; the Passion is forgot.
'Tis below Wit, they tell you, to admire;
And ev'n without approving they desire.
Their private Wish obeys the publick Voice,
'Twixt good and bad Whimsey decides, not Choice.
Fashions grow up for taste, at Forms they strike;
They know what they wou'd have, not what they like.
Bovy's[17] a Beauty, if some few agree
To call him so, the rest to that degree
Affected are, that with their Ears they see.
Where I was visiting the other Night,
Comes a fine Lady, with her humble Knight,
Who had prevail'd with her, through her own Skill,
At his Request, though much against his Will,
To come to *London*———
As the Coach stopt, I heard her Voice, more loud
Than a great-bellied Woman's in a Croud;
Telling the Knight that her Affairs require
He, for some Hours, obsequiously[18] retire.
I think she was asham'd he shou'd be seen,
Hard Fate of Husbands! the Gallant had been.
Though a diseas'd, ill-favour'd Fool, brought in:
Dispatch, says she, the Business you pretend,
Your beastly Visit to your drunken Friend.
A Bottle ever makes you look so fine:

[15] gambling [16] sharpers
[17] a coarse banker and merchant acceptable only for his wealth [18] dutifully

Methinks I long to smell you stink of Wine.
Your Country-drinking Breath's enough to kill:
Sour Ale corrected with a Limon-Pill.[19]
Prithee, farewel: We'll meet again anon.
The necessary thing bows, and is gone.
She flies up stairs, and all the haste does show
That fifty antick Postures will allow,
And then burst out———Dear Madam, am not I
The strangest, alter'd, Creature: Let me die
I find my self ridiculously grown,
Embarrast with my being out of Town:
Rude and untaught like any Indian Queen;
My Country Nakedness is plainly seen.
How is Love govern'd? Love that rules the State;
And pray who are the Men most worn of late?
When I was marry'd, Fools were à-la-mode;
The Men of Wit were held then incommode.[20]
Slow of Belief, and fickle in Desire,
Who, e're they'll be perswaded, must enquire;
As if they came to spy, and not to admire.
With searching Wisdom, fatal to their ease,
They still find out why, what may, shou'd not please:
Nay, take themselves for injur'd, when we dare
Make 'em think better of us than we are:
And, if we hide our Frailties from their sights,
Call us deceitful Jilts, and Hypocrites:
They little guess, who at our Arts are griev'd,
The perfect Joy of being well deceiv'd.
Inquisitive, as jealous Cuckolds,[21] grow;
Rather than not be knowing, they will know,
What being known, creates their certain woe.
Women should these, of all Mankind, avoid;
For Wonder, by clear Knowledge, is destroy'd.
Woman, who is an arrant Bird of Night,
Bold in the dusk, before a Fool's dull sight,
Must fly, when Reason brings the glaring Light.
But the kind easie Fool, apt to admire
Himself, trusts us, his Follies all conspire
To flatter his, and favour our Desire.
Vain of his proper Merit, he, with ease,
Believe we love him best, who best can please:
On him our gross, dull, common Flatteries pass;
Ever most happy when most made an Ass:
Heavy to apprehend; though all Mankind
Perceive us false, the Fop, himself, is blind.
Who, doating on himself,———
Thinks every one that sees him of his mind.
These are true Womens Men—here, forc'd to cease
Through want of Breath, not will, to hold her peace;
She to the Window runs, where she had spy'd
Her much-esteem'd, dear Friend, the Monkey ty'd:
With forty Smiles, as many antick Bows,

[19] lemon-peel [20] Frenchified term: unsuitable, not the thing
[21] husbands of unfaithful wives

As if't had been the Lady of the House:
The dirty, chatt'ring Monster she embrac'd;
And made it this fine tender Speech at last.
Kiss me, thou curious Miniature of Man;
How odd thou art, how pretty, how japan:[22]
Oh! I could live and die with thee: Then on,
For half an hour, in Complements she ran.
I took this time to think what Nature meant,
When this mixt thing into the World she sent,
So very wise, yet so impertinent.
One that knows ev'ry thing, that God thought fit
Shou'd be an Ass through choice, not want of Wit.
Whose Foppery, without the help of sense,
Cou'd ne'er have rose to such an excellence.
Nature's as lame in making a true Fop
As a Philosopher; the very Top,
And Dignity, of Folly we attain
By studious search, and labour of the Brain:
By observation, Counsel, and deep Thought:
God never made a Coxcomb worth a Groat.
We owe that Name to Industry and Arts;
An eminent Fool must be a Fool of Parts.
And such a one was she; who had turn'd o'er
As many Books as Men; lov'd much, read more:
Had a discerning Wit; to her was known
Every one's Fault, or Merit, but her own.
All the good Qualities that ever blest
A Woman so distinguish'd from the rest,
Except Discretion only, she possest.
But now *Mon Cher*, dear Pug, she cries, adieu,
And the Discourse, broke off, does thus renew:
You smile to see me, who the World perchance,
Mistakes to have some Wit, so far advance
The Interest of Fools, that I approve
Their Merit more, than Men of Wit, in love.
But, in our Sex, too many Proofs there are
Of such whom Wits undo, and Fools repair.
This, in my time, was so observ'd a Rule,
Hardly a Wench in Town but had her Fool.
The meanest, common Slut, who long was grown
The jeast, and scorn, of ev'ry Pit-Buffoon;[23]
Had yet left Charms enough to have subdu'd
Some Fop or other; fond to be thought lewd.
Foster[24] could make an *Irish* Lord a *Nokes;*[25]
And *Betty Morris*[24] had her City Cokes.[25]
A Woman's ne'er so ruin'd, but she can
Be still reveng'd on her undoer, Man:
How lost soe'er, she'll find some Lover more,
A more abandon'd Fool than she a Whore.
That wretched thing *Corinna*, who has run
Through all th' several ways of being undone:

[22] Japanese wares, especially black japaned or lacquered objects and porcelain were just becoming fashionable.

[23] vulgar jester who sits in the pit [24] well-known bawds (Hayward) [25] ninny

Cozen'd at first by Love, and living then
By turning the too dear-bought Cheat on Men——
Gay were the Hours, and wing'd with Joy they flew,
When first the Town her early Beauties knew:
Courted, admir'd, and lov'd, with Presents fed;
Youth in her Looks, and Pleasure in her Bed:
Till Fate, or her ill Angel, thought it fit
To make her doat upon a Man of Wit:
Who found 'twas dull to love above a day;
Made his ill-natur'd Jeast, and went away.
Now scorn'd of all, forsaken and opprest,
She's a *Memento Mori*[26] to the rest:
Diseas'd, decay'd, to take up half a Crown
Must mortgage her long Scarf, and Manto[27] Gown:
Poor Creature, who unheard of, as a Fly,
In some dark hole must all the Winter lie:
And want, and dirt, endure a whole half Year,
That, for one Month, she Tawdry[28] may appear.
In *Easter*-Term she gets her a new Gown;
When my young Master's Worship comes to Town:
From Pedagogue, and Mother, just set free;
The Heir and Hopes of a great Family:
Who with strong Beer, and Beef, the Country rules;
And ever since the Conquest, have been Fools:
And now, with careful prospect to maintain
This Character, lest crossing of the Strain
Shou'd mend the Booby-breed; his Friends provide
A Cousin of his own to be his Bride:
And thus set out———
With an Estate, no Wit, and a young Wife:
And the cold Comforts of a Coxcomb's Life:
Dunghill and Pease forsook, he comes to Town,
Turns Spark, learns to be lewd, and is undone:
Nothing suits worse with Vice than want of sense:
Fools are still wicked at their own expence.
This o'er-grown School-Boy lost *Corinna* wins;
At the first dash to make an Ass begins:
Pretends to like a Man that has not known
The Vanities or Vices of the Town:
Fresh in his Youth, and faithful in his Love,
Eager of Joys which he does seldom prove:
Healthful and strong, he does no pains endure,
But what the Fair One he adores, can cure.
Grateful for Favours, does the Sex esteem,
And libels none for being kind to him.
Then of the Lewdness of the Town complains,
Rails at the Wits, and Atheists, and maintains
'Tis better than good Sense, than Pow'r, or Wealth
To have a Blood untainted, Youth, and Health,
The unbred Puppy, who has never seen
A Creature look so gay, or talk so fine,
Believes, then falls in love, and then in debt:

[26] reminder of death; death's head [27] cut in the Italian or Spanish fashion
[28] cheaply showy

Mortgages all, ev'n to the ancient Seat,
To buy his Mistress a new House for Life:
To give her Plate, and Jewels, robs his Wife.
And when to th' height of Fondness he is grown,
'Tis time to poison him, and all's her own.
Thus, meeting in her common Arms his Fate,
He leaves her Bastard Heir to his Estate:
And, as the Race of such an Owl deserves,
His own dull, lawful Progeny he starves.
Nature (that never made a thing in vain,
But does each Insect to some end ordain)
Wisely provokes kind-keeping Fools, no doubt,
To patch up Vices Men of Wit wear out.
Thus she ran on two hours, some grains of Sense
Still mixt with Follies of Impertinence.
But now 'tis time I shou'd some pity show
To *Cloe,* since I cannot chuse but know,
Readers must reap what dullest Writers sow.
By the next Post I will such Stories tell,
As, join'd to these, shall to a Volume swell;
As true as Heaven, more infamous than Hell.
But you are tir'd, and so am I.

Farewel.

A SATYR AGAINST MANKIND[29]

Were I, who to my cost already am,
One of those strange, prodigious Creatures *Man,*
A Spirit free, to chuse for my own share,
What sort of Flesh and Blood I pleas'd to wear,
I'd be a Dog, a Monkey or a Bear,
Or any thing, but that vain Animal,
Who is so proud of being rational.
The Senses are too gross; and he'll contrive
A sixth,[30] to contradict the other five:
And before certain Instinct, will preferr
Reason, which fifty times for one does err—
Reason, an *Ignis fatuus* of the Mind,
Which leaves the Light of Nature, Sense behind.
Pathless, and dangerous, wand'ring ways, it takes,
Through Errour's fenny Bogs, and thorny Brakes:
Whilst the misguided Follower climbs with pain,
Mountains of Whimseys, heapt in his own Brain,
Stumbling from thought to thought, falls headlong down
Into Doubts boundless Sea, where like to drown,
Books bear him up a while, and make him try
To swim with Bladders of Philosophy:
In hopes still to o'ertake the skipping Light:
The Vapour dances, in his dazzled sight,
Till spent, it leaves him to eternal night.
Then old Age, and Experience, hand in hand,
Lead him to Death, and make him understand,

[29] printed in a broadside, 1675 (Hayward)
[30] common sense, the step between sensation and reason

After a search so painful, and so long,
That all his Life he has been in the wrong.
Huddled in Dirt, [the][31] reas'ning Engine lies,
Who was so proud, so witty, and so wise:
Pride drew him in, as Cheats their Bubbles[32] catch,
And made him venture to be made a wretch:
His Wisdom did his Happiness destroy,
Aiming to know the World he should enjoy.
And *Wit* was his vain frivolous pretence,
Of pleasing others at his own expence.
For *Wits* are treated just like *Common Whores;*
First they're enjoy'd, and then kickt out of doors.
The Pleasure past, a threatning Doubt remains,
That frights th' Enjoyer with succeeding Pains.
Women, and *Men of Wit,* are dang'rous Tools,
And ever fatal to admiring Fools.
Pleasure allures, and when the Fops escape,
'Tis not that they're belov'd, but fortunate;
And therefore what they fear, at heart they hate.
But now methinks some formal Band and Beard[33]
Takes me to task; Come on, Sir, I'm prepar'd:
Then by your favour, any thing that's writ
Against this gibing, gingling knack, call'd *Wit,*
Likes me abundantly; but you'll take care
Upon this point, not to be too severe.
Perhaps my Muse were fitter for this part:
For I profess, I can be very smart
On *Wit,* which I abhor with all my heart.
I long to lash it, in some sharp Essay,
But your grand Indiscretion bids me stay,
And turns my Tide of Ink another way;
What Rage ferments in your degen'rate Mind,
To make you rail at Reason and Mankind?
Blest glorious Man, to whom alone kind Heav'n
An everlasting Soul hath freely giv'n;
Whom his great Maker took such care to make,
That from himself he did the Image take,
And this fair Frame in shining Reason drest,
To dignifie his Nature above Beast—
Reason, by whose aspiring Influence,
We take a flight beyond material Sense,
Dive into Mysteries, then soaring pierce
The flaming limits of the Universe,
Search Heav'n and Hell, find out what's acted there,
And give the World true grounds of hope and fear.
Hold, mighty Man, I cry; all this we know,
From the pathetick Pen of *Ingelo,*
From *Patrick*'s Pilgrim, *Sibb*'s Soliloquies,[34]

[31] to supply an omission in the text [32] dupes

[33] A clergyman bearded and in clerical neck-band; note that the following lines are in dialogue: l. 47, the *I* of the poem; 48–51, the clergyman; 52–57, *I,* perhaps to himself; 58–71, the clergyman; and then *I* through to the end.

[34] Ingelo, a writer of a religious romance and several sermons; Bishop Patrick, author of the *Parable of the Pilgrim;* Richard Sibbs, a voluminous Puritan writer (Hayward)

And 'tis this very Reason I despise,
This supernat'ral Gift, that makes a Mite
Think he's the Image of the Infinite;
Comparing his short Life, void of all rest,
To the eternal and the ever Blest;
This busie puzling stirrer up of doubt,
That frames deep Mysteries, then finds 'em out,
Filling with frantick Crouds of thinking Fools,
The reverend Bedlams,[35] Colleges and Schools;
Born on whose Wings, each heavy Sot can pierce
The Limits of the boundless Universe:
So charming Ointments[36] make an old Witch fly,
And bear a cripled Carkass through the Sky.
'Tis this exalted Pow'r whose Business lies
In Nonsense and Impossibilities:
This made a whimsical Philosopher,[37]
Before the spacious World his Tub prefer:
And we have many modern Coxcombs, who
Retire to think, 'cause they have nought to do.
But Thoughts were giv'n for Actions Government;
Where Action ceases, Thought's impertinent.
Our Sphere of Action is Lifes happiness,
And he that thinks beyond, thinks like an Ass.
Thus whilst against false reas'ning I inveigh,
I own right Reason, which I would obey;
That Reason, which distinguishes by Sense,
And gives us rules of good and ill from thence;
That bounds Desires with a reforming Will,
To keep them more in vigour, not to kill:
Your Reason hinders; mine helps to enjoy,
Renewing Appetites, yours would destroy.
My Reason is my Friend, yours is a Cheat:
Hunger calls out, my Reason bids me eat;
Perversely yours, your Appetite does mock;
This asks for food, that answers what's a Clock?
  This plain distinction, Sir, your doubt secures;
'Tis not true Reason I despise, but yours.
Thus, I think Reason righted: But for Man,
I'll ne'er recant, defend him if you can.
For all his Pride, and his Philosophy,
'Tis evident Beasts are, in their degree,
As wise at least, and better far than he.
Those Creatures are the wisest, who attain
By surest means, the ends at which they aim.
If therefore *Jowler* finds, and kills his Hare
Better than *Meres*[38] supplies Committe-Chair;
Though one's a Statesman, th' other but a Hound,
Jowler in Justice will be wiser found.
You see how far Man's Wisdom here extends:
Look next if Human Nature makes amends;
Whose Principles are most generous and Just;
And to whose Morals, you wou'd sooner trust.

[35] hospitals for the insane, Bethlehem [36] ointments that could cast a charm or spell
[37] Diogenes, the Cynic [38] Sir Thomas Meres, M.P. for Lincoln (Hayward)

Be judge your self, I'll bring it to the Test,
Which is the basest Creature, Man, or Beast:
Birds feed on Birds, Beasts on each other prey;
But savage Man alone, does Man betray.
Prest by Necessity, *They* kill for Food;
Man undoes Man, to do himself no good.
With Teeth, and Claws, by Nature arm'd *They* hunt
Nature's allowance, to supply their want:
But Man with Smiles, Embraces, Friendships, Praise,
Inhumanely, his Fellows Life betrays,
With voluntary Pains, works his Distress;
Not through Necessity, but Wantonness.
For Hunger, or for Love *They* bite or tear,
Whilst wretched Man is still in Arms for Fear:
For Fear he arms, and is of Arms afraid;
From Fear, to Fear, successively betray'd.
Base Fear, the Source whence his best Passions came,
His boasted Honour, and his dear-bought Fame:
The Lust of Pow'r, to which he's such a Slave,
And for the which alone he dares be brave:
To which his various Projects are design'd,
Which makes him gen'rous, affable, and kind:
For which he takes such pains to be thought wise,
And scrues his Actions, in a forc'd Disguise:
Leads a most tedious Life, in misery,
Under laborious, mean Hypocrisie.
Look to the bottom of his vast Design,
Wherein Man's Wisdom, Pow'r, and Glory join;
The Good he acts, the Ill he does endure,
'Tis all from Fear, to make himself secure.
Meerly for safety, after Fame they thirst;
For all Men would be Cowards if they durst:
And Honesty's against all common sense—
Men must be Knaves; 'tis in their own defence,
Mankind's dishonest; if they think it fair,
Amongst known Cheats, to play upon the square,[39]
You'll be undone——
Nor can weak Truth, your Reputation save;
The Knaves will all agree to call you Knave.
Wrong'd shall he live, insulted o'er, opprest,
Who dares be less a Villain than the rest.
Thus here you see what Human Nature craves,
Most Men are Cowards, all Men shou'd be Knaves.
The Difference lies, as far as I can see,
Not in the thing it self, but the degree;
And all the subject matter of Debate,
Is only who's a Knave of the first Rate.

[39] strictly, honestly

John Oldham

JOHN OLDHAM was born at Shipton Moyne in Gloucestershire in 1653. He matriculated at St. Edmund Hall, Oxford, 1670, and took his B.A. in 1674. Probably after teaching in his father's school, he became in 1676 usher at Croydon School. Here his poetical talents are said to have attracted a visit from the Earl of Rochester and several friends from Woodstock Park. In February, 1679, he left Croydon to become a private tutor until 1681. He then tried life in London for a brief period and returned a second time after another tutorship. In 1683 he went to live under the patronage of the young Earl of Kingston at Holme-Pierpont near Nottingham. His poems (particularly his early *Satire, Address'd to a Friend that is about to . . . Come Abroad in the World*, immortalized in the use made of it as social history by Macaulay and Thackeray) are the best record of his determination to be a poet and of his struggle for independence in a world that, as he bitterly notes, offered little to teacher, to clergyman without influence, or to poet. He died of small-pox at Holme-Pierpont within a year of his going there. At some time not long before his death he became acquainted with Dryden, whose lines on his death form the best comment on his significance.

Oldham began publishing in 1677 with an ode on the marriage of Princess Mary to William of Orange, which failed to attract attention. *Garnet's Ghost*, the first of his *Satyrs Upon the Jesuits*, was published in 1679 (without author or date) and all were finished by the end of that year. *A Satyr Against Vertue* and *The Clarret Drinker's Song* (*The Careless Good-fellow*) appeared in 1679 and 1680; the complete *Satyrs upon the Jesuits . . . with some Other Pieces*, in 1681. Several other publications, which included imitations and translations, led up to *The Works of Mr. John Oldham, together with his Remains*, 1684, and a number of following editions through 1722. This was largely a gathering of volumes already in print, with the *Remains* in a fresh text. E. Thompson published in 1770 the first volume of a proposed three volumes of *Compositions in Prose and Verse*. Robert Bell's edition of the *Poetical Works*, 1854, reissued in 1871, is incomplete and bowdlerized. *A Bibliography of John Oldham*, including consideration of two important autograph manuscripts and some others was published in the *Proceedings & Papers of the Oxford Bibliographical Society* (1936) by Harold F. Brooks. This contains also a biographical and critical introduction. Mr. Brooks's edition remains in manuscript.

Oldham is important for his contribution to the development of formal neoclassical satire. His *Satyrs upon the Jesuits*, called forth by the Popish Plot, lives and even achieves a breadth of effect by the energy of its vituperation and by the particularity of its reference to the varied vices which he delineates as illustrations or parallels of Jesuit malice. One of his favorite themes is the exposé of the philosophy and manners common among the court wits, which he treats in this satire; in imitations of Boileau, Horace, and Juvenal, remarkable for lively telling detail; in the heavily ironic *Satyr Against Virtue* which he imagines as spoken by one of the wits (Rochester) in the form of an awkward ode; and in the drinking song we publish. The lines of the delineation of the wit are firm and penetrating, though the portrait is without subtlety or aesthetic distance. For Rochester on his death it is to be noted that Oldham expressed a deep admiration.

Oldham's most significant contribution to the form of satire is his "imitations," his adaptations, that is, of earlier satires to contemporary persons and situations, imitations which have the peculiar depth that is given by reminiscence and implicit contrast of the original situation and its later recurrence. His favorite device of casting his satire into the mouth of a speaker from another age, which he owes to Jonson, did not become significant in later satire, except as it may have contributed in some measure to stimulate the epic tones and dramatic forms and the respect for earlier native satiric tradition of *Absalom and Achitophel* and *The Hind and the Panther*. In manner, Oldham is essentially bludgeoning. He had none of Rochester's genius for comic situation or dramatic irony in characterization. His poems lack larger design, and he has no memorable lines. That is forbidden by his roughness and by the untempered gusto which gives his poems their vitality. It may be noted, finally, that his *Spencer's Ghost* repeats exactly the charges of indifference to poetry and lack of patronage which had been voiced by Spenser and echoed by Wither; it affords, accordingly, by its treatment in a different manner of the same subject matter, a very neat illustration of the shift in poetry from the Renaissance to the Age of Reason. Weldom M. Williams has studied "The Genesis of John Oldham's *Satyrs upon the Jesuits*," *PMLA* LVIII (1943), with important inferences from the Oldham manuscripts, and "The Influence of Ben Jonson's Catiline" upon the same work, *ELH* XL (1944). Previté-Orton includes him in his general study. For discussion of his relation to Dryden's *MacFlecknoe*, see Monk's Dryden bibliography.

SATYRS UPON THE JESUITS[1]

PROLOGUE

For who can longer hold? when every *Press*,
The *Bar* and *Pulpit* too has broke the Peace?
When every scribling *Fool* at the alarms
Has drawn his Pen, and rises up in Arms?
And not a dull *Pretender* of the Town,
But vents[2] his gall in *Pamphlet* up and down?
When all with licence *rail*, and who will not,
Must be almost suspected of the *PLOT*,
And bring his *Zeal* or else his Parts in doubt?
   In vain our *Preaching Tribe* attack the *Foes*,
In vain their weak *Artillery* oppose;
Mistaken honest men, who gravely *blame*,
And hope that *gentle Doctrine* should reclaim.
Are *Texts*, and such exploded trifles fit
T'impose, and sham upon a *Jesuit?*
Would they the dull old *Fisher-men*[3] compare
With mighty *Suarez*, and great *Escobar?*[4]
Such thred-bare proofs, and stale *Authorities*

[1] Text: third edition, 1685 [2] gives passage to
[3] The Apostles [4] Jesuit theologians

May *Us* poor simple *Hereticks* suffice:
But to a fear'd *Ignatian*'s[5] Conscience,
Harden'd, as his own Face, with Impudence,
Whose Faith in contradiction bore, whom Lies,
Nor Non-sense, nor Impossibilities,
Nor shame, nor death, nor damning can assail:
Not these mild fruitless methods will avail.
'Tis pointed *Satyr*, and the *sharps* of Wit
For such a *prize* are th' only Weapons fit:
Nor needs there *Art*, or *Genius* here to use,
Where *Indignation* can create a muse:
Should Parts, and Nature fail, yet very spite
Would make the arrant'st *Wild*, or *Withers*[6] write.
It is resolv'd: henceforth an endless War,
I and my Muse with them, and theirs declare;
Whom neither open *Malice* of the *Foes*,
Nor private *Daggers*, nor *St. Omers*[7] *Dose*,
Nor all, that *Godfrey*[8] felt, or *Monarchs* fear,
Shall from my vow'd, and sworn revenge deter.
Sooner shall false *Court Favourites* prove just,
And faithful to their Kings, and Countrys trust:
Sooner shall they detect the tricks of *State*,
And knav'ry, suits, and bribes, and flatt'ry hate:
Bawds shall turn *Nuns, Salt* D——s grow chast,
And Paint, and Pride, and Lechery detest:
Popes shall for *Kings Supremacy* decide,
And *Cardinals* for *Huguenots*[9] be try'd:
Sooner (which is the great'st impossible)
Shall the vile Brood of *Loyola*, and *Hell*
Give o'er[10] to Plot, be Villains, and Rebel;
Than I with utmost spite, and venegeance cease
To prosecute, and plague their cursed race.
The rage of *Poets* damn'd, of *Womens Pride*
Contemn'd, and scorn'd, or *proffer'd lust* denied:
The malice of *Religious* angry *Zeal*,
And all, *cashier'd*[11] *resenting States-men* feel:
What prompts dire *Hags* in their own blood to write
And sell their very souls to Hell for spite:
All this urge on my rank envenom'd spleen,
And with keen Satyr edg my stabbing Pen:
That its each home-set thrust their blood may draw,
Each drop of Ink like *Aquafortis*[12] gnaw.
Red hot with vengeance thus, I'll brand disgrace
So deep, no time shall e'er the marks deface:
Till my severe and exemplary doom
Spread wider than their guilt, till it become
More dreaded than the *Bor*, and frighten worse
Than damning *Pope's Anathema's*, and curse.

[5] Jesuit, after their founder, Ignatius Loyola
[6] Notorious poor poets; see Dryden's *Essay of Dramatick Poesie.*
[7] a Jesuit college; its dose, its doctrine (Crane)
[8] See general introduction.
[9] French Protestants [10] cease
[11] dismissed [12] brandy

from SATYRS UPON THE JESUITS

SATYR III

[Satire III, entitled "Loyola's *will*," imagines the founder of the Jesuit order from his death bed advising his order how to proceed to success. After instructing them to welcome converts brought to the order by need, the exhaustion of vice, despair, etc., he instructs them how (in contrast to the other orders) to succeed in the world.]

When shaven Crown, and hallow'd Girdle's Power
Has dub'd him Saint, that Villain was before;
Enter'd, let it his first Endeavour be
To shake off all remains of Modesty,
Dull sneaking Modesty, not more unfit
For needy flatt'ring Poets, when they write,
Or trading Punks,[13] than for a *Jesuit:*
If any Novice feel at first a blush,
Let Wine, and frequent converse with the Stews[14]
Reform the Fop, and shame it out of Use,
Unteach the puling[15] Folly by degrees,
And train him to a well-bred Shamelessness.
Get that great Gift, and Talent, Impudence,
Accomplish'd Mankind's highest Excellence:
'Tis that alone prefers, alone makes great,
Confers alone Wealth, Titles, and Estate:
Gains Place at Court, can make a Fool a Peer,
An Ass a Bishop, can vil'st Blockheads rear
To wear Red Hats, and sit in Porph'ry Chair.[16]
'Tis Learning, Parts, and Skill, and Wit, and Sense,
Worth, Merit, Honour, Vertue, Innocence.
Next for *Religion,* learn what's fit to take,
How small a Dram do's the just Compound make.
As much as is by th' Crafty *States-men* worn
For Fashion only, or to serve a turn:
To bigot Fools its idle Practice leave,
Think it enough the empty Form to have:
The outward Show is seemly, cheap, and light,
The Substance Cumbersom, of Cost, and Weight:
The Rabble judge by what appears to th' Eye,
None, or but few the Thoughts within descry.
Make't you an Engine[17] to ambitious Pow'r
To stalk behind, and hit your Mark more sure:
A Cloak to cover well-hid *Knavery,*
Like it, when us'd, to be with ease thrown by:
A shifting Card,[18] by which your course to steer,
And taught with every changing *Wind* to veer.
Let no Nice, Holy, Conscientious Ass
Amongst your better Company find place,
Me, and your Foundation to disgrace:
Let Truth be banisht, ragged Vertue fly,
And poor unprofitable Honesty;
Weak Idols, who their wretched Slaves betray;

[13] prostitutes [14] brothels [15] queruously whining
[16] as a cardinal [17] instrument [18] chart

To every Rook, and every Knave a Prey:
These lie remote, and wide from Interest,
Farther than Heaven from Hell, or *East* from *West*,
Far, as they e'er were distant from the brest.
Think not your selves t' Austerities confin'd,
Or those strict Rules, which other Orders bind,
To *Capuchins, Carthusians, Cordeliers*[19]
Leave Penance, meager Abstinence, and Prayers:
In lousie Rags let *Begging Fryars* lye,
Content on Straw, or Boards to mortifie:
Let them with Sackcloth discipline their Skins,
And scourge them for their madness, and their Sins:
Let pining *Anchorets*[20] in Grotto's starve,
Who from the Liberties of Nature swerve:
Who mak't their chief *Religion* not to eat,
And place't in nastiness, and want of Meat:
Live you in *Luxury*, and pamper'd *Ease*,
As if whole Nature were your *Cateress.*
Soft be your Beds, as those, which Monarchs *Whores*
Lye on, or *Gouts* of *Bed-rid Emperors:*
Your *Wardrobes* stor'd with choice of Suits, more dear
Than *Cardinals* on high Processions wear:
With Dainties load your Boards, whose every *Dish*
May tempt cloy'd *Gluttons*, or *Vitellius*[21] *Wish.*
Each fit a longing[22] *Queen:* let richest *Wines*
With *Mirth* your Heads inflame, with *Lust* your Veins:
Such as the Friends of dying *Popes* would give
For *Cordials to prolong* their *gasping Life.*

THE CARELESS GOOD FELLOW

Written March 9, 1680[23]

A pox of this fooling, and plotting of late,
What a pother, and stir has it kept in the state?
Let the Rabble run mad with Suspicions, and Fears,
Let them scuffle, and jar, till they go by the ears:
Their Grievances never shall trouble my pate,
So I can enjoy my dear Bottle at quiet.

What Coxcombs were those, who would barter their ease
And their Necks for a Toy,[24] a thin Wafer and Mass?
At old *Tyburn*[25] they never had needed to swing,
Had they been but true Subjects to Drink, and their King;
A Friend, and a Bottle is all my design;
He has no room for Treason, that's top-full of Wine.

[19] members of orders of monks and friars, the first and last, Franciscan
[20] anchorite, a religious, living in retirement
[21] Roman emperor famous for consumption of food and drink
[22] be fit for, referring to a supposed longing for special foods during pregnancy, long a subject of comedy
[23] Text: *Poems and Translations*, 1683
[24] trifle (the mass)
[25] where heretics were hung, or burned

I mind not the Members[26] and makers of Laws,
Let them sit or Prorogue, as his Majesty please:
Let them damn us to Woollen,[27] I'll never repine
At my Lodging, when dead, so alive I have Wine:
Yet oft in my Drink I can hardly forbear
To curse them for making my Claret so dear.

I mind not grave Asses, who idly debate
About Right and Succession, the trifles of State;
We've a good King already: and he deserves laughter
That will trouble his head with who shall come after:
Come, here's to his Health, and I wish he may be
As free from all Care, and all Trouble, as we.

What care I how Leagues[28] with the *Hollander* go?
Or Intrigues betwixt *Sidney*, and Monsieur *D' Avaux?*[29]
What concerns it my Drinking, if *Casel* be sold,
If the Conqueror take it by Storming, or Gold?
Good *Bordeaux*[30] alone is the place that I mind,
And when the Fleet's coming, I pray for a Wind.

The Bully of *France*, that aspires to Renown
By dull cutting of Throats, and vent'ring his own;
Let him fight and be damn'd, and make Matches and Treat,
To afford the News-mongers, and Coffee-house Chat:
He's but a brave wretch, while I am more free,
More safe, and a thousand times happier than He.

Come He, or the Pope, or the Devil to boot,
Or come Faggot, and Stake; I care not a Groat;
Never think that in *Smithfield* I Porters will heat:
No, I swear, Mr. *Fox*,[31] pray excuse me for that.
I'll drink in defiance of Gibbet, and Halter,
This is the Profession, that never will alter.

[26] of parliament
[27] alluding to a law requiring burial in woolen
[28] See general introduction and *Absalom and Achitophel.*
[29] Algernon Sidney, (beheaded 1682) for intrigues with France, a politician; D'Avaux, a French diplomat
[30] where wine was made
[31] author of the *Book of Martyrs,* or story of the martyrs of the English Church, some burned at Smithfield

INDEX OF AUTHORS

INDEX OF TITLES AND FIRST LINES

Titles of poems and prose are printed in italics, and first lines of poems in roman.